D0713658

Career Development and Counseling

This book is dedicated to the memory of my father, Jifang Tang,
who made me believe I can do anything I want, even if I am a girl.

Career Development and Counseling

Theory and Practice in a Multicultural World

Mei Tang

University of Cincinnati

Los Angeles | London | New Delhi
Singapore | Washington DC | Melbourne

FOR INFORMATION:

SAGE Publications, Inc.
2455 Teller Road
Thousand Oaks, California 91320
E-mail: order@sagepub.com

SAGE Publications Ltd.
1 Oliver's Yard
55 City Road
London EC1Y 1SP
United Kingdom

SAGE Publications India Pvt. Ltd.
B 1/I 1 Mohan Cooperative Industrial Area
Mathura Road, New Delhi 110 044
India

SAGE Publications Asia-Pacific Pte. Ltd.
3 Church Street
#10-04 Samsung Hub
Singapore 049483

Acquisitions Editor: Abbie Rickard
Editorial Assistant: Elizabeth Cruz
Production Editor: Kimaya Khashnobish
Copy Editor: Michelle Ponce
Typesetter: C&M Digitals (P) Ltd.
Proofreader: Alison Syring
Indexer: Kathy Paparchontis
Cover Designer: Candice Harman
Marketing Manager: Susannah Goldes

Copyright © 2019 by SAGE Publications, Inc.

All rights reserved. No part of this book may be reproduced or utilized in any form or by any means, electronic or mechanical, including photocopying, recording, or by any information storage and retrieval system, without permission in writing from the publisher.

Printed in the United States of America

Library of Congress Cataloging-in-Publication Data

Names: Tang, Mei, (Counselor educator), author.

Title: Career development and counseling : theory and practice in a multicultural world / Mei Tang, University of Cincinnati, USA.

Description: Thousand Oaks, California : SAGE Publications, Inc., [2018] | Includes bibliographical references and index.

Identifiers: LCCN 2018016814 | ISBN 9781452230863 (pbk. : acid-free paper)

Subjects: LCSH: Career development. | Vocational guidance. | Multiculturalism.

Classification: LCC HF5381 .T2335 2018 | DDC 650.14—dc23
LC record available at https://lccn.loc.gov/2018016814

This book is printed on acid-free paper.

18 19 20 21 22 10 9 8 7 6 5 4 3 2 1

DETAILED CONTENTS

Chapter 7 • Assessment — 177

SERIES EDITORS' PREFACE

Introduction to the Series

COUNSELING AND PROFESSIONAL IDENTITY IN THE 21ST CENTURY

Career Development and Counseling: Theory and Practice in a Multicultural World by Dr. Mei Tang is a text that distinguishes itself from all other books on career counseling. In her book, Dr. Tang not only presents the knowledge, skills, techniques, and intervention strategies essential for career counseling but also addresses professionalism and career counseling issues from a global perspective. *Career Development and Counseling: Theory and Practice in a Multicultural World* is unique, among all other career counseling texts in a number of ways.

First, *Career Development and Counseling* has aligned all its content with the requirements of CACREP standards on career counseling. This unique feature will effectively assist those graduate students in the CACREP programs and those in the graduate programs that intend to get CACREP accreditation to meet all the requirements of CACREP standards.

Second, *Career Development and Counseling* has a unique feature in that it discusses career planning in a global and multicultural context. As the trend of economic, cultural, social, political, environmental, and informational globalization continues its strength, integrating multicultural and global issues into career planning and career counseling has never been as critical as it is now. This text certainly helps future counselors prepare themselves in this capacity.

Third, *Career Development and Counseling* distinguishes itself from all other texts in that it contains a comprehensive body of rich content. For example, the text emphasizes career development prevention and intervention not only with students in K-12 school settings and postsecondary settings but also with adults in community settings. Furthermore, the text underlines various career counseling theories, techniques, strategies, assessments, technology, and information resources.

Lastly, *Career Development and Counseling* has a distinct dimension of application and professional identity development. This dimension of application and professional identity development has been reflected throughout the content of the text. The text provides readers with the most recent knowledge, skills, and techniques about career counseling, which they have the opportunity to apply while learning and developing their professional identity.

While we are proud of the content and topics covered within this text, we are more than aware that one text, one learning experience, will not be sufficient for the development of a counselor's professional competency. The formation of both your professional identity and practice will be a lifelong process. It is a process that we hope to facilitate through the presentation of this text and the creation of our series: *Counseling and Professional Identity in the 21st Century.*

Counseling and Professional Identity in the 21st Century is a new and pedagogically sound series of texts targeting counselors in training. This series is NOT simply a compilation of isolated books matching that which is already in the market. Rather, each book, with its targeted knowledge and skills, will be presented as a part of a larger whole. The focus and content of each text serves as a single lens through which a counselor can view his or her clients, engage in his or her practice, and articulate his or her own professional identity.

Counseling and Professional Identity in the 21st Century is unique not just in the fact that it is packaged as a series of traditional texts but also in that it provides an *integrated* curriculum targeting the formation of the readers' professional identity and efficient, ethical practice. Each book within the series is structured to facilitate the ongoing professional formation of the reader. The materials found within each text are organized in order to move the reader to higher levels of cognitive, affective, and psychomotor functioning, resulting in his or her assimilation of the materials presented into both his or her professional identity and approach to professional practice. While each text targets a specific set of core competencies (cognates and skills), competencies identified by the professional organizations and accreditation bodies, each book in the series will emphasize each of the following:

a. The assimilation of concepts and constructs provided across the text found within the series, thus fostering the reader's ongoing development as a competent professional

b. The blending of contemporary theory with current research and empirical support

c. A focus on the development of procedural knowledge with each text employing case illustrations and guided practice exercises to facilitate the reader's ability to translate the theory and research discussed into professional decision making and application

d. An emphasis on the need for and means of demonstrating accountability

e. Fostering of the reader's professional identity and with it the assimilation of the ethics and standards of practice guiding the counseling profession

We are proud to have served as co-editors of this series feeling sure that all of the texts included, just like *Career Development and Counseling: Theory and Practice in a Multicultural World* by Dr. Mei Tang, will serve as a significant resource to you and your development as a professional counselor.

Richard Parsons, PhD

Naijian Zhang, PhD

PREFACE

PURPOSE FOR WRITING THE TEXT

Writing this book is filling a sense of need and obligation. As a counselor educator, I often struggle to find a textbook that covers all the content required by CACREP standards. I end up selecting one textbook and providing supplemental readings from other sources. Having taught a career development course for about 20 years, I occasionally have a few students showing interests in the topic, but more common trends are "why do we need this class?" or "I don't see the usefulness of this course to my counseling practice" or "I am not going to be a career counselor, but I will be a mental health counselor, why is this class not an elective?" After answering such questions in class for so many years, I knew I needed to write a career development textbook that addresses these doubts of students. Through reviewing the roots of the counseling profession; interconnection of work, health, and wellness; career development theories; and intervention approaches, students will see the value of career development to counseling process and to becoming an effective counselor regardless of their work settings and populations.

Thus, the purpose of this book is to provide a comprehensive overview of career development in the framework of educating future helping professionals be well prepared for serving clients as whole persons, in addition to covering the curriculum standards for career development, one of the eight foundation areas required by the CACREP. I hope students, after reading this book, will develop an integrated view of career development and counseling intervention. Career development is not just about career choice. It is about self-concept, meaning making, identity, and life span development. Counselors without sufficient understanding of the intertwined nature and complex interrelationship of work, family dynamics, physical and mental health, and impact of sociocultural, economic, and other contextual factors to career development, will not be adequately equipped to help clients effectively. I want this book to be a useful resource for both students in training and working helping professionals.

ORGANIZATION AND FEATURES

In order for students to acquire the necessary background information and the foundation knowledge of sociocultural factors in relation to career development, the first three chapters provide the historical context for the emergence, evolution, and current status of career development intervention, meaning of work in cross-cultural settings, and sociocultural factors pertaining to career development. Chapter 3 on cross-cultural career development provides a lens to examine and analyze how a variety of factors from a multicultural counseling perspective are applicable in individual career trajectory and how counselors need to be mindful in developing cultural competency to provide career intervention.

Chapters 4 and 5 provide overviews of major career development theories that students need to gain understanding of for their future license examination; these two chapters are also helpful for learning about the subsequent chapters that focus more on application of theories and career intervention approaches in various settings. Chapters 6, 7, and 8 introduce the process, assessment, and strategies of career intervention so that students can develop skills in providing career intervention to individuals. Chapter 9 focuses on technology and information sources that are essential for career intervention. This chapter also incorporates the use of technology for extending or enhancing career counseling practice. Chapter 10 describes the principles and specific steps of developing career intervention programs to benefit more people across different settings. Chapters 11, 12, and 13 provide information pertaining to career intervention with students in K-12 and postsecondary educational settings and diverse people in community settings. Chapter 14 introduces theory and practice of adult career development. These chapters give students more in-depth information about how career intervention can be implemented to help the target population. Chapter 15, the last chapter, integrates key components of this book to reinforce the theme of the book—interaction of intrapersonal and contextual factors that influence career development as well as association of career and wellness.

Each chapter has the same format and component. The learning objectives with emphasis on student competency are provided at the beginning, and the summary/keystones are provided at the end of the chapter. These features provide the outline and quick overview of the most important concepts covered in the chapter. Each chapter also has case illustrations, learning activities, and additional resources. These learning tools can be used for engaging students in active learning and real-world applications.

The uniqueness of this book is its infusion of a multicultural framework throughout the entire book. The other distinct features are integration of mental health and career development and multiple case illustrations to demonstrate the concepts.

ACKNOWLEDGMENTS

I want to take this opportunity to thank several people who have supported writing this book in various ways. Jane Goodman edited several chapters with great detail, wrote a few case illustrations, and provided encouragement when I experienced difficulties. I want to thank Kassie Graves for her trust in me and her understanding. I could not have completed this book without Abbie Rickard, who provided a lot of support and care, and has tremendous patience with my tardiness. I bow to Naijian Zhang and Richard Parsons for their direction and commitment to helping me complete writing this book.

Many thanks extend to my colleagues and students at the University of Cincinnati and particularly those students who took my career development class, who shared their stories about their life journey with me in and outside of the classroom, and who inspired me by their own career paths. I certainly cannot thank enough the contributors of this book, Mary Anderson, Kimberly Gilliam, Julia Larson, Rhonda Norman and Norman Townsel. I also want to thank all the reviewers who provided many helpful comments and suggestions in their reviews. My gratitude also goes to everyone who has influenced my career path in my discovery journey.

SAGE would like to acknowledge and thank the following reviewers for their thoughtful feedback and constructive comments:

Angela Cleveland, Caldwell University

David Julius Ford, Jr., James Madison University

Stephen P. Joy, Albertus Magnus College

Tara Malone, Fairfield University

Damara Goff Paris, Emporia State University

Elizabeth A. Roumell, Texas A&M University, College Station

E Mackenzie (Ken) Shell, Clark Atlanta University

ABOUT THE AUTHOR

Mei Tang, PhD, LPC, is in the counseling program in the School of Human Services at the University of Cincinnati (UC). She has been a faculty member at UC and a counselor educator since 1996. Her teaching areas include career development, group testing, internship, counseling theories, and doctoral seminars in ecological counseling and research. Dr. Tang's research focus includes cross-cultural career development, cultural identity and acculturation, counselor education and supervision, assessment and evaluation, and application of ecological counseling. Her publications appear in journals such as *Journal of Vocational Behavior*, *Career Development Quarterly*, *Journal of Career Assessment*, *Journal of Multicultural Counseling and Development*, *Counselor Education and Supervision*, and *Professional School Counseling*. She currently is the associate editor of the *Journal of Counseling and Development* and is an editorial board member of *Career Development Quarterly*. She served as vice president-AAPI of Association of Multicultural Counseling and Development from 2014 to 2016. She is also a member of the NCDA/ACES Commission.

ROOTS, GROWTH, AND TRENDS OF CAREER DEVELOPMENT AND INTERVENTION

As the first and introductory chapter in the book, this chapter provides a background for understanding career development from both historical and contextual perspectives. Though the focus of discussion of milestone development is on the United States, we will keep the cross-cultural perspective in the entire book to recognize the sociocultural contexts for one's career development in cross-cultural settings as well. This chapter will introduce the roots of career development, review the historical milestones that shaped career development and intervention in the United States today, and discuss current and future trends for the profession.

LEARNING OBJECTIVES

After completing the reading and exercises provided in this chapter, you will be able to:

- summarize how career development evolved in the past 100 years,

- describe social and economic milestones in the history of career development and career development professionals,

- elucidate the roles and services provided by career development professionals currently,

- summarize the relevant training and competency requirements, and

- gain a vision of some future trends of career development interventions.

OVERVIEW OF HISTORICAL DEVELOPMENT

Pioneering Work in Early Days

For thousands of years of human history, people's choices of what to do to make a living were severely restricted. Hunter gatherers needed to hunt and gather—tasks that were often gender segregated it is believed—and even with some division of labor, choice was limited. Later, due to the limited social mobility of the time, most people followed the family occupation without really having an opportunity to change the pattern. The need to make a decision regarding occupation only occurred when choices became available. As more distinct career specialties emerged, some even needing specialized training that went beyond family apprenticeship (Gibson & Mitchell, 2006), making a choice about one's future work became a necessity. By the time of historical record, a large number of discrete occupations existed in many societies.

In many ancient societies, probably still true in some areas, elders were viewed as wise and capable of knowing many things. Elders were therefore looked at as able to provide guidance to youth as they chose their life directions. When options were few and necessities or resources for training were limited, this was not a difficult task. Documented occupational descriptions can be traced back to the 15th century (Zytowski, 1972). Zytowski (1972) also concluded that because the books printed then were not really accessible to a largely illiterate population, the task of guiding young people in their choice of life and work was mainly done by priests when parents and family were unable to be of help.

The change came when many unprecedented new jobs emerged as the result of industrialization. The newly increased jobs demanded a skillful workforce, and further, higher demand of more skillful workers prompted the need for public education to become available to more common people. With a large number of graduates from secondary schools and a changing economic structure, the conventional guidance about entering into work from family and people in the church was not sufficient anymore.

Emergence of Vocational Guidance in the United States

In our previous discussion, we attempted to be global in our perspective, but as we continue, we will focus on the United States. As stated above, when there was little division of labor and few people worked outside of family endeavors, there was little need for helping people make a decision about their occupations. However, at the dawn of industrialization, starting in Europe and soon spreading to the North American continent, the traditional entrance into the workforce through family inheritance and apprenticeship was no longer adequate. There were many new, unprecedented jobs becoming available, and people needed help to understand these new opportunities as well as knowing about and acquiring the training and skills required for fulfilling these new job positions. Herr (2001) stated,

> The rise of what was first identified as vocational guidance in the United States in the late nineteenth and early twentieth centuries was directly associated with major shifts from a national economy that was primarily based on agriculture to an economy that was . . . increasingly based on manufacturing and industrial processes. (p. 197)

The changing occupational structure, which demanded a large number of laborers in the newly created factories, led to urbanization and concurrently domestic migration from rural areas to cities.

Social and Economic Context: The other contextual factor that influenced the emergence of vocational guidance in the late 19th century and early 20th century, in addition to urbanization and increased diversification of occupations as a result of industrialization, was the huge influx of immigrants to the United States. The new immigrants mainly settled in urban areas, which intensified the pressure on resources in the cities created by the domestic migration. This large wave of immigrants, along with industrialization and urbanization, served to "shape the world of work of America for the rest of the century" (DeBell, 2001, pp 77). These new immigrants, lacking the education or skills needed for jobs, encountered tremendous challenges to making a living. They had limited resources to help them adjust to the new environment and their living conditions were not adequate. For those who could find a job, the working conditions were generally poor and unsafe. All of these factors led to the organized effort to seek better working conditions and assistance for youth and adults toward finding employment (Gibson & Mitchell, 2006).

There were other major changes in the world of work at turn of the 20th century. Technology was changing, for example, the development of the telegraph, photograph, and the expansion of the railroad system. The nation also was witnessing the rising of a new middle class, namely professionals well educated and trained to be engineers, doctors, and technicians, and there was an increased gap between the poor and the rich (Zytowski, 2001), leading to discontent and political disruptions. In response to these issues of poverty, unemployment, and social unrest, a progressive social reform movement began. Centered at first largely in the Northeast, social reformers began several programs to help children and adults make good vocational choices. As the same time, several government policies and legislation in the earlier days also shaped the development of vocational guidance. For instance, the landmark Smith-Hughes Act of 1917 supported vocational education training in secondary schools (Pope, 2000).

Parsons's Landmark Work

It is widely known in the counseling profession that Frank Parsons is the pioneer of vocational guidance and that he laid down principles and foundations for modern career counseling. Although there were precursors to his work in the "friendly visitors" of the YMCA, Parsons's posthumously published *Choosing a Vocation* (1909) had an influence that has lasted until the present. Though theories, strategies, and tools have multiplied since Parsons's era, his philosophy of helping individuals find work that accommodates their abilities and needs still applies. Parsons's pioneering work represents the social reformers' intention to provide a solution to the unprecedented problems in society at the time and to advocate for the less fortunate people lost in the rapidly changing social and economic context.

Frank Parsons was recruited in 1905 to head the Breadwinner's Institute, an evening and weekend educational institution to help those who could not afford to go to college obtain the education and skills to become employable. Later in 1908, the Vocation Bureau was founded in Boston with an aim to provide systematic vocational guidance to youth. Parsons proposed the plan for the bureau and was the first director. He also drafted the training plan for counselors who would take the positions at the Bureau or

YMCA where many educational classes were offered to help people gain job-related skills through a variety of vocational classes (Zytowski, 2001). Parsons believed youth needed guidance in choosing a vocation upon graduating from high school so that their talents were not wasted, and he also advocated for such guidance to be provided in a systematic way by competent professionals. That set forth the groundwork for the evolution of guidance and subsequently, counseling.

The three steps of Parsons's approach of vocational guidance functioned as the guidelines of career counseling for many years, and they were also considered the basis of trait-and-factor theories that were later practiced by many counselors in variety of settings. The following are Parsons's three steps:

1. Develop a clear understanding of yourself, abilities, interests, resources, limitations, and other qualities.

2. Develop knowledge of the requirements and conditions of success, advantages and disadvantages, compensation, opportunities, and prospects in different lines of work.

3. Use "true reasoning" on the relations of these two groups of facts (Parsons, 1909, p. 5).

The detailed information of Parsons's principles and trait-factor approach will be discussed in Chapter 4 when theories in the trait-factor categories are presented. Basically, Parsons's approach illustrates that self-knowledge and knowledge of work are the essential elements in mapping out a fitting occupation for individuals.

Parsons's approach and its influence on the practice of career counseling is far-reaching for both career development theories and practices. The three-step approach shaped not only the "trait-and-factor" theoretical approaches but also the practice of career counseling to help clients making career choices. The principles of Parsons's approach were reflected in the book *Choosing a Vocation* published in 1909 one year after his death. In the book, he suggested the importance of systematic methods of understanding lines of work and careful study of both individuals and work; he believed that everyone must receive honest and adequate guidance before choosing a vocation. Parsons also suggested "it is better to choose a vocation than merely to hunt a job," and similarly, that "the youth should have a large survey to the field of vocations, and not simply drop into the convenient or accidental position" (Parsons, 1909, pp. viii). Current career development thought still embraces these ideas.

Evolution of Vocational Guidance

If progressive social reform gave birth to vocational guidance, educational reform in public schools, development of standardized testing, and passing of legislation related to vocational guidance and career education were clearly other contextual factors that shaped the evolution of career counseling.

Progressive Education: Until late 19th century, education was available only to a few elite groups in society and never meant to prepare students for job hunting or employment. There was no such need as people who could afford education either did not need a job to make a living or were destined to work in certain limited fields such as the church, medicine, teaching, or law. Because child labor was still legal at that time, very few children went to school beyond two or three years. As the social and economic structure was rapidly changing as a result of the Industrial Revolution, so was the need to have more people with appropriate education and training for the work. Thus, there was a greater need to not only provide education to the mass of people but also revise the curriculum to be more pertaining to the work world. The curriculum in the public schools was criticized for "bookish" content and not appropriately training students to be prepared for work. The criticism was not unjustified, since secondary education was limited to a few elite groups of people for a long time, and the purpose of it was to prepare graduates to go to college rather than enter into the workforce. The new lines of work and increased need for skilled labor prompted the need to reform secondary education. Jesse Davis, another pioneer in the vocational guidance movement, introduced the idea of incorporating vocational guidance into the school curriculum in Grand Rapids, Michigan, in the first decade of 20th century (Brewer, 1942). Davis, a school administrator, believed that youth needed to understand themselves and occupations to make better career choices and that development of moral consciousness, character, and ethical behavior would influence individuals' career choices (Capuzzi & Stauffer, 2006). Under Davis's leadership, vocational guidance was taught in English classes in the city schools across Grand Rapids. This was significant in the history of both vocational guidance and school counseling because it set the groundwork for fully integrating career development and academic development as well as social/personal development into the school system. The national school counseling model developed by the American School Counselor Association (ASCA) shared Jesse Davis' concepts, that is, that schools should educate students in academic, career, and personal/social/emotional areas, rather than just academic content.

The impact of progressive education reform occurring in schools in late 19th century and early 20th century America was far-reaching and influential even until today. American education has never ended the debate about the role of public education in regard to preparing students for society—teaching merely the basics or academic content or teaching beyond basics and incorporating other critical skills, for example, personal and social skills and decision-making skills, into curriculum. Nonetheless, advocates for progressive education such as John Dewey (1916) made significant contributions to the evolution of vocational guidance because of their efforts on behalf of providing comprehensive education to all students regardless of whether they were college-bound or in vocational tracks.

By the 1930s, fewer than half of the schools in American urban cities had vocational guidance programs (Brewer, 1942). Along with the introduction and experiment of teaching career development in classrooms came the need for adequately trained professionals to deliver the services. Teachers in New York City schools could earn a special

LEARNING ACTIVITY 1.1
COMPARISON OF HISTORICAL CONTEXT

Find three factors in current social and economic context that share similar features with the beginning of the 20th century. Find three factors that are different from then. In small groups, discuss the impact of these factors on career development.

guidance certificate by going through the training program related to guidance activities (Tang & Erford, 2010). The first university course about vocational guidance was taught at Harvard in 1911 (Aubrey, 1977, as cited in Capuzzi & Stauffer, 2006).

Though not systematic or widely available yet, vocational guidance and career development education were on a trajectory of becoming a major force in education and becoming a profession with a focused mission in the following years. The evolution process also was significantly influenced by the emergence of psychometric measurement and legislation related to guidance and education.

Development of Standardized Testing: When Parsons began his pioneering work in Boston to help youth understand themselves and occupations, there were few tools available for him to use (Herr, 2001). Parsons (1909) asked the clients to read biographies and interview workers to understand the world of work and asked counselors to observe clients' characteristics and teach clients self-reflection skills to map out the appropriate occupations for their characteristics. This self-assessment served the purpose well for implementing Parsons's three-step approach to help persons use "true reasoning," but it might be subject to the criticism that it lacked a scientific base. One reason for criticism of subjective self-assessment was the rise of testing, particularly standardized testing.

The first objective test was recorded as the intelligence test developed by Alfred Binet and Theophile Simon in France in 1905 (Zunker, 2002). The objective and standardized testing made it possible to administer the tests in group settings, an advantage to reduce the cost and increase efficiency. As the student population grew and the number of occupational titles increased, the tasks of understanding both individuals and the nature of work became immense. World War I (WWI) also accelerated the need for standardized, objective, and group administered assessment tools to determine efficiently who would be officers and who would be front line soldiers. The Army Alpha and Army Beta tests were developed and widely used during the WWI. The use of psychometrics for developing standardized tests "helped to establish the credibility of vocational guidance as a profession and justified its presence in schools" (Capuzzi & Stauffer, 2006, pp. 10).

Legislation: Vocational guidance emerged as a response of progressive social reformers to social and economic challenges at the turn of the 20th century, but without funding sources becoming available through federal legislation, vocational guidance probably would have had a slower development. According to Herr (2001), landmark legislation made significant contributions to the evolution of career guidance and counseling, particularly in regard to youth and other subgroups of the population. For example, there were the National Defense Education Act of 1958, which was fueled by a reaction to the Russians launch of Sputnik, funded training and placement of huge number of school counselors in K-12 settings; the Career Education Incentive Act of 1976, which enabled the full incorporation of career development content into the educational curriculum; and the School to Work Opportunities Act of 1994, which reemphasized the linkage of school and work for students. More recently, information that the United States is falling behind our global competitors in technology related areas has led to legislation related to encouraging students to enter science, technology, engineering, and math (STEM) careers. This legislation has had an impact again on guidance and counseling in schools and institutions of postsecondary education.

CASE ILLUSTRATION 1.1

JOHN MCCOY

John McCoy knew that he wanted to be a journalist as long as he could remember knowing what they did. He grew up admiring journalists on the radio and on television, but his strongest admiration was for print journalists. He loved movies about early 20th-century newspapers, like *The Front Page*, and imagined himself in a trench coat smoking cigarettes—although he didn't smoke—covering crime and corruption. John worked on his school newspaper, read every paper he could get his hands on, and hoped to major in journalism in college. But, just as he was entering his senior year in high school, the bottom dropped out of the newspaper business. Papers were laying off staff, not hiring; many papers ceased publishing; and the job prospects for John were very poor. His parents and his high school counselor urged

him to consider other majors, such as something in the STEM field, in which there are more career opportunities due to high demand for workers, but journalism had been John's dream his whole life.

Discussion Questions

1. What are the reasons for his parents and high school counselor urging John to think about different occupations than journalism?

2. Do you think going to a STEM field is a wise choice for John or not?

3. How could he reconcile his desire to pursue journalism with the fact that there are more opportunities for STEM careers?

Early legislation related to career counseling was the Vocational Rehabilitation Act of 1918, which was established to provide job training for WWI veterans (Heppner, Casas, Carte, & Stone, 2000 as cited in Capuzzi and Stuffer, 2006). The Smith-Hughes Act of 1917 provided funding for vocational education and organized guidance programs in schools (Pope, 2000). The George Barden Act in 1946 also had a significant impact on vocational guidance and evolution of career development as a profession. This act authorized salaries and travel expenses of vocational counselors and supported counselor-training courses, and therefore, led to certification of counselors and ultimately the professionalization of counselors (Herr & Shahnasarian, 2001).

Professional Organization and Publication: The first professional organization of vocational guidance was founded in 1913 in Grand Rapids, Michigan, at the third National Conference on Vocational Guidance. The name of the organization was National Vocational Guidance Association (NVGA), which is now the National Career Development Association (NCDA). Another national association that had a significant impact on the evolution of vocational guidance was the National Occupational Conference, which was a clearinghouse for the study of occupations, the measurement of individual differences, and information about vocational guidance practices (Savickas, Pope, & Niles, 2011). These two organizations played critical roles in unifying nine associations related to guidance, student personnel, and adult education into one organization in 1934, then titled American Council of Guidance and Personnel Associations (Brewer, 1942) and now known as the American Counseling Association.

The primary journal of NCDA, *Career Development Quarterly*, traces its origin to the newsletter of Boston Vocational Bureau first published in 1911 and then published as the journal of NVGA in 1915 as the *Vocational Guidance Bulletin* (Savickas et al., 2011). When the journal celebrated its centennial publication in 2011, three previous editors of the journal, Mark Savickas, Mark Pope, and Spencer Niles noted the legacy of its long history of providing occupational information, guidelines for vocational practice, research of career development theories, and leadership in public policy and social justice. They also discussed the contribution of journal articles focusing on diversity and issues of career development in a global setting. There is also an annual review of the year's articles relating to career development from many related journals, allowing readers to update their knowledge in an easily digestible fashion.

The Dictionary of Occupational Titles (DOT), first published by the Bureau of Labor Statistics of the U.S. Department of Labor in 1939, was the first publication of its kind that provided comprehensive information about all jobs that could be classified. In the subsequent year, Occupational Outlook Services was established as a division of the Bureau of Labor Statistics (BLS). In 1948, the *Occupational Outlook Handbook* was first published by the Bureau of Labor Statistics and has been published regularly since then. It is revised and updated every two years and provides pertinent information of an occupation for individuals in career decision making. The DOT was replaced by O*NET (Occupational Information Network), which was initiated in 1998 and is a database, not a print book like DOT (Bureau of Labor Statistics, n.d.). These publications, in addition to publication of vocational assessment instruments and standardized aptitude tests, gave vocational guidance counselors more resources and tools for use and propelled the establishment of career development practice.

Establishment of Vocational Guidance as a Profession

By the time of World War II (WWII) and the next few years after the war, several contextual factors influenced the development of career counseling as a specialty and profession. There began to be wide use of standardized tests, including vocational assessment instruments and publications pertaining to information about occupations as well as information about vocational guidance practice. Veterans returning home also needed both educational and vocational advising. As Pope (2000) stated, "The post-WWII period led to the rise of the professional practice of counseling, especially career counseling" (pp. 199).

The period from 1940 to 1959 witnessed the expansion of vocational guidance into colleges and universities (Pope, 2000). In addition to the George Barden Act that authorized funding for salaries and travel expenses of vocational counselors, the GI Bill of 1946 allocated funding for veterans to go to college and receive job training, and thus propelled a huge influx of veterans as students to colleges and universities across the nation. These veterans brought many unprecedented challenges to higher education, one of which was academic and career advising for these nontraditional students. With the passing of the National Defense Education Act of 1958, counselor training programs mushroomed. Many counselor training programs in the country were founded during the 1950s. They trained many school teachers for postgraduate certification in guidance so that they would be qualified to work in elementary and secondary schools, as well as in higher education settings.

During this time, several other factors were noteworthy for their impact on vocational guidance. Psychological testing experienced another booming period with many new tests developed and existing instruments revised. For example, the Strong Interest Inventory, a commonly used assessment of occupational interests first developed in 1927, went through a major revision during this period. Another popular test used in career counseling field, the Myers and Briggs Type Indicator, was developed by a mother-daughter team, not as an assessment for career counseling but for understanding individual personality differences. The emphasis of vocational guidance began to be attending to individual characteristics, individual differences, and individual well-being, rather than simply addressing social problems. The new definition of vocational guidance by NVGA changed

> the focus of vocational guidance from a concentration on what is to be chosen to increasing attention on the characteristics of the chooser. . . . [I]t diminished the emphasis on matching individual to job and on the provision of occupational information at a particular point in time. Instead, it emphasized the psychological nature of vocational choice, accented the developmental influence on career behavior across the life span, blended the personal and vocational dimensions of guidance into a whole, and elevated the importance of self-understanding and self-acceptance. (Herr, 2001, p. 204)

Broadened Role of Career Counseling and Services

With the changing focus of vocational guidance, the definition of vocational guidance was changed from "the process of assisting the individual to choose an occupation, prepare for it, enter upon it, and progress in it" to "the process of helping a person to develop and accept an integrated and adequate picture of himself [sic] and of his role in the world of work, to test this concept against reality, and to convert it into a reality, with satisfaction to himself and to society" (Super, 1951, p. 89, as cited in Herr, 2001). It is evident from this changing definition that vocational guidance was not just a job placement service anymore; rather, it entailed the concept of developing self-understanding and satisfaction. In other words, it is not only about finding a job but more importantly finding a job that is satisfying and meets the needs of society.

Pope (2000) characterized the history of career counseling as consisting of six stages, each of which has a theme. The first stage (1819-1919) was labeled Job Placement Services. The second stage (1920-1939) was summarized as providing educational guidance in the schools and the solidified role of vocational guidance in school. The third stage (1940-1959) was characterized as the expansion of vocational guidance in colleges and universities and the training of counselors. In the fourth stage (1960-1979), Pope described the theme of vocational guidance as "meaningful work" (p. 200). Young people in the 1960s and 1970s wanted more than an income-generating job; they wanted a job that would fulfill their ideals of improving the well-being of society. Pope also discussed the launch of career counseling services in other settings than schools and universities such as governmental agencies, nonprofit community agencies, and business and industrial settings during this period. The last two stages of Pope's classification were the fifth stage (1980-1989), a time when there was a growing number of career counseling professionals engaged in independent practice and a demand for career counseling services related

CASE ILLUSTRATION 1.2
HELPING STUDENTS GET MOTIVATED

Lin Tsu had become a high school counselor after 12 years of teaching English in an inner-city school, home to the poorest children in the Rust Belt city where she made her home. In those 12 years, she had become increasingly convinced that the relationships she built with her students were more useful than the literature she was required to teach, which often felt irrelevant to the students' lives. After receiving her master's degree in counseling, she was fortunate to move into a position in the same high school in which she had been teaching. She was committed to the ASCA model of personal, academic, and career domains in her work. Although all three were important to Lin, it was the career aspect of her job that really gave her the most satisfaction. She firmly believed that without good job opportunities, her students were condemned to remain in poverty. So, she took advantage of all opportunities for classroom guidance and lobbied strongly for computer-assisted career guidance programs and for a career development facilitator available to the students at least part time. She hoped that by motivating her students to seek satisfying work, she could motivate them to stay in and succeed in school.

Discussion Questions

1. How can a school counselor effectively help the students lacking motivation become engaged in learning?

2. Why does Lin so strongly believe in helping her students to be motivated to seek satisfying work? Do you agree with her or not?

to job outplacement, an inevitable outcome of economic decline in 70s; and the sixth stage (1990 to present) with a focus on the school-to-job transition, increasing internationalization of career counseling, emphasis on multicultural career counseling, and the prevalence of technology advancement and complexity in career counseling. Pope (2015) classified historical development of career intervention into three periods, namely, vocational guidance, career education, and life design. The emergence of life design career intervention is the new reality of insecure and anxious workers due to the project-based model of employment that does not provide stability or loyalty. The life design proposed by Savickas (2012) will be elaborated in Chapter 5.

A merger of NVGA, the American College Personnel Association, and the Guidance Supervisors and Counselor Trainers led to the foundation of the American Personnel and Guidance Association (APGA) in 1952. As a founding division of APGA (now American Counselors Association [ACA]), NVGA played a key role in advocating and providing leadership in seeking professional identity for career development practice practitioners. As a result, career development and counseling remains one of the core training requirements of counselor certification and licensing. The broadened role and services of vocational guidance were solidified when the name of the organization NVGA was changed to National Career Development Association (NCDA) in 1985 as *career development* captures the changing nature and mission of the profession better than vocational guidance.

BOX 1.1
CHRONICLE OF VOCATIONAL GUIDANCE AND CAREER DEVELOPMENT

Year	Events
1908	The Vocational Bureau in Boston was founded; Frank Parsons played a major role in establishing this first organization to provide vocational guidance and counseling.
1909	Parson's book *Choosing a Vocation* was published posthumously. This book provided the concepts and procedures of vocational guidance.
1910–1903	Jesse Davis introduced the vocational and moral guidance in the city schools of Grand Rapids, Michigan.
1910	The first national conference on vocational guidance was held in Boston.
1913	The National Vocational Guidance Association (NVGA) was formed in Grand Rapids, Michigan.
1915	The first publication of NVGA, the *Vocational Guidance Bulletin*, was started.
1918	The U.S. government instituted programs in 1918 for World War I veterans with disabilities, marking the beginning of vocational rehabilitation counseling.
1933	The U.S. Employment Service was created by the Wagner-Peyser Act.
1939	The *Dictionary of Occupational Titles* was published by the Bureau of Labor Statistics.
1940	The Occupational Outlook Services was established in the Bureau of Labor Statistics.
1946	The George Barden Act authorized the salaries and travel expenses of vocational counselors and supported counselor-training courses.
1948	The *Occupational Outlook Handbook* was first published.
1951	The historic NVGA definition of vocational guidance was changed from an emphasis on what is to be chosen to the nature of the chooser.
1951	The NVGA, merged with several student personnel and guidance organizations, and formed American Personnel and Guidance Association, the predecessor of the American Counseling Association.
1958	The National Defense Education Act was passed, providing funds for training school counselors
1963	The Vocational Education Act was passed, providing students vocational guidance and counseling.

(Continued)

(Continued)

Year	Events
1964	Civil Rights Act was passed; the civil rights movement accelerated the democratization of educational and occupational opportunities for minority groups.
1968	Vocational Education Act Amendment was passed, advocating for career programs, responses to the disadvantaged and physically handicapped, and the expansion of a broadened concept of guidance and counseling.
1971	Career education was introduced as a priority of the U. S. Office of Education
1984	The Carl D. Perkins Vocational Education Act advocates programs designed to improve, extend, and expand career guidance and counseling programs to meet the needs of vocational students.
1985	The NVGA changed its name to National Career Development Association.
1992	The Americans with Disability Act (ADA) was passed, requiring employers to provide reasonable work accommodations to persons with disabilities.
1994	The School-to-Work Opportunities Act provided funds for supporting career exploration for all students in school settings.

Adapted from Herr and Shahnasarian, 2001

Career Development Theories Boom: Starting in the late 1940s and continuing to today, many career development theories came into existence. These career development theories became major sources for enrichment of practice, research, and professional identity for career development professionals. The trend of career development theories in the last five decades also reflected the changing nature of career development practice. The early model of the trait-factor approach focused on matching the people to the work. Holland's (1985) typology model is an example of trait-and-factor theoretical approaches in modern time. In the 1950s, Super (1957) started his 50 years of work on career development from a developmental perspective and emphasized that the goal of career counseling is self-understanding and self-acceptance. In the 1970s and 1980s, Krumboltz's Learning Theory (Krumboltz, 1976) brought attention to addressing cognitive learning experiences and situational factors to understand career development of individuals. The late 1970s and early 1980s were the time when researchers and practitioners started to attend to the differences among diverse populations. Research about women and ethnic minorities began to appear in scholarly journals (e.g., Betz and Hackett's [1981] work on women entering nontraditional occupations, Leong [1995] on ethnic minority career development). From the 1990s until the first decade of the 21st century, multiple career development theories have emerged. The common feature of these new emerging career development theories is the focus on the interaction of person and environment, and they are a more comprehensive and integrated approach to career development and counseling. Some examples include Social Cognitive Career Development (Lent, Brown, & Hackett, 1994), Hansen's Integrated Life Planning (1997), and Ecological Career Counseling (Cook, Heppner, & O'Brien, 2002).

PROFESSIONALISM

When Parsons started the first vocational guidance in Boston at the beginning of the 20th century, the goal was to help youth and new immigrants to find a job. At that time, there was no theoretical approach or guidelines for those guidance workers at the bureau to follow, no empirically tested assessment tools to use in the helping process, or any comprehensive occupational information readily available to share with clients. There was no systematic training or credentials for vocational guidance workers then. The professional organizations to provide leadership and guidelines did not exist either. One hundred years later, vocational guidance has transitioned to career development and intervention; career development theories and strategies flourish; career assessment for various career development areas is widely used; and information about occupations is not only comprehensive but also available to everyone who needs it. Professionals need not only training but also credentials to practice career counseling. Professional organizations certainly played a key role in moving the practice of career counseling as a profession to its current status and continue to provide leadership in advancing career development intervention.

Training and Credentials

Career development is a fundamental component of the curriculum for counselor education. It is one of the eight foundations of CACREP (Council of Accredited Counseling and Related Education Programs) standards (CACREP, 2016). The CACREP Standards about career development are as follows:

CAREER DEVELOPMENT—studies that provide an understanding of career development and related life factors, including all of the following:

- Theories and models of career development, counseling, and decision making

- Approaches for conceptualizing the interrelationships among and between work, mental well-being, relationships, and other life roles and factors

- Processes for identifying and using career, avocational, educational, occupational and labor market information resources, technology, and information systems

- Approaches for assessing the conditions of the work environment on clients' life experiences

- Strategies for assessing abilities, interests, values, personality, and other factors that contribute to career development

- Strategies for career development program planning, organization, implementation, administration, and evaluation

- Strategies for advocating for diverse clients' career and educational development and employment opportunities in a global economy

- Strategies for facilitating client skill development for career, educational, and life-work planning and management

- Methods of identifying and using assessment tools and techniques relevant to career planning and decision making

- Ethical and culturally relevant strategies for addressing career development

In addition to the foundation areas, the CACREP also has a specialty in career counseling, which means counselor training programs can seek accreditation to offer a master's degree in career counseling. The details of accreditation standards can be found at the CACREP website: www.cacrep.org. The National Board of Certified Counselors (NBCC), an organization providing national certification and a variety of counseling certification and license exams, also offers National Certification of Career Counselors.

Persons interested in career development occupations may obtain a graduate degree in counseling, career counseling, student personnel, rehabilitation counseling, or counseling psychology. The National Career Development Association is the leading organization in career development, and has stated that, "Career professionals practice only within the boundaries of their competence, based on their education, training, supervised experience, state and national professional credentials, and appropriate professional experience" (National Career Development Association, 2015). Thus, a person without appropriate training or credentials should not claim to be a career development professional.

There are several certification or credentialing offered by the NCDA. Certified Career Services Provider (CCSP) is the credential for individuals from a wide range of backgrounds to deliver services and demonstrate core competency in the field of career services. The other credentials include Certified Master of Career Services (CMCS), Certified Career Counselor (CCC), Certified Clinical Supervisor of Career Counseling (CCSCC), Certified Career Counselor Educator (CCCE), and Certified School Career Development Advisor (CSCDA). More details can be found at the NCDA website (https://www.ncda.org/aws/NCDA/pt/sp/credentials_ccsp).

LEARNING ACTIVITY 1.2
CAREER DEVELOPMENT AND MY COUNSELING SPECIALTY

Review the NCDA career counseling competencies (located at https://www.ncda.org/aws/NCDA/pt/sd/news_article/37798/_self/layout_ccmsearch/true). Discuss each area in relation to your personal goal now as a student in a counselor training program. Choose the ones that you think are most relevant to your future role as a counselor (be specific to your program now, e.g., mental health counselor, school counselor, marriage and family counselor, career counselor, substance abuse counselor, etc.). Provide a rationale for your choice.

Work Settings

There are multiple work settings for career development practitioners. Vocational guidance started in community settings to reach new immigrants and migrants from farms to cities who needed help to seek jobs. One hundred years later, career development services are available to diverse groups of individuals in a variety of settings. In K-12 settings, licensed school counselors are primarily responsible for helping students with career related issues, including identifying students' career aspirations, helping students understand themselves and the world of work, providing assistance in postsecondary planning, and implementing students' plans for postsecondary career options. At colleges and universities, career counseling professionals usually work in the career development center, sometimes named career planning and placement centers, on campus. They help students with issues such as deciding on a major that can lead to the career in which they are interested, dissemination of employment information, and coordination between employers and students for job placement. Career development facilitators often work in career centers, providing the informational counterpart to counselors' work and administering assessments. They also help students with job search skills such as resume writing, networking, and interviewing.

Though K-12 and postsecondary educational settings are the two predominant places where career development practice occurred during much of the 20th century, career counseling practitioners work nowadays in many diverse settings. Career counseling practitioners can work in government agencies, military settings, and organizations such as those in business and industry. They can also work in nonprofit social service agencies or community-based mental health services agencies. In recent years, an increasing number of career counseling professionals have worked in private practice settings or contracted with large agencies to provide career counseling services. The massive layoffs of recent decades have also created a need for career counselors who work in outplacement firms or directly for the organizations that are downsizing. Employee assistance programs (EPAs) are an example of workplace-based career and mental health services provided by career counselors. The expansion of EPAs also attests to the interconnection of health and work.

A new horizon for career counseling practice is moving from face-to-face meetings with clients to the virtual world. Career counselors might work with clients through an online platform, or even computer-assisted career counseling programs, as a result of information technology advancement. The increased use of and availability of the Internet and media technology enables people to become less dependent on an office space to provide services, and consequently, more people to become independent practitioners. Social media is used by career practitioners as a means for delivering information, a medium for interpersonal communication, and a working space for interaction (Kettunen, Vuorinen, & Sampson, 2015). It becomes clear that information and communication technology (ICT) provides alternative tools for career service practitioners to extend services to reach more people.

Professional Organizations

The premier professional organization for career development professionals is the NCDA, a founding division of the American Counseling Association. NCDA, formerly NVGA, founded in 1913, continually provides leadership in guidance and direction of career development practice (Savickas et al., 2011). NCDA publishes the journal, the *Career Development Quarterly*; a magazine, *Career Developments*; and an online publication, *Career Convergence*, as well as many books for members and other professionals interested in career development issues. It also sponsors an annual convention, connecting educators, researchers, and practitioners at one location.

The other relevant professional organizations for career development include the American School Counselor Association, American Counseling Association, American College Counseling Association, American Rehabilitation Counseling Association, National Employment Counseling Association, and the Society of Counseling Psychology and its subgroup, Society of Vocational Psychology. These organizations represent different focuses, but each has a focus on one or more aspects of career development. Also, at an international level, the International Association of Educational and Vocational Guidance provides information through their journal, newsletter, and annual conferences.

Career Counseling Competencies

According to NCDA, professionals engaged in career services must demonstrate minimum competencies in 11 areas (National Career Development Association, 2009), which are as follows:

- **Career Development Theory:** Theory base and knowledge considered essential for professionals engaging in career counseling and development

- **Individual and Group Counseling Skills:** Individual and group counseling competencies considered essential for effective career counseling

- **Individual/Group Assessment:** Individual/group assessment skills considered essential for professionals engaging in career counseling

- **Information/Resources:** Information/resource base and knowledge essential for professionals engaging in career counseling

- **Program Promotion, Management, and Implementation:** Skills necessary to develop, plan, implement, and manage comprehensive career development programs in a variety of settings

- **Coaching, Consultation, and Performance Improvement:** Knowledge and skills considered essential in enabling individuals and organizations to impact effectively upon the career counseling and development process

- **Diverse Populations:** Knowledge and skills considered essential in providing career counseling and development processes to diverse populations

- **Supervision:** Knowledge and skills considered essential in critically evaluating counselor performance, maintaining and improving professional skills, and seeking assistance for others when needed in career counseling

- **Ethical/Legal Issues:** Information base and knowledge essential for the ethical and legal practice of career counseling

BOX 1.2
VARIOUS TERMS RELATED TO CAREER DEVELOPMENT

Career:	The course of events constituting a life (Super, 1980); the total constellation of roles played over the course of a lifetime (Herr & Cramer, 1996)
Career Development:	Refers to lifelong psychological and behavioral process as well as a contextual influences shaping one's career over the life span; involves the person's creation of a career pattern, decision-making style, integration of life roles, values expression, and life-role self-concepts (Herr & Cramer, 1996)
Career Development Intervention:	Involves any activities that empower people to cope effectively with career development tasks (Spokane, 1991)
Career Counseling:	Involves a formal relationship in which professional counselors assist a client or group of clients to cope more effectively with career concerns
Career Education:	A systematic effort through academic curriculum that connects classroom learning and the work world to help all students develop knowledge and skills needed for employment and to function in society (Hoyt, 2005)
Career Development Programs:	A systematic program of counselor-coordinated information and experiences designed to facilitate individual career development (Herr & Cramer, 1996, p. 33)
Vocational Guidance:	Specific activities targeted at assisting individuals in making decisions, developing plans, and learning skills to enter into the workforce and implement the plan; 1937 definition by NVGA: the process of assisting individuals to choose an occupation, enter upon it, and progress in it (Super, 1951, p. 92)
Work:	Blustein's (2006) definition: integrated social, psychological and contextual aspects, work as a means for survival and power, for social connection, a means for self-determination (p. 22)
Vocation:	A term used interchangeably with job and occupation but associated with the idea that people are "called" (Isaacson & Brown, 2000)
Job:	A group of similar positions in a single business (Isaacson & Brown, 2000)
Occupation:	A group of similar jobs in several businesses (Isaacson & Brown, 2000)
Life Style and Planning:	Systematic preventions and interventions to help individuals develop a plan that incorporates multiple roles they have at various settings
Career Coaching:	A specific intentional effort to help individuals enter or advance in organizations (Isaacson & Brown, 2000)

- **Research/Evaluation:** Knowledge and skills considered essential in understanding and conducting research and evaluation in career counseling and development
- **Technology:** Knowledge and skills considered essential in using technology to assist individuals with career planning

Meeting these competencies is an ongoing ethical obligation on the part of career professionals, mandating reading current literature, attending training and conferences, and engaging in supervision.

CURRENT STATUS AND FUTURE TRENDS OF CAREER DEVELOPMENT

Changing Workforce

The American population has become increasingly diverse over the last few decades. Immigrants have and will continue to come from diverse countries and regions, rather than from predominantly European counties as a century ago. With the changing demographics of the country, the American workforce also will become even more diverse. The trend of racial and ethnic diversity in the workforce is expected to continue in the next 10 years (Bureau of Labor Statistics, 2016). As the Hispanic population continues to increase at faster rates, so does the group's labor force. BLS projects that the share of Hispanics in the total labor force over the next decade will continue to increase and will make up nearly 20% of the labor force in 2024.

The largest two groups contributing to the diverse workforce are women and ethnic minorities. The number of women in the workforce, particularly the women with school-aged children, changed dramatically from the 1960s to the mid-1990s, and change also occurred in where women worked (DeBell, 2001). Starting in the 1960s, women entered into occupations that had in the past been predominantly held by men. An increasing number of women since civil rights movement in the 1960s hold high-level positions in both business and professional organizations as well as in other arenas such as medicine and law. The income gap between women and men has reduced, but there is still a gap, with women making 82% of men's earning for the same job (Bureau of Labor Statistics, 2017a). The glass ceiling is cracked but not entirely broken yet.

Racial and ethnic minority groups in the United States have a similar history of work experiences as women, often working in low paid, hard-labor jobs with poor working conditions in the past and now moving to more professional jobs. A higher proportion of Hispanic and African American males hold jobs in service and sales than White and Asian American males. Hispanic women have the lowest participation in the labor force than any other ethnic minority group (Bureau of Labor Statistics, 2017a).

Structure and Meaning of Work

At the beginning of the 20th century, the United States experienced a major change in the occupational structure from agricultural dominance to industrial dominance as the result of industrialization and urbanization. In the last decade of the 20th century and now, the first two decades of the 21st century, the U.S. economy has again gone through a substantial change, from manufacturing jobs to service jobs, largely due to the Information Age (DeBell, 2001; Bureau of Labor Statistics, 2017a). As put by DeBell (2001), the majority of the American workforce used to be farmers. They then worked in manufacturing and recently have become clerks. Along with these changes came emergence of some new jobs, for instance, database administrators and many computer- or information-related new job titles; simultaneously, some jobs became obsolete. The changed economic structure was influenced by computer and telecommunication technology advancement, globalization, collapse of many communist states and the rise of American-style capitalism, and domestic deregulations (Whittman, 1999 as cited in DeBell, 2001). These factors changed the American economic structure from manufacturing to service and information provision to the world.

Changes in the work structure have significant impacts on the relationship or meaning associated with work for many people. In the past, one could have a career built upon one occupation and even, in many cases, one job over a life span. In today's work environment, few people can hold one job for their entire adult work life, and the trend is for people to hold many contract-based, freelance-style or project-based jobs, sometimes across various occupations. See Box 1.2 for the definition of *career, occupation,* and *jobs.* One consequence of the changing work structure is loss of job security. When downsizing, reorganization, layoff, and outsourcing become routine daily news, few people are free from the fear of being the next one who could face unemployment. The economic recession in the last 10 years simply worsened the hardship experienced by many average American families. There are few supportive work environments or systems that reward workers' loyalty; instead, workers feel insecure or are overworked due to the loss of colleagues. The meaning of *work* common in the last century is fading. We are losing the aspect of working that, "functions to provide people with a way to establish an identity and a sense of coherence in their social interactions. . . . [and] furnishes at least part of our external identity in the world" (Blustein, 2006, p. 3).

Technology and Social Media

Technological innovation in the last 100 years has had an enormous impact. Originally innovations such as steam engines and automobiles were welcomed because they brought people at a distance together closer and faster. Others such as washing machines and dishwashers were appreciated and sought after because they freed people from laborious duties at home and work. Interestingly enough, the new innovative computer technology created a very different psychological impact on people. On the one hand, those benefits enjoyed at the last technical innovation boom are still there: Automation of almost everything makes banking services and clerical assistance available 24 hours/ 7 days per week, and social media technology connects people across the globe at any time. On the other hand, because of newer technical innovations, many people have lost their jobs or have become isolated or alienated at work settings (Blustein, 2006). It is ironic and perplexing that social media, with the intention and means to bring people closer despite distance, in fact, makes people feel the loss of human connection at work or sometime even at home.

Technology advancement and sophistication have changed not just the human interaction part of work; they have also changed the ways that business is done. Face-to-face communications are greatly reduced and often only used when e-mail or text messaging channels are inoperative. Work from home is possible and becoming more common due to the advancement of information and communication technologies. Osborn Kronholz, Finklea, and Cantonis (2014) added called for technology savvy career intervention practice and summarized functions of available technologies as enhancing decision making, job search, and expanding service delivery. Social media such as Facebook and LinkedIn are used by both job seekers and job hirers. Osborn et al. also raised ethical concerns for professionals to be mindful of, such as access and social equity.

Globalization

Globalization is not just a concept or buzzword in business literature; the consequences of globalization are extensive and far-reaching (Blustein, 2006). Blustein (2006) analyzed the definition of globalization by Friedman (1999), which basically indicated that globalization means the spread of free-market capitalism to everywhere in the world and concluded that competitiveness of economies changed the priority of the organization from the loyalty between worker and organization to the company's viability (remaining competitive). Further he stated that globalization created a labor market without national or linguistic boundaries, therefore, jobs move to wherever high quality and low cost can be accomplished.

Competitiveness and the free market economy in conjunction with technology has led to a growing number of international businesses. Some large multinational corporations with annual profits greater than the gross national products of some countries have the power to create and destroy the local economy (DeBell, 2001). Social cultures, national security, and the environment are all tremendously affected by globalization (DeBell, 2001). "On a more individual level, globalization has created vast pockets of despair and social disengagement" (Blustein, 2006, p. 44).

Multiple Life Roles and Adaptive Roles Across the Life Span

The experience of having one occupation for one's entire life in one organization is probably unknown to younger generations. Because of technology advances and the globalization of the economy, many new jobs are contract and freelance jobs, requiring people to provide the services needed for the company at the time but without longevity or commitment from the employer to the workers. This uncertainty creates stress and harms health. Research has supported the notion that unemployment or underemployment impacts both physical health (Kramer & Chung, 2015) and mental health (Olesen, Butlerworth, Leach, Kelaher, & Pirkis, 2013). The relationship of health and work will be further discussed in Chapter 2.

Gibson and Mitchell (2006) listed seven traditional expectations about work by Americans in the past:

1. America is the land of opportunity.

2. One should enter a career at least as good as, but preferably better than, one's parents.

3. One prepares for and enters into a career choice for life.

4. With honest and hard work, one will advance in one's career.

5. Many careers are more suitable and primarily limited to men and some—a much smaller number—are more suitable and primarily limited to women.

6. The vast majority of available jobs are in the business and industrial sectors.

7. The level of education one achieves is related to level of career opportunities available.

How many of these expectations are still valid remains uncertain. It is assured, though, that one cannot prepare for and enter a career choice for life. What is also certain is that growth employment is in the health care industries and associated occupations (Bureau of Labor Statistics, 2017b). It becomes questionable whether people can do better than their parents as more and more young people are underemployed after graduation from college. That makes the seventh expectation questionable, too.

It is often believed that higher education should lead to jobs or better jobs, but that is not always true, because as stated earlier, many of the available jobs are service oriented, seasonal, or temporary, such as personal care aides or home health aides (the two fastest growing jobs from 2016 to 2026 according to BLS, 2017b), and do not require a four-year college degree. At the same time, a higher percentage of college graduates are underemployed or even unemployed, and this discrepancy between job skill requirements from employers and education/training preparation led to the Career Pathways initiative to address the gap in workforce preparation (Schwartz, 2016).

The changing world of work no longer provides stability; therefore, the challenge for workers is not only to seek a meaningful job but also to find ways to keep themselves mobile and adaptive to new work requirements. "Multiple careers across the life span are now the norm" (Capuzzi & Stauffer, 2006, p. 29). Thus, lifelong learning is now necessary for people to keep up with the changes and to be competitive. Individuals need the skills of mobility, adaptability, flexibility, and transferability in order to be successful in their careers. Career development professionals, accordingly, should expand their roles to effectively help their students and clients (Herr, 2001). Career development professionals need to help clients develop awareness, attitudes, and competencies in planning and managing their careers across the life span. The traditional role of only helping people make career decisions is no longer sufficient in the context of today's world of work. Career decision is only one dimension of career counseling. Counselors can help clients with such tasks as implementation of choices, managing multiple roles at work and home, becoming a

LEARNING ACTIVITY 1.3
MULTIPLE ROLES

Chart your roles at different settings and at different times. Discuss the implications of multiple and adaptive roles across the life span for you as an individual citizen and as a helping professional as well.

lifelong learners, and managing transitions. Life design (Savickas, 2012) approach seems to fit more to the needs of career counseling in the midst of the unpredictable work world. Or in other words, career counseling is an integral part of counseling.

Multiculturalism, Social Justice, and Advocacy

The career development profession has its roots in progressive social reform, out of a need to help youth and new immigrants to find jobs. A century later, the need for career development professionals to help the less fortunate remains the same. And, as the workforce becomes more diverse, there is increasing need for career counselors to become culturally competent.

When envisioning the future of career development practice, Herr (2001) stated the importance of addressing ageism, sexism, racism, and diminished feelings of self-worth and called for career development professionals to help people achieve human dignity. Yes, indeed, human dignity for everyone. To achieve this goal, culturally appropriate career intervention is needed to help individuals. As Leong and Flores (2015) stated, despite the progression in career research, more studies are needed to understand marginalized groups and underserved populations. Counselors are expected by professional code of ethics to advocate for clients' benefits. The various forms of discrimination based on personal characteristics and backgrounds and their impact on one's career development will be discussed in more detail in Chapter 3. Social justice and advocacy were the driving forces of Parsons's work over 100 years ago and continue to be the mission of career intervention in the 21st century.

Summary: Challenges and Opportunities

In today's Information Age, we are overloaded with information and face many unprecedented challenges. These challenges often coexist with opportunities. Although globalization and technology present challenges for workers everywhere, career development professionals have the possibility of turning these challenges to the opportunity to broaden services and roles. Technology can be helpful or hurtful. In other words, everything is relational. Helping people gain awareness of the relational nature of their struggles, develop positive and hopeful perspectives of career paths across the life span, acquire adaptive and transferrable skills to manage their multiple careers, and become advocates for themselves are a few things that career development professionals can do in the future.

Keystone

- The change in our approach to career and vocations came when many unprecedented new jobs emerged as the result of industrialization.

- The long history of career development illustrates the core functions of the career counseling profession: to respond to the social and economic situation, particularly for people who are disadvantaged.

- Frank Parsons laid out the foundations of career counseling that still influence the practice and research today. Parsons's approach aimed at helping people find work that accommodated their abilities and needs.

- Progressive education, development of standardized testing, and legislation had great impacts on the evolution of vocational guidance.

- The merger of professional organizations, publications about career-related information and practice, and necessary services for veterans after WWII led to the establishment of career counseling as a specialty and profession.

- The focus of career counseling is no longer a job placement; instead, it is broadened to help individuals develop self-understanding and engage in a satisfying work and life across the life span.

- Career development professionals work in various settings, including K-12 schools, colleges, government and nonprofit agencies, private practices, the military, and businesses.

- The changing workforce and occupational structure, advancement of technology and social media, globalization of the economy, and the need for multicultural competency and social justice have significant impacts on people's life and work, resulting in people having multiple and adaptive life roles across the life span.

Additional Resources

American Counseling Association: http://www.counseling.org

American School Counselor Association: https://www.schoolcounselor.org

Bureau of Labor Statistics: http://www.bls.gov

CACREP: http://www.cacrep.org/template/index.cfm

International Association of Educational and Vocational Guidance: http://iaevg.net/

NCDA: http://associationdatabase.com/aws/NCDA/pt/sp/guidelines

National Board of Certified Counselors: http://www.nbcc.org

Society of Vocational Psychology: https://www.div17svp.org

U.S. Department of Labor: http://www.dol.gov

U. S. Bureau of Census: http://www.census.gov

References

Betz, N. E., & Hackett, G. (1981). The relationship of career-related self-efficacy expectations to perceived career options in college women and men. *Journal of Counseling Psychology*, *28*, 399-410.

Blustein, D. L. (2006). *The psychology of working: A new perspective to career development, counseling and public policy*. Mahwah, NJ: Lawrence Erlbaum Associates.

Bureau of Labor Statistics, U.S. Department of Labor. (2016). Hispanics will make up nearly 20 percent of the labor force in 2024. *Ted: The Economics Daily*. Retrieved from https://www.bls.gov/opub/ted/2016/

hispanics-will-make-up-nearly-20-percent-of-the-labor-force-in-2024.htm.

Bureau of Labor Statistics, U.S. Department of Labor. (2017a). A look at women's education and earnings since the 1970s. *TED: The Economics Daily.* Retrieved from https://www.bls.gov/opub/ted/2017/a-look-at-womens-education-and-earnings-since-the-1970s.htm.

Bureau of Labor Statistics. (2017b). *Employment projections—2016-26 USDL-1429.* Retrieved from www.bls.gov/emp.

Bureau of Labor Statistics. (n.d.). *Revising the standard occupational classification system.* Retrieved from https://www.bls.gov/soc/socrpt929.pdf.

Brewer, J. M. (1942). *History of vocational guidance.* New York, NY: Harper.

Capuzzi, D., & Stuffer, M. D. (2006). *Career counseling: Foundations, perspectives, and applications.* Boston, MA: Allyn and Bacon.

Cook, E. P., Heppner, M. J., & O'Brien, K. M. (2002). Career development of women of color and white women: Assumptions, conceptualization, and interventions from an ecological perspective. *Career Development Quarterly, 50,* 291-304.

Council for Accreditation of Counselor and Related Educational Program. (2016). *2016 Standards.* Retrieved from http://www.cacrep.org/for-programs/2016-cacrep-standards.

DeBell, C. (2001). Ninety years in the world of work in America. *Career Development Quarterly, 50,* 77-88.

Dewey, J. (1916). *Democracy and education: An introduction to philosophy of education.* New York, NY: Macmillan.

Friedman, T. L. (1999). *The Lexus and the olive tree: Understanding globalization.* New York, NY: Farrar, Strauss, & Giroux.

Gibson, R. L., & Mitchell, M. H. (2006). *Introduction to career counseling for the 21st century.* Upper Saddle River, NJ: Pearson Merrill Prentice Hall.

Hansen, L. S. (1997). *Integrative life planning—Critical tasks for career development and changing life patterns.* San Francisco, CA: Jossey-Bass.

Herr, E. L. (2001). Career development and its practice: A historical perspective. *Career Development Quarterly, 49,* 196-211.

Herr, E. L., & Cramer, S. H. (1996). *Career guidance and counseling through the life span: Systematic approaches* (5th ed.). New York, NY: HarperCollins.

Herr, E. L., & Shahanasarian, M. (2001). Selected milestones in the evolution of career development practices in the twentieth century. *Career Development Quarterly, 49,* 225-232.

Holland, J. L. (1985). *Making vocational choices: A theory of vocational personalities and work environments* (2nd ed.). Englewood Cliffs, NJ: Prentice Hall.

Hoyt, K. B. (2005). *Career education: History and future.* Tulsa, OK: National Career Development Association.

Hoyt, K. B., Evans, R. N., Mackin, E. F., & Mangum, G. L. (1972). *Career education: What it is and how to do it* (2nd ed). Salt Lake City, UT: Olympus.

Isaacson, L. E., & Brown, D. (2000). *Career information, career counseling and career development* (7th ed.). Boston, MA: Allyn & Bacon.

Kettunen, J., Vuorinen, R., & Sampson, J. P. J. (2015). Practitioners' experiences of social media in career services. *The Career Development Quarterly*, *63*(3), 268-281. 10.1002/cdq.12018

Kramer, A., & Chung, W. (2015). Work demands, family demands, and BMI in dual-earners families: A 16-year longitudinal study. *Journal of Applied Psychology*, doi:10.1037/a0038634.

Krumboltz, J. D. (1976). A social learning theory of career choice. *Counseling Psychologists*, *6*, 71-80.

Lent, R. W., Brown, S. D., & Hackett, G. (1994). Toward a unifying social cognitive theory of career and academic interest, choice ad performance. *Journal of Vocational Behavior*, *45*, 79-122.

Leong, F. T. L. (1995). *Career development and vocational behavior of racial and ethnic minorities*. Hillsdale, NJ: Erlbaum.

Leong, F. L., & Flores, L. Y. (2015). Career interventions with racial and ethnic minority clients. In P. J. Hartung, M. L. Savickas, W. B. Walsh, P. J. (Eds.), *APA handbook of career intervention: Vol. 1. Foundations* (pp. 225-242). Washington, DC: American Psychological Association. doi:10.1037/14438-013

National Career Development Association. (2009). *Career counseling competencies*. Retrieved from https://www.ncda.org/aws/NCDA/pt/sd/news_article/37798/_self/layout_ccmsearch/true.

National Career Development Association. (2015). *2015 NCDA code of ethics*. Retrieved from https://www.ncda.org/aws/NCDA/asset_manager/get_file/3395.

Niles, S. G., & Harris-Bowlsbey, J. (2002). *Career development interventions in the 21st century*. Upper Saddle River, NJ: Pearson Merrill Prentice Hall.

Olesen, S. C., Butterworth, P., Leach, L. S., Kelaher, M., & Pirkis, J. (2013). Mental health affects future employment as job loss affects mental health: Findings from a longitudinal population study. *BMC Psychiatry*. Retrieved from http://www.biomedcentral.com/1471-244X/13/144.

Osborn, D. S., Kronholz, J. F., Finklea, J. T., & Cantonis, A. M. (2014). Technology savvy career counseling. *Canadian Psychology*, *55*, 258-265.

Parsons, F. (1909). *Choosing a vocation*. Boston, MA: Houghton-Mifflin.

Pope, M. (2000). A brief history of career counseling in the United States. *Career Development Quarterly*, *48*, 194-211.

Pope, M. (2015). Career intervention: From the industrial to the digital age. In P. J. Hartung, M. L. Savickas, W. B. Walsh, P. J. Hartung, M. L. Savickas, & W. B. Walsh (Eds.), *APA handbook of career intervention: Vol. 1. Foundations* (pp. 3-19). Washington, DC: American Psychological Association.10.1037/14438-001.

Savickas, M. L. (2012). Life design: A paradigm for career intervention in the 21st century. *Journal of Counseling and Development*, *90*, 13-19.

Savickas, M. L., Pope, M., & Niles, S. G. (2011). The career development quarterly: A centennial retrospective. *Career Development Quarterly*, *59*, 528-538.

Schwartz, R. B. (2016). The Career pathways movement: A Promising strategic for increasing opportunities and mobility. *Journal of Social Issues*, *72*, 740-759. doi: 10.1111/josi.12192

Spokane, A. R. (1991). *Career intervention.* Englewood, NJ: Prentice Hall.

Super, D. E. (1951). Vocational adjustment: Implementing a self-concept. *Occupations, 30,* 88-92.

Super, D. E. (1957). *The psychology of careers.* New York, NY: Harper & Row.

Super, D. E. (1980). A life-span, life-space, approach to career development. *Journal of Vocational Behavior, 16,* 292-298.

Tang, M., & Erford, B. T. (2010). History of school counseling. In B. T. Erford (Ed.), *Handbook of school counseling, theory, programs, and practices* (2nd ed., pp. 9-22). Austin, TX: Pro-ED.

Zunker, V. G. (2002). *Career counseling: Applied concepts of life planning* (6th ed.). Pacific Grove, CA: Brooks/Cole.

Zytowski, D. G. (1972). Four hundred years before parsons. *Personnel and Guidance Journal, 50*(6), 443.

Zytowski, D. G. (2001). Frank Parsons and the progressive movement. *Career Development Quarterly, 50,* 57-65.

WORK IN GLOBAL CONTEXT

After introducing the history and current status of career development and intervention in the last chapter, it is necessary to discuss several pertinent issues to further understand why it is important to understand career development of individuals and why counselors need to gain knowledge and skills in career intervention. What does work mean to individuals? How is work related to a person's self-concepts and life in general? What factors have a significant impact on individuals' career development? There may not be readily available consensus in the answers to these questions; however, presenting various views and updated research findings to these questions assists us to gain better understanding what kind of role work plays in our lives and how it influences our well-being. Thus, this chapter will explore these fundamental issues from both historical and cross-cultural perspectives and present a synthesis of how work is related to individuals' self-concepts, life roles, and health in the global context.

LEARNING OBJECTIVES

After completing the reading and exercises provided in this chapter, you will be able to:

- describe the meaning of work across historical contexts and various cultures,

- recognize the relationship between the global economy and the changing work environment,

- explain the relationship between work and health,

- identify the interrelatedness of work and family roles,

- examine the personal and contextual factors influencing career development,

- develop an integrated view of career development in the diverse and changing work world, and

- apply an ecological career counseling perspective to career intervention for personal growth and change.

MEANING OF WORK

Defining *work* is not as easy as it seems to be. Does work have to be paid or compensated? Is taking care of family members without pay considered work? How about volunteering work? The definition of *work* is probably different for different people at different times. Back in the early days when women did not have the right to vote or work outside of the home, women might not have been compensated for their contribution to taking care of family members and house chores, but would their share of the family responsibilities have been considered work? It seems that we need to define work first before discussing the meaning of work.

Definition of Work and Related Terms

"What do you do for a living?" "Where do you work?" and "What kind of job do you have now?" are typical questions asked when people try to get acquainted at social occasions. Occupation is a popular item as part of the demographic background on almost any survey. These questions solicit the information about one's occupation, and the expected responses imply information such as social status, income level, and educational background. Therefore, the terms *work*, *job*, and *occupation* are used in daily life interchangeably to indicate one's employment status. In Chapter 1, we provided definitions of these terms without much elaboration. The following definitions provide more discussion from the perspective of how these terms are conceptualized in the discourse of career development.

> *Job*—an activity people do to satisfy basic needs, for instance, to pay the bills so that people can support themselves and families for a living. A job requires certain qualifications, or otherwise, the employer would not be satisfied with the performance, so paid employment is the core of *job*.

> *Occupation*—occupation is a title given to a type of job that a group of people share. In other words, the nature of the job is similar, the entry requirements are the same, and the occupation can be across different organizations and settings.

> *Work*—an activity people do to satisfy multiple needs of life; can be paid or unpaid, but with a purpose to produce something. David Jepsen (2013) listed three hallmark qualities of work: (1) work involves purposeful effort; (2) work requires skills and talent; and (3) work yields a lasting product (p. 24). From this perspective, work is certainly more than a paid employment although it can be one's employment. Blustein said, "working involves effort, activity and human energy in given tasks that contribute to the overall and economic welfare of a given culture. This includes paid employment as well as work that one does in caring for others within one's family and community" (p. 3).

Therefore, *job* and *occupation* can be conceptualized as the terms to mean paid work one does, while *work* may be paid or unpaid and can be either in employment settings or at home. Work provides more than just financial compensation; it provides a purpose of life for people, or it provides meaning of one's deeds that may satisfy multiple dimensions for individuals. The next sections will review the meaning of work from both historical and cross-cultural perspectives.

Meaning of Work From Historical Perspectives

Most people agree that work and one's identity are closely connected in the modern world; however, this connection has only existed for a little over one hundred years, as people began to have a choice in regard to occupation. Before the Industrial Revolution at the end of the 19th century, people were identified not by their occupation, but rather, by their last name or residence or class (Niles & Harris-Bowlsbey, 2013). The classification of occupation emerged only after more jobs become available as a result of urbanization and industrialization. For centuries, people inherited their family's tradition of making a living, whether it was farm work or craftsmanship. Niles and Harris-Bowlsbey (2013) also stated that in classical societies, one worked for survival and that work was viewed as a curse as it involved hard labor. Therefore, the association of work and individual identity was not warranted.

One important influence on the meaning of work is the Christian belief that work is a will of God to help the less fortunate and for spiritual purification. This tradition has dominated Western civilization for a long time until the Reformation initiated by John Calvin. The predestation of Calvin's doctrine has influenced the meaning of work to be shifted to success oriented (Niles and Harris-Bowlsbey, 2013). In other words, working hard to pursue upward mobility is accepted as the norm and morally justified. This value was known as "Protestant work ethic," which emphasized diligence, independent effort, and self-sufficiency as virtuous. Prior to big corporations emerging as the result of industrialization, people worked for themselves, and personal and family needs could be met usually through their own work. Savickas (2013) referred to this kind of value as "vocational ethic." In contrast, once people migrated to urban cities and worked for organized companies, self-sufficiency was no longer valued; instead, climbing the corporate ladder became expected for successful workers. According to Savickas, this change from working for oneself to working for hierarchical organizations set the discourse of the "career ethic" in the 20th century. People strive to move up the corporate ladder and reach tenure within the organization. One's occupational status therefore defines one's identity as well.

The link between work and one's worth, a commonly accepted social norm that still dominates the 21st century, is another important aspect of meaning associated with work since the end of the 19th century. The kind of work individuals do indicates their social identity and economic status. In other words, one's work or occupation is a reference for others to judge his or her socioeconomic status. Work was often associated with success, good character, and hard work when dual bonding (i.e., loyalty to each other and taking care of each other's needs) from employers and employees was still available (Gibson & Mitchell, 2006). However, as stability of work is no longer a common phenomenon, people have less control over their careers, and they may involuntarily have to frequently change jobs.

In such a situation, the centrality of work in one's life as well as the link between work and self-worth create a stressful situation as people without work experiences not only experience a loss of financial security but also harmed self-esteem and identity (Herr, Cramer, & Niles, 2004). Thus, it is necessary to examine the meaning of work to individuals from a contextual perspective.

In the modern society, working functions to provide people with a way to establish an identity and as sense of coherence in their social interactions and furnishes part of their external identity in the world (Blustein, 2006). Blustein (2006) further stated that working has very personal meaning that is influenced to a great extent by individual constructions and by socially mediated interactions with others. Working has been one of the constants in our lives. According to Blustein, work serves several psychological functions: (a) it provides means to survival and power; (b) it provides means for people to build social connections and interpersonal relationships; and (c) it provides a means to achieve self-determination, regardless of whether the motivation is intrinsically or extrinsically driven. In summary, work fulfills economic functions, survival needs, and sociological functions and provides individuals with a means of fulfilling needs for connection, achievement, structure, and purpose.

It is human nature to search for meaning, and people need to have a purpose for living and to get answers to the following questions for themselves: Who am I? Where do I stand in these many relationships? What is my worth? Do I make a difference? Guevara and Ord (1996) stated that these questions basically reflect the three types of meaning that work can provide to people. One is a sense of belonging; work provides a social network for people. How many people have social relationships with coworkers or build social connections through work? The answer to this question probably provides a glimpse of people's social lives. Another way to understand how work plays such an important role in one's social life is to calculate the percentage of his or her friends that are known through work relationships and how much of one's time is spent with colleagues. For some people, work provides the only means of interpersonal connection (Blustein, 2006). Similarly, Goldsmith (1995) asserted that people have a need for endorsement or social acceptance and that work provides an avenue to satisfy this need. The second meaning associated to work noted by Guevara and Ord is that people find or establish their self-concept through work. In other words, through one's work, one can find an answer to the question "Who am I?" Many career development theories (See Chapters 4 and 5) actually view work as the outlet of self-concept. People often feel more satisfied with work if they find their values and interests are rewarded through their work. In a sense, if work provides an opportunity for us to fully satisfy our needs and implement self-concept, we find the purpose for going to work and the meaning of why we work, beyond making ends meet. The third aspect of meaning given to work is a sense of worth, or in other words, the sense of making a difference or impact on this world. This sense of making a difference in this world is similar to human nature of wanting to leave a legacy or the desire to see one's worth. The work produces an outcome or product, which in essence provides a sense of making a contribution for the benefit of society. For example, a grandma at age 85 is much happier when she can do some sewing jobs for her children or grandchildren. Knowing this, her children find some alterations or repairs for her do, even though they don't actually need these jobs completed. However, this work gives the grandma fulfillment when she thinks or feels her work is useful to others. Finding a position in relation to the outside world, making connections with others, and contributing to the common good of society also reflect social identity and social gratification individuals can achieve through work (Goldsmith, 1995).

To some people, the meaning of work is their response to *calling*. A *calling* was traditionally referred to as being called by God to serve. In modern times, a *calling* is defined as work that is motivated by a divine drive to integrate one's work with some overall purpose or meaningfulness of life (Dik & Duffy, 2009). People often feel much joy when they find their calling, and finding one's calling means that one's personal characteristics can be applied to work that benefits the common good of society (Block & Richmond, 1997). Similarly, the spirituality of work has gained much attention in recent years because many people feel a loss of self at work and like to find an integration of spirituality in the workplace. Research has found that for those people who felt a calling in their work, the subjective and self-referred criteria were more salient than external criteria set by others (Heslin, 2005). This finding illustrates the importance of having a sense of meaning in work.

Work, for most people, first satisfies the needs of survival; once the survival needs are accommodated, people need to find purpose and meaning in work to feel motivated and inspired. Work, therefore, provides direction, meaning, relationships, and identity for individuals. The trend in work went from having no choice (in the agricultural economy), to choosing an occupation (during industrial context), to finding meaning in work (postmodern time). This evolution accounted for the relationship between people and work in the United States and many Western cultures.

Meaning of Work From Cross-Cultural Perspective

The meaning of work exhibits variability across different times, geographic locations, and social strata (Hall & Mirvis, 1996). If there is one common feature of work across different cultures, it might be supporting oneself and family to live when basic living has to be supported through work. In other words, when survival is still a challenge, making ends meet is what work should and needs to be. Beyond satisfying survival needs, the meaning of work is subjective perception; therefore, the sociocultural context in which people live and work inevitably influences how work is viewed and its implications to people. Work then has a unique meaning that is derived from and embedded within specific cultural contexts and is shaped by individual experiences of working.

Social, economic, and political structure changes all impact the meaning of work or attribution to work experiences (Ardichvili & Kuchinke, 2009). For instance, in Russia, the centrality of work was less important during the economically stable period and became increasingly critical post breakdown of the Soviet Union when the economy underwent transition. Another example is the reunited Germany where the meaning of work shifted from a duty-bound morality to an individualistic value orientation. These kinds of changing implications of work to individuals were the result of changing socioeconomic contexts. When everyone was assigned a job in the state planning economy (e.g., in former Soviet Union and China before economic reform), choice and autonomy was limited, which led people to view work more as a duty and responsibility than self-fulfillment. Similarly, individuals in a collectivism-oriented culture often feel more responsibility to contribute the family or group interests rather than personal satisfaction.

Even in the same socioeconomic environment, people from various cultural backgrounds or socioeconomic statuses may experience working differently, and therefore their perception of work is different. When people have no or limited choices, like some new immigrants in the United States or people without a lot of resources (e.g., education, support from family, network), work provides a means to satisfy basic human needs. Thus, the meanings of work, such as identity or purposefulness as discussed previously, may or may not be endorsed by people in this situation.

LEARNING ACTIVITY 2.1

Divide the class into an even number of groups, and then give each group a different task. Even-numbered group members will respond to the question "If I win $10 million in the lottery, will I quit my job?" Odd-numbered group members will role play as cocktail party attendees, and each member can choose anybody they want to be (including themselves), and at the end, the group will discuss what information they are interested in knowing about others and what information they feel comfortable sharing.

A multinational study on the meaning of work (Meaning of Work International Research Team, 1987) examined the centrality of work in Belgium, Britain, China, Germany, Hong Kong, Israel, Japan, Netherlands, the United States, and Yugoslavia and found that the importance of centrality of work is much higher in China, Japan, and Hong Kong than European countries except Yugoslavia, which was in the middle range along with the United States and Israel. The data also showed that among six valued work outcomes, *Income* was ranked first for all locations. China is the only country ranking *Serving the Society* second and *Interesting and Satisfying* the sixth, which was almost the reversed order for other locations (Westwood & Lok, 2003). It is noted that the MOWIRT data was collected in the mid-1980s and that a lot of changes have occurred in the world economy since then. These changes in some regions, for example in China, were dramatic and significantly influenced people's lives; therefore, it is unknown whether the same pattern of valued work outcome would still exist.

The meaning attributed to work varies depending on social, economic, political, and cultural context. As the work economy is increasingly globalized, the impact of the changing global economy is worthy of examination. The next section will discuss the occupational structure change in global context and a changing work environment.

WORK AND GLOBAL CHANGING ECONOMY

Traditional work is typically geographically specified and time restricted. In other words, your work setting can be described as Ames, Iowa, or Bangkok, Thailand. Your work schedule is 7 to 3 or 9 to 5, depending on whether you work as a school teacher or office worker. However, in today's world, one might work from home in Ames, Iowa, but for a company with its main office in London, England, and further, one does not have a set schedule from 9 to 5 but rather works whenever it fits the time allowance of colleagues in a global setting. The changing occupational structure, advancement of technology, and globalized economy make this scenario possible.

Changing Occupational Structure on Global Context

For the last two decades, the United States, as well as the world, has witnessed significant changes in occupational trends, with some jobs phasing out and new jobs surfacing on a very fast pace. Being employed in the post office was considered, for a long time, to be secure, as it is almost a lifelong guaranteed job. However, post office service clerk is one of the fastest declining jobs in the United States according to the labor statistics of the U.S. Bureau of Labor Statistics (2017). The other fastest or largest declining occupations are related to machine operation, textile fields, switch board operator, farmers, data entry, and word processing typists. The recently published employment projection for 2016-2026 by the Bureau of Labor Statistics (2017) revealed that health care and associated occupations accounted for a larger share of new jobs and are on a rising trend. Occupations with faster than average employment growth include personal care and service occupations, community and social service occupations, and computer and mathematical occupations. Of the fastest growing occupations, 18 require some level of postsecondary education for entry. It becomes apparent that the diminishing jobs are all being replaced by technology innovations; in other words, what used to be done by humans can now be more efficiently done by machines or computers.

Technology advancement and globalization are the main reasons for occupational structural change. Outsourcing has become a household term in the new millennium. Outsourcing is an example of globalization but also another example of the impact of technology. With information technology, a customer service call from the United States can be answered by a contract worker in the Philippines. In the late 20th century, many manufacturing jobs were moved from the United States to developing countries in South America or Asia. An occupational growth projection in 1999 stated that the fastest growing occupations for the future were computer engineers, computer support specialists, database administration, data processing, equipment repairs, desktop publishing specialists, medical assistants, paralegals, and personal care and health aides (Bureau of Labor Statistics, 1999). The top five were all jobs related to application of computer science and engineering. Almost 20 years later in 2017, a computer-related occupation is still on the top of the list of fastest growing occupations, but at the ninth place, and it is software developer. The top 10 fastest growing occupations are in new technology (solar photovoltraic, wind turbine service technician), health care (e.g., personal care aides, home health aide), and data analysis and management (statistician, mathematician) (Bureau of Labor Statistics, 2017). The reasons for this change could be due to the aging population (need for health care), and these health care and service jobs cannot be outsourced because they require geographic proximity. One cannot have someone across the ocean aid a senior for bathing, for instance. The projected increase in jobs in data analysis and management is largely due to emerging needs of using big data for business decisions and services.

The shift of growth in manufacturing occupations to technology jobs and then to health and service-related jobs in the last five decades in the United States reflects the structural change in the economy, as result of technology and a globalized market and society (Andersen & Vandehey, 2012). Consider two of the most well-known products of the United States: iPhone and Hollywood movies. The production of both involves multinational professionals across the globe. However, outsourcing, downsizing, and corporate mergers have created unprecedented challenges for workers, as with the changes come the instability. The impact of instability on individuals will be illustrated in the later part of this chapter.

CASE ILLUSTRATION 2.1
JOSHUA AND SOPHIA

Joshua Wright, a 46-year-old White male, worked in a large equipment manufacturing company for close to 23 years. He started as an engineer, and then became a project manager, and then a sales manager. Five years after he began working for the company, he started an MBA program, and the company paid 90% of his tuition. At the beginning of the new millennium, he was assigned to work in South America as the regional director. He met his second wife there. Joshua and his wife moved back to the United States after working in South America for four years. Joshua could not find an appropriate position within the company. There were not a lot of higher level managerial positions available, and he seemed overqualified or even "outdated" for engineering jobs. He became a project manager again, but he often felt unsatisfied because he did not think his skills and experience were fully used. He started to consider finding a different job and did not mind relocation. Sophia, his wife, was native speaker of Spanish and had a college degree in literature. She tutored students in Spanish for some time, but she couldn't find a full-time job with health care coverage. Joshua has to stay in his project manager position because his family needs the medical insurance. Then, a headhunter approached Joshua and asked him if he was interested in working for a computer hardware manufacturing company as the sales director. The position did not require relocation but did require extensive travel both domestically and internationally, which meant that he would not be home for most of the time, sometimes including holidays because of the different holiday schedules in other countries. Joshua and Sophia had two teenage children, and they lived in a city where they didn't have other family members nearby (Sophia's family is in South America). Joshua took the position

because (1) it was a position that could provide him opportunity to fully use his abilities, which would make him happier; (2) it provided a higher income and fringe benefits, plus the perks related to being a frequent flyer provided by airlines and hotels; and (3) it also provided an opportunity for career advancement. Joshua worked in this position for six years, then, at age 52, he lost his job due to the company being purchased by another company from Europe and the international sector was totally reorganized and consolidated with the new parent company. Joshua tried very hard to find a new job but to no avail. Meanwhile, Sophia began receiving more requests for her tutoring work. She tutored not only high school and college students who took Spanish classes, but her largest group of clients was actually adults who wanted to learn the language, either for personal enrichment or for advancing careers. Many of her adult students told her that proficiency in Spanish could help them get a job or a better job. Sophia thought maybe it was the time for her to look for a full-time job.

Discussion Questions

1. How would you describe Joshua's career path in relation to globalization? What are advantages and disadvantages of the global economy for Joshua and his family?

2. What would you have recommended Joshua do when he was laid off from his second employer?

3. Would you suggest Sophia look for a new full-time job? Or, would you recommend she maintain the same flexible, part-time tutoring job and encourage Joshua to find a similar job to what he did before? What are the reasons for your recommendation?

Changing Workplace

Technology and globalization did not simply have an impact on the patterns of occupations shifting from industrial to service; the workforce is becoming more divers than ever, too. Since the early 1960s, more women and racial/ethnic minority members have entered the workforce, and the participation rate by diverse groups in the labor force is increasing. According to the Bureau of Labor Statistics (2017), the labor force continues to change in racial and ethnic composition with the percentage Asian and Hispanic workers growing much faster than the average; workers of Hispanic origin are expected to make up about 1 out of 5 workers in 2026. In addition, despite the forthcoming big wave of retirement of baby boomers, more workers actually postpone retirement for various reasons. Some delay retirement due to financial situations, as the economic crisis in 2008 adversely affected many people's pension plans and retirement investments, and some push back the timeline of retirement because they still enjoy the fulfillment that work brings them. In some cases, particularly in the declining fields, there are simply not enough qualified young people to fill the positions. The diverse workforce is also a result of globalization (e.g., cooperate mergers, outsourcing) with people representing different countries of origin, languages, religions, ethnicities, and other aspects of culture in one workplace. The diversity issues of career development and intervention will be further analyzed in Chapter 3.

Change is also occurring in work styles because of the technology availability and diverse workforce. An example is flexible work hours, due to various time zones and working from home. The Internet makes work more mobile and accessible to people. A teacher can grade her students' assignment via an online platform even when she is at a Virginia beach and her students are in California. The younger generation workers bring a very different style to work settings, as they are more technology savvy and used to instant gratification. A *60 Minutes* episode, "The Millennials Are Coming," reported that companies need to hire consultants to train new millennial employees to learn the basics of being a professional while at the same time training managers to work with millennials who grew up with the belief that they are special and can do anything they want. For younger generation workers, their priority is not necessarily work, as their parents or boomers have chosen; instead, they choose their lifestyle and friends as their priority.

The demand of work performance is also changing, as the result of the occupational trend change from manufacturing to technology to service. Traditional skills such as memory, typing, and mechanical abilities are no longer as valued as before because volumes of information can be easily searched on the Internet in one click. It is more important to know how to locate and navigate the information than remembering the information. Thirty years ago, a secretary needed skills in typing and dictating; today, a secretary needs to be able use computer software for word processing, spreadsheets, and databases well to qualify for the work. No office workers today can survive without using e-mail. Communication is essential in work settings considering the diverse workforce, multidisciplinary approach often required to solve problems, and distant locations of colleagues.

The changes in economy, work settings, workforce, and work styles signal the constant need for learning new skills to keep up with change. The interconnectedness of a global market shaped the structure of economies to be interdependent; therefore, one event at a region could cause a series of events in many nations. The uncertainty could negatively impact individuals' sense of safety and emotional status. The following section will explain the relationship between work and health.

WORK AND HEALTH

The relationship between work and health is complex and multidimensional. The World Health Organization (WHO) defines health as "complete physical, mental, and social well-being and not merely the absence of disease or infirmity" (World Health Organization, n.d.). What role does work play in achieving such-defined health? How does health impact one's work? Or verse versa, how does work impact one's health? It is commonly understood that one needs good health to perform work duties. In fact, poor health conditions, or limiting physical and mental health, negatively affects individuals' likelihood of being employed (Pacheco, Page, & Webber, 2014). On the other hand, work demands and conditions can also affect individuals' overall health (Kramer & Chung, 2015; Oginska-Bulik, 2005).

Work and Physical Health

In the modern work world, almost everyone feels stressed and tired regardless of what kind of occupations they have. Think of yourself as an example. When was the last time that you felt relaxed, energetic, and full of creative ideas that you wanted to try at work? The high demand for efficiency and productivity in work settings in the 21st century means that everyone needs to be held accountable for achieving efficiency and productivity. As a result, many workers have to work long hours to keep up with the demand. Another factor for people putting in more work hours is the increased or higher cost of living. Many people need to work more than one job to make ends meet, which means they need to work longer hours. Longer work hours means that there is less time to take care of one's other needs, for example, sleep time, interaction time with family and friends, and leisure activities. Research has found that longer work hours were likely to elevate body mass index (BMI) over time (Kramer & Chung, 2015). It is no surprise then that one's health could be compromised if work leads to deprivation of a healthy lifestyle.

The relationship between work and physical health is certainly not a one-way direction. Just as longer time and higher demands at work can potentially create stress and negatively affect health, unemployment or underemployment was found by the researches to be harmful to physical health (Anderson & Winefield, 2011). Losing jobs means interruption of steady income and possibly health insurance through the employer. Underemployment created uncertainty to individuals as well because of inability to provide sufficient resources. The issues as result of unemployment or underemployment, such as financial security, sense of identity, and connection to the others, can be overwhelming for people. The researchers found that both unemployment and underemployment are strongly associated with unhealthy behaviors, particularly with drinking (Anderson & Winefield, 2011). The cutback of healthy behavior (exercise) and the surge of risky behavior (binge drinking) can increase the likelihood of chronic illnesses such as hypertension, diabetes, and mental health.

Physical health is not only related to the loss of a job or inadequate employment but also to people who are working as well. Specifically, it seems that cardiovascular disease and digestive ulcers were commonly found among people who have job-related stress or job misfit (Faragher, Cass, & Cooper, 2005; Siegrist, 1996). It is interesting to note that the correlation between cardiovascular disease seems more robust with people who feel that they have made great efforts but received fewer rewards. This could be an indication of interrelationship between mental health and physical health. As people feel less recognized or rewarded for their hard work, stress or negative feelings could impact their physical health. Job characteristics can affect one's physical health as well. For instance, a common understanding (perhaps a stereotype also) is that people working in manufacturing or other labor-intensive occupations tend to drink and smoke more often. Some researchers did find differences between workers in different fields in regard to risky behaviors and health conditions; that is, workers with more people interaction and responsibility for others' welfare were more likely to have hypertension and reduced risk of drinking (Alterman et al., 2008). On the other hand, physical health status can impact work performance. Fatigue can impair one's function. A meta-analysis of the relationship between job performance and one's overall health indicated that somatic complaints, high blood pressure, and obesity all negatively impacted employees' task performance either by self-reported evaluation or supervisors' ranking (Ford, Cerasoli, Higgins, & Decesare, 2011). Ford et al. (2011) further explained that high blood pressure had the most consistent negative impact on task performance compared to the other physical symptoms.

Work and Mental Health

As stated earlier, as physical and mental health are interrelated, it is not surprising then that an association between work and mental health exists as well. The relationship between mental health and employment status is, however, reciprocal, meaning mental health issues can be risk factors for unemployment but can also be the consequences of unemployment or underemployment (Olesen, Butterworth, Leach, Kelaher, & Pirkis, 2013). Many studies have found that loss of jobs or inadequate employment resulted in depression, anxiety, and increased drinking and drug abuse (Faragher et al., 2005; Mossakowski, 2008; Oginska-Bulik, 2005; Tsutsumi, Kayaba, Theorell, & Siegrist, 2001). Further, people with full-time employment had lower levels of stress and depressive symptoms, had healthier eating habits, exercised more, and consumed less alcohol or cigarettes (Rosenthal, Carroll-Scott, Earnshaw, Santilli, & Ickovics, 2012). These research findings provided support to the concept discussed earlier in this chapter about the centrality of work to individuals' lives and identities. Therefore, unemployment is even more detrimental to one's mental health than physical health. Some researchers have argued that the impact of losing a job bears similarities to one going through grief process (Herr, 1989). Unemployment and underemployment not only affect mental health of individuals but also families and communities (Pedulla & Newman, 2011).

Work performance is another area that has been examined for its association with psychological well-being. An old cliché, "Happy workers are more productive," is actually true in reality. Ford et al. (2011) verified that psychological well-being is more strongly related to work performance than physical health. Their findings based on meta-analysis of multiple studies found that depression, anxiety, and fatigue were negatively correlated to work performance and that life satisfaction is positively related to work performance. According to Ford et al., work performance is impaired probably because poor psychological health leads to cognitive deficits—for example, memory problems, learning, and executive functioning—typically required at work. Neglecting mental health then can jeopardize work productivity. Even more challenging is the invisibility of mental health disorders perceived in the workplace, resulting in a lack of support or intervention (Denman, 2015).

LEARNING ACTIVITY 2.2

Ask students to design a work environment they think would help workers feel happy and productive. Then, review the elements they included in their designs, and discuss why these elements are important to have for a satisfying work environment. The design should be comprehensive, in other words, the work environment is not limited to physical environment or work settings; it should also include policies and procedures to make workers perform to their best.

If work performance is more of a concern for employers, job satisfaction certainly is more of an individual concern and mission of career counselors. A satisfying job gives people a sense of happiness and fulfillment. Too often we have witnessed the same individual presents totally different attitudes about life and himself or herself when his or her job situation changes. For instance, a woman who enjoys interacting with people and fashion design was miserable when she worked at a printing factory where she had to wear a uniform and performed repeated tasks on a machine daily with minimum communication with coworkers. The same woman changed jobs and became a sales clerk in the woman's department of a department store, and she figuratively glowed at work and home. Unsatisfying jobs can lead to several mental health disorders, including depression, anxiety, and low self-esteem (Edwards & Rothbard, 1999; Faragher et al., 2005; Oginska-Bulik, 2005; Tsutsumi et al., 2001). A variety of situations at work settings may contribute to one's lack of job satisfaction. Misfit of the personal characteristics and job requirements can make people feel less satisfied, just as the woman who worked in a printing factory, illustrated earlier. If the job demands are high, yet the rewards are not, people may feel unsatisfied. If people work in an environment with no or low autonomy, they tend to feel less satisfied, as their sense of independence and control is not accommodated.

The complex and reciprocal relationship between mental health and work may require workers be aware of work-related stress or anxiety. In order to alleviate work-related stress and anxiety, in addition to being attentive to work schedules, workloads, and time balance, it is also important to seek support from families, colleagues, and supervisors. Relationships in work settings could be critical to the support and resources one needs to combat job-related stress. Research found that feedback received from supervisors about employees' work increased levels of job satisfaction and that workers receiving support from their supervisors had improved mental health compared to those who did not (Martin & Schinke, 1998; Stansfeld, Fuhrer, Shipley, & Marmot, 1999). In a similar fashion, harsh criticism was negatively related to job performance and satisfaction. Constructive feedback and support from supervisors signals care for workers and makes them feel valued and respected. Transparency is also essential. It is important for both employees and employers to engage in dialogue to understand each other's perspectives. In this respect, workers can see how their work performance is related to the entire organization's welfare and develop a sense of belonging, an element for meaning of work (Blustein, 2006).

As Herr (1989) once stated, "unemployment, problematic work relationships, and stressful work conditions play a significant role in the development of physical and mental health problems" (p. 8). The multi-aspect and multilevel relationship between work and health reveals the importance of work in one's life and its central role in one's psychological well-being. It is evident that a happy and satisfied worker would have better performance at work and would suffer from a variety of physical and mental health problems if becoming unemployed or underemployed. At work, job-related stress and anxiety could impact one's health as well. The following section will discuss the relationship between job satisfaction and job stress.

Job Satisfaction and Occupational Stress

Since work plays such a central role in one's life and health, it is valuable for both organizations and workers to become aware of contributing factors to job satisfaction and job-related stress. Such information should be helpful to prevention and intervention of occupational stress, burnout, and health problems. According to the WHO, work-related stress is the response people may have when the work demands are beyond their knowledge and abilities to deal with or incompatible to their values and skills (WHO, n.d.). Occupational stress becomes a national and international concern as the cost of occupational stress is estimated to be huge (Dollard & Winfield, 1996). Workers' health, if compromised, leads to more absence from work, then to low productivity, and also higher costs of health insurance (WHO, n.d.). On the other hand, happy and satisfied workers can be not only productive but also creative and then generate more positive outcomes for themselves and their employers.

The risk factors for occupational stress can be classified into two categories. One is the work characteristics, meaning the work has high demands of attention, effort, hours, and emotional investment. For instance, working at emergency departments in hospitals typically is highly stressful because of the nature of the work. Some people might find such highly demanding jobs fit their personal characteristics and abilities well and do not feel the stress level is more than normal, but for some people, working at an emergency department is too stressful because of the lack of routine and stability. The risk factor category is the work environment, which includes two subcategories: organization support and interpersonal relationships. Research has found that employees feel anxious when no clear structures, expectations, or feedback are provided and when there is no predictable or clear information shared with workers for policy, decision, or career and professional development opportunities (Burke, 1976, 1993). The interpersonal relationships among coworkers, particularly, the relationship between supervisors and supervisees, could determine one's perception of friendly or unfriendly work environment.

Two theoretical models have been widely used for accounting for occupational stress: Karasek's Demand-Control-Support Model and Siegrist's Effort-Reward Imbalance Model. The Demand-Control-Support Model posits that high demand, low control, and low social support at workplace would most likely cause people to experience occupational stress. When individuals are requested to perform a task that is not within their capacity, are not in the position to make any changes, and receive no support from supervisors or colleagues and are still expected to deliver the product, they feel no way out. An example of this type of situation could be a school receptionist at the front desk made to deal with an angry parent who demands her child be placed in a different classroom, with an administrator who insisted that the staff in the principal's office should handle the issue, and this receptionist received no support from the school counselors or other colleagues. Mark and Smith (2012) found that managers' support did have mediating effects on the relationship between work demands and stress level of workers. The same study also found that rewards and coping skills could have impact on one's mental health. The Effort-Reward Imbalance model proposed that workers would have work-related stress and health problems if their effort in the workplace does not result in adequate rewards. This proposition can be evidenced by the research about job satisfaction that identified opportunities to learn and advance up the career ladder, good salary, and respect of colleagues as the reasons for job satisfaction (Burke, 1976; Jawahar, 2012). It is evident that occupational stress occurs if the demands and tasks are beyond people's knowledge and skills and when they perceive lack of support, decision-making power, or rewards for their effort and performance. Simply put, when demands are high, and the rewards are low, workers tend to have decreased job satisfaction.

Not surprisingly, contributing factors to job satisfaction include reasonable work demands, some sense of control over what and how individuals accomplish the work, and receiving support from the organization and others. In addition, research has confirmed that job satisfaction is more likely when individual needs, values, and expectations were matched to the workplace (Dawis & Lofquist, 1984). This fitness between personal characteristics and work environment exemplifies another theoretical framework on occupational stress—the person and environment fit model (Caplan & Harrison, 1993), which depicts that poor fit between personal characteristics and the workplace increased the possibility of developing stress. Job satisfaction is more than just the absence of risk factors, and it reflects the meaningfulness one can find in his or her effort at work. Robert, Young, and Kelly (2006) argued that meaningfulness, a component in spiritual well-being, is associated with job satisfaction as it provides fulfillment and sense of accomplishment for individuals. Thus, job satisfaction, more than just the nonexistence of negative feelings in the workplace, provides people a sense of worthiness and sense of belonging. When satisfaction is absent, mental and physical health could be compromised.

Prevention of work-related illness is important to both individuals and society at large. A national organization, the National Institute of Occupational Safety and Health (NIOSH), as a section within Centers for Disease Control and Prevention (CDC), has the mission to address occupational stress and hazards. The coping strategies for preventing occupational stress should target building a better fit between individual expectations and work demands, providing channels for individuals to have their voices heard at workplaces, and offering support and promoting collegiality. Empowerment was found to positively reduce work-related stress and to improve job satisfaction (Andrew & Kacmar, 2014). Increasing individuals' problem-solving skills, resources, and coping strategies and soliciting support from work and social networks would help workers achieve job satisfaction as well (Mark & Smith, 2012). It is also important to make any prevention and intervention programs be appropriate in the multicultural workplace with a diverse workforce (Pasca & Wagner, 2011).

Employee assistance programs (EAP) are prevention and intervention programs at the workplace to help both employees and employers identify and resolve personal concerns; EPAs are a vital tool for maintaining and improving worker health and productivity (ODEP, 2018). EPA services typically include mental health services, referrals, substance abuse counseling, career counseling, counseling services for personal issues and family relationship, work/life support, and wellness and health promotion. Several researchers suggest EAPs can set up policies, procedures, and practices to increase mental health literacy in the workplace, provide mental health training for employees, and promote the use of workplace support (Denman, 2015; Hancock & Page, 2013). Despite the evidence of EAPs to benefit workers in regard to retention, performance, and decreased medical costs, EAPs are underused (Hancock & Page, 2013). Counselors trained within wellness and strength-based models are well positioned to advocate for and promote implementation of EAPs in work settings.

PERSONAL AND CONTEXTUAL FACTORS FOR CAREER DEVELOPMENT

The impact of the changing work environment and the complex relationship between work and health leads us to believe that a person's career development is shaped and influenced by both personal and contextual factors. Understanding the interaction of personal and contextual factors and their impact would better assist counselors conceptualize the challenges and barriers, as well as assets and resources of individuals in their career development and career decision-making process. Individual career development is a product of the interactive impact of psychological, biological, sociocultural, political, economic, educational, and historical influences.

Personal Factors

Personal factors are either innate characteristics from individuals' biological background or developed as the result of their growing up experiences, including family background and educational accessibility. Individuals' career paths might be variant depending on the extent to which they can implement or find an outlet for these features at work. These factors are important for individuals to become aware of since good understanding of oneself is a critical part of the career exploration process and essential for career development across the life span.

Genetic Factors

The physique of a person, such as height, weight, and skin color, are examples of genetic factors that are easily identified from appearance. There are some other genetic factors that are not so obvious. One's sensibility, motor skills, and disability categories and status, for instance, may not be easily known to the others or sometimes even to individuals themselves and may require professional evaluation. For instance, many people do not know that they have a learning disability until high school or college. In a general sense, most people have sufficient physical capacities required by common occupations; however, some occupations require such specific physical prowess that only certain people with innate talents can succeed (Isaacson & Brown, 2000). Almost everyone can play basketball for fun or exercise, but not everyone can play basketball as a profession; meanwhile, professional basketball players can do many other vocations after retirement. Gender, race, ethnicity, and sexual orientation all can influence how people make their career decision and path.

Psychological Characteristics

Whether one feels satisfied with her or his career choice and, consequently, whether she or he decides to stay or leave a job, is largely related to whether the job provides an avenue for the person to meet the needs, outcomes, and values one expects of work. Many of the career development theories (see Chapters 4 and 5) explain how one makes a career choice to fulfill needs out of personal desire and family obligation and expectations for one's life. Isaacson and Brown (2000) stated the personal psychological characteristics affecting one's career success include aptitude, interests, personality, and values. Aptitude, and specifically intelligence, and information processing ability are considered by the researchers to have an impact on one's career aspiration and path (Gottfredson, 2005; Sampson, Peterson, Lentz, & Reardon, 1992). Interests, a common studied and measured characteristic in career development research, is often viewed as the utmost factor for one's career aspiration, or at least the initial motivating factor. Many of the career intervention strategies also focus on discovering and defining one's interests in various occupations and then finding a career in which people can realize these interests. Despite the positive relationship between one's interests in occupations and chosen occupations, not everyone can work in a job in which they are fully interested in due to many other factors that can affect their career development. Personality and values are the other two common psychological constructs theorized and assessed by researchers to explain career choice behavior and work performance (e.g., Holland's Typology Theory and Super's Developmental Approach, which will be reviewed in Chapter 4). A very shy person probably will not choose sales as an occupation, just as an extroverted individual cannot imagine working all day alone in a cubicle without any human interaction.

Personal Resources

Personal resources can be understood as personal background factors that would influence individuals' access and preparation for entering into the workforce. These factors include a person's socioeconomic status, the sociocultural and socioeconomic backgrounds of the family, access to education and training, and the social network of individuals and their families. Socioeconomic status significantly influences a person's career planning and success through education opportunities and other learning enrichment opportunities (Isaacson & Brown, 2000). Extracurricular programs typically require investment by the parents; those students whose parents have higher earning power are more likely to be involved in off-school learning activities such as private tutoring, study abroad programs, and skill development classes (e.g., piano, ballet, figure skating). Access to education determines what kind of curriculum and learning experiences one has, which has been found by research to significantly influence self-efficacy and career choices (Brown & Lent, 2013). Because of the importance of educational levels and quality to career development, people's learning experiences are critical to their career aspirations and paths. Family dynamics and parents' work experience can provide vicarious learning experiences for children, too. In sum, personal resources are determined by many contextual factors in a person's life.

Contextual Factors

Sometimes people cannot choose the occupations they are interested in, not because they do not have interests or abilities, but because they do not have sufficient training or credentials to meet the requirements. Or, even if they are able to make a career choice they like, by the time they complete the necessary training and are ready to enter the workforce, there is no job for them because the economy is gloomy. These contextual factors are beyond the control of individuals.

Work Requirements

The nature of work itself is a factor for individuals to consider in making career decisions. Some basic skills such as reading and writing are necessary for most jobs; and as discussed before, some minimum skills in using computer and online communication (e.g., e-mail, online posting) are becoming increasingly essential at workplaces now. Some jobs require specialized training, for example, being an aircraft pilot; some require much longer time in education before entering into the profession, for example, being a cardiologist; and some require certain physical or cognitive abilities, for example, being able to lift 75 pounds or being able to detect a pattern in a seemingly random string of numbers. The work environment can also influence individuals' career decisions—for example, outdoor versus indoor work, a routine time schedule versus a changing every day schedule, or working with machines versus working with people. These work requirements and conditions cause people to either consider or avoid choosing the occupation. Related to the work environment is the relationship and interaction among coworkers, or the organizational culture. The characteristics of the work environment, that is, if the work setting provides autonomy, support, respect, and comfort, are important to many people. Some people like to work in a relaxed work environment where codes for attire and communication style are more informal; however, not everyone likes a laid-back work environment. The nature of work requirements and working conditions as well environments are factors people consider in making their career choices.

Sociocultural Influence

There is nothing more important than sociocultural influences on people's career development as career development is a process of socialization. When one asks the question "What do you do for living?" at a cocktail party, people often use the answers given to evaluate the person's social status, because the type of occupations has certain ascribed values by society. People have developed stereotypes of occupations in regard to their typical characteristics, income, and prestige in the society. These stereotypical understandings of occupations are developed through observation of people working in the field either in reality or media. Accordingly, people are influenced by these sociocultural factors in their selection of careers (see details of Gottfredson's career development theory in Chapter 4). People typically choose an occupation that they feel is acceptable to their perceived self-identification in social status, including prestige level, gender role, and ethnic group. An example of sociocultural influence on one's career development can be found in the case that many women in the early decades of the 20th centuries worked as teachers, nurses, and secretaries if they chose to work, because back then, the social norms for women at work were in these occupations. As of today, young girls have many more choices than their grandparents because the society in most industrialized countries has evolved to accept female leaders, female doctors, female scientists, and female professional athletes, for example.

CASE ILLUSTRATION 2.2
TERESA'S DILEMMA

Teresa is a 48-year-old female, divorced and currently unemployed. She has three children, and two of her children are married and living on their own; the youngest is in her late teens. Teresa was born with a congenital heart defect, which was initially believed would prevent her from living beyond infancy. She underwent an experimental heart surgery at age three. She has had to exercise some caution about the type of physical activities she performs.

Her family was from the Appalachian mountain region and moved to an urban area for better job opportunities. She described her family as poor, uneducated, and living hand-to-mouth; her parents did not finish high school and did not seem to expect her to have any further education after high school.

She attended six different high schools in four years; she reported that she took mainly college preparatory courses because she enjoyed them. She earned acceptable grades and spoke to a school counselor about her wish to attend college, but the counselor was unsupportive. Even though she earned 27 on the ACT, she did not go to college; instead, she married right after her high school graduation. She married a man who had just completed army training and was sent to Vietnam after the wedding. After military service, her husband made his living either as a semiskilled construction worker or as a truck driver. He never provided a steady income and a continuity of benefits, especially health insurance, which made Teresa's heart condition worsen.

Teresa scored high enough on the civil service test to be hired at the post office for a period of two and a half years. She became pregnant and took a leave from the post office. After the child was born, she was rehired by the post office full time as a night worker and had to care for her child during the daytime. When forced to leave the post office, she joined a local dog club and began to give private lessons in dog obedience. This work schedule was flexible and allowed her to take care of her children. However, her long hours of work over an extended period of time aggravated her heart condition; she collapsed at work one day and then she had to cut back to part-time work, and later, she had to quit her job altogether. A year later, she went back to work as a courier for a multilocation automobile dealer. Even this job became too much for her, and she collapsed again at work due to a third-degree heart block. She underwent open heart surgery to correct her heart condition.

After her surgery, it was clear that she could not do any job involving physical labor. Her friends at the local dog club encouraged her to attend college. She then enrolled at a local college. During her junior year, her marriage fell apart. She and her husband were divorced during her senior year. She graduated with a double major in social work and sociology and GPA of 3.98. Her employment goal is to become a rehabilitation counselor. She is currently working full time on a master's degree in rehabilitation counseling at a state university. Teresa is worried about whether she can work full time again and if her health and her family situation can accommodate that.

Discussion Questions

1. What individual and contextual factors do you see from this case illustration that affected Teresa's career development?

2. If you were Teresa's counselor, what would you do to help her? What are some potential issues you think need to be addressed?

3. What are the assets and barriers Teresa has in her ecological system?

Socioeconomic Influence

During the graduation seasons of 2009 to 2012, if one watched the TV news on major channels such as NBC, ABC, or CBS, one would have seen pretty consistent reports: College graduates have a tough time securing a job; their starting salary is lower than expected or than their counterparts of the previous years. With the housing market crash, and changes discussed in the section about work and the global economy, the U.S. economy went into recession. So many people lost their jobs that everyone knew someone either in their family or social network that got laid off from work. The labor market is a significant factor because people cannot enter the workforce if the demand for new workers is nonexistent, or people's careers are interrupted if their positions are cut. Besides economic factors, significant events could impact the supply and demand as well. For instance, there was an increasing need for hiring workers in transportation security after the September 11 tragedy in 2001 and in Internet security as online databases and business transactions become more commonly practiced. The labor market, economic situation, and historical context that individuals encounter during their life spans influence their career trajectories tremendously.

INTEGRATED VIEW OF CAREER DEVELOPMENT

As evidenced in the previous sections on the centrality of work in individuals' lives and its impact on health, career development cannot be separated from the development of a whole person and should not be viewed only for finding a matching career for the person; it should be viewed as an integral part of human development. The multifaceted nature of the relationship of work and other aspects of life needs to be understood. Career services to individuals also need to be integrated, addressing the dynamics and complexities of work and life.

Work and Other Aspects of Life

Family and Work

Family and work have a reciprocal relationship with each other. A happy family life could be helpful to satisfying and productive work; and fulfilling and satisfying work could result in a happy family life and quality relationships. This reciprocal relationship can be explained by the compensatory model, which indicates that better adjustment in one area compensates for poor adjustment in another area; or the spill-over model, that is, an individual's behavior and attitudes can be carried over between work and home settings (Schultz & Henderson, 1985). Better coordination of the conflict between family and work demand, such as work hours, schedule conflicts, spouse career, change in family structure, fatigue and irritability, can lead to high productivity. Having family members use EAPs could help to alleviate some domestic stressors and family-to-work conflict and eventually help work performance (Hancock & Page, 2013).

People who have supportive families and who have help with the household chores and who are able to obtain appropriate childcare tend to be more satisfied with their jobs (Rudd & McKenry, 1986). These people have more of a balance between work and home life, with support in the activities they engage in at work and home (Rudd & McKenry, 1986), have decreased impairment at work (Casey & Grzywacz, 2008), and less intention to leave their jobs (Haar, 2004). More dissatisfaction occurred when there was too much work that overflowed into home life, than when the balance was weighted with more family involvement that might influence work life (Haar, 2004). If one can maintain a balance between work and home, the general health of the family is improved (Rudd & McKenry, 1986). If a person is able to have a supportive and intimate relationship with his or her family, he or she has an enhanced sense of well-being.

What occurs at home can sometimes interfere with work. If there is a lot of stress at home, it can lead a person to have a decreased sense of job satisfaction (Frone, Russell, & Barnes, 1996). Work can also interfere with family life, which in return can affect the way one feels about his or her job. If a person feels as though he or she is unable to commit enough time to being with his or her family, both physically with them in person and emotionally being there, then mentally, he or she has a decreased sense of wellness (Stevanovic & Rupert, 2009). Sandberg, Yorgason, Miller, and Hill (2012) found that marital distress is a significant predictor for depressive symptoms, health, and work satisfaction. Similarly, Sandberg et al. (2013) found that a high level of negative couple interaction is associated with less job satisfaction as these individuals tended to have more mental and physical problems. It is interesting that spouse work hours and size of the family can increase the chances of BMI elevation over time, indicating the importance of family interdependence in dealing with family and work demands and allocating time and resources (Kramer & Chung, 2015).

It is evident that separation of work and family life is not helpful to conceptualize one's career development. Work and family life affect each other positively or negatively depending on the attitudes and approaches used to manage the demands and challenges from each and how one coordinates the various roles one plays at these two different settings.

Work and Life Roles

Changes in the labor force lead to changes of labor division at home. With more women working outside of the home, men have increased their share of the household duties (Goldenberg & Goldenberg, 2008). Similarly, with an increasing number of dual-career families, the traditional gender role identification and designation for work and family is changing as well (Whiston, Campbell, & Maffini, 2012). People are more accepting of men staying home and taking care of children while women are the breadwinners of the family. However, the division of household labor is far from equal (Fitzgerald, Fassinger, & Betz, 1995); women still do the majority of household tasks and are the primary caretakers of the family, even in the dual-career families (Newman & Newman, 2009). Role overload, role conflict, and career-family conflict is the reality and challenge that modern workers need to face. "Hence assumptions about an ideal worker that link time at work and continuous availability with productivity need to be questioned and challenged. But such changes will only help gender equity if they also legitimize the personal responsibilities of all employees" (Bailyn, 2011, p. 107).

Role overload means that one has more responsibilities and duties than time and energy permits; in other words, time-related demands exceed the time management resources an individual has (Schultz & Henderson, 1985). For a working mother juggling the parent role, wife role, and worker role on a routine basis, any unanticipated event, for example, overtime at work, emergency business trip, sick child, or senior parent getting ill, could add an extra load to the already full plate. As a result, role conflict becomes inevitable. Role conflict is "competing demands from different roles" (Zunker, 2012, p. 245). Balancing work and family roles is a task for men and women in dual-career families, in fact, for everyone in modern society. Unfortunately, not many organizations are family friendly (Reardon, Lentz, Sampson, & Peterson, 2000). Compared to other industrialized countries, the United States has the least favorable work environment and policy for working families. Despite the changing labor force composition, the world of work is still functioning with the mentality that one member of the family stays home and plays the single role of caregiver (Halpern, 2005). Suggested accommodations for making organizations more family friendly include emergency care, onsite childcare, flexible work arrangements and schedule, and childcare benefits (Zunker, 2012).

Role overload and role conflict do not only apply to dual-career families. As a matter of fact, many people deal with this struggle regardless of family status. Many people nowadays work and study full time at the same time. The juggling between various roles—student, worker, family member, and friend—is everyone's issue. Understanding the roles one has in addition to the role as a worker is helpful for a counselor to develop appropriate intervention strategies.

Certainty, Change, Transition, and Adjustment

The previous section reviewed the psychological impacts of unemployment or underemployment. The uncertainty and consistent change in the economy and labor market has a similar impact on one's psychological well-being. The traditional concept of work and home life being entirely separate entities with clear boundaries of time spent at work and at home is questionable. Technology, for instance, enables 24/7 access to work, and consequently, distress if workers cannot effectively cope with technology (Atanasoff & Venable, 2017). Use of technology and the global workforce also mean some employees have to work constantly due to different time zones. Hard work and loyalty to one's employer would pay off; such belief was probably true in the past but not anymore. Working at one place until retirement becomes less likely. Instead, chronic job insecurity, corporate restructuring, and discomfort associated with different role designations at work and home than tradition roles are reality; however, rules and practices are not catching up (Moen & Roehing, 2005). Counselors cannot follow the old framework of vocational guidance, making a career choice for the lifetime. Rather, counselors need to help clients develop life span transitioning.

According to Fouad and Bynner (2008), there are two kinds of transition: voluntary transition is driven by personal goals, and people usually have time to prepare for it; involuntary transition is typically enforced by situational or environmental constraints, and people often have no choice or time for the transition. Due to economic changes, the school-to-work transition often takes longer for youth nowadays than it did for their parents or grandparents. In addition, the younger generation will encounter more transitions as well, meaning people will move from one job to another and will move in and out of employment more often because of the instability of the work world. People experiencing these changes face multiple psychological challenges. Fouad and Bynner (2008) suggested that helping professionals should help individuals build capacities, including higher adaptability and self-awareness to prepare for transitions, and also that institutions need proactive programming for youth and adults to make voluntary transitions.

Integrated Services

The interconnectedness of various roles people have during their life span and the complex relationship of work and family life requires counselors to view career development beyond just occupation choice and career decision making; instead, helping clients with career concerns a framework that integrates personal and contextual factors that would impact a person in his or her exploration of self, identity, and meaning of life, as well as making a living. Artificial separation of various aspects of people's lives is not helpful to clients (Blustein, 2008). The counseling profession is distinct from other helping professions with its roots in vocational guidance and helping people at disadvantages to adjust to contextual demands (as illustrated in Chapter 1). Counselors are in the unique position among all the helping professionals to be able to provide integrated services to clients because counselors are the only helping professionals who are trained to understand both career and mental health issues as required by the training standards within the professional organization and accreditation standards (Council for Accreditation of Counseling and Related Educational Programs, 2016).

The call for integrated services that address both mental health needs and career issues has been ongoing for a long time. Spokane (1989) proposed that personal adjustment and career adjustment need to be addressed simultaneously when making a difficult career decision; a well-adjusted career decision leading to a good job will lead to psychological well-being. From a different perspective but with the same goal, Herr (1989) called for career counseling as a mental health modality because mental disorder symptoms might be due to poor personal work environment fit (Herr, 1989). For instance, a worker who experienced lack of appetite, difficulty sleeping, and low energy seemed to have depression, but with further exploration, it was found that his boss was demanding, aggressive, micromanaging, and often assigned him work that he did not have the capacity or resources to accomplish. He had these symptoms because he was constantly worried that he would be fired. This scenario illustrates that counselors need to conceptualize clients' presenting issues from a more integrated perspective of both mental health and career issues. Niles and Yoon (2011)

MULTICULTURAL BOX 2.1

In Case Illustration 2.2, Teresa had good score on the ACT but chose not to go to college. In fact, when she went to her school counselor in high school and wanted to learn what majors she should consider in college, her school counselor said, "I don't think attending college is a good choice for you. You should consider a trade school and get a job within a year or two. College is not for girls like you." What is your reaction to her school counselor's words? Why? What was wrong with Teresa's school counselor's words? Reviewing Teresa's occupational history, what factors influenced her decisions? How would you categorize these factors?

Tips for Consideration: sex, socioeconomic status, gender role, values, social expectation, historical context, interaction of personal and contextual factors.

also discussed the opportunities for mental health counselors to help clients in a more holistic approach.

To promote career counseling integrated with mental health counseling, competency development is needed in counselor training programs. Niles and Pate Jr. (1989) suggested the following: (1) foster a sense of enthusiasm about career counseling; (2) help students to understand that work influences clients' lives; (3) do more research about the interrelationship and outcome with and without integration; and (4) provide professional development opportunities for developing the knowledge and skills in comprehensive counseling services. A national commission for promoting this competency development in counselor education programs was founded by the National Career Development Association (the national professional organization of career development) and the Association of Counselor Education and Supervision (ACES; the national organization for counselor education) to advocate for enhancing integrated services to all clients.

THE ECOLOGICAL PERSPECTIVE OF CAREER INTERVENTION

Integrated services require the counselor to conceptualize the client's presenting issues from a broad perspective, taking into consideration the various personal and contextual factors that would influence one's career development and career decision making. With the ever-changing work environment, helping clients become their own advocates and agents to navigate the complex and changing dynamics of the economy, workforce, and work settings is essential. The ecological career counseling model proposed by Cook, Heppner, and O'Brien (2002) suggested that optimal career intervention should find the accordance of individual and contextual factors of a person's ecosystem, in other words, help individuals become change agents to use their resources to maximize their potential and minimize the barriers to live a fulfilling life. Ecological career counseling emphasizes the importance of change agency and the meaning-making process for individuals in their career development.

Change Agency of Individuals

The concept of being a change agent for oneself, proposed by the ecological career counseling model, echoed the idea of several other scholars to address the instability of the work environment in the 21st century. Savickas (2013) recommended that life-design and developing life-course competency, not planning, should be the goal of career intervention. It is clear from the previous discussion that matching a fit career for a person is not sufficient anymore (Russo, Guo, & Baruch, 2014), as rarely can one hold a job for a lifetime. To be prepared for uncertainty requires self-awareness and adaptability (Savickas, 2013). Another way to conceptualize the goal of career intervention is to enhance *flexicurity*, flexibility and security, particularly for those who are at risk of being in and out of jobs because of lack of resources (Sultana, 2012). It is equally important to encourage lifelong learning and to be aware of the resources and assets as well as barriers in the ecosystem one has or needs to develop so that one can increase his or her career adaptability and flexicurity. For instance, the policy for career education in the European community requires the curriculum to provide guidance for youth to gain learning and application skills that will benefit them to be lifelong learners and workers. The acknowledgment of the necessity of lifelong learning would help policy makers endorse and implement policies to facilitate prevention and intervention programs targeting development of attitudes and skills for lifelong learning.

Understanding one's assets and barriers in the ecosystem is necessary for becoming a self-change agent. What constitutes assets and barriers varies for different people at different settings and times. It is contextualized and time bound. For instance, having the skills and training in nuclear technology during the cold war period in the United States was an asset for securing a job; however, at the end of the 20th century, those working in the nuclear industry lost jobs and had a difficult time finding other jobs because of the downturn of that industry. Age and experience could be assets or barriers depending on what kind of career or specific positions one is trying to find. Ecological career counseling could be helpful for individuals developing adaptability and flexibility by identifying barriers and turning the barriers into assets.

Meaning Making in Changing Environment

Earlier sections of this chapter illustrated the meaning of work to people from historical and cross-cultural contexts. Work evolves from meeting survival needs to a choice, and to meaning search and identification (Blustein, 2006). With the changing economy and technology advancement, the work world is becoming increasingly unpredictable and unstable. One job for a lifetime is not realistic anymore, from either a societal or personal perspective. People are in constant search of meaning of their worth in this world through work and other aspects of life. In other words, career development is a journey to live one's autobiography (Savickas, 2005). The construction of this journey is personal, and satisfaction must be determined by one's own meaning-making process (Cook, Heppner, & O'Brien, 2002). Both personal characteristics and contextual influences, as well as the interaction of the two, shape individuals' meaning-making process.

In the midst of the constantly changing work world of the 21st century, one needs to identify his or her niche in this dynamic and diverse world. As noted previously, work and health have a complex and reciprocal relationship. The research also found that a meaningful and purposeful life could lead to positive role identity and role salience, which ultimately impacts mental and physical health (Thoits, 2012), and particularly, that subjective career success mediates one's physical and mental health (Russo, Guo, & Baruch, 2014). Blustein (2006) also suggested that internal criteria for success lead to greater autonomy and control and allow for a protean career (Hall & Mirvis, 1996), an individualized career path unique to each person. It is clear that career counseling is no different than mental health counseling; that is, counselors need to empower clients to find their own voices and meaningful connection to the outside world and to thrive beyond survival.

Summary: Challenges and Opportunities

The centrality of work to humans indicates the importance of having a satisfying career as it provides for survival needs, sense of worth, self-identity, and health. With the changes in work environment, due to technology, globalization of the economy, and diverse labor force, unpredictability and uncertainty have become the norm for career development. Transitions, from nonwork to work, from work to no-work or underemployment, between family roles and work roles, are inevitable. The interaction of individual characteristics and contextual factors presents both challenges and opportunities for people to explore their purposeful and meaningful career and life. To address these challenges, individuals need to develop an understanding of their personal niche in relation to others in the multisystem affecting their career development; and counselors should work with individuals to create opportunities for constructing meaningful careers that effectively optimize their resources and reduce the barriers.

Keystones

- Work plays a central role in people's lives and provides people a sense of belonging, identity, and recognition, in addition to financial rewards.

- The meaning of work changes over time and varies in different cultural contexts.

- The globalization of the economy and technology advancement have led to drastic changes in occupational structure and trends of requirements for entering into the workforce.

- The workforce is increasingly diverse in regard to almost every aspect of demographics, with the younger generation of workers demonstrating different work styles.

- Work and health have a multilayered, complex, and possibly reciprocal relationships; and lack of one impacts the other.

- Both personal and contextual factors, and interplay of these factors, influence the trajectory of a person's career development.

- Because of the complex interaction of individuals in relation to work and other roles of life, career development needs to be understood from an integrated view, and career services need to be integrated as well.

- The ecological career counseling model, advocating for self as a change agent and meaning searching and identification, provides a framework for integrated career intervention.

Additional Resources

Hall, D. T., & Associates. (1996). *The career is dead— Long live the career: A relational approach to careers.* San Francisco, CA: Jossey-Bass.

Job Stress Network: http://www.workhealth.com

Millennial workers: http://www.cbsnews.com/news/the-millennials-are-coming

NIOSH (National Institute of Occupational Safety and Health): http://www.cdc.gov/niosh/topics/stress

World Health Organization: http://www.who.int/occupational_health/topics/stressatwp/en

References

Alterman, T., Grosch, J., Chen, X., Chrislip, D., Petersen, M., Kreig, E. Jr., Chung, H., & Muntaner, C. (2008). Examining association between job characteristics and health: Linking data from the occupational information 10 (O*Net) to two U.S. national health surveys. *Journal of Occupational Environmental Medicine, 50*, 1401-1413. doi:10.1097/JOM.0b013e318188e882

Andersen, P., & Vandehey, M. (2012). *Career counseling and development in global economy* (2nd ed). Belmont, CA: Brooks/Cole.

Anderson, S., & Winefield, A. H. (2011). The impact of underemployment on psychological health, physical health, and work attitudes. In D. C. Maynard, D. C. Feldman, D. C. Maynard, & D. C. Feldman (Eds.), *Underemployment, psychological, economic, and social challenges* (pp. 165-185). New York, NY: Springer Science + Business Media.

Andrews, M. C., & Kacmar, K. M. (2014). Easing employee strain: The interactive effects of empowerment and justice on the role overload strain relationship. *Journal of Behavioral and Applied Management, 15*, 43-58.

Ardichvili, A., & Kuchinke, K. P. (2009). International perspectives on the meaning of work and working: Current research and theory. *Advancement in Developing Human Resources, 11*, 155-167. doi:10.1177/1522309333494

Atanasoff, L., & Venable, M. A. (2017). Technostress: Implications for adults in the workforce. *The Career Development Quarterly, 65*(4), 326-338. doi:10.1002/cdq.12111

Bailyn, L. (2011). Redesigning work for gender equity and work-personal life integration. *Community, Work and Family, 14*, 97-112. doi:10.1080/13668803.2010.532660

Block, D., & Richarmond, L. (Eds.). (1997). *Connecting between spirit and work in career development: New approaches and practical perspectives*. Palo Alto, CA: Davies-Black.

Bureau of Labor Statistics. (1999). *Employment projects program: Table 1.1, Employment by major occupational groups, 2010 and projected 2020*. Retrieved from www.bls.gov.

Bureau of Labor Statistics. (2017). *Employment projections—2016-26 USDL-1429*. Retrieved from www.bls.gov/emp.

Blustein, D. L. (2006). *The psychology of working: A new perspective for career development, counseling, and public policy*. Mahwah, NJ: Lawrence Erlbaum Associates.

Blustein, D. L. (2008). The role of work in psychological health and well-being: A conceptual, historical, and public policy perspective. *American Psychologist, 63*(4), 228-240. doi:10.1037/0003-066X.63.4.228

Burke, R. J. (1976). Occupational stress and job satisfaction. *Journal of Social Psychology*, *100*, 235-244.

Burke, R. J. (1993). Organizational-level interventions to reduce occupational stressors. *Work and Stress*, *7*, 77-87.

Caplan, R. D., & Harrison, R. V. (1993). Person-environment fit theory: Some history, recent development, and future directions. *Journal of Social Issues*, *49*, 253-276.

Casey, P. R., & Grzywacz, J. G. (2008). Employee health and well-being: The flexibility and work-family balance. *The Psychologist-Manager Journal*, *11*, 31-47.

Cook, E. P., Heppner, M. J., & O'Brien, K. M. (2002). Feminism and women's career development: An ecological perspective. In S. G. Niles (Ed.), *Adult career development: Concepts, issues, and practices* (3rd ed., pp. 168-189). Columbus, OH, US: National Career Development Association.

Council for Accreditation of Counseling and Related Educational Programs (CACREP). (2016). *2016 CACREP Standards SECTION 2: Professional counseling identity*. Retrieved from http://www.cacrep.org/section-2-professional-counseling-identity.

Dawis, R. V., & Lofquist, L. H. (1984). *A psychological theory of work adjustment: An individual differences model and its application*. Minneapolis: University of Minnesota.

Denman, S. J. (2015). Mental illnesses are not invisible: An insight into workplaces. *International Journal of Disability, Development and Education*, *62*(3), 339-345. doi:10.1080/1034912X.2015.1027520

Dik, B. J., & Duffy, R. D. (2009). Calling and vocation at work: Definitions and prospects for research and practice. *Counseling Psychologist*, *37*, 424-450. doi:10.1177/0011000008316430

Dollard, M. F., & Winefield, A. H. (1996). Managing occupational stress: National and international perspective. *International Journal of Stress Management*, *3*, 69-83.

Edwards, J. R., & Rothbard, N. P. (1999). Work and family stress and well-being: An examination of person-environment fit in the work and family domains. *Organizational Behavior and Human Decision Processes*, *77*, 85-129. doi:https://doi.org/10.1006/obhd.1998.2813

Faragher, E.B, Cass, M., Cooper, C. L. (2005). The relationship between job satisfaction and health: a meta-analysis. *Occupational and Environmental Medicine*, *62*, 105-112. doi:10.1136/oem.2002.006734

Fitzgerald, L. F., Fassinger, R. E., & Betz, N. E. (1995). Theoretical advances in the study of women's career development. In W. B. Walsh & S. H. Osipow (Eds.), *Handbook of vocational psychology: Theory, research, and practice* (2nd ed., pp. 67-109). Mahwah, NJ: Erlbaum.

Frone, M. R., Russell, M., & Barnes, G. M. (1996). Work-family conflict, gender, and health-related outcomes: A study of employed parents in two community samples. *Journal of Occupational Health Psychology*, *1*, 57-69. doi:10.1037/1076-8998.1.1.57

Ford, M. T., Cerasoli, C. P., Higgins, J. A., & Decesare, A. L. (2011). Relationships between psychological, physical, and behavioural health and work performance: A review and meta-analysis. *Work & Stress*, *25*, 185-204. doi.org/10.1080/02678373.2011.609035

Fouad, N. A., & Bynner, J. (2008). Work transitions. *American Psychologist, 63*(4), 241-251. doi:10.1037/0003-066X.63.4.241

Gibson, R. L., & Mitchell, M. H. (2006). *Introduction to career counseling for the 21st Century.* Upper Saddle River, NJ: Pearson Merrill Prentice Hall.

Goldenberg, H., & Goldenberg, I. (2008). *Family therapy: An overview* (7th ed.). Belmont, CA: Brooks/Cole.

Goldsmith, W. (1995). Task performance and fulfillment: Work and career tribal and peasant societies. In F. Gamst (Ed.), *Meaning of work* (pp. 79-89). Albany: State University of New York Press.

Gottfredson, L. S. (2005). Applying Gottfredson's theory of circumscription and compromise in career guidance and counseling. In S. D. Brown & R. W. Lent (Eds.), *Career development and counseling: Putting theory and research to work* (pp. 71-100). Hoboken, NJ: John Wiley and Sons.

Guevara, K., & Ord, J. (1996). The search for meaning in a changing work context. *Future, 28,* 709-722.

Haar, J. M. (2004). Work-family conflict and turnover intention: Exploring the moderation effects of perceived work-family support. *New Zealand Journal of Psychology, 33*(1), 35-39.

Hall, D. T., & Mirvis, P. H. (1996). The new protean career: Psychological success and the path with a heart. In D. T. Hall (Ed.), *The career is dead—Long live the career: A relational approach to careers* (pp. 15-45). San Francisco, CA: Jossey-Bass.

Halpern, D. F. (2005). Psychology at the intersection of work and family: Recommendations for employers, working families, and

policymakers. *American Psychologist, 60,* 397-409. doi:10.1037/0003-066X.60.5

Hancock, F., & Page, F. (2013). Family to work conflict and the usefulness of workplace support. *Occupational Medicine, 63,* 373-376.

Herr, E. L. (1989). Career development and mental health. *Journal of Career Development, 16*(1), 5-18. doi:10.1007/BF01354263

Herr, E. L., Cramer, S. H., & Niles, S. G. (2004). *Career guidance and counseling through the life span: Systematic approaches* (5th ed.). New York, NY: Harper Collins.

Heslin, P. (2005). Conceptualizing and evaluating career success. *Journal of Organizational Behavior, 26,* 113-136.

Isaacson, L. E., & Brown, D. (2000). *Career information, career counseling, and career development* (7th ed.). Needham Heights, MA: Allyn & Bacon.

Jawahar, I. M. (2012). Mediating role of satisfaction with growth opportunities on the relationship between employee development opportunities and citizenship behaviors and burnout. *Journal of Applied Social Psychology, 42,* 2257-2284.

Jepsen, D. A. (2013, Summer). What exactly is your work? *NCDA Career Developments, 29* (3), 24-24.

Kramer, A., & Chung, W. (2015). Work demands, family demands, and BMI in dual-earners families: A 16-year longitudinal study. *Journal of Applied Psychology,* doi:10.1037/a0038634.

Lent, R. W. (2013). Social cognitive career theory. In S. D. Brown & R.W. Lent (Eds.), *Career development and counseling: Putting theory and research to work* (pp. 115-146). Hoboken, NJ: John Wiley.

Mark, G., & Smith, A. P. (2012). Effects of occupational stress, job characteristics, coping, and attributional style on the mental health and job satisfaction of university employees. *Anxiety, Stress and Coping*, *25*, 63-78.

Martin, U., & Schinke, S. P. (1998). Organizational and individual factors influencing job satisfaction and burnout of mental health workers. *Social Work Health Care*, *28*, 51-62. doi: 10.1300/J010v28n02_04

Meaning of Work International Research Team (MOWIRT). (1987). *The meaning of working*. London, UK: Academic Press.

Moen, P., & Roehling, P. (2005). *The career mystique: Cracks in the American dream*. Lanham, MD: Rowman & Littlefield.

Mossakowski, K. N. (2008). Is the duration of poverty and unemployment a risk factor heavy drinking? *Social Science & Medicine*, *67*, 947-955.

Newman, B. S., & Newman, P. R. (2009). *Development through life: A psychological approach* (9th ed.). Belmont, CA: Wadsworth.

Niles, S. G., Harris-Bowlsbey, J. (2013). *Career development interventions in the 21st century* (4th ed). Upper Saddle River, NJ: Pearson Merrill Prentice Hall.

Niles, S. G., & Pate, R. H., Jr. (1989). Competency and training issues related to the integration of career counseling and mental health counseling. *Journal of Career Development*, *16*, 63-71.

Niles, S. G., & Yoon, H. J. (2011). Career counseling: Current challenges and opportunities for mental health practitioners. In A. J. Palmo, W. J. Weikel, & D. P. Borsos (Eds.), *Foundation of mental health counseling* (4th ed.) (pp. 135-153). Springfield, IL: Charles C. Thomas.

Office of Disability Employee Policy (ODEP). (2018). *Employee assistance programs for a new generation of employees: Defining the next generation*. Retrieved from https://www.dol.gov/odep/documents/employeeassistance.pdf.

Oginska-Buiik, N. (2005). Emotional intelligence in the workplace: Exploring its effects on occupational stress and health outcomes in human service workers. *International Journal of Occupational Medicine and Environmental Health*, *18*, 167-175.

Olesen, S. C., Butterworth, P., Leach, L. S., Kelaher, M., & Pirkis, J. (2013). Mental health affects future employment as job loss affects mental health: findings from a longitudinal population study. *BMC Psychiatry*. Retrieved from http://www.biomedcentral.com/1471-244X/13/144.

Pacheco, G., Page, D., & Webber, D. J. (2014). Mental and physical health: Re-assessing the relationship with employment propensity. *Work, Employment and Society*, *28*(3), 407-429. doi:10.1177/0950017013491450

Pasca, R., & Wagner, S. L. (2011). Occupational stress in the multicultural workplace. *Journal of Immigrant Minority Health*, *13*, 697-705.

Pedulla, D. S., & Newman, K. S. (2011). The family and community impacts of underemployment. In D. C. Maynard, D. C. Feldman (Eds.), *Underemployment, psychological, economic, and social challenges* (pp. 233-250). New York, NY: Springer Science + Business Media.

Reardon, R. C., Lentz, J. G., Sampson, J. P., & Peterson, G. W. (2000). *Career development and planning: A comprehensive approach*. Pacific Grove, CA: Brooks/Cole.

Robert, T. E., Young, S., & Kelly, V. A. (2006). Relationship between adult workers' spiritual well-being and job satisfaction: A preliminary study. *Counseling and Values*, *50*, 165-175.

Rosenthal, L., Carroll-Scott, A., Earnshaw, V. A., Santilli, A., & Ickovics, J. R. (2012). The importance of full-time work for urban adults' mental and physical health. *Social Science & Medicine*, *75*(9), 1692-1696. doi:10.1016/j.socscimed.2012.07.003

Rudd, N. M., & McKenry, P. C. (1986). Family influences on the job satisfaction of employed mothers. *Psychology of Women Quarterly*, *10*, 363-372.

Russo, M., Guo, L., & Baruch, Y. (2014). Work attitudes, career success and health: Evidence from china. *Journal of Vocational Behavior*, *84*(3), 248-258. doi:10.1016/j.jvb.2014.01.009

Sampson, J. P., Jr., Peterson, G. W., Lenz, J. G., & Reardon, R. C. (1992). A cognitive approach to career services: Translating concepts into practice. *The Career Development Quarterly*, *41*, 67-74.

Sandberg, J. G., Harper, J. M., Hill, E. J., Miller, R. B., Yorgason, J. B., & Day, R. D. (2013). 'What happens at home does not necessarily stay at home': The relationship of observed negative couple interaction with physical health, mental health, and work satisfaction. *Journal of Marriage and Family*, *75*(4), 808-821.

Sandberg, J. G., Yorgason, J. B., Miller, R. B., & Hill, E. J. (2012). Family-to-work spillover in Singapore: Marital distress, physical and mental health, and work satisfaction. *Family Relations: An Interdisciplinary Journal of Applied Family Studies*, *61*(1), 1-15. doi:10.1111/j.1741-3729.2011.00682.x

Savickas, M. L. (2005). The theory and practice of career construction. In S. D. Brown & R. W. Lent (Eds.), *Career development and counseling: Putting theory and research to work* (pp. 42-70). Hoboken, NJ: Wiley.

Savickas, M. L. (2013). The theory and practice of career construction. In S. D. Brown & R.W. (Eds.), *Career development and counseling: Putting theory and research to work* (2nd ed., pp. 147-183). Hoboken, NJ: Wiley.

Schultz, J. B., & Henderson, C. (1985). Family satisfaction and job performance: Implications for career development. *Journal of Career Development*, *12*(1), 33-47.

Siegrist, J. (1996). Adverse health effects of high-effort/low-reward conditions. *Journal of Occupational Psychology*, *1*, 27-41.

Spokane, A. R. (1989). Are there psychological and mental health consequences of difficult career decisions? *Journal of Career Development*, *16*, 19-23.

Stansfeld, S. A, Fuhrer, R., Shipley, M. J., & Marmot, M. G. (1999). Work characteristics predict psychiatric disorder: prospective results from the Whitehall II study. *Occupational and Environmental Medicine 56*, 302-307.

Stevanovic, P., & Rupert, P. (2009). Work-family spillover and life satisfaction among professional psychologists. *Psychology: Research and Practice*, *40*, 62-68.

Sultana, R. G. (2012). Flexibility and security? "Flexicurity" and its implications for lifelong guidance. *British Journal of Guidance and Counseling*, 1-19. doi:10.1080/03069885.2012.721125

Thoits, P. A., (2012). Role-identity salience, purpose and meaning in life, and well-being among volunteers. *Social Psychology Quarterly*, *75*, 360-384.

Tsutsumi, A., Kayaba, K., Theorell, T., & Siegrist, J. (2001). Association between job stress and depression among Japanese employees threatened by job loss in a comparison between two complementary job-stress models. *Scandinavian Journal of Work Environmental Health*, *27*, 146-153. doi:10.5271/sjweh.602

Westwood, R., & Lok, P. (2003). The meaning of work in Chinese contexts: A comparative study. *International Journal of Cross Cultural Management*, *3*, 139-165.

Whiston, S. C., Campbell, W. L., & Maffini, C. S. (2012). Work-family balance: A counseling psychology perspective. In N. A. Fouad, J. A. Carter, & L. M. Subich (Eds.), *APA handbook of counseling psychology: Vol. 2. practice, interventions, and applications* (pp. 75-102). Washington, DC: American Psychological Association.

World Health Organization. (n.d.). *Stress at the workplace*. Retrieved from http://www.who .int/occupational_health/topics/stress atwp/en.

Zunker, V. G. (2012). *Career counseling: A holistic approach* (8th ed.). Belmont, CA: Brooks/ Cole.

CROSS-CULTURAL PERSPECTIVES IN CAREER DEVELOPMENT

The U.S. society has become more diverse than ever in the 21st century, and increasingly diverse populations will be growing steadily in the future. Counselors, regardless of whether they work in school or community settings, work with diverse clientele daily. Understanding the complexity of multicultural perspectives to individual well-being and to one's career development is critical for counselors to provide culturally appropriate intervention services. In this chapter, we will introduce some critical concepts related to multicultural issues in career development and intervention. It is important to understand these concepts and their implications to career development because sociocultural contexts influence people's career trajectory. In addition, developing cultural competency is the ethical obligation of every counselor. This chapter includes current demographic information on workforce and change in the work settings, cultural differences in regard to different dimensions, intersection of various dimensions of diversity and their implication to individuals' career development, multicultural issues related to career development in work settings, and development of multicultural competency in working with diverse population. The illustrations of the career-related issues in multicultural work environment should inspire students to better understand theories and strategies of individuals' career development to be presented in the following chapters.

LEARNING OBJECTIVES

After completing the reading and exercises provided in this chapter, you will be able to:

- describe the changing profile of the labor force in the workforce;

- identify social barriers such as gender, ethnicity, race, socioeconomic status, religious background, sexual orientation, able-status, and other personal factors in relation to one's career development;

- describe the definition and meaning of issues pertaining to multicultural career development in work settings such as occupational stereotypes, occupational segregation, occupational discrimination, and glass ceiling;

- examine cultural identity and acculturation and their relationship to career development;

- analyze how the intersection of contextual factors and personal inputs influences individuals' career development and decision-making process;

- develop cultural competency in working with diverse populations; and

- translate cultural competency and social justice awareness to advocate for disadvantaged groups for their career development needs.

CHANGING WORKFORCE

The labor force in the United States has experienced significant changes since the middle of the 20th century as the result of civil rights movement. More minority members and women entered the workforce beginning in the 1960s and continue to be the fastest growing groups in the labor force. The diverse workforce is a reflection of the American population change in the last two decades as well. According to the U.S. Census Bureau (2016), the Hispanic population grew 43% from 2000 through 2010, four times faster than the growth rate for the United States as a whole, and is the largest numerical minority group in United States. The census data from the American Community Survey (U.S. Census Bureau, 2016) shows that Hispanic or Latino individuals comprise 17.8% of entire the U.S. population, Black/African American 12.3%, Asian American 5.4%, Native American 0.7%, and Native Hawaiian and other Pacific Islander 0.2%. In regard to labor force participation, Hispanic Americans also surpass White Americans in labor force participation, and Hispanic men have the highest participation rate (74.4%) among all ethnic groups (Bureau of Labor Statistics, October 2017a). African-American men have had consistently lower rates than the rate of for all men; African-American women generally had higher rates than rates for all women and much higher rates than African-American men; rates for both Black men and women are projected to decline from 2016 to 2026. (Bureau of Labor Statistics, 2018). The participation distribution between men and women in 2016 was 53.2% and 46.8%, and in 2026 this ratio is projected to be 52.6% and 47.4% respectively (Bureau of Labor Statistics, October 2017b). The labor force continues to change in racial and ethnic composition, with the percentage of Asians and people of Hispanic backgrounds expected to grow much faster than the average annual rate from 2016 to 2026. One in five workers by 2016 is projected to be an individual of Hispanic origin (Bureau of Labor Statistics, 2017a). It is also noticed that more and more dual income families emerge due to not only the women's liberation movement but also economic necessity as the cost of living has also been on the rise in the recent decades. The traditional, average family with the husband being the breadwinner and the wife the caregiver is not necessarily the norm anymore.

There are several factors contributing to the growing diversity in the labor force. The American population experiences demographic changes over time, as illustrated by the census data. The composition of the U.S. population includes people representing diverse cultural backgrounds. Another factor impacting the increasingly diverse workforce is the rising number of immigrants in the last few decades. Unlike the first wave of immigrants at the beginning of the century that were mainly from Europe, the majority of new immigrants since the mid 1960s were from various continents, with more from Central and South American countries and Asian regions. Immigrants often filled low-paid positions requiring minimum language skills and education credentials. As stated above, women's rising participation in the labor force is mainly the result of the civil rights movement and education opportunities accessible to girls. In addition, more women choose to work outside of home due to the financial situation where additional income is needed to support the family. Similarly, some women have to work because they are the sole breadwinner for the family. Some families, on the other hand, make the decision that men stay at home and women work outside of home.

In summary, with the demographic changes in the American population; an influx of immigrants from various parts of the world; the civil rights movement resulting in awareness of equality for minorities, women, and other oppressed groups; and changes in education and employment, lifestyle choices, and financial necessity, more women and minority members have entered the labor force. As the workforce is becoming diverse in various dimensions, it is necessary to understand the implications of the diverse labor force to individuals in their career exploration so that counselors can better serve their clients.

SOCIAL BARRIERS TO CAREER DEVELOPMENT

Career development is personal, yet it is also social, as working involves interaction with the outside world beyond one's individual space. However, not everyone has equal access and resources to opportunities for satisfying career development. "The existence of social barriers such as racism, sexism, classism, heterosexism, and ableism function to create very disparate conditions that consign many individuals to a life of despair and want" (Blustein, 2006, p. 194). Though disparate conditions in the work environment have changed, conditions are still far from equitable. These barriers still significantly influence and can be impediments for individuals' career development.

Gender

Women's participation in the labor force has experienced significant changes in the past 50 years, evidenced by not only more women entering into the work world but also women holding more diverse occupations and positions than their counterparts in the earlier years. Women had access to education at the beginning of the 20th century, but their career choices were limited to a few service related fields such as teaching, nursing, and possibly secretarial or clerical jobs. Very few women at the beginning of the 20th century could work outside of home or hold any professional positions other than in educational or service-oriented settings. This kind of occupational limitation for women gradually changed as a result of the women's liberation movement at the turn of the last century and the civil rights movement in the mid 20th century. As of today, a large number of women work in various positions, including occupations traditionally dominated by males (e.g., engineers, scientists, factory workers). However, even with an unprecedented number of women entering the workforce, women are still less represented in science, technology, math, and engineering (STEM) fields and in top administrative positions in any organizations (Betz, 2005). It is argued that persistent underrepresentation of women and ethnic minorities in STEM fields across different levels of schools and professions is a complex social problem that requires more systematic intervention (Syed & Chemers, 2011).

A long time stereotypical view of roles for women is that they are innate caretakers and nurturers. The implied meaning is that women are better suited for domestic work and taking care of family rather than working outside of home. In fact, many researchers have found that multiple roles are important to women's mental and physical health and protect against unfavorable mental health (Barnett & Hyde, 2001). Betz (2005) argued that women, just like men, need satisfaction of achievement and interpersonal relationships outside of the home. In addition to psychological needs and well-being, working also provides women independence and economic security that could not be possible if women still relied on others for meeting their basic needs. With the high cost of living and depressed economic situations in modern society, dual incomes are sometimes a necessity for families rather than an option. However, participation in the labor force, though making significant progress in the historical context, does not mean women have equal access, opportunity, and compensation as men. Equity is still a critical issue for women in regard to career choice and advancement.

Women by far still do not have equal opportunities to highly paid or prestigious jobs as men. There are many fewer females holding top administrative positions in all types of organizations. For instance, there were only 40 female college presidents out of 254 American college presidents (Newman, 2014). Women disproportionately work in low-paid, less stable jobs and have less mobility (Niles & Harris-Bowlsbey, 2013). For the same jobs (exact same job duties and responsibilities, requiring the same credentials), females are paid only 82% of males' compensation, a progressive growth from 65% in the 1970s (Bureau of Labor Statistics, 2017c). Such inequality has been addressed by various professionals over a long time period and progress has been made, compared to even bigger discrepancies in pay for women in earlier years. Nonetheless, women still do not have equality in opportunity or rewards. For instance, women veterans had lower employment rates than their male counterparts (Greer, 2017).

Barriers to equality in work settings for women involve restricted choices, ability utilization, opportunities for advancement, and equal pay. The traditional gender role as homemaker and mother might be still an important factor for many women when making career decision and choices (Fitzgerald, Fassinger, & Betz, 1995). The restricted choices might be due to gender role stereotyping like women being in service-related occupations. Research has found that this traditional gender role identification was the result of socialization of belief and behavior patterns (see Gottfredson, 1981; Farmer, 1997; Betz, 2006). Girls and boys had similar career aspirations when they were young and progressively showed changed as they aged, with female adolescents adjusting their career aspirations to be more consistent with the traditional female-dominated occupations. Similarly, the educational system in the United States reinforced this socialized belief through implicit or sometime even overt messages in classroom activities and learning experiences. The early studies about college students found that only 30% of the females believed they could complete a degree in engineering compared to 70% of the males who thought so (Betz & Hackett, 1981). More recent studies found a similar pattern of discouragement for women choosing STEM occupations. Female engineering graduate students were found to gradually adapt their occupational aspirations and career identities to fit socio-cultural expectations and struggle in their early yeas as female employees in STEM fields (Papafilippou & Bentley, 2017). Parents probably also play a role in shaping children's beliefs about gender stereotypes of occupations. Further, this socialization could be internalized by females, causing them to avoid male-dominated occupations, thinking that they are not fit for these occupations (Betz, 2005; Cook, 1993).

According to Betz and Hackett (1981), the reason for females avoiding science and technology occupations was related to lack of role models, encouragement from others, and self-efficacy. Self-efficacy, denoted in Bandura's (1977, 1986) social learning theory, influences people in their choice of behaviors. For example, when young girls see few female adults working as engineers or lawyers, when they receive messages from teachers, parents, and other people constantly that girls are not suited for certain jobs, and when they see more boys than girls are given opportunities to try hard math problems, they begin to doubt their own abilities in these areas and accept the belief of female inadequacy in math and science themselves; consequently, girls avoid occupations that require abilities in math and science. Interventions addressing gaps in gender role identification and equality need to provide supportive learning experiences for female students, such as living learning programs in which female college students interact with peers to discuss academic and career issues (Szelenyi, Denson, & Inkelas, 2013).

Race and Ethnicity

A pluralistic society as in the United States, with people from multicultural, multiethnic, and multilingual backgrounds, presents complexity for understanding the career development needs of each individual. Though this section will describe some characteristics of racial/ethnic minority groups in regard to their career-related needs, it does not mean that only between-group differences are important to understand in order to provide culturally appropriate career intervention; in other words, it is equally important to be aware of within-group differences and individual characteristics. In the section Intersection of Diversity, we will discuss in more detail the interrelatedness of various dimensions of one's cultural background.

The disparity for females in the work environment also occurs to racial and ethnic minority members. For instance, labor statistics showed that African Americans have the lowest labor force participation among all racial groups (63.6%, compared to national average at 70.2% and 71% for White Americans). Regarding education levels, Hispanic Americans had the lowest rate of completing bachelor's or higher degrees among all ethnic groups (17%) and had the highest rates of high school dropout (Bureau of Labor Statistics, 2013). African Americans had a high rate of school dropout, too, at the level of 26%; and

African-American males had the highest rate of unemployment (14.2%,), according to recent labor statistics (Bureau of Labor Statistics, 2013). African and Hispanic Americans were also overrepresented in service and laborer intensive occupations as compared to White Americans. It is noticed that Asian Americans had the highest percentage of completing undergraduate degree (58%) and the fewest high school dropouts. However, Asian Americans were less represented in top administrative positions and were disproportionately overrepresented in technology fields. What these data and research findings reveal is that racial/ethical minorities, regardless of their educational credentials, face barriers in career attainment. As a matter of fact, when college students were interviewed about their perceptions of barriers to career development, racial and ethnic status was identified as one of the barriers (Luzzo, 1993). A meta-analysis of race and ethnicity in career development research found that there is no significant difference among racial/ethnic groups in regard to career aspiration or career decision making; however, racial and ethnic minorities perceived more barriers and fewer opportunities than their White American counterparts (Fouad, Byars, & Winston, 2005). Racial and ethnic minorities have similar aspirations, but they are not properly represented in all levels and types of work as compared to White Americans; this may be due to barriers as a result of discrimination (Fouad & Kantamneni, 2008).

The barriers to minority members in regard to career choices and career advancement are multiple. In addition to limited access to quality educational opportunities and resources, occupational stereotypes, occupational discrimination, occupational segregation, and the glass ceiling were considered as having impacts on minority members' career development (Leong and Serafica, 2001). The next section will discuss these concepts in detail.

The following reviews some major characteristics of racial/ethnic minorities in regard to career development. It needs to be noted that these are just common features shared by many members of the groups and, in some cases, also are indications of stereotypes. It does not mean that every single member within the group will perfectly fit to these characteristics. In other words, one needs to be careful not to stereotype any individuals because she or he belongs to a certain ethnic group.

Hispanic Americans

Hispanic Americans are actually a very diverse group representing various race, ethnicity, language, immigration status, and religious backgrounds. Often referred to as Latino/a Americans, this indicates one historical characteristic associated with this group—most have origins related to Latin American continents. This is the fastest growing and largest minority group in the United States and will grow from currently 9% of the population to 22% by 2050 (Zunker, 2012). Hispanic Americans, especially Hispanic women, were underrepresented at all educational levels and had lower high school graduation rates. Consequently, they had restricted employment and were more likely to work in lower paid, less skilled occupations (Flores & O'Brien, 2002). Hispanic Americans value family unity and prioritize family goals over individuals ones; strong family relationships and interdependence are treasured; family members as well as community members usually show deference to authority figures who typically are older male adults (Brown, 2012). The male dominance in Hispanic-American culture intensifies the challenges for Hispanic women in regard to their career development because the traditional role designation for Hispanic women is being a mother, caretaker of the family, not pursuing career success outside of the home (Rivera, Chen, Flores, Blumberg, & Ponterotto, 2007). Hispanic women have to reconcile inconsistencies between their career aspiration and their family expectations when they pursue nontraditional career choices, for example, requiring more education, higher income, and status (Flores & O'Brien, 2002). When examining Mexican-American girls' career decision-making process, career self-efficacy, perceived support and barriers, along with acculturation were found to be influential for choosing nontraditional career choices (Flores & O'Brien, 2002).

Language and immigration status are two important factors that influence Hispanic Americans' career path. The majority of the Hispanic population in the United States is of Mexican heritage (Gibson & Mitchell, 2006). As an increasing number of Hispanics are migrating from the southern states to the Midwest and northern states in the United States, there are changing trends for the workforce, economy, and cultural interactions with both the Hispanic community and the entire society. For instance, bilingual signs in public arenas are more available beyond border states in the South.

African Americans

African Americans are the second largest minority group in the United States and have historically been the victims of oppression and discrimination for a long time. African Americans are the most researched minority group (Miller & Brown, 2005) in educational and career development areas. African Americans are overrepresented in poverty, unemployment, and lower level occupations with little room for professional growth and career advancement; however, the data also show that a high percentage of African-American workers are in managerial and administrative positions (Herr & Cramer, 1996). Middle-class and college-educated African-American parents are more likely to encourage and aspire for their offspring to attain higher educational achievement and occupational accomplishment. Family support and strong parental expectations are the motivation for many young African Americans to achieve highly in academic performance and professional advancement (Miller & Brown, 2005). Their accomplishments do not overshadow the discrimination and racism experienced by African Americans in education and work domains. The low rate of high school graduation is still prevalent in urban schools where there is a disproportionately large number of African-American youth. African Americans are still overrepresented ■ in labor-intensive, low-paid, low-skilled occupations.

Asian Americans

The term *Asian American* is simply a convenient label to lump together everyone whose ancestors or who themselves come from Asia; however, in terms of race/ethnicity, language spoken, religious background, and cultural background, there is more diversity than commonality within this group. For example, people from central Asia (e.g., an Arab-speaking Turkish Muslim) and Southeast Asia (e.g., a French-speaking Vietnamese Buddhist) do not share anything in common except that their origin is in the Asia continent. Diversity among Asian Americans also occurs in their generation status, place of birth, and acculturation levels. One of the misconceptions of Asian Americans is the model minority stereotype. Though some or even many Asian Americans have achieved success in academic domains—the basis on which this model minority label is mainly based on—it does not mean that every Asian American has accomplished the same level of success. Such an incorrect label, in fact, overshadows the needs of Asian Americans because lacking awareness of the true situation blocks the access and availability of resources to help members in need; thus, Asian Americans are more likely to be underserved. For example, Asian-American high school students have difficulty securing college scholarships or financial aid compared to other racial groups because of model minority myth. The model minority myth is detrimental to the interests of many Asian Americans because this empirically inaccurate discourse masks the diversity (in regard to socioeconomic status, educational attainment, academic achievement, and need for services) within the group (Tang, 2008; Tsunokai, 2005), and consequently, difficulties (limited English skills, miscommunication, discrimination, and alienation) experienced by Asian Americans have become invisible to policymakers (Yang, 2004).

Research about Asian Americans' career development has recently become more available than before. Many studies have found that family and acculturation are two significant factors influencing career choices and decision making of Asian Americans (Leong & Chou, 1994; Patel, Salahuddin, & O'Brien, 2008; Tang, Fouad, & Smith, 1999). Family influences individuals in multifaceted ways. Filial piety is a core value in traditional Asian culture, which indicates that parents have the authority to make decisions for their children, including educational and career plans, and sometimes marriage. Though in modern society, not many parents would make decisions for their children or demand absolute obedience; however, the expectation of children's deference to their parents' authority is still prevalent not only among parents but also among children. Young people feel obligated to fulfill their parents' expectations or feel guilty if they disobey. The parental expectation and influence on Asian American youth's career choice was evidenced in many studies (Tang et al., 1999). Therefore, when an Asian-American teenager says he or she wants to be a physician, career counselors cannot assume this decision is out of his or her own interests, because the decision may have been made based on his or her perceived responsibility to the family as well as to live up to parents' expectation. In general, the conflict between Asian-American parents and their offspring is often the parents' priority on stability and secure financial rewards by the occupation versus their children's priority on personal interests and aspirations, particularly when the stability or security of employment is shaky.

Native Americans

Native Americans are probably the least researched and most overlooked group among all minority groups. One of the reasons for less attention from scholars and practitioners could be because Native Americans are the smallest in number yet the within-group differences are huge (Brown, 2012). There is a wide variety of languages spoken and different tribes with distinct cultural characteristics, which presents challenges to study and generalize the findings of any studies. Due to the history and government policy of preservation, few Native Americans participate in work outside of their tribes, and therefore, have limited knowledge of the world of work or have a narrow range of occupational choices (Martin, 1991; Miller & Brown, 2005).

Despite the diversity within the group, Native Americans share some common cultural values that could potentially impact their career development. According to Miller and Brown (2005), Native Americans emphasize tribal community over personal career development; or in other words, career choice cannot jeopardize the relationship to the family and community. It is of utmost importance that individuals' career choices should benefit the family and tribal community as well. Another value that is significant in understanding Native Americans is their time orientation. Traditional Native Americans tend to be present oriented rather than future oriented (Sue & Sue, 2013). One main goal of most career development intervention is to have a concrete career plan with goals identified and action steps to accomplish the goals. However, Native American may not conform to this rigorous, structured future planning, as many Native Americans may focus more on the flexibility rather than stability in regard to planning and view family, home, and community as more important than a job or career (Martin, 1991; Martin & Farris, 1994).

Because many children in Native American families learn English and native languages at the same time, they encounter a challenge of mastering both languages with proficiency. Low perceived social status was another barrier for Native Americans, and coping and self-efficacy could buffer system and personal classism experienced (Thompson, 2013). Native American high school students with learning disabilities were found to be less likely to live independently and to experience more difficulty in transitioning to adult life (Ramasamy, Duffy, & Camp, 2000). When examining life-role salience, Brown and Lavish (2006) found that home/family participation and commitment were more salient than work participation and commitment, and that youth decided to attend college for fighting the issue of low employment rate. The research also found that mentoring in the school settings and informal mentoring in communities for science experiences would help Native American students develop interests in STEM fields (Stevens, Andrade, & Page, 2016). Native Americans living in two cultures were found to be constantly trying to balance between the two cultures that often have different values (Sanchez, Poll-Hunter, Stern, Garcia, & Brewster, 2016). Thus, understanding their self-concept and cultural identity is beneficial to comprehending Native Americans' career development. Counselors working with Native Americans need to consider the importance of working with clients' family and extended families and the possibility of cultural conflict influencing career decision making (Martin, 1991).

Religious Background

The U.S. population includes many varieties of religious backgrounds; however, not all faiths have the equal voice in the society. The work environment may or may not accommodate workers from diverse religious backgrounds. Thus, it is necessary for counselors to be aware of the potential issues related to clients' religious backgrounds and the impact on their decision-making processes, career choices, and vocational behaviors. Unfortunately, there are few studies about the relationship between one's religious background and career development, despite the fact that most literature on multicultural counseling and career development as well as the Council of Accredited Counseling and Related Education Programs (CACREP) standards include religious background as one of the areas for multicultural competency (Flores & Bike, 2014; CACREP, 2016). The limited number of studies did find a relationship between religious background and career decisions. For instance, Rich & Golan (1992) found that high school girls in religious settings were more likely to choose male-dominated occupations than their counterparts in secular schools. In another study about work ethics in business, it was found that people with Muslim backgrounds scored higher than people from Protestant and Catholic backgrounds on Protestant Work Ethics characterized by "hard work and success," "internal locus of control," and "negative attitude toward leisure" (Zulfikar, 2012). The same study did not find statistical differences on the "work as an end itself" dimension among three groups, although Protestant groups scored the highest.

The role of religion and spirituality to individuals' mental health and career development has been increasingly recognized by counseling professionals (Duffy, 2006). While religion and spirituality could vary in definition and measurement in research, belief in and relationship with faith or higher power(s) are usually encompassed. Duffy (2006) summarized that religion and spirituality had a positive impact on how individuals coped with career-related challenges such as career decision making, higher job satisfaction, and finding coherence of values and careers. Another growing research on a related topic is calling. "Calling refers to a personally or socially meaningful engagement with one's work, sometimes linked to one's religious or spiritual perspective, sometimes to a sense of passion or giftedness, and sometimes to a deeply held set of values for making a difference or leaving a legacy" (Dik & Duffy, 2015, p. 305). Dik and Duffy (2015) concluded that a sense of calling provides more satisfaction, motivation, and commitment in the work and more meaningfulness of career and life.

Socioeconomic Status

The impact of social class and classism on career development is well documented in many studies and considered one of the key barriers for individuals' pursuit of educational and career attainment (Ali, 2013; Fouad & Brown, 2000; Blustein et al., 2002; Liu, 2001). Socioeconomic status, or SES, typically is understood as one's position in social and economic ranks characterized by educational and occupational achievement and income level. It is well evidenced in research that low SES can limit one's opportunities to access resources, occupational aspiration, or attainment (Fouad & Kantamneni, 2008; Blustein et al., 2002). Smith (2005) found that SES was a robust impact factor for clients' psychological behaviors when other demographic variables were controlled. People in poverty and the working class often could not fully explore their potentials and capacities due to limited resources, and therefore, viewed work as a means to obtain income for a living rather than for self-concept implementation or self-expression (Blustein, Kozan, Connors-Kellgren, & Rand, 2015). Work, specifically unemployment or underemployment, could have a reciprocal relationship with poverty; in other words, work or unemployment might be the reason for many people in mobile poverty situations, that is, in and out of poverty because of dependence on employment income (Smith, 2005), which could be harmful for health.

Classism is defined as prejudice and discrimination against others to maintain one's own perceived social status (Liu & Ali, 2005), and consequently, it reinforces social and economic stratification. Liu and Ali (2005) also discussed how classism could hinder professionals fully understanding individuals who had different life paths than their own (e.g., attending college and obtaining a meaningful and financially rewarding job).

Upward mobility and achieving career success valued by the middle class may not be the core values for other groups; however, the dominant discourse of the U.S. society is that everyone needs to work hard to attain higher occupational status, but resources are not readily available to everyone to be adequately prepared for entry into the workforce.

Disability

The American Disability Act defines disability as physical, mental, or emotional impairment that substantially limits functioning in a major life activity, including work. There is a huge heterogeneity among people with disability, depending on the nature of disability. In general, participation in the workforce by people with disabilities is low with a decreasing trend (Newman, Wagner, Cameto, Knokey, & Shaver, 2010). Further, there was a discrepancy between wanting to work and actual employment. The type and severity of disability are significant determinants of employment outcome (Fabian & Liesener, 2005, p. 562). Barriers to workforce participation include: employer attitudes and discrimination, lack of adequate preparation for the workplace, lack of postsecondary education and vocational training, lack of available community employment services, and perceived difficulties of services by the professionals (Fabian & Liesener, 2005). Zunker (2006) also stated the following factors could present barriers to people with disability: difficulties in accepting and adjustment to disabilities due to traumatic experiences, misconceptions and attitudes toward disability by others, lack of role models, threatened self-concept, and coping skills.

Many federal legislation, policies, and vocational programs at schools aim at addressing barriers. The Individuals with Disabilities Education Act (Public Law 101-476) was established in 1976 to help individuals transition from school to adult life, to include postsecondary education and vocational training, employment, independent living, and social and community participation. The Americans with Disabilities Act (PL 101-336), passed in 1990, prohibits discrimination against people with disabilities in various settings, for example, employment, public services, transportation, and telecommunication. In addition, "reasonable accommodation" is another important part of this act. Some other recent legislation aims at providing opportunities and incentives for people with disabilities to be prepared and ready for work participation. Functional vocational assessment, as alternative career assessment tool, would do a better job in understanding the strengths and limitations of students with severe disabilities (Dewlen & Spires, 2000). In the same vein, vocational rehabilitation programs shift away from a deficit model to a person-environment fit model and to transition services leading to employment (IDEA, 2004).

Despite the legislation promoting assistance offered to people with disabilities to transition to employment, there is still lacking applicable theory or sufficient education programs to prepare youth for career planning and performance (Fabian & Liesener, 2005). At the same time, the percentage of children classified as having a serious emotional disturbance has increased considerably (U.S. Department of Education, National Center for Educational Statistics, 2012). It is necessary then for educators and counselors to examine the specific challenges encountered by these children with mental health issues and emotional disturbances and to develop appropriate career planning and transition services. The barriers experienced by adolescents with disabilities include insensitivity, discrimination, lack of accommodation, and responsive services (Geenen, Powers, Vasquez, &

Bersani, 2003); family values and desire for optimum capacity for successful transition were found in the same study as critical to transition to adult life.

To effectively help individuals with disabilities, counselors need to gain competencies in the following areas: (a) gain knowledge of federal and state laws, guidelines, policies, and institutional rules; (b) understand basic types and characteristics of disabilities; (c) become aware of barriers and issues from employers as well as the public about needs and abilities of people with disabilities in relation to work; (d) gain knowledge and skills to perform career assessments that are ecologically fit to clients with disabilities with goals; (e) become familiar with resources in the community for educational and employment opportunities for people with disabilities; (f) understand the policies and methods of providing appropriate accommodations in work settings; and (g) have knowledge of vocational rehabilitation programs and career intervention services in the community. Polo Sanchez and Lopez Justicia (2016) found that training programs for job search strategies along with the student initiatives help college students with disabilities secure jobs. Career service professionals at college settings need to collaborate with staff members in disability services to make career intervention programs accommodate the needs of students with disabilities.

Sexual Identity and Orientation

Another socially oppressed group is the LGBTQ (lesbian, gay, bisexual, transgender, queer) population. Like other oppressed minority groups, the LGBTQ individuals have gone through an identity development process for self-concept development (Cass, 1979; Chapman & Brannock, 1987; Pope, Prince, & Mitchell, 2000). Common themes for LGBTQ identity development are characterized by the beginning stages of confusion and questioning, as they see differences between themselves and others. The middle stages typically refer to their effort of comparing, seeking answers, and feeling an incongruence of who they are and how they feel. The late stages include progressive self-acceptance, pride, and synthesis of their identity. Understanding the LGBTQ identity stages is important for counselors when working with LGBTQ clients on career development issues because failing to recognize the level of development of the LGBTQ client can potentially risk the trust by clients.

Although there is scant research about career development and intervention among the LGBTQ population, the effort to apply and examine career development theories to the population has been ongoing for decades (Chung, 2003; Chen & Vollick, 2013). For college LGBTQ students, seeking help and using career assessment tools might be a concern because they are afraid of being exposed as gay when going through the tests (which may have questionable fairness and validity to the population) or being misdiagnosed (Pope et al., 2000). Discrimination against sexual minority college students can be subtle or blatant, but a campus-wide antidiscrimination and inclusion policy would reduce the occurrence of verbal threats (Hong, Woodford, Long, & Renn, 2016). The difficulties for sexual minority workers include sexual identity disclosure and management, workplace discrimination, negotiation of benefits, and lack of resources and services (Chung, 2003; Pope & Barrett, 2002). One study found that Black, queer college students felt that their visible aspects of identity such as race, gender expression, and degree of disclosure influenced their perception of career development (Harris, 2014). The workplace discrimination could be overt, such as official policies against the rights of LGBTQ employment and limited career choice, or it could be covert, such as a hostile work environment (Chung, 2001).

LEARNING ACTIVITY 3.1

WHAT HAVE YOU EXPERIENCED?

Have the students list their personal demographic information on a piece of paper, for example, male, able, middle class, Christian and so on, on one side of a paper. Then list the schools they have attended, colleges they have attended, any extracurricular activities they have participated in, and any jobs they have had on the other side of the paper. Now review the two lists, and identify the privileges they have that led them to where they are today, and identify the barriers/hurdles they have experienced that have prohibited them from accomplishing their goals so far. The students should do this task alone and quietly (allowing them to process the information). After everyone completes the task, the instructor facilitates the class to discuss how the identified privileges and barriers impact their own career paths and how these privileges and barriers are related to their personal demographic characteristics.

Despite progress in gender identity inclusion in educational settings and in the workplace, there are still prevalent social and institutional discrimination for people of gender nonconforming identity and trans people (Restar & Reisner, 2017). The unemployment rate for trans people is three times higher than for the general population and four times higher for trans people of color (Mennicke & Cutler-Seeber, 2016), and the poverty rate is also higher for trans people (Restar & Reisner, 2017). Discrimination in the workplace could be in the form of overt assault or even violence, or removal from direct contact with customers, or denial of promotion (Mennicke & Cutler-Seeber, 2016). Antidiscrimination policies, professional training of employees, and formal and informal inclusion organizational procedures are suggested by the scholars to help people of gender nonconforming identity in the workplace. Chung (2001) also recommended that LGBTQ people could consider self-employment, look for LGBTQ friendly and supportive work settings, or take risks in facing discrimination as coping strategies for career choices. The model of dealing with discrimination proposed by Chung includes quitting, remaining silent, soliciting social support, and confronting discrimination. Counselors working with LGBTQ clients need to be mindful that not everyone is ready for confrontation, so it is critical to understand LGBTQ identify development status and apply the intervention strategies that fit clients' level of LGBTQ identity. Counselors should engage in activities promoting social justice, advocate for LGBTQ rights, and become familiar with LGBTQ culture (Pope & Barrett, 2002).

MULTICULTURAL CAREER DEVELOPMENT ISSUES

Occupational Stereotypes

Occupational stereotypes refer to the widespread and overgeneralized perception of certain characteristics associated to a group of people in career domains. For instance,

Hispanic women work as hotel cleaning staff, Asian Americans are engineers, and African-American males work as garbage collectors; all these are examples of occupational stereotypes. Another example is when a boy was injured in a car accident, the emergency room doctor could not operate on him because the doctor was the boy's parent. Most people assume this doctor is the boy's father, but in fact, the doctor is his mother. The story tells us an example of gender stereotype of occupations as people see more males as doctors and females as nurses. The occupational stereotypes exist for multiple reasons: the traditional view of gender roles or ethnic groups in the occupations, the presence of certain people in presumed occupations for a long time, and media coverage with stereotypical images of people working in certain occupations. In addition, occupational stereotypes are reflections of the fact that there is overrepresentation of certain demographic groups working in limited occupations, and one sees very few ethnic minority members or women in some other occupations, for example, few women in managerial and administrative positions in organizations or few Asian Americans in legal occupations. Native Americans, African Americans, and Latina women have persistent underrepresentation in STEM fields (Syed & Chemers, 2011). Occupational stereotypes can negatively impact both individuals and organizations by limiting individual career choices and selection of future workforce.

Occupational Segregation

Occupational segregation refers to the unbalanced distribution of members of an ethnic group across occupations, that is, overrepresented in certain occupations and underrepresented in other occupations. Occupational segregation is related to occupational stereotypes because the reasons why people have a stereotype of ethnic groups in certain occupations is due to what they consistently see in the media as well as their surroundings. The research has found that significantly higher numbers of minority members held jobs that are predominantly lower level, low paid, and with less career mobility (Leong & Hayes, 1990; Leong & Serafica, 2001; Bureau of Labor Statistics, 2017a). For instance, Hispanic Americans accounted for 13.7% of the total labor force, but a much higher percentage of them work in miscellaneous agriculture, and a higher proportion of Hispanic women work in service or sales areas (Bureau of Labor Statistics, 2017b). It is not known whether occupational stereotypes lead to occupational segregation or occupational segregation reinforces occupational stereotypes; regardless of which is true, the reality is that occupational segregation puts minority people at risk of being denied their capacities because of the restricted opportunities. Occupational segregation might also be the result of occupational discrimination.

Occupational Discrimination

The relationship among occupational stereotypes, occupational segregation, and occupational discrimination is interrelated. It can be understood as three dimensions of one issue—equality for people from cultural backgrounds different from the dominant group in the society. Occupational discrimination refers to the overt or subtle unfair treatment against targeted groups. Discrimination can be in subtle forms such as by-passing a minority member for promotion or giving poorer reviews, or it can be in blatant forms including verbal bulling or violence against minority members. Prejudice out of racism, sexism, and so on can negatively influence the self-image of those groups oppressed and discourage people from pursuing their dream careers (Bowman & Evans, 2006). People's perceived discrimination in work settings is evidenced in a Gallup survey that showed that 46% of African Americans, 34% of Asian Americans, 27% of Hispanic Americans, and 17% of White Americans reported discrimination and prejudice in work settings (Fukuyama & Cox, 1992). Actual or perceived discrimination may lead minority members to develop poor vocational self-concepts and consequently avoid some occupational choices (Miller & Brown, 2005). According to Miller and Brown (2005), the long history of oppression toward people of color through displacement, restricted opportunities to education and occupation, economic exploitation, social marginalization, and segregation policy could not be easily or quickly changed despite the effort of addressing the equality issues since the Civil Rights movement in the 1960s. Professional counselors still have a long course of effort to address the inequality issues in educational and work settings. Social justice and advocacy are needed to make the change to the level and magnitude necessary for achieving equity. The competency section will discuss the skills and strategies counselors can apply in promoting social justice and advocating for clients.

Microaggressions in the Workplace

Although the law of the United States clearly bars racism and hate crimes, and many people do not believe they are racist, it does not mean racism or discrimination against people based on race, ethnicity, gender identity, religion, sexual orientation, disability, or other personal characteristics are nonexistent; as Sue (2010) argued, racism appears in subtle and covert forms in daily life. This indirect form of racism is *microaggression*, defined by Sue et al. (2007) as "verbal, behavioral, and environmental indignities, whether intentional or unintentional, that communicate hostile, derogatory, or negative racial slights and insults to the target person or group" (p. 273). The research on microaggressions later was extended to other marginalized groups—people of color, women, LGBT, and trans people (see Sue, 2010; Nadal, 2011, 2013). The implied message from various microaggression behaviors conveys the theme of marginalized groups being alien in one's own land, being inferior, denial of racial reality/sexism/cisgender privilege, and pathologizing/abnormality (Nadal, 2013). Microaggressions may not violate the law but they still create a harsh and hostile work environment (Mizzi, 2017), and most often, coworkers, supervisors, and administrators are the offenders. Workplace microaggressions have been experienced by ethnic minority members and found to be related to withdrawal from work, intention to quit, and negative job satisfaction (DeCuir-Gunby & Gunby, 2016; Nadal, Mazzula, Rivera, & Fujii-Doe, 2014).

Awareness and recognition of microaggressions are needed for counselors to develop cultural competency in working with diverse populations. As cultural competency is not an end product but rather an ongoing process of improvement, keeping open minds for learning and humbleness would be helpful. To address microaggressions in the workplace, systemwide change (e.g., creating or updating codes of conduct, workplace policies, legal reform, or staff development in the organization) is necessary (Mizzi, 2017). Counselors can help clients from marginalized groups by being advocates and engaging in professional training for all workers on the topic of microaggressions and building supportive and inclusive work environments.

Glass Ceiling

The glass ceiling refers to "artificial barriers based on attitudinal or organizational bias that prevent some groups of people from advancing in an organization" (Betz, 2005, p. 265). Betz (2005) also stated that for women of color, subtlety of the glass ceiling did not even exist; what they encounter is concrete ceiling or walls, which indicates forceful barriers for women to take leadership roles in corporate America. In a study about female and male executives, it was found that female executives had less opportunities for promotion, less benefits, and less rewards, despite having exactly the same credentials and experiences as their male counterparts (Lyness & Thompson, 1997). The Department of Labor's Federal Glass Ceiling Commission (1995) reported that a glass ceiling existed based on the fact that women held only 3% to 5% of senior corporate leadership positions. It confirmed the "existence of invisible, artificial barriers, women and minorities from advancing up the corporate ladder to management and executive positions" (p.iii). The commission report revealed that a glass ceiling existed due to (1) societal barriers—gender role stereotypes, biases, and prejudice; (2) institutional barriers—isolated women workers, lack of pipeline of women leaders, lack of mentoring and management training for women, and lack of advancement opportunities; and (3) inadequate government policies and guidelines.

Though the term *glass ceiling* originally referred to the phenomenon of women being limited from earning top leadership positions, the similar pattern applies to minority groups as well (Wilson, 2014). It is well evidenced that racial/ethnic minority members experience glass ceilings across many settings (Phelps & Constantine, 2001; Chen, 2005). Since the civil rights movement and federal initiatives of eliminating artificial barriers for women and minorities, there has been some increase of women and minorities taking top executive positions, but there has not been a lot of significant changes since the commission report, and there is still a large disparity in women and minorities in leadership positions (Wilson, 2014). When discussing her experiences of overcoming the glass ceiling, McCrady (2012) said,

> In many ways, it is a far, far better world for women professionals today than it was 40 years ago. We have laws against sexual harassment and sexual discrimination; we have better maternity leave policies and better child care facilities; and we have women professionals at all levels of accomplishment and influence—women no longer have to take a solitary journey. Importantly, women today do not experience the same sense of vulnerability to lost opportunities, and do not have to fight battles for legitimacy on a daily basis. Women, though, still have choices that loom larger than the choices men make about career and family; and while institutional sexism has largely gone underground, I believe that prejudices against women continue to exist in subtle but still demoralizing ways. (p. 720)

Yes, indeed, overt gender marginalization and discrimination may not be as common today, but achieving total equality for women has a long way to go. Gender equality could be perceived as women's greed, and the success of women leaders could be perceived as an easy task or luck; or in other words, women in leadership positions were expected to deliver the job yet at the same time they were minimized for their competence (Isaac, Kaatz, & Carnes, 2012). The complexities of the glass ceiling on women need careful consideration in career intervention.

LEARNING ACTIVITY 3.2
STEREOTYPES

Do this prompt response exercise to witness how we all have stereotyped images of certain groups in regard to their work certain occupations being held by certain groups of people. Pair the students who sit across from each other. One person states ethnicity, race, gender, or names of countries or products randomly, and the other person responds immediately with an occupation, without time to think about the prompt. For instance,

"Asian American" as the prompt, and "engineers" as the response. Then switch the role, one gives the prompt using the occupational titles, and the other responds with the group of people holding the occupation; for instance, "nurses" as the prompt and "women" as the response. After a few rounds, the instructor asks the class to debrief about the common theme in each pair and discuss how we function when time to think is limited.

The concepts reviewed in this section reveal the multicultural issues that influence the choice, development, advancement, and support for people of minority status in this society. These issues are interrelated and could impact independently or interactively individuals at different stages of their life span. Understanding the constructs of these issues and their implications to minority members in their career development would help counselors develop appropriate awareness and competency so that they can more effectively help clients live up to their aspirations and potentials.

INTERSECTION OF DIVERSITY

As stated above, our society is becoming unprecedentedly diverse and multifaceted in nature regarding individual characteristics. People often assume diversity refers to ethnic or racial minority groups, in fact, diversity encompasses many different aspects. We have reviewed gender issues, racial/ethnicity issues, socioeconomic status, disability issues, and so on; these aspects do not exist in an isolated manner; instead, they coexist in an interactive way. For instance, socioeconomic status, race/ethnicity, and gender were found as single factor or interactively with each other to have impacts on career aspirations of youth (Howard et al., 2011). These factors influence one's career development and path in a confluent fashion rather than disparately; therefore, it is important for counselors to understand the interaction of these factors and their impact on one's career development in order to develop more culturally appropriate understanding and interventions. Acculturation and cultural identity are two concepts pertaining to understanding the nature of intersection and interaction of multifactors. Thus, prior to discussing convergence of multicultural issues, acculturation and cultural identity are reviewed.

Acculturation

When a person moves from one context to a different context, for instance, people migrating from rural Mexico to urban Chicago, they encounter a new culture different from their original culture. This experience of living in one cultural context yet being influenced by another culture has individuals encountering two cultures simultaneously. A widely known definition of acculturation is "the dual process of cultural and psychological change that takes place as a result of contact between two or more cultural groups and their individual members" (Berry, 2005, p. 698). Therefore, acculturation involves the original and the new culture that one needs to constantly negotiate and adjust to in their interaction with the outside world. Berry (2003) described four types of attitudes toward both cultures: assimilation—more inclined to acquiring new culture than retaining traditional culture; separation—more inclined to retaining traditional culture than acquiring new culture; marginalization—not interested in retaining traditional culture or acquiring new culture; and integration—effectively acquiring new culture while retaining traditional culture. The expectation for acculturation outcome was changed from assimilation to integration over time, reflecting the recognition of a multidimensional, bidirectional acculturation process instead of a linear, unidirectional process (Tang & Bashir, 2012). Another view of acculturation depicts it as adaptation to the host culture: one is psychological adaptation, the affective aspect including self-concept and perceived well-being; and the other is sociocultural adaptation, the behavior aspect regarding one's interaction with others and society (Ward, Bochner, & Furnham, 2001). Since the 1980s, there has been an increasing number of studies about acculturation and its impact on behaviors, values, identity, and socialization (Yoon, Langrehr, & Ong, 2011).

Acculturation is also one of the frequently studied variables in career development research for its significance on many aspects of career development (Miller & Kerlow-Myers, 2009). Miller and Kerlow-Myers (2009) concluded, through a content analysis of acculturation research in career development, that acculturation was studied for its relationship and influence on career choice, self-efficacy, interests, aspiration, job satisfaction and performance, and work values and attitudes; however, the results were mixed, except that career self-efficacy and acculturation were found to be positively associated consistently. For instance, several studies found that higher levels of acculturation led people to be more confident to choose an occupation based on their own interests and aspiration instead of an occupation that was more accepted by their original cultural groups (e.g., Flores & O'Brien, 2002; Leong & Tata, 1990; Tang et al.,1999). The studies also found that highly acculturated Asian Americans, that is, typically indicated by being more identified with mainstream culture, strong English proficiency, and mainstream behavior and values, would be more likely to choose an occupation that is more consistent to their own interests and preferences rather than their parents' choices for them or involuntary choice made to satisfy others' expectations or needs (Leong & Chou, 1994). Similarly, low acculturated individuals might experience more struggles because they tried to fulfill their traditional roles in a society with different values and expectations than their tradition. Leong (2001) found that acculturation was positively related to job satisfaction and negatively associated to occupational stress and strain for Asian Americans. In general, acculturation is an important factor for the career development of immigrants and minority members and needs to be considered for its impact on one's career decision-making process and choice.

CASE ILLUSTRATION 3.1

ALICE'S CHALLENGES

Alice is a junior in an urban high school. She has a 3.5 GPA, and scores 2100 on the SAT. She wants to go to college and become a neurologist. However, her parents told her that she could only go to a two-year college, at least for the time being, because they do not have enough money to support a four-year college tuition, particularly the prestigious private university where the neuroscience program is top ranked. Alice was disappointed but understood, so she made an appointment with her school counselor to discuss the options she has and whether she should go to the local community college and later transfer or go to a state university that is about 200 miles away. Besides tuition, living cost is a concern, too. Both her parents are working, and she is not qualified for any federal assistance programs. Alice is biracial with her mother being White and her father being Hispanic. She is the oldest of five children, and her parents want her to get some vocational training and then find a job that would help the family financially. Alice was diagnosed with dyslexia when she was in middle school and needs accommodation for testing. She wants to study neuroscience to understand how the brain functions so that she can help people dealing with challenges as she has. When she met with her school counselor, she expressed her frustration of not being able to go to her desired college, not because she is not capable but because she could not afford it. She also expressed her torn feelings between pursuing her own aspirations and getting a job sooner to help her family. She asked the school counselor if she attended a community college what the likelihood would be that she could transfer to a neuroscience program two years later. She is also concerned about whether she could succeed in obtaining a college degree or a job in the neuroscience field as she does not see many women, let alone biracial women, working in this field. She wants more information on financial aid and to explore the possibilities of getting financial aid, although her father does not like the idea.

Discussion Questions

1. What are some social barriers you anticipate that are influencing or would impact Alice's career development? Which ones are at the individual level? Which ones are at the societal level? Which ones are at the group level?

2. If you were Alice's school counselor, what would you do to help her?

3. Please list the possible challenges Alice will encounter if Alice becomes a neurologist. Will these challenges be different or the same if Alice changes her work settings or occupations? Why, or why not?

Racial/Ethnic Identity

Acculturation and racial/ethnic identity, though viewed as the same or similar concepts in the helping profession, actually are different in meaning and implications. *Cultural identity* is another term used often to indicate racial or ethnic identity. While racial identity refers to one's identification with a group based on shared physical and hereditary characteristics, ethnic identity refers to one's identification with a group based on shared ancestry, history, and cultural traditions (Byars-Winston, 2010). Racial and ethnic identity is part of individuals' self-identity, and it generally reflects an evolution from no intention of knowing one's heritage to achieving a pride of one's race and ethnicity (Phinney, 1990). If *acculturation* pertains to immigrants or people who move from one culture to another culture (voluntarily or sometime involuntarily), *racial identity* applies to everyone, as it is part of self-concept, and everyone has a racial and ethnic background that is shared within one group and different from other groups. Understanding clients' racial identity is valuable for counselors to build a work alliance with clients and to develop culturally appropriate career interventions.

The earlier racial identity models focused on African Americans, but with increased attention to minority members and multicultural issues in counseling research, racial identity models have been applied to many minority groups (Sue & Sue, 2013). The Black Identity model by Cross (1971, 1995) set the groundwork for research of development of racial identity. The Cross model described five stages of development of identity for African Americans: Pre-encounter, Encounter, Immersion-Emersion, Internalization, and Internalization-Commitment. Each stage is as follows: Pre-encounter—negative or minimizing one's race (Black) and preference to mainstream reference (White American); Encounter—feeling torn between one's own race and others, questioning one's identity because of a shocking person or social event; Immersion-Emersion—idealizing African racial group and renouncing everything that is White; Internalization—beginning to achieve inner peace and objectively viewing one's own race with reasoning rather than being emotional; Internalization-Commitment—after achieving inner peace and security, action for social changes follows. Helms (1990) developed a measurement of Cross's identity model but with only the first four stages and also articulated that one's racial identity is both a developmental process and a stage or status. Each status of racial identity includes beliefs and attitudes of membership in one's own and others' racial groups and guides the person to organize racial information about themselves, other people, and institutions (Helms, 1990). According to Helms, people can move in a linear fashion from the Pre-encounter stage to the Internalization stage or between these statuses depending on the situation. Racial identity is an important factor for African Americans as the history of slavery, oppression, segregation, and discrimination has impacted perceptions, emotions, and behavior significantly.

Racial identity development models for other minority groups (e.g., Asian American, Latino/Hispanic Americans) have been developed but were not as well documented or researched extensively as for African Americans (see Sue & Sue, 2013 for details). Some scholars made efforts to develop a pan-race/ethnicity identity model (e.g., Phinney, 1992, 1996; Atkinson, Morten, & Sue, 1998) to capture the common themes of racial identity development. The Minority Identity Development model (MID) by Atkinson, Morten, and Sue (1998) is an example of such efforts. The MID has five stages—conformity, dissonance, resistance and immersion, introspection, and integrative awareness—that depict the early stages of believing in the values of the dominant group, to conflict between self-appreciation and group appreciation, to appreciation of both self and others (Sue & Sue, 2013). The importance of understanding one's racial identity is because racial identity influences people's career trajectory.

Racial identity was found to be significantly related to vocational identity for African Americans (Jackson & Neville, 1998). Perry (2008) studied students of color in urban settings and found that high levels of racial internalization, low levels of dissonance, and career planning led to better school engagement. Carter and Constantine (2000) found a significant relationship between racial identity and life role salience for African-American college students and between career maturity for Asian Americans. However, Lease (2006) did not find racial identity to be related to occupational choices among African-American high school students. Similarly, one study found that minority students with higher levels of ethnic identity perceived a higher level of career decision-making difficulties (Carlo, 2000). As summarized by Byars-Winston (2010),

> earlier racial identity statuses (e.g., Preencounter) are associated with less confidence in making career decisions, and later statuses of racial identity (e.g., immersion/emersion and internalization) correspond to more advanced career development including career exploration, positive career outcome expectations, and narrowing of career options. (p. 449)

The status and/or stages of individuals' racial/ethnic identity impacts their perception of the work environment and interaction with others in work settings (Helms & Piper, 1994) Minority Identity Development model (MID), and incorporating ethnic identity status into one's self concept may help individuals develop cognitive mapping of their career possibilities, interests, self-efficacy, and abilities (Byars-Winston, 2010).

Intersectionality and Interaction

People have multiple roles, like being a worker, parent, and sister; and similarly, one's identity involves many facets, such as being a Christian, middle-class, female, African American dealing with ADD, and having the internalization stage of racial identity. These roles and identities cannot be isolated; in fact, they interact with each other constantly; therefore, self-concept is actually the intersection of all these dimensions of one's roles and identities. Robinson-Wood (2009) argued that the multiple identities people develop are the product of contextual and socially constructed discourses and are not static; rather, they might shift in different contexts. The research found evidence of the impact of multiple identities on career decision making and process, and multiple identities may include gender, sexual orientation, ethnicity, and acculturation, which is connected to career identity of LGBTQ immigrants (Chen & Vollick, 2013). For African-American and Latina girls in high school, both ethnic identity and gender role attitudes were found to have influenced their career choices (Gushue & Whitson, 2006); similarly, immigrant women of color experienced triple jeopardy for their career development pursuit (Mighty, 1997). African-American women working in predominantly White work environments adopted the coping strategies of identity shifting to battle the negative consequences of discrimination (Dickens & Chavez, 2017). It is evident that self-concept is multifaceted or multilayered, dynamic, and ever-changing as the environment changes. Therefore, to understand the career development needs of a person, counselors need to consider the interaction and intersection of the multiple roles one has and multiple identities one develops. Further, these constructs of self are shaped as people interact with others in the multisystems in their contexts (Cook, 2012). The contextual factors influencing one's self-concept are also interactive and multidimensional (Fouad & Kantamneni, 2008).

The Model of Contextual Factors in Vocational Choice by Fouad and Kantamneni (2008) proposed that there are three dimensions of how contextual factors influence career

CASE ILLUSTRATION 3.2
SARA IS NOT SURE ABOUT HER POSITION

Sara is a 32-year-old accountant and works in a medium-sized company in the Midwest. She was born to parents who migrated to the United States from Pakistan when she was 5 years old. She could understand Urdu when her parents and grandparents were talking, but she could not speak the language. When she was living with her parents, she studied the Koran written in English with youth in her church. Actually, most of her friends were peers in her high school and church. She had a hard time making friends at college and often felt isolated because there was no support system like she had back home (i.e., closely tied families and churches in the small town). There was a student association for Asian Americans on campus, but she found most members were Chinese or Korean Americans. She also found a South Asian student organization, but most students were international students from the area, and she could not connect with them very well, except that they looked alike in appearance. At her work settings, she was often assigned to assist a White male colleague on major projects despite the fact that she has a CPA and her male colleague is still working toward his CPA. Her fiancé owns a family business and often expects her to help

his operation whenever he needs it regardless of whether she has time or not. Sara actually wants to open a tax service herself, but her parents and friends often say she should just join others rather than having her own practice. She feels that she is often misunderstood by others because people often see only parts of her but not the wholeness of her. She is seeing a counselor now, and her counselor told her she should be assertive and not let the men in her life take advantage of her. The counselor planned to coach Sara to be assertive and request a promotion to her supervisor as she certainly is qualified and deserves the promotion.

Discussion Questions

1. Why do you think Sara often feels misunderstood by others? What could lead to the misunderstanding?

2. What factors in Sara's growing-up experiences influenced her worldviews? How do these factors shape her current feelings?

3. What do you think of the plan Sara's counselor designed for her?

development: Individual Dimension—interests, needs, values, personality, abilities, self-efficacy, and aspiration; Group Dimension—gender, race/ethnicity, family relationship, role models, social class, religion, sexual orientation, and specific demographic groups; and Societal Dimension—acculturation, cultural values, opportunity structure, discrimination, schooling, barriers, labor market, culture of origin, and differences from mainstream culture. These three dimensions are interactive, and one may become more salient than the others depending on the individual's developmental stages. Cook, Heppner, and O'Brien (2005) described the similar interactive and multilayered contextual factors in shaping women and minority members' career development. In Cook et al.'s ecological perspective on career development, individual traits are significantly influenced by the microsystem (such as family, schools, and communities one lives in) and macrosystem (such as cultural values, government policies, gender or race stereotypes, and biases). For instance, a teenage girl believes that her occupational options are teacher, secretary, or nurse, and a teenage boy would think these occupations are not fit for him for the same reason, that is, they see very few men and many women in these occupations. These are the macrolevel contextual influences. If a girl grows up in a family where the mother works at a national lab, and if many women in their church work as engineers, managers in local banks, or doctors, and if she is encouraged by her school counselor to pursue her interests in career choices, she might have broader considerations than the gender-stereotyped occupations in the society; these are microlevel contextual influences. Well, what if this girl's parents were recent immigrants, and they wanted their daughter to have a secure job with steady income rather than pursuing a designing job that the daughter is aspiring to because they do not think this job is secure or financially rewarding? What if the acculturation levels are different for the girl and for her parents? What about her personal characteristics such as interests, abilities, and personality? All these factors do not influence career development in isolated ways; instead, they act in a confluent way.

MULTICULTURAL COMPETENCY IN CAREER COUNSELING

As discussed in this chapter, as workers are diverse and many social barriers and multiple contextual factors interactively influence individuals' career development, it is then critical for counselors to develop competency in working with diverse clients. Professional organizations have both competency standards and training standards to promote multicultural competency for counselors. Many scholars have also developed various models of culturally appropriate career interventions. These competency and training guidelines are helpful for counselors in developing multicultural competency in career development intervention to better serve the diverse population. The following summarizes the key components of becoming culturally competent in working with diverse population on career issues.

Professional Standards

The most widely acknowledged and endorsed multicultural counseling competencies, Multicultural Counseling Competencies (MCC; Sue, Arrendondo, & McDavis, 1992), were first jointly published by the American Counseling Association (ACA) and the Association for Multicultural Counseling and Development (AMCD) with an aim of emphasizing the importance of standardizing the necessary components of culturally valid counseling intervention and research. The concepts of developing competencies in knowledge, attitudes, and skills in counselors, clients, and intervention strategies have set the foundations for many other domain-specific multicultural counseling competencies in the last two decades. Recently, the AMCD has endorsed the Multicultural and Social Justice Counseling Competencies (MSJCC) in 2015, which expands and revises the MCC to reflect different layers that lead to multicultural and social justice competencies (Ratts, Singh, Nasssar-McMillan, Butler, & McCullough (2015). The expanded MSJCC adopts the socioecological model that emphasizes interaction of identities and dynamics of power, privilege, and oppression of both counselors and clients in the counseling process.

The MSJCC requires that counselors develop self-awareness of their own social status including privileges and barriers, their attitudes and beliefs, and their strengths and limitations; that counselors develop process skills to become mindful of their social status and implications of it to counseling; and that counselors take actions to increase their self-awareness. Counselors need to acquire knowledge, develop process skills, and take actions in understanding clients' worldviews, social statuses, attitudes and beliefs, values, social identities, and experiences with power, privilege, and oppression. Counselors then need to apply self-awareness and understanding of clients' worldviews to enrich the counseling relationship and dynamics and deliver culturally responsive intervention. Finally, the MSJCC expect that counselors intervene with and advocate for clients at various levels of the ecological system (e.g., individual, institutional, community, and societal). In essence, it is necessary to develop knowledge, attitudes, skills, and actions to increase self-awareness and awareness of clients in regard to cultural and social identities, attitudes, values, and experiences with social group status; to translate the awareness to enhance the counseling relationship; and to take actions to advocate for clients.

In addition, the CACREP 2016 standards also require that qualified and competent counselors need to have strategies for identifying and eliminating barriers, prejudices, and processes of intentional and unintentional oppression and culturally relevant strategies for addressing career development of diverse population. The National Career Development Association (NCDA) also has a committee on diversity and cultural inclusion to provide cross-cultural competency-based standards, tools, and training for career development professionals. Multicultural competency for career development and intervention is necessary not only because the professional organizations demands it but also because the service to clients could be inadequate or inappropriate if counselors do not have competency to provide culturally appropriate intervention. Becoming a multiculturally competent counselor requires lifelong active examination of and participation in personal and social change (Metzger, Nadkarni, & Cornish, 2010).

Culturally Appropriate Career Intervention

To develop culturally appropriate career intervention, cultural validity and cultural specificity are needed (Leong & Brown, 1995). According to Leong and Brown (1995), *cultural validity* refers to whether theoretical constructs have the same meaning across different cultures and have the same implications for people from various cultural backgrounds; *cultural specificity* refers to concepts and constructs that are specific to certain cultural groups. For instance, does career self-efficacy mean the same to White Americans, Asian Americans, Canadians, and Germans? This is a cultural validity concern. How does *machismo* impact Hispanic Americans in their career exploration? This is an example of a cultural specificity concern. Effective career counseling intervention needs integration of both cultural validity and specificity (Leong & Brown, 1995). In other words, counselors need to be mindful of whether the career theories and constructs are applicable to culturally different clients and at the same time consider the cultural values that are specific to clients. Leong, Hardin, and Grupta's (2011) cultural formulation approach listed five components that guides career intervention: (1) cultural identity of the individuals, (2) cultural conceptions of career problems, (3) cultural contexts and psychosocial environment, (4) cultural dynamics of the therapeutic relationship, and (5) overall cultural assessment. As seen in this approach, cultural factors need to be incorporated to understand clients and issues presented and to build trust in the counseling relationship.

MULTICULTURAL BOX 3.1

Alex Bahl is an Indian-American student who is interested in becoming a social worker. He is actually enrolled in a pre-med program because his family wants him to be a physician. He is not very happy with his current major because he does not like the courses in biology or chemistry, even though he can manage to earn good grades in these courses. He came to the career service center on his campus for career counseling. The session went well, and the counselor encouraged Alex to pursue his own career aspiration, said his high GPA would make it easy to transfer, and gave him the contact person in the school of social work to understand the admission procedure. They made an appointment to follow up two weeks later. However, Alex never returned to counseling. The counselor called and e-mailed Alex a few times and got no response. Why did Alex not return to counseling? Why didn't he respond to the calls? What could have gone awry in the counseling session? What can the counselor do differently so that Alex will return to the counseling?

Tips for Consideration: What kind of cultural values do Alex and his family have? What is his family relationship and dynamic? Why would his family insist on Alex being a physician? What does multicultural competency entail?

Flores and Heppner (2002) suggested the following process for culturally appropriate career counseling: developing a strong working alliance; maintaining a stance of "creative uncertainty"; assessing the client's level of racial salience (i.e., how clients see race as a factor in conceptualizing the interaction with outside world); determining the locus of the client's worldview, level of acculturation, and racial identity status; exploring how the roles of racism, sexism, and poverty have influenced the client's self-efficacy beliefs; encouraging the use of social networks and role models; considering using group work and even including extended family; and encouraging the client to return for additional assistance if he or she experiences obstacles after counseling has terminated. To build the working alliance, counselors need to examine their own worldviews and be open to exploring their own identities. Counselors also need to recognize social barriers and contextual influences on one's career development and ensure career assessment and interventions align with clients' cultural values (Leong & Flores, 2015).

Summary: Challenges and Opportunities

As the American population becomes increasingly diverse, so does the labor force in work settings. A more diverse workforce presents both challenges and opportunities for counselors. The challenges are embedded in the layers of sociocultural context in which occupational stereotypes, discrimination, and segregation could hamper minority groups' career aspirations. Multidimensional contextual factors interactively influence career development and decision making in a complex and dynamic way; therefore, a narrow and static view of people and their career development could lead to misconceptions and underservice, which presents another challenge for career intervention. Despite the challenges, career intervention incorporating multifaceted and dynamic sociocultural influences on individuals' cultural identity and self-concept have great potential to benefit clients from diverse cultural backgrounds. Culturally appropriate intervention needs to adequately address the impact social barriers have on individuals' career development and to develop culturally accommodating strategies.

Keystones

- The American workforce is more diverse than ever in many dimensions as a result of immigration and more women and minority members entered into the labor force.

- Social barriers such as racism, sexism, classism, and other forms of biases against certain groups present great challenges for people from nondominant groups to fully implement their potentials.

- Occupational stereotypes, segregation, and discrimination at work settings limit minority members' career aspirations and opportunities.

- Factors influencing individuals' career development are multifaceted at various levels of one's ecological system, and these factors are interactive and dynamic.

- Acculturation and cultural identity have been important in shaping one's self-concept and interaction with others and how people make career decisions.

- Equality and social justice are long-term goals and require multisystem intervention and effort.

- Multicultural competency for career intervention is required by counseling professional organizations and accreditation standards, and counselors need to develop self-awareness of and understanding of clients' worldviews, attitudes, and skills when working with diverse population.

- Developing multicultural competency requires counselors to provide culturally accommodating interventions that have cultural applicability of career constructs and incorporate specific cultural constructs for the certain group.

Additional Resources

Multicultural and Social Justice Counseling Competencies: http://www.multiculturalcounseling .org/index.php?option=com_content&view=article& id=205:amcd-endorses-multicultural-and-social- justice-counseling-competencies&catid=1:latest& Itemid=123

National Glass Ceiling Commission: http:// nationalglassceilingcommission.org

References

Ali, S. R. (2013). Poverty, social class, and working. In D. L. Blustein (Ed.), *The Oxford handbook of* *the psychology of working* (pp. 127-140). New York, NY: Oxford University Press.

Atkinson, D. R., Morten, G., & Sue, D. W. (1998). *Counseling American minorities* (5th ed.). Boston, MA: McGraw-Hill.

Bandura, A. (1977). Self-efficacy: Toward a unifying theory of behavioral change. *Psychological Review, 84*, 191–215.

Bandura, A. (1986). *Social foundations of thought and action: A social cognitive theory*. Englewood Cliffs, NJ: Prentice-Hall.

Barnett, R. C., & Hyde, J. S. (2001). Women, men, work, and family: An expansionist theory. *American Psychologist, 56*, 781-796.

Berry, J. W. (2003). Conceptual approaches to acculturation. In K. M. Chun, P. B. Organistra, & G. Martin (Eds.), *Acculturation: Advances in theory, measurement, and applied research* (pp. 17-37). Washington, D. C: American Psychological Association.

Berry, J. (2005). Acculturation: Living successfully in two cultures. *International Journal of Intercultural Relations, 29*, 697-712. doi:10.1016/j.ijintrel.2005.07.013

Betz, N. E. (2005). Women's career development. In. S. D. Brown, & R. W. Lent (Eds.), *Career development and counseling: Putting theory and research to work* (pp. 253-277). Hoboken, NJ: Wiley & Sons.

Betz, N. E. (2006). Basic issues and concepts in the career development and counseling of women. In W. B. Walsh, & M. J. Heppner (Eds.), *Handbook of career counseling for women* (2nd ed.) (pp. 45-74). Mahwah, NJ: Lawrence Erlbaum Associates.

Betz, N. E., & Hackett, G. (1981). The relationship of career-related self-efficacy expectations to perceived career options in college women and men. *Journal of Counseling Psychology, 28*, 399-410.

Blustein, D. L. (2006). *The psychology of working: A new perspective for career development, counseling, and public policy*. Mahwah, NJ: Lawrence Erlbaum.

Blustein, D. L., Chaves, A. P., Diemer, M. A., Gallagher, L. A., Marshall, K. G., Sirin, S., & Bhati, K. S. (2002). Voices of the forgotten half: The role of social class in the school-to-work transition. *Journal of Counseling Psychology, 49*, 311-323. Cited in SES section

Blustein, D. L., Kozan, S., Connors-Kellgren, A., & Rand, B. (2015). Social class and career intervention. In In P. J. Hartung, M. L. Savickas, W. B. Walsh, P. J. (Eds.), *APA handbook of career intervention: Vol. 1. foundations* (pp. 243-257). Washington, DC: American Psychological Association. doi:10.1037/14438-014

Bowman, S. L., & Evans, G. L. (2006). Career and lifestyle planning with visibly recognizable racial and ethnic groups. In D. Capuzzi & M. Stauffer (Eds.), *Career and lifestyle planning: Theory and application*. Boston, MA: Allyn & Bacon.

Brown, D. (2012). *Career information, career counseling, and career development* (10th ed.). Boston, MA: Pearson

Brown, C., & Lavish, L. A. (2006). Career assessment with Native Americans: Role salience and career decision-making self-efficacy. *Journal of Career Assessment, 14*(1), 116-129. doi:10.1177/1069072705281368

Bureau of Labor Statistics, U.S. Department of Labor. (2013, November). Racial and ethnic characteristics of the U.S. labor force in 2012. *TED: The Economics Daily*. Retrieved from http://www.bls.gov/opub/ted/2013/ted_20131119.htm.

Bureau of Labor Statistics, U.S. Department of Labor. (2017a, October). *Table 3.1 Civilian labor force participation rate, by age, sex, race, and ethnicity.* Retrieved from https://www.bls.gov/emp/ep_table_303.htm.

Bureau of Labor Statistics, U.S. Department of Labor. (2017b, October). *Table 3.3 Civilian labor force participation rate, by age, sex, race, and ethnicity.* Retrieved from https://www.bls.gov/emp/ep_table_303.htm.

Bureau of Labor Statistics, U.S. Department of Labor. (2017c, December). A look at women's education and earnings since the 1970s. *TED: The Economics Daily.* Retrieved from https://www.bls.gov/opub/ted/2017/a-look-at-womens-education-and-earnings-since-the-1970s.htm.

Bureau of Labor Statistics, U.S. Department of Labor. (2018). *Blacks in the labor force.* Retrieved from https://www.bls.gov/spotlight/2018/blacks-in-the-labor-force/home.htm.

Byars-Winston, A. (2010). The vocational significance of Black identity: Cultural formulation approach to career assessment and career counseling. *Journal of Career Development, 37,* 441-464. doi:10.1177/0894845309345847

Carlo, A. M. (2000). *Career development of ethnic minorities: The effects of ethnic identity and acculturation on perceived career barriers.* (International Dissertation Abstract 2000-95014-130).

Carter, R. T., & Constantine, M. G. (2000). Career maturity, life role salience, and racial/ethnic identity among Black and Asian American college students. *Journal of Career Assessment, 8*(2), 173-187. doi:10.1177/106907270000800206

Cass, V. C. (1979). Homosexual identity formation: A theoretical model. *Journal of Homosexuality, 7,* 219-235.

Chapman, B. E., & Brannock, J. C. (1987). Proposed model of lesbian identity development: An empirical examination. *Journal of Homosexuality, 14*(3-4), 69-80. doi:10.1300/J082v14n03_05

Chen, C. P., & Vollick, S. (2013). Multiple identities and career development of GLB immigrants. *Counselling Psychology Quarterly, 26*(2), 208-224. doi:10.1080/09515070.2012.735892

Chen, T. T. (2005). A longitudinal test and a qualitative field study of the glass ceiling effect for Asian Americans. *Dissertation Abstracts International, 65,* 3755.

Chung, Y. B. (2001). Work discrimination and coping strategies. Conceptual framework for counseling lesbian, gay, and bisexual clients. *The Career Development Quarterly, 50,* 33-44.

Chung, Y. B. (2003). Career counseling with lesbian, gay, bisexual, and transgendered persons: The next decade. *The Career Development Quarterly, 52,* 78-86.

Cook, E.P. (1993). The gendered context of life: Implications for women's and men's career life plans. *The Career Development Quarterly, 41,* 227-237.

Cook, E. P. (2012). *Understanding people in context: The ecological perspective in counseling.* Alexandria, VA, US: American Counseling Association.

Cook, E. P., Heppner, M. J., & O'Brien, K. M. (2005). Multicultural and gender influences in women's career development: An ecological perspective. *Journal of Multicultural Counseling and Development, 33,* 165–179. doi:10.1002/j.2161-1912.2005.tb00014.x

Council for Accreditation of Counseling and Related Educational Program (CACREP). (2016). *2016*

CACREP standards section 2: Professional counseling identity. Retrieved from http://www.cacrep.org/section-2-professional-counseling-identity.

Cross, W. E. (1971). The Negro-to-Black conversion experience: Towards a psychology of Black liberation. *Black World, 30*, 13-27.

Cross, W. E. (1995). The psychology of Nigrescence: Revisiting the Cross model. In J. G. Ponterrotto, J. M. Casas, L. A. Suzuki, & C. M. Alexander (Eds.), *Handbook of multicultural counseling* (pp. 93-122). Thousand Oaks, CA: Sage.

DeCuir-Gunby, J. T., & Gunby, N. W. (2016). Racial microaggressions in the workplace: A critical race analysis of the experiences of African American educators. *Urban Education, 51*(4), 390-414. doi:10.1177/0042085916628610

Dewlen, B., & Spires, H. L. (2000). Students with severe disability. In N. Peterson & R. C. Cortez Gonzalez (Eds.), *Career counseling models for diverse populations: Hands-on application by practitioners*. Belmont, CA: Brooks/Cole.

Dickens, D. D., & Chavez, E. L. (2017). Navigating the workplace: The costs and benefits of shifting identities at work among early career U.S. Black women. *Sex Roles*. doi:10.1007/s11199-017-0844-x

Dik, B. J., & Duffy, R. D. (2015). Strategies for discerning and living a calling. In P. J. Hartung, M. L. Savickas, W. B. Walsh, P. J. Hartung, M. L. Savickas, & W. B. Walsh (Eds.), *APA handbook of career intervention, Volume 2: Applications* (pp. 305-317). Washington, DC: American Psychological Association. doi:10.1037/14439-023

Duffy, R. D. (2006). Spirituality, religion, and career development: Current status and future directions. *The Career Development Quarterly, 55*, 52-63.

Fabian, E. S., & Liesener, J. J. (2005). Promoting the career potential of youth with disabilities. In S. D. Brown & R. W. Lent (Eds.), *Career development and counseling: Putting theory and research to work* (pp. 551-572). Hoboken, NJ: John Wiley & Sons.

Farmer, H. (1997). Women's motivation related to mastery, career salience, and career aspiration: A multivariate model focusing on the effects of sex role socialization. *Journal of Career Assessment*, 355-381.

Federal Glass Ceiling Commission. (1995). Good for business: Making full use of the nations human capitol. Retrieved from https://www.witi.com/research/downloads/glass-ceiling.pdf.

Fitzgerald, L. F., Fassinger, R. E., & Betz, N. E. (1995). Theoretical advances in the study of women's career development. In W. B. Walsh, & S. H. Osipow (Eds.), *Handbook of vocational psychology: Theory, research, and practice* (2nd ed., pp. 67–109). Mahwah, NJ: Erlbaum.

Flores, L. Y., & Bike, D. H. (2014). Multicultural career counseling. In F. T. L. Leong, L. Comas-Díaz, G. C. Nagayama Hall, V. C. McLoyd, & J. E. Trimble (Eds.), *APA handbook of multicultural psychology, Vol. 2: Applications and training* (pp. 403-417). Washington, DC: American Psychological Association.

Flores, L. Y., & Heppner, M. J. (2002). Multicultural career counseling: Ten essentials for training. *Journal of Career Development, 28*, 181–202. doi:10.1023/A:1014018321808

Flores, L. Y., & O'Brien, K. M. (2002). The career development of Mexican American adolescent women: A test of social cognitive career theory. *Journal of Counseling Psychology, 49*, 14–27. doi:10.1037/0022-0167.49.1.14

Fouad, N. A., & Brown, M. T. (2000). Race and class in development: Implications for vocational psychology. In S. D. Brown & R. W. Lent (Eds.), *Handbook of counseling psychology* (3rd ed., pp. 379-410). New York, NY: Wiley.

Fouad, N. A., & Byars-Winston, A. M. (2005). Cultural context of career choice: Meta-analysis of Race/Ethnicity differences. *Career Development Quarterly, 53*(3), 223-233. doi:10.1002/j.2161-0045.2005.tb00992.x

Fouad, N. A., & Kantamneni, N. (2008). Contextual factors in vocational psychology: Intersections of individual, group, and societal dimensions. In S. D. Brown & R. W. Lent (Eds.), *Handbook of Counseling Psychology* (4th ed.). Hoboken, NJ: Wiley.

Fukuyama. M. A., & Cox, C. I. (1992). Asian-Pacific Islanders and career development. In D. Brown & C. Minor (Eds.), *Career needs in a diverse workforce: Implications of the NCDA Gallup survey* (pp. 27-50). Alexandria. VA: National Career Development Association.

Geenen, S., Powers, L., Vasquez, A. L., & Bersani, H. (2003). Understanding and promoting the transition of minority adolescents. *Career Development for Exceptional Individuals, 26*(1), 27-46. doi:10.1177/088572880302600103

Gibson, R. L., & Mitchell, M. H. (2006). *Introduction to career counseling for the 21st century.* Upper Saddle River, NJ: Pearson Merrill Prentice Hall.

Gottfredson, L. S. (1981). Circumscription and compromise: A developmental theory of occupational aspirations. *Journal of Counseling Psychology, 28*, 545–579.

Greer, T. W. (2017). Career development for women veterans: Facilitating successful transitions from military service to civilian employment. *Advances in Developing Human Resources, 19*(1), 54-65. doi:10.1177/1523422316682737

Gushue, G. V., & Whitson, M. L. (2006). The relationship of ethnic identity and gender role attitudes to the development of career choice goals among Black and Latina girls. *Journal of Counseling Psychology, 53*(3), 379-385. doi:10.1037/0022-0167.53.3.379

Harris, L. N. (2014). Black, queer, and looking for a job: An exploratory study of career decision making among self-identified sexual minorities at an urban historically Black college/university. *Journal of Homosexuality, 61*(10), 1393-1419. doi:10.1080/00918369.2014.928170

Helms, J. E. (1990). Measurement of black racial identity attitudes. In J. E. Helms (Ed.), *Black and White racial identity: Theory, research, and practice* (pp. 33-47). Westport, CT: Praeger.

Herr, E. L., & Cramer, S. H. (1996). *Career guidance and counseling through the life span: Systematic approaches* (5th ed.). New York: HarperCollins.

Hong, J. S., Woodford, M. R., Long, L. D., & Renn, K. A. (2016). Ecological covariates of subtle and blatant heterosexist discrimination among LGBQ college students. *Journal of Youth Adolescence, 45*, 117-131. doi:1007//s10964-015-0362-5.

Howard, K. A. S., Carlstrom, A. H., Katz, A. D., Chew, A. Y., Ray, G. C., Laine, L., & Caulum, D. (2011). Career aspirations of youth: Untangling race/ethnicity, SES, and gender. *Journal of Vocational Behavior, 79*, 98-109.

The Individuals with Disabilities Education Act. (IDEA) (2004). *About IDEA*. Retrieved from https://sites.ed.gov/idea/about-idea.

Isaac, C. A., Kaatz, A., & Carnes, M. (2012). Deconstructing the glass ceiling. *Sociology Mind*, *2*(1), 80-86. Retrieved from http://search.proquest.com/docview/928098695?accountid=2909.

Jackson, C. C., & Neville, H. A. (1998). Influence of racial identity attitudes on African American college students' vocational identity and hope. *Journal of Vocational Behavior*, *53*(1), 97-113. doi:10.1006/jvbe.1997.1611

Lease, S. H. (2006). Factors predictive of the range of occupations considered by African American juniors and seniors in high school. *Journal of Career Development*, *32*(4), 333-350. doi:10.1177/0894845305283003

Leong, F. L. (2001). The role of acculturation in the career adjustment of Asian American workers: A test of Leong and Chou's (1994) formulations. *Cultural Diversity and Ethnic Minority Psychology*, *7*(3), 262-273. doi:10.1037/1099-9809.7.3.262

Leong, F. L., & Flores, L. Y. (2015). Career interventions with racial and ethnic minority clients. In P. J. Hartung, M. L. Savickas, W. B. Walsh, P. J. (Eds.), *APA handbook of career intervention: Vol. 1. foundations* (pp. 225-242). Washington, DC: American Psychological Association. doi:10.1037/14438-013

Leong, F. T. L., & Brown, M. T. (1995). Theoretical issues in cross cultural career development: Cultural validity and cultural specificity. In W. B. Walsh & S. H. Osipow (Eds.), *Handbook of vocational psychology: Theory, research, and practice* (2nd ed., pp. 143–180). Mahwah, NJ: Erlbaum.

Leong, F. T. L., & Chou, E. L. (1994). The role of ethnic identity and acculturation in the vocational behavior of Asian Americans: An integrative review. *Journal of Vocational Behavior*, *44*, 155-172.

Leong, F. T. L., Hardin, E. E., & Gupta, A. (2011). Self in vocational psychology: A cultural formulation approach. In P. J. Hartung, & L. M. Subich (Eds.), *Developing self in work and careers: Concepts, cases, and contexts* (pp. 193–211). Washington, DC: American Psychological Association. doi:10.1037/12348-012

Leong, F.T.L., & Hayes, T.J. (1990). Occupational stereotyping of Asian Americans. *The Career Development Quarterly*, *39*, 143-154. doi:10.1002/j.2161-0045.1990.tb00835.x

Leong, F. T. L., & Serafica, F. C. (2001). Cross-cultural perspective on Super's career development theory: Career maturity and cultural accommodation. In F. T. L. Leong, & A. Barak (Eds.), *Contemporary models in vocational psychology: A volume in honor of Samuel H. Osipow* (pp. 167-205). Mahwah, NJ: Lawrence Erlbaum.

Leong, F. T. L., & Tata, S. P. (1990). Sex and acculturation differences in occupational values among Chinese-American. *Journal of Counseling Psychology*, *37*, 208-212.

Liu, W. M. (2001). Expanding our understanding of multiculturalism: Developing a social class worldview model. In D. B. Pope-Davis, & H. L. K. Coleman (Eds.), *The intersection of race, class, and gender in counseling psychotherapy* (pp. 127-170). Thousand Oaks, CA: Sage.

Liu, W. M., & Ali, S. R. (2005). Addressing social class and classism in vocational theory and practice: Extending the emancipatory approach. *The Counseling Psychologist*, *33*, 189-196. doi:10.1177/0010000042772269

Luzzo, D. A. (1993). Ethnic differences in college students' perceptions of barriers to career development. *Journal of Multicultural Counseling and Development, 21,* 227-236.

Lyness, K. S., & Thompson, D. E. (1997). Above the glass ceiling? A comparison of matched samples of female and male executives. *Journal of Applied Psychology, 82*(3), 359-375. doi:10.1037/0021-9010.82.3.359

Martin, W. E. (1991). Career development and American Indians living on reservations: Cross-cultural factors to consider. *The Career Development Quarterly, 39*(3), 273-283. doi:10.1002/j.2161-0045.1991.tb00399.x

Martin, W. E., & Farris, K. K. (1994). A cultural and contextual decision path approach to career assessment with Native Americans: A psychological perspective. *Journal of Career Assessment, 2*(3), 258-275. doi:10.1177/106907279400200305 cited

McCrady, B. S. (2012). Overcoming the glass ceiling: Views from the cellar and the roof. *Behavior Therapy, 43*(4), 718-720. doi:10.1016/j.beth.2012.03.007

Mennicke, A., & Cutler-Seeber, A. (2016). Incorporating inclusivity: How organizations can improve the workplace experiences of trans people across the trans spectrum: A U.S. perspective. In T. Kollen (Ed.), *Sexual orientation and transgender issues in organizations* (pp. 513-523). doi:10.1007/978-3-319-29623-4_30

Metzger. L. L. H., Nadkarni, L. I., & Cornish, J. A. E. (2010). An overview of multicultural counseling competencies. In J. A. E. Cornish, B. A. Schreier, L. I. Nadkarni, L. L. H. Metzger, & E. R. Rodolfa (Eds.), *Handbook of multicultural counseling competencies.* Hoboken, NJ: John Wiley & Sons.

Mighty, E. J. (1997). Triple jeopardy: Immigrant women of color in the labor force. In P. Prasad, A. J. Mills, M. Elmes, A. Prasad, P. Prasad, A. J. Mills, . . . A. Prasad (Eds.), *Managing the organizational melting pot: Dilemmas of workplace diversity* (pp. 312-339). Thousand Oaks, CA: Sage. doi:10.4135/9781452225807.n13

Miller, M. J., & Brown, S. D. (2005). Counseling for career choices: Implications for improving interventions and working with diverse populations. In S. D. Brown, & R. W. Lent (Eds.), *Career development and counseling: Putting theory and research to work* (pp. 441-465). Hoboken, NJ: Wiley & Sons.

Miller, M. J., & Kerlow-Myers, A. E. (2009). A content analysis of acculturation research in the career development literature. *Journal of Career Development, 35*(4), 352-384. doi:10.1177/0894845308327739

Mizzi, R. C. (2017). Tough times: Adult educators, microaggressions, and the work context. *New Horizons in Adult Education and Human Resource Development, 29*(2), 54-59. doi:10.1002/nha3.20179

Nadal, K. L. (2011). The racial and ethnic microaggressions scale (REMS): Construction, reliability, and validity. *Journal of Counseling Psychology, 58*(4), 470-480. doi:10.1037/a0025193

Nadal, K. L. (2013). *That's so gay: Microaggressions and the lesbian, gay, bisexual, and transgender community.* Washington, DC: American Psychological Association. doi:10.1037/14093-000

Nadal, K. L., Mazzula, S. L., Rivera, D. P., & Fujii-Doe, W. (2014). Microaggressions and Latina/o Americans: An analysis of nativity, gender, and ethnicity. *Journal of Latina/o Psychology, 2,* 67-78. doi:10.1037/lat0000013

Newman, J. (May 14, 2014). Women are underrepresented as college chiefs but may get higher pay. *Chronicle of Higher Education*. Retrieved from http://chronicle.com/blogs/data/2014/05/18/women-are-underrepresented-as-college-chiefs-but-may-get-higher-pay.

Newman, L., Wagner, M., Cameto, R., Knokey, A. M., and Shaver, D. (2010). *Comparisons across time of the outcomes of youth with disabilities up to 4 years after high school. A report of findings from the National Longitudinal Transition Study (NLTS) and the National Longitudinal Transition Study-2 (NLT2)* (NCSER 2010-3008). Menlo Park, CA: SRI International.

Niles, S. G., Harris-Bowlsbey, J. (2013). *Career development interventions in the 21st century* (4th ed). Upper Saddle River, NJ: Pearson Merrill Prentice Hall.

Papafilippou, V., & Bentley, L. (2017). Gendered transitions, career identities and possible selves: The case of engineering graduates. *Journal of Education and Work, 30*(8), 827-839. doi:10.1080/13639080.2017.1375088

Patel, S. G., Salahuddin, N. M., & O'Brien, K. M. (2008). Career decision-making self-efficacy of Vietnamese adolescents: The role of acculturation, social support, socioeconomic status, and racism. *Journal of Career Development, 34*(3), 218-240. doi:10.1177/0894845307308488

Perry, J. C. (2008). School engagement among urban youth of color: Criterion pattern effects of vocational exploration and racial identity. *Journal of Career Development, 34*(4), 397-422. doi:10.1177/0894845308316293

Phelps, R. E., & Constantine, M. G. (2001). Hitting the roof: The impact of the glass-ceiling effect on the career development of African Americans. In W. B. Walsh, R. P. Bingham, M. T. Brown, C. M. Ward, W. B. Walsh, R. P. Bingham, . . . C. M. Ward (Eds.), *Career counseling for African Americans* (pp. 161-175). Mahwah, NJ: Lawrence Erlbaum.

Phinney, J. (1990). Ethnic identity in adolescents and adults: A review of research. *Psychological Bulletin, 108*, 499–514.

Phinney, J. S. (1992). The multigroup ethnic identity measure: A new scale for use with diverse groups. *Journal of Adolescent Research, 7*(2), 156-176. doi:10.1177/074355489272003

Phinney, J. S. (1996). Understanding ethnic diversity: "The role of ethnic identity." *The American Behavioral Scientist, 40*(2), 143.

Polo Sánchez, M. T., & López Justicia, M. D. (2016). Transition to employment of university students with disabilities: Factors for success. *Universitas Psychologica, 15*(2), 15-27. doi:10.11144/Javeriana.upsy15-2.teus

Pope, M., & Barret, B. (2002). Counseling gay men toward an integrated sexuality. In L. D. Burlew & D. Capuzzi (Eds.), *Sexuality counseling* (pp. 149-176). Hauppauge, NY: Nova Science.

Pope, M. S., Prince, J. P., & Mitchell, K. (2000). Responsible career counseling with lesbian and gay students. In D. A. Luzzo (Ed.), *Career counseling of college students: An empirical guide to strategies that work* (pp. 267-282). Washington, DC: American Psychological Association. doi:10.1037/10362-015

Ramasamy, R., Duffy, M., & Camp, J. L. J. (2000). Transition from school to adult life: Critical issues for Native American youth with and without learning disabilities. *Career Development for Exceptional Individuals, 23*(2), 157-171. doi:10.1177/088572880002300204

Ratts, M. J., Singh, A. A., Nassar-McMillan, S., Butler, S. K., & McCullough, J. R. (2015). *Multicultural and social justice counseling competencies*. Retrieved from http://www.multiculturalcounseling.org/index.php?option=com_content&view=article&id=205:amcd-endorses-multicultural-and-social-justice-counseling-competencies&catid=1:latest&Itemid=123.

Restar, A. J., & Reisner, S. L. (2017). Protect trans people: Gender equality and equity in action. *The Lancet, 390*(10106), 1933. doi:10.1016/S0140-6736(17)31823-8

Rich, Y., & Golan, R. (1992). Career plans for male-dominated occupations among female seniors in religious and secular high schools. *Adolescence, 27*(105), 73-86.

Rivera, L. M., Chen, E. C., Flores, L. Y., Blumberg, F., & Ponterotto, J. G. (2007). The effects of perceived barriers, role models, and acculturation on the career self-efficacy and career consideration of Hispanic women. *The Career Development Quarterly, 56*(1), 47-61. doi:10.1002/j.2161-0045.2007.tb00019.x

Robinson-Wood, T. L. (2009). *The convergence of race, ethnicity, and gender* (3rd ed.). Columbus, OH: Pearson Education.

Sánchez, J. P., Poll-Hunter, N., Stern, N., Garcia, A. N., & Brewster, C. (2016). Balancing two cultures: American Indian/Alaska native medical students' perceptions of academic medicine careers. *Journal of Community Health: The Publication for Health Promotion and Disease Prevention, 41*(4), 871-880. doi:10.1007/s10900-016-0166-x

Smith, L. (2005). Psychotherapy, classism, and the poor: Conspicuous by their absence. *American Psychologist, 60*, 687-696. doi:10.1177/0011000007309861

Stevens, S., Andrade, R., & Page, M. (2016). Motivating young Native American students to pursue STEM learning through a culturally relevant science program. *Journal of Science Education and Technology, 25*(6), 947-960. doi:10.1007/s10956-016-9629-1

Sue, D. W. (2010). *Microaggressions in everyday life: Race, gender, and sexual orientation*. Hoboken, NJ: Wiley.

Sue, D. W., Arredondo, P., & McDavis, R. J. (1992). Multicultural counseling competencies and standards: A call to the profession. *Journal of Multicultural Counseling and Development, 20*, 64–88.

Sue, D. W., Capodilupo, C. M., Torino, G. C., Bucceri, J. M., Holder, A. M., Nadal, K. L., & Esquilin, M. E. (2007). Racial microaggressions in everyday life: Implications for counseling. *American Psychologist, 62*, 271–286. doi:10.1037/0003-066X.62.4.271

Sue, W., & Sue, D. (2013). *Counseling the culturally diverse: Theory and practice*. Hoboken, NJ: John Wiley & Sons.

Syed, M., & Chemers, M. M. (2011). Ethnic minorities and women in STEM: Casting a wide net to address a persistent social problem. *Journal of Social Issues, 67*(3), 435-441. doi:10.1111/j.1540-4560.2011.01708.x

Szelényi, K., Denson, N., & Inkelas, K. K. (2013). Women in STEM majors and professional outcome expectations: The role of living-learning programs and other college environments. *Research in Higher Education, 54*(8), 851-873. doi:10.1007/s11162-013-9299-2

Tang, M. (2008). Psychological impacts of "Model Minority" on Asian Americans. In G. Li & L. Wang (Eds.), *Model minority myth revisited: An interdisciplinary approach to demystifying*

Asian American educational experience (pp. 117-132). Charlotte, NC: Information Aging.

Tang, M., & Bashir, H. (2012). Diversity from the ecological perspective. In Cook, E. P. (Ed.), *Understanding people in context: The ecological perspective in counseling* (pp. 161-178). Alexandria, VA: American Counseling Association.

Tang, M., Fouad, N. A., & Smith, P. L. (1999). Asian Americans' career choices: A path model to examine factors influencing their career choices. *Journal of Vocational Behavior*, *54*(1), 142-157. http://dx.doi.org/10.1006/jvbe.1998.1651

Thompson, M. N. (2013). Career barriers and coping efficacy among Native American students. *Journal of Career Assessment*, *21*(2), 311-325. doi:10.1177/1069072712471501

Tsunokai, G.T. (2005). Beyond the lenses of the "model" minority myth: A descriptive portrait of Asian gang members. *Journal of Gang Research*, *12*, 37-58.

U.S. Census Bureau. (2016). *American community survey 1-year estimates*. Washington, DC: Author.

U.S. Department of Education, National Center for Education Statistics. (2012). *Fast facts*. Retrieved from https://nces.ed.gov/fastfacts/display.asp?id=64.

Ward, C, Bochner, S., & Furnham, A. (2001). *The psychology of cultural shock* (2nd ed.). London, UK: Routledge.

Wilson, E. (2014). Diversity, culture and the glass ceiling. *Journal of Cultural Diversity*, *21*(3), 83-9.

Yang, K. (2004). Southeast Asian American children: Not the "model minority." *The Future of Children*, *14*, 127-133.

Yoon, E., Langrehr, K., & Ong, L. Z. (2011). Content analysis of acculturation research in counseling and counseling psychology: A 22-year review. *Journal of Counseling Psychology*, *58*(1), 83-96. doi:10.1037/a0021128

Zulfikar, Y. F. (2012). Do Muslims believe more in Protestant work ethic than Christians? Comparison of people with different religious backgrounds living in the U.S. *Journal of Business Ethics*, *105*, 489-502. doi:10.1007/s10551-011-0981-z

Zunker, V. G. (2006). *Using assessment results in career counseling* (7th ed.). Monterey, CA: Brooks/Cole.

Zunker, V. G. (2012). *Career counseling: A holistic approach* (8th ed.). Belmont, CA: Brooks/Cole.

CAREER DEVELOPMENT THEORIES I

Theory provides a framework for practitioners to conceptualize clients' issues in order to develop an appropriate intervention plan. A theory is like a roadmap for counselors to find the most efficient route to help clients. People often think theories are abstract and do not necessarily see the value of understanding theories in their daily counseling practice. This is a misconception. Understanding theories gives practitioners a framework to organize, analyze, and evaluate the information available or to be collected and to conceptualize how to proceed with counseling.

The chapter will begin by introducing the groundwork laid by early professionals, since it is important for students to understand the context and evolution of career development theories. Then the major career development theories known for theoretical contribution, research, or practice will be presented. Each theory section will include contextual information, theoretical constructs and prepositions, and applications and current status.

This chapter and the next will cover the fundamental knowledge of career development theories and their applications in career counseling and intervention.

LEARNING OBJECTIVES

After completing the reading and exercises provided in this chapter, you will be able to:

- describe the main propositions and key concepts of major career development theories,

- explain the contribution of each theory to career counseling practice and intervention,

- contrast the similarities and differences of the career development theories,

- identify the intervention strategies associated with each theory,

- analyze the applicability of each theory to diverse populations, and

- critique the advantages and disadvantages of each theory.

EARLIER APPROACHES

Prior to Parsons starting the vocational guidance for youth in the Boston area in the late 19th century, some books on occupations and trades were traced back to the 15th century (Zytowski, 1972), but using the scientific methods to assist people in finding jobs is attributed to Parsons's true reasoning method (Herr, 2013). Parsons laid the foundation of vocational guidance in the early 1900s. His approach and its influence on the practice of career counseling and intervention are still relevant in the 21st century (Zytowski, 2001). Frank Parsons's (1909) three-step approach has influenced vocational guidance for over 100 years and is still the major cornerstone for trait-and-factor career development theories.

Parson's concept of vocational guidance was described in his book *Choosing a Vocation,* published in 1909, one year after his death. The principles he stated for providing vocational guidance to youth became the foundation for what later evolved into trait-and-factor theory. The term *trait* refers to a characteristic of an individual that can be measured through questioning and interviewing. *Factor* refers to a characteristic of the job, required for job performance to be successfully accomplished. The core aspect of the trait-and-factor approach is to find a match between individuals' characteristics and specific requirements of work settings, and the greater the fit between the two, the better is the outcome expected for the satisfaction of both individuals and employers.

Parsons (1909) proposed that choosing an occupation requires a clear understanding of both oneself and the occupation being considered, and that an assessment of each is necessary for making the choice. The information about oneself is referred to as a characteristic of an individual or *trait*, which can be measured through questioning and interviewing. The information about the occupation is conceptualized as a *factor*, a characteristic of the job and work setting. The assessment of an occupation involves clear knowledge of job requirements, conditions, advantages, disadvantages, and compensation structure. Parsons's approach laid out the following prerequisites for good decision making:

1. a clear understanding of yourself, your attitudes, abilities, interests, ambitions, and resource limitations and their causes;

2. a knowledge of the requirements and conditions of success, advantages and disadvantages, compensation, opportunities, and prospects in different lines of work; and

3. true reasoning on the relations of these groups of facts.

In this approach, later termed as *trait-and-factor*, the emphasis is on the collection of information of individuals' characteristics and occupational demands for job performance; therefore, testing and other forms of information gathering become critical in the helping process. To help clients make a sound career decision, counselors need to gain knowledge about clients regarding their aptitude, skills, personality, interests, and values. They also need to help clients gain knowledge about the job requirements. Before formal assessment tools became available, the process of identifying the characteristics of each was through interviewing and observation and then analyzing the information by reasoning.

Another early approach in career counseling is Williamson's (1939) model, which articulated that the counseling goal was to help clients understand and organize personal and other resources so that they could identify an appropriate occupation that matched their individual characteristics. Williamson articulated that clients typically either have difficulty in making a choice, have no choices, or have poor choices, meaning there is a discrepancy between their individual characteristics and the work requirements. In order to help resolve these issues, counselors need to provide directions and resources for clients in their search for an occupation that would satisfy both individual and work expectations.

The significance of these early approaches is their pioneering work on fulfilling the need of providing vocational guidance to individuals who faced unprecedented challenges in finding an occupation. In the past, most people followed the work done by their parents, often in a family farm or working on the farm of a landowner. After the Industrial Revolution, as people migrated to the cities, this tradition broke down, and the need for career choice grew. In the United States of the early 20th century, this trend was exacerbated by large numbers of immigrants who also needed help in finding employment. Institutions called settlement houses arose to help these two types of migrants—from the farms and from other countries—settle into their new environment. It is in this context that career development as a formal process grew and flourished. However, there has been criticism about the trait-and-factor approach in recent decades. There is concern about its emphasis on testing and lack of consideration of differences in the career development of people with diverse backgrounds. Another issue with this approach is its static rather than developmental view of an individual's career development. The world of work in the 21st century requires multiple career decisions, and the trait-and-factor approach implies a unitary, single moment in time process. Nonetheless, the trait-and-factor approach has the merit of providing a foundation to understand the relationship between individual characteristics and work requirements.

TRAIT-AND-FACTOR APPROACHES

The career development theories in this category have a common theme in their account for individuals' reasons and behaviors in choosing a vocation—a relationship between one's personal characteristics and the characteristics of the work environment. The trait-and-factor approach emphasized the correspondence between the two sets of information that would make one's career choices be a sound one, that is, the information about oneself and work requirements. We will choose two career development theories that not only are representative of the trait-factor approach but also had significant impact in the development of career counseling practice in the 20th century. The first one to be introduced is Holland's vocational choice theory, and the second one to be introduced is work adjustment theory.

Holland's Vocational Choice or Typology Theory

Holland's career development theory (1985a, 1996a, 1997) is probably the most well-known and widely used theory in career development. It has influenced the practice of career counseling and intervention for decades since its emergence. Its popularity might be because of its ease of implementation in helping clients solve their career-related problems as well as the availability of associated assessment tools to assist clients identify their personal characteristics.

One of the most significant of Holland's contributions to career development intervention is his Holland's Codes of Occupations (Holland, 1996b). Before Holland's Codes, there was only the complicated Department of Labor Dictionary of Occupational Titles for classifying occupations into an easy and understandable system that counselors and clients could use for career counseling purposes. Few scholars or career counseling practitioners would disagree that Holland had an unprecedented impact on career development counseling theory, practice, and research.

Beginning in 1966 and continually to 1997, Holland wrote extensively to explain his approach to understanding human behavior in regard to making a career choice and as to how individual and work environmental characteristics interact with each other and influence individuals' decisions on career choice and adjustment. Through extensive empirical studies measuring vocational interests, Holland developed his approach to explain why people are attracted to certain occupations and thrive in certain work situations but are not as happy in some work environments. Continuous effort of conducting research throughout the years led to Holland's revising and refining his typology. The fundamental principle of his theory is his belief that people possess certain personalities and that work environments also possesses certain personalities; the individual personalities and work personalities are categorized into six types. These six types were drawn from numerous empirical studies and can be described as follows:

Realistic: The realistic personality type typically tends to like activities involving mechanical or physical abilities, motor skills, and manipulating machines and prefers to avoid activities requiring building strong interpersonal relationships or expression of meaning or feelings. Realistic type people usually prefer natural, concrete, and practical work environments and like to engage in agricultural, technical, or engineering occupations. The realistic type is often described as practical, less flexible, conforming, materialistic, self-effacing, frank, natural, asocial, thrifty, genuine, normal, uninsightful, hardheaded, persistent, and uninvolved (Holland, Powell, & Fritzsche, 1994).

Investigative: The investigative personality type typically likes to find solutions to problems through scientific methods, logic, analytical skills, and critical thinking. This type enjoys activities involving ideas, symbols, and words; they do not like problem solving via mechanical or social interaction. Investigative type people usually prefer such classes as reading, science, and foreign languages and occupations such as scientists, anthropologists, geologists, and researchers. The investigative type is often described as analytical, independent, rational, cautious, intellectual, reserved, complex, introspective, critical, unassuming, curious, precise, and unpopular (Holland, Powell, & Fritzsche, 1994). Investigative type people are often perceived as lacking social abilities or leadership qualities.

Artistic: The artistic personality type likes activities involving the use of creativity and free expression, and likes doing things in an unsystematic way. People in this type usually prefer to work in an environment that does not restrict their ability to create, that does not require routine or structured work schedules, and that does not demand mechanical abilities. The typical occupations liked by people of the artistic type are artists, writers, composers, musicians, and stage directors. Artistic-type individuals are usually described as complicated, impractical, open, disorderly, impulsive, original, emotional, independent, sensitive, expressive, introspective, idealistic, intuitive, imaginative, and nonconforming.

Social: The social personality type is typically characterized by an inclination to interact with people and help others. Individuals of this type often are attracted to a work environment that provides warmth, support, and care to people, particularly people who need help. They prefer activities involving the use of their knowledge and skills to educate, help, and empower others. Social personality type people are attracted to work in occupations such as teachers, counselors, church workers, and youth camp directors. People with social personalities see themselves as sociable, responsible, and nurturing. The characteristics of this type also include helpful, responsive, cooperative, idealistic, empathic, kind, tactful, friendly, patient, understanding, generous, and persuasive.

Enterprising: The enterprising personality type is more likely to appreciate an influential and powerful position in organizations and likes to use leadership skills in decision making. They like to convince and persuade others, to lead organizations, and to sell products. People in the enterprising personality type are attracted to occupations like managers, salespersons, business executives, and lobbyists. The personal characteristics of the enterprising type include energetic, inquisitive, adventurous, excitement-seeking, optimistic, agreeable, self-confident, ambitious, exhibitionistic, sociable, domineering, extroverted, and verbal.

Conventional: The conventional personality type is likely to engage in structured and organized activities that are consistent and systematic. People in this category enjoy work environments that are orderly, routine, and dependable. They are drawn to occupations such as bookkeepers, accountants, bankers, stenographers, and cost estimators. The personal characteristics of the conventional include careful, inflexible, persistent, conforming, inhibited, practical, conscientious, methodical, prudish, defensive, obedient, thrifty, efficient, orderly, and unimaginative.

These six types apply to both individuals and work environments. According to Holland (1985a), people are satisfied with their jobs if they can work in the environment that is the same or very similar to their personality types. The relationship between these six types can be depicted in a hexagon (see Figure 4.1). According to Holland, the types next to each other on the hexagon have a close relationship, meaning they share some similarities; and the types across from each other on the hexagon have the least relationship between the two types and also have the least common characteristics. They may even be the complete opposite. For instance, the realistic type is closest on the hexagon to the investigative and conventional types, but it is opposite of the social type. It means that the realistic type (practical work environment, technical) has the least similar characteristics to the social type (prefer people interaction).

Holland's theory (1985b, 1996a, 1997) has several important concepts that guide career counseling assessment and interventions. The basic assumptions are listed below, and then the major concepts are introduced.

FIGURE 4.1 ■ Holland's Hexagonal Model of the Relationship Among Personality

Holland, J. L., Whitney, D. R., Cole, N. S., & Richards, J. M., Jr. (1969). *An empirical occupational classification derived from a theory of personality and intended for practice and research* (ACT Research Report No. 29). Iowa City, IA: ACT, Inc.

Basic Assumptions

1. People expresses their personality through choice of a vocation.

2. Each person holds stereotypical views of various vocations, and people are guided by these stereotypical views in their career choices.

3. As individuals have personalities, vocations have similar personalities.

4. Vocational satisfaction, stability, and achievement depend on the extent to which the individual's personality and the work environment are compatible.

Important Concepts

Congruence: the degree of fit between personal traits and work environment factors. If one's personality is consistent with her or his work environment, congruence exists; otherwise, there is a lack of congruence. A highly congruent career choice leads to job satisfaction and likelihood of success on the job. For instance, if one's personality types are social and enterprising, and her or his work environment also has the characteristics of social and enterprising, congruence is achieved. Both individual and work environment personality types can usually be represented by two or three of the six types on the hexagon.

Differentiation: the distinctiveness of individuals' personality profile (Spokane & Cruza-Guest, 2005). In other words, it refers to how clearly the individual could identify his or her preferred types. A person with differentiated personality types has her or his preferred type(s) close in distance on the hexagon, and these preferred types are also highly distinct from the other personality types. For instance, if one has clearly identified interests in realistic and investigative types and no or significantly low interest in the other four types, this person has a differentiated personality profile. If one has similar level of interests across all six types (aka flat profile), this person does not have differentiation.

Consistency: refers to the degree of similarity of one's personality types on the hexagon. It could be conceptualized as the coherence of individuals' types. One has consistency if the preferred personality types are close or adjacent to each other on the hexagon. On the other hand, if the preferred types are opposites on the hexagon, there is no consistency. For instance, realistic and investigative or social, artistic, and enterprising types are examples of consistency; realistic and social, enterprising, and investigative types are examples of lacking consistency.

Identity: the degree of clarity and stability of one's goals, interests, and talents (Holland, 1997). One would have higher vocational identity if she or he has consistency, differentiation, and congruency of the personality types, and as a result, according to Holland, would be more satisfied with work and life. A stronger and clearly defined identity is more likely to lead to an easier career decision-making process and choices.

Holland's theory has generated many vocational assessment tools that have been applied in career counseling practice across various settings, from K-12 schools to college settings and community agencies. The most well-known and widely used one is the *Self-Directed Search* (SDS; Holland, Powell, & Fritzsche, 1994). The SDS gains its popularity from its self-explanatory features, ease of administration and interpretation, and associated occupational and educational information. It consists of the Assessment booklet, Interpretative Guide, and Occupational Information booklet. The SDS is designed for self-administration, self-scoring, and self-interpretation, which reduces the cost and increases the accessibility so that more people can use it. The other measurements developed to apply Holland's concepts for career counseling include My Vocational Situation (Holland, Daiger, & Power, 1980), Vocational Identity (Holland, Gottfredson, & Power, 1980), and Vocational Preference Inventory (Holland, 1996b). These tools help to apply Holland's theoretical constructs in career counseling practice.

Holland's hexagon model led to the codes known as RIASEC for not only signifying Holland's career personality types but also occupational classification for organizing occupations. The Holland's codes typically are represented by two or three letter combinations, such as AE, SEA, or RIC, and the first letter indicates the primary code, which is the dominant code. The Holland's codes have become the classification system for many vocational assessments and measures. These instruments are not developed based on Holland's theory, but they use the classification of Holland's codes to organize the assessment results. These vocational measures include the Strong Interest Inventory, The Harrington-O'Shea Career Decision Making Systems, Find Your Interests (part of the revised Armed Services Vocational Aptitude Battery), and the O'Net System. Since Holland's codes have been available, it has become simpler for clients to understand the meaning of vocational assessment results and to apply the information to their career planning. Similarly, counselors have found that using Holland's classifications simplifies communicating the results of vocational assessments. Holland's contribution to the career development and intervention field is substantial, and the typology theory has been a research topic for numerous scholars in the almost half century since it was first proposed.

The research about Holland's theory can be categorized into two major types: one examines the structure of the typology and determines if the hexagon shape and relationship among the six types are as Holland proposed, and the other kinds of research mainly examine the validity of the theoretical concepts, particularly the concept of congruence. Many studies have examined whether there is truly congruence among one's personality or vocational interests and career choice, actual work, and career aspirations. Though not all the studies supported Holland's concepts consistently, many studies did provide strong support to the circular structure of the six types and to a lesser degree the validity of the congruence proposition (Spokane & Cruza-Guet, 2005). Most criticism of Holland's theory centers around its static view of career development and that it is based on a male, middle-class framework of career development. However, many cross-cultural studies of Holland's theory have been conducted in the last three decades and found that there was a surprisingly large amount of evidence to support the basic theoretical construct for both men and women, as well as for ethnic minorities (Day, Rounds, & Swaney, 1998). It seems that there may be different underlying meanings of some personality types, for instance, realistic and conventional, for females and males (e.g., Fitzgerald, Fassinger, & Betz, 1995; Betz & Schifano, 2000). Similarly, though many studies found that the hexagon model was applicable to different cultural groups, the order of RIASEC was not necessarily identical, and the degree of the relationships were different from the norm groups in the United States (Leong, Austin, Sekarant, & Komarraju, 1998; Tang, 2001). In sum, empirical studies supported Holland's major propositions of RIASEC typology and the interrelationship among the types and Holland's prediction about work satisfaction being related to congruence and identity, although the magnitude might not be as robust as Holland predicted (Nauta, 2013).

The purpose of career counseling in Holland's paradigm is to help clients identify and clarify their personality types and interests and then to explore the work environment that corresponds to or fits with as closely as possible these personality types. The SDS can be helpful in this process as it is designed to help clients discover their interests in occupational areas, and to use RIASEC to codify their self-estimates of abilities in accomplishing tasks expected in a variety of occupations.

LEARNING ACTIVITY 4.1

Review the descriptions of the six Holland's Codes. Ask the students to identify three codes that closely describe who they are. Then ask the students to list one or two jobs or volunteer work they have done before that they enjoyed a lot. Ask the students to review the characteristics of that job and find the Holland's Codes that related to that job. Ask the students to think of work they have done before that they hated and couldn't imagine doing again. Identify the Holland's Codes for this job. Next ask the class to generate a report that shows (a) the number of students who had congruence between their own codes and the codes of their favorite work, (b) the number of students whose codes showed consistency, and (c) the number of students whose least likeable work showed the opposite codes of their own codes.

Work Adjustment Theory

The other major representative of the trait-and-factor approach career development theory is the Theory of Work Adjustment (TWA; Dawis & Lofquist, 1984). The TWA theory emerged as looking at the fit between person and environment but more recently became focused on the interaction of person (P) in an environment (E), focusing on the action and reaction to each other in mutual ways (Dawis, 2005). According to TWA, work adjustment is a continuous and dynamic process by which workers seek to achieve and maintain correspondence with a work environment. If workers find satisfaction from the work environment, they would continue to work in the same work environment; otherwise, they may feel unsatisfied and consider changing jobs or finding an alternative work setting. In TWA, *P* stands for the worker and employee, and *E* stands for the work environment and organization.

Basic Assumptions

1. As a living organism, people (P) have requirements that have to be met through their environment (E); the most important P requirements are needs: biological or survival and psychological well-being.

2. E's requirements can be met by P just as P's requirements can be met by E. In other words, work environments have "requirements" that are analogous to the needs of individuals.

3. P and E are conceptualized as parallel and complementary; fulfillment of their requirements results in satisfaction for P and E.

4. Both individuals and environments develop mechanisms for satisfying their needs. When the needs of individuals in an environment (work) and those of the environment are satisfied, correspondence exists.

5. Three variables—skills, aptitudes, and personality structure—can be used to predict the success of the worker if the reinforcement pattern of the work environment is known.

6. The tenure, or time spent in a job by workers, is the result of their satisfaction with the job and satisfactoriness in performance.

7. The three outcomes, the satisfaction, satisfactoriness, and tenure of P in a given work E, are the basic indicators of work adjustment.

Key Concepts

Some important theoretical concepts in the TWA need to be defined here before further explaining the theory. These concepts are critical elements for understanding the theoretical propositions of the TWA. The following definition is based on Dawis (2005):

Satisfaction—a state variable that refers to an affective response to the cognitive evaluation of P-E correspondence. It also refers to P being satisfied with the reinforcers provided by E.

Satisfactoriness—satisfaction by E. It refers to the employer's satisfaction with the individual's performance.

Correspondence—a fit between person and environment; if both P's and E's requirements are met, correspondence exists. It also refers to the extent to which an individual's needs and requirements are fulfilled by the work that he or she does that also meets the expectations and requirements of the job.

Tenure—length of stay on the job. It can also be categorized as position tenure, job tenure, occupational tenure, and organizational tenure. When both satisfaction and satisfactoriness correspond to each other, tenure is more likely to occur.

Dawis (2005) summarized the major propositions of the TWA as follows:

1. Work adjustment at any time is indicated by the concurrent levels of P satisfaction and P satisfactoriness.

2. P satisfaction is predicted from E reinforcers to P values correspondence, provided that there is P abilities to E ability requirements correspondence.

3. P satisfactoriness is predicted from P abilities to E ability requirements correspondence, provided that there is E reinforcers to P values correspondence.

4. Satisfactoriness moderates the prediction of P satisfaction from E reinforcers to P values correspondence.

5. Satisfaction moderates the prediction of P satisfactoriness from P abilities to E ability requirements correspondence.

6. The probability of P quitting E is inversely related to P satisfaction.

7. The probability that E will fire P is inversely related to P satisfactoriness.

8. P tenure is predicted from P satisfaction and P satisfactoriness.

Basically, the TWA theory explains the reasons why people stay in one position (in some cases, job, or occupation) and factors for their decision to stay or leave. Tenure needs both satisfaction and satisfactoriness. When the person's values are reinforced by the work environment, satisfaction occurs; when the person's abilities and skills meet the requirements of the work environment, satisfactoriness occurs. If one has only satisfaction but not satisfactoriness, it is very likely he or she will be fired. On the other hand, if one has only satisfactoriness but no satisfaction, he or she will probably quit the job. In other words, people have needs, and work has rewards, when these two sets correspond concurrently, tenure will be the outcome. Otherwise, if the work environment does not provide the compensation the worker expects, two possible adjustment behaviors could occur: The employer could change the reinforcers, or the individual could change their expectations of rewards. For instance, a woman who needs to have a flexible work schedule so that she can take care of her aging parents, is currently employed in a job that requires a tight schedule from 9 to 5 daily, without any flexibility at all. Even though she can satisfy the employer because she has the skill sets they need, her needs are not met.

She can ask the employer to give her some flexibility, such as a different work schedule, as long as she delivers the product or allow her to work from home when needed, but if these needs cannot be met by the employer, that is, the reinforcer does not satisfy her needs, she is likely to look for a different job that can satisfy her needs.

In practice, the TWA has generated two sets of assessment that practitioners could use for career intervention. One type is to assess the needs and values, and the most frequently used and researched is the Minnesota Importance Questionnaire (MIQ; Rounds, Henley, Dawis, Lofquist, & Weiss, 1981). The MIQ profile contains 20 needs and 6 values that are compared to reinforce patterns at various occupations. This process of comparison results in a list of occupations with which individuals might feel satisfied (Swanson & Schneider, 2013). Another example—the Work Importance Profiler (WIP), which also assesses needs and values—is based on the ranked version of the MIQ, and is part of the O*NET managed by the U.S. Department of Labor. The other set of assessment tools aims at measuring the correspondence of personal needs and work requirements. According to Dawis (2005), the General Aptitude Test Battery (GATB; a multiple-ability assessment developed by the U.S. Employment Services, a division of the U.S. Department of Labor) is used to measure skills and abilities. It has 12 skill tests that could be used for all occupations. Work satisfaction and satisfactoriness have been measured through the Minnesota Satisfaction Questionnaire and the Minnesota Satisfactoriness Scale that were developed by the research team at the University of Minnesota and are available at the institute website (http://www.psych.umn.edu/psylabs/vpr/default.htm). These assessment tools help individuals gain understanding of their needs and values as well as the fitness to work demands.

The research about the TWA has mainly supported the roles of satisfaction and satisfactoriness in work adjustment and has supported the significance of role satisfaction in predicting tenure (Dawis, 2005). Most of the research focused on the person-environment fit and used the measures developed from the TWA constructs. There is some research that supports the utility of TWA to diverse populations, for instance, African Americans and LGBT population (Swanson & Schneider, 2013). The application of TWA extends to various settings and life development stages due to its focus on work adjustment; that is, it can be useful to help adolescents to identify their work needs, values, skills, and possible occupations for fulfilling these needs, or it can help dissatisfied workers to find reasons for their dissatisfaction and possible solutions (Dawis, 2005).

CASE ILLUSTRATION 4.1
FINDING THE NEXT FIT

John McNeill comes to the government office to register for his unemployment benefits. The receptionist informs him that a requirement of receiving unemployment compensation is that he must be actively seeking work. She asks him if he knows how to do that and in what area he will

(Continued)

(Continued)

be looking. He replies that he has no idea. He had worked at the same furniture factory since he left high school, without a diploma, at age 16, and he worked there for 20 years until they moved their operations to Vietnam. She then offers to make an appointment for him to meet with their career specialist to help him plan for his future.

The career specialist discusses with John his work history and draws out from him what he liked about his job and what he did well. They discuss his satisfaction with being involved in making a product he could be proud of as well as his increasing skill level and satisfaction with learning new techniques. He was particularly satisfied with being able to tell his children that he could run the computerized quality control system. John believes that his work was satisfactory to his employers as he consistently received good ratings and compliments from his immediate supervisors. As he worked in a traditional unionized environment, he did not receive increased pay based on learning these new skills, but he did receive a raise each time a new contract was negotiated based on his seniority. He is very sad that this job is gone and extremely worried about his future.

The specialist spent some time letting John vent about his feelings and then moved him to a discussion of how he could apply the skills and abilities developed on his previous job to new work. They also discussed what kind of work environment John enjoys. It turns out that John likes to work with equipment or machines, and to have a routine work schedule and a clear structure of work duties and specific instructions from the supervisor.

They also discussed the modern application process, and she helped him use the state computer program for developing a resume. They then discussed how to prepare and conduct oneself on a job interview and set up a time for John to attend a group session offered at the agency for practicing interview skills. Their focus in this part of the session was on helping John articulate how he had been satisfactory to his employer and how he could convey this through the paperwork and during an interview with potential employers. They ended their time together with the specialist showing John how to use the computer listings of job openings in the office and at home.

Discussion Questions

1. What do you think the career specialist tried to accomplish with John? What theoretical framework does he follow?

2. What would be John's Holland's Codes? What would be possible occupations for John to explore in your view?

DEVELOPMENTAL APPROACHES

If the core idea of trait-and-factor approaches focuses on individual characteristics and their role in making satisfactory career decisions, the developmental approach in career development theories emphasizes the importance of self-understanding and its role in career exploration and decision making. In this category, Super's career development theory is the most influential one, and it has had a significant impact on career development theory and research. Another well-known developmental approach is Gottfredson's theory that describes the process of making a career choice in childhood and adolescence.

Super's Life Span, Life-Space Theory

Donald Super was a leading scholar who provided an alternative to the trait-and-factor approach to career development. The main idea of Super's developmental career development theory is that individuals' career choice is the outcome of self-exploration and the implementation of one's self-concept. We will introduce Super's basic assumptions first, then the key theoretical concepts, and lastly, the application and use of Super's theory in career counseling.

The following summarizes Super's basic assumptions (1953, 1954, 1957, 1980, 1990):

1. People differ in their abilities, personalities, needs, values, interests, traits, and self-concept.

2. People are skilled, by virtue of these characteristics, for a number of occupations.

3. Each occupation is associated with a characteristic pattern of abilities and personality traits—with tolerances wide enough to allow both some variety of occupations for each individual and some variety of individuals in each occupation.

4. Vocational preferences and competencies, the situations in which people live and work, and hence their self-concept, change with time and experience, although self-concept, as a product of social learning, is increasingly stable from late adolescence until late maturity, providing some continuity in choice and adjustment.

5. This process of change may be summed up in a series of life stages (a "maxicycle") characterized as a sequence of growth, exploration, establishment, maintenance, and decline, and these stages may in turn be subdivided into (a) the fantasy, tentative, and realistic phases of the exploratory stage and (b) the trial and stable phases of the establishment stage. A small (mini) cycle takes place in transitions from one stage to the next or each time an individual is destabilized by a layoff due to a reduction in force, changes in personnel needs, illness or injury, or other socioeconomic or personal events. Such unstable or multiple-trial careers involve new growth, re-exploration, and re-establishment (recycling).

6. The nature of the career pattern—that is, the occupational level attained and the sequence, frequency, and duration of trial and stable jobs—is influenced by the individual's parental socioeconomic level, mental ability, education, skills, personality characteristics (needs, values, interests, traits, and self-concepts), and career maturity as well as by the opportunities to which he or she is exposed.

7. Success in coping with the demands of the environment and of the organism in that context at any given life-career stage depends on the readiness of the individual to cope with these demands (that is, on his or her career maturity).

8. Career maturity is a hypothetical construct. Its operational definition is perhaps as difficult to formulate as is that of intelligence, but its history is much briefer and its achievements even less definite.

9. Development through the life stages can be guided partly by facilitating the maturing of abilities and interests and partly by aiding in reality testing and in the development of self-concept.

10. The process of career development is essentially that of developing and implementing occupational self-concepts. It is a synthesizing and compromising process in which the self-concept is a product of the interaction of inherited aptitudes, physical makeup, opportunity to observe and play various roles, and evaluations of the extent to which the results of role playing meet the approval of superiors and colleagues (interactive learning).

11. The process of synthesis of or compromise between individual and social factors, between self-concept and reality, is one of role playing and of learning from feedback, whether the role is played in fantasy, in the counseling interview, or in such real-life activities as classes, clubs, part-time work, and entry-level jobs.

12. Work satisfaction and life satisfaction depend on the extent to which the individual finds adequate outlets for abilities, needs, values, interests, personality traits, and self-concept. They depend on establishment in a type of work, a work situation, and a way of life in which one can play the kind of role that growth and exploratory experiences have led one to consider congenial and appropriate.

13. The degree of satisfaction people attain from work is proportional to the degree to which they have been able to implement their self-concept.

14. Work and occupation provide a focus for personality organization for most men and women, although for some persons this focus is peripheral, incidental, or even nonexistent. Then other foci, such as leisure activities and homemaking, may be central. (Social traditions, such as gender-role stereotyping and modeling, racial and ethnic biases and opportunity structure, as well as individual differences, are important determinants of preferences for such roles as worker, student, leisurite, homemaker, and citizen.)

Key Concepts

According to Super, there are two sets of factors that shape persons' career development: one set includes their psychological characteristics including needs, values, interests, intelligence, ability, and special attitudes; the other set includes the socioeconomic factors that define the context in which individuals interact with the world. The factors in this latter category include school, family, peer groups, community, the economy, society, and the labor market. These two sets of factors influence the development of one's self-concept, the core concept in Super's theory. Several key concepts are fundamental to understanding the career development process described by Super.

Self-Concept: how individuals view themselves and their situations; a combination of biological characteristics, roles played in various settings, and evaluation of their interactions with others and external environments. Super stated that vocational development is the process of developing and implementing a self-concept. This process involves self-differentiation, role playing, exploration, and reality testing through interactions with family, school, community, and society. In other words, the self-concept is developed through exploration of different roles at different times and settings.

Life Roles: Super proposed that each person plays different roles throughout his or her life and that each role may be played with more priority at different times. For instance,

FIGURE 4.2 ■ Super's Life Stages and Life Space Model

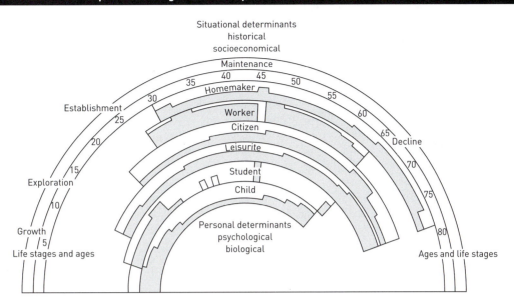

Super, D. E., & Harris-Bowlsbey, J. A. (1979). *Guided career exploration*. U.S.A.: Psychological Corp.

the role of child is more dominant during early childhood and less so in young adulthood time, when individuals are focusing on work and their own family building; however, the role of child becomes important again in later adulthood when children are expected to take care of their aging parents. Super described six major roles people play in their lives: worker, homemaker, citizen, student, child, and leisurite. Worker and citizen are major roles that everyone has from adolescence to the ending age. The homemaker's role usually does not start until young adulthood, when people are living independently, in a relationship, or starting a family. In essence, we all have multiple roles, but at different time periods, we may emphasize certain roles more than the others. The variation of role salience is influenced by life stages, another important concept of Super's theory.

Life Stages: Life stages, essential to life span and life-space theory, depict Super's core idea about the lifelong process of self-concept exploration and implementation. From birth to death, people experience these life stages:

Growth: refers to physical and psychological growth during the time from birth to middle childhood. This is also the time when children show curiosity and have fantasies about occupations and when preteens start to develop interests and capacities. During the growth stage, children develop their sense of self and fantasize about work through interacting with their parents and other adult figures at home, at school, and in the community.

Exploration: refers to the life stage when individuals become more aware of themselves and the world of work and start to explore some career choices. There are three substages during this phase: *crystallizing, specifying,* and *implementing.* According to Super, these tasks take place approximately between the ages of 14 to 24. *Crystallizing* is the process of gaining further knowledge of the work world and clarifying the information about the types of work that individuals were interested in during their growth stage. The *specifying* substage refers to the process of making decisions using information gathered, and this is the phase that requires individuals to develop the skills and ability to evaluate information, make career choices, and plan accordingly. *Implementing* is the substage in which people either prepare themselves (e.g., gaining necessary education and training or experiences) to enter the workforce or directly enter an occupation. These three mini-cycles, as Super described them, can be recycled if needed. For instance, if one develops new interests, or is forced to look for a new job, the entire or part of these processes may be necessary for reentry into the workforce.

Establishment: This refers to the stage in which people secure a job and become successful in a particular occupation. Establishment in one's selected career usually indicates that one has mastered three components in sequential order: *stabilizing, consolidating,* and *advancing.* Stabilizing indicates being safe and secure in one's position after entering into the occupation. Once individuals become confident in their positions within the occupation, consolidating is the next step, meaning that they find contentment in work and have a desire to be recognized and appreciated for their performance. Because of this successful performance, the next natural step is advancing. Advancing refers to the final ministage in establishment, which is defined by higher level status with more responsibility and recognition.

Maintenance: This stage refers to the circumstance when people may face the decision to either continue in the same job or find an alternative job if no more fulfillment can be attained. There are three substages within the maintenance stage: holding, updating, and innovating. Holding means keeping up with the current job and staying in the same position without much change. According to Niles and Harris-Bowlsbey (2013), "those who decide to say in their current occupations but not to update their skills often become poor performers and stagnate in their work" (p. 52). In today's job market, it may also mean losing their jobs. Updating and innovation means people make an effort to update their skills, improve their performance, and explore new and innovative ideas for better results. These people usually remain active and productive in their professions and feel satisfied and happy.

Disengagement/Decline: If physical and mental capacities begin to decline and one cannot maintain the same level of activity in work as before, then, according to Super, it is the time to think about retirement. There are *decelerating, retirement planning,* and *retirement living* substages. Decelerating refers to the pace and intensity of work performance beginning to decline. One becomes more concerned about post-retirement life, thus, retirement planning is another substage of this disengagement stage. The other one is retirement living; needless to say, this is the time when people actually retire from work, or at least paid employment.

Life Spaces: Super posits that each life role also has its life space in which each particular role plays a dominant part at different time. The life space can also be understood as the theatres in which roles are performed. For instance, the role of children is played primarily at home and in school.

Role Salience: This concept is based on Super's idea (1990) that life structure consists of multiple roles with a focus at different stages. It indicates that the importance or the values assigned to work and other life roles varies across the life span and across different life-spaces. The rainbow diagram (Figure 4.2) illustrates this concept through a changing array of life roles, with dark colors implying more focus at the time.

Career Maturity: Super (1955) described vocational maturity as mastery of these tasks: orientation to vocational choice, information and planning about a preferred occupation, consistency and wisdom of vocational preference, and crystallization of traits. It means that one needs to have a clear understanding of individual characteristics and attitudes toward work, know how to collect and evaluate information regarding preferred occupations, and know how to prepare to enter into the chosen field. Individuals with career maturity show stability in an occupational field over time and understand the relationship between vocational choice and various aspects of personal characteristics. Career maturity has been extensively researched, and most research involved examining the validity of Super's theoretical constructs and predictability of career maturity to career satisfaction, career decision self-efficacy, and career outcome (Hartung, 2013). The two most influential ones are the Career Development Inventory (see more details in Chapter 7), an assessment tool that measures the level of career maturity, and the Career Maturity Inventory (CMI), first developed by Crites (1965) and then updated by Crites and Savickas (1995). The role of career maturity to career exploration behavior, particularly in adolescence and young adulthood, was well supported by the research (Hartung, 2013).

No other career development theory has generated so many constructs as Super's life span and life-space theory. It has had significant influence on the career development research and practice for many decades. It provided an alternative approach to trait-and-factor career development theories, which emphasized matching individuals' abilities, or interests, to pertaining occupations. Super's developmental career theory introduced the concept that helping individuals choose a career is more than just finding a matching career, and that the process of exploring career options facilitates awareness of self-identity and needs. In the developmental approach, people are more cognizant of themselves in regard to making career choices. Super and his associates have conducted sustained and systematic research over 60 years and provided ample empirical support of the life-space and life-stage theory across nations (Super & Sverko, 1995). The theory has been updated and revised over the years to attend to the criticism on lack of gender and cultural context consideration (Hartung, 2013).

LEARNING ACTIVITY 4.2

Divide the class into small groups. Within each group, ask the members to share with each other the following:

1. Roles they spend the most time in now

2. Roles they spend the least time in now

3. Roles they ideally want to spend the most time in

Then ask the group members about the developmental stages they are currently at and life space in which they are spending most of their time. Discuss if life stage and life space have any impact on their time spent on each role Super listed.

Gottfredson's Theory of Circumscription and Compromise

Another career theory that fits within the developmental approach is Gottfredson's circumscription and compromise theory (Gottfredson, 1981, 2005). Her theory focuses on how career aspirations develop, particularly in childhood and adolescence. Gottfredson believed that people seek occupations that satisfy their interests, goals, and abilities, and that this process is evolving and involves development processes that require growing mental capacity, constructing self-concept, eliminating choices (circumscription), and compromising. The four developmental tasks are particularly important for the career development process: age-related cognitive growth, self-directed development of self, progressive elimination of least favored vocational alternatives, and recognition of and adjustment to external constraints on vocational choice.

According to Gottfredson (2005), the career development process begins in childhood as children grow in their ability to learn and reason. Cognitive growth increases from thinking intuitively in preschool years, to thinking more concretely at pre-adolescent years, and thinking abstractly at adolescence. As children grow in their mental ability, they increasingly become capable of understanding, analyzing, and evaluating information around them. In regard to career development, they begin by looking at the most visible and concrete attributes of people and occupations and later can narrow their choices by making multidimensional comparisons. Gottfredson claimed that children's cognitive growth also yielded to two major products: the cognitive map of occupations and the self-concept. Career aspirations are the attempts then to implement one's self concept; therefore, the process of choosing occupations is the process of finding a matching occupation that is consistent with their self-concept.

Self-concept, in Gottfredson's definition, is self-directed construction of self, based on one's own perception of self in relation to the world around him or her. In other words, we are born with certain genetic traits that are relatively independent of environmental influences. However, as children grow, they increasingly select, shape, and interpret their environments (Gottfredson, 2005) as well; therefore, self-concept is the constellation of genetically conditioned self and culturally contingent self. Neither is necessarily fixed and can be changed. Vocational traits such as personality, interests, and values are more culturally bound and experience dependent because individuals' living and educational experiences play a major role in shaping their activation and awareness of their likes and dislikes, abilities, and inadequacies. For instance, children growing up in a family with resources versus children growing up in disadvantaged families would have different exposure to learning and occupational information and therefore would have a different understanding of self and the occupational world. On the other hand, siblings growing up with the same parents in the same household can also develop totally different self-concepts, because each individual reacts to the same environment differently. This process of making a career choice involves two components: circumscription and compromise.

Circumscription

People develop occupational maps that guide them in the selection process. According to Gottfredson (2005), this process of circumscription of eliminating occupations that conflict with our self-concepts has four developmental stages:

Stage 1: Orientation to Size and Power (ages 3 to 5); young children at this stage understand that work is part of adult life and that someday they too will become adults and workers. They choose occupations that are perceived to be big or powerful, for instance, police officer or fire fighter.

Stage 2: Orientation to Sex Roles (ages 6 to 8); children at this stage begin to see differences in gender and sex roles related to occupations. They rely on the most visible attributes to distinguish who performs different occupations, looking at the gender of the workers observed, their clothing, and the activities being performed. An early study of gender-related attitudes among children of this age (Schlossberg & Goodman, 1972) found that while children were verbally open to men and women performing a variety of occupations, even those typically performed mostly by men or mostly by women, they were completely gender stereotyped in their own occupational choices. The only exception in four groups of children was one kindergarten girl who wanted to be an astronaut.

Stage 3: Orientation to Social Valuation (ages 9 to 13); by this stage, children become aware of the status hierarchies outlined by society and are sensitive to social evaluation of status; therefore, they may be critical of lower status occupations. Children during this stage also can think more abstractly and arrange their occupational choices on two dimensions: prestige level and sex type. By this time, a large number of occupations are eliminated if they are perceived as too low in status, wrong sex type, or too difficult to enter. Children began to build boundaries that are consistent with their viewed levels of social valuation, sex, and academic ability.

Stage 4: Orientation to Unique Self (ages 14 and older); adolescents and young adults during this stage become more conscious of their search for occupations within the tolerable boundaries (or the available choices after the elimination in the previous stages) that are more personally fulfilling and compatible with their self-concept. The search process is more complex since it is multidimensional and has other factors besides the vocational domains (e.g., family obligations, accessibility, and affordability of preparation to attain the goal) that are affecting career planning. Idealistic and realistic aspirations then become the focus of their career exploration.

Compromise

Career aspirations are the result of the interaction between estimates of accessibility and compatibility estimates. As children grow and develop perceptions of themselves and occupational fields, they begin to narrow or circumscribe their range of occupations based on their estimates of compatibility (sex-type, prestige, and interests) and accessibility. The final choice is a compromise as adolescents and adults give up their most preferred choices in favor of those that are more accessible. When people are forced to compromise, the order is sex-type, prestige, and interests (Gottfredson, 2005).

Gottfredson's theoretical approach to career development emphasizes the importance of being provided with adequate learning and experiences in early years and to engaging in activities that are important to develop individuals' ability and self-insights. Self-insights are valuable to appropriate self-investment that leads to career decision implementation. Gottfredson (2005) suggested that career counselors can help clients optimize learning, experiences, self-insights, and self-investment through these strategies: reduce task complexity; accommodate cognitive diversity; provide a variety of experiences; promote self-agency in shaping experiences; facilitate inventory and integration of information about self; promote sound conception of a fitting and feasible career life; facilitate assessment of accessibility of preferred career life; and promote self-agency in enhancing self, opportunity, and support.

CASE ILLUSTRATION 4.2
WHEN CAN DOROTHY SETTLE DOWN?

Dorothy Pike made an appointment with a career counselor because she felt stuck and was not able to figure out her next steps regarding her occupational choices. She had graduated from college with a degree in English that is the butt of so many jokes about its lack of connection to work. But for her, it wasn't a joke, it was a real problem. She had loved her studies, especially modern poetry, but the only jobs she had been able to find in the three years since graduation had been in retail sales. Not only were these jobs not satisfying but the pay was close to minimum wage—not enough to begin saving for the house she wanted to buy or the lifestyle she hoped to achieve. In Super's terms, she was in the exploration stage. Even though at 25 she should be nearing the end of the substages, she was still at the crystallization phase and was very pleased when she heard that there was someone who could help her move ahead.

The counselor began her work with Dorothy by taking a history and exploring with Dorothy her experiences during the fantasy stage experienced during her childhood and early adolescence—what Super termed growth—and considering what she was thinking about the roles she hoped to play as her life continued. Dorothy shared that when she was about 5, she wanted to be a fire fighter, then gave up that idea when she found out that there were not many women fire fighters. Then she wanted to work at summer camps but gave up that idea when she heard from her cousins that those jobs do not have high income or esteem. Dorothy has thought about being a doctor, but she eliminated that option because she

was afraid that her grades were not good enough. She chose English as a major, thinking she would have wide-open options. On learning that Dorothy was engaged and hoped to have children, that she was an active member of her local political party, and that she enjoyed reading and photography as hobbies, the counselor began to help Dorothy see a picture of how her interests and abilities might play out in the workplace. Her extensive avocational roles, including the anticipated marriage and motherhood, meant that she would need to be looking at work that accommodated these interests.

Dorothy and her counselor developed a plan for focusing on exploration and speeding up the processes of crystallization and implementation. They drew up a list of possible occupations, aided by her taking the Value Scale and the Strong Interest Inventory, and made plans to explore each through reading, occupational information interviews, and job shadowing. They made an appointment for three weeks later to give Dorothy time to follow up and provide a deadline to encourage action.

Discussion Questions

1. Why do you think Dorothy keep eliminating her career choices? What factors do you think influenced her choice?

2. Why do you think the counselor wants to speed up the crystallization process? Do you agree with this action?

SOCIAL COGNITIVE APPROACHES

There are two common features of the career development theories in this category: the fundamental ideas of the theories derived from Bandura's (1977, 1986) social cognitive learning theory and the importance of learning experiences to career aspiration and career intervention. The two social cognitive career development theories presented below are the two best known.

Krumboltz's Learning Theory

John Krumboltz and his colleagues in the past three decades have attempted to explain how people make career choices and in recent years, have looked at how career counselors can help. Krumboltz's learning theory of career development has been extended from the original "social learning theory of career decision making" (SLTCDM) to "learning theory of career counseling" (LTCC) (Krumboltz, 1979, 1996; Mitchell & Krumboltz, 1996), the former focusing on explaining factors that influence individuals' career decision making and the latter providing intervention strategies for counselors to work with clients in searching for a career choice. The latest addition to Krumboltz's theory is Planned Happenstance (Krumboltz, 2009)

Krumboltz identifies four factors that influence individuals in career decision making:

1. Genetic endowment and special abilities: inherited characteristics such as race, gender, physical conditions, intelligence, and musical ability. Some of these inherited abilities can be partially restrictive to learning outcome. For example, if one does not have musical ability, one may learn to read music and pass a music class but would not be likely to become a skilled musician.

2. Environmental conditions and events: factors beyond individuals' control that exist in their living context, such as the existence of learning opportunities, job opportunities, educational systems, family resources, social-political context, natural disasters, and the changing labor market.

3. Learning experiences: any prior learning experiences occurring before making educational and career decisions; there are two kinds of learning experiences. The first is instrumental learning experiences—individuals' reactions to environmental stimuli and their consequences, which involve three components: antecedents, behaviors, and consequences. For example, a student who wants to choose a major entering college engages in talk with school counselors and parents and obtains occupational information, perhaps by completing a job shadow day with someone in a field of interest. He or she may like what he or she finds and is then more likely to choose a major associated with this job. In this case, the behavior of engaging in exploration yielded positive experiences and therefore would influence the person to do more exploration in the future. The other kind of learning experience is associative learning, which involves observation and classical conditioning. Through observing someone in work settings, career explorers

can develop their understanding and potentially decide whether this is a job that they might like to hold. A bad experience with one nurse, for example, might be generalized to all nurses, which might influence the person to avoid being a nurse.

4. Task approach skills: the skills applied to each new task or problem, such as work habits, perceptual and cognitive processes, ways of learning, and ways of responding to environmental conditions.

Krumboltz claims that these four factors interactively and constantly influence people as they encounter learning experiences; consequently they have impacts on how people make career decisions in these four ways: (1) self-observation generalization, (2) generalization about the world, (3) task approach skills, and (4) action. Through observing one's own behavior, interests, and beliefs, one develops a sense of self and then draws conclusions about abilities, performances, and expectations from behaviors. Observation about the work world come from actual experience or associated learning experiences, which then lead to generalized knowledge of occupations. After developing an impression of self and the world, one applies task approach skills to combine and evaluate this information. Taking actions involves implementation of career decisions made to prepare oneself to enter the workforce or make changes.

Planned Happenstance

This refers to the situation in which people take advantage of the unplanned events that occur in their lives. Krumboltz and his colleagues (Mitchell, Levin, & Krumboltz, 1999) believe that many factors in our lives such as social, political, economic, educational, and occupational conditions are ever changing and unpredictable. Therefore, career counseling should not just help clients make one career choice; rather, the goal should be to learn to take actions to benefit from opportunities and to achieve a satisfying life (Krumboltz, 2009).

Krumboltz's social learning theory of career development emphasized the importance of learning in shaping one's experiences and understanding of self and the work world. Krumboltz (1996) believes that the goal of career counseling is to facilitate learning about oneself and the work environment so that one has the ability to create a satisfying life. He and his colleagues later developed the learning theory of career counseling, which provides a framework of how counselors can help clients' career-related problems. The problems related to career development, according to Krumboltz, are due to clients' faulty cognitive constructs and faulty reasoning. Some examples of self-defeating thoughts are changes couldn't happen, viewing life in general as negative, and blaming others, and some examples of faculty reasoning include overgeneralization, single or narrow focus, and unreasonable standards for self-evaluation (Andersen & Vandehey, 2012). Krumboltz (1996) criticized the static view of career development and intervention and stated that counselors should help clients be prepared through lifelong learning to manage the change that is endemic in the modern world. In applying learning theories of career counseling, Mitchell and Krumboltz (1996) stated the following:

1. People need to expand their capabilities and interests, not base decisions on existing characteristics only. Interest inventories assess what we know and what we have experienced. To maximize a client's career choice options, counselors must encourage the client to explore new activities, develop new interests, and consider new options based on newly formed interests and capacities.

2. People need to prepare for changing work tasks and not assume that occupations will remain stable. Because change is constant, career counselors must help their clients identify new skills to learn and develop strategies for coping with the stress inherent in an everchanging world of work.

3. People need to be empowered to take action, not merely to be given a diagnosis. For some clients, implementing a career choice is more challenging than making the choice. Many clients need ongoing assistance from their career counselors as they attempt to adjust to the career choice they have made and implemented.

4. Career counselors need to play a major role in dealing with all career problems, not just career selection. Career-related concerns exist beyond this concern of identifying a career choice. Many clients struggle with burnout, underemployment, relationship problems with coworkers, family member's reactions to career choices, and low self-efficacy.

Therefore, the career intervention based on Krumboltz's learning theories of career development has two main goals: facilitate learning (developmental and preventive) and restructure faulty cognition to make necessary changes (intervention on targeted population or remedial). To facilitate learning, career counseling practitioners should identify, provide, and create learning opportunities for clients to acquire self-knowledge and knowledge about the world of work. These learning opportunities can be job shadowing, internships, observations, career information resources in print or online, or career education classes (Niles & Harris-Bowlsbey, 2013). Krumboltz (1996) also suggested the strategies in career counseling for intervention purpose: goal clarification, role models, role playing, simulation, cognitive restructuring, cognitive rehearsal, narrative analysis, countering a troublesome belief, and reinforcement. In order to help clients identify troublesome beliefs, Krumboltz (1991) developed the Career Beliefs Inventory (CBI). This instrument helps counselors assess clients' career beliefs and assumptions, so that counselors can work on clients' problematic beliefs.

Social Cognitive Career Theory by Lent, Brown, and Hackett

Social Cognitive Career Theory (SCCT) was another career development theory derived from Bandura's (1977, 1986) social cognitive learning theory. Bandura's theory has been applied in many fields since its development. The first application of Bandura's social cognitive learning theory to career development was Betz and Hackett's (1981) work on women's career development. Betz and Hackett argued that few women entered science and technology related careers because there was a lack of supporting resources for women to develop self-efficacy and positive outcome expectations, as they also were lacking role models, encouragement from others, or actual learning or work experiences for them to be inspired to enter into those occupations. Later, many empirical research studies examined the role of self-efficacy and outcome expectations to educational achievement and career choice behaviors (Lent, Brown, & Larkin, 1984; Lent & Hackett, 1987). Lent, Brown, and Hackett proposed SCCT in 1994, and they have revised the model several times since then. The following will introduce the main constructs of SCCT, its application, and its current status.

There are three major constructs in SCCT model that are critical to career choice behavior and performance. As stated earlier, SCCT applied Bandura's (1977, 1986) general principles to account for the career development process. These three constructs are self-efficacy beliefs, outcome expectations, and personal goals. SCCT highlights the interplay of these three variables as they shape the action in career development.

Self-efficacy beliefs are conceived as a "dynamic set of self-beliefs that are linked to particular performance domains and activities" (Lent, 2005, p. 104). According to Bandura (1997), there were four sources influencing one's self-efficacy beliefs: personal performance accomplishment, vicarious learning, social persuasion, and physiological and affective states. For example, we usually feel more confident engaging in activities if (1) we have previously successfully done the same or similar activities, (2) we see someone else who is similar to us do it, (3) our family members and friends encourage us to do so, and (4) simply because we are inspired and excited by the activity itself. On the other hand, if we do not have any of the above supporting resources, we are more likely to avoid the task than to attempt the task.

Outcome expectation refers to belief about the consequences of pursuing certain behaviors (Lent et al., 1994). The outcome expectation is not about one's capacity; rather, it is about the anticipated outcome as a result of the behavior. For instance, I think I can have a comfortable lifestyle if I become a banker. The outcome expectation in this case is the comfortable lifestyle, and this anticipation comes from observation of others and learning from a variety of sources.

Personal goals refer to an individual's intention to engage in a particular activity or to produce a particular outcome (Lent, 2005). The SCCT also distinguishes two kinds of goals: One type relates to choice-content and the other to performance. The former is about the intent of choice, and the latter is about the intent of quality of implementation of choice. According to SCCT, goals affect the actions individuals take in occupational and educational pursuit. The relationships among self-efficacy beliefs, outcome expectations, and personal goals are reciprocal, meaning self-efficacy and outcome expectation influence personal goals, and personal goals in return would influence self-efficacy and outcome expectation.

The main principles of SCCT include the following:

1. The interaction of people with their environments is highly dynamic; individuals are influenced by and also influence their environments.

2. Career-related behavior are influenced by four aspects of the person: behavior, self-efficacy beliefs, outcome expectations, and goals, in addition to genetically determined characteristics.

3. Self-efficacy beliefs and expectations of outcomes interact directly to influence interest development. People become interested in things that they believe they can perform well, which will produce valued outcomes.

4. Personal factors such as gender, race, physical health, disabilities, and dispositions and contextual factors such as family background, family or personal social economic status, and opportunities influence self-efficacy development as well outcome expectations, and ultimately, goals and performance.

5. Actual career choice and implementation will be influenced by a number of direct and indirect variables in individuals' context, in addition to self-efficacy, outcome expectation, and goals. Some of the contextual factors, for example, occupational discrimination, economic variables such as supply and demand, and the culture of the decision maker could directly influence career choice, goals, and performance.

6. Performance in educational activities and occupations is the result of the interactions among ability, self-efficacy beliefs, outcome expectations, and the goals that have been established. All things being equal, people with the highest level of ability and the strongest self-efficacy beliefs will perform at the highest level. However, self-efficacy beliefs and outcome expectations are altered continuously as individuals interact with their environment.

Figure 4.3 illustrates the SCCT model. As shown in the diagram, learning experiences play an important role in development of self-efficacy and outcome expectation that directly influence interest development. Therefore, the intervention strategies of SCCT focus on facilitating development of self-efficacy and outcome expectation through providing relevant learning experiences. Specifically, Lent (2005, 2013) suggested the following strategies: organizing structured psychoeducational programs, cognitive restructuring to recognize attribution of performance, modeling, encouraging trial of new tasks and focusing on skill growth rather than ultimate success, building self-efficacy on domain-specific tasks, fostering career decision-making skills and goal setting, teaching self-regulation skills, facilitating career choice making and implementation by expanding choice options, coping with barriers and building support, examining the discrepancies between perceived self-efficacy and task performance, and providing mastery experiences.

The SCCT has been extensively studied in the last two decades. Since it is a comprehensive theory that incorporates trait-and-factor approach, developmental, and social cognitive learning career development theory, it attracts many studies examining its applicability to diverse populations. The research findings thus far have supported most of the propositions (Lent, 2005, 2013). In summary, self-efficacy is strongly related to interest and outcome expectations; past successful experiences are correlated to building stronger self-efficacy; self-efficacy and outcome predict career choice both directly and indirectly through interests; and the applications to cross-cultural populations were found consistent to the propositions of SCCT (Sheu & Lent, 2009).

FIGURE 4.3 ■ SCCT Model

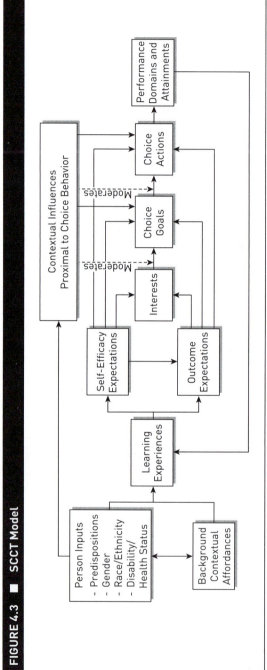

Copyright 1993 by R. W. Lent, S. D. Brown, and G. Hackett.

CASE ILLUSTRATION 4.3
SUSAN IS PLANNING FOR COLLEGE

Susan Chu makes an appointment with her high school counselor to discuss college and career planning. She expects to go to college and wants help deciding on a major field of study. Her counselor informs her that most colleges allow students to defer this decision until they have had an opportunity to take classes in a variety of areas, but Susan is anxious to know where she is heading before she begins. Her counselor agrees to help her and begins by giving her the Self-Directed Search to take home, complete, and score. The counselor asks Susan to compute her three-letter code and look through the occupations listed in the occupations finder for all the permutations of that code. They set a meeting for the following week.

When Susan returns to the counselor, she informs her that she has SAE as her code, but she is not exactly sure whether she wants the occupations listed under this code or similar codes (e.g., AES, EAS) because she does not know what these occupations actually entail. The counselor asks Susan first if she thinks that her code is representative of her, and Susan says yes, she feels that it captured her combination of interests and skills. The counselor then suggests that Susan find someone from her extended family who is working in those fields suggested by the code, or anybody's job that is appealing to her, and shadowed that person. She also encourages Susan to look for opportunities to do a summer internship where she could learn about those occupations. The counselor also suggests Susan get involved in school clubs or student organizations to gain some experiences.

They plan to continue to meet after Susan has done the suggested activities. Meanwhile, Susan starts to gather information from the Internet regarding those occupations as well. Three months later, when Susan talks to her counselor again, she wants her counselor to tell her steps she needs to take to major in psychology because she finds a lot of interesting people she meets through those activities have a background in psychology.

Discussion Questions

1. What theoretical framework does Susan's counselor try to follow to help Susan? Why is it seemingly working?

2. What would you recommend Susan do next? What theoretical framework would you choose to conceptualize your plan?

3. What tasks do you think Susan needs to accomplish before high school graduation according to Super's theory? As her counselor, how you would facilitate completing that task?

MULTICULTURAL BOX 4.1

Fitzgerald and Betz (1994) stated "Career development theories have always had the most to say about the smallest segment of the populations, that is, white middle class heterosexual men" (p. 105). Cook, Heppner, and O'Brien (2005) said that "Traditional models of career development evolved at a time when the typical worker was visualized as young, male, White, able bodied, publicly heterosexual, and ethnically homogenous (White immigrants from Western Europe)" (p.165). The labor force and structure dramatically changed from the beginning of the 20th century to the 21st century. How would you evaluate the theories reviewed in this chapter in regard to their applicability to the diverse workforce discussed in Chapter 2?

Tips for Consideration: Is the life stages theory proposed by Super applicable to non-White, low socioeconomic populations? How about women? Will the reinforce pattern be the same for men and women? Will the vocational personality be perceived the same across different cultures?

Summary: Challenges and Opportunities

The emergence of vocational guidance was the response to the social and economic change at the end of the 19th century. Parsons's approach of understanding personal traits in relation to work characteristics laid the foundation not only for trait-factor theories of career development but also career counseling practice. Though each theory reviewed in this chapter has its own unique features and different focus, the commonalities exist. These theories aim to explain vocational behavior, making decisions about career choice, and the relationship between individual characteristics and work environment features. These theories provide a helpful framework and tool for career intervention and will continue to influence research and practice, despite the concern about their contemporary application to diverse and changing population. With more recognition of the importance of work to health and human development and more research conducted to examine the theories, these theories actually have been continually modified and updated to address the changes and enhance their applicability for appropriate intervention.

Keystones

- Career development theories were built on the foundation laid by Parsons's approach to help individuals who need vocational guidance and evolved to become comprehensive in explaining vocational behavior.

- The core of all the theories is understanding the dynamic relationship between person and work environment, that is, how a person is related to the outside world through work.

- The theories in the trait-factor category focus on consistency between personal characteristics, including interests, needs, personality, and abilities, and work requirements, including skill sets and characteristics of work environment.

- The theories in the developmental framework emphasize the developmental nature of career development and the importance of self-concept expression through careers.

- The theories in the social cognitive learning category shared the root of Bandura's social cognitive learning theory and emphasize the impact of learning and experiences to one's vocational behavior.

- These career development theories have had a significant impact on career intervention and research over a long period of time.

Additional Resources

Fitzgerald, L. F., & Betz, N. E. (1994). Career development in cultural context: The role of gender, race, class, and sexual orientation. In M. L. Savickas & R. W. Lent (Eds.), *Convergence in career development theories: Implications for science and practice* (pp. 103-107). Palo Alto, CA: CPP Books.

Savickas, M. L. (1994). Donald Edwin Super: The career of a planful explorer. *Career Development Quarterly, 43*, 4-24.

Swanson, J. L., & Fouad, N. A. (2010). *Career theory and practice: Learning through case studies* (2nd ed.). Thousand Oaks, CA: Sage.

University of Minnesota Vocational Psychology Research Institute: http://vpr.psych.umn.edu

References

Andersen, P., & Vandehey, M. (2012). *Career counseling and development in global economy* (2nd ed.). Belmont, CA: Brooks/Cole Cengage Learning.

Bandura, A. (1977). Self-efficacy: Toward a unifying theory of behavioral change. *Psychological Review, 84*, 191–215.

Bandura, A. (1986). *Social foundations of thought and action: A social cognitive theory*. Englewood Cliffs, NJ: Prentice-Hall.

Bandura, A. (1997). *Self-efficacy: The exercise of control*. New York, NY: Freeman.

Betz, N. E., & Hackett, G. (1981). The relationship of career-related self-efficacy expectations to perceived career options in college women and men. *Journal of Counseling Psychology, 28*, 399-410.

Betz, N. E., & Schifano, R. S. (2000). Evaluation of an intervention to increase realistic self-efficacy and interests in college women. *Journal of Vocational Behavior, 56*, 35-52.

Cook, E. P., Heppner, M. J., & O'Brien, K. M. (2005). Multicultural and gender influences in women's career development: An ecological perspective. *Journal of Multicultural Counseling and Development, 33*, 165–179. doi:10.1002/j.2161-1912.2005.tb00014.x

Crites, J. O. (1965). Measurement of vocational maturity in adolescence. *Psychological Monograph, 79*(Whole No. 595).

Crites, J. O., & Savickas, M. L. (1995). Revision of the Career Maturity Inventory. *Journal of Career Assessment, 4*, 131-138.

Dawis, R. V. (2005). The Minnesota theory of work adjustment. In S. D. Brown & R.W. Lent (Eds.), *Career development and counseling: Putting theory and research to work* (pp. 3-23). Hoboken, NJ: John Wiley.

Dawis, R. V., & Lofquist, L. H. (1984). *A psychological theory of work adjustment: An individual differences model and its application.* Minneapolis: University of Minnesota.

Day, S. X., Rounds, J., & Swaney, K. (1998). The structure of vocational interests for diverse racial-ethnic groups. *Psychological Science, 9,* 40–44.

Fitzgerald, L. F., & Betz, N. E. (1994). Career development in cultural context: The role of gender, race, class and sexual orientation. In M. L. Savickas & R. W. Lent (Eds.), *Convergence in career development theories: Implications for science and practice* (pp. 103–117). Palo Alto, CA: Consulting Psychologists Press.

Fitzgerald, L. F., Fassinger, R. E., & Betz, N. E. (1995). Theoretical advances in the study of women's career development. In W. B. Walsh & S. H. Osipow (Eds.), *Handbook of vocational psychology: Theory, research, and practice* (2nd ed., pp. 67–109). Mahwah, NJ: Erlbaum.

Gottfredson, L. S. (1981). Circumscription and compromise: A developmental theory of occupational aspirations. *Journal of Counseling Psychology, 28,* 545–579.

Gottfredson, L. S. (2005). Gottfredson's theory of circumscription, compromise, and self-creation. In D. Brown & Associates (Eds.), *Career choice and development* (4th ed., pp. 85–148). San Francisco, CA: Jossey-Bass.

Hartung, P. J. (2013). The life-span, life-stage theory of careers. In S. D. Brown, & R. W. Lent (Eds.), *Career development and counseling: Putting theory and research to work* (2nd ed., pp. 83-114). Hoboken, NJ: Wiley & Sons.

Herr, E. L. (2013). Trends in the history of vocational guidance. *Career Development Quarterly, 61,* 277-282. http://dx.doi:10.1002/j.2161-0045:2013.00056.x

Holland, J. L. (1985a). *Making vocational choices: A theory of career* (2nd ed.). Englewood Cliffs, NJ: Prentice Hall.

Holland, J. L. (1985b). *Manual for the Vocational Preference Inventory.* Odessa, FL: Psychological Assessment Resources.

Holland, J. L. (1996a). Exploring careers with a typology: What we have learned and some new directions. *American Psychologist, 51*(4), 397-406. doi:10.1037/0003-066X.51.4.397

Holland, J. L. (1996b). *The occupational finder.* Odessa, FL: Psychological Assessment Resources.

Holland, J. L. (1997). *Making vocational choices: A theory of vocational personalities and work environments* (3rd ed.). Odessa, FL: Psychological Assessment Resources.

Holland, J. L., Daiger, D. C., & Power, P. G. (1980). *My vocational situation.* Palo Alto, CA: Consulting Psychologists Press.

Holland J., Gottfredson D. C., & Power P. G. (1980). Some diagnostic scales for research in decision making and personality: Identity, information, and barriers. *Journal of Personality and Social Psychology, 39,* 1191–1200.

Holland, J. L., Powell, A. B., & Fritzsche, B. A. (1994). *The SDS technical manual*. Odessa, FL: Psychological Assessment Resources.

Krumboltz, J. D. (1979). A social learning theory of career decision making. In A. M. Mitchell, G. B. Jones, & J. D. Krumboltz (Eds.), *Social learning and career decision making* (pp. 19-49). Cranston, RI: Carroll Press.

Krumboltz, J. D. (1991). *Manual for the Career Beliefs Inventory*. Palo Alto, CA: Consulting Psychologists Press.

Krumboltz, J. D. (1996). A learning theory of career counseling. In M. L. Savickas, & W. B. Walsh (Eds.), *Handbook of career counseling theory and practice* (pp. 55-80). Palo Alto, CA: Davies-Black.

Krumboltz, J.D. (2009). The happenstance learning theory. *Journal of Career Assessment*, *17*(2), 135-154.

Lent, R. W. (2005). A social cognitive view of career development and counseling. In S. D. Brown, & R.W. Lent (Eds.), *Career development and counseling: Putting theory and research to work* (pp. 101-127). Hoboken, NJ: John Wiley.

Lent, R. W. (2013). Social cognitive career theory. In S. D. Brown & R. W. Lent (Eds.), *Career development and counseling: Putting theory and research to work* (pp. 115-146). Hoboken, NJ: John Wiley.

Lent, R. W., Brown, S. D., & Hackett, G. (1994). Toward a unifying social cognitive theory of career and academic interest, choice, and performance [Monograph]. *Journal of Vocational Behavior*, *45*, 79–122.

Lent, R. W., Brown, S. D., & Larkin, K. C. (1984). Relation of self-efficacy expectations to academic achievement and persistence. *Journal of Counseling Psychology*, *31*(3), 356-362. http://dx.doi.org/10.1037/0022-0167.31.3.356.

Lent, R. W., & Hackett, G. (1987). Career self-efficacy: Empirical status and future direction. *Journal of Vocational Behavior, 30*, 347-382.

Leong, F. T. L., Austin, J. T., Sekaran, U., & Komarraju, M. (1998). An evaluation of the cross-cultural validity of Holland's theory: Career choices by workers in India. *Journal of Vocational Behavior, 52*, 441-455.

Mitchell, L. K., & Krumboltz, J. D. (1996). Krumboltz's learning theory of career choice and counseling. In. D. Brown, L. Brooks, & Associates (Eds.), *Career choice and development* (3rd ed.) (pp. 233-276). San Francisco, CA: Jossey-Bass.

Mitchell, L. K. Levin, A. S., & Krumboltz, J. D. (1999). Planned happenstance: Constructing unexpected career opportunities. *Journal of Counseling and Development, 77*, 115-124.

Nauta, M. M. (2013). Holland's theory of vocational choice and adjustment. In S. D. Brown, & R. W. Lent (Eds.), *Career development and counseling: Putting theory and research to work* (2nd ed.) (pp. 55-82). Hoboken, NJ: Wiley & Sons.

Niles, S. G., Harris-Bowlsbey, J. (2013). *Career development interventions in the 21st century* (4th ed.). Upper Saddle River, NJ: Pearson Merrill Prentice Hall.

Parsons, F.A. (1909). *Choosing a vocation*. New York, NY: Houghton Mifflin.

Rounds, J. B, Jr., Henly, G. A., Dawis, R. V., Lofguist, L. H., & Wiess, D. J. (1981). *Manual for the Minnesota Importance Questionnaire: A measure of needs and values*. Minneapolis: Vocational Psychology Research, University of Minnesota.

Schlossberg, N. K., & Goodman, J. (1972). A woman's place: Children's sex stereotyping of occupations. *Vocational Guidance Quarterly, 20*(4), 266.

Sheu, H., & Lent, R. W. (2009). A social cognitive perspective on well-being in educational and work settings: Cross-cultural considerations. *International Journal for Educational and Vocational Guidance, 9*, 45-60.

Spokane, A. R., & Cruza-Guet, M. C. (2005). Holland's theory of vocational personalities in work environment. In S. D. Brown & R. W. Lent (Eds.), *Career development and counseling: Putting theory and research to work* (pp. 24-41). Hoboken, NJ: Wiley.

Super, D. E. (1953). A theory of vocational development. *American Psychologist, 8*, 185-190.

Super, D. E. (1954). Career patterns as a basis for vocational counseling. *Journal of Counseling Psychology, 1*(1), 12-20.

Super, D. E. (1955). The dimensions and measurement of vocational maturity. *Teachers College Record, 57*, 151-163.

Super, D. E. (1957). *The psychology of careers.* New York, NY: Harper and Row.

Super, D. E. (1980). A life-span, life-space, approach to career development. *Journal of Vocational Behavior, 16*, 292-298.

Super, D. E. (1990). A life-span, life-space approach to career development. In D. Brown & L. Brooks (Eds.), *Career choice and development: Applying contemporary theories to practice* (2nd ed., pp. 197-261). San Francisco, CA: Jossey-Bass.

Super, D. E., & Sverko, B. (Eds.), (1995). *Life roles, values and careers: International findings of the work importance study.* San Francisco, CA: Jossey-Bass.

Swanson, J. L., & Schneider, M. (2013). Minnesota theory of work adjustment. In S. D. Brown, & R. W. Lent (Eds.), *Career development and counseling: Putting theory and research to work.* (pp. 29-53). Hoboken, NJ: John Wiley.

Tang, M. (2001). Investigation of the structure of vocational interest of Chinese college students. *Journal of Career Assessment, 9*, 365-379.

Williamson, E. G. (1939). *How to counsel students: A manual of techniques for clinical counselors.* New York, NY: McGraw-Hill.

Zytowski, D. G. (1972). Four hundred years before parsons. *Personnel and Guidance Journal, 50*(6), 443.

Zytowski, D. G. (2001). Frank Parsons and the progressive movement. *Career Development Quarterly, 50*, 57-65.

5

CAREER DEVELOPMENT THEORIES II

In Chapter 4, we provided an overview of three major career development theories: trait and factor, developmental, and social cognitive learning. In this chapter, we will introduce some important theories that have either made a significant contribution to career development interventions or have offered alternative ways of understanding the career development process. Some of the theories reviewed in this chapter have existed for a while and have had a significant impact on the evolution of career development theories; some represent the most recent career development theories. As in Chapter 4, the major concepts and constructs of the theories will be presented first, then their use and application in career counseling will be illustrated.

LEARNING OBJECTIVES

After completing the reading and exercises provided in this chapter, you will be able to:

- describe the main propositions and key concepts of major career development theories,

- explain the contribution of each theory to career counseling practice and intervention,

- contrast the similarities and differences of the career development theories,

- identify the intervention strategies associated with each theory,

- analyze the applicability of each theory to diverse populations, and

- critique the advantages and disadvantages of each theory.

THEORIES WITH FOCUS ON PROCESS

The theories to be reviewed in this section are distinct from each other and are not understood typically as belonging to one category; however, these theories do share one commonalty: the propositions of these theories focus on the process of making a career decision. How people make decisions about their career choices and vocational behaviors, rather than the reasons and factors for career choices, is what these theories emphasize in understanding vocational behavior.

Tiedeman's Decision-Making Model

David Tiedeman's career decision-making model views career development as a continuous, nonlinear, multidirectional, and parallel process; and the decision evolves from integration of different factors in one's personal and common realities. Several developmental theories influenced Tiedeman's development of his own theory of career development, including Erikson's (1950) theory of human development, Ginsberg's (Ginsberg, Ginsburg, Axelrad, & Herma, 1951) vocational development, and Super's (1957) developmental stage theory approach (Jepsen, 2008; Savickas, 2008). Tiedeman described the process of career development as involving individual choice and meaning making in response to changes (Duys, Warsd, Maxwell, & Eaton-Comerford, 2008). Tiedeman's view of the career development process was complex in that it involved continuously differentiating ones' ego identity, processing developmental tasks, and resolving psychological crises. Tiedeman believed that the process of career development is also the process of trying to evaluate self or self-in-world through identification and exploring various aspects of occupations. Individuals are trying to integrate within society, or in other words, search for acceptance by members of the selected field (Zunker, 2002). One important concept of Tiedeman's career decision-making model is the constant change and instability of the job market and necessity of individual awareness, acceptance, and readiness to navigate these changes. Savickas (2008) referred to Tiedeman as the first postmodern theorist and engineer of career construction theory.

Tiedeman and O'Hara (1963) proposed that people continually redefine their career interests and commitment through decision-making phases, and that there are two phases in the decision-making process: anticipating a choice and adjusting to a choice. Within each phase, there are several specific stages.

Anticipating a Choice

This is the phase that typically occurs in one's pre-entry to the workforce and involves four phases that facilitate individuals gaining clarity of themselves and the work world, choice of a goal, and planned action to achieve the goal. The four phases are as follows:

Exploration—individuals during this stage consider possible actions, may follow their imagination in different directions, try out certain behaviors, and then have tentative goals; they reflect on aspirations, abilities, interests, and future societal implications pertaining to a career choice.

Crystallization—represents a stabilization of thought. Individuals during this stage need to continually evaluate alternatives, narrow alternatives to a few choices, and generate tentative goals and actions. The characteristic of this step is that there is a firm move toward stability of choices.

Choice—a definite goal is identified, and a course of actions is planned to accomplish the goal. The choice may not necessarily be entirely conscious or clear, yet a choice is made.

Clarification—the characteristic of this period is more certainty and less doubt about one's career decision; one develops stronger self-identity in the chosen occupation and ends the anticipatory phrase. People may also question their choices and need to repeat the previous phases.

Adjusting to a Choice

The phase of anticipation leads to the implementation of and adjustment to a choice. Once a choice is made and is implemented, the next phase, adjusting to a choice, begins. This phase is a continuous process of implementing, reevaluating, and adjusting one's choice until satisfaction is achieved. The satisfaction is based on the integration of oneself into the career chosen.

Induction—further identification of self and defense of self within the career social system. During the induction phase there is further progression of an individualized goal in relation to social context this is also the stage in which one implements his or her choice.

Reformation—being accepted into the career group and receiving acknowledgment by the other members of the group. During this step, people also become more assertive about their identity in the career group and can become an advocate.

Integration—the excitement about the new choice may diminish and become an integral part of self; satisfaction of a committed action is attained (could change as conditions change), and the career group and individual accept each other.

Application

Tiedeman's career decision-making model focused on the importance of finding meaning in the process of selecting a career. He saw the process of career choice as similar to the process of self-development because in both one is looking to being accepted and integrated into an occupational group and into society in general. The idea that development could be inverse is unique but truly reflects the reality of many people who do not have linear progression in the ever-changing job market. Interventions based on Tiedeman's model centered on creating hope, flexibility, resourcefulness, and adaptive cognitive processes so that individuals gain new perspective and adjust career decisions in response to the change (Duys et al., 2008). Considering the uncertainty and unpredictability of the work world in the 21st century, this conceptual framework is even more applicable for career counseling.

Cognitive Information Processing Approach

This is another theoretical approach focusing on the process of decision making and implementing a career choice. The Cognitive Information Processing theory (CIP) was developed by Peterson, Sampson, and Reardon (1991) and has gained recognition in recent years as an emerging career development theory. Unlike most other career development theories that are primarily descriptive of individuals' career decision-making process, CIP is a prescriptive approach and offers ideas for improving career decision making (Sharf, 2002). The aim of CIP is to help people improve problem-solving and decision-making skills and apply these skills to solve career-related problems (Sampson, Lentz, Reardon, & Peterson, 1999). There are four assumptions of CIP, and the key concepts include the "Pyramid of Information Processing Domains" and the CASVE Cycle, which is an acronym for Communication, Analysis, Synthesis, Valuing, Execution.

The four assumptions are as follows:

1. Career decision making involves both cognitive and affective processes. CIP emphasizes the importance of cognitive processing in career decision making but does not deny the role of emotions in the process.

2. The capacity to make appropriate career decisions depends on the availability of cognitive operations and knowledge. Knowledge of career decision making helps individuals recognize, find, and analyze occupational information as well as information about themselves.

3. Career development involves continual growth and change in knowledge structures. Both the work world and individuals themselves are ever changing; thus, a life span process is necessary.

4. The goal of career counseling is to enhance the client's career decision-making capacities through facilitating the growth of information-processing skills. Individuals can improve their career decision-making skills if they can develop specific decision-making skills as well as higher-level executive control processes.

The Pyramid of Information Processing: There are three components of cognitive processing. The base of the pyramid is knowledge of oneself and occupations, then the second level is decision-making domains, and finally, the top of the pyramid is executive processing domains.

The knowledge about self involves common personal traits that other career development theories also identify, such as values, interests, skills, preferences for employment, and family situations. People store this information in their memories, interpret and reconstruct them, and apply them in their current context (Peterson, Sampson, Reardon, & Lentz, 1996). The knowledge about occupations refers to information about occupational classifications, about specific industries, and about jobs. People organize this information into related concepts and make meaningful connections each time they acquire new information.

The decision-making domain is also referred to as generic information-processing skills and known as the CASVE cycle. The CASVE cycle depicts the process and skills required to make decisions. Peterson et al. (1996) believed that a problem is a gap between an existing and a desired state of affairs and that problem solving involves acquiring information and strategies to remove the gap. The outcome of the problem solving is a choice that possibly can remove the gap. Decision making then is to transform the choice into actions. The knowledge domain is to prescribe what people need to know, and the decision making or the CASVE cycle prescribes how to solve problems and make decisions. The CASVE cycle uses five skills described as follows:

- Communication (C): identify the problem through both internal and external input that signals the need for a decision. People become aware of the necessity to act on the information learned to make a decision. The example questions and statements are: "How can I help you with your concern on choosing/changing a major?" "What happens that concerns you so much now?"

- Analysis (A): examine the self-knowledge and occupational knowledge and interrelate the components of the identified problem. Reexamining the information gained from this phase leads to an idea how best to close the gap between where they are now and where they would like to be in their career. Counselors can facilitate clients' self-assessment by asking these sample questions "What do you think your strengths and weaknesses are in regard to communication?" or "What factors are prohibiting you from making a decision?"

- Synthesis (S): generating likely solutions through elaboration and crystallization. The purpose of elaboration is to expand their career options, and the aim of crystallization is to narrow their options to a manageable number of feasible choices. For example, counselors can use a statement like this: "Tell me what options you have considered so far." and "What else can you do with your strength?" or "Out of these options, what is the one that you feel most attracted to?"

- Valuing (V): prioritize alternatives through evaluating the already narrowed choices against one's value system and other contextual factors. This could mean weighing the benefits and drawbacks of several options from the synthesis phase. The purpose is to identify optimal options. A sample question can be "What are the pros and cons of each option we have generated so far?"

- Execution (E): form a plan or strategy to implement the choice. People need to identify specific steps to transform the career decision into action. This might mean small steps such as enrolling in certain courses or developing a resume, or it can also be a strategic plan such as choosing a college major or planning a series of career moves. The sampling statements could be "What is your first step after our session?" and "List three actions you will take in the next few weeks."

Once the execution phase has taken place, individuals need to return to the communication phase to evaluate whether or not they successfully have closed the gap or career problem. If the evaluation outcome turns to be favorable, they can continue the implementation of the plan. Otherwise, they need to proceed through the process of the CASVE cycle again.

The executive processing domain is at the top of the pyramid, which represents the metacognition function of the CPI approach, meaning that people examine how they think and how they act. This domain refers to the function of initiation, coordination, monitoring the storage and retrieval of information, and related metacognitive skills (Peterson et al., 1991). The specific tasks involve self-talk, self-awareness, and monitoring and control. *Self-talk* refers to the internal dialogue we have within ourselves regarding career-related issues. Positive self-talk such as "I am interested in biology, and I have good grades in academics, so I can apply to biology programs in college" is expected for solving career problem. Negative talk (e.g., "I can never do anything well.") is an issue that counselors help clients to address in counseling. *Self-awareness* is necessary because addressing the gap and problem solving requires one's understanding of his or her values, interests, and skills and being aware of one's actions and reasons for why he or she is acting in a particular way. If one has self-awareness, one can recognize one's own negative self-talk and then accordingly make an effort to change it. *Monitoring and control* are necessary for more effective problem solving, as it is necessary to monitor engagement in each phase of the CASVE process and to control the time and effort in each phase.

Application

The CPI, when applied in career development interventions, involves identification of thoughts about career decision making, particularly negative thoughts that hamper the decision-making process. An assessment tool, the Career Thoughts Inventory, was developed by Sampson, Peterson, Lenz, Reardon, and Saunders (1996) to help clients gain understanding of their thoughts during career decision making. The Career Thoughts Inventory can be used in the recommended seven step approach described below:

Step 1: Conduct initial interview—establish the relationship, clarify client career concerns, explain the pyramid of information and the CASVE process.

Step 2: Conduct preliminary assessment—determine the readiness of clients for career decision making; the Career Thoughts Inventory can be used for assistance.

Step 3: Define problems and analyze causes—collectively clarify the problem and analyze the reasons for the problem.

Step 4: Formulate goals—collectively identify and set the goals of career counseling. The goals become the basis for an individual learning plan (ILP).

Step 5: Develop individual learning plan—counselors work with clients to create a plan that lays out the activities for clients to achieve the goals.

Step 6: Implement the individual learning plan—clients complete the ILP with the support of counselors.

Step 7: Evaluation of goal attainment and summative review—help clients review the progress toward reaching the goals and using the knowledge and skills learned through the process in future applications.

The application of CIP mainly focuses on assessing readiness of individuals in making sound career decisions. Through the use of the Career Thoughts Inventory and ILP in following the CASVE process, counselors facilitate clients' knowledge and skill development in career decision making. Since the first publication of the CIP in 1991, most of the research studies on the theory were conducted by the authors; however, there has been more research in recent years done by other scholars (Brown, 2012). These studies examined the theory in various settings and with different populations and found some evidence of effectiveness in reducing negative career thoughts and usefulness with people with special needs (Niles & Harris-Bowlsbey, 2013). Sampson, Reardon, Peterson, and Lentz (2004) suggested the application of the CIP in a variety of settings and across different development stages, from helping adolescents in identifying career paths, to helping clients seek employment, and to strategic planning for staff development.

THEORIES FOCUSING ON NEEDS AND VALUES

The two theories in this section focus more on the content rather than process, in regard to factors and influences on individuals' career development. The first one, proposed by Ann Roe, emphasizes the importance of needs developed from early childhood experiences to one' career aspiration. The other one proposed by Duane Brown views values as central to one's career decision making. These two theories have different beliefs of what factors are critical for shaping career development, but both theories examine the influences to one's career decision, instead of the process of reaching the decision.

Roe's Needs Approach

Ann Roe's scholarship was mainly in the psychology of child development, but her contribution to career development is no less significant. Roe emphasized the relationship between needs and vocational selection. She also looked at the impact of early childhood experiences, particularly the parent-child interaction, on individuals' development of interests, attitudes, and capacities in future career behavior. Roe also proposed the occupational classification system that has influenced interest inventory development and applications in career counseling (Sharf, 2002).

Roe (1957) believed that intelligence and special abilities were largely hereditary and involuntary. In other words, people do not choose their parents or the environment in which they grow up. Roe based her research of personality development theory on Maslow's hierarchy of needs. She hypothesized that unsatisfied needs or partially fulfilled needs can be determinants of interests, and that individuals are more motivated to have accomplishment if the needs are more intense. Unconscious or conscious needs become motivators in career choice. Roe also hypothesized that the development of needs is influenced by early childhood experiences, parenting style, and parent-child interaction.

Parent-Child Interaction: One of the core concepts of Roe's approach is that parenting behavior and the interaction between parents and child has a significant influence on one's future career behavior. She believed that the pattern of relationships, family dynamics, and parents' attitudes toward children shaped the development of children's orientation toward people and, consequently, their career choices. Specifically, Roe (1957) listed three types of parental attitudes.

Concentration on the child—this type ranges from an overprotective to an overdemanding style. An overprotective parent fosters dependence in the child and limits the child's curiosity and exploration. An overdemanding parent sets high expectations and standards for the child in regard to skills and performance. This type of parent typically requests perfection and may be punitive to children if excellence is not achieved. Children brought up in either overprotective or overdemanding homes tend to become self-centered. Children with overprotective parents seek others' approval, develop a positive sense of self (Niles and Harris-Bowlsbey, 2013), and are likely to choose careers in which the orientation is toward others; and children with overdemanding parents are likely to develop rigid thought patterns and the attitude that only perfection is acceptable.

Avoidance of the child—Roe stated that there are two kinds of avoidance: rejection and neglect. Rejection refers to emotionally rejecting children by parents who intentionally provide no love or affection. Neglect also lacks emotional or physical attention to children but is not intentional from parents. Children growing up with avoidance style parenting are likely to develop aggressive or defensive attitudes toward people. They are more likely to choose careers involving data and things versus people.

Acceptance of the child—accepting parents neither overlook or overconcentrate on children and are neither coercive nor restrictive (Roe, 1957). Accepting parents encourage independence rather than dependence of their children. Roe said that if acceptance comes by default and provides minimum love it is casual acceptance. The other kind is loving acceptance, which means parents show warmer attitudes and do not interfere with children's own resources. Children brought up in homes with acceptance are more interested in people rather than data or things in occupational choices.

Occupational Classification System

Roe (1956), in her early book, *The Psychology of Occupations*, developed a detailed system to classify occupations to characterize the variety of occupations that share similarities. The system has eight groups and six levels. The six levels indicate the complexity and responsibility of each occupation. For instance, in the same service group, the lowest level includes occupations such as maids and watchmen, and the highest level involves the jobs such as social worker supervisor and personal therapists.

The eight occupational groups in Roe's system are service (generally people-oriented occupations), business contact (involving interpersonal interactions in a business environment), organization (involving management and administration), technology (making, producing, and maintaining products), outdoors (application of science in outdoor environment), science (creation and discovery of knowledge, development and application of science in various areas), general culture (involving human activity and culture), and arts and entertainment (create or perform art). The six levels are classified based on the degree of difficulty and complexity of decision making as well as responsibility. The higher level involves more independent responsibility, and the lower level typically has less responsibility and usually involves following directions. The six levels are (from high to low): professional and managerial 1, professional and managerial 2, semiprofessional and small business, skilled, semiskilled, and unskilled. The difference between professional and managerial 1 and 2 is level 2 encompasses less independence or less important responsibility, for instance social workers versus social worker supervisors.

Application

The occupational classification system created by Roe (1956) contributed significantly to organizing the variety of occupations in an easy comprehensible way for researchers, practitioners, and individuals. The associated education and skill requirements for each type of occupations provide useful information for those who make career plans and decisions. This occupational classifications system is widely used in career research and assessment. Roe was the first to examine the impact of parent-child interaction on career development and explain how needs influence career development.

The criticism about Roe's theory is that all of her research was retrospective, based on individuals' recollections, and that it lacked validity (Sharf, 2002, Niles & Harris-Bowlsbey, 2013). Although some research (e.g., Roe & Lunneborg, 1990) supported the influence of early childhood experiences on future occupational choice, it only applied within occupations rather than across occupations. The research in general about her theory did not support it (Osipow & Fitzgerald, 1996). However, Brown and Voyle (1997) suggested that lack of research support for Roe's theory might be due to insufficient research methodologies. Roe's theory was not developed for career intervention, yet it inspired research and influenced the development of interest inventories (Sharf, 2002).

Brown's Value-Based Holistic Model of Career and Life-Role Choices

The unique feature of Brown's value-based holistic model of career and life-role choices is its emphasis on the role of values in career choice. As the name of the theory indicates, Brown's theory aimed at providing a comprehensive approach to explaining the variety of life roles. However, its complexity and its many propositions made it difficult to use. The theory does not therefore meet the test stated in the beginning of Chapter 4 to provide a schema for understanding career development and provide a guideline for helping clients with career and career-related issues. The author also noticed this problem and modified the theory in 2002 to focus on the role of values in career choice, satisfaction, and success.

"Values are beliefs that are experienced by the individual as standards regarding how he or she should function" and "Work values are the values that individuals believe should be satisfied as a result of their participation in the work roles" (p. 37, Brown, 2012). According to Brown (2012), work values, along with cultural values, play a central role in the career decision-making process, career choice, and satisfaction with, as well as success in, the chosen occupations. In other words, values are an important factor in the process of decision making, the actual decision made (career choice), and the outcome of the decision (success in the work chosen and satisfaction with the choice).

People develop their value systems through a process Brown refers to as *enculturation*. Enculturation is the process by which individuals incorporate the beliefs/values of their cultural group and form a value system (Brown, 2012). During this process, people clarify and crystalize the values that can be applied to their own behavior and that can meet their needs in socially acceptable ways. Thus, enculturation is influenced by social and cultural factors (e.g., gender, ethnic group, family, socioeconomic status), and the behavioral aspect of values is shaped by the cultural context in which they develop.

People may not fully implement their values in their selected careers if they suffer from mental health problems, are discriminated against because of being in a nonmainstream cultural group, have limited access to information, struggle with poverty, or lack self-efficacy in career-related tasks. Brown's updated valued-based approach has incorporated these factors in the propositions.

Propositions of Brown's Value-Based Theory

1. Highly prioritized work values are the most important determinants of career choices if (a) individuals perceive that they are unconstrained to act on their values; (b) at least one option available will satisfy the values held by the individual; (c) the individual has values-based information about his or her options and accurate information about values; (d) the difficulty level of implementing the options is approximately the same; and (e) the financial resources available to the individual are sufficient to support the implementation of values-based options.

2. Individuals who hold collective social values defer to or are significantly influenced by the expectations of the group or family members. As a result, their career choice is less related to their individual choices than is the case of people who hold individualistic values. The impact of their value systems also influences people's decision-making strategies, processes, and results.

3. For individuals who make their own career decisions, the process of choosing a career involves a series of "estimates"—one's values, the skills and abilities required to be successful in an occupation, and the work values that would be met within the occupational alternatives being considered. Individuals who hold collective values will (a) underestimate their ability if humility is one of their cultural values or (b) simply be less able to make these estimates because there is less emphasis in their group on providing feedback about individual strengths and weakness.

4. Individuals who highly prioritize collective relationships and value cooperative achievement will experience greater stress in roles characterized by conflict and will be less satisfied in those roles than people who value individualism and competitive achievement.

5. Success in the work role depends upon a combination of factors including scholastic aptitude, special aptitudes, the quality and number of educational opportunities available, family socioeconomic status, participation in the work role, having a past-future or future time orientation, and the barriers in the workplace resulting from discrimination.

6. Occupational tenure is partially the result of the match between the cultural and work values of the worker, supervisor, and colleagues.

(adapted from Brown, 2012)

LEARNING ACTIVITY 5.1
VALUE CLARIFICATION

Have the entire class do a brainstorming exercise to generate a long list of what they think is important for them regarding work. To facilitate the exercise, the instructor can ask the class to review their previous work experiences and identify what elements in those work experiences made them feel contented, happy, and energized. Have two volunteers record the list on the blackboard (whiteboard or flip chart). Once no more new items are identified by the class, ask each member to sort the items on the list into four categories: absolutely important (valued), very important (prefer to have it), important (but can compromise), and not so important (does not matter if not having it). Then divide the class into several small groups, and discus their rationale for making their lists. All members have a chance to review their list after discussion and make changes if they want. Finally, ask a few volunteers to share and discuss their lists in the big group.

Application

Helping clients identify values could be accomplished through quantitative approaches such as inventories, for example, "Value Scales" (Rokeach, 1973) and "The Life Values Inventory" (Crace & Brown, 2004). The other approaches to help clients clarify and crystalize their values include projective approaches, interactive activities such as asking clients to describe daydreams, the use of discretionary time and money, peak experiences, completing unfinished sentences, and the use of imagery. These activities can also be used for prioritization of values. Additional strategies to help clients prioritize their values suggested by Brown (1995) included asking clients to choose between two conflicting situations such as "becoming rich" versus "being accepted by others"; ranking the values identified as important to clients; and creating stimuli for clients to respond without much time (to avoid social desirability). Brown also suggested that one needs to determine role relationships and resolve any role conflicts to prepare for planned and unplanned transitions. The value-based approach is relatively a new theory and has not generated many empirical studies yet.

THEORIES FROM A HOLISTIC VIEW

The two theories to be discussed in this section provide alternative perspectives of conceptualizing one's career development. Both theories disagree with most traditional career development theories for their separation of life roles and work roles. Both theories believe that career cannot be separated from other aspects of life and every aspect of life should be integrated into a whole self.

Hansen's Integrative Life Planning

The Integrative Life Planning theory (ILP) by Sunny Hansen emphasizes the multidimensionality of career development and the role of career counselors as change agents in helping people address the wholeness of development. It is a holistic approach that focuses on integrating various life roles and work in career planning. It views work in relation to other life roles, thus, work is part of life. It criticized a fragmented view of work and life. Hansen (2001) believed that changes in the workplace and work itself call for an integrative approach to career development. One significant feature of ILP is its integrated view of body, mind, and spirit in lives and diversity in a person's life roles, culture, community, ways of thinking, and behavior. It draws upon the meaning work brings to individuals' lives based on their culture. Hansen frequently uses a quilt metaphor to describe the process of career development. Counselors help their clients fit pieces together to create a meaningful whole.

ILP suggests that career counselors need to be aware of the following: (1) dramatic changes that require people to broaden the thought and practice about how we work with employees, students, and clients; (2) helping clients develop skills in integrative thinking rather than linear or reductionist thinking; (3) understanding their own culture and prioritizing the critical life tasks; (4) the contexts and themes of a changing society; and (5) recognition that need and commitment to change are essential to the ILP process.

The ILP approach to career counseling views planning as an inclusion of all of the various parts of a client's life. It identifies six critical life tasks (Hansen, 2011; Hansen and Suddarth, 2008), all of which are part of what was, in Hansen's original formulation, one of the tasks—weaving our lives into a meaningful whole:

1. Finding work that "needs doing" in a changing global context

2. Attending to our health

3. Connecting family and work, emphasizing life-role integration and importance of negotiating roles and relationships

4. Valuing inclusivity and pluralism

5. Exploring spiritual and life purpose, the important part in self-actualization

6. Managing transitions and organizational change; this ability is important to cope effectively with transitions in the uncertainty

Application

ILP emphasizes community, democracy, and a global worldview. It was frequently used in higher education with juniors and seniors (Hansen, 2011). Hansen suggests that counselors work with students on how to create a meaningful, fulfilling life using critical life tasks while improving society, and that personal change will lead to societal change. Counselors can ask their clients to identify the life tasks most important to them and take the time to work on them. Hansen suggests service learning as a possible means to explore societal concern and as a skill-development tool (Hansen, 2001). Though ILP was developed in the United States, it has been applied in many other countries (Hansen, 2011).

CASE ILLUSTRATION 5.1

Maria Wright has been trying to, as she puts it, find her place in the world. She graduated from a two-year program at the local community college that prepares students to be medical transcriptionists. But with new technologies, the demand for these positions has dropped off, and she never really liked it much anyway. She tells the counselor that she always thought she would do something to make a difference in the world, but she doesn't know what that is. Her counselor has studied ILP and the importance of spirituality in career development and thinks that Maria would benefit from using that approach. She first explains that she thinks that Maria should think about her decision making as being life planning rather than simply career planning. She then goes over the six parts of ILP with Maria, emphasizing finding work that needs doing and exploring spirituality and life purpose. Maria agrees that both of those principles make sense, but she still doesn't know what she wants to do! The counselor begins to use some more traditional techniques with Maria, giving her an interest inventory and helping her look at her values and preferences with a card sort. She also encourages Maria to think about the meaning behind the word *vocation*, which comes from the root *to call*. She asks Maria to think about what calls to her, what she is doing when she feels "in the zone," when she feels really alive. She suggests that Maria keep a journal for the week before their next meeting and record these kinds of times. They will then look for themes and begin the process of coming up with some possible occupations for Maria to investigate.

Discussion Questions

1. Why do you think Maria's counselor chose ILP? Do you agree or disagree that using ILP is a good idea?

2. What tasks from ILP do you think are the most for Maria to resolve?

3. What other theoretical approach would you choose if you were Maria's counselor? Please state why you believe this approach would work effectively with Maria.

This theory was developed in response to societal and economic changes in global settings. It is one of the few theoretical models that includes spirituality in considering individual career development. It also values social action and advocacy on the part of both counselors and clients. More research is needed to examine the effectiveness of applying this model to career intervention practice.

Lifecareer Theory

This theory was developed from the developmental and process perspective but is unique in its viewing of career and life as the same entity rather than two separate parts. Miller-Tiedeman and Tiedeman (1990) stated "life is a career." The lifecareer theory (Miller-Tiedeman, 1988, 1997) asserted that individuals do not need a counselor to use other people's theories to help their career issues, instead, they should tell their own stories and become their own career development theorists. Miller-Tiedeman criticized most traditional theories as failing to understand the role of individualized experiences each person has to his or her career development, and fail to empower clients to live their own experiences. Thus, lifecareer theory encourages each person to become his or her

LEARNING ACTIVITY 5.2
LIFE ROLES DISTRIBUTION

One a blank paper, draw a circle first, then slice the circle into pieces as one would slice a pizza. The number of slices is based on the life roles you see yourself playing currently. Name each piece for a role you play. Slice the pieces proportionally according to how you see the importance of each role. Then draw another circle, and slice the circle again, but this time, slice the number and proportion based on the ideal life roles you want to play. Then compare the two circles and see if they are identical or different. Discuss what it is consistent between the two circles or what and why the two circles are different.

own career theorists, or in other words, become conscious of his or her experiences and capitalize on those experiences.

This theory is very different from other career development theories in regard to conceptualizing career development. It views life as career, stating that one does not need to look for a career because there is already one that just needs to be lived. By trusting the inner wisdom that comes from one's intellectual ability, previous experiences, and intuition, you can experience your career. Individuals are able to process information and make decisions in a process that flows. The theory suggests people should not work against flow; rather, they should let the process evolve itself. Admittedly, this theory is quite philosophical, thus, it can be criticized for impracticality or be acclaimed for unlimited possibilities as Miller-Tiedeman (2008) argued.

Spiritual Perspective

The role of spirituality to human functioning has been researched with increasing attention in recent years (Duffy, 2006). The two theories reviewed earlier (i.e., Hansen's ILP and Miller-Tiedeman's Lifecareer) addressed the spiritual aspect to one's life and importance of spirituality to wholeness of oneself. Bloch and Richmond (1997) explored the meaning of work through examining the connection between spirituality and work and stated that wholeness can be achieved through infusing work with values and spirit. Bloch and Richmond (1998) proposed seven connectors between work and spirituality, described as follows:

Change—inevitable; internal or external

Balance—balance between work and relationship, play

Energy—when individuals love their work, the work generates energy

Community—work is a means of interacting with one's community

Calling—calling is about hearing your own song and singing it out loud and clear

Harmony—finding a true sense of appreciation and understanding

Unity—a sense of flow or being totally involved in one's work, to be a part of the work not apart from it

MULTICULTURAL BOX 5.1

Cascade is a 45-year-old Caucasian woman who has worked in retail for seven years and is currently graduating from a doctoral program in a social science field. She has been a research assistant during her graduate study and earned a good evaluation by her supervisor. She enjoys doing research, assisting teaching, and being actively involved in professional organizations. Cascade has been married to Joe for 20 years, and their two children are in high school and middle school respectively. Cascade was a stay-at-home mom for about 10 years while the kids were little. She has a bachelor's degree in psychology, but she did not pursue any career with her degree. She started a part-time retail job when her children were in grade school. By the time her two children were in middle school, she began to get more involved in church. She was encouraged by one of the members in the church to attend graduate school and then find a full-time job. She thought this was a good idea but wasn't sure if her husband would support the idea. Joe is actually very supportive, since he thinks it would be good for Cascade when their two children go to college in a few years. Joe works as a financial consultant and is always very busy. Cascade wants to be a faculty member after graduation, but she can not relocate due to Joe's job and her younger child who is still in high school. But there are not many faculty positions available in the area if she does not relocate. Both Cascade and Joe need to work to support the family expenses, including college tuition for two children. If not working as a faculty member, Cascade can work as a research associate for some organizations or work as a freelance consultant on research projects, but she would miss a lot of things she enjoys at a university setting, and there is no stability or security either. What is Cascade's dilemma? What career development theory or theories would be helpful to help Cascade resolve her issues?

Tips for Consideration: What if Joe is the one who graduated from a doctoral degree? What kind of social messages have Joe and Cascade internalized? Which theories address the issues presented in Cascade's situation with a more culturally appropriate perspective?

These connectors enable people to develop a sense of connectedness, an important part of wholeness. Seeing career as spiritual keeps individuals from being self-centered and helps them find ways to contribute to the world (Bloch, 2005). Niles and Harris-Bowlsbey (2013) summarized that spiritual approaches in general emphasized the following themes:

- Career development intertwines with human development. Life cannot be compartmentalized into "silos" of activity; thus, careers should be viewed holistically.

- Clients should be encouraged to embrace and celebrate their life journeys, rather than judging past experiences negatively. All life experiences provide opportunities for learning and growth.

- Maintaining an attitude of flexibility and openness fosters development as well as the opportunity to identify new opportunities for growth and learning.

- Change should be celebrated and embraced rather than feared and avoided.

- Career development interventions that actively and collaboratively engage the client in career counseling; incorporate intuition as well as reason in decision making; and draw upon subjective assessment activities, imagery, meditation, and positive self-affirmations also engage the spirit in the career development process.

In summary, the spiritual perspective of career development recognizes that change is necessary and should be welcomed rather than feared; career development is an integral part of one's entire identity; and one should be open and flexible minded to learn and grow when provided with opportunities. Spirituality is one part of the whole self and, therefore, should be incorporated into the career development process and exploration. A holistic approach is necessary because work, life, and spirituality are all interconnected.

THEORIES OF CONSTRUCTION PERSPECTIVE

The changes in economy, technology, and workforce significantly shifted the traditional pathways of career development for most people. Making one career choice and maintaining the chosen occupation for a lifetime is almost nonexistent in the 21st century. With all these changes, many scholars challenged the practicability of conventional career development theories to helping people in the everchanging world of work. One common theme of the postmodern theories is that they all are influenced by constructivism, recognizing the contextual influence and individual changing agency. The theories derived from constructivism shared some basic assumptions such as lifelong career development, interconnected of self and others in a dynamic interaction, and active agency (Mahoney, 2003). The following three theories are examples of recently emerging theories with the construction perspective.

Career Construction Theory

Career construction theory aims at integrating various theoretical concepts in career development to a convergent or metatheoretical approach that addresses the evolution of career development theories and impact of unprecedented changing work world on the person. The theory was developed by Mark Savickas in the process of updating Super's developmental approach (Andersen & Vandehey, 2012), and the theory has been evolving during the last two decades. In addition to the trait and factor, developmental, and social cognitive learning perspectives, career construction theory represents a new focus of career development theory—constructivism or meaning making in the process of career development. As Savickas (2005) said, "viewing career from constructionist and contextual perspectives focuses attention on interpretive processes, social interaction and the negotiation of meaning" (p. 43).

According to Savickas (2013), career construction theory addresses how individuals build careers through personal construction and social construction, how people grow by adapting to an environment, and how career development contemplates self-construction. There are three fundamental perspectives that outline career construction theory: self as actor, self as agent, and self as author. Savickas adapted the tripartite mode of personality theory of McAdams (1995) and explained how three layers of self (as object, as subject, and as project) can be applied in vocational behavior and career construction. Self as object fits with the objective view of person-environment fit tradition of vocational guidance. This aspect focuses on the fitness between individual personalities and associated occupations. Self as subject indicates the major propositions of humanistic and developmental approaches that emphasize self-discovery and self-actualization. This aspect supplements the objective view of self and focuses on a subjective view of self and self-determination within hierarchical structures of organizations and societies. Self as project emerged as a new perspective in response to the changing economy, the digital revolution, the information society, and the global economy. Savickas suggested that workers must be flexible in maintaining employability through lifelong learning and adapting to occupational transitions and must prepare themselves for possibilities. Because of the changing and unpredictable situation of the work world of the 21st century, career construction theory proposes that there needs to be a transformation of the conception of career from seeing it as a linear and stable path to constructing a subjective career that fits the meaning of work and life. Accordingly, career construction theory asserts that,

> individuals, through their actions in the family, compose a social role as an actor, then adapt this role for use in the theaters of the school and community, and eventually author an autobiographical story that explains the continuity and coherence in occupational experiences. (Savickas, 2013, p. 151)

These concepts—self as actor, as agent, and as author—reflect the progression of one's self-making or self-construction in both career and life. During early childhood, people internalize their role models and social interactions to guide their behaviors and actions. Through imitation and repeated role playing, individuals form temporal stability of traits or personalities. These traits are usually understood as personalities, and career construct theory views personality as located in the person but *reputation* as located in the person's social network. In other words, "reputation is specific to the unique network of people with whom individuals interact. Reputation, or trait ascription, will eventually be located in the network of coworkers in their occupations" (Savickas, 2013, p. 153). Therefore, reputation could be used for evaluating the potential of individuals to join certain occupational groups. Career construction theory also posits that using personality types such as those in Holland's RIASEC taxonomy is a useful and efficient classification system for professionals to use to communicate with each other. However, instead of viewing these types as contents only, career construction theory claims that these are also self-construction strategies internalized from interpersonal experiences and cultural discourse.

Self as agent indicates the self-regulating agency that people need to pursue goals of their choice. Starting in middle childhood, individuals extend their self-construct beyond family settings, to school and community settings. This agency is necessary for individuals to adapt to the external environment and changes so that they can accomplish their goals. According to Savickas (2013), there are three challenges or vocational tasks that need individuals' adaptation: vocational developmental tasks (age-related, social norm expectations), occupational transitions (willingly or unwillingly transition from one job to another), and work trauma (unwanted or unplanned job loss or interruption). With the current lack of certainty in occupations, individuals must adapt and be ready for everchanging work environments. Career construction theory suggests adaption is the outcome of adaptivity, adaptability, and adapting in sequential order. "Adaptivity denotes the personal characteristic of flexibility or willingness to meet career tasks, transitions, and traumas with fitting responses. Adaptability denotes an individual's psychosocial resources for coping with current and anticipated vocational tasks, occupational transitions, and work traumas" (Savickas, 2013, p. 157). Adapting is using coping behaviors to address changing conditions.

Self as author connotes identity narratives that individuals develop as they make meaning out of their career stories and their interactions with society. People are expected by society to integrate their actions and agency into a theme that runs through life. This career theme unifies the occupational plot and helps people remain congruent with self even though the conditions might vary; the theme also helps the narrative continue with "a purposive attitude towards life" (Savakis, 2013, p. 165). "The identity narrative expresses uniqueness of an individual in her or his particular context by articulating goals, directing adaptive behavior, and imposed meaning of activities. The individual uses this self-sustaining narrative to evaluate career opportunities and negotiate social constraints" (Savakis, 2013, p. 163).

Career Intervention Strategies

Based on the three layers of self-construct, there are three major career intervention services for individuals depending on their needs. They are vocational guidance to help individuals identify career fit, career education or coaching to help people learn coping strategies to adapt to transitions and cultivate preparedness, and career counseling for individuals to develop a vocational identity and design a life (Savickas, 2012). Vocational guidance and career education have been practiced since the evolution of career development and follow the career development theories reviewed in Chapter 4. Career construction theory proposed a new model of career intervention—that is, life design—specifically to help clients construct and deconstruct career stories, reconstruct a career theme, and coconstruct the next chapter of the story. Savickas (2013) suggested that practitioners follow these steps in career construction counseling: ask clients to describe the incident that makes them feel disconnected from their career theme and assess the adaptive readiness, resources, and goals they want to coconstruct with counselors. The Career Construction Interview (CCI) (originally developed by Savickas, 1989) is a tool that counselors can use to facilitate clients telling stories that reveal how they have constructed self, identity, and career. Some sample questions from the CCI are, "Who do you admire?" "Who would you like to pattern your life after?" "What do you like to do in your free time?" The details of using this interview can be found in Chapter 7. The last step is action. Counselors and clients together create an action plan to transform the undesired situation to an intended one and act on the plan. A recent development based on career construction theory is a career counseling model—Life Design (Savickas, 2015), which emphasizes the role of agency and active role of individuals in developing their own career trajectory.

This theory represents a new trend in career development and intervention in the 21st century. It was built on existing career development theories and incorporated other personality, social psychology, and human development theories. Career construction theory introduced a paradigm shift to career intervention, namely, instead of prescribing a road map for individuals, coconstructing a guide for individuals to walk the path unfolding. It emphasizes the active role individuals can play in building a career for themselves.

CASE ILLUSTRATION 5.2

Leonard Burgess comes to a career counselor because he is anticipating losing his job when his company relocates to a distant state. He is 45, a mid-level executive, and has been offered a job in the new location, but his wife has a good job where they are, his children are in middle and high school, and he does not want to move. Leonard's counselor has recently attended several workshops about career construction theory, and it made sense to him, particularly for this client. Before beginning any further exploration, the counselor asks Leonard to state his situation as a problem or a question. After some thought, Leonard replies, "Should I keep doing the same thing as I have been doing but in a different place, or Shall I use my severance money to change fields?"

The counselor asks Leonard to talk for a while about his life up to this point, focusing on what has made him happiest and where he has struggled. When Leonard gets stuck, the counselor encourages him to think about early experiences and favorite magazines, TV shows, or books.

As Leonard talks, the counselor reflects what he is hearing and asks Leonard to summarize what he has heard the counselor saying. For example, when Leonard describes an early childhood memory of playing catch with his father, the counselor asks him to caption the experience as if it were a drawing. Leonard replies, "Boy happy to be pleasing dad." When discussing his favorite magazine, Leonard says he reads *Sports Illustrated*, even though he is not that interested,

because it gives him a topic of conversation with his father who is a "sports nut."

As Leonard talks about his job, the one he will be losing soon, it appears that he struggled to please his boss, an authoritarian type of supervisor, and that he is actually a bit relieved to have an excuse to leave the position. Leonard says he has no idea what he is interested in. He majored in business in college because his parents, his dad really, told him that was best, and he has worked for his present employer since graduating. He has few recollections of self-directed enjoyable activities, but the ones he does have center around abstract problem solving—brain teasers in the newspaper and figuring out how to fix things around the house. He confesses that he even enjoys doing his taxes as he likes figuring out how to make the most of his deductions. The counselor encourages Leonard to think about how he would construct his life if it were up to him.

Discussion Questions

1. What are the unspoken issues for Leonard? How would you conceptualize his issues described in the case?

2. If different approaches were used for Leonard than the approach illustrated in the case, what would be the most likely outcome? Why so? What difference will there be for Leonard in the long run?

Chaos Theory of Careers

Chaos theory was applied by Pryor and Bright (2003, 2011) to career development to address the complexities of factors influencing one's career development. The Chaos Theory of Career (CTC) emphasizes nonlinear, interactive, and dynamic systems affecting individuals and the role of chance to a person's career development (Bright, Pryor & Harpham, 2005). Pryor and Bright introduced four constructs to explain the cornerstones of their theory: complexity, change, chance, and construction.

- **Complexity:** Numerous influences in career development are interconnected. Parents, social media, sexual orientation, politics, gender, health, and cultural tradition all constitute contextual factors that sometimes behave unpredictably.

- **Change:** These contextual systems are quite sensitive to change and may cause clients to veer from their desired path of career development. The authors state that traditional theories ignore the influence of change on career decision making.

- **Chance:** The authors argue that change is the norm. Individuals cannot predict or control events within the systems noted above.

- **Construction:** Due to the lack of control individuals have over the complex, interconnected systems, they must be proactive in directing their lives.

The new concepts proposed by Pryor and Bright include attractors, fractals, nonlinearity, emergence, and phase shifts. *Attractor* refers to systems functioning in a certain way that could affect career development. There are four types of attractors: *point attractor*—the system is destined to move toward a clearly defined point (e.g., water flows from high point to low point); *pendulum attractor*—the system operates between two defined points (e.g., making a career decision between being a teacher and being an artist); *torus attractors*—a system moves in repetitive fashion over time (e.g., habitual, routine pattern of working); and *strange attractors*—a system operating in steady, self-repeating, familiar pattern with possibility for radical nonlinear change, like "edge of chaos," meaning "constant flux between the stability of closed systems and complete breakdown of the systems into chaos" (Bright & Pryor, 2011, pp. 164). According to Pryor and Bright, *fractals* indicate the trajectory of strange attractor's functioning, that is, people's behavior has dynamically stable patterns but is subject to unpredictable change. *Nonlinearity* means that small changes in one system can result in overwhelmingly large changes in another system. For instance, a typo in a statistical report by one decimal point seems small but could lead to totally different findings. *Emergence* is finding patterns from complex and dynamic systems at different times and contexts. *Phase shift* refers to the change due to unplanned events.

Application

The purpose of CTC-driven intervention is to identify clients' fractal patterns or to identify familiar patterns to oneself and the readiness one has to respond to unpredictable events. The *Luck Readiness Test, Complexity Perception Text*, and *Creative Thinking Strategies Card Sort* were all created by the authors to use in CTC counseling. The authors suggest using as many approaches as possible to identify the client's fractal pattern. Narrative personal account and metaphors may also be used to identify patterns. Another goal of intervention is to help clients be open to exploration and feel comfortable with uncertainty. Pryor and Bright (2014) stated that research supported the effectiveness of CTC in reducing stress and increasing self-efficacy in career decision making as compared to traditional approaches and that students were more satisfied with the outcome and higher sustainability as they had the opportunities to reflect on the complexities and unplanned events on their career trajectories.

LEARNING ACTIVITY 5.3
TRANSFERABLE SKILLS IDENTIFICATION

During the last semester of your graduate program for counselor education, many students become worried about their job prospects. This exercise can help students identify what skills they have developed during counselor education program that can be useful in other work settings if not being a counselor.

Step 1: List the competencies and skills to work as a counselor.

Step 2: Identify the occupations that require the identified competencies and skills.

Step 3: Select the ones that are most appealing and go to the Occupational Outlook (http://www.bls.gov/ooh), and discuss how they can explore other occupations in which they can use their skills.

Systems Theory

The System Theory Framework (SFT; Patton & McMahon, 1999, 2006) is a metatheory that incorporates many concepts from earlier career theories and provides an integrated framework for career development and intervention. It holds that career development is influenced by three systems: individual system, social system, and environmental-societal system. The *individual system* is more than personal characteristics; it is a whole, including gender, values, health, sexual orientation, disability, ability, interests, beliefs, skills, personality, world-of-work knowledge, age, self-concept, physical attributes, ethnicity, and aptitudes. The *social system* refers to the proximal social system composed of family, peers, community groups, education institutions, media, and, workplace. The *environmental-societal* system is the distal social context to individual system, including political climate, historical trends, employment market, geographic location, socioeconomic status, and globalization (Patton, 2008).

In addition to incorporating the system theory of Bronfenbrenner (1979) as seen in the previous descriptions of a variety of systems, Patton and McMahon based their theory on constructivism as a guiding philosophy. It emphasizes the centrality of individuals in career exploration and decision, that is, individuals construct the meaning of their life. The STF also focuses on process that is characterized by recursiveness, change over time and chance. Recursiveness, which connotes nonlinearity, multidirectionality, and mutuality across different times, interacts with other systems. The STF values storytelling as an effective approach to recount the pattern and relationships within the systems, and therefore, to empower individuals to construct their career path.

Application

As the core part of STF is personal agency and an ongoing process of exploration, the practice of STF emphasizes meaning making and storytelling. Therefore, the assessment and career counseling processes are more integral parts rather than sequential steps.

A qualitative career assessment was developed by the McMahon, Watson, and Patton (2005), "My System of Career Influences," to consider contextual influences on one's career choice. It was created for use with adolescents and adults. Individuals construct a diagram that includes all of the systems that influence them. This helps them understand how all the pieces of their lives are connected and helps them identify life themes for use in future stories.

Summary: Challenges and Opportunities

The theories reviewed in this chapter exemplified the trend of evolution of career development theories toward holistic, integrated, and systematic theorizing of people's vocational behavior. Compared to the theories in Chapter 4, the career development theories in this chapter shift the focus from helping people find a fit career to helping people fit to a career. The theories about the process of making career decisions explains how people reach a decision on career choices, transitions, and response to work-related demands. The needs, values, spirituality, and contextual influences are recognized for their significance in shaping one's career development. The most recent development is the increasing attention to the constructive perspective of vocational behavior and intervention. The recognition of self-agency, meaning-making, interaction of multilevel systems, nonlinear process of development, and fluctuation in dynamic environment in these recent theories provide a new outlook of career development in the unpredictable work environment as unfolding in the 21st century. Despite the broadened career theories and effort of convergence of theories, challenges still exist. There are still too many theories for any professional to keep abreast of realistically (not all the theories proposed in the history and literature can be presented in this book, for example, theories that focus on relational aspects such as Relational Theory of Working by Blustein [2011] and Richardson's work on relationship practice [2000]), yet there is no theory that is found to be applicable and valid to every aspect of career development or every person in the diverse world. More research is needed to consolidate the constructs of various theories and to translate the theoretical concepts to practice ideas.

Keystones

- Tiedeman's career decision-making model posits that career development parallels to ego development and that people continually redefine their career commitment through decision-making process involving exploration, crystallization, choice, clarification, and adjusting to a choice.

- The Cognitive Information Process approach focuses on the cognitive process of making a career decision in a cycle of gathering, analyzing and communicating information, executing, and evaluating the action.

- Roe's approach is the only model that articulates the impact of the parent-child

- relationship and needs to career choice, and it introduces the occupational classification system.

- Brown's Value-Based theory views values influenced by individuals' cultural backgrounds playing a central role in shaping one's career choice; consistency of individual values and work environment.

- The theories addressing the spiritual aspect of career development emphasize the importance of interconnection of spirituality and work to reach wholeness of oneself.

- Savickas's Career Construction Theory proposes that people are actors of their own career development and adaptability is crucial for mastery of interaction with variable world.

- Chaos Theory of Career emphasizes the necessity of openness to experiences and importance of identifying patterns amidst an irregular work world.

- The Systems theory, a metatheory, provides a combined theoretical framework to account for career development.

Additional Resources

Gunz, H., & Peiperl, M. (Eds.) (2007). *Handbook of career studies*. Thousand Oaks, CA: Sage.

Savickas, M. L. (1993). Career counseling in the postmodern era. *Journal of Cognitive Psychotherapy: An International Quarterly, 7*, 205–215.

Savickas, M. L. (1995). Current theoretical issues in vocational psychology: Convergence, divergence, and schism. In W. B. Walsh & S. H. Osipow (Eds.), *Handbook of vocational psychology* (pp. 1–34). Mahwah, NJ: Erlbaum.

Savickas, M. L. (2000). Renovating the psychology of careers for the twenty-first century. In A. Collin & R. A. Young (Eds.), *The future of career* (pp. 53–68). Cambridge, UK: Cambridge University Press.

Savickas, M. L. (2001). Towards a comprehensive theory of career development: Dispositions, concerns and narratives. In F. T. L. Leong & A. Barak (Eds.), *Contemporary models in vocational psychology* (pp. 295–319). Mahwah, NJ: Erlbaum.

References

Andersen, P., & Vandehey, M. (2012). *Career counseling and development in global economy* (2nd ed.). Belmont, CA: Brooks/Cole Cenage Learning.

Bloch, D. P. (1997). Spirituality, intentionality and career success: The quest for meaning. In D. P. Bloch, & L. J. Richmond (Eds.), *Connections between spirit and work in career development*. Palo Alto, CA: Davies-Black.

Bloch, D. P. (2005). Complexity, chaos, and nonlinear dynamics: A new perspective on career development theory. *The Career Development Quarterly, 53*(3), 194-207.

Bloch, D. P., & Richmond, L. J. (1998). *Soul work: Finding the work you love, loving the work you have.* Palo Alto, CA: Avies-Black.

Blustein, D. L. (2011). A relational theory of working. *Journal of Vocational Behavior, 79,* 1-17. doi:10.1016/jvb.2010.10.004

Bright, J. E. H., Pryor, R. G. L., & Harpham, L. (2005). The role of chance events in career decision making. *Journal of Vocational Behavior, 66,* 561–576.

Bright, J., & Pryor, R. (2011). The chaos theory of careers. *Journal of Employment Counseling, 48*(4), 163-166.

Bronfenbrenner, U. (1979). *The ecology of human development.* Cambridge, MA: Harvard University Press.

Brown, D. (1995). A values-based approach to facilitating career transitions. *The Career Development Quarterly, 44*(1), 4.

Brown, D. (2012). *Career information, career counseling, and career development* (10th ed.). Boston, MA: Pearson.

Brown, M., Lum, J., & Voyle, K. (1997). Roe revisited: A call for the reappraisal of the theory of personality development and career choice. *Journal of Vocational Behavior, 51*(2), 283-294.

Crace, R. K., & Brown, D. (2004). *Life values inventory.* Williamsburg, VA: Applied Psychology Resources.

Duffy, R. D. (2006). Spirituality, religion, and career development: Current status and future directions. *The Career Development Quarterly, 55,* 52-63.

Duys, D. K., Ward, J. E., Maxwell, J. A., & Eaton-Comerford, L. (2008). Career counseling in a volatile job market: Tiedeman's perspective revisited. *The Career Development Quarterly, 56*(3), 232-241.

Erikson, E. H. (1950). *Childhood and society.* New York, NY: Norton.

Ginsberg, E., Ginsburg, S. W., Axelrad, S., & Herma, J. L. (1951). *Occupational choice: An approach to a general theory.* New York, NY: Columbia University Press.

Hansen, L. (2001). Integrating work, family, and community through holistic life planning. *The Career Development Quarterly, 49*(3), 261-274.

Hansen, L. S., & Suddarth, B. (2008). Integrative life planning. *Career Developments, 24*(4), 5-9.

Hansen, S. (2011). Integrative life planning: A holistic approach. *Journal of Employment Counseling, 48*(4), 167-169.

Jepsen, D. A. (2008). A tribute to David Tiedeman. *The Career Development Quarterly, 56*(3), 225-231.

Mahoney, M. J. (2003). *Constructive psychotherapy.* New York, NY: Guildford.

McAdams, D. P. (1995). What do we know when we know a person? *Journal of Personality, 63,* 365-396.

McMahon, M., Watson, M., & Patton, W. (2005). Qualitative career assessment: Developing the my system of career influences reflection activity. *Journal of Career Assessment, 13,* 476-490. doi:10.1177/106 9072705277930

Miller-Tiedeman, A. L. (1988). Lifecareer Process Theory: A healthy choice. In D. P. Bloch, & L. J. Richarch (Eds.), *Connecting between spirit and work in career development* (pp. 87-114). Palo Alto, CA: Davies-Black.

Miller-Tiedeman, A. L. (1997). *The Lifecareer: The quantum leap into a process theory of career.* Vista, CA: LIFECAREER Foundation.

Miller-Tiedeman, A. (2008). Essential Tiedeman: Anchoring the north star for human development. *The Career Development Quarterly, 56*(3), 242–245.

Miller-Tiedeman, A. L., & Tiedeman, D. V. (1990). Career decision making: An individualistic perspective. In D. Brown, L. Brooks, & Associates (Eds.), *Career choice and development: Applying contemporary theories to practice* (2nd ed., pp. 308-337). San Francisco, CA: Jossey-Bass.

Niles, S. G., Harris-Bowlsbey, J. (2013). *Career development interventions in the 21st century* (4th ed.). Upper Saddle River, NJ: Pearson Merrill Prentice Hall.

Osipow, S. H., & Fitzgerald, L. F. (1996). *Theories of career development* (4th ed.). Boston, MA: Allyn & Bacon.

Patton, W. (2008). Recent developments in career theories: The influences of constructivism and convergence. In J. A. Athanasou, R. Van Esbroeck (Eds.), *International handbook of career guidance* (pp. 133-156). Retrieved from https://doi-org.proxy.libraries.uc.edu/10.1007/978-1-4020-6230-8

Patton, W., & McMahon, M. (1999). *Career development and systems theory: A new development.* Pacific Grove, CA: Brooks/Cole.

Patton, W., & McMahon, M. (2006). *Career development and systems theory: Connecting theory and practice* (2nd ed.). Rotterdam, The Netherlands: Sense.

Peterson, G. W., Sampson, J. P. Jr., Lenz, J. G., & Reardon, R. C. (2002). A cognitive information processing approach to career problem solving and decision making. In D. Brown & Associates (Eds.), *Career choice and development* (4th ed., pp. 312–372). San Francisco, CA: Jossey-Bass.

Peterson, G. W., Sampson, J. P., Jr., & Reardon, R. C. (1991). *Career development and services: A cognitive approach.* Pacific Grove, CA: Brooks/Cole.

Peterson, G. W., Sampson, J. P., Jr., Reardon, R. C., & Lentz, J. G. (1996). Becoming career problem solvers and decision makers: A cognitive information processing approach. In D. Brown, L. Brooks, & Associates (Eds.), *Career choice and development* (3rd ed., pp. 423-475). San Francisco, CA: Jossey-Bass.

Pryor, R. G. L., Bright, J. E. H. (2003). The chaos theory of careers. *Australian Journal of Career Development, 12,* 12–20.

Pryor, R. G. L., Bright, J. E. H. (2011). *The chaos theory of careers: A new perspective on working in the twenty-first century.* New York, NY: Routledge.

Pryor, R. G. L., & Bright, J. E. H. (2014). The chaos theory of careers (CTC): Ten years on and only just begun. *Australian Journal of Career Development, 23*(1), 4-12. doi:10.1177/1038416213518506

Richardson, M. S. (2000). A new perspective for counsellors: From career ideologies to empowerment through work and relationship practices. In A. Collin & R. A. Young (Eds.), *The future of career* (pp. 197–211). Cambridge, UK: Cambridge University Press.

Roe, A. (1956). *The psychology of occupations.* New York, NY: Wiley.

Roe, A. (1957). Early determinants of vocational choice. *Journal of Counseling Psychology, 4*(3), 212-217.

Roe, A., & Lunneborg, P. W. (1990). Personality development and career choice. In D. Brown, L. Brooks, & Associates (Eds.), *Career choice and development: Applying contemporary theories to practice* (2nd ed., pp. 68-101). San Francisco, CA: Jossey-Bass.

Rokeach, M. (1973). *The nature of human values.* New York, NY: Free Press.

Sampson, J. P., Jr., Lentz, J. G., Reardon, R. C., & Peterson, G. W., (1999). A cognitive information processing approach to employment problem solving and decision making. *The Career Development Quarterly, 48,* 3-18.

Sampson, J. P., Jr., Peterson, G. W., Lentz, J. G., Reardon, R. C., & Saunders, D. E. (1996). *Career thoughts inventory.* Odessa, FL: Psychology Assessment Resources.

Sampson, J. P., Reardon, R. C., Peterson, G. W., & Lentz, J. G. (2004). *Career counseling and services: A cognitive information processing approach.* Belmont, CA: Brooks/Cole-Thomson Learning.

Savickas, M. L. (1989). Career-style assessment and counseling. In T. Sweeney (Ed.), *Adelerian counseling: A practical approach for a new decade* (3rd ed., pp. 289-320). Munice, IN: Accelerated Development Press.

Savickas, M. L. (2005). The theory and practice of career construction. In S. D. Brown & R. W. Lent (Eds). *Career development and counseling: Putting theory and research to practice* (pp. 42-70). Hoboken, NJ: Wiley & Sons.

Savickas, M. L. (2008). David V. Tiedeman: Engineer of career construction. *The Career Development Quarterly, 56*(3), 217-224.

Savickas, M. (2012). Life design: A paradigm for career intervention in the 21st century. *Journal of Counseling and Development, 90*(1), 13-19.

Savickas, M. L. (2013). Career construction theory and practice. In S. D. Brown & R. W. (Eds), *Career development and counseling: Putting theory and research to practice* (2nd ed., pp. 147-183). Hoboken, NJ: Wiley & Sons.

Savickas, M. L. (2015). Career counseling paradigms: Guiding, developing and designing. In P. Hartgung, M. Savickas, & W. Walsh (Eds.), *The APA handbook of career intervention* (Vol. 1, pp. 129-143). Washington, DC: APA Books.

Sharf, S. R. (2002). *Applying career development theory to counseling* (3rd ed.). Pacific Grove, CA: Brooks/Cole.

Super, D. E. (1957). *The psychology of careers.* New York, NY: Harper & Row.

Tiedeman, D. V., & O'Hara, R. P. (1963). *Career development: Choice and adjustment.* Princeton, NJ: College Entrance Examination Board.

Zunker, V. G. (2002). *Career counseling: Applied concepts of life planning.* Pacific Grove, CA: Brooks/Cole-Thomson Learning.

6

CAREER COUNSELING PROCESS

Is career counseling process the same or different from personal counseling? This might be a question that many people wonder and want an answer to. This chapter will provide comprehensive information on the process of career counseling so that students will understand how career counseling is practiced from the beginning to the end. The definition and framework of career counseling will be reviewed. It is important to understand the process of career counseling because it requires a trusting relationship and appropriate procedures to help students and clients resolve their concerns about career issues. In the previous chapters, we have reviewed the variety of career development theories. These theories aim to explain the trajectories of one's career development and factors shaping one's career decision making. In this chapter, the focus is not about the reasons or factors that account for individuals' career development; rather, the focus is about the process in which counselors help clients resolve issues or achieve the goals identified through the process. The processes described in this chapter should be used more as a guideline for students to develop their own practice that best fit clients' needs and to apply their multicultural competency in helping clients. It is not meant to provide specific intervention strategies (which will be reviewed in Chapter 8) that counselors could use. It aims at providing an overview of career intervention from the beginning to the end so that a counselor could conceptualize his or her work with clients pertaining to career development and career-related concerns.

LEARNING OBJECTIVES

After completing the reading and exercises provided in this chapter, you will be able to:

- define career counseling, career intervention, and the career counseling process;
- describe the roles and functions counselors play in career counseling and intervention;

- explain client factors in the career counseling process;

- illustrate principles and procedure of providing career counseling;

- explain the decision-making process and skills in the context of career intervention;

- apply the career counseling process in assisting clients working on resolving career related issues; and

- develop competencies for implementing the process and conducing outcome evaluation.

OVERVIEW OF CAREER COUNSELING

There is a common misconception about career counseling: it is only conducted in high school and college settings, and counselors working in mental health agencies or community settings do not need to understand career development theories because their clients seek services on mental health issues rather than career issues. Another misconception is that career counseling is directive, and guidance oriented, and involves a lot of testing, therefore, building trust relationships between counselors and clients is not important. These are just some examples of some misconceptions of career counseling. The fact is that career counseling is far more complex than what is perceived as merely giving advice on career decisions. As we discussed in Chapters 1 and 2, career development involves multiple dimensions of a person's role and cannot be separated from one's self-identity or meaning of life; therefore, career counseling is essentially personal counseling. Because vocational guidance is the root of the counseling profession itself, it exemplifies the integral nature of career counseling as part of counseling rather than a separate entity. Thus, it is important to review the process of providing career counseling for effective career intervention.

Definition of Career Counseling

The National Career Development Association (NCDA) defines career counseling as "the process of assisting individuals in the development of a life-career with focus on the definition of the worker role and how that role interacts with other life roles" (NCDA, 2009). From this definition, it is evident that career counseling focuses on helping individuals' development as a worker but also emphasizes the importance of integrating other life roles in the process in order to achieve this goal. Many other views of career counseling have similar standpoints and also stress the importance and inseparability of career and personal counseling. For instance, Brown and Brooks (1991) suggested that if clients lack motivation or show an inability to make reasonable assessments of themselves and their environment, counselors need to address these issues before they can work on career decision issues. In their suggested process of career counseling, establishing a relationship is the first step before one can do other tasks, such as objective assessment of individuals' personal characteristics and evaluating the relationship between personal characteristics and occupational possibilities (Brown & Brooks, 1991). Gysbers and Moore (1987) suggested three phrases necessary for career counseling: establishing a working relationship, which involves defining roles and developing an understanding of the client's characteristics and environment; making a diagnosis of the client's problem to guide choices of interventions; and lastly, evaluating the impact of the intervention and terminating the relationship.

Crites (1981) suggested that career counseling can be therapeutic and should have the same process as psychotherapy, but it is beyond personal counseling in terms of scope and effectiveness as work is a central and major role of one's life. From these views of career counseling, it is evident that career counseling does involve relationship building and a process that helps clients fully develop their potentials to live a satisfying life. Accordingly, helping, educating, and guiding are the common features that are expected in career counseling to help clients have successful career development across the life span.

Helping

Isaacson and Brown (2000) pointed out that various definitions of career counseling share one common feature, that is, interpersonal process with a goal of facilitating career development by eliminating barriers including mental health problems. Therefore, it is an essential purpose and function of career counseling to help clients, just as any other counseling specialty would do. The counseling aspect of career counseling requires counselors to (1) develop a trusting relationship with clients through basic counseling skills, including listening, empathy, and attending skills; (2) address emotional and behavior issues arising in the process of career exploration and decision making; (3) facilitate clients' development of self-awareness and efficacy in regard to making a career related decision; and (4) assist clients to construct meaningful and satisfying work that integrates the various roles they play in their life across the life span. Niles and Harris-Bowlsby (2013) proposed that career development needs to be counseling-based career assistance, affirming the importance for career counselors to build therapeutic relationships and be collaborators with clients to achieve the goal of empowering clients to articulate their experiences, clarify their self-concepts, and construct their own lives. According to Niles and Harris-Bowlsby, counseling-based career assistance requires counselors to use basic counseling skills to forge a working alliance regardless of the theoretical framework of the career development approach. In other words, it does not matter whether the intervention approach is based on Holland's hexagon theory or Super's developmental theory, the counselor needs to first establish a trusting relationship with the client. This working alliance is even more critical when clients have resistance to working with counselors, to change, or to implementing the intervention plan. No effective work can be accomplished if clients are not engaged in the counseling process or motivated to take any actions. Therefore, the perceptions that career counselors would not need basic counseling skills or that empathy is not needed in career counseling are misrepresentative.

Providing emotional support to clients is essential to effective career counseling because individuals often feel lost or unsure when they come for career counseling. In the event of becoming unemployed, feeling hopeless, defeated, and that the situation is unfair is common; and the research has documented a strong association of loss of jobs to depression and other forms of mental health disorders (Olesen, Butterworth, Leach, Kelaher, & Pirkis, 2013). Amundson (1995) suggested counselors working with people going through unemployment could benefit from cognitive reframing by focusing on the positive experiences in the past and creating hope by showing them transferable skills they have for new prospective work. The support can also be extended by expressing encouragement and praise to help clients feel valued and by providing solution-focused strategies to transition to reenter workforce (Amundson, Harris-Bowlsbey, & Niles, 2005).

Education

Career intervention has another aspect that is critical and necessary to optimal development of individuals, particularly children and youth. Though vocational guidance was originated and had long history in public schools, it was considered more as a supplemental service to the school curriculum for many years. However, this situation was changed when the concept of career education was first introduced in the 1970s as part of the educational reform (Hoyt, 2005). From its inception, career education was significantly impacted by the federal legislature with the goal of reforming K-12 curriculum so that students acquired academic skills required and expected in the work settings. The connection between academic learning and the work world has since influenced some other federal legislature such as the School to Work initiative and career development intervention practice in educational settings (Hoyt, 2005).

According to the Career Education ACT of 1974 and the Career Education Incentive Act of 1977, career education should increase the relationship between schools and society; provide opportunities for counseling, guidance, and career development for all children; relate the subject matter of the curricula of schools to the needs of the persons to function in society; extend the education process beyond the school into the area of employment and community; foster flexibility in attitudes, skills, and knowledge to cope with changes and obstacles; make education more relevant to employment and functioning in society; and eliminate any distinction between education for vocational purpose and general academic education. These components of the career education movement are still applicable in the 21st century, especially when job security and stability is rare anymore in the everchanging economy. The evaluation of career education predominantly supported the value and positive impacts on students' academic achievement and career-related behaviors, including increased self-awareness and work values, career decision making and job searching skills, and specific occupational skills (Hoyt, 2005). As of today, career education, despite the loss of the federal funding, has been infused broadly in practice at various forms by educational systems, business, government, and community. As Hoyt (2005) stated, the future of career education relies on continued conceptualization, validation, funding, collaboration, and implementation by both leaders and shareholders at the local level, and school counselors are well positioned to coordinate the needed changes across K-16 educational settings.

Guidance

The aspect of guidance in career counseling is rooted in the vocational guidance implemented in Boston by Parsons at the turn of the 20th century. It has the clear goal of guiding youth through the career exploration process so that they can make sound decisions for occupational choices. Career guidance is different from helping or educating, yet is an important function of career counseling, because guidance can provide clarity for what directions and actions should be taken to achieve the identified goals. Depending

LEARNING ACTIVITY 6.1
COUNSELORS' ROLES

Divide the class into small groups with each group consisting of at least one school counseling and one mental health counseling student. List the roles and functions of school counselors and mental health counselors in their respective work settings in regard to clients' career development needs. Have each group summarize their discussion and report to the entire class. The points for the class discussion are the different roles counselors could play at variety of settings and the functions of career counseling in helping clients in various settings.

on the development stage, maturity level, and cultural context, directive intervention might be needed. In the past, school counselors played the role of vocational guidance. Within the current American School Counselor Association (ASCA) model (American School Counselor Association, 2012), career development is one of the three domains in which school counselors have responsibilities to help students develop competency; the other two are academic and social/emotional development. Career intervention with a focus on guidance could be beneficial for implementing career decisions such as college application for high school students or job application for people in pre-entry into the labor force. The differences between career education and guidance are that (1) guidance focuses on targeted areas of career-related knowledge, skills, and activities that would help students to be ready for making career and educational decisions, while career education aims at having the entire educational experiences integrated so that students can gain a better understanding of the connection between academics and work world, and (2) guidance can be done outside of the classroom and in the absence of teachers' participation, but career education has to incorporate teachers and total curriculum integration.

Career guidance also emphasizes the importance of prevention since all the guidance efforts are meant to help students gain an understanding of self and the world of work in order to make sound decision on educational and occupational plans. Guidance, different from counseling that is individualized intervention, focuses on application of self-knowledge to occupational choices. Another purpose of guidance is to provide help for individuals to balance individual and societal needs and to achieve social inclusion (Gothard, Mignot, Offer, & Ruff, 2001). For example, in the era of the cold war, school counselors were introduced to the elementary schools to identify and guide talented young students to pursue a career in science and technology fields with the aim of keeping the United States competitive. A more recent version of this initiative is science, technology, engineering, and math (STEM) programs across K-16. Similarly, the career pathway movement is an effort to address the needs of more skilled workers to fill the gap in the workforce. Nearly half of jobs require education beyond high school but not necessarily a four-year college degree; for instance, the most-needed yet hard-to-fill jobs are those skilled technician positions in STEM fields (Schwartz, 2016). Community colleges are positioned as significant national pathways to meeting the growing and diverse needs of a global workforce critical to the nation's competitiveness and future (more details can be found at https://www.aacc.nche.edu). A successful pathway project requires collaboration between high schools and community colleges.

ROLE OF COUNSELORS

In career counseling, depending on the setting and population served, counselors could play a variety of roles such as consultant, coach, supervisor, mentor, or instructor. These different roles may not be exclusive to each other, since some functions and duties overlap or are similar, yet understanding these roles would help counselors consolidate the services they can provide to meet the client's needs. For example, in a community-based career counseling service agency, if the clientele are mainly recent laid-off workers from a major employer in town, counselors would play a consultant role to the employer, be counselors to the clients receiving the direct services at their agency, and possibly function as coaches to those people who already had plans to look for new jobs. Each of these roles are needed to serve the clients better, and they are not replacing the counseling role, but rather complement or expand the typical scope of services provided by counselors. Each of these roles are reviewed next.

The consultant role is actually the most frequent duty of counselors, as many counselors are expected to provide their expertise on certain issues to help other counselors or organizations solve a problem and help clients through indirect services. Therefore, consultants possess the extensive and in-depth knowledge and experiences for the area that they will provide consultation for, and they usually do not serve the clients directly; instead, they often observe the dynamics of the clients' behavior in the work settings and interaction with others to assess the problem, make evaluations, and then make recommendations for solutions (Simpson, 2006). The goal of consultation is to advise and educate the consultee to develop an action plan for helping the client or for program improvement (Simpson, 2006). In the earlier example of laid-off workers, the counselors in the community agencies are invited by the major employer to provide solution plans to human resources staff and managers who would be on the front line in helping employees address the anxiety, frustration, uncertainty, and other emotional struggles prior to and post lay-off. This is an example of counseling playing a consultant role.

Job coaching, though, is not recognized by professional counselors as adequate counseling. The main goal of career counseling or the counselor's role is to facilitate the life span career development through prevention and intervention activities; however, the goal of coaching is to assist people to identify skills, goals, and talents that will maximize potential (Simpson, 2006). According to Simpson, the function of coaching for counselors focuses on action-oriented and solution-focused intervention for individuals who want to optimize their potential from the current work settings. For example, a mid-life worker wants to change his career from retail management to human resource management. He is not sure what steps he needs to take to make a smooth and advantageous transition. A career coach can help this person develop and implement a plan of action leading to his desirable outcome.

Supervision is an important role all counselors need to play during their professional life, with two aims: one is to help colleagues continually develop professional competency, and the other is to help the counseling profession in general (Simpson, 2006). The common functions of supervisors include monitoring, evaluating, advising, and supporting (Bernard & Goodyear, 2004). The role of supervisor requires counselors to provide feedback and evaluation to other counselors about their skills and delivery of services to clients. In the case of career counseling, counselors could need supervision when they encounter clients presenting issues beyond their competence comfort zone, and vice versa, can provide assistance to their colleagues on topics and issues in which they have expertise. The difference between consultation and supervision is the former focuses on helping the consultee identify solutions to clients' problems, while the latter focuses on supervisees' development of skills to help clients solve their issues. Using the same example above, a counselor with additional training on career counseling (e.g., Global Career Facilitation Certification) could supervise other colleagues who counsel the laid-off employees at the community agency and help them transition to the next possible jobs.

CLIENT FACTORS

Personal factors have a significant influence not only on individuals' choice of occupations but also on the career counseling process. The personal factors pertaining to career development trajectory and occupational choices have been extensively discussed in many career development theories as reviewed in the previous chapters. These stable individual characteristics such as personality, interests, values, abilities, and aptitudes have been mainly associated with fitness of career choices (Creed & Hood, 2015); that is, these personal traits are conceptualized to influence the outcome of one's career choices. The other type of personal factors, understood as process variables reflecting individual characteristics pertaining to motivation, maturity level, and capacity to make decisions and changes, could have influence on the process and outcome of a career decision as well. The following will illustrate how these individual characteristics would play a role in the process of career decision making.

Expectation and Motivation

Many people might think that career counseling process is different than personal counseling and that career counseling focuses only on finding a major or occupation for clients. If clients have these kinds of expectations toward career counseling, they may not be willing or ready to explore emotional and personal issues in life during the counseling session. Many individuals come to career counseling expecting to talk about specific career concerns or to solidify their decisions, and thus, prefer to have a task-oriented approach rather than person-focused counseling (Galassi, Grace, Martin, James, & Wallace, 1992). Therefore, counselors need to be mindful of clients' expectations for career counseling and meet the clients where they are; otherwise, not meeting their expectations might negatively affect the counseling process or even the outcome, eventually.

Clients' expectations and attitudes have important influences on the career counseling process, yet there is no sufficient research to determine the exact impact of client factors on the process or outcome of career counseling (Whiston & Rose, 2015). Research found that attitudes toward career counseling influence their effort and commitment to attend the counseling session. People with more positive attitudes toward career counseling are more motivated to seek help on their career-related issues and anticipate that the career counseling process could be beneficial. On the other hand, people might lack motivation to follow up on activities assigned or come back to the session if their attitudes are not so positive.

Maturity Level

According to the developmental approach of career development (e.g., Super's theory), people go through various stages to explore career options, identify their self-concepts, and grow in maturity of making decisions and implementing choices. There are different challenges at each stage, and a person who could meet these challenges at the age or developmentally appropriate level is considered to have achieved maturity; and on the other hand, if one cannot develop understanding of or master the developmentally appropriate tasks of career exploration and decision making, she or he would be viewed as lacking in career maturity. Career maturity is supposed to be related to mastering the age appropriate career-related tasks, and as a result, lead to career adjustment and adaptability (Creed & Hood, 2015). In other words, a child should gain some basic understanding of what kinds of occupations exist what she or he likes, and an adolescent needs to understand what specific occupations entail and what they are inclined to plan for the future, including college or other occupational options, and be capable of gathering information and making a decision. When a situation calls for a change—for instance, the entrance for the labor market has significantly changed and requires new skill sets—one can make a plan accordingly to keep updated with the skill requirements. A person with career maturity would have a relatively easy time to make the adjustment and smoothly manage the career tasks. Similarly, maturity level would also impact the process of career counseling intervention. A client with an age-appropriate maturity level would be more open and responsive to the counseling intervention and engage in actions because of his or her readiness to explore and set goals. If the counselor is unaware of the maturity level of the client, the counseling session might not be as helpful as it could be because of inconsistency of the goals for the career counseling and capacity the client has to handle the task. For instance, if the goal is to decide a major in college, but the client has an unrealistic view of himself or the world of work, the counseling process would not benefit the client if the counselor insists the client to follow the typical procedure—that is, assessment, identification of options, and implementation of choices—without addressing the client's unrealistic expectation first. Put in another way, if the client is not ready for career intervention yet, the counseling process needs to meet the client where he or she is.

Readiness for Change

The primary goal of career counseling is to help clients develop clear understanding of themselves and optimize their potential to live a fulfilling and productive life. To achieve this goal, clients themselves need to be an active participant in the process and also be willing to take actions to follow up on the tasks generated from the counseling process. However, if the clients are not ready psychologically or emotionally, and if they are not clear about their career identity yet, counselors should take these factors into consideration for conducting the career counseling process. As Rochlen, Milburn, and Hill (2004) stated, "clients who are largely uncertain of their career choice may not be ready for action-related interventions" (p. 273). Rochlen et al. also found that clients with both career-related uncertainty and presence of distress illustrated more concerns for emotional distress and anxiety for current status and future planning and shared more similarities as clients for personal counseling. From this finding, we can concur that the career counseling process cannot ignore client factors such as attitudes and emotional status

CASE ILLUSTRATION 6.1
PETER: LACK OF MOTIVATION

Peter is a 21-year-old junior in a state university and currently majors in business, but he needs two more years to graduate, if everything goes well for the next two years. The reason for his taking longer than four years in college is because he has changed majors three times so far. He has not earned enough credits in each of these prior majors to graduate with the respective major, but rather only as a minor. In addition, he does not feel interested in completing a degree with those majors or seeking jobs working in those fields, either. He started the college as a music major, as he is very interested in playing guitar and wanted to be a song writer and performer at that time, or he thought he could at least be a music teacher in middle school. After just one semester, he found that he was not as gifted as he thought he was in music nor did he want to teach music to adolescents. He could not imagine himself standing in a classroom with 20 teenagers. He then changed his major twice, but each time he could not find passion in learning or commitment to pursuing a career in the field. He simply could not find the energy to start looking for internships or other opportunities that could lead to jobs. His grades are fine, and he likes to read and enjoys spending time on the Internet. Right now, his parents are paying his tuition, but they told him that he has to graduate in two years, otherwise, he has to pay his own tuition. Peter gets anxious because he is afraid that he cannot get enough credits again and consequently cannot graduate. He came to the counseling center on campus to seek help. Peter's counselor is an intern who is in the graduate program of counselor education. She tried to understand why Peter could not stay in one degree program to earn enough credits, so she asked Peter "What makes you switch majors so frequently?" Peter said, "I don't know, I guess I am just a weird person." The intern counselor assured Peter that he is not a weird person, and as a matter of fact, he is smart because he earned good grades in each of his degree programs and can handle these different disciplines. Peter then asked, "Why did I get excited for a new major at first and then get bored after a few courses? I just don't want to enter into an occupation that I am not even interested in, but now it seemed that I have to get a degree regardless. Can you tell me what I should do, complete a B. A. in business or switch to a major that guarantees I will graduate? I am so anxious, just tell me what I should do. I don't mind going to graduate school if I have to." The intern counselor told Peter that she needed to conduct a few career assessments before she could give him an answer to his question. The assessment included an interest inventory, an aptitude test, and a career decision-making self-efficacy. The results showed that Peter's interests are AEI by Holland's code, he has a high level of abilities in music, math, reasoning, and communication; his self-efficacy in making decisions is average, compared to other college students. The counselor shared these results with Peter and said, "It looks like a business major is a good fit for you, and you just need to stay focused and finish this degree."

Discussion Questions

1. How do you conceptualize Peter's problem?

2. How do you view Peter's counselor's approach?

3. If you were Peter's counselor, what would you do differently? Why?

and cannot only focus on career-related issues, as personal and career issues are probably intertwined. Narrow focus or failure to recognize the emotional and attitude problems of clients could negatively affect the career process or outcome. Therefore, counselors should not push too much if clients are not ready for change; instead, they should explore what factors contribute to the lack of motivation and action.

In addition, in the midst of never-ending changes in technology and the economy, uncertainty and instability become the new norm; therefore, individuals need to have tolerance of ambiguity for the future (Andersen & Vandehey, 2012). In the same vein, counselors need to prepare clients to become aware of their own attitudes toward, as well as ways of dealing with, uncertainty during the career counseling process so that distress related to uncertainty can be effectively addressed in the intervention. Helping clients become ready for change and transition, then, serve well for client benefits.

PROCESS OF CAREER COUNSELING

The process of career counseling is not different from other kinds of counseling; that is, it is a process involving counselors and clients working collaboratively to achieve the identified goals. Many scholars contend that personal counseling and career counseling are very similar in regard to the process of intervention (e.g., Betz & Corning, 1993; Niles & Pate, 1989). A study about the personal and career counseling differences actually found little difference between the two in terms of working alliance, outcome measures, and counseling process, and that the only difference is clients' expectation about the counseling (Lewis, 2001). Advocates for integration of personal and career counseling argue that separation of personal and career counseling is artificial (Blustein, 2008) and urge the counseling profession to adopt an integrated approach of mental health and career counseling. Thus, it is apparent that counselors helping clients with career concerns go through the same process as counselors helping clients with mental health issues or any other kind of issue. In the early ages, Williamson (1939, 1965) proposed a six-step process for career counseling. These six steps involve analyzing of individuals, summarizing the data gathered, diagnosing the problem, identifying established goals, counseling for smooth and successful implementation, and following up and planing evaluation. This suggested process follows the procedure of diagnosis, goal setting, action, and follow up, a similar process that most counseling approaches entail. Additional evidence that career counseling shares similar principles of personal counseling is that the major relevant professional organizations of career development (e.g., NCDA, Society of Vocational Psychology [SVP], International Association of Education and Vocational Guidance [IAEVG], and CACREP) require counseling and assessment skills as one of the competency standards for practitioners (Juntunen & Martin, 2015). All these facts lead to the conclusion that career counseling has the same process as personal counseling, which requires counselors to build rapport with clients, facilitate clients' awareness and actions to reach the goals, and follow up to evaluate the progress. In this section, the specific, detailed steps of each stage in the career counseling process will be described.

Establishing a Working Alliance

As stated above, career counseling is a specialized intervention within the counseling field; therefore, relationship building is critical to the process (Heppner et al., 2004). The trusting relationship is important not only to the process but also to the effective counseling intervention because career counseling is not just about a making a career choice, which was mistakenly perceived by many counselors and allied helping professionals; it is a process of helping clients identify their meaning of life and their life trajectory. Without a trusting relationship in place, how can clients be open and honest with their own true emotions and engage in searching for values and interests that are significant in shaping their satisfactions and success in the world of work? Thus, the beginning stage of the career counseling process requires counselors do the following to build a working alliance:

(a) Explain the structure of career counseling, including expectations, clients' responsibilities, and counselors' roles; informing the client about the nature of career counseling process is important for the clients to engage in the collaboration (Amundson, Harris-Bowlsbey, & Niles, 2005).

(b) Explain the ethical obligations that counselors must follow and what clients need to be aware of regarding ethical behavior.

(c) Provide time for clients to ask questions and share their concerns.

(d) Provide emotional support; demonstrating care and empathy is necessary for the entire process but particularly important for the initial stage to establish a working alliance (Amundson, 1995). If no emotional support is shown to clients, some important aspects of clients' information could be missed or misunderstood, which then leads to inappropriate goal setting or interventions (Leong, 1993).

(e) Recognize clients' personal and contextual background; ignoring clients' perspectives and subjective experiences minimizes opportunities for providing effective emotional support (Amundson, 2003).

Information Gathering

Providing emotional support and building a working alliance is necessary but not sufficient to effectively helping career counseling clients (Niles & Harris-Bowlsbey, 2013). Niles and Harris-Bowlsbey (2013) suggested that informational and appraisal support are also needed in order to help clients achieve their goals. After a trusting relationship is built and a working alliance is achieved, gaining information is the next step. This phase involves identifying the concerns clients have, collecting information to clarify personal needs and characteristics, and gathering information pertaining to careers.

Problem Identification

This part of the information gathering is aimed at making a diagnosis about the nature of the presenting issues clients bring to the career counseling session. For some individuals, the issues could be a work and family balance challenge or decisions to be made about relocation, and for some individuals, the issues could be life stage transition, for example, from school to work, or from staying home back to labor force, or sometimes involuntarily being out of job. Because of the variety of these reasons why people need to seek career counseling, it is important for counselors to clarify the nature of the problems so that appropriate intervention can be implemented. Williamson (1965) stated that the problems for career choice fall into one of the three kinds: no choice, uncertain choice, or unwise choice. Similarly, Crites (1981) emphasized the importance of diagnosing and suggested that career problems can be categorized to adjustment problems (well-adjusted versus maladjusted), indecision problems (multipotential, undecided, and uninterested), and unrealism problems (unrealistic, unfulfilled, and coerced individuals). For instance, a person who has multiple interests and talents tends to have difficulty in choosing a major or an occupation; however, this kind of indecision is quite different from the individuals who could not decide due to anxiety of making a decision; the former is indecision because of too many appealing options, and the latter is lack of psychological capacity to make a decision. The third situation pertains to someone who shows no interest or motivation to plan for his or her future and simply cannot make a decision because he or she does not care. Counselors encounter this type of client in mental health counseling, too. A familiar phrase from these clients is, "I don't know." For these clients, if counselors fail to identify the reasons and background issues for the lack of motivation, simply stressing the importance of making a career plan would not help clients effectively, and instead, counselors may lose clients after the first session. Thus, understanding the nature of the clients' problems is critical to conceptualizing an appropriate approach for the career counseling process and outcome. Counselors should consider the specific nature of the problem before choosing assessment and intervention strategies.

In some cases, the problems could be a combination of psychological adjustment and career indecision. If individuals are psychologically healthy, adjustment problems and indecision problems may be resolved by helping clients identify the possible contributing factors to indecision and by assisting clients to develop skills in making career decisions; however, if the individuals experience psychological distress along with indecision, career intervention then requires counselors to work with clients on both reducing the distress and facilitating career decision-making skills to fulfill the career goals (Multon, Wood, Heppner, & Gysbers, 2007). Again, without clarification of the nature of the problem, the intervention could totally miss the target or be ineffective.

Another factor to consider in problem identification is the developmental stage of individuals. If the difficulties and challenges experienced by the clients are developmentally appropriate, counselors could play a dominant role as a consultant or educator to facilitate self-exploration of individuals. For instance, if a high school junior is anxious about making a postsecondary plan, which is developmentally appropriate as one is still in the exploration stage according to Super's developmental theory, the school counselor could provide guidance to help the student develop awareness of self in relation to work and competency in making career decisions. If a high school junior still has a fantasy about work and does not have a reasonable understanding of his or her relationship among self, schooling, and the world of work, and further, if this student has an unrealistic career choice and is not aware of the reasons why this career choice is unrealistic, it is then necessary to consider whether the student has a developmentally inappropriate maturity level and, therefore, needs more intensive services than just career guidance and decision making.

Appraisal/Assessment

Once the nature of the problem is clarified, in order to gain clear understanding of individuals' needs, values, interests, aptitudes, self-efficacy, career decision-making skills, maturity level, outcome expectations, and other factors that may influence one's career

LEARNING ACTIVITY 6.2

INFORMATION GATHERING AND GOAL SETTING

Complete the form below and discuss with your peers:

Long-term goal _____

Five-year goal _____

One-year goal _____

I want to be _____ because I am interested _____ and value

_____ and this career choice will allow me to _____. I need to do

_____ so that I can become _____.

My strength lies in _____

My weakness is _____

Resources for achieving the goal _____

Pathways, steps to achieve the goal _____

Alternative short-range plan _____

Time needed to enter this career alternative _____

choice and decision making, a formal or informal assessment is needed. More details about career assessment will be reviewed in Chapter 7. This section will focus on introducing how assessment needs to be incorporated in the process of information gathering.

Assessment is the subsequent step after the counselor clarifies with the client the problems hindering his or her career development. Depending on the nature of the problem, the assessment tools are selected to further confirm or explore the issues. For instance, a client experiences stress because of anticipated change in the organization, and he is not sure if he should wait until the final announcement of change and act accordingly or should consider finding another job to avoid uncertainty. The assessment in this case should focus on clarifying role resilience and life themes as well as coping skills, because understanding where clients are in these areas would be useful to generate the goals and intervention that benefit clients going through this stressful period. In other situations where individuals have no or few clues regarding occupations or college majors they should choose, the assessment of interests, values, and needs, as well as the outcome expectation would be helpful. For clients experiencing indecision, the assessment tool for career decision-making skills, self-efficacy, and related personality assessment tools would be helpful. For those clients who have unwise or unrealistic career choices, assessing their traits as well as gathering the information about the desirable occupations, for example, educational requirements, job market outlook, and work conditions, might help them gain a better understanding of the realistic picture of the occupations of their choice, and thus allow them to engage in career exploration activities leading toward more feasible paths that would provide them both fulfillment and expected lifestyle.

While the standardized, normed, and objective assessment is useful in gaining information about the characteristics of clients, it may not necessarily be the best or appropriate approach to do assessment or sufficient for a complete and in-depth gathering of information of clients. The same results of interest inventories or value assessment could have different meanings to different individuals, and the counselor's role is not to relay the testing results but to facilitate clients' self-awareness and knowledge of the world of work through the assessment process, in which only objective assessment is not sufficient because all individuals have unique life experiences that shape their understanding of themselves and careers (Niles & Harris-Bowlsbey, 2013). Assessment is not only about obtaining a series of test results; rather, it is an important and necessary step in the career counseling process to provide support and opportunities to clients to clarify their career concerns and identify career counseling goals (Niles, 1996). Therefore, using nonstandardized assessment, taking the subjective experiences of clients into consideration, and facilitating clients' own meaning making are equally important to the assessment phase and should be considered as an option when choosing the objective assessment tools.

Gathering Information About the World of Work

Gathering information also involves gaining knowledge of the world of work, such as the nature of the work itself, work settings, job outlook, and the requirements of entering a variety of occupations. From a trait-and-factor theoretical approach, both self-knowledge and world-of-work knowledge are necessary to explore the fit occupation for individuals. From developmental and construction approaches, understanding of the work world would be helpful for people to determine if the target occupation would be appropriate for them to express their self-concept and if they could find meaning out of working a particular occupation. In other words, gaining knowledge about the world of work is a necessary part of gathering information in the process of career counseling, as it provides an important source of data for people to see the connection of their own characteristics to the occupations in the world of work. Without the information about the world of work, the process of helping clients understand the relationship between oneself and work would have a missing link; therefore, it is critical for counselors to provide the sources of and avenues to look for such information. More importantly, counselors should educate clients about how to use the information systems on various platforms to discover the information.

In the 21st century, information is not too little; to the opposite, it is often too much. As Internet technology advances, there are volumes of information available online, which creates a dilemma for counselors and clients alike. On the one hand, it is great that everyone has access to the information; but on the other hand, there is little censorship of the accuracy and quality of the information. Further, without proper guidance or assistance, people might be misinformed or may not make the best use of the information; therefore, career counselors need to not only provide the sources of data but also teach clients how to filter through the materials and make meaning of the data to be informative.

To obtain the information on the nature of work and requirements for entering the occupation, a long-standing tool is the *Dictionary of Occupational Titles* (DOT). The DOT was first published in 1939 and has been updated consistently for the past 70 years. Now it is also available online (http://www.occupationalinfo.org/contents.html). Besides the published materials on occupational information, counselors can also help clients gain an understanding of work environments through experiential activities such as information interview, job shadowing, and volunteering. These activities give individuals the learning and insight that written materials are not able to offer, such as feeling the atmosphere at work settings. These activities are particularly beneficial to gain hands-on and real-world experiences for youngsters without much actual work experiences. Information regarding job outlook and requirements of entering a variety of occupations can be found through a publication of the Bureau of Labor Statistics (http://www.bls.gov/ooh/) and through state job and employment units.

Goal Identification

After the problems are clarified, the subsequent step is to identify the goals that would help clients address these identified problems effectively. Depending on the nature of the problems, the goals of the career counseling process could target making a reasonable educational or occupational choice, developing a plan for transition (e.g., from overseas deployment to home), finding work-life balance, or enhancing personal attainment or performance. The goals need to be based on the synthesis of the information gathered; in some cases, further assessment might be needed for generating intervention strategies. For instance, a 30-year-old veteran tried to find a new path after returning from deployment but was not sure what occupations would be fit for him. Through the information-gathering phrase, it was determined that he was interested in student affairs related jobs in higher education institutions; therefore, the goals were to help him develop an action plan so that he could enter into this occupational field. One part of the plan was obtaining a bachelor degree, but the client showed hesitance to enroll in a local college. In this case, further assessment is needed to understand the reasons and factors for his reluctance and how to overcome these barriers.

The goals also need to be in accordance with the ecological system of the individual, particularly the resource and assets versus barriers in regard to the goal attainment. If individuals do not have support from their ecological system or resources to implement the identified goals, achieving the goals or sustaining outcome of the goal achievement could be difficult. Therefore, the goals need to be attainable and may need modification as one's resources and barriers are often changing or could be varied depending on the time and settings. If clients show lack of effort or failure to complete the assigned tasks, it is possible that the goals of career counseling are not appropriately identified and should be reexamined (Amundson, 1995). An ecologically compatible goal would be more likely to be implemented with success and motivate individuals to take actions.

Generating Options Toward Goal Attainment

This phase is the logical step after the goals are identified and clarified. If the goal identification process takes into consideration multiple perspectives and a variety of sources of information, this step should be relatively smooth. Even so, careful planning for actions to be taken to achieve the goal is still needed. When discussing the options for action plans, counselors need to keep in mind two factors: (1) clients' factors, that is, their readiness to change, motivation, resilience, and so on as reviewed in the earlier section and (2) the possibility or need for modification due to the changing dynamics of the ecological system of clients. It is critical for counselors to keep these two perspectives while generating options with clients for action planning because absence of these perspectives could lead to failure of career intervention. As a matter of fact, the specific action plans need evaluation and reevaluation of the goals if clients come across new situations. As Amundson (1995) stated, achieving success requires both personal confidence and encouragement from others; therefore, one task for counselors is to help clients attain necessary personal and social strength to follow through their action plans.

In working with clients on developing action plans, the following elements are critical to the execution completion. First, the chosen actions for clients to implement need to be positively oriented, strength based, and easily used; second, the intervention strategies need to be specific and concrete and also should include as much detail as possible, so that clients can start the action with foreseeable effort and outcome expected, and therefore, more motivated to take actions; third, the actions and plans should be within clients' control (Walter and Peller, 1992), or in other words, the suggested intervention should be compatible with clients' capacity and resources; fourth, counselors need to help clients prepare for unexpected barriers that might arise to avoid giving up when they encounter difficulties (Amundson, 1995); and finally the counselor must allow clients to reflect and evaluate each option thoroughly, including giving them the opportunity to try some options before full implementation; after all, it is important for clients to learn and grow from these experiences.

Implementation

Once clients fully and thoroughly evaluate their options and decide on the action plans, it is the time to move to the actual implementation phrase. All the previous steps are necessary preparation for a smooth transition to this phase with an aim of successful execution of the plan. Depending on the identified goals, the action may mean enrolling in educational programs, specific job training for entry into the workforce directly, changing occupations, or reentering the workforce after absence or finding a balance between work and life. These actions may take a short time to complete (e.g., specific job training) or a long time (e.g., enrolling in educational programs) or even could be an ongoing process without a clear ending point (e.g., finding balance of work and life or preventing work-related burnout). In any case, this is the phase that requires clients to take actions and follow through with the plans; therefore, support from counselors to keep clients motivated, encouraged, and committed to accomplish the plan is critical.

The importance of counselor involvement in career intervention has been recognized by the research and, in particular, counselors could provide a more effective career counseling process that generates better and more sustainable outcome (Whiston, Brecheisen, & Stephens, 2003). A counselor's role as facilitator and coordinator in addition to being a counselor could be helpful for successful implementation of the action plans and intervention strategies. Counselors could gather resources and coordinate services for clients so that they can optimize their assets and overcome barriers. Counselors could do the following to help clients during the implementation phrase:

Problem solving appraisal support: Very often people cannot proceed to take actions, not because they are not motivated, but because they are afraid of failure or lack problem-solving skills. Through working with clients on their problem-solving confidence, approach behaviors, and personal control during the career counseling process, clients are more likely to gain positive outcome and changes such as becoming more decisive (Heppner et al., 2004). Thus, counselors could help clients analyze their problem-solving approach and identify the barriers that could hamper their action plans, and then if necessary, assist them in developing a better problem-solving style during the counseling process.

Practice for specific situation: Another possible barrier for clients' actions is lack of skills to act on the suggested intervention strategies. For instance, one part of the action plan is to do an informational interview to understand more details of a selected occupation; however, the client is anxious to make a phone call to the organization or to make the request. Counselors could help clients practice how to make such a phone call during the session and then give homework for clients to practice on their own. Practicing the skills in a familiar and trustworthy environment (such as the counselor's office or the clients' own home) would help clients be willing to try something they do not feel comfortable doing otherwise. Mock interviews are another example that is often used to help clients in the implementation phase for a better outcome. Counselors, after working with clients through previous phases, are in the position to know strengths and weaknesses of clients, and therefore, should be able to determine what kinds of assistances clients need to become better prepared for taking actions.

Giving feedback and monitoring: After all, the counseling intervention is to help clients become self-sufficient in making decisions and change in a positive direction; for clients to accomplish these goals, it is important to develop the capacity to learn from their performance and past experiences. During the implementation phase, since clients are actively engaged in the various action-oriented activities, it is the best time for counselors to monitor their progress as well as to give feedback about their performance and skills. Giving feedback could also lead to iterative learning, which is critical to developing capacity to continual growth. Counselors could start the session by asking, "What have you done, and what do you think you do well and what do you think you don't do well?" and then "What do you learn from these differences?" Finally, counselors can ask clients, "What would you do differently next time?" Intentionality is a critical component in learning and growth. Counselors should help clients become more aware of the intentionality of their behaviors and what they can learn from their errors. Monitoring and giving feedback can also keep clients engaged and empowered to complete the implementation.

Stress management and anxiety reduction: As stated before, prior to implementation, counselors need to assess if clients are ready to make decisions or changes. It is stressful to make important decisions such as choosing a major or an occupation, or changing a lifestyle; therefore, continually providing emotional support is critical to successful implementation. As a matter of fact, many intervention components in career counseling need the counselors' presence and support that were found to increase the effectiveness of career counseling intervention (Brown et al., 2003). Brown et al. (2003) suggest counseling intervention could include interpretations of information gathered, modeling, and support. Counselors need to understand and assess the source of anxiety and stress and then work collaboratively with clients to develop individualized strategies for reducing anxiety and managing stress.

Follow Up

This is the last phase before ending the career counseling process. Summary and evaluation are two components during this phase. This step is helpful for two reasons: first of all, it is beneficial for both counselors and clients to know if the intended outcome is actually achieved and what other interventions might be needed to sustain the outcome; second, it is helpful for clients to identify the insights and learning gained through the career counseling intervention and to apply in their future situations. In other words, it is helpful to identify transferable skills that would benefit one in a different work environment. Finally, evaluation gives clients the opportunity to reflect their own development and move to a new stage of life.

DECISION-MAKING PROCESS AND SKILLS

In the previous section, we described the general process of career counseling that could be applied for addressing a variety of career development aspects, ranging from choosing a career to adjusting to career transitions. In each of the steps of the career counseling process, clients are faced with information and many options about which they need to make decisions. Indeed, one important goal of career counseling is to help clients make sound decisions for their optimal career development. Thus, helping clients gain career decision-making skills is a must. It is reasonable to say that the career counseling process is also a process of assisting individuals with making a decision pertaining to career development.

Three models of career decision making are presented to illustrate how counselors can help clients in the career counseling process to reach a decision and gain skills through the process. The career decision-making model of Tiedeman and O'Hara (1963) described that there are two stages, namely anticipating choice and adjusting to a choice. The first stage delineated the components of career decision making (exploration, crystallization, choice, and clarification), and the second stage is implementation and adjustment to a choice (induction, reformation, and integration). According to Tiedeman and O'Hara, individuals begin the decision process in unsystematic ways, and counselors need to help them strengthen self-awareness and explore these options rather than running away (exploration). The continual exploration leads to better understanding of each option's advantages and disadvantages and eventually stability of the thinking process (crystallization). Following a clearer examination of options is the decision (choice), and the choices being tried and reexamined (clarification) for insurance.

Another approach with a focus on the decision-making process and skills is the Cognitive Information Processing (CIP) model (Sampson, Reardon, Peterson, & Lenz, 2004). Sampson et al. (2004) proposed a guide to good decision making, which goes in a cycle following this order: knowing I need to make a choice—become aware of the difficulties or situation requiring a decision to be made; understanding myself and my options—analyzing and clarifying self-knowledge in relation to career options; expanding and narrowing my list of options—to make sure I am not being limited by options yet at the same time to narrow the options to a manageable list; choosing an occupation, program of study, or job—comparing cost and benefits of the final list and prioritizing the options; implementing my choice—committed to take actions on the top choice; and knowing I made a good choice—evaluating the situation to determine if the desirable status is achieved.

The PIC Model for Career Decision Making was proposed by Gati and Asher (2001) as an application of decision theory to career development. The three stage of the model are prescreening, in-depth exploration, and choice. The prescreening stage has three substages: preparing for sequential elimination involving two tasks—locating career-related aspects important to clients, ranking aspects by importance; sequential elimination involving two tasks—locating the range of compromise in the aspects, comparing preferences with alternatives' characteristics, eliminating incompatible ones; and testing sensitivity to changes involving three tasks—verifying reported preferences, verifying elimination of previously appealing alternatives, and locating almost promising alternatives. The in-depth exploration stage involves a series of activities to test the suitability of the promising alternatives against four conditions: compatibility of alternatives with individual preferences, compatibility in less important aspects, fit in core aspects, and probability of actualization. Gati and Asher also suggested reexamining eliminated promising alternatives. The final stage, choice, is to choose the most suitable alternative after comparing and evaluating the suitable alternatives.

In sum, despite their distinctions of each model reviewed above, there are three themes that show commonality of these three models. One is the importance of information; all three models recognizes that a sound decision is based on comprehensive and valid information, and all three listed an initial stage of decision-making process as preparation to be ready for accessing and understanding the information. The second

LEARNING ACTIVITY 6.3
COMPARISON AND ELIMINATION

The instructor asks the students to brainstorm 10 important factors that they want to have in their future jobs. It could be anything, such as meaningful to one's self-concept, sense of fulfillment/rewarding, income, prestige, supportive work environment, location, career ladder opportunities, interesting/fun, collegial relationship, and so on. The alternative option is to have the entire class brainstorm as many as possible factors important to their decisions on choosing a job; then ask each student to choose 10 of the most important ones to himself or herself. The next step is for each student to eliminate 5 of 10 factors. Then eliminate 3 out of 5, and finally, to choose 1 of 2 remaining options. Allow sufficient time for the class to process their decisions.

After everyone has reduced their factors to 1, the instructor facilitates class discussion by asking these questions:

1. What are the top 5? What is the last 1 remaining?

2. How do you make your decision in eliminating?

3. Why is the remaining 1 the most important?

The class discussion can also be around the common or unique choices the class makes in regard to what is most important to work situation.

common feature in all includes the process of broadening the options to avoid missing hidden alternatives and eliminating the alternatives to keep the task manageable. The third commonality is the role of self-awareness and cognitive functioning in the process of making a career decision.

Summary: Challenges and Opportunities

The career counseling process is defined by Heppner and Heppner (2003) as "the overt and covert thoughts, feelings, and behaviors of both client and counselors during a career counseling session" (p. 430). From the topics and issues discussed in this chapter, it is apparent that the career counseling process is not devoid of personal counseling process. However, the research about career counseling process and outcome is lacking (Heppner & Heppner, 2003), which further mystifies the nature of career counseling or misleads people to think career counseling does not entail emotions. Nonetheless, career counseling was found to have positive impacts on career indecision and to be effective for helping clients with career concerns (Perdix, Stauffer, Masdonati, Massoudi, & Rossier, 2012) and improving clients' career-directedness (Verbruggen & Sels, 2008). One of the challenges is the need to have more empirical studies about the long-term effects in addition to the increasing research on the short-term effectiveness of career counseling. The other challenges include the misconception about the nature of career counseling, tendency to separate mental health and career counseling, and lack of funding at various settings to employ more qualified and appropriately credentialed professional counselors to do the job. When more research has been conducted to examine the efficacy of the working alliance and counseling technique to the career process and outcome, we will have more understanding of career counseling leads to the changes and consequently has the potential to design more effective interventions.

Keystones

- Career counseling is a process built upon the working alliance between counselors and clients with a goal of helping clients to achieve their potential.

- Counselors could play a variety of roles depending on the goals identified through the counseling process and needs of clients.

- Counselors need to be aware of clients' expectations, motivations, maturity levels, and readiness to change.

- The procedure of career counseling typically follows these steps: establishing a working alliance; gathering information, including problem identification, appraisal of clients, and information about the world of work; identifying goals; generating options toward goal attainment; implementing, and following up.

- The decision-making process is similar and requires counselors to help clients gather relevant information and evaluate the pros and cons of options before making a decision.

Additional Resources:

ASCA Model: https://www.schoolcounselor.org/school-counselors-members/asca-national-model

Dictionary of Occupational Titles: http://www.occupationalinfo.org/contents.html

Pathway Model: https://www.aacc.nche.edu/wp-content/uploads/2018/01/12PathwaysModelDescriptionFinal1616.pdf

O*Net Website: https://www.onetonline.org

References

American School Counselor Association. (2012). *The ASCA national model: A framework for school counseling programs* (3rd ed.). Alexandra, VA: Author.

Amundson, N. E. (1995). An interactive model of career decision making. *Journal of Employment Counseling, 32*, 11-21.

Amundson, N. E. (2003). *Active engagement: Enhancing the career counselling process* (2nd ed.). Richardmon, B.C: Ergon Communications.

Amundson, N. E., Harris-Bowlsbey, J., & Niles, S. G. (2005). *Essential elements of career counseling.* Upper Saddle River, NJ: Merrill/Prentice Hall.

Andersen, P., & Vandehey, M. (2012). *Career counseling and development in global economy* (2nd ed.). Belmont, CA: Brooks/Cole Cenage Learning.

Bernard, J. M., & Goodyear, R. K. (2004). *Fundamentals of clinical supervision* (3rd ed.). Boston, MA: Allyn & Bacon.

Betz, N. E., & Corning, A. F. (1993). The inseparability of career and personal counseling. *The Career Development Quarterly, 42*, 137-142.

Blustein, D. L. (2008). The role of work in psychological health and well-being: A conceptual, historical, and public policy perspective. *American Psychologist, 63*(4), 228-240. doi:10.1037/0003-066X.63.4.228

Brown, D., & Brooks, L. (1991). *Career counseling techniques.* Boston, MA: Allyn & Bacon.

Brown, S. D., Krane, N. E. R., Brecheisen, J., Castelino, P. Budisin, I, Miller, M., & Eden, L. (2003). Critical ingredients of career choice interventions: More analyses and new hypotheses. *Journal of Vocational Behavior, 62*, 411-428.

Creed, P. A., & Hood, M. (2015). Process variables: Maturity, identity, decision-making, and adjustment. In P. J. Hartung, M. L. Savickas, W. B. Walsh (Eds.), *APA handbook of career intervention: Vol. 1. foundations* (pp. 351-372). Washington, DC: American Psychological Association. doi:10.1037/14438-019

Crites, J. O. (1981). *Career models: Models, methods, and materials.* New York, NY: McGraw-Hill.

Galassi, J. P., Crace, R. K., Martin, G. A., James, R. M., & Wallace, R. L. (1992). Client preferences and anticipations in career counseling: A preliminary investigation. *Journal of Counseling Psychology*, *39*, 46-55. doi:10.1037/0022-0167.39.1.46

Gati, I., & Asher, I. (2001). Prescreening, in-depth exploration, and choice: From decision theory to career counseling practice. *Career Development Quarterly*, *50*(2), 140-156. doi:10.1002/j.2161-0045.2001.tb00979.x

Gothard, B., Mignot, P., Offer, M., & Ruff, M. (2001). *Career guidance in context*. Thousand Oaks, CA: Sage.

Gysbers, N. C., & Moore, E. J. (1987). *Career counseling: Skills and techniques for practitioners*. Englewood Cliffs, NJ: Prentice Hall.

Heppner, M. J., & Heppner, P. P. (2003). Identifying process variables in career counseling: A research agenda. *Journal of Vocational Behavior*, *62*, 429-452.

Heppner, M. J., Lee, D., Heppner, P. P., McKinnon, L. C., Multon, K. D., & Gysbers, N. C. (2004). The role of problem-solving appraisal in the process and outcome of career counseling. *Journal of Vocational Behavior*, *65*(2), 217-238. doi:10.1016/S0001-8791(03)00100-3

Hoyt, K. B. (2005). *Career education: History and future*. Tulsa, OK, National Career Development Association.

Isaacson, L. E., & Brown, D. (2000). *Career information, career counseling, and career development*. Boston, MA: Allyn & Bacon.

Juntunen, C. L., & Martin, E. L. (2015). Standards, competencies, and guidelines in career interventions. In P. J. Hartung, M. L. Savickas, W. B. Walsh (Eds.), *APA handbook of career intervention: Vol. 1. foundations* (pp. 389-402). Washington,

DC: American Psychological Association. doi:10.1037/14438-021

Leong, F. T. L. (1993). The career counseling process with racial/ethnic minorities: The case of Asian Americans. *Career Development Quarterly*, *42*, 26-40.

Lewis, J. (2001). Career and personal counseling: Comparing process and outcome. *Journal of Employment Counseling*, *38*, 82-90.

Multon, K. D., Wood, R., Heppner, M. J., & Gysbers, N. C. (2007). A cluster-analytic investigation of subtypes of adult career counseling clients: Toward a taxonomy of career problems. *Journal of Career Assessment*, *15*, 66-86. doi:10.1177/1069072706294508

National Career Development Association. (2009). *Career counseling competencies*. Retrieved from http://www.ncda.org/aws/NCDA/pt/sd/news_article/37798/_self/layout_ccmsearch/true.

Niles, S. G. (1996). Offering appraisal support within career counseling. *Journal of Employment Counseling*, *33*(4), 163-173.

Niles, S. G., Harris-Bowlsbey, J. (2013). *Career development interventions in the 21st century* (4th ed.). Upper Saddle River, NJ: Pearson Merrill Prentice Hall.

Niles, S. G., & Pate, R. H. (1989). Competency and training issues related to the integration of career counseling and mental health counseling. *Journal of Career Development*, *16*, 63-71.

Olesen, S. C., Butterworth, P., Leach, L. S., Kelaher, M., & Pirkis, J. (2013). Mental health affects future employment as job loss affects mental health: Findings from a longitudinal population study. *BMC*

Psychiatry. Retrieved from http://www.biomedcentral.com/1471-244X/13/144.

Perdix, S., Stauffer, S., Masdonati, J., Massoudi, K., & Rossier, J. (2012). Effectiveness of career counseling: A one-year follow-up. *Journal of Vocational Behavior, 80*, 565-578.

Rochlen, A. B., Milburn, L., & Hill, C. E. (2004). Examining the process and outcome of career counseling for different types of career counseling clients. *Journal of Career Development, 30*(4), 263-275. doi:10.1023/B:JOCD.0000025115.25272.66

Sampson, J. P., Reardon, R. C., Peterson, G. W., & Lentz, J. G. (2004). *Career counseling and services: A cognitive information processing approach*. Belmont, CA: Brooks/Cole-Thomson Learning.

Schwartz, R. B. (2016). The career pathways movement: A promising strategy for increasing opportunity and mobility. *Journal of Social Issues, 72*(4), 740-759. doi:10.1111/josi.12192

Simpson, L. R. (2006). Consultation, coaching and supervision. In D. Capuzzi, & M. D. Stuffer (Eds), *Career counseling: Foundations, perspectives, and applications* (pp. 230-253). Boston, MA: Allyn and Bacon.

Tiedeman, D. V., & O'Hara, R. P. (1963). *Career development: Choice and adjustment*. New York, NY: College Entrance Examination Board.

Verbruggen, M., & Sels, L. (2008). Can career self-directedness be improved through counseling? *Journal of Vocational Behavior, 73*, 318-327. doi:10.1016/j.jvb.2008.07.001

Walter, J. L., & Peller, J. E. (1992). *Becoming solution-focused in brief therapy*. New York, NY: Brunner/Mazel.

Whiston, S. C., Brecheisen, B. K., & Stephens, J. (2003). Does treatment modality affect career counseling effectiveness? *Journal of Vocational Behavior, 62*, 390-410. doi:10.1016/S0001-8791(02)00050-7

Whiston, S. C., & Rose, C. S. (2015). Career counseling process and outcome. In P. J. Hartung, M. L. Savickas, W. B. Walsh (Eds.), *APA handbook of career intervention: Vol. 1. foundations* (pp. 43-60). Washington, DC: American Psychological Association. doi:10.1037/14438-003

Williamson, E. G. (1939). *How to counsel students: A manual of techniques for clinical counselors*. New York, NY: McGraw-Hill.

Williamson, E. G. (1965). *Vocational counseling: Some historical, philosophical, and theoretical perspective*. New York, NY: McGraw-Hill.

ASSESSMENT

Career assessment is an important aspect of career development intervention because it assists the process of information gathering about clients' characteristics as well as their preferences regarding the world of work. Career assessment provides tools to counselors to help clients understand themselves better and identify intervention strategies. It is necessary for counselors to understand the concepts of assessment and its application in the career development domain so that they can effectively decide on the best approach to help their clients. The process and outcome of assessment can be helpful for both counselors and clients in developing the intervention plan.

LEARNING OBJECTIVES

After completing the reading and exercises provided in this chapter, you will be able to:

- explain the purposes and roles of assessment in career development intervention,

- discuss the procedure of administering an instrument and interpreting the results of such an instrument in the career counseling process,

- select the appropriate assessment tools to meet the needs of clients,

- compare the strengths and weakness of a variety of assessment methods including formal and nonformal tools and techniques,

- describe the major areas and contents of career assessment tools commonly used in the career counseling process,

- analyze the appropriate and inappropriate uses of assessment in career development,

- identify the legal and multicultural issues in career assessment and their implications for helping people from diverse backgrounds, and

- recognize bias issues in assessment related to diversity (e.g., gender, race, culture, and socioeconomic status) and how that can affect the use of assessment in career counseling.

ROLE OF ASSESSMENT IN CAREER DEVELOPMENT INTERVENTION

When Parsons helped immigrant youth and others in Boston at the beginning of the 20th century, he did not have the readily available assessment tools we have today, but the first two steps of his triadic approach were gathering information about the self and the world of work through analysis, which in essence is assessment. The trait-and-factor approach, built upon Parsons's proposed vocational guidance model, heavily relies on assessing personal characteristics that may influence career aspiration, career choices, and satisfaction. For many years, the trait-and-factor model was the dominant career counseling approach, and its focus on the development of instruments and inventories "became such a pervasive influence on vocational counseling that they became inextricably linked" (Isaacson and Brown, 2000, p. 345). Standardized assessment to guide people in the career decision-making process became prevalent because of the fundamental principles of finding fitness between individual characteristics and the occupational structure (Niles & Harris-Bowlsbey, 2002). While it is debatable whether standardized assessment is an integral part of career intervention, it is noteworthy that assessment did play an important role in intervention history and is still currently used in providing career assistance to a wide variety of populations.

The role of assessment in career counseling is multilayered. First, it is a useful component in the career counseling process because the assessment results provide practical information for counselors and clients in making career-related decisions. More importantly, the process of conducting assessment itself can be helpful in facilitating self-awareness and self-exploration. Facilitating exploration of individuals' self-understanding is critical for career development and intervention, because understanding self in relation to the world of work is an important component in all theoretical approaches to career development. Finally, career assessment tools are useful in examining the applicability of career development theories (Starkey & Rasmus, 2006). Indeed, many career instruments have been developed to either validate the constructs in career development theories or apply the career development theories in helping clients. A well-designed and empirically tested valid career assessment tool can assist in using the pertaining theory to help the targeted population, can better serve clients, and can potentially help clients effectively manage their careers and other life roles. However, if not appropriately used, assessment can harm rather than benefit clients.

From this case illustration, it becomes clear that *appropriate* use of career assessment is critical to career development and intervention. Let us enumerate the errors in Susan's story. First, assessment and inventories were administered without finding out anything about Susan, her needs, what she already knew about her interests, abilities, past experiences, and so forth. Second, results were mailed, denying her the opportunity to fully understand their meaning and how the results might apply to her. Thirdly, and perhaps

CASE ILLUSTRATION 7.1
RECEIVING ASSESSMENT RESULTS BY MAIL

Susan came to see a career counselor because she was expecting to complete college with a bachelor's degree in English in about three months and was not sure how or where to look for a job after graduation. It was the custom at the career center where she went to school to give all clients a battery of tests when they came for help. She was given five of these tests and inventories and then told to schedule an appointment with a career advisor. Because this was a busy time of year for the career center, as many students wait until the last minute to seek help, she was mailed her results while waiting for her appointment, four weeks later. Susan noticed that "editor" appeared as a career option several times in her results. This sounded like a good idea to her, so she ignored her appointment and registered for a class in editing being offered that summer. About halfway through the class, she realized that she hated editing, so she dropped the class. Back where she started, she again contacted the career office. When asked to take the tests again, because there had been a several months lapse since last she took them, she gave up in despair.

Discussion Questions

1. What could be the reasons for Susan's feeling of despair?

2. What are factors that could contribute to Susan's decision not to come to her appointment?

3. What are some potential issues in this case in terms of professional best practice?

LEARNING ACTIVITY 7.1

Divide the class into small groups. Even-numbered groups role-play inappropriate use of tests in the career counseling process; odd-numbered groups role-play appropriate use of tests in the career counseling process.

a. Have each group demonstrate their role-plays to the entire class, and then discuss the possible ways to potentially harm clients if assessment is used inappropriately.

b. Have the class generate a list of precautions they can use in the future to avoid any potential harms.

all too common in times of tight budgets, her wait to see an advisor was so long that she felt compelled to act on inadequate information. And finally, being asked to retake the assessments, still without seeing an advisor, drove her away from the career center completely. When help is not useful, it is worse than neutral, because it sends the message to an individual that there really is no help possible.

Demystifying assessment results in career counseling is necessary, especially when there is a variety of assessment methods that could achieve the goal of providing useful and helpful information in increasing self-understanding. The following sections of this chapter will explain how assessment can be used appropriately to avoid misuse and the common areas of assessment in career intervention.

PURPOSE OF ASSESSMENT

Although assessment plays an important role in career counseling, it does not mean that administering a test is always beneficial or even necessary. Giving a test without a clearly defined goal or without considering the advantages or disadvantages is poor practice. It is in fact unethical for counselors to administer tests without taking the responsibility to consider the welfare of clients (American Counseling Association, 2014). As test publishing is a profit-driven industry, counselors need to be mindful of the influence of marketing and public relations that could potentially impact the decision making. Counselors should not give an instrument to a client without examining whether the instrument serves the purpose of helping the client. Therefore, the first thing counselors need to consider is whether assessment is necessary or beneficial for their clients. They then need to decide what kinds of assessment would best serve their purposes.

The purposes of career assessment are multiple and can vary depending on the issues individuals bring to career counseling. If a high school student goes to a school counselor for postsecondary planning and wants to know what major he or she should choose for college, the purpose of assessment may be to help him or her understand interests and career aspirations or maybe to help sort out several options already considered; however, if the student's issue is related to lack of decision-making skills, the purpose of assessment might be finding out about the difficulty in making decisions and if there are particularly problematic areas. The purposes of career assessment are organized into three areas by Niles and Harris-Bowlsbey (2002): the first category is identifying needs of individuals and groups; the second is identifying personal characteristics and increasing self-understanding; and the third category is determining the change and progress in career development domains. The specific purposes of career assessment can be summarized as the following:

- To increase clients' self-understanding and self-awareness

- To understand clients' career beliefs, life styles, work attitudes, and needs for career development

- To identify abilities and skills in relation to academic achievement and work-related domains

- To identify occupational interests, needs, values, expectations, and outcome expectations

- To help clients understand their personality traits in relation to the world of work

- To examine one's developmental stages in regard to career development and career maturity

- To recognize career decision-making styles in order to help clients address the challenges they face

- To help clients make career decisions based on the information gained through assessment

- To facilitate career planning that would benefit clients across the life span

AREAS AND CONTENTS OF ASSESSMENT

Early in the modern career development era, there was an emphasis on matching personal characteristics and work environment. This emphasis led to a focus on skills and personality traits. Beginning in the 1950s, career development theories flourished, leading to more aspects of career development being assessed and leading to a variety of methods being used. This section introduces the most commonly used career assessment tools classified into the following categories: *interests, values/needs, decision making, aptitudes, self-efficacy, career maturity/development, career beliefs/thoughts,* and *personality*.

Career Interests

Assessment of interests has been heavily examined and has a long history. The earliest interest inventory was developed in 1927 (i.e., The Strong Interest Inventory). Wide use of interest inventories in secondary schools and colleges reflected the long-standing belief that people choose and enjoy an occupation because they are interested in the activities involved in this occupation, and these scales measure people's likes and preferences for certain occupations (Brown, 2012). The following are some examples of commonly used interest inventories:

Strong Interest Inventory (SII): The SII was first published in 1927, and the latest version was published in 2004. It is published by Consulting Psychology Press. It was designed to measure people's interests in a broad range of occupations, work activities, and leisure interests. The most recent revision is shortened from the previous 1994 version, from 317 items to 291 items (Donnay, Thompson, Morris, & Schaubhut, 2004). It provides scores on six General Occupational Scales (GOT), which are organized by Holland's hexagon theory; 30 Basic Scales (BIS), which measure clusters of interests related to the GOT; and 244 Occupational Scales (OS). It also has five Personal Style Scales (i.e., Learning Style, Work Environment, Leadership Style, Risk Taking, and Team Orientation). One of the advantages of the SII is that it is frequently updated to make the instrument reflect the current status of the workforce as closely as possible. More details about the SII can be found at the website https://www.cpp.com/products/strong/index.aspx. The SII is not only widely used but also heavily researched with both high reliability and validity (See Hansen & Swanson, 1983; Larson & Borgen, 2002; Jenkins, 2013). The newest development of SII was used in conjunction with the Skills Confidence Inventory (SCI; Betz, Borgen, & Harmon, 2005). The SCI provides the confidence level individuals perceive on the six GOTs. This provides a useful tool for counselors to help clients identify more promising areas (high confidence and high interests) and address the areas where high interests and low confidence occur. It has been translated into different languages as well. The cross-cultural studies about the SII showed that it is a valid instrument to be used in different cultures (Hansen & Lee, 2007; Tang, 2009). Earlier criticisms that the SII (Schlossberg and Goodman, 1972) is gender biased have been partially addressed in more recent versions. The separate reporting of norms both manages this concern and avoids it. Careful interpretation can help individuals understand the disparity in scores for their gender and the opposite.

Self-Directed Search (SDS, Holland, 1994): The SDS was developed to measure Holland's typology theory, and the test items were categorized into the six Holland's types: realistic, investigative, artistic, social, enterprising, and conventional. It is based on the assumption that individuals and jobs can be categorized into the same six categories. It is published by Psychological Assessment Resources. The advantages of the SDS are its ease of administration (taking 10 minutes to complete the instrument) and that it is self-administered, self-scored, and self-interpreted. The scoring is straightforward and based on raw scores. Individuals can generate a three-letter code—for example, RIA: realistic, investigative, artistic—by summing the raw scores of each category. The highest three (rank ordered) are the personal profile. Then one can use the Occupational Finder (part of the SDS package) to find what occupations fit the same or similar codes. The SDS has been translated into more than 25 languages, and there are over 600 research studies on the SDS (Ciechalski, 2009), including examining its reliability and validity in cross-cultural settings (e.g., Yang, Lance, & Hui, 2006). More details can be found at the PAR website at http://www4.parinc.com/Products/Product.aspx?ProductID=SDS_R.

Kuder Career Interest Assessment (KCIA-32): The KCIA-32 was originally developed by Kuder and went through several versions (e.g., an earlier version codeveloped with Zytowski, known as the Kuder Occupational Interest Survey), and the current version was published by Kuder, Inc. in 2012. It contains 32 triads of interest items that one needs to rank by preference from most preferred to third most preferred. The KCIA-32 provides two sets of scores; one presents occupational scales of the 16 career clusters and pathways, and one presents the Holland RIASEC codes. The six Holland areas of interests can be used to identify the O*NET occupations and 16 national career clusters (Harris-Bowlsbey, Niles, Zytowski, Rayman, & Trusty, 2013). The KCIA-32 is part of the Kuder Career Planning System developed to help students and adults with career and education planning. The Kuder system has versions for preK-12 and was endorsed by many school districts as a tool for career exploration and postsecondary career planning. More details can be found at http://www.kuder.com. The advantage of the Kuder system is that it is easily accessible (the Internet-based assessment), and results are immediately available; a personal portfolio can be created for tracking and comparison (Gibbons, 2013). The other benefits, according to Gibbons, are its user-friendly online information and one-stop platform for many career development needs.

O*NET Interest Profiler: The O*NET Interest Profiler was developed by the U.S. Department of Labor, Employment and Training Administration as part of the O*NET database. It is a self-administered and self-scoring assessment of one's

LEARNING ACTIVITY 7.2

Instruct students to go to the O*Net website and explore the tests and other information provided at the site. Then ask them to each write a brief report to list the pros and cons of their experiences taking the instruments. Divide the class into dyads, and have them practice interpreting the results to each other. Then discuss as a whole class how these instruments and websites are helpful or not helpful for their career development needs.

work-related interests at no cost. It has both a paper (IP) and a computerized interest profiler (CIP). It can be administered alone or in conjunction with other O*Net Career Exploration tools. The Interests Profiler results are organized by Holland's six types, and the highest code among the six codes is viewed as the primary interest area. The score report guides users to explore their primary interest areas, including information about levels of preparation necessary for each job listed. One can find more information about O*Net at their website at http://www.onetcenter.org/overview.html?p=3. The IP and CIP have strengths in their easy and accessible use as well as to being applicable for a variety of people (Crockett, 2013).

Personality

Personality is considered to be a major factor related to one's career aspiration and career decision-making. Roe (1956), Super (1990), and Holland (1985) all stressed the impact of personality development on career development. The research studies about the relationships among personality, career interests, self-efficacy, decision making, career success, and satisfaction were popular for a long time (see Borgen & Lindley, 2003; Wang, Jome, Haase, & Bruch, 2006). However, very few instruments were developed for the purpose of career counseling per se; they were usually developed for personality research but used as a tool in studies about the relationship between personality and career related behaviors. In other words, the majority of personality instruments were not used by career counseling practitioners in their practice. One exception, however, is the increasing use of the Myers-Briggs Type Indicator (MBTI) in the career counseling field.

Myers-Briggs Type Indicator (MBTI): The MBTI was originally designed by Isabel Briggs Myers and Katherine Briggs in 1942 to measure personality types described by Jung and was used as a tool for understanding personal characteristics and interpersonal relationships. It has been used frequently in business settings for organizational improvement, team building, and reducing workplace conflict (Briggs Myers, McCaullery, Quenk, & Hammer, (2009). The MBTI is currently published by Consulting Psychology Press, and the most recent forms are Form M and Q. The MBTI report includes a profile with a 4-letter code indicating one aspect of four dichotomies—Extraversion (E)-Introversion (I), Sensing (S)-Intuition (N), Thinking (T)-Feeling (F), and Judging (J)-Perceiving (P). It is available in 21 different languages and has been studied globally. The MBTI can be jointly used with the SII for career counseling purposes (O'Hara, Thompson, Donnay, Morris, & Schaubhut, 2006). More details can be found at the CPP website: https://www.cpp .com/products/mbti/index.aspx.

Values and Needs

In this category, the assessment focuses on identifying the work values and needs that individuals want to satisfy through their work experiences. Brown (2012) noted that needs and values may be confused and that "values are learned or grow out of needs and are assumed to be a basic source of human motivation" (p. 152). Zunker (2002) classified value assessment into two types: (1) measuring work values and (2) measuring values associated with broader aspects of lifestyle. For example, regarding work values, it may be important to some clients to have work that allows them to be creative. Others may have a deep need to work where appreciation is expressed frequently and where they receive recognition for their efforts. Lifestyle values may include values such as wanting to work in a setting where one can bike to work or work at home. Other lifestyle values may have to do with work family balance or being able to live in a particular climate.

Minnesota Importance Questionnaire (MIQ): The MIQ (Rounds, Henly, Dawis, & Lofquist, 1981) was developed to apply the Theory of Work Adjustment that was based on the philosophy that persons' needs affect their choices of work environment, and the degree to which those needs are being met will directly affect individuals' satisfaction in that environment. The MIQ measures individual needs and values or occupational preference. It has six scales: achievement, comfort, status, altruism, safety, and autonomy, and each scale has associated needs. More information about the MIQ is located at http://www.psych.umn.edu/psylabs/vpr/miqinf.htm. The hierarchical taxonomy of MIQ allows counselors to use the results with clients at different career development stages, from general exploration to specific decisions on career choice or transition (Rounds & Jin, 2013). Despite the excellent reliability and validity of MIQ, the instrument is outdated in both research and application; however, the MIQ was revised for the O*NET system, generating the Work Importance Profiler and Work Importance Locator (WIP and WIL; Rounds & Jin, 2013).

The Value Scale: The Value Scale (Super & Neville, 1985 Work Importance Profiler and Work Importance Locator (WIP and WIL) was based on Super's Lifespan Career Development theory and measures one's occupational values including *ability utilization, economic security, personal development, economic rewards, lifestyle, altruism, social relations, working conditions, advancement, creativity, aesthetics, autonomy, prestige, cultural identity, social interactions, authority, variety, physical activity, risk,* and *physical prowess*. This instrument assesses general values one seeks to satisfy through various life roles. If these values cannot be satisfied through one's career, they would be satisfied via other life roles people assume. It has 105 items and has both ipsative and normative interpretations.

Kuder Work Values Assessment: The Kuder Work Values Assessment (KWVA) was formerly known as Super's Work Values (SWVI). There are subscales: workplace, innovation, accomplishment, income, and prestige. The KWVA is part of the Kuder

Career Planning System and available to middle school students as well as the adult population. It is also available in Spanish, Arabic, Korean, and Chinese. It is an Internet-based assessment, and the most recent user manual was published in 2012 (Harris-Bowlsbey et al., 2013). It was published by Kuder, Inc., and details can be found at https://www.kuder.com/solutions/kuder-career-planning-system/.

Decision Making

Sometimes people find it difficult to make a career decision not because they are unaware of their personality, needs, interests, or values but because they have difficulty making a decision or lack skills in the decision-making process. The three instruments introduced below aim to identify the issues related to making a career decision or function as diagnostic tools (Brown, 2012).

Career Decision Scale (CDS): The CDS developed by Samuel H. Osipow, aims to measure indecision and its antecedents. It has two subscales (certainty and indecision), but 16 out of 19 items are for scale indecision, and the certainty scale is more for a validity check (Osipow & Winer, 1996). The recent version was published in 1987 by Psychological Assessment Resources.

My Vocational Situation: This assessment developed by Holland, Daiger, and Power was developed to measure vocational identity, occupational information, and barriers. It is particularly designed to identify the lack of vocational identity. It has norm groups for both high school students and adults. It has been one of the most widely used career assessment tools for both practice and research. It also has been translated into many other languages. The latest source for this instrument publication is Psychological Assessment Resources.

Career Decision Self-Efficacy Scale (CDSES): The original form of the CDSES was developed by Taylor and Betz (1983) and a shortened form by Betz, Klein, and Taylor (1996). The original form contains 50 items with five subscales: self-appraisal, occupational information, goal setting, planning, and problem solving. The shortened form has 25 items and measures the same five domains as in the original form (Betz & Taylor, 2001). The CDSES is also widely used and researched (Luzzo, 1993) and has been researched in cross-cultural settings frequently as well (see Creed, Patton, & Watson, 2002; Zhang-Hampton, 2005).

Aptitudes, Skills, and Abilities

The assessment tools in this category share one common feature: measuring the competency of individuals to master job-related tasks in work settings. The term *aptitude* indicates potential to acquire knowledge and skills; however, as Brown (2012) argued, in reality, the aptitude tests still measure what is learned. These kinds of assessments were used widely in the early period of vocational guidance, particularly during the WWII, when matching people to the job dominated the field. The assessments in this category often are in the form of batteries. The following are two examples in this category:

Armed Services Vocational Aptitude Battery (ASVAB): The ASVAB was developed by the United States Department of Defense and is the most widely used multiple aptitude test battery in the world (Patrick, Samide, Muth, Comito, & Gross, 2013). The most recent update was the ASVAB Career Exploration Guide in 2012. The ASVAB Career Exploration program is a free and comprehensive career exploration and planning program including aptitude, interest inventory, and other structured career-related activities. The results could help individuals to explore occupations fit with their abilities and interests. It is also aimed at helping high school students or adults in planning a career in the military through finding the suitability of individuals to military careers. The ASVAB has seven composite scores and 10 subset scores. The seven composite scores are academic ability; math; verbal; mechanical and crafts; business and clerical; electronics and electrical; and health, social, and technology. The ASVAB is administered by a U.S. Department of Defense or U.S. Office of Personnel Management employee though security and school counselors typically coordinate the schedule with students. Taking the ASVAB is also exempt from the Family Education Rights and Privacy Act, but participation is voluntary (Patrick et al., 2013). Their website is located at http://www.official-asvab.com/index.htm.

O*NET Ability Profiler: The Ability Profiler developed by the U.S. Department of Labor, Employment and Training Administration, is part of the O*NET system with a whole-person approach. It is a multiple-aptitude battery that replaced an earlier Department of Labor instrument of ability, the General Aptitude Test Battery (GATB), and has timed measurement on nine basic abilities valuable in the workforce (Metz & Jones, 2013). The nine measured areas are the skills required in most occupations such as verbal ability, arithmetic reasoning, computation, spatial ability, form perception, clerical perception, motor coordination, finger dexterity, and manual dexterity. The score report has both a summary score and percentile ranks compared to the normed sample representing diverse gender, ethnicity, age, education levels, and employment status. The score report also provides a list of occupations that fit to their ability profile, but Kinnier and Gorin (2013) cautioned that the results of the ability profiler should not be used to rule in or out any specific occupations; rather, they should be used with other career assessment tools to guide further self-exploration and information seeking. More information can be found at the O*NET website at www.onetcenter.org.

Self-Efficacy

The application of Bandura's (1977) self-efficacy to career development was first done by Betz and Hackett in 1981 to account for women's underrepresentation in science and technology related careers. The measurement and research of self-efficacy in career development have been one of the most popular topics in the last three decades. One distinctive feature of measuring self-efficacy is that it should measure task specific or domain specific behaviors (Betz, 2000). So, instead of asking the individuals "How confident are you about becoming a teacher?" ask "How confident are you about instructing 9-year-old students in a classroom?" The CDSES, which focuses on skills for making a career decision, was described earlier. Other measures of self-efficacy are:

Skills Confidence Inventory: The inventory developed by Betz, Borgen, and Harmon (2005) is published by Consulting Psychology Press and measures specific activities involved in Holland's six occupational types. It has been found that combined use of Skills Confidence Inventory and Strong Interest Inventory results provided stronger prediction of career choice (Betz et al., 1996).

Career Counseling Self-Efficacy: The Career Counseling Self-Efficacy assessment was developed by O'Brien, Heppner, Flores, and Bikos (1997). This is not about career choice but measures the self-efficacy level of counselors in regard to providing career counseling. For instance, there is an item "Select an instrument to assess a career client's interests." From the sample items, one can tell that it also follows the concept that self-efficacy measurement needs to be task specific.

Career Maturity and Development

Assessing career maturity is often viewed as the same process as assessing career development. Based on Super's (1957) theory, the distinction can be made that career development is a continuous process, and career maturity is viewed as having age appropriate understanding and attitudes toward accomplishing career-related goals. Two instruments are well-known in this area:

Career Development Inventory (CDI): This inventory was developed by Super, Thompson, Lindeman, Jordaan, and Meyers (1981). The CDI's purpose is to measure readiness to make vocational and educational decisions, and it has five subsets: career planning, career exploration, decision making, knowledge of the world of work, and knowledge of preferred occupations. The fifth subset—knowledge of preferred occupations—is not recommended to be used with people who have not completed the eleventh grade (Glavin, 2013). This instrument is now available free at the website vocopher.com. There is a long history of using and researching CDI for application of Super's theory, but it seems an update of the instrument and research is needed (Pietrzak, 2013).

Career Maturity Inventory (CMI): The CMI (Crites & Savickas, 1995) was designed to be used mainly with sixth to twelfth graders. It aims to determine how ready a student is to make a career decision. More information can be found at the website vocopher.com.

Career Belief and Thoughts

The inventories and instruments in this category measure the views and thoughts held about career, career decision making, and barriers to career success. They can be used as diagnostic tools to understand the factors that make it difficult for people to make career decisions. Two examples are provided below:

Career Beliefs Inventory (CBI): The CBI by Krumboltz was designed to help people identify career beliefs that may hamper their accomplishment of career goals. It is published by Consulting Psychologists Press. The 10-page booklet provides immediate interpretation of scores and suggested action steps for overcoming barriers.

Career Thought Inventory: The Career Thought Inventory developed by Sampson, Peterson, Lenz, Reardon, and Saunders (1996) identifies dysfunctional thinking in career problem solving and decision making. It has three construct scales: decision-making confusion, commitment anxiety, and external conflict. It also provides recommendations for identified problems. It is published by Psychological Assessment Resources.

APPROPRIATE USE OF ASSESSMENT

Deciding whether assessment is the appropriate approach to help clients in making career decisions is often not that easy. Counselors need to be mindful of multiple factors before they make recommendations to clients. The client is the most important factor to consider in determining what kind of instruments should be chosen for career assessment. Because the purpose of assessment is to help clients understand themselves better, make reasonable career decisions, and effectively implement their career aspirations, assessment tools need to meet clients' needs and to accommodate clients' test-taking capacities. To accomplish these two goals, counselors need first to understand their clients. As stated before, it is not a good or ethical practice to administer a test without considering clients' welfare. For this reason, we caution against procedures that administer a prechosen set of instruments to all clients without any intake procedures that determine client needs. To maximize client benefits, counselors are expected to (a) carefully review the assessment options available, that is, whether a formal or informal assessment will serve the purpose better; (b) learn about clients' attitudes toward and conceptions of testing, because either too much or too little faith in the testing process and results could be problematic (If clients idolize inventoried results, it could cause distress when the results do not confirm their thinking. On the other hand, if clients do not believe in testing, it presents a challenge for counselors as well); and (c) gather information about clients' educational level, socioeconomic background, and cultural background, as these factors can have a significant impact on the trustworthiness of test results. For instance, if the client has an eighth grade reading level, but the test items require a twelfth grade reading level, it becomes questionable whether the assessment tool could accurately provide the reliable result that the client can use. The importance of considering clients' cultural backgrounds in determining assessment tools has been advocated by many researchers (see Leong & Hartung, 2000; Flores, Spanieman, & Obasi, 2003). The research on test validity has considerable evidence that many tests are subject to cultural bias; therefore, understanding clients' cultural values and beliefs, particularly about career, life, family, and gender roles, would be helpful in making career assessment decisions.

Counselors' theoretical orientation and frame of reference affect what kind and type of assessments they choose (Lonborg & Hackett, 2006; Lowman and Carson, 2000). Further, counselors' attitudes toward and understanding of career assessment in relation to helping clients could affect the process and interpretation of instruments and other assessment tools. Finally, but not least at all, counselors need to be mindful about their own qualifications and competency to administer and interpret the specific instruments chosen. Counselors should be familiar with the professional ethical codes as well as the state regulations regarding use of tests in counseling to ensure that the use of tests is within their scope of practice (Wilson, Tang, & Wilson, 2013).

CASE ILLUSTRATION 7.2
UNSURE WHAT TO DO NEXT

Dwane MacNeil came in the spring to the career center at his community college because he had completed a year of general education classes and wasn't sure what he should take in the upcoming fall semester. Dwane was an African-American 28-year-old man who presented himself confidently and had a professional appearance. He had worked for nine years as a clerk in a record store after completing high school. He was a responsible employee and was rewarded by promotions to assistant manager and later to manager of his branch. Recently, store sales have been dropping precipitously due to iTunes and similar Internet-based music. Dwane has enjoyed his job but thinks he would be wise to have alternate career plans. He is knowledgeable about and likes music but has little information about what else he might be interested in or in what else he might do well. He is clear about his transferable skills of dedication, persistence, and good verbal communication. He is less clear about his academic skills. He was a poor student in high school—though he says he didn't work very hard—and he has been an average student at the community college. His counselor decided that an interest inventory would be useful to help him identify some other possible career avenues. She decided that his college experience gave them enough information about his abilities that an ability test was not necessary. She also planned on spending time with Dwayne using some informal assessment tools such as a values card sort and a strengths check list. She also planned to use the transition model (Anderson, Goodman, & Schlossberg, 2012) to evaluate his needs as he faces the changes he anticipates.

Discussion Questions

1. What resources does Dwane possess? What barriers does he face?

2. Based Dwane's background, what assessment methods should be considered appropriate for him?

3. What kind of assessment tools would you select for Dwane if you were his counselor?

Technical quality and meaningfulness of the assessment to clients are two additional important factors to consider. More details about technical quality will be discussed in the subsequent section on selecting instruments. Regarding the meaningfulness of assessment to clients, we want to emphasize that a client's meaning-making process about career assessment and its outcome cannot be ignored. Why should the meaningfulness be considered for career assessment? Perhaps an example is helpful to explain the points here. A woman experiencing a mid-career change asks her counselor to explore her career options that combine her previous job skills and her current interest of changing to a different career path. It seems logical to assess her interests and values as well as her skill sets in order to help her find the next occupation she might enjoy. However, this woman has a negative view of standardized testing because of her past experiences, and she believes that those test results are only for young people who know nothing about the world of work and themselves. Should the counselor insist on using a test? What benefits will there be for this client if a formal assessment is forced? From the ecological counseling perspective (Cook, 2012), it is important for counselors to facilitate the meaning-making process with clients. If the testing is not meaningful to clients, how can clients' welfare be respected? Therefore, if the test process or results do not make sense to clients, counselors should consider alternative routes to help clients. Informal assessment is often more acceptable to clients who have been burned by past testing experiences.

PROCEDURE OF ASSESSMENT

Once the purposes of career assessment are determined, counselors need to decide what kind of assessment would be appropriate for their clients. In making this important decision, counselors should be mindful of both individual and contextual factors, the administration of assessment tools, and the process of interpretation of test results. The following discusses in detail the procedures involved in career assessment.

Process of Assessment

The process of career assessment can be linear or circular, depending on the goal and contextual factors that might influence the outcome of career counseling. The linear process means that there is a clearly defined beginning and ending phase for career assessment. Once the assessment is completed, it is done, and there is no need to revisit the process. Such a model is probably more prevalent in the trait-and-factor career counseling approach. The circular process indicates that the process of career assessment might be ongoing and recurrent along with the process of career counseling. In other words, career assessment is an integral part of career planning and intervention, and therefore, it cannot be totally isolated from the entire process of career counseling, which may repeat the assessment-implementation-evaluation-reassessment cycle several times until the clients are ready to move on. The relationship of assessment to the career planning process is illustrated by Niles and Harris-Bowlsbey (2009) in their 7-step career planning process:

1. Become aware of the need to make career decisions.

2. Learn about or reevaluate vocational self-concept.

3. Identify occupational alternatives.

4. Obtain information about the identified alternatives.

5. Make tentative choices from among available occupations.

6. Make educational choices.

7. Implement a vocational choice.

It is apparent that assessment is involved in the first 5 steps of this model in order to make educational and career decisions. Thus, depending on the goals and needs of clients, assessment could be performed at multiple times during the career counseling process and may be continuous as well. When we consider the kind of assessment done by counselors through observing, reflecting on thoughts and feelings, and checking the accuracy of perceptions, it becomes clear that assessment is an ongoing aspect of all counseling.

While it is necessary to keep in mind the integral role of career assessment in the career counseling process, it is also necessary to become aware of the process of performing career assessment with a client or a group of clients. The order of the process is as follows:

- Identify the needs of individuals: The first step is to determine what issues clients bring to the counseling; based on these presenting issues, counselors and clients collaborate to identify the goals and needs for career intervention that would benefit clients.

- Explore options for assessment tools: Once the needs and goals are identified, it is necessary to investigate the available assessment tools and evaluate which ones are appropriate for each client. It is important for counselors to carefully consider all the possible options and then choose the most appropriate ones. It is not a good practice to choose only the ones that counselors are familiar and comfortable with but that may not necessarily be the best ones for clients.

- Selecting the instruments: After carefully evaluating the possible instruments to use, counselors should select the most appropriate ones for the client, based on multiple factors. The details on how to select the instrument are discussed in the following section.

- Preparing the client for the assessment: It is important to discuss the assessment with the client to determine his or her expectations, readiness, preconceived ideas about the results, and so forth. Clients who are striving for the "right answers" during an interest inventory, for example, will have less useful results.

- Administer the assessment: Once the decision on what kind of assessment tool to use is made, counselors need to make arrangements for clients to take the test, which may or may not involve counselors themselves being the administrator. Some concerns need to be addressed in test administration (see the discussion later).

- Interpret the results of assessment: When the results of assessment become available, counselors need to schedule at least one and most often more sessions to explain and make meaning of the results with clients. This phase of testing is very critical, and it is not ethical to administer an instrument to clients without proper orientation or interpretation. Counselors should consider clients' views and readiness in their preparation for the interpretation session.

- Work with clients to make a decision about educational and career choices: The goal of interpretation is to make meaning of test scores and incorporate the information into the educational and career decisions; therefore, this phase should focus on how to use the insight gained through assessment and develop a plan that will help clients achieve their educational and career goals.

- Evaluation and follow up: This step is necessary for a complete process of assessment since it provides feedback about the outcome of implementation of the career decision, which is useful for modifying or revisiting the choice when needed. At a minimum, counselors can check on the status and progress of clients' career planning and action.

Issues in Administering Assessment Tools

It is essential that counselors build a trusting relationship with clients during the process of assessment since this is a critical element for a smooth and effective counseling process. Counselors should provide a safe environment and create a relaxing atmosphere for clients to be at their best during administration. By providing a friendly and interference-free testing environment, counselors fulfill their ethical responsibility of taking care of client welfare. In the same vein, if clients need accommodation for testing due to their disability status, counselors should ensure that such accommodation is provided. This effort may require collaboration with disability services in the organization.

During the test administration, counselors also need to be mindful of the use of unbiased language and avoid any misleading statements that could influence clients' behavior. Counselors should carefully conduct their demeanor to model professional behavior and show respect to clients.

Importance of Interpretation

The importance of interpretation cannot be emphasized enough. Without interpretation, scores or results are meaningless and will fail to serve the purposes of assessment. "Assessment is a waste of time and money if its results are not used to inform decision making" (Niles & Harris-Bowlsbey, 2005, p. 165). In order to inform decision making, counselors and clients jointly need to understand the meaning of scores from the instruments and draw inferences by integrating the results of the assessment with the personal and contextual factors pertaining to the client. Nile and Harris-Bowlsbey (2005) also suggested thinking about educational, occupational, and lifestyle implications of the assessment results for clients. They also stressed that there are no prescriptive answers as to how to do interpretation. Indeed, the poorest practice of interpretation is to tell clients this is the occupation that this inventory tells you to choose. This is irresponsible interpretation that counselors should avoid. Instead, counselors should get proper training to fully understand the instruments and be qualified to actually interpret the tests rather than being simply a message deliverer. It is important to be aware, however, that clients are hoping for answers. They may therefore hear, "This is the job for you" unless extreme care is taken to avoid that conclusion.

In regard to the specific steps in interpreting the assessment results, Anderson and Vandehey (2012) recommended the following four steps of interpretation:

(1) Review the results before the client comes in.

(2) Ask the client what it was like to take the inventory.

(3) Prepare a brief report with highlights in the first result-sharing session, and go over the results in several sessions, providing clients with time to digest the information.

(4) Interpret the instruments from the general to the specific.

Sometimes, clients may hold unrealistic hopes or focus too much on testing results, wishing that all their issues and questions will be answered by the test results. In this case, it is necessary for counselors to educate clients about the true nature of testing and explain why test results may not be the solution but only a tool to help counselors and clients find a solution. Anderson and Vandehey (2012) stated that interpretation should "facilitate a learning experience in which the client discovers how to apply assessment results for self-exploration and for integrating external information with career self-concept" (p 208).

SELECTING ASSESSMENT TOOLS

Selecting an appropriate instrument is critical to accomplishing the goal of career assessment. Besides the factors discussed above, it is important to do a thorough and careful test review of the instruments before making recommendations for clients. The test review provides counselors information about the technical properties of the test, thus making the selection more evidence-based. A thorough review of an assessment instrument should consider the following:

(a) The purpose of the test should fit the needs of the client, or the content of the instrument should pertain to the goals of assessment for the client.

(b) Psychometric properties of the instrument should be adequate for valid inferences. As the ACA ethical codes state, "counselors carefully consider the validity, reliability, psychometric limitations, and appropriateness of instruments when selecting assessments" (American Counseling Association, 2014, p. 11). Reliability and validity are the two most frequent psychometric qualities that counselors need to carefully review to ensure the technical quality of the tests. Reliability of a test gives information about how consistent the test scores are across time (Whiston, 2009). It is important to review the reliability coefficient of a test so that counselors and clients can interpret whether the test scores can be trusted or how much they can feel confident about the test results. Equally important is the validity of a test. Validity provides the information about whether the test measures what it is supposed to measure. For example, suppose a client needs to be assessed for her maturity in career development. The instrument needs to deliver information about individuals' maturity level on career development domains. No matter how reliable the results from this test are across time, it is not a valid instrument for career maturity unless it measures that construct. There are different kinds of validity as well, face, content, construct, and predictive being the most important. These are complicated concepts, and we recommend the reader consult a measurement text. What is most important to remember is that it is dangerous to use assessment results to prescribe career choice. They are appropriately used to open discussion, provide information, and encourage exploration.

(c) The assessment tools should be appropriate to clients' backgrounds including their age, developmental level, and gender and cultural background. To evaluate whether an assessment tool is appropriate for a particular client, counselors should read the manual carefully and pay particular attention to the norm group for various scales. It is also recommended for counselors to read relevant literature about the use of the instrument with different populations and subgroups.

MULTICULTURAL COUNSELING BOX 7.1

Alisia was a 40-year-old African-American female. She dropped out of high school and later earned her GED. She worked in various seasonal jobs since she was 16. Her longest job experiences was working in a fast food restaurant (10 years). She has done cleaning, housekeeping, landscaping, and worked as a nanny and nursing aid. Her last job was at a retail store, helping customers who had questions about finding particular merchandise. She loved this job, enjoyed the interaction with people, and was happy to see that her assistance truly helped people, but she was laid off last month. Now she came to a community service agency seeking some help to get her a more stable job. The counselor at the agency decided to do an assessment first before helping Alisia.

He decided to use the Strong Interest Inventory as it is a well-esteemed instrument in the field. He also decided to let Alisia take the MBTI because he is qualified to administer and interpret the test, and he thought the information gained from MBTI would be good for understanding Alisia's work styles.

What are potential violations of ethical obligations and multicultural competencies in this scenario? What would be your choice of assessment tools for Alisia that demonstrate cultural competency?

Tips for Consideration: Reading levels of clients, external validity of the instrument, purpose of the instrument, and the welfare of clients are critical.

(d) Consider practical issues, including ease of taking the assessment tools, trouble-free accessibility to scoring and reporting, reasonable costs within the budget range, and helpfulness of the test manual. These elements do not necessarily affect the psychometric quality of the instruments but will influence the test-taking performance and welfare of clients. If assessment tools are too difficult to take, clients might make errors that could affect the results or discourage clients from engaging in the testing process at all. If the test manual does not provide sufficient information about reliability, validity, or norm groups, it is difficult for counselors and clients to interpret the results adequately. Cost effectiveness is again an ethical responsibility that counselors should abide by to take care of clients. Having clients pay unnecessary expenses for testing is not in compliance with the ACA ethical codes.

Table 7.1 summarizes the elements counselors need to evaluate in test review. One can also check the National Career Development Association (NCDA) guidelines for career assessment review at the NCDA website (http://associationdatabase.com/aws/NCDA/pt/sp/guidelines).

Locating Assessment Information

Where can counselors find information about testing and assessment? How can counselors obtain a review copy of the actual assessment tool? To do a thorough test review, answering these questions is necessary. For wide-ranging information and review of assessment tools, the *Mental Measurements Yearbook*, published by Buro's Institute of Mental Measurement, is the most acknowledged database that hosts

TABLE 7.1 ■ Test Review Structure	
Test Review Structure	
General Information	Technical Considerations
Title, author, publisher	Normative sample
Test forms	Reliability
Type of test	Validity
Date of publication	General utility, evaluation
Cost, accessibility	Usefulness of the manual
Time required to administer	Comments of other reviewers
Purpose and nature of instrument	Additional comments
Purpose (as stated in test materials)	
Description of test (content, items, scores)	
Practical features (administrative requirements, format)	
Grade/age levels	
Use in counseling	

comprehensive information about all kinds of instruments, not just restricted to career assessment. Another source for locating test information is *Tests in Print*, which provides basic information about tests; however, it does not have detailed reviews available as in the *Mental Measurements Yearbook*. Other databases that do not focus on assessment but hold comprehensive scholarly products such as PsychInfo, ERIC, and Psychological Abstracts are also good sources for identifying instrument and test review information.

For assessment information specifically for career development, a very helpful resource is the NCDA publication, *A Counselor's Guide to Career Assessment Instruments* (Whitfield, Feller, & Wood, 2009; Wood & Hays, 2013). It contains test reviews and a comprehensive list of career assessment tools. The benefits of this book, compared to other sources, are that it is focused on only the career counseling domain and is specifically developed for career counseling and counselors.

Test publishers can also be another source for locating tests; however, one needs to be careful about this source because test publishers' marketing materials may not be as objective as they should be. Therefore, it is important to request an actual copy of the test before making a purchase decision. It is critical for counselors to review the independent reviews in addition to the information provided by the publisher. The following are the most common test publishers that have products relating to career development:

Consulting Psychologists Press: https://www.cpp.com/en/index.aspx

Educational Testing Service: https://www.ets.org

Pearson Assessments: http://www.pearsonassessments.com

Psychological Assessment Resources: http://www4.parinc.com

Western Psychological Services: http://www.wpspublish.com/app/authors/wpsauthors.aspx

Scholarly journals are another source for locating test information, particularly for noncommercial tests. Newly developed instruments usually will appear first in scholarly journals. Many test reviews as well as reliability and validity studies are also published in scholarly journals. The journals that most likely contain career assessment information are *Measurement and Evaluation in Counseling and Development, Educational and Psychological Measurement, Journal of Career Assessment, Journal of Vocational Behavior,* and *Career Development Quarterly.*

VARIETY OF METHODS FOR ASSESSMENT

For a long time, assessment was predominantly focused on objective and standardized assessment methods. The use of tests and inventories in counseling, and particularly to predict vocational satisfaction, was criticized by Goldman (1972) for its failure, and he advocated for alternatives. More recently, Healy (1990) noted that clients undergoing traditional testing and assessment were put into a passive role and had little voice in the process of career assessment. Healy also stated that this use of assessment was finding a fit between a person and a work environment without considering the contextual influence on a person's career behavior. These criticisms and the emergence of new career development theories have prompted the development of a variety of career assessment methods, including many nonstandardized assessment tools. The wide range of assessment methods not only provides diversity of types of assessment but also broadens the content of assessment. It also expanded theoretical frameworks and career counseling strategies, because some of the assessment procedures are an integral part of career intervention rather than a separate step in career counseling. The advancement in computer and Internet technology diversified assessment methods as well. This section presents various views of assessment types and the subsequent section will present examples of assessment content.

Formal Assessment

Formal assessment usually refers to tests or inventories that are standardized, and objective, and possess sound psychometric qualities. Alternative terms referring to this type of assessment include *traditional* and *quantitative*. These assessments are designed with scientific rigor (Niles & Harris-Bowlsbey, 2005). The advantages of this type of assessment are the empirical support of their psychometric qualities, which, lend more information about reliability and validity of these instruments. Accordingly, they are more trustworthy. However, these instruments have costs and require specific training to appropriately use and interpret them. The clients may depend on counselors to understand the meaning of the results. The clients are passive receivers of the information and have an active role in the process.

Informal Assessment

Informal assessment, also referred to as *qualitative, nontraditional, constructive,* or *integrative* assessment, typically focuses on meaning making associated with clients' development process. Both counselors and clients are actively involved in the assessment and interpretation process (Goldman, 1992; Neimeyer & Neimeyer, 1993). It often entails use of real-life experiences and is active, dynamic, and reconstructive (Peavy, 1996). As such, informal assessment has been shown to have a positive impact on clients' increased understanding and meaning making (Schultheiss, 2005; Whiston & Rahardja, 2005). Recently, efforts are underway to use established procedures to provide data for analysis for informal assessment (McMahon, Patton, & Watson, 2003). Whiston and Rahardja (2005) also suggested integration of both quantitative and qualitative methods in assessment, that is, helping clients explore meanings of scores from standardized instruments.

The category of informal assessment in career development is a broad one. It includes semiformal activities such as card sorts and checklists as well as interview protocols and observation. It can encompass art therapy techniques and outdoor activities. In other words, with this nomenclature, we are including all of the ways we assist clients to more clearly understand themselves and their options.

Let us provide some examples:

1. Card sorts: These are available commercially or can be homemade. One form is for each card to state the name of an occupation. A more detailed explanation, its Holland code, or other information may be on the back. The client is asked to sort the cards into three or five piles from most interesting to least. Some counselors like to use a fourth (or sixth) pile for "don't know enough to decide." Many find it best to force the distribution, allowing, for example, no more than one third of the cards to be in the middle. If a client shows few interests, you might want to ask them to put at least one third into the "might be interested" pile. If they are interested in everything, the reverse strategy might be useful. One idea is to begin the discussion with the rejected occupations, as there can be a lot learned from discovering why they are in that category. For example, many clients reject occupations they think they are not good at—perhaps an inaccurate self-image. Or they may believe that the work requires more education than they have or wish to get—which can open up a discussion of similar work in other settings or with lower educational requirements. The purpose of this assessment is to encourage discussion, not to arrive at a decision. Card sorts can also be used with values, interests, or other aspects of the career decision-making process.

2. Interview protocol: Savickas (September 4, 2003) described a process of helping clients understand their deepest needs and desires through a series of questions about early recollections and current activities. The questions are as follows:

a. Who do you admire? Who would you pattern your life after? Who did you admire growing up? How are you like this person? How are you different from this person?

b. Do you read any magazines regularly? Which ones?

c. What do you like to do in your free time?

d. Do you have a favorite saying or motto?

e. What are (were) your three favorite subjects in high school? What subjects did (do) you hate?

f. What is your earliest recollection?

Using these questions and follow-up discussion, counselors can help clients uncover what is important to them and create a narrative that describes the past and present and creates a future scenario. This kind of assessment bears little resemblance to taking a computer-scored instrument but can often achieve the same aims, that is, to assist clients in making career decisions.

3. Art therapy techniques: One example is to have clients create collages, from magazines or from their photo collections, on paper or on the computer. These collages can be representations of their past and their desired future. They can be videos or any of a number of other artistically oriented techniques. There is not space here to give complete instructions; we are presenting the idea here just to give you an idea of the range of creative options for informal assessments.

Finally, it is important to understand in looking at informal assessment vis a vis formal assessment, that it is not an either/or situation. Skilled career counselors use both as and when appropriate.

Computerized and Online Assessment

The use of computer technology in career assessment in the early days was mainly for scoring, storage, and data management. Increasingly sophisticated computer programming enables test developers to perform complex tasks in test construction, such as item analysis, individual response analysis, and generating profile reports based on the normed database. In fact, the Computer Assisted Career Guidance System (CACGS) has more than 40 years of history, and by now most of the CACGS programs are delivered via the

---

LEARNING ACTIVITY 7.3

Have the students create a deck of cards that lists needs and another deck that lists values that they believe are important for work settings. Ask the students to compare the two decks and determine if there is overlap in them.

Have the class discuss how these cards can be used in assessment for career exploration. Discuss advantages and disadvantages of using such card games versus taking a standardized instrument.

Internet. With personal computers and the Internet becoming more available to most people in the 21st century, administering tests via computer is more prevalent than ever before. Online testing or web-based testing also prompted many poor instruments, lacking in research or scrutiny. A more detailed presentation of information technology and its application in career development intervention will be presented in Chapter 9. Here we simply wish to remind readers that computer and Internet technology has provided more resources and choices for test development, administration, results presentation, and interpretation and that careful scrutiny needs to be applied to ensure that the tools used are appropriate and well done.

CULTURAL, ETHICAL, AND LEGAL CONCERNS OF USE OF ASSESSMENT

With the increasing diversity in educational settings and the labor force, it becomes central that counselors need to use assessment tools carefully to effectively serve the needs of a diverse population. Ethical, legal, and culturally competent use of career assessment is not only imperative because of the ethical codes of the professional organizations and the requirements of licensing boards but also because of the nature of the counseling profession, that is, to help individuals develop their potential to be productive citizens. Inappropriate use of career assessment can be detrimental to clients' welfare, as we illustrated in Case Illustration 7.1. In order to effectively use career assessment and

MULTICULTURAL COUNSELING BOX 7.2

Mariam is a 16-year-old high school student with average academic performance. She is interested in pursuing a career in marketing, but she is not sure if this is a good choice for her as she perceives herself as introverted and not very good at speaking in public. Mariam sees many of her Latina friends working in the health services fields and thinks she probably should do the same, but she is afraid she does not have the ability to take math and science courses. She became anxious after attending the college fair at her high school because she felt lost in the volume of information and options provided. She came to her school counselor for help.

As her school counselor, what factors would you consider in working with Mariam? What additional information would you need to be able to conceptualize her presenting issues? What approaches would you take to help Mariam so that she won't feel so anxious? How would you explain about taking these tests to Mariam?

Tips for conceptualization: As a Hispanic female teenager, Mariam probably faces some challenges of developmental and cultural issues, and her gender role development is still evolving, which may be in conflict between the mainstream and her traditional gender role definitions. Her family's socioeconomic status, educational levels of her parents, her personal characteristics, her style of problem solving, and why she is interested in marketing are not known. The college fair is supposed to help her, but instead, makes her more anxious. So, might assessment be used to be helpful rather than be harmful?

be mindful about cultural, ethical, and legal issues in using career assessment, counselors need to consult their professional associations' guidelines and codes of ethics, such as the following:

- Standards for Multicultural Assessment by Association for Assessment in Counseling and Education: http://aarc-counseling.org/assets/cms/uploads/files/AACE-AMCD.pdf

- Multicultural Counseling Competencies by the Association of Multicultural Counseling and Development, authored by Arredondo, Toporek, Brown, Jones, Locke, Sanchez, and Stadler (1996): https://www.counseling.org/Resources/Competencies/Multcultural_Competencies.pdf

- Career Counselor Assessment and Evaluation Competencies, a joint effort by both NCDA and the Association for Assessment in Counseling and Education, providing comprehensive details about career assessment competencies: http://aarc-counseling.org/assets/cms/uploads/files/AACE-NCDA.pdf

In addition, counselors need to keep abreast of the current literature on multicultural issues in career assessment. Many scholars advocated for considering cultural context in using career assessment and counseling (Blustein & Ellis, 2000; Flores et al., 2003; Leong & Hartung, 2000; Watson, Duarte and Glavin, 2005), and for translating, applying, and interpreting career assessment tools into various languages other than the original language in cross-cultural settings (Duarte & Rossier, 2008). A culturally appropriate assessment model, proposed by Flores et al. (2003), recommended that multicultural competencies, career competencies, and basic counseling skills should all be integrated in the career assessment process. Specifically, counselors should engage in culturally encompassing information gathering, formulating tentative hypotheses, culturally appropriate selection of instruments, culturally appropriate administration, cultural interpretation of assessment data, testing hypotheses, and recycling, if necessary.

Summary: Challenges and Opportunities

Assessment was considered a strength when a special issue of *Career Development Quarterly* in 2002 invited scholars to do a SWOT (strengths, weaknesses, opportunities, and threats) analysis of the career counseling field. The strength lies in the fact that it has a long history of using a variety of assessment tools in the career intervention procedure and that extensive research has supported development and application of assessment tools. Appropriate use of assessment in career counseling would help counselors facilitate better understanding of clients; it should broaden the outlook for clients rather than limit.

As the focus and definition of a career is changing along with the labor market's changing demand for skilled employees, so will career assessment need to expand and change (Lock & Hogan, 2000). Assessment methods and content have already increased over the last three decades as a result of the emergence of new career development theories and innovative technologies. This trend will continue because reliable and valid, and more importantly, *meaningful* assessments assist clients and counselors to develop better understanding of career development needs and action plans. Another trend is that assessment can encompass more than matching a person to a job. Rather, it can be used as a stimulus for new learning (Krumboltz and Jackson, 1993) or to expand learning opportunities (Krumboltz & Vidalakis, 2000). In addition, future assessments should provide information on personal flexibility, willingness and ability to multitask, self-initiative, and motivation (Harrington & Long, 2013).

In sum, career assessment is an integral part of the career counseling process and can be helpful in understanding clients, exploring career options, and evaluating the effectiveness of career interventions when the assessment is applied with cultural, legal, ethical, and contextual compliance.

Keystones

- Assessment is an integral part of career counseling and intervention and has historically played an important role in career intervention.

- Appropriate use of assessment following the ethical guidelines of both ACA and NCDA is required for all counselors.

- The purposes of career assessment are multiple and vary depending on individuals' needs and issues. Counselors need to use assessment only as is appropriate and beneficial to clients. It is highly recommended for counselors to understand clients' needs first and then determine whether or what assessment tools can be helpful to clients' career exploration and decision.

- Career assessment is not for prescribing a career choice but for facilitating exploration of individuals' career development. It is suggested that counselors need to demystify the testing results.

- Counselors need to consider both individual and contextual factors in selecting assessments as well as the psychometric properties.

- The procedure of assessment should include identifying the needs of individuals, exploring options for assessment tools, selecting the instruments, administering the instruments, interpreting the results, developing an action plan, and evaluating and following up.

- There are varieties of formal and informal assessment methods that measure various career development constructs. Counselors need to be aware of the advantages and disadvantages of each type and not be biased against either.

- It is important for counselors to consider clients' welfare in making a decision of whether, what, and how career assessment should be used for helping clients' career concerns.

Additional Resources

ERIC Clearinghouse of Assessment and Evaluation: http://ericae.net/testcol.htm

Mental Measurements Yearbook: http://buros .org/mental-measurements-yearbook

The Buros Center for Testing: http://www.unl .edu/buros

References

American Counseling Association. (2014). *ACA code of ethics*. Alexandria, VA: Author.

Anderson, M. L., Goodman, J., & Schlossberg, N. K. (2012). *Counseling adults in transition: Linking Schlossberg's theory with practice in a diverse world* (4th ed.). New York, NY: Springer.

Anderson, P., & Vandehey, M. (2012). *Career counseling and development in a global economy*. Belmont, CA: Brooks/Cole.

Arredondo, P., Toporek, M. S., Brown, S., Jones, J., Locke, D. C., Sanchez, J., & Stadler, H. (1996). *Operationalization of the multicultural counseling competencies*. Alexandria, VA: AMCD.

Bandura, A. (1977). Toward a unifying theory of behavior change. *Psychological Review, 89*, 191-125.

Betz, N. E. (2000). Self-efficacy theory as a basis of career assessment. *Journal of Career Assessment, 8*, 205-222.

Betz, N. E., Borgen, F. H., & Harmon, L. (2005). *Skills confidence inventory applications and technical guide* (2nd ed.). Palo Alto, CA: Consulting Psychologists Press.

Betz, N. E., & Hackett, G. (1981). The relationship of career-related self-efficacy expectations to perceived career options in college

women and men. *Journal of Counseling Psychology, 28*, 399-410.

Betz, N. E., Klein, K. L., & Taylor, K. M. (1996). Evaluation of a short form of the Career Decision-Making Self-Efficacy Scale. *Journal of Career Assessment, 4*, 413-428.

Betz, N. E., & Taylor, K. M. (2001). *Career Decision Self-Efficacy Scale: Technical manual*. Worthington, OH: Author.

Blustein, D., & Ellis, M. V. (2000). The cultural context of career assessment. *Journal of Career Assessment, 8*, 379-390.

Borgen, F. H., & Lindley, L. D. (2003). Optimal functioning in interests, self-efficacy, and personality. In W. B. Walsh (Ed.), *Counseling psychology and optimal human functioning* (pp. 55-91). Hillsdale, NJ: Lawrence Erlbaum Press.

Briggs Myers, I., McCaullery, M. H., Quenk, N. L., & Hammer, A. L. (2009). *MBTI manual: A guide to the development and use of Myers-Briggs type indicator instrument* (3rd ed.). Mountain View, CA: Consulting Psychology Press.

Brown, D. (2012). *Career information, career counseling, and career development* (10th ed.). Boston, MA: Pearson.

Ciechalski, J. C. (2009). Self-Directed Search (4th ed.). In E. A. Whitfield, R. W. Feller, & C.

Wood (Eds.), *A counselor's guide to career assessment instruments* (5th ed., pp.304-308). Broken Arrow, OK: National Career Development Association.

Cook, E. P. (2012). *Understanding people in context: The ecological perspective in counseling.* Alexandra, VA: American Counseling Association.

Creed, P. A., Patton, W., & Watson, M. B. (2002). Cross-cultural equivalence of the Career Decision-Making Self-Efficacy Scale and career commitment: An Australian and South African comparison. *Journal of Career Assessment, 10*, 327-342.

Crites, J., & Savickas, M. (1995). *Career Maturity Inventory.* Boulder, CO: Crites Career Consultation.

Crockett, S. A. (2013). O*Net interest profiler and computerized O*Net interest profiler. In C. Wood, & D. G. Hays (Eds.), *A counselor's guide to career assessment instruments* (6th ed., pp. 262-267). Broken Arrow, OK: National Career Development Association.

Donnay, D. A. C., Thompson, R. C., Morris, M. L., & Schaubhut, N. A. (2004). *Technical brief for the newly revised STRONG INTEREST INVENTORY® ASSESSMENT: Content, reliability, and validity.* Retrieved from https://www.cpp.com/Pdfs/StrongTechnicalBrief.pdf.

Duarte, M. D., & Rossier, J. (2008). Testing and assessment in an international context: Cross-and multicultural issues. In J. A., Athanasou, & R. Van Esbroech (Eds.), *International handbook of career guidance* (pp. 489-510). New York, NY: Springer.

Flores, L. Y., Spanierman, L. B., & Obasi, E. M. (2003). Ethical and professional issues in career assessment with diverse racial and ethnic groups. *Journal of Career Assessment, 11*, 76-95.

Gibbons, M. M. (2013). Kuder career planning system: Kuder career interest assessment, Kuder career confidence assessment, and Kuder work values assessment. In C. Wood, & D. G. Hays (Eds.), *A counselor's guide to career assessment instruments* (6th ed., pp. 208-210). Broken Arrow, OK: National Career Development Association.

Glavin, K. (2013). Career Development Inventory. In C. Wood, & D. G. Hays (Eds.), *A counselor's guide to career assessment instruments* (6th ed., p. 319). Broken Arrow, OK: National Career Development Association.

Goldman, L. (1972). Tests and counseling: The marriage that failed. *Measurement and Evaluation in Guidance, 4*, 213-220.

Goldman, L. (1992). Qualitative assessment: An approach for counselors. *Journal of Counseling and Development, 70*, 616-622.

Hansen, J. C., & Lee, W. V. (2007). Evidence of concurrent validity of SII scores for Asian American College students. *Journal of Career Assessment, 15*, 1-11.

Hansen, J. C., & Swanson, J. L. (1983). Stability of interests and the predictive and concurrent validity of the 1981 Strong-Campbell Interest Inventory for college majors. *Journal of Counseling Psychology, 30*, 194-201.

Harrington, T., & Long, J. (2013). The history of interest inventories and career assessment in career counseling. *The Career Development Quarterly, 61*, 83-92. doi:1002/j.2161-0045.2013.00039.x

Harris-Bowlsbey, J., Niles, S, Zytowski, D., Rayman, J., & Trusty, J. (2013). Kuder career planning system: Kuder career interest assessment, Kuder skills confidence assessment, and Kuder work values assessment. In C. Wood, & D. G. Hays (Eds.), *A counselor's guide to career assessment instruments* (6th ed., pp. 203-208). Broken Arrow, OK: National Career Development Association.

Healy, C. C. (1990). Reforming career appraisals to meet the needs of clients in the 1990s. *The Counseling Psychologists*, *18*, 214-226.

Holland, J. L. (1985). *Making vocational choices: A theory of career* (2nd ed). Englewood Cliffs, NJ: Prentice Hall.

Holland, J. L. (1994). *Self-directed Search (SDS), Form R*. Odessa, FL: Psychological Assessment Resources.

Isaacson, L. E., & Brown, D. (2000). *Career information, career counseling, and career development*. Boston, MA: Allyn & Bacon.

Jenkins, J. A. (2013). Strong interest inventory and skills confidence inventory. In C. Wood & D. G. Hays (Eds.), *A counselor's guide to career assessment instruments* (6th ed., pp. 280-284). Broken Arrow, OK: National Career Development Association.

Kinnier, R. T., & Gorin, J. (2013). O*net ability profiler. In C. Wood, & D. G. Hays (Eds.), *A counselor's guide to career assessment instruments* (6th ed., pp. 143-145). Broken Arrow, OK: National Career Development Association.

Krumboltz, J. D., & Jackson, M. A. (1993). Career assessment as a learning tool. *Journal of Career Assessment*, *1*, 393-409.

Krumboltz, J. D., & Vidalakis, N. K. (2000). Expanding learning opportunities using career assessment. *Journal of Career Assessment*, *8*, 315-327.

Larson, L. M., & Borgen, F. H. (2002). Convergence of vocational interests and personality: Examples in an adolescent gifted sample. *Journal of Vocational Behavior*, *60*, 91-112.

Leong, F. T. L., & Hartung, P. J. (2000). Cross-cultural career assessment: Review and prospects for the new millennium. *Journal of Career Assessment*, *8*, 391-401.

Lock, J., & Hogan, R. (2000). Expanding the focus of career assessment. *Journal of Career Assessment*, *8*, 411-417.

Lonborg, S. D., & Hackett, G. (2006). Expanding the focus of career assessment. *Journal of Career Assessment*, *8*, 411-417.

Lowman, R. L, & Carson, A. D. (2000). Integrating assessment data into career counseling. In D. Luzzo (Ed.), *Career counseling of college students: An empirical guide to strategies that work* (pp. 121-136). Washington DC: American Psychology Association.

Luzzo, D. A. (1993). Reliability and validity testing of the career decision-making self-efficacy scale. *Measurement and Evaluation in Counseling and Development*, *26*, 137-142.

McMahon, M. Patton, W., & Watson, M. (2003). Developing qualitative career assessment process. *Career Development Quarterly*, *51*, 194-202.

Metz, A. J., & Jones, J. (2013). Ability and aptitude assessment in career counseling. In S. D. Brown, & R. W. Lent (Eds.), *Career development and counseling: Putting theory and research to work* (2nd ed., pp. 449-476). Hoboken, NJ: Wiley.

Neimeyer, G. J., & Neimeyer, R. A. (1993). Defining the boundaries of constructivist assessment. In G. J. Neimeyer (Ed.),

Constructivist assessment: A casebook (pp. 1-30). Newbury Park, CA: Sage.

Niles, S. G., Harris-Bowlsbey, J. (2002). *Career development interventions in the 21st century.* Upper Saddle River, NJ: Pearson Merrill Prentice Hall.

Niles, S. G., Harris-Bowlsbey, J. (2005). *Career development interventions in the 21st century* (2nd ed.). Upper Saddle River, NJ: Pearson Merrill Prentice Hall.

Niles, S. G., Harris-Bowlsbey, J. (2009). *Career development interventions in the 21st century* (3rd ed.). Upper Saddle River, NJ: Pearson Merrill Prentice Hall.

O'Brien, K. M., Heppner, M. J., Flores, L. Y., & Bikos, L. H. (1997). The Career Counseling Self-Efficacy Scale: Instrument development and training applications. *Journal of Counseling Psychology, 44,* 20-31.

O'Hara, J. M., Thompson, R. C., Donnay, D. A. C., Morris, M. L., & Schaubhut, N. A. (August, 2006). *Correlating the newly revised Strong Interest Inventory® with the MBTI®.* Poster presented at the American Psychological Association Annual Conference, New Orleans, LA.

Osipow, S. H., & Winer, J. L. (1996). The use of the Career Decision Scale in career assessment. *Journal of Career Assessment, 4,* 117-130.

Patrick, J., Samide, J., Muth, D. L., Comito, N. S., & Gross, C. L. (2013). Armed services vocational aptitude battery career exploration program. In C. Wood, & D. G. Hays (Eds.), *A counselor's guide to career assessment instruments* (6th ed., pp. 127-133). Broken Arrow, OK: National Career Development Association.

Peavy, R. V. (1996). Constructivist career counseling and assessment. *Guidance and Counseling, 11,* 8-14.

Pietrzak, D. (2013). Career Development Inventory. In C. Wood, & D. G. Hays (Eds.), *A counselor's guide to career assessment instruments* (6th ed., pp. 320-323). Broken Arrow, OK: National Career Development Association.

Roe, A. (1956). *The psychology of occupations.* New York, NY: Wiley.

Rounds, J. B., Jr., Henly, G. A., Dawis, R. V., Lofquist, L. H., & Wiess, D. J. (1981). *Manual for the Minnesota Importance Questionnaire: A measure of needs and values.* Minneapolis: Vocational Psychology Research, University of Minnesota.

Rounds, J., & Jin, J. (2013). Nature, importance and assessment of needs and values. In S. D. Brown & R. W. Lent (Eds.), *Career development and counseling: Putting theory and research to work* (2nd ed., pp. 417-447). Hoboken, NJ: Wiley.

Sampson, J. O., Peterson, G. W., Lenz, J. G., Reardon, R. C., & Saunders, D. E. (1996). *Career Thoughts Inventory.* Odesa, FL: Psychological Assessment Resources.

Savickas, M. L. (2003, September 4). *The career theme interview.* Oral presentation to the International Association of Educational and Vocational Guidance, Berne, Switzerland.

Schlossberg, N. K., & Goodman, J. (1972). A woman's place: Children's sex stereotyping of occupations. *Vocational Guidance Quarterly, 20*(4), 266.

Schultheiss, D. E. P. (2005). Qualitative relational career assessment: A constructivist paradigm. *Journal of Career Assessment, 4,* 381-394.

Starkey, D. S., & Rasmus, S. D. (2006). Individual and group assessment and appraisal. In D. Capuzzi & M. D. Stauffer (Eds.), *Career counseling: Foundations, research, perspectives, and applications* (pp. 113-151). Boston, MA: Allyn & Bacon.

Super, D. E. (1957). *The psychology of careers*. New York, NY: Harper.

Super, D. E. (1990). A life-span, life-space approach to career development. In D. Brown & L. Brooks (Eds.), *Career choice and development: Applying contemporary theories to practice* (2nd ed.) (pp. 197-261). San Francisco, CA: Jossey-Bass.

Super, D.E., Thompson, A.S., Lindeman, R. H., Jordaan, J. P., & Meyers, R. A. (1981). *The Career Development Inventory*. Palo Alto, CA: Consulting Psychologists Press.

Tang, M. (2009). Examining the application of Holland's theory of vocational interests and choices of Chinese college students. *Journal of Career Assessment, 17,* 86-98.

Taylor, K. M., & Betz, N. E. (1983). Application of self-efficacy theory to the treatment of career indecision. *Journal of Vocational Behavior, 22,* 63-81.

Wang, N., Jome, L. M., Haase, R. F., & Bruch, M. A. (2006). The role of personality and career decision-making self-efficacy in the career choice commitment of college students *Journal of Career Assessment, 14,* 312-332.

Watson, M., Duarte, M. E., & Glavin, K. (2005). Cross-cultural perspectives on career assessment. *The Career Development Quarterly, 54,* 29-35.

Whiston, S. C. (2009). *Principles and application of assessment in counseling* (3rd ed.). Belmont, CA: Brooks/Cole-Cengage Learning.

Whiston, S. C., & Rahardja, D. (2005). Qualitative career assessment: An overview and analysis. *Journal of Career Assessment, 13,* 371-380.

Whitfield, E. A., Feller, R. W., & Wood, C. (Eds.). (2009). *A counselor's guide to career assessment instruments* (5th ed.). Broken Arrow, OK: National Career Development Association.

Wilson, F. R., Tang, M., & Wilson, C. R. (2013). Selecting career assessment instruments. In C. Wood & D. G. Hays (Eds.), *A counselor's guide to career assessment instruments* (6th ed., pp. 85-99). Broken Arrow, OK: National Career Development Association.

Wood, C., & Hays, D. G. (2013). *A counselor's guide to career assessment instruments* (6th ed.). Broken Arrow, OK: National Career Development Association.

Yang, W., Lance, C. E., & Hui, H. C. (2006). Psychometric properties of the Chinese Self-Directed Search (1994 ed.). *Journal of Vocational Behavior, 68,* 560-576.

Zhang-Hampton, N. Z. (2005). Testing for the structure of the Career Decision Self-Efficacy Scale-Short Form among Chinese college students. *Journal of Career Assessment, 13,* 98-113.

Zunker, V. G. (2002). *Career counseling: Applied concepts of life planning* (6th ed.). Pacific Grove, CA: Brooks/Cole.

CAREER COUNSELING STRATEGIES AND TECHNIQUES

After reading the first seven chapters, students should have a solid understanding of foundations of career development theories and practices. The career counseling process outlined in Chapter 6 illustrates how career intervention could be done from a procedure and structure perspective. This chapter will provide information on concrete and innovative strategies and techniques to facilitate career awareness, self-understanding, clarification of roles in life, and many other tasks clients encounter in their career development across the life span. These techniques can be used as parts of the career counseling process or alone for a particular career intervention with a specific goal. The implementation of these techniques requires counselors to be mindful of the cultural context of clients for a successful outcome.

LEARNING OBJECTIVES

After completing the reading and exercises provided in this chapter, you will be able to:

- describe the purpose of using career counseling techniques to help individuals explore and make their career choices,

- apply career counseling strategies to facilitate individuals' knowledge of self and the world of work,

- apply career counseling strategies to assist individuals to make optimal decisions for their education and career choices,

- identify strategies and techniques that would help individuals to be motivated and committed to take actions,

- develop action plans to help individuals implement their career decisions,

- design intervention strategies aimed at enhancing individuals' capacity for career entry and advancement,

- apply career development theories to use with facilitating life span career resilience, and

- recognize the ethical and multicultural implications to application of career counseling techniques to diverse populations in various settings.

PURPOSE OF CAREER COUNSELING TECHNIQUES

From the previous chapters, in which we have reviewed career development theories and the career counseling process, it is apparent that strategies and techniques are needed to apply the theoretical concepts during the career counseling process to help clients. Techniques and strategies are the practical tools for counselors to engage and empower clients to accomplish the goals identified for their career development. It is important to gain competency in using the techniques, but it is even more critical to be aware of the purpose of using these techniques, because any tools cannot be effective unless the persons using them have a clear understanding of what these techniques are aiming for and whether the design of these techniques aligns with the goals of intervention. It is similar to the example that a screwdriver is a wonderful tool, but it will not work well if you want to connect electronic wires in the basement. Most career development theories focus on explaining the constructs pertaining to career choice behavior, career decision making, and personal and contextual factors influencing vocational behavior and provide associated assessment tools to understand personal traits and behaviors pertaining to these aspects of career development. However, counselors need to be equipped with counseling techniques to actually apply these theories and assessment tools to help clients make their decision on career choices, to engage them in the career counseling process, and to motivate clients to take actions to implement their decisions. Techniques are helpful for counselors to be effective in the process of career counseling and to have successful career intervention with clients. It is necessary for counselors to gain competency in applying career counseling techniques so that they can accomplish the career counseling goals set for their clients; yet, it is equally important for clients to understand the purpose behind these techniques so that they can adapt, modify, and tailor the techniques to accommodate the clients' needs. In the same vein, career counseling techniques can only be effective when counselors understand the purpose of using techniques.

The purposes of using career counseling techniques are multifold, and some are based on certain career development theories; some are not. These objectives are typically aimed for by variety of techniques used in career counseling:

1. To facilitate clients' self-awareness about one's personality and related traits to career development

2. To increase clients' self-knowledge about the world of work for a better understanding of the interaction between the person and environment

3. To engage clients in exploring various roles and the intersection of these roles to career and life satisfaction

4. To motivate clients in challenging and difficult situations

5. To facilitate clients in developing knowledge and skills in career decision making

6. To assist clients to make a decision on educational, occupational, and life transition options

7. To encourage clients to take actions toward their career planning and implementation

8. To help clients be cognizant of and find solutions to career barriers

9. To assist clients to develop career capacity and resilience that are necessary to career development in the 21st century

The ultimate goal of career counseling is to facilitate individuals' awareness of career development needs, to develop competency in career decision making and implementation of choices, and to become capable of navigating and managing one's work and life to satisfaction. To accomplish these goals, a variety of strategies and techniques could be applied to help clients in the career counseling process. The first category of career counseling techniques focuses on career exploration with an aim to increase awareness of their own personal attributes and knowledge of the world of work as well as the interaction of personal and contextual influences on one's career development. The second category of career counseling techniques pertains to making career decisions, overcoming barriers, and taking actions to fulfill one's career aspirations. The third category is about preparing for entrance into the workforce and building one's career resilience and career adaptability.

STRATEGIES FACILITATING CAREER EXPLORATION

In this section, the career counseling techniques focusing on facilitating exploration of one's own characteristics and exploration of the work environment are reviewed. One of the major career development tasks is to understand oneself and how one's personal characteristics could be applied in the world of work for a satisfactory outcome for both individuals and the work environment. To do so, it is critical to have as much as possible accurate knowledge of individuals' own interests, values, needs, and aspirations as well as of requirements, expectations, and rewards of occupations. As discussed in Chapter 2, work and life are intertwined, so therefore, various roles one plays and how these roles interact with one's career identity needs to be clarified. Clearer understanding of oneself and world of work is essential for career decision making and other career development tasks.

Broaden Self-Awareness

A variety of standardized assessment tools are available that provide information about personal traits such as interests, values, needs, skills, and so on, which has been reviewed in Chapter 7. In this section, we will focus on career counseling techniques that can facilitate exploration and understanding of oneself in relation to career aspects that could have impacts on career choice and behavior. Some are structured interviews, and some are drawing exercises, but all are designed by their authors to engage clients in examining more closely who they are, the important aspects of their lives, and the capacities they have that may be unrecognized.

Career System Interview (McIlveen, McGregor-Bayne, Alcock, & Hjertum 2003): This structured interview is based on System Theory Framework (McMahon & Patton, 2006). The aim is to create a space in which the client can hear his or her voice openly talking about careers, so it is semistructured and requires counselors to use their basic counseling skills to guide the process for clients to share their understanding of how their interests, values, and self-concepts are influenced by various systems (e.g., family, school, community, culture, etc.). The Career System Interview also follows the construction theory; therefore, having clients make their meaning is what counselors need to do, or they let the client reach his or her own interpretation of the themes derived from the conversation.

The Life Career Assessment (LCA): This is a structured interview for career counseling proposed by Gysbers and Moore (1987) that aims to increase clients' career planning abilities. This approach requires counselors to use their knowledge of career development theories and counseling skills to identify and analyze life career themes and to understand and interpret the words and statements clients use to express their ideas, values, attitudes, and beliefs about themselves, others, and the world. The LCA structure (pp. 74-75) is presented as follows:

Career Assessment

1. Work experience (part/full-time, paid/unpaid)
   a. Last job
   b. Liked best about
   c. Disliked most about
   d. Same procedure with another job

2. Education or training progress and concerns
   a. General appraisal
   b. Liked best about
   c. Disliked most about
   d. Repeat for levels or types

3. Recreation
   a. Leisure-time activities
   b. Social life (within leisure context)
   c. Friends (within leisure context)

Typical Day

1. Dependent-independent

    a. Relies on others

    b. Insists on someone else making decisions

2. Systematic-spontaneous

    a. Stable routine

    b. Persistent and attentive

Strength and Obstacles

1. Three main strengths

    a. Resources at own disposal

    b. What do resources do for clients

2. Three main obstacles

    a. Related to strengths

    b. Related to themes

Summary

1. Agree on life themes

2. Use client's own words

3. Relate to goal setting

The goals of this interview guide are to identify a theme of clients' existing work and life and then to help clients translate these themes to the career domain. Gysbers and Moore (1987) did not suggest following the structure mechanically; instead, counselors should incorporate these formats into their own style and flow of the career counseling process. They also emphasized the importance of having clients summarize the interview information obtained because it would increase clients' self-awareness and motivation to work on their career planning.

People's needs actually are multifaceted and may not always be satisfied through work (Super, 1990). For instance, one loves music and enjoys artistic types of activities but chooses to work as an accountant to satisfy the needs for living and supporting family; this person may join a band or church choir as a hobby or leisure activity to satisfy his passion for music. Vice versa, someone may have a hard time figuring out his or her career interests, even after having done many career interest assessments. In this case, exploring one's hobby or leisure activities could be useful to understand one's needs, as one's leisure activities might provide insights to what kinds of career interests are implied.

The Lifelong Leisure Graph: This is a tool to help counselors discover one's leisure needs (Burlew, 1989). First, clients create a chart with a horizontal axis representing the

CASE ILLUSTRATION 8.1
STRUCTURED INTERVIEW

Ann was laid off from her previous job as a marketing director of a mid-sized company in a Midwest state. She is 38 years old, has a bachelor's degree in communications, and worked as a journalist before joining the marketing research company. Ann is married with two children, and her husband works at a local bank. She has been out of a job for three months, and at first, she enjoyed the down time since she had been busy all her life until this layoff occurred. However, she is becoming more and more irritated that she does not have a routine schedule, and she cannot bring income to the family so that they have to cut down their expenses. She tried to look for another marketing job but did not secure one. So, she sought career counseling and hoped to figure out what she should do—continue to look for a job or go back to school to change career tracks. The following illustrates the structured interview her counselor did with her:

Co: Tell me what you like best at your previous jobs.

Ann: I actually enjoyed the time I spent with customers, trying to understand their needs and expectations for our services. I also like to be around my colleagues who are creative and brainstorm ideas for projects. I like the team effort spirit. I can do management, but it drains my energy rather than giving me a sense of accomplishment.

Co: How about the parts you don't like about this job or the other previous jobs?

Ann: Well, like I said, the management part, I don't like to assume the responsibility for others, and don't like the pressure from my boss to control the budget and manage my subordinates. I also didn't like the frequent traveling I had to do. I'd rather stay home with my kids who need me more as they are in school now.

Co: What do you see as your strength from previous work experiences?

Ann: I am good at organization, building a collaborative and functional team, and I can also gain trust from my customers, and as matter of fact, most people I encountered. I seem to have a natural ability to make people feel comfortable and trusted. Because of my work, I can do budgeting and manage people and publication relations well.

Co: Anything else? How about your strength on school subjects or in other settings?

Ann: When I was in high school, I liked psychology, and I once considered majoring in psychology in college but eventually majored in communications because I heard that with a bachelor's degree in psychology you couldn't find good jobs, and you have to go all way to get a PhD, and I am not sure if I want to get a PhD. At my last work, I found I could understand others' problems easily; don't know if it's because I am good at listening to others or because I have better communication skills.

Co: What do you like to do during your off work time?

Ann: I like reading, watching movies, and, if there is time, I like the reading club in my community. We are a tight family; I like the family gathering time during the holidays. I like cooking and organizing a nice party for my family and friends.

Co: Describe an ideal way to spend your day.

Ann: That's hard. I think on a typical day, if I can work for some hours, no long commute, have a supportive and efficient work environment, enjoy my work, have a good relationship with colleagues, have interesting conversation at work, then come home, prepare meals for my family, spend fun time with kids, it's best not to worry about work at home.

Co: Use three words to describe your likes and dislikes, use three words to describe your strength and weakness, what are they?

Ann: Connection, creativity, freedom, and three dislikes would be authority, pressure, and lack of flexibility. Strength: understanding, organization, relating, and weakness, maybe fear of failure, cannot handle conflict, and hesitant.

Co: What are the resources that help you in your life? And what are the barriers in your life at this moment?

Ann: I have a supportive family, both my spouse and my extended family. I have many years of work experience, well this could be my barrier, too, since I have been in one industry for so long, and this industry is changing dramatically due to social media and the Internet. I am not sure my skill sets are still useful. I cannot relocate because of my family.

Discussion Questions:

1. What would you do next after this structured interview?
2. How would you help Ann to develop a plan for her next move?

age when the leisure activity first occurred, and the vertical axis representing their current level of interests, with the initials of the activity to the corresponding position on the chart. Secondly, the counselor and client review the chart together to identify which leisure activities remain at a high level of interest and which activities have dropped. Lastly, the counselor probes further about the parts of the activity or the specific activities that are interesting to the client. Burlew (1989) suggested that counselors could give this tool as an assignment for the client and discuss the graph at a later session to explore the meaning of it and how the information could be transformed to understand one's interests.

My Life and My Book: This activity is modified from several similar ideas based on a narrative approach, such as storied approach and my career chapter (McIlveen & Patton, 2007). The aim of this exercise is to inspire individuals to revisit where they come from and where they want to go, who influences them and what kind of life and person they want to be in the future. This writing exercise can be done as a homework assignment for an individual career counseling session and then the product can be reviewed by counselors and clients, or it can be done in groups where counselors or instructors facilitate the discussion about what everyone has learned from this exercise. The guideline for *My Life and My Book* is as follows: (a) Write a book about yourself; the first part is about your past up until today, give this section a title; (b) Besides you, who are the main characters of this section and what is your relationship to these people; (c) Write a memorable moment of your life during this time, and be sure to describe who was there with you; (d) Write about your current life, and give a title to this section; (e) Who are the main characters of this section, and what is your relationship with these people; (f) How would you describe your current daily life? Describe your favorable parts and your least favorable parts; (g) The last section of your book is about your future, give a title to this section; (h) Describe a scene that you envision yourself being part of and feeling really proud of, and who you are with at that scene; (i) What phrase would you like to be engraved on your tombstone? (j) Finally, what is the title of your book? After clients complete their book writing, counselors can discuss the reasons why they write the book the way they write, and what this writing exercise means to them.

Expand Knowledge of the World of Work

Most people acquire their understanding of occupations through their parents and other family members in early childhood and then probably through watching TV and other mass media. If you ask a preschool child what she or he wants to do in the future, the typical answer is some kind of work she or he has known from family members or a character learned from media. Many high school seniors or even college students have limited knowledge of existing occupations. While it may not be feasible for any individuals to know every single occupation available, it is necessary to know the major classifications of occupations and more importantly where and how one can gain more information about the occupations such as educational requirements, nature of the work involved, work conditions, and so on. Knowledge about the world of work is critical to making informed decisions on one's career choices. Career counselors need to create opportunities and assist clients to understand the nature of work and work environments so that they can gain a better understanding of the options they have.

Education-Based Activities

Gaining information about the work is better done earlier than later because it takes time and resources to obtain more and in-depth information. Starting early gives structure and time for young children to be exposed to as wide as possible variety of occupations and for adolescents and youth to explore and clarify the occupations appealing to them. School counselors can collaborate with school teachers to incorporate career awareness and exploration into class projects. For instance, an English teacher can ask students to write a report on three jobs, one from their family members, one from a favorite character in a movie or TV show, and one that they have never heard of before. Students can complete this report by interviewing the people or through doing the search on the Internet or both. The aggregate information can be shared with the entire class or grade for students to learn about more available jot titles and pertaining information. Besides infusing career exploration into class projects, school counselors can also organize schoolwide events for career awareness such as career day. Integrating career development content into education curriculum, for example, a career project on a selected industry or profession, through a career course or other subject courses, is implemented in Hong Kong high schools and has increased students' awareness and readiness for career exploration and planning (Cheung, 2015).

Other strategies that could increase knowledge of the world of work include co-op education and service learning. Service learning can be done in both high school and college settings and can be part of a single class or part of the entire curriculum. The advantage of service learning is twofold: on the one hand, students have the opportunity to apply their classroom learning to the real world for better knowledge acquisition and application; on the other hand, students can understand more about the work environment and relevant occupations in a particular setting. To successfully launch a service learning project, careful planning and coordination between instructors and partnering work sites is must. The aim of co-op education is for students to develop work ethics and skills through real jobs in the actual work settings. The co-op education is implemented more frequently in higher education settings because it focuses on linking work experiences in job settings to the discipline in which students are pursuing their degrees, so that students are ready to work after graduation. In a sense, it might be good for gaining comprehensive information of a particular occupation rather than obtaining basic information on variety of occupations.

Observation and Inquiry Activities

The above-suggested activities are all integrated as part of an educational curriculum. There are some strategies that require individuals to take initiative on their own to collect the information about the work world. Counselors can give these activities as homework assignments for clients and ask them to bring the results back to the subsequent session for discussion. One strategy is job shadowing. Through following a worker on a typical working day from the start to the end, individuals can get a glimpse of both the occupation of the person followed and work environment. This activity would be beneficial to adolescents who are exploring and clarifying their occupational choices or to those people who are considering a career change. Another common strategy is information interview. The aim of conducting an information interview is to collect the relevant information about a specific occupation through interviewing a person currently working in the field. To accomplish this activity, counselors need to provide some guidance on the sources where clients can contact to conduct the interview and questions that should be asked during the interview to obtain pertinent and valuable information. A practice interview in a counseling session might be helpful for those individuals who have anxiety of talking to a stranger.

While information interviews and job shadowing create the opportunity to obtain information about occupations, it takes a lot of time to be prepared and gather information on a few occupations, which means it would be ideal for someone who has already done exploration and needs clarification in the process of decision making. For those individuals who are still exploring, it might be more beneficial to gain more wide-ranging information in a relatively short time as the first step. To accomplish this goal, one can look into the resources for occupational information via printed materials or online publications. One reliable and comprehensive source is *Occupational Outlook Handbook* (OOH), first published in 1939 and continually published to date and now available as an online resource (http://www.bls.gov/ooh). The OOH lists information about occupation categories such as arts and design, business and finance, computer and information technology, and healthcare. One can search for specific job titles such as graphic designer, budget analyst, computer programmer, or nurse. Each occupational group or title presents information on median pay, entry level education required, job market projection, and summary of what this occupation does as well as work environment. Other helpful resources are O*NET Online (www.onetonlline.org), which is a comprehensive online service with career assessment, educational, and occupational information, and an education and career planning guide by ACT that provides interactive guidance about career exploration including assessment and descriptions of occupational categories classified by Holland's codes.

Clarification of Roles

Understanding oneself and the world of work is necessary but not sufficient to make a sound decision about one's career choice, because one still needs to understand her or his needs in relation to the world of work, or in other words, whether the roles a person plays or decides to play could be accommodated by the work world is an important aspect for making a career decision. Further, whether one can integrate her or his identified life roles with work is critical for career development and success. "How one presents oneself at work in different ways could be seen as a form of identity performance as individuals seek to shape, maintain, or revise their occupational identities" (Brown & Bimrose, 2015, p. 243). Therefore, clarifying one's identify or roles played at various settings is a must for one to find a healthy relationship between oneself and the outside world, including the work environment. As a matter of fact, many strategies in the career development literature do pay much attention to role clarification, value clarification, examining the contextual influences on one's role identification, and career identity.

LEARNING ACTIVITY 8.1
INFORMATION INQUIRY

Divide the class into small groups, and give each group a task to independently complete. The task is to locate information about a particular occupation of their choice. They can choose one or more of the following approaches: social media platform, online occupational outlook, state or federal government agencies, or websites from the university career development. Each group needs to report their findings regarding educational requirements, job outlook, income, characteristics and nature of work, location and/or work environment, advantages and disadvantages of this work, and who is in this occupational field and their satisfaction or views of the job.

After all the groups have completed the task, ask the class to discuss the following questions:

1. What is your learning about the occupation? Were there any surprises? What impresses you the most?

2. What was the process of obtaining the information? Which source tends to be more useful?

3. What insights did you gain from this exercise in regard to helping clients gather information about work?

FIGURE 8.1   ■   The Flower of Identity

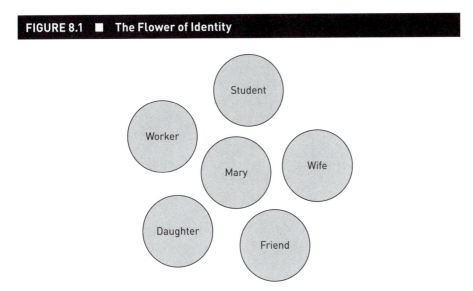

The Flower of Identity: This technique helps clients explore their career identities. It was developed by Cinamon (2015), with an aim to explore clients' identities and other roles in family and social life; to clarify values, importance, and personal meanings associated to these roles; and to help clients envision their work and family roles in the future. First, draw six circles, with one circle in the center, and have one's own name written in the central circle; for the other five circles, write different roles he or she holds currently (e.g., spouse or family member, student, friend). Then ask the individual to mark the most important role to him or her. Counselors should discuss with clients how they make their ranking order of the importance of roles and the meaning of these roles to clients.

The following illustrates three strategies that are commonly used in career counseling; the first two are also used as assessment tools as they provide a platform for clients to engage in exploring and clarifying their career aspirations. The third one is group work, the nature of which is optimal for persons to gain understanding of interaction of people and environment.

Career Genogram

Genogram is usually known as a technique in family counseling to visually illustrate the family relationships and dynamics. The career genogram is an adaptation of the family genogram (Bowen, 1980) to gather information about occupational status of family members. It is particularly useful in career counseling because the career genogram could generate in-depth information about work world views, possible environmental barriers, family-work role conflicts in the context of family tradition, and cultural heritage (Gysbers, Heppner, & Johnston, 2003). The career genogram, also known as occupational family tree, can also be used in K-12 school settings by school counselors and classroom teachers to help students become aware of the family influence on one's career choice (Dickson & Parmerlee, 1980). The process of constructing the genogram is as important as the actual product because individuals gain not only the family history regarding occupational information but also enhanced understanding of themselves in relation to their family members and family dynamics. Constructing a career genogram is particularly useful with students who struggle with work-family-socialization-identity issues as "career genograms provide real-life frameworks on which clients can visually organize and map perceptions of personal, work, and family concerns, task and stresses into meaningful representations in the context of overall family life and family history" (Gysbers et al., 2003, p. 209).

The method of constructing a career genogram has three steps according to Gysbers et al. (2003). First, explain the purpose of career genogram, for example, the influences of family to clients' values, barriers, and self-concepts. Second, explain how to construct the genogram showing the three generations of family members' occupational titles; start with oneself along with siblings, then add parents and uncles and aunts next to each parent (their siblings), and add grandparents from each side of parents. The square symbol is for male members and circle symbol is for female members; in each symbol, write name, age, occupational title (e.g., teacher, accountant, homemaker), and the relationship to oneself. The third step is to analyze the career genogram; counselors could help clients explore career issues by asking questions such as "What is your role in the family both now and when you grow up?" or "What are the dominant values in the family of origin?" or "Who are you most like in your family?" The questions are meant to facilitate clients to explore and clarify their needs, aspirations, values, and expectations and can be tailored to have a different focus depending on the nature of clients' presenting issues and career counseling goals.

The career genogram is a useful tool for people at the exploration stage of career development or for those who are not clear about themselves in regard to career choices. By examining the pattern of family members' careers, one can understand how historical, cultural, socioeconomic contexts, and family traditions could have impacts on their values and aspirations. Further, the career genogram can assist clients in exploring their identities in the context of their relationship to family and work. The interactive process of constructing and analyzing the career genogram can strengthen the working alliance between counselors and clients as well.

LEARNING ACTIVITY 8.2
CAREER GENOGRAM

Assign homework for class to develop a career genogram following the guidelines in the chapter. Then ask students in class to discuss the following questions:

(a)   Whose occupation from the genogram is most appealing to you, and why?

(b)   How do you view your career path in the context of your family and the society you grew up in (e.g., do you see any change in roles, functions, expectations of individuals)?

(c)   Reflect on what you have learned from developing this genogram.

Card Sort

Card sort is an example of a nonstandardized, nonnormed assessment tool, but it can also be used as a career counseling tool because both counselors and clients need to be actively engaged in activities in order to do card sort. It is interactive so that it is helpful to build working relationships; it is flexible so that it can be tailored to clients' needs; it has a structure that everyone is familiar with so that it is easy to use for both counselors and clients; and it is open-ended so that there are endless possibilities for counselors and clients to make the process meet their needs (Gysbers et al., 2003). Another advantage is immediacy, as the interaction between counselors and clients at the time of counseling intervention provides the opportunity for discussing the meaning and implications while sorting the cards.

Though card sort is typically designed as an assessment tool, it can also be used as an exploration activity because of its interactive and flexible characteristics. Some examples like The Missouri Occupational Card Sort (Gysbers et al., 2003) and The Career Values Card Sort (Knowdell, 1995) are developed to assess the occupational interests, values, or aspirations, but they can be used to facilitate clarification of roles for clients, too. For instance, when discussing the piles for "dislikes" and "likes" in occupational titles while using The Missouri Occupational Card Sort, counselors could ask the reasons for dislikes and likes and common themes for each pile; as a result, the clients may gain better understanding of what types of occupations they enjoy and how their perception and other factors of their life could influence their choices. As a matter of fact, counselors could even design their own card sort games to better serve the needs of their clients (Chope, 2015). The essential feature of card sort is to facilitate clients to sort a large number of options to a few manageable categories; therefore, counselors could work with clients to generate all the possibilities first and then create the titles for categories such as "never," "maybe," and "likely" to consider or to pursue; "always enjoy," "often enjoy," "seldom enjoy," and "never enjoy" for activities, academic subjects, topics, and so on. One can use construction paper or even recycle old business cards (assuming printed on one side only) to create card decks.

The benefits of using card sort as a tool to help clients explore their career options are multiple: increase individual's engagement, stimulate discussion about the reasons for choices, provide a supportive and relaxing environment for clients to work on career exploration, and provide immediate feedback (Gysbers & Moore, 1987). It reinforces the intuitive feelings when the visual presentation of the classified card deck is shown to the clients. It enhances work alliance and creativity, and it is cost effective.

Group Work

Group work has been an effective counseling approach widely used in many settings for various populations (Trotzer, 2006). Using groups for career education, guidance, and intervention is recognized as efficient because it allows for dissemination of the information to more people during the same time frame (Pyle, 2007). The group work also has the advantage of offering participants a platform to practice communication skills and interaction with diverse people in a safe environment, which is very critical to the development of work ethics in the future. Receiving and giving feedback to each other in groups is another benefit for individuals seeking career counseling because they can see the multiple perspectives and appreciate the variety of thoughts.

Career groups are commonly used in K-12 and college settings for career exploration and learning about career decision making. Groups can be used in elementary schools for increasing awareness of the world of work, for understanding self and the world of work in middle school, and for exploration and choice in high schools (Pyle, 2007). In community settings, large groups are used for workshop presentations to deliver training for job search assistance, and small groups are more often provided to individuals who need career exploration. More recently, corporations offer enhancement or career growth groups for employees to promote wellness and prevent burnout (Pyle, 2007). Not only can groups be applied at various settings, it is also conducive to apply to career theories. For instance, career construction theories have been implemented in group structure with adults (Di Fabio, 2013). Groups have been found to be effective with diverse populations (Pope, 1999). Pope (1999) argued that the nature of group work concords with Asian culture that values collaboration and team building.

Group work is particularly helpful for role clarification because the group setting provides opportunities for interpersonal connection, structured activities, experiential learning, and feedback exchange for one to explore, examine, and validate the cores issues and crystalize the options. It could help participants develop resilience, overcome barriers, and decrease career decision-making difficulties.

STRATEGIES FOR CAREER DECISION MAKING

Indecision and Decision Difficulties

As we all have experienced in our daily life, making a decision is not always easy. The difficulties of decision making could be due to multiple reasons. On one side, there are enormous volumes of information that people need to process in order to make an informed decision; on the other hand, decision making requires knowledge and skills that people may or may not have. Therefore, it becomes necessary to counselors to first understand what kinds of difficulties that impede clients making a decision and then help clients develop proper decision-making skills so that clients can apply the skills in the future. Although counselors can help clients make a choice for occupations, it would be better if not only a decision is made but clients could develop the competency in making a decision themselves for the future.

Factors Contributing to Decision-Making Difficulties: As stated above, there are many factors that contribute to the decision-making process. Gati and Levin (2014) have summarized six difficulties in career decision making. These six factors are as follows: (1) the large number of alternatives to choose from: this could be overwhelming especially in the midst of unprecedented accessibility because of the Internet and information system technology; (2) the many aspects of work that need to be taken into consideration for a decision: for example, work conditions, compensation, preparation time, and so on; (3) uncertainty about oneself and the world of work; (4) most career decisions require some compromise but people often are not ready to make the compromise; (5) external barriers such as societal expectation or parental expectation, particularly when these expectations are not the same as one's own aspiration; and (6) worry about the "wrong" decision: often one cannot decide because of fear of making a mistake when the cost of a mistake is too high, for example, spending too much money and time on a college degree that may not lead to a job.

In addition, the difficulties of making a decision could be related to emotional and personality factors. *Indecision* is viewed as a normative phase of development in the process of decision making and is temporary (Osipow, 1999). Most of the areas measured by the Career Decision Making Difficulties Questionnaire (CDDQ, Gati, Krausz, & Osipow, 1996) are examples of indecision: lack of readiness due to lack of motivation; lack of information about the decision-making process; lack of information about self; lack of information about occupations; lack of information about additional sources of information; and inconsistent information due to unreliable information, internal conflicts, and external conflicts. One category in CDDQ is general indecisiveness and dysfunctional belief. *Career indecisiveness* is viewed as related to emotional and personality-related characteristics and is chronic, pervasive, and much more difficult to change (Gati & Levin, 2014). Career indecisiveness involves three clusters: pessimistic view of decision making process and outcome, negative ramification of anxiety in career decision making (e.g., anxiety about process of making a decision, anxiety about the uncertainty and commitment to a choice, and anxiety about outcome), and developmental and personality-related aspects including general trait anxiety, low self-esteem, crystalized identity, and conflictual attachment and separation (Gati & Levin, 2014).

Understanding the reasons why people have difficulties in making a decision and factors that contribute to their difficulties would benefit counselors to better serve clients because the intervention could be more on target. Several assessment tools could be used to gain better understanding of the difficulties experienced by clients. For instance, CDDQ (Gati et al., 1996) would provide understanding about the kinds of difficulties that impede clients' decision making. Career Decision Scale (Osipow, Carney, & Barak, 1976) could assess the level of difficulties. Career Decision Making Profile (Gati, Gadassi, & Mashiah-Cohen, 2012), on the other hand, characterizes the decision-making behavior in 12 dimensions and integrates both personal and contextual influences to decision-making styles. With the information gathered through these tools, counselors can help clients more effectively.

Decision-Making Process

CIP Approach

The Cognitive Information Processing model developed by Sampson, Peterson, Lentz, and Reardon (1992) emphasizes the role of cognitive functioning in decision making and choices for educational options and occupations. The CASVE (communication, analysis, synthesis, valuing, execution) cycle (Peterson, Sampson, & Reardon, 1991), a guide to the decision-making process, aims at helping clients increase their problem and career decision-making skills and can be applied to educational, training, and occupational choices. The CASVE cycle starts by bringing the clients' awareness of the gap between their current status and desirable status in regard to internal and external cues. In other words, either external cues such as graduating from high school, losing employment, or relocating or internal cues such as unhappiness at work or guilt of neglecting family due to excessive work load, prompt people to become more aware of the gap between where they are and where they need to be; therefore, they need to make a choice to close this gap. The cycle ends at the time when people execute their decisions. The CASVE is the abbreviated name for each step of the approach as follows (based on Sampson, Reardon, Peterson, & Lentz 2004).

Communication: Identifying a gap between one's current state and desirable state, or awareness of need to make a choice. The choice could be educational or occupational or could be a decision to take an employment offer or not.

Analysis: Clarify their knowledge about themselves, including interests, values, skills, and knowledge about the work world and educational options, clarify their preferred or typical way of reaching a decision and solving problems, gain understanding of how career decision-making style influences their approach to solve the career-related problem, and then reflect and integrate what they have learned through the process. Thus, clients need to understand themselves and their options during this phase.

Synthesis: Expand or narrow the options so that there are no missing options and the number of options is manageable. In other words, the goal of synthesis is to generate many options from various sources and assessments to avoid missing any possible options and then review these options to narrow them down to manageable numbers for further evaluation.

Valuing: At this phase, clients evaluate the costs and effects of their short list of options (suggested by Sampson et al., 2004, to be three to five) pertaining to oneself and significant others in their life space. Then prioritize these options based on the optimal balance of cost and effects and set the first ranked option as the tentative choice.

Execution: Also known as implementing my choice and the final phrase of the cycle until starting a new cycle. At this time, clients need to act on their tentative first choice, which means enrolling in educational programs or finding a job, or moving to a different location. Execution could be reality testing before the final choice is made.

The CASVE approach was developed for making a decision on educational or occupational choices, but it can be applied to help individuals with other career-related decisions, such as employment problems or decisions, and it can be used to increase individuals' general decision-making and problem-solving skills (Sampson, Lentz, Reardon, & Peterson, 1999). This approach provides a step-by-step guide for clients to follow so that they can generate a few optimal options that integrate their own needs and other factors in their life for them to further explore and then implement their top choices. It is structured, logical, and sequential, and therefore, it is conducive to people and settings requiring systematic and planned intervention (e.g., K-12 career planning intervention). For some people, if motivation is an issue, other approaches may be applicable.

Resolution of Splits

This technique is useful when clients are torn between two or more choices. The purpose is to help people clarify the pros and cons of each choice through dramatic reenactment of two chairs and using chairs to represent the different parts of oneself. As described by Amundson (2003), counselors discuss with the client the elements of the activity and roles of counselors and clients first, and then ask the clients to identify the two aspects of self. Each chair represents the different competing aspects. Clients name the chair, and when siting in the chair, clients need to speak, feel, and act in the position of that perspective. Clients are encouraged to externalize their various issues and start the resolution process. Amundson (2003) stated that

> the interesting part of the back-and-forth movement is that clients often begin to experience change as the dialogue continues. At some point, the under-dog may speak out more forcefully or the top-dog begins to soften. Whatever the process, there can be a coming together of the two chairs into a more unified and integrated whole. Part of the difficulty for many counselors is waiting for this shift in perspective to occur. (p. 145)

It is important for counselors to set up appropriately without time pressure and to process the feelings and experiences clients have during the exercise. Sometimes it is more valuable to process the conflicting self needs than to actually find a solution.

Making a Decision for Educational and Occupational Choice

Even if people do not have indecision issues, making a choice on what occupations one should pursue or what majors one should choose when entering college is still a challenge for most people. Counselors can use a variety of intervention strategies and techniques to help K-16 students develop understanding and competency in making educational and occupational decisions. The techniques reviewed in the previous section focus on the process and clarifying a variety of roles. This section will review the strategies in identifying a reasonable decision for the future educational or career plan.

For a long time, the approaches to helping individuals make career choices were based on the trait-and-factor model, which focuses on matching personal traits and requirements of the work. These approaches aim at making a career choice by logic and rational process through assessment and solving problems. In these approaches, counselors play more direct roles, and clients are the recipients of the intervention. Other approaches, emerging in recent years, focus on the agency of individuals and acknowledge the influences of multisystems to one's career choice.

College students may be unprepared or underprepared for college study or life, and consequently face financial stress, longer time in college, and struggling in career decision making (Hughes, Gibbons, & Mynatt, 2013). Many traditional trait-factor approaches and techniques described in the career development theories have the advantage of helping those students who are more prone to standardized assessment and intervention based on trait-and-factor approach, but not everyone can be benefitted from such approaches; thus, more nonlinear or constructive methods might be helpful.

The narrative approaches have the advantages of empowering clients to use their own language and reflect on their own life experiences, gaining a broadened view and adaptability by clients, and allowing counselors and clients to work in collaboration to adjust to the changing dynamics of the work world. The intervention strategies that adopt the narrative approaches through online activities such as autobiography, role models, and personal mythology have had more positive impacts on individuals in regard to increasing certainty of making career decisions and reducing indecision (Severy, 2008).

The storied approach (Brott, 2001) is a postmodern career counseling approach that is based on the theory of constructivism and emphasizes the counseling relationship and process to generate story development. During the career counseling process, counselors use facilitating and clarifying questions to help clients to coconstruct, deconstruct, and construct stories. Coconstruction allows for counselors and clients to collaboratively reveal the past and present experiences; deconstruction is to unpack the stories to help clients gain different perspectives on their experiences; and construction is for clients to rewrite the stories for their future experiences. Brott (2001) suggested facilitating questions might be "What is your earliest memory before you began school?" and "Tell me about where you lived and the people you remember." These questions are meant to facilitate coconstruction of clients' stories about their beliefs, feelings, and attitudes. Reflective questions might include "What does that experience say about what's important to you?" and "What is the significance of that moment in your life?" or "What have you learned from that experience?" The reflective questions are for clients to explore and identify the meaning of their stories. Following the facilitating and reflective questions, counselors could help clients unpack the stories by asking about the space, time, and significant persons in their life experiences. During the construction phrase, preference questions ("Are you moving in your preferred direction?" "Pick between two possibilities.") can be asked to expand the stories to future directions. It is also suggested by Brott to ask *why* questions to understand clients' motivation and meaning of their stories, as well as the context in which these stories develop and are meaningful to clients.

Using the storied approach could be particularly helpful to those people who do not like standardized assessment or very directive approach for career decision making. The narrative nature of the storied approach facilitates clients' roles and responsibilities in exploration, identification, and direction of their own life experiences. It also focuses on collaboration between counselors and clients rather than giving diagnosis and solving problems for clients. Individuals' life stories are their experiences with the world, and clients are empowered by reauthoring their stories for their future.

Making a Decision for Life Transition

To help individuals clarify their career needs and concerns, one tool is systematic classification of career concerns (Niles, 1996). Help clients identify their career concerns on two dimensions: either important now or important later, controllable or uncontrollable. With this clarification, clients can then develop an action plan that falls in the important now and controllable category

Life Portrait

This strategy is based on Savickas's (2005, 2013) career construction theory and can help clients identify a theme from prior experiences. It is particularly helpful to those individuals who are not satisfied with their current jobs but uncertain of changes or directions of changes. Counselors listen to the stories and facilitate the process for clients to reconstruct the storylines that are hidden in their narratives; through this process, one can find the meaning of his or her life. Through asking clients to provide responses to these questions, counselors facilitate clients to craft a life portrait that connects their past to the future. According to Savickas (2011), the first step is to ask, "how can I be useful to you?"; career counseling goals are determined by clients' responses to this question. Then ask clients about their early recollections to identify core problems. The third step is to ask whom people admired before age 6 to understand self-concepts. The fourth step is to ask about favorite magazines, TV shows, and websites for information to determine settings that fit their lifestyle. The fifth question is to ask about their favorite character in a movie or story book; the responses provide information about how to solve a similar problem or transition to preferred settings. The sixth step is the analysis of favorite quotes or mottos clients provide, which gives hints to clients' self-help strategies. The last two steps are analysis of different fields of study and occupations that might be fitting and a review of the response to the original request for career counseling. The life portrait helps career counselors transform stories of clients into a grand narrative that expresses identity, current transition needs, and the envisioned future (Savickas, 2011).

The Pattern Identification Exercise

This technique could be used as an exploration exercise or as a tool to help clients identify their life theme, which may not be readily known to them. In Amundson's (2003) work on active engagement, the Pattern Identification Exercise has the following 4 steps:

1. Identify an activity from leisure, education, or work that is particularly enjoyable. Think about a specific time when it was very enjoyable or positive and a specific time when it was very negative.

2. Describe sequentially in detail these positive and negative experiences. List the descriptions in parallel columns on either side below the name of the activity. Then use questions to facilitate a full description of events, people involved, feelings, challenges, successes, outcomes, motivations, dynamics, and so on.

3. What does this information say about you as a person? Seek to draw out the client's goals, values, skills, personal style, interests, and so on. Look for patterns. List these points between the columns of information on the two experiences.

4. What does this suggest regarding your career choice or career planning? List these findings below the general characteristics

When career transition is anticipated and well planned, people have time to prepare and get ready for the transition. However, in the economic context nowadays, people often involuntarily change jobs or even are forced out of jobs. Involuntary transition is stressful and presents many challenges to individuals and their families. To help people deal with involuntary transition, counselors need to address both emotional and career issues. The immediate needs should be met by encouragement, support, and specific job search skills with a goal of securing a job. As a lifetime job is now rare, it is necessary for career counselors to help clients develop lifelong transition capacity by capitalizing on unplanned events to create learning opportunities and build their assets and confidence from past experiences (Krumboltz, Foley, & Cotter, 2013).

STRATEGIES FOR ACTION

To achieve identified career goals, one needs to take actions. The previous sections discussed strategies and techniques that aim to help people explore, understand, and clarify their career aspirations and then make a sound decision for their future. Once the decision is made, action is the natural next step to implement the decision. In many cases, the action is actually an integral part of the exploration and decision-making process, in which clients need to follow the plans and counselors' suggestions as part of the counseling process. Therefore, how to motivate clients to actively engage in action for a better career counseling intervention outcome becomes necessary for counselors to take into consideration. This section will review the counseling techniques that would assist counselors to motivate and engage clients in career exploration actions so that they are ready for career planning and implementation of the plans.

Enhancing Motivation and Overcoming Barriers

Engagement

Amundson (2003) proposed the idea of active engagement to enhance the career counseling process so that clients would be empowered to rediscover their creativity and reframe their thought and behavior. By this active engagement in the career counseling process, clients would have better sense of ownership and responsibility to take actions for their career exploration and decision making. Amundson used the term *careercraft* as a framework to explain that the career counseling process needs three elements—functionality, skills, and creativity—to make it beneficial for clients; in other words, career counseling needs to be practical (functionality), help clients achieve their goals and find their life and work satisfaction (skills), and be creative to facilitate clients' mastery of living their life (creativity). Active engagement is needed because the traditional structured, organized, logical process focuses on the results too much and neglects the innovation and flexibility that are equally important for career development, particularly in the fast-changing society of the 21st century. As the stability and loyalty of work settings has decreased, it is necessary for individuals to be in charge of their careers. Thus, having a mastery of developing one's career rather than being told to take a career path is a must.

Overcome Barriers

Career barriers could be both internal or external factors that impede one's career development (see, Crites, 1969; Luzzo, 1993) or, in many cases, the interaction of both intrapersonal and environmental conditions that make the career development trajectory difficult (Swanson & Tokar, 1991). The intrapersonal barriers could be lack of interests, lack of motivation, lack of maturity, lack of decision-making skills, or lack of urgency to take actions. The external barriers could be lack of resources; lack of support; discrimination based one's gender, race, class, religion, sexual orientation, or so on; or socioeconomic context at the time. Many of these external factors limit one's educational opportunities that are critical to understand and enter the workforce. Creating hope and more educational opportunities for people at disadvantages are recommended by many scholars

(Niles, Amundson, & Neault, 2011). In the realm of personal factors contributing to barriers, people sometimes cannot make decisions or take actions simply because they just feel stuck or cannot see how to make a change. In this case, creativity is needed; one needs to think outside of the box and move outside of his or her comfort zone. "Metaphors are one of the ways in which counselors can nurture and expand imagination and creative problem solving" (Amundson, 2015, p. 301). Using metaphors in the career counseling process can help clients describe more accurate feelings and enlighten an innovative way to gain insight to their problems as well as solutions.

Solution-focused therapy is a counseling approach that has become more recognized as an effective approach in mental health and school counseling settings. As this approach focuses on positive change and clients' strength and resources, it lends itself to being an efficacious method to work with clients lacking motivation. Burwell and Chen (2006) suggested that scaling questions, such as "What would be different if your . . . was at five instead of four?" to motivate clients take small steps for change. Counselors can use compliments to normalize clients' feelings and use bridging statements to link potential next steps with problem solutions. Counselors can also ask clients to identify exceptions to their problems to help clients build on their assets and miracle questions to encourage them aspire to their career potentials.

Once the barriers and decision-making difficulties are addressed, the next step is to take actions. After all, the goal of career counseling is to help clients implement their career decisions and move toward living a fulfilling life. All the theories of career development are helpful to understand vocational behavior and the decision-making process, but clients need to take actions to make the decision and change.

Taking Actions

Individual Career Plans

An individual career plan (ICP; Gysbers & Moore, 1987) is a comprehensive, developmental, person-centered, person-directed, and competency-based action plan for guiding clients in career planning. It is critical to consider both personal and contextual factors in one's life, one's maturity level, and readiness to change and to empower clients in the process of making this plan. The plan is organized around major life roles: worker role, consumer/citizen role, learner role, personal role, and family member role. In each section, record information, task performance, and action plan about the next step. Another component is the career growth action plan, which involves analyzing and synthesizing information recorded in the life role section and generating current and future actions. The action plan is for both short-range and long-range goals. Both resources such as support groups, role models, and barriers such as lack of experiences should be identified and noted. Each specific step for each area should be noted and monitored.

Individual Learning Plan

According to Happenstance Learning Theory (Krumboltz, 2015), learning occurs everywhere anytime if one takes action, meaning people should participate and use every opportunity presented to them, planned or unplanned, to explore their purpose of life. Krumoltz (2015) also stated that learning from one's action not from passive listening is the best way to solve one's career problems. The counselor's role in career counseling is therefore to help clients identify their concerns, empower clients to see their own learning from past actions, and learn to frame unplanned events into career opportunities and overcome barriers to action (Krumboltz, 2009). To overcome barriers to action, Krumboltz (2009) suggested asking these questions: "What do you believe is a first step you could take now to move closer to what you want?", "What action will you take before we meet next?", and "By what date and time will you e-mail me a report of your action?" It is apparent that these questions aim at holding individuals accountable to start taking actions leading toward change.

Commitment

Key Questions Technique

Guerriero and Allen (1998) proposed the use of asking key questions to mobilize the career counseling process that creates awareness and leads to solution. The way of asking these key questions is meant to bring clients' deeper understanding of the career issues and need to change. To ask a key question, the counselor needs to keep in mind that these questions should bring the results desired, either facilitating exploration or leading to solutions. Some key questions that a counselor could use to follow this technique include the following:

- What are your reasons for seeking career counseling?

- What are your expectations?

- What two or three career questions would you like to have answered as a result of the career counseling?

- What career path have you been following?

- What did we learn from your career history and career assessment process?

- What resources do you need to reach your goal?

- What is the next action you will take after today's session?

- What could be the barriers?

- How would you resolve them?

Experiential Learning

The importance of actively participating in activities for learning has been discussed previously. It is believed that experiential learning is more conducive to retaining and constructing knowledge than passive receiving of messages from instructors. Similarly, learning about career development and understanding oneself in regard to needs, values, interests, and career aspirations would also be better achieved through experiential learning. Coutlter-Kern et al. (2013) did a study about the impacts of service learning on college students' career decision making and found that those students who participated in service learning—helping high school students take career assessment tools and interpreting the results to high school students—have a better understanding of the career decision-making process than those who did not participate in the service learning activities. Another study found that middle school students who participated in service learning activities have shown an increase in career development, academic learning, and social/personal development (Stott & Jackson, 2005). Along with the notion of the social cognitive learning theory perspective (Lent, Brown, & Hackett 1994, 2002; Krumboltz, 1996), actual experiences in work-related activities are the optimal ways for people to obtain career-related knowledge and skill; therefore, counselors can encourage clients to participate in more activities in communities or work settings, to volunteer in various setting, and to shadow someone at work for a day. The experiential learning can also be accomplished through internships, cooperative education, service learning, class projects, and seasonal paid jobs. The learning-focused experiences expand the views of the work world and deepen understanding of the reality of working; it is not just a good item to be added to the resume, which certainly is helpful for job searching; it truly can provide valuable lessons for people to understand themselves and work environments. Counselors can collaborate with educators to create experiential learning opportunities for youth.

BUILDING CAREER RESILIENCE

In the context of the current socioeconomic structure, that is, increasing barriers for youth to secure stable and rewarding jobs, it is necessary for career intervention to go beyond conventional identifying of personal traits to corresponding work, decision making, and planning. While all the techniques reviewed in this chapter so far are useful, it is still necessary to consider helping individuals develop capacity and skill sets that are helpful through difficult times. As a matter fact, with the changing labor market becoming so volatile, career resilience and adaptability have become essential for everyone who wants to have a satisfying career development trajectory. The research has supported that proactive career behavior is helpful for managing careers in the adversity of the job market. Building one's assets or career resilience and career adaptability are two kinds of proactive career behaviors to be reviewed in this section.

Building Assets

Building assets refers to developing and strengthening skill sets and professionalism that are required in work settings. Engaging in proactive behavior in the process of career building increases employability. *Employability* is understood as individuals' likelihood of satisfactory performance in relation to employment prospects (Rothwell, 2015). The traits to enhance employability include knowledge, metacognition, skill requirement, social recognition, growth and flexibility, ability to cope with new job assignments, being fully engaged in work settings, and proactively creating and realizing opportunities (Rothwell, 2015). According to Greenleaf (2014), proactive career-building behaviors can significantly generate new or unforeseen opportunities for individuals that would eventually increase their chances of gaining employment. Examples of career-building behaviors are networking, interning, using career services on campus, obtaining work experiences via a part-time job or in different fields than one's academic training, and actively connecting with alumni. Greenleaf also suggested strategic action taking for college students, that is, taking initiatives to learn new knowledge about work and themselves and then becoming prepared for unplanned events. Taking initiative also means doing more than just what is expected or required in the work setting; by going beyond standard requirements, one takes an active and self-starting approach to work. Personal initiative, consistent with the organization's mission, has a long-term focus, is goal- and action-oriented, requires persistence in the face of barriers and setbacks, and is self-starting and proactive (Frese, Fay, Hilburger, Leng, & Tag, 1997).

In the midst of an uncertain job outlook, as we see in the 21st century, developing career resilience becomes essential. Career resilience, proposed by Borgen, Amundson, and Reuter (2004), is how people "cope with the everyday stress of working life" (p. 52), and is associated with internal locus of control, flexibility and creativity, sense of purpose, sense of hope and optimisms, courage and determination, positive self-talk, less self-blaming and feelings of guilt, and problem-solving skills. Borgen et al. used career portfolio in a training workshop to promote career development and enhance career resilience and found that the process, that is, explaining what artifacts should be included in the portfolio, the reasons for selected artifacts, and how to present and share them with others, is actually more helpful than the final product of the portfolio. The process, referred to by Borgen et al. as "portfolio thinking," enables people to see the breadth and depth of their past accomplishments, develop a vision to future possibilities, expand the ideas for use of portfolio, and become more aware of their own control, or in other words, career self-management.

Work-based education is another approach to foster resilience, particularly for disengaged youth (DeLuca et al., 2010). Work-based education serves as a protective factor for youth struggling with engagement in schools and learning. Having students learn the subject matter through participation in the actual work world not only provides engaging learning experiences for youth but also increases their school performance. The nature of work-based education is a guided and planned learning; therefore, it is effective for students to become motivated, engaged, and action oriented to delivering good performance, which helps them develop resilience that eventually helps youth in the context of difficulties. To have a successful work-based education, communication and peer and family support are essential.

Career Adaptability

In today's world of work, it has become unlikely that one can hold a job in one organization for a lifetime. More people change jobs more frequently, either out of choice or involuntarily. On average, the majority of people change jobs every five to seven years (Mulins, 2009). Career adaptability is a "psychological construct that denotes an individual's readiness and resources for coping with current and imminent vocational developmental tasks, occupational transitions, and personal traumas" (Savickas, 2005, p. 51). When a normative, linear career development path is no longer available, and no bonding or loyalty between employers and employees exists, and instead, short-term, part-time, project-based, and contingent contracts become the norm, individuals need to be their own agents and manage their careers (Savickas, 2015). Preparing individuals to expand possibilities and adapt to changes is how career counseling practitioners can help individuals become resilient in the midst of uncertainty and adversity.

Life design (Savickas, 2015) is a career counseling approach to help clients become more active and intentional in their own career development; therefore, it is a counseling process that empowers individuals to be prepared for uncertainty and adversity as they find the meaning of their life and identity even though holding various jobs and projects rather than being defined by their work.

> Life designing involves clients in a quest for a different perspective from which to review their lives and revise their narratives. Career counselors collaborate with clients to position a new perspective from which they may selectively and creatively reinterpret the past to shape an identity narrative that addresses transition and transformation. This reconstruction cumulates insights by repositioning client micronarrative or small stories into a macronarrative or autobiography. Revision should amplify the theme in a client's identity narrative to better direct, regulate, and sustain efforts to cope with current concerns, challenges, and choices. (Savickas, 2015, p. 138)

Counselors can use a career construction interview to facilitate clients telling their stories and understanding their life themes through these stories, and then forming intentions, setting goals, and making an action plan.

Adaptability is an attitude and capability that is helpful for individuals to acquire employability and resilience in the context of an unstable and uncertain world of work in the 21st century. The life design career counseling approach helps individuals identify their life themes, which are guide posts for their career paths despite adversity and a changing job environment. Life transition is the norm rather than a derail for the new generation workers, therefore, counselors need to help people develop adaptability to be prepared for change and transition.

Summary: Challenges and Opportunities

In the last few decades, career intervention has evolved from matching people to a job to guiding people to explore their options through various life stages, to helping them identify who they are and how they manage their career development. The career counseling strategies are more diversified and creative as the result of an emergence of many construction and system-oriented approaches in career intervention. In the same vein, with an increasing recognition of the importance of work and life integration, career counseling techniques are applied in various settings with diverse populations for multiple purposes. In other words, career counseling techniques are not merely for choosing an occupation or finding a job; they are actually a counseling intervention that can help people find meaning in their life and integrate life and work across the life span. Thus, counselors are well positioned to implement career intervention approaches that are truly based on wellness, prevention, and a strengths-based counseling model. The techniques reviewed in this chapter aim at increasing people's capacity to do better in self exploration, decision making, planning and action, transition, and employability; all these approaches are for career counseling but also beyond—they are also for helping people live a meaningful and flourishing life with purpose and autonomy.

It is also important to remember that career counseling techniques can only be beneficial when they are applied with ecological validity, that is, the techniques are appropriate to the personal and contextual characteristics of clients. Though the research in general supported that career intervention techniques can be applied cross-culturally (Feller, Russell & Whichard, 2005), it does not mean that individual differences can be neglected. For example, not everyone has access to technology or resources for career intervention; equitable and affordable services may not be available to some groups and communities. While these present challenges, there also lies the opportunities for counselors to advocate for expansion of career intervention to more people in a wide range of settings.

Keystones

- The goal of career intervention is to increase individuals' self-awareness of their own characteristics in relation to work environment and career development.

- To facilitate clients' understanding of their roles and the interaction of a variety of roles pertaining to their lives and work satisfactions, counselors can use formal assessment, structured interviews, informal assessment tools, and exploration activities.

- Counselors need to equip clients with knowledge and skills of the decision-making process in regard to planning, selecting, and implementing career choices.

- It is necessary for counselors to empower clients with understanding of and coping strategies to the barriers, obstacles, and unexpected events that can impede the implementation of their career decisions.

- Transition, whether voluntary or involuntary, is inevitable in one's career path; thus, it is important to help clients broaden career options and transferrable skills through engagement and intended effort of learning.

- Career adaptability and career resilience are critical for people to develop in order to thrive in the unstable work environment.

Additional Resources

Pope, M., & Minor, C. (2000). *Experiential activities for teaching career counseling classes and for facilitating groups*. Broken Arrow, OK: National Career Development Association.

References

Amundson, N. E. (2003). *Active engagement: Enhancing the career counseling process* (2nd ed.). Richmond, BC, Canada: Ergon Communications.

Amundson, N. E. (2015). Using metaphor in career intervention. In P. J. Hartung, M. L. Savickas, W. B. Walsh, P. J. Hartung, M. L. Savickas, & W. B. Walsh (Eds.), *APA handbook of career intervention, Volume 2: Applications* (pp. 293-304). Washington, D.C.: American Psychological Association. doi:10.1037/14439-022

Borgen, W. A., Amundson, N. E., & Reuter, J. (2004). Using portfolios to enhance career resilience. *Journal of Employment Counseling, 41*(2), 50-59. doi:10.1002/j.2161-1920.2004.tb00878.x

Bowen, M. (1980). *Key to the genogram.* Washington, DC: Georgetown University Hospital.

Brott, P. E. (2001). The storied approach: A post-modern perspective for career counseling. *Career Development Quarterly, 49*(4), 304-313. doi:10.1002/j.2161-0045.2001.tb00958.x

Brown, A., & Bimrose, J. (2015). Identity development. In P. J. Hartung, M. L. Savickas, W. B. Walsh, P. J. Hartung, M. L. Savickas & W. B. Walsh (Eds.), *APA handbook of career intervention: Vol. 1. foundations* (pp. 241-254). Washington, DC: American Psychological Association. doi:10.1037/14439-019

Burlew, L. D. (1989). The life-long leisure graph: A tool for leisure counseling. *Journal of Career Development, 15,* 164-173. doi:10.1177/0894845 38901500303

Burwell, R., & Chen, C. P. (2006). Applying the principles and techniques of solution-focused therapy to career counselling. *Counselling Psychology Quarterly, 19*(2), 189-203. doi:10.1080/09515070 600917761

Cheung, R. (2015). Fostering career exploration. In P. J. Hartung, M. L. Savickas, & W. B. Walsh, (Eds.), *APA handbook of career intervention* (pp. 157-169). Washington, DC: American Psychological Association. doi:10.1037/14439-012

Chope, R. C. (2015). Card sorts, sentence completions, and other qualitative assessments.

In P. J. Hartung, M. L. Savickas, & W. B. Walsh (Eds.), *APA handbook of career intervention, Volume 2: Applications* (pp. 71-84). Washington, DC: American Psychological Association. doi:10.1037/14439-006

Cinamon, R. G. (2015). The Synergy Project: A group career counseling intervention to enhance work-family management. In P. J. Hartung, M. L. Savickas, W. B. Walsh (Eds.), *APA handbook of career intervention, Volume 2: Applications* (pp. 413-425). Washington, DC: American Psychological Association. doi:10.1037/14439-030

Coulter-Kern, R.G., Coulter-Kern, O.E., Schenkel, A. A., Walker, D. R., and Fogle, K. L. (2013). Improving student's understanding of career decision making through service learning. *College Student Journal,* 306-311.

Crites, J. O. (1969). *Vocational psychology.* New York, NY: McGraw-Hill.

DeLuca, C., Hutchinson, N. L., deLugt, J. S., Beyer, W., Thornton, A., Versnel, J., . . . Munby, H. (2010). Learning in the workplace: Fostering resilience in disengaged youth. Work: *Journal of Prevention, Assessment & Rehabilitation, 36*(3), 305-319.

Di Fabio, A. (2013). Applying career construction in group-based contexts with adults. In A. Di Fabio, & J. G. Maree (Eds.), *Psychology of career counseling* (pp. 83-99). Hauppauge, NY: Nova Sciences.

Dickson, G. l, & Parmerlee, J. R. (1980). The occupational family tree: A career counseling technique. *School Counselor, 28,* 99-104.

Feller, R. W., Russell, M., & Whichard, J. A. (2005, September). Career techniques and interventions: themes from an international conversation. *Career Development Quarterly, 54*(1), 36. Retrieved from http://go.galegroup

.com.proxy.libraries.uc.edu/ps/i.do?p=
EAIM&sw=w&u=ucinc_main&v=2.1&it=r&
id=GALE%7CA136113357&sid=summon&
asid=91adab63b6829840ba6d5ad6261796fe.

Frese, M., Fay, D., Hilburger, T., Leng, K., &
Tag, A. (1997). The concept of personal initiative: Operationalization, reliability and
validity in two German samples. *Journal of
Occupational and Organizational Psychology,
70,* 139-161. doi:10.1111/j.2044-8325.1997
.tb00639.x

Gati, I., Gadassi, R., & Mashiah-Cohen, R.
(2012). Career decision-making profiles vs.
styles: Convergent and incremental validity. *Journal of Vocational Behavior, 81,* 2-16.
doi:10.1016/j.jvb.2012.03.004

Gati, I., Krausz, M., & Osipow, S. H. (1996). A taxonomy of career decision making. *Journal
of Counseling Psychology, 43,* 510-526.
doi:10.1037/0022.43.4.510.

Gati, I., & Levin, N. (2014). Counseling for career decision making difficulties: Measures and methods. *The Career Development Quarterly, 62*(2),
98-113. doi:10.1002/j.2161-0045.2014.00073.x

Greenleaf, A. T. (2014). Making the best of a bad
situation: Career counseling young adults in
the aftermath of the great recession. *Journal
of Employment Counseling, 51*(4), 158-169.
doi:10.1002/j.2161-1920.2014.00049.x

Guerriero, J. M., & Allen, R. G. (1998). *Key
questions in career counseling: Techniques
to deliver effective career counseling services.* Mahwah, NJ: Lawrence Erlbaum
Associates.

Gysbers, N. C., Heppner, M. J., & Johnston,
J. A. (2003). *Career counseling: Process,
issues, and techniques* (2nd ed.). Boston, MA:
Pearson.

Gysbers, N. C., & Moore, E. J. (1987). *Career
Counseling: Skills and techniques for practitioners.* Englewood Cliffs, NJ: Prentice Hall.

Hughes, A. N., Gibbons, M. M., & Mynatt, B.
(2013). Using narrative career counseling
with the underprepared college students.
Career Development Quarterly, 61, 40-49.

Knowdell, R. L. (1995). *Values card ad sort planning kit.* San Jose, CA: Career Research and
Testing.

Krumboltz, J. D. (1996). A learning theory of
career counseling. In M. L. Savickas &
W. B. Walsh (Eds.), *Handbook of career counseling theory and practice* (pp. 55-80). Palo
Alto: Davies-Black.

Krumboltz, J. D. (2009). The happenstance learning theory. *Journal of Career Assessment, 17*(2),
135-154. doi:10.1177/1069072708328861

Krumboltz, J. D. (2015). Practical career
counseling applications of the happenstance learning theory. In P. J. Hartung,
M. L. Savickas, W. B. Walsh (Eds.), *APA
handbook of career intervention, Volume 2:
Applications* (pp. 283-292). Washington,
DC: American Psychological Association.
doi:10.1037/14439-021

Krumboltz, J. D., Foley, P. F., & Cotter, E. W.
(2013). Applying the happenstance learning
theory to involuntary career transitions.
The Career Development Quarterly, 61, 15-26.
doi:10.1002/j.2161-0045.2013.00032.x

Lent, R. W., Brown, S. D., & Hackett, G. (1994).
Toward a unifying social cognitive theory
of career and academic interest, choice,
and performance [Monograph]. *Journal of
Vocational Behavior, 45,* 79–122.

Lent, R. W., Brown, S. D., & Hackett, G. (2002).
Social cognitive career theory. In D. Brown &

Associates (Eds.), *Career choice and development* (4th ed., pp. 255–311). San Francisco, CA: Jossey-Bass.

Luzzo, D. A. (1993). Value of career decision-making self-efficacy in predicting career decision-making attitudes and skills. *Journal of Counseling Psychology, 40*, 194-199.

McIlveen, P. McGregor-Bayne, H., Alcock, A., & Hjertum, E. (2003). Evaluation of a semi-structured career assessment interview derived from systems theory framework. *Australian Journal of Career Development, 12*, 33-41.

McIlveen, P., & Pattton, W. (2007). Narrative career counselling: Theory and exemplars of practice. *Australian Psychologist, 42*(3), 226-235. doi:10.1080/00050060701405592

McMahon, M., & Patton, W. (2006). The systems theory framework: A conceptual and practical amp for career counseling. In M. McMahon, & W. Patton (Eds.), *Career counseling: Constructive approaches* (pp. 94-109). London, UK: Routledge.

Mulins, J. (2009, Summer). Career planning the second time around. *Occupational Outlook Quarterly*. Retrieved from https://www.bls.gov/careeroutlook/2009/summer/art02.pdf.

Niles, S. G. (1996). Offering appraisal support within career counseling. *Journal of Employment Counseling, 33*(4), 163-173.

Niles, S. G., Amundson, N. E., & Neault, R. A. (2011). *Career flow: A hope-centered approach to career development*. Columbus, OH: Pearson.

Osipow, S. H. (1999). Assessing career indecision. *Journal of Vocational Behavior, 55*, 147-154. doi:10.1006/jvbe.1999.1704

Osipow, S. H., Carney, C. G., & Barak, A. (1976). A scale of educational and vocational undecidedness: A typological approach. *Journal of Vocational Behavior, 9*, 233-243.

Peterson, G. W., Sampson, J. P. Jr., & Reardon, R. C. (1991). *Career development and services: A cognitive approach*. Pacific Grove, CA: Brooks/Cole.

Pope, M. (1999). Applications of group career counseling techniques in Asian cultures. *Journal of Multicultural Counseling and Development, 27*, 18-30.

Pyle, K. R. (2007). *Group career counseling: Practice and principles*. Broken Arrow, OK: National Association of Career Development.

Rothwell, A. T. (2015). Employability. In P. J. Hartung, M. L. Savickas, W. B. Walsh (Eds.), *APA handbook of career intervention, Volume 2: Applications* (pp. 337-350). Washington, DC: American Psychological Association. doi:10.1037/14439-025

Sampson, J. P. Jr., Lentz, J. G., Reardon, R. C., & Peterson, G. W., (1999). A cognitive information processing approach to employment problem solving and decision making. *The Career Development Quarterly, 48*, 3-18.

Sampson, J. P. Jr., Peterson, G. W., Lentz, J. G., & Reardon, R. C. (1992). A cognitive approach to career services: Translating concepts into practice. *The Career Development Quarterly, 41*, 67-74.

Sampson, J. P., Reardon, R. C., Peterson, G. W., & Lentz, J. G. (2004). *Career counseling and services: A cognitive information processing approach*. Belmont, CA: Brooks/Cole-Thompson Learning.

Savickas, M. L. (2005). The theory and practice of career construction. In R. W. Lent, & S. D.

Brown (Eds.), *Career development and counseling: Putting theory and research to work* (pp. 129-143). Hoboken, NJ: John Wiley & Sons.

Savickas, M. L. (2011). *Career counseling.* Washington, DC: American Psychological Association.

Savickas, M. L. (2013). Career construction theory and practice. In S. D. Brown & R. W. Lent (Eds), *Career development and counseling; Putting theory and research to practice* (2nd ed., pp. 147-183). Hoboken, NJ: Wiley & Sons.

Savickas, M. L. (2015). Career counseling paradigms: Guiding, developing and designing. In P. J. Hartung, M. L. Savickas, & W. B. Walsh (Eds.), *APA Handbook of career intervention, Vol 1* (pp. 129-143). Retrieved from http://dx.dot.org/10.1037/14438-008.

Severy, L. E. (2008). Analysis of an online career narrative intervention: "What's My Story?" *Career Development Quarterly, 56,* 268-273.

Stott, K. A., & Jackson, A. P. (2005). Using service learning to achieve middle school comprehensive guidance program goals. *Professional School Counselor, 9*(2), 156-159.

Super, D. E. (1990). A life-span, life-space approach to career development. In D. Brown, & L. Brooks (Eds.), *Career choice and development: Applying contemporary theories to practice* (2nd eds., pp. 197-261). San Francisco, CA: Jossey-Bass.

Swanson, J. L., & Tokar, D. M. (1991). College students' perception of barriers to career development. *Journal of Vocational Behavior, 38,* 92-106.

Trotzer, J. P. (2006). *The counselor and the group: Integrating theory, training, and practice* (4th ed.). New York, NY: Routledge.

INFORMATION, TECHNOLOGY, AND CAREER INFORMATION RESOURCES

Julia Larson

In the 21st century, technology plays a critical role in our work and in our lives. However, it is important to keep in mind that technology, in all of its forms, is merely a tool to help you and your clients achieve your goals. New tools and resources can enrich the intervention experience for counselors as well as for clients, which means career practitioners need to retain a level of curiosity about the quality, applicability, and accessibility of these tools with a diverse client base. This chapter will introduce a variety of career-related resources and ways in which they might be used in career intervention. Though computer- and Internet-based resources grow in number and scope daily, counselors can evaluate resources in part by assessing how well the technology helps one achieve one's goals.

LEARNING OBJECTIVES

After completing the reading and exercises provided in this chapter, you will be able to:

- identify how technological tools and resources can play a role in career development engagement and practice;

- describe families of technologies that can be used to benefit a counseling practice;

- identify comprehensive vocational research sites to help clients to identify potential career options and make more informed career decisions;

- recommend technology resources to clients to address assessment, research, portfolio management, and social media and personal branding needs;

- evaluate a client's access to and literacy with technology; and

- assess the challenges and opportunities technology brings to both the client and counselor.

ROLE OF TECHNOLOGY IN CAREER DEVELOPMENT

The role of technology in counseling is as diverse as the tools and resources available. Career counselors routinely use technology in their work with individuals and groups; a range of educator and practitioner guidelines have been developed. These resources guide the development of programming, policies, and procedures for career counseling professionals. The Council for Accreditation of Counseling and Related Education Programs (CACREP; 2016) requires that prospective career counselors be capable of training others to use technology in the acquisition of career-related information. Competencies expected at both master's and doctoral degree levels are detailed by the Association for Counselor Education and Supervision (ACES, 2017). The National Board of Certified Counselors (NBCC, 2016) defines standards of practice for distance counseling, defining terms and listing methods of service delivery. Among the professional responsibilities of career development professionals are knowledge of these guidelines and awareness of changes and updates across time.

Ongoing technical training and integration of online and computer-based resources are required if career professionals are to maintain a high standard of service (Barak, 2003; Gati & Asulin-Peretz, 2011; Gore & Leuwerke, 2000; Kirk, 2000; Sampson & Lumsden, 2000). Training sources can be identified through professional organizations including NBCC, National Career Development Association (NCDA), and National Association of Colleges & Employers (NACE). Professional associations are also an excellent source for current information on the ever-evolving pool of resources, helping career professionals identify interventions appropriate for the population and situation.

As technology evolves, it also raises ethical issues. For example, e-mail, Skype, and FaceTime facilitate communication between counselor and client—regardless of distance. They also raise privacy and other issues that have the potential to compromise their use. Again, the guidelines put forth by CACREP, ACES, and NBCC provide career practitioners with the information needed to appropriately steer their actions—as well as establish policies, procedures, and best practices.

Another technology-centric issue is access. Access to computers, portable devices, smartphones, and the Internet varies widely. As a result, it is important for a counselor to learn the points of access in one's own organization and in the community of one's clients. Two organizations to include in this survey that offer wide community access are the public library system and the state workforce agency.

COUNSELOR-FOCUSED TECHNOLOGY

Distance communications technology, mentioned earlier, is not the only facet of career counseling that can benefit from technological advances. Whether practicing in a clinical, educational, or private practice setting, technology can enhance a counselor's

LEARNING ACTIVITY 9.1

Have the class divide into small groups. Ask the students to develop a group presentation for math majors at your institution called "Careers in Math." Ask the students to discuss the resources they will use to structure the presentation, the different tools they will introduce to the prospective students, and the format they will use to keep the group engaged.

group information delivery, administrative and management efficiency, program evaluation, and outcome measurement. This section is designed to share ways in which counselors may use familiar technology in a career counseling and education context, as well as introduce new possibilities. It is by no means an exhaustive review of all technologies that may be beneficial to a counseling practice.

- Presentation Software: Microsoft PowerPoint, still a dominant presentation platform, is being challenged by relative newcomers, including Prezi and SlideShare. Tools like Poll Everywhere may be used gather live audience or class presentation survey data in real time via text.

- Project Management: Cloud-based software including Zoho and Teamwork facilitate individual and team project management and collaboration, as well as daily tasks.

- Data Collection, Management, and Reporting: There are many reasons a counselor or practice may want to collect information electronically, including intake surveys, reflection assignments, and program evaluation surveys. Online programs including Survey Monkey and Qualtrics allow you to conduct surveys through a variety of mediums and develop reports that include statistical calculations and charts where appropriate. Data collected through these mediums can also be exported into software including Microsoft Excel or Access or Filemaker Pro. Organizations are also beginning to use dashboard technology like iDashboards to present data graphically.

Each of the technologies discussed above may be used in a variety of ways. As a counselor one has a responsibility to research any technological decision. Professional organizations and peer institutions can provide a wealth of information when one is weighing a decision about technology and invaluable support upon implementation. Only the earliest adopters need to experience a technology's pros and cons in a counseling practice alone.

CLIENT-FOCUSED TECHNOLOGY AND RESOURCES

Client-focused technology and resources can be divided into several categories: accessibility, assessment and reflection, research, document and portfolio development and management, and social media and personal branding. As systems become more integrated and complex, these are not the clearest of divisions, but they will be used in this section as a lens to better see how technology can enrich a counselor's engagement, support, and education of one's clients.

Computer-assisted career guidance is only one area of career counseling in which technology is useful. Web-based resources add significantly to the counselor's tools for assisting clients with aspects of job search ranging from identifying websites with relevant job listings to building an effective professional network. Following are some current web-based resources.

Accessibility Software

A variety of technologies have been developed to support individuals who have physical limitations that would otherwise limit or prohibit use of software programs and the Internet. For example, visually impaired clients may use Jaws® screen-reading software (Freedom Scientific, 2013) to surf the web, and those unable to use a keyboard may use Dragon speech recognition software to write career-related documents. Other technologies allow counselors to present information in diverse ways using a variety of mediums. When working with special needs clients, consult with a professional who has expertise in this area.

Assessment and Reflection

Assessment plays such a key role in career counseling, as discussed in Chapter 7, it is no surprise that it was one of the earliest areas of the field to employ technology. Technological advancement in the 1960s paved the way for the automation of portions of the career planning process (Harris-Bowlsbey & Sampson, 2001). Though we are fortunate to have moved beyond punch cards and bubble sheets in this arena, an understanding of the history and origins of such systems allows a counselor to make a more educated decision when recommending a particular assessment to a client.

Computer-Assisted Career Intervention Programs

Computer-Assisted Career Guidance Systems (CACGS) feature tools to assist clients in building knowledge of self and the world of work, evaluating and choosing from a variety of occupational options, planning for education, and entering the workforce. Tracing the development of these systems illustrates their dynamic and sometimes ephemeral nature. As an example, DISCOVER® (American College Testing Program, 1984), a preferred career-guidance system for decades, evolved into DISCOVER II during the 21st century and was decommissioned in 2012. Career decision makers now may access different career-guidance systems; following is a select list of options:

- Focus 2 (1987) includes assessment of client readiness, interests, values, personality, skills, and even leisure interests; information on college majors (customizable for your institution's majors) and over 1,000 careers; and planning and decision-making resources. College students are the target population for Focus 2. More information is available at https://www.focuscareer2.com. Focus 2 traces its roots to the 1967 Education and Career Exploration System (ECES) for which Donald Super served as lead architect (Tirpak & Schlosser, 2013).

- The Kuder® Career Planning System™ (KCPS) includes assessment of interests, skills, and values; information on career and postsecondary options; and tailored content for instructors of career development courses. Parental access, e-portfolio options, and lifelong account retention are among the features of this system. The products in the KCPS include Kuder® Galaxy™ for pre-kindergarten through fifth-grade students, Kuder® Navigator™ for middle school through high school students, and Kuder® Journey™ for postsecondary through adult users. KCPS has implemented research-based adaptations for numerous cultures outside the United States. The Kuder® Career Planning System™ traces its roots all the way back to the 1938 publication of the Kuder Preference Record.

- The System of Integrated Guidance & Information, SIGI³® (2004, Valpar International Corporation, http://www.valparint.com/sigi3.htm) began as SIGI (Katz, 1975), produced by Educational Testing Service, and became SIGIPlus before it was purchased in 2004 by Valpar, who "refreshed, updated, and renamed the program SIGI³" (http://www.valparint.com).

- TypeFocus™ Internet Inc. (1997) targets English-speaking career explorers ages 15+ and includes assessment of personality, interests, and values; and exploration of occupations (including green career options and growing careers). Users have access to a portfolio, goal-setting tools, job search resources, and work-life success tips.

Qualified practitioners may also access fee-based online assessments through the websites of Consulting Psychologists Press and Psychological Assessment Resources, Inc. These assessments address career-relevant variables ranging from interests and personality preferences to factors affecting major and career choice. Below are a few of the assessments to consider and their respective sources:

- Career Attitudes and Strategies Inventory (CASI)

- Career Decision Scale (CDS)

- Career Thoughts Inventory (CTI)

- Job Stress Survey (JSS)

- Myers Briggs Type Indicator (MBTI)

- Self-Directed Search (SDS)

- Strong Interest Inventory (SII)

- Vocational Preference Inventory (VPI)

Advantages and Disadvantages

Online resources for career intervention, including those introduced here, have distinct advantages and disadvantages. Betz and Turner (2011) detail advantages of Internet-based assessment as "online administration of measures, immediate scoring and profiling,

CASE ILLUSTRATION 9.1

Jìng Zhang came to career counseling for the first time. She is 40 years old and stepped out of the workforce 15 years ago to raise her three children. Prior to that time, she completed an associate's degree in liberal arts studies. While raising her three children, she has worked various part-time jobs: bank teller, substitute teacher, and partner in a small craft booth. She is comfortable using a computer and owns both a computer and smartphone.

Discussion Questions

1. Do you suggest that she take an online assessment?

2. If so, which one(s), and what assignment structure and follow-up do you suggest to Jìng?

and immediate access to relevant occupational information and to placement aids" (p. 275). Possible advantages noted by Gati and Asulin-Peretz (2011) include the following:

> First . . . the intervention can be carried out at the time, place, and pace most convenient for the individual. Second, interventions that are conducted online can eliminate or significantly reduce some of the factors discouraging individuals from seeking career counseling (e.g., lack of anonymity and stigma). Third, more sophisticated interventions provide documentation of the dialogue between the client and the system, which is available not only to the clients but also to the counselor. Fourth, online interventions are structured; thus, as opposed to face-to-face counseling, standardized evaluation can be carried out rather easily (Gati, Kleiman, Saka, & Zakai, 2003). Specifically, since every element of the intervention has a specific goal and procedure, it is clear what the expected change is. Finally, such interventions can be delivered at a fairly low cost (Herman, 2010). (p. 263)

Disadvantages emphasized by Gati and Asulin-Peretz (2011) range from limitations of the intervention to lack of client guidance in choosing the appropriate intervention to the absence of human expertise to guide the process. This list of disadvantages offers the career practitioner insights into potential prompts and follow-up that may help increase the benefits realized through completion of self-guided interventions.

From cumbersome and expensive in the 1960s to affordable and accessible today, computer-based career planning systems now face the challenges of the ongoing cost of development and the challenge of maintaining funding in an atmosphere where expectations of free or low-cost Internet resources are the norm and in which commercially developed applications of unverified validity proliferate (Harris-Bowlsbey & Sampson, 2001).

Research

The roots of vocational guidance actually implied the importance of information in the process of making career decisions, as Parsons's three-step approach requires gathering information about the work world and oneself. Individuals in the initial stages of identifying and exploring careers benefit from access to high-quality career-specific information. Gathering information on the careers under consideration allows individuals to identify career options with the greatest degree of correlation with their own interests, values, abilities, and the other essential personal characteristics and preferences.

Emerging technologies have the potential to significantly improve the quality and accessibility of career information. Access to information was once limited to the local library reference desk through large, indexed volumes or locally accessible newspapers; now similar information—and more—is available at the touch of a finger. From job banks featuring wide-ranging positions for a broad audience to career- and diversity-specific sites, the Internet brings access to resources to an entirely new level. Gone are the days of only searching the classified advertisements for jobs and asking friends for networking contacts. This section will identify resources for field, organization, role, individuals and networking contacts, position, salary, and research resources, as well as resources for specific populations. As explained at the opening of this section, many of the resources described below cross these boundaries. This section will begin with the more complex resources and transition to the more specialized.

Comprehensive

Comprehensive resources are available from the federal government as well as the private sector. These resources are inclusive of a variety of categories of information and are an excellent starting point for a counselor and client. The most commonly used resources from the federal government include the following:

- The *Dictionary of Occupational Titles* (DOT), now O*Net, provides career development professionals and consumers with essential data on a wide range of careers and job titles. Sponsored by the United States Department of Labor, O*Net (http://www.onetonline.org) has resources tailored to Spanish-speaking users, veterans, and career changers. O*Net has gone beyond basic career information to include interest assessment, training resources, and job listings.

- The *Occupational Outlook Handbook* (http://www.bls.gov/ooh) is produced by the United States Bureau of Labor Statistics. Its content, also available in Spanish, includes essential information about each career ranging from daily activities and typical environment to estimated income and requisite preparation.

- National and state labor data are available from the Department of Labor via the website of the Bureau of Labor Statistics and in the Occupational *Outlook Handbook*, mentioned above. National and state labor data are recommended as an integral part of career exploration and decision making; researching the existence of accessible and appropriate job opportunities is an important element in considering career options. Therefore, career exploration must include adequate attention to job outlook: Will the career exist when the job seeker is ready to begin working in the field of choice? Will there be sufficient position openings to ensure a reasonable chance of employment? How does geographic preference factor into the equation?

Comprehensive resources available from private companies include Career Builder and Monster. One resource worthy of particular mention is The Riley Guide. Founded in 1994 by a university librarian, Margaret Riley, now Margaret F. Dikel, while serving as a librarian at Worcester Polytechnic Institute, The Riley Guide™ is a career resource cornucopia that is well organized and comprehensive.

Field

Professional organizations' websites and LinkedIn pages often provide the best resources about their field and are as diverse as the fields they represent. The National Association of Social Workers, Society for Human Resource Management, and American Institute of Biological Sciences are but a few examples of field-focused sites. Professional organizations may be identified using O*Net or The Riley Guide. Vault and WetFeet are two commercial sites dedicated to providing multifield-specific information.

Organization

There are a variety of resources to research potential organizations for which to work. Directory resources include ReferenceUSA and LexisNexis, as well as field-specific directories, for example, *The Marketing Fact Book*. Community and university reference librarians and library sites can serve as excellent resources to navigate the many publications available.

Individual organizations may be initially researched on their own websites and social media channels. However, it is important to remember that their public face is purposefully designed by their marketing teams, so though they may be informative, their goal is to present the organization in the best possible light. Private companies like Glassdoor, Vault, and Wetfeet provide external reviews about specific corporate cultures and may also provide details about the organization's interviewing and hiring practices.

Role

The *Occupational Outlook Handbook* and O*Net provide the most comprehensive descriptions of specific jobs. Additional resources are available within professional organization websites; clients can also match skills and review job descriptions using LinkedIn, which will be more extensively addressed later in the chapter.

Individuals and Networking Contacts

Of course, individuals can be "Googled," but there are specific sites where you can find more comprehensive professional information. The most prominent is LinkedIn, which based on its own description in 2018 includes, "562 million members in over 200 countries and territories worldwide." It is an excellent site to research particular individuals and find individuals with whom to network. Also, high schools and colleges are increasingly hosting alumni networks and directories online, which can be valuable resources.

Position

There are hundreds of thousands of job posting websites, including organizations' recruiting pages. However, a significant number of sites are of poor quality and others are aggregators, like Indeed, pulling together many websites' openings in one place. Counselors may turn to workforce centers and libraries to learn about nationally and locally focused listings of vetted sites. National posting sites include:

- USAJobs
- Simply Hired
- Indeed
- Idealist

Professional organization websites, mentioned earlier in the chapter, can also be a resource for postings as are field-specific posting sites. For example, sources for health care include Nurse.com, the National Assembly of Health and Human Services, and the National Institutes of Health. When it comes to pursuing job postings, leave no stone unturned.

Salary

Many sites include salary information, including those that have already been mentioned, including the Department of Labor, Glassdoor, and Salary.com. For new college graduates, the National Association of Colleges and Employers produces comprehensive U.S. salary data by area of study and field.

Specific Populations

There are also a variety of resources for diverse populations, including professional groups, like the National Association of Black Journalists; overarching diversity-focused sites including the Black Collegian and WorkplaceDiversity; population-focused sites like Out and Equal, focused on LGBT and allies jobseekers; and Getting Hired for individuals with disabilities.

Document and Portfolio Management

Job search involves numerous tools including a targeted resume and effective correspondence. Depending upon the career aspiration, recent additions to the job search

LEARNING ACTIVITY 9.2

Have the class work in small groups to work on the case of Tiana Jason. Tiana is a sophomore in college interested in pursuing a career that connects with her astronomy and astrophysics major. Her employment experience to date includes a research internship with a physics professor and volunteering at an animal shelter.

Over the course of multiple meetings with Tiana, she shares that she has been diagnosed with Asperger Syndrome. The counselor will be meeting with Tiana on a weekly basis to help her move forward in her career development. Create a two-month work plan for Tiana that incorporates online research tools and resources.

have gone far beyond the basic tools and may include candidate-developed websites or portfolios, some including blogs, video content, charts, graphs, or the ability to integrate links to social media, just to list a few. Users are advised to review terms of use and policies for all online resources. While many commercial options exist, the following list highlights a few resources offering users basic online portfolio development services free of charge:

Beyond.com (http://www.beyond.com) provides tools to build an online portfolio, with options to integrate functions such as blogging, an online store, social media, and job search.

College Central (http://www.collegecentral.com) integrates the job search function with online portfolio development tools with resources for students, alumni, employers, and career services.

Google sites (http://sites.google.com) facilitates the development of a website, with options to include wikis and to enable video chats and document sharing. The availability of site templates and access in 38 languages are among the Google sites features.

Visual CV (http://www.visualcv.com) facilitates development of an online resume with options to include videos, charts, and data. Visual CV also allows the user to build more than one online resume in order to target a variety of career objectives.

Weebly (http://www.weebly.com) features drag-and-drop website construction, blogging, and online store options. Weebly is available in 11 languages.

WordPress (http://www.wordpress.org) began as a blogging tool but now offers users a wide array of tools to create websites, portfolios, and more. Available in 70 languages, WordPress continues to expand in functionality while remaining free of charge.

Social Media and Personal Branding

Social media has brought new tools to the discovery process whether discovery refers to career exploration and choice or to job opportunities. Resources like LinkedIn and Twitter offer ways to initiate and expand your professional network, gather important company and industry information, and increase visibility within your field of choice. Due to the dynamic nature of social media, the following information has the potential to be outdated before it is even published. This section, therefore, will focus primarily on

LEARNING ACTIVITY 9.3

Choose a website/online-portfolio-building resource, and build a personal website that integrates at least one additional function (blog, online store, other).

LEARNING ACTIVITY 9.4

Search for your own name on the Internet. Stay on top of your online presence by setting up a Google Alert for yourself, so that you are notified any time your name appears on the web.

two resources: LinkedIn and Twitter. Career development professionals are encouraged to continue building knowledge, understanding, and use of these tools (as well as related or future tools) for personal professional growth, as well as for the improvement of services to clients.

Digital footprint is a term that describes a wide range of Internet-based transactions, from LinkedIn profile content and Tweets to Facebook photographs and newspaper articles. Careful and consistent use of social media—and a positive, professional social media presence—may elevate one candidate above a close rival. Consider the results when an employer uses Google to search the Internet for your name.

Launched in 2003, LinkedIn currently sports over 562 million users. Used by individuals across 200 countries and territories worldwide (LinkedIn, 2018), LinkedIn is primarily used for professional networking, offering users the opportunity to go beyond sharing resume-typical personal information and work history. LinkedIn adds options to incorporate personal information (a professional-quality photograph and list of personal interests), accomplishments (lists of awards and honors), as well as presentations and projects. The benefits of using this resource may include the following:

1. Connecting with professionals in your field or intended field for purposes of facilitating career exploration or professional networking

2. Maintaining and building professional collegial relationships over time

3. Following the activity of select companies, organizations, or institutions of interest

4. Joining LinkedIn groups in your areas of interest to further your knowledge of the field, increase awareness of industry trends and activity, and establish yourself within your field by actively participating in discussions

5. Maintaining a positive, professional online presence and a degree of visibility that may open doors to future opportunities

Adding LinkedIn to current job search strategies can be accomplished by using instructional content from a higher-education-oriented page on the LinkedIn website (http://university.linkedin.com). This content provides guidance ranging from basic profile creation to complex directions for optimizing use of this social media tool to increase the power and reach of networking and job search efforts.

ERE Media (2013) reports that 96% of recruiters surveyed use LinkedIn to seek out candidates. While Twitter did not approach LinkedIn's popularity for sourcing, it still stands as a helpful tool for job search. Individuals may use Twitter to monitor or "follow"

CASE ILLUSTRATION 9.2

In the spring, Dwayne MacNeil visited the career center at his community college because he had completed a year of general education classes and wasn't sure what he should take in the upcoming fall semester. An African-American 28-year-old man, Dwayne presented himself confidently and had a professional appearance. After an initial intake conversation (outlined in Chapter 7), his counselor conducted an interest inventory, spent time with Dwayne using some informal assessment tools such as a values card sort and a strengths check list, and used the transition model (Anderson, Goodman, & Schlossberg, 2012) to evaluate his needs as he faces the changes he anticipates. Dwayne returns in the fall and is considering diverse career options, including sound engineering technician, general and operations manager, and administrative services manager.

Discussion Questions

1. As you consider referring Dwayne to online resources and tools, what issues should you address, and what questions should you ask Dwayne?

2. What online sources of data would you recommend to Dwayne to allow him to understand the responsibilities of each role, and assess the projected salary and outlook for each career option?

3. What tools would you recommend Dwayne use to identify professionals with whom to network in his fields of interest?

4. What recommendations would you make to Dwayne regarding his online presence?

the "tweets" of companies in which they are interested; users may also choose to maintain a regular stream of thoughtful and relevant tweets to project a positive professional image. Incorporated in 2007, Twitter reports use by over 336 million monthly active users and over 500 million tweets sent per day. Twitter's users also span the globe, with only 20.5% of Twitter accounts being U.S. based (Twitter, 2018).

MULTICULTURAL COMPETENCY AND TECHNOLOGY USE ENHANCES CAREER COUNSELING

Feller, Russell, and Whichard (2005) discuss cross-cultural application of career interventions, stating that,

> best practices are those that combine activities into comprehensive career planning and development programs. Self-knowledge and career exploration; interactive, diverse, and integrated methods of delivery; and a supportive environment are noted by this group as primary components universal to programs that lead to sound career decision making. (pp. 38-39)

They also discuss what can be done to adapt resources and programming as well as perceived challenges in doing so.

BOX 9.1
IMPACT OF TECHNOLOGY ON INDIVIDUALS' CAREER DEVELOPMENT

The transition from print materials to online resources has resulted in a significant impact on the career development process. Career centers previously lined with well-stocked bookshelves now offer relatively few print resources. Where career-related publications once proliferated, computers, touchpads, and smartphones now connect individuals with an electronic library far more extensive and diverse.

Before technology became such an integral part of career centers, assessment of a client's literacy may have been a rare occurrence for the career development professional. Now, initial contact with a new client requires assessment of that individual's familiarity with and ability to use technology to his or her best advantage. The assumption, in many cases, is that all clients are computer savvy and capable of navigating the Internet to achieve a full range of career-related goals, from exploring career fields, to identifying appropriate educational options, to networking effectively and completing a successful job search. This is a risky assumption. In fact, clients fall along a continuum of familiarity and expertise; when working with clients, one individual may look with great confusion at the perceived complexity of a website, while the next navigates quickly and confidently! Proficiency in the use of specific software and social media tools is another important assessment task as clients begin building resumes and cover letters, developing professional profiles and websites, and creating online portfolios. Career counselors are increasingly expected to be aware of the tools required to accomplish these tasks—and of the resources for learning new software and social media outlets to accomplish the tasks of career development.

LEARNING ACTIVITY 9.5

Investigate the software courses/training available on your campus. Where can a student go to learn basic word processing software to complete a resume? What courses are offered for other career-relevant software?

Issues of technology competency are not the only consideration; access is another factor to consider. While some clients have extensive access to technology, others may have limited access; again, it is important to assess these factors rather than assume that all clients are fully connected by means of multiple electronic devices. Even in our current culture, there are those who access the Internet only through local libraries.

Client beliefs about computer-based information also must be assessed. Some clients may believe that Internet-based information is limited or that career-related information is accessed primarily through casual use of an online search engine. Other clients may believe that the Internet is the single source for any and all information they could possibly need. Introduction of targeted, research-based websites helps clients begin to discern important differences between various sources of online information. Every career counselor bears the responsibility of helping clients develop a more accurate perception of computer-based information and an awareness of the need to be discriminating in the selection of career resources.

Summary: Challenges and Opportunities

Any tool can be used poorly or well. As a counselor, it is important to see the pros and cons of any tool, for each client.

Client challenges may include the following:

- Aversion to using technology

- Unwillingness to disclose technology skills deficits

- Lack of access to training or development of computer skills, real or perceived

- Risks associated with online assessment ranging from lack of Internet assessment oversight to the corresponding proliferation of inferior assessment tools (Lock & Hogan, 2000)

- Need for human interaction in the form of support from and interpretation by a career counselor after completing computer-based assessment (Betz & Borgen, 2009; Kirk, 2000; Tirpak & Schlosser, 2013)

- Fixation on specific career options generated by computer-based assessments; assessment results may indicate occupational titles that represent a "good fit" with an individual's interest but a "poor fit" with the individual's level of education

Counselor challenges may include the following:

- Training to keep practitioners current and collaborative in their use of technology (Barak, 2003; Gati & Asulin-Peretz, 2011; Kirk, 2000; Lock & Hogan, 2000; Sampson & Lumsden, 2000) and aware of risks to confidentiality (Kirk, 2000; Sampson & Lumsden, 2000)

- Need to clarify the goals and outcomes of computer-based interventions (Osborn, Peterson, Sampson, & Reardon, 2003) and to tailor the intervention to client need (Sampson, 1999)

- Complications of studying the impact and effectiveness of computer-based systems with minors (Fowkes & McWhirter, 2007)

Opportunities for clients might include the following:

- Integration of "fit" elements beyond the basic interpersonal characteristics to environmental/workplace considerations (Lock & Hogan, 2000)

- Improved career counseling outcomes when counselor involvement augments the time invested in online assessment (Harris-Bowlsbey, 2013; Whiston, Brecheisen, & Stephens, 2003)

Opportunities for counselors may include the following:

- Cost effectiveness of online resources may increase the number and range of resources that can be offered (Harris-Bowlsbey, 2013; Sampson, 1999; Whiston, Sexton, & Lasoff, 1998)

- A decrease in cost with corresponding increases in use of online interventions and in the amount of time counselors can spend in direct contact with clients (Gati & Asulin-Peretz, 2011)

- The ability to extend career counselors' reach through electronically facilitated career services. "The rapid growth of web connectivity via smartphones is a technological development that makes the delivery of career guidance systems feasible in developing countries where people do not have access to computers" (Harris-Bowlsbey, 2013, p. 185).

- With increased counselor involvement, the interrelationships between career and life elements can be more easily integrated into the process of career counseling.

Keystones

- Technological tools and resources play a critical role in career development engagement and practice.

- Appropriate use of technology (following the professional standards set by NCDA, NACE, CACREP, ACES, and NBCC) is required for all counselors.

- The purposes and uses of technology are diverse. To be effective, counselors need to stay up-to-date with established, new, and emerging technologies and online resources.

- Technology is solely a tool to be used in career counseling, and not a replacement of it. It is suggested that counselors work closely with clients to recommend and evaluate technologically based resources.

- It is important for counselors to assess clients' access to and familiarity with technology when making a decision of whether, what, and how technology should be used for helping clients address career concerns.

Additional Resources

Career Counselor Technology Forum on LinkedIn: https://www.linkedin.com/grp/home?gid=1870624

LinkedIn © 2018: http://www.linkedin.com/about-us

LinkedIn Corporation © 2013, LinkedIn for Higher Education: http://university.linkedin.com

Microsoft PowerPoint: https://www.microsoft.com

Prezi, Inc. © 2013: http://prezi.com

Twitter, Inc. © 2018: https://about.twitter.com/company

References

ACES. (2017). *ACES guidelines for online learning in counselor education technology*. Retrieved from https://www.acesonline.net/sites/default/files/Online%20Learning%20CES%20Guidelines%20May%202017%20%281%29.pdf.

American College Testing Program. (1984). *DISCOVER*. Iowa City, IA: Author.

Anderson, M. L., Goodman, J., & Schlossberg, N. K. (2012). *Counseling adults in transition: Linking Schlossberg's theory with practice in a diverse world* (4th ed.). New York, NY: Springer.

Barak., A. (2003). Ethical and professional issues in career assessment on the internet. *Journal of Career Assessment, 11*(1), 3-21.

Betz, N. E., & Borgen, F. H. (2009). Comparative effectiveness of CAPA and FOCUS online: Career assessment systems with undecided college students. *Journal of Career Assessment, 17,* 351-366.

Betz, N. E., & Turner, B. M. (2011). Using item response theory and adaptive testing in online career assessment. *Journal of Career Assessment, 19*(3), 274-286.

Council for Accreditation of Counselor and Related Educational Program. (2016). *2016 standards.* Retrieved from http://www.cacrep.org/for-programs/2016-cacrep-standards.

ERE Media. (2013). *About ERE Media.* Retrieved from http://www.ere.net/about.

Feller, R. W., Russell, M., & Whichard, J. A. (2005). Career techniques and interventions: Themes from an international conversation. *Career Development Quarterly, 54*(1), 36-47.

Fowkes, K. M., & McWhirter, E. H. (2007). Evaluation of computer-assisted career guidance in middle and secondary education settings: Status, obstacles, and suggestions. *Journal of Career Assessment, 15*(3), 388-400.

Freedom Scientific. (2013). *JAWS screen reader.* Retrieved from http://www.freedomscientific.com.

Gati, I., & Asulin-Peretz, L. (2011). Internet-based self-help career assessments and interventions: Challenges and implications for evidence-based career counseling. *Journal of Career Assessment, 19*(3), 259-273.

Gati, I., Kleiman, T., Saka, N., & Zakai, A. (2003). Perceived benefits of using an Internet-based interactive career planning system. *Journal of Vocational Behavior, 62,* 272-286.

Gore, Jr., P. A., & Leuwerke, W. C., (2000). Information technology for career assessment on the internet. *Journal of Career Assessment, 8,* 3-19.

Harris-Bowlsbey, J. (2013). Computer-assisted career guidance systems: A part of NCDA history. *Career Development Quarterly, 61,* 181-185.

Harris-Bowlsbey, J., & Sampson, Jr., J. P. (2001). Computer-based career planning systems: Dreams and realities. *Career Development Quarterly, 49*(3), 250-260.

Herman, S. (2010). Career HOPES: An Internet-delivered career development intervention. *Computers in Human Behavior, 26,* 339-344.

Katz, M. R. (1975). *SIGI: A computer-based system of interactive guidance and information.* Princeton, NJ: Educational Testing Service.

Kirk, J. J. (2000). Web-assisted career counseling. *Journal of Employment Counseling, 37,* 146-159.

LinkedIn. (2018). *About LinkedIn.* Retrieved from https://about.linkedin.com.

Lock, J. D., & Hogan, R. (2000). Expanding the focus of career assessment. *Journal of Career Assessment, 8*(4), 411-417.

NBCC. (2016). *The NBCC policy regarding the provision of distance professional services.* Retrieved from http://www.nbcc.org/Assets/Ethics/NBCCPolicyRegardingPracticeofDistanceCounselingBoard.pdf.

Osborn, D. S., Peterson, G. W., Sampson, Jr., J. P., & Reardon, R. C. (2003). Client anticipations about computer-assisted career guidance system outcomes. *Career Development Quarterly, 51*(4), 358-367.

Sampson, Jr., J. P. (1999). Integrating internet-based distance guidance with services provided in career centers. *Career Development Quarterly, 47*(3), 243-254.

Sampson, Jr., J. P., & Lumsden, J. A. (2000). Ethical issues in the design and use of Internet-based career assessment. *Journal of Career Assessment, 8*(1), 21-35.

Tirpak, D. M., & Schlosser, L. Z. (2013). Evaluating FOCUS-2's effectiveness in enhancing first-year college students' social cognitive career development. *Career Development Quarterly, 61*, 110-123.

Twitter. (2018). *Q1 letter to shareholders.* Retrieved from http://files.shareholder.com/downloads/AMDA-2F526X/6283368086x0x978181/2FD6D58F-A930-4EB2-90B0-9C3A120648DE/Q1_2018_Shareholder_Letter.pdf.

Whiston, S. C., Brecheisen, B. K., & Stephens, J. (2003). Does treatment modality affect career counseling effectiveness? *Journal of Vocational Behavior, 62*, 390-410.

Whiston, S. C., Sexton, T. L., & Lasoff, D. L. (1998). Career-intervention outcome: A replication and extension of Oliver and Spokane. *Journal of Counseling Psychology, 45*, 150-165.

DESIGNING AND EVALUATING CAREER DEVELOPMENT INTERVENTION PROGRAMS

From the previous chapters, it is evident that helping individuals embark on a successful journey leading to satisfactory work and life requires plans and actions, and it is critical to develop the plans and actions proactively rather than reactively; therefore, it is necessary to intentionally reach out to more people through programming so that career intervention can benefit larger groups of people. This chapter will explain the importance of prevention in career development. The definition of prevention and its application in career development domain will be reviewed. This chapter will also describe and explain the concepts of program development and evaluation for career prevention and intervention purposes. The essence of developing, implementing, and evaluating career development programs will be illustrated. After reading this chapter, students will gain the necessary knowledge and skills to develop appropriate career development programs for prevention or intervention purposes in various settings. Multicultural consideration is crucial in developing successful career development programs. The chapter will discuss how contextual and cultural factors are incorporated in developing and evaluating ecologically valid and effective prevention or intervention programs for career development.

LEARNING OBJECTIVES

After completing the reading and exercises provided in this chapter, you will be able to:

- describe the rationale of developing career prevention and intervention programs,

- articulate the importance of having career intervention program at various settings,

- comprehend the role and impact of prevention on life span career development,

- describe the principles of program development and evaluation,

- apply the principles of program development evaluation to career prevention and intervention in various settings,

- evaluate program effectiveness and outcome, and

- identify critical elements to enhance program development and implementation.

RATIONALE OF CAREER DEVELOPMENT PROGRAMS

Rene was a high school junior and wanted to go to college, but she was not sure how she should proceed in regard to the application process, major choices, financial aid, and colleges she should consider because her parents did not attend college and could not provide any suggestions or guidance. Rene talked to her English teacher about her thoughts of going to college, and the teacher suggested that she could talk to the school counselor. Rene went to the school counselor's office and became anxious when she found that her designated school counselor had 400 other students under her watch. Rene's situation was not so uncommon for many high school students, and in fact, many college students face similar challenges, too. Because it is unlikely Rene's high school could hire more school counselors, what would be the realistic and reasonable way to help Rene with her college exploration needs? Or in other words, are there alternative approaches for helping Rene and her fellow students to navigate the system so that they can have adequate services for their college and career exploration needs? A proactive and systematic approach could potentially accomplish the goal effectively and efficiently. Such intervention also should reach a larger audience and benefit more people who may not otherwise be served. In Rene's situation, if there was a career prevention and intervention program available at her high school, she would have access to the information she needs to explore her options. The following section will review the reasons why career development programs are needed and what career development programs can accomplish in regard to helping individuals in career exploration, decision making, career readiness, and career transition.

Necessity of Career Development Programs

The primary reason for having career development programs is accessibility and effectiveness. Considering Rene's case, when there are a large number of high school students and only a handful of school counselors, a well designed and implemented program would help Rene and her peers to gain the necessary skills and access to resources for career exploration. As programs are meant to provide systematic and preventive interventions to help people with anticipated needs and challenges, they lend themselves to serve more people. The expected outcome of reaching more people can be seen in the historical movement of career intervention in school settings. Back in the 1970s, when career education movement led to the establishment of a variety of career prevention and intervention programs in K-12 settings in the United States, the aim was to offer students curriculum and services that help them to broaden their career horizon and to acquire knowledge, skills, and attitudes needed for a productive and satisfying life (Isaacson & Brown, 2000). The core of the career education movement is to integrate classroom learning and real-world work capacity so that all students are ready for making sound career decisions and competent in work settings. As of today, though career education programs may not exist exactly as they were in the seventies and eighties, the essence of the program, that is, incorporating career development into education, is reflected in the comprehensive school counseling program advocated by the American School Counselor Association, which targets helping all students in K-12 settings to become contributing citizens to society by developing knowledge, attitudes, and skills to be ready to learn, to develop socially and emotionally, and to make decisions for postsecondary planning (American School Counselor Association, 2004). Thus, career development programs with systematic efforts to use resources effectively seem like a reasonable approach to benefit more individuals.

The other reason for needing career development programs is out of consideration of many career development theories that emphasize life span development and the role of learning experiences in shaping one's career identity and choices (e.g., Super, 1990; Krumboltz, 1996; Lent, Brown, & Hackett, 1994). Similarly, constant changes in work environment and transitions from one life stage/ life space to another (e.g., from school to work, from employment to unemployment, or from homemaker to the labor force) present challenges to people. To help people be prepared for these challenges and meet their needs at various life stages, proactive and systematic career development programs are necessary.

Further, despite the good intention of policy and visionary effort to help individuals with life career development tasks, in many cases, there is a gap between policy and practice with many individuals not having access to services or being underserved (Bloch, 1996; Goodman & Hansen, 2005). A survey of middle school principals and school counselors in regard to how the American School Counselor Association (ASCA) model was implemented found that students' needs on career planning, specifically understanding the world of work, the relationship between school learning and career, and making informed career decisions, were not adequately met (McCotter & Cohen, 2013). This gap in policy and practice is exactly why systematic career development programming is needed, because such programs could be useful to fill the gaps by reinforcing the policy and vision to reach more people. For instance, career readiness is one of the national standards advocated by ASCA, however, without comprehensive and systematic programming, this goal is simply impossible to be achieved because not every school counselor or teacher has the time or ideas to help all students. It then becomes an issue of accessibility and privilege, that is, those students with better resources in any form (e.g., parental support, being on a certain team or project that happens to have funding for more services) probably will navigate the system better and can get their needs served, but those students who do not have such resources can easily fall through the cracks and be neglected.

The research findings from many studies also verified the benefits of having a comprehensive career development program. The benefits included gaining more accurate information about career development needs and options (Herr, 1999), increased self-efficacy in making career decisions, and fewer needs for intervention (Herr, Cramer, & Niles, 2004). Feller (2006) summarized the research findings from America's Career Resources

Network Association report of 2003 in regard to benefits of comprehensive career development programs as the following:

Educational: (a) improved educational achievement; (b) improved preparation and participation in postsecondary education; (c) better articulation among educational levels; (d) higher graduation and retention rate

Social: (a) higher levels of work satisfaction and career retention; (b) short paths to primary labor markets for young workers; (c) lower incidents of work-related stress and depression; (d) reduced likelihood of work-related violence

Economic: (a) lower rates and shorter periods of unemployment; (b) lower costs of worker turnover; (c) lower incarceration and criminal justice costs; (d) increased worker productivity (p. 181)

In summary, career development programs are needed because these programs can provide more accessible and high-quality services to more people, and they are also cost effective, compared to individual advising and counseling. There is evidence for the efficacy of comprehensive career development programs benefiting people and society. The career development programs are needed also due to the life span developmental needs everyone has in regard to their career and life roles. Many career development theories have posited the necessity of proactive and systematic intervention to help people learn and manage their life roles and career tasks at various life stages. Proactive and systematic intervention targeting all (i.e., as many as possible) is the reason for the necessity of career development programs and also the purpose of such programs.

Purpose of Career Development Programs

As stated above, the purpose of career development is to systematically and proactively help students and workers have smooth transitions and satisfying work and life. Planning, particularly planning with an informed decision-making process, is critical to accomplish these goals. Therefore, the overall goal of a career development program is not just to help individuals make a choice in regard to career decision making (e.g., choosing a major, selecting an occupation, deciding to find a new job, etc.); rather, it should focus more on facilitating individuals' knowledge and skill development so that they know how to make decisions and manage career and life tasks. This is also the difference between comprehensive program interventions and individual counseling, as the former focuses on prevention and the latter focuses more on individualized intervention.

The national standards of ASCA for career development have laid the foundation for comprehensive career development programs in K-12 settings with an aim to enable students make a successful transition from school to work, across the life span. The standards include three major standards and 43 specific standards for career development. The three major standards are as follows: (1) Students will acquire the skills to investigate the world of work in relation to knowledge of self and to make informed career decision; (2) Students will employ strategies to achieve future career goals with success and satisfaction; and (3) Students will understand the relationship between personal qualities, education, training, and the world of work. The details of the national standards as seen in Appendix A clearly show the intent and effort of targeting students' development on knowledge and skills to identify awareness of themselves and understanding of the relationship between personal characteristics and careers; to develop knowledge skills in making career decisions to achieve career goals; and to apply knowledge and skills to be transition and employment ready.

The purposes of career development programs are varied depending on the population and setting where the program is implemented. For school and college students, it is important to help them understand the relationship between learning in the classroom and job performance in work settings, to have a comprehensive career plan that assists them to acquire the necessary academic training and experiences leading to college and career readiness, and to develop competency in acting on the plan. For adults, a career development program could focus on identifying the meaningfulness of work and life, assisting professional development and growth to deal with life situations through employee assistance program (Feller, 2006), and training for transition preparedness (Trainor, Smith, & Kim, 2012). In organizations and community settings, career development programs could also target enrichment activities that help people identify their strengths and transferrable skills to either advance their careers or reenter the workforce if becoming unemployed involuntarily.

PRINCIPLES OF CAREER DEVELOPMENT INTERVENTION PROGRAMS

Role of Prevention to Life Span Career Development

If career development is simply for choosing an occupation, comprehensive programming probably is not as critical as discussed in the previous section. There are many assessment tools and counseling strategies that can assist individuals in making sound career choices; however, the goal of career development intervention is not just making a choice about occupations or majors or whether one should stay in a job or move or relocate, it is about identifying and living a fulfilling life across the life span. To be prepared for this life span process, prevention at early stages paves the way for later stages. Therefore, prevention is the essence of career development programs after all.

Prevention is defined as preventing a problem behavior from ever occurring or minimizing the negative impact of problematic behavior (Romano & Hage, 2000) and promoting healthy behavior and well-being from both individuals and institutions (Chronister, McWhirter, & Kerewsky, 2004). The previous chapters have reviewed the relationship of work and health, family dynamic, and life roles. It is evident that an unsatisfactory career trajectory can negatively influence a person's life in general; thus, career development programs with the goal of readiness for employment and transition attempt to prevent unemployment or unhappy employment. The potential of prevention in the career development intervention has been articulated by many scholars (Brown, Lamp, Telander, & Hacker, 2013; Donelly & Given, 2010; Nota, Ginevra, & Santilli, 2015; Schultheiss, 2005). It is commonly known that with prevention, the earlier the better. This is also why ASCA promotes comprehensive career development programs as early as in elementary schools. Elementary school children certainly cannot make any decision about their careers, but exposure to occupations, learning the appropriate behaviors such as discipline, social skills, respect to rules, and so on, help them succeed in future work settings. If comprehensive career development programs could help K-12 and college students develop problem solving and transferrable skills across fields, it would prepare them to be resilient in adverse situations in the future. For instance, children typically acquire their conception of gender stereotypes of occupations in elementary school years (Gottfredson, 2002). If school counselors could develop and implement comprehensive career development programs with a components on dispelling occupational stereotypes on gender, race, ethnicity, and other social constructs, it would benefit more children gain better understanding of occupational stereotypes and barriers to career development for nondominant groups and better prepare them for future career readiness. The core value of prevention is to empower people with the capacity to manage their careers and to avoid possible problems.

Important Elements in Career Development Programs

The early efforts of systematic programming such as career education highlighted the importance of awareness and skill development. The program elements of career education included awareness of a wide range of career options, of one's own personality, of industry (production, distribution, and consumption), and attitudes toward life roles, self, and others (Brown, 2012). The recent ASCA model also emphasizes the importance of self-awareness and the application of knowledge in real work settings. For adults, transitions and balancing life role and work demands; communication with others, including family members and coworkers; and meaningful and accountable development/growth plans are considered to be critical issues impacting employees' satisfaction (Feller, 2006). Therefore, comprehensive, developmental, and systematic prevention should be the principle of career development programs in any context, either in school settings or in employment or community settings. With this principle, there should be variation to accommodate the needs of the population the program serves.

Comprehensiveness refers to the need for career programs to serve individuals with an integration of all aspects of life rather than just solving one problem or job placement (Carr, 1996). The nature of systematic and developmental prevention efforts are parallel to each other because systematic intervention needs to be based on a developmental framework so that prevention and intervention can be steady, corresponding to the level and needs of the population served. Lacking systematic or development ingredients in programming underserves the individual because career development itself occurs across the life span and links to every aspect of a person's life, as we have discussed in previous chapters. The comprehensiveness is also the guiding framework for career development programs, or in other words, the foundation and philosophy is needed to direct the goal and scope of the programming. Without a solid foundation, the program development could be groundless or at the risk of reacting to situational problems rather than systematic, developmental, and comprehensive prevention. In addition, an effective program requires infrastructure that supports the design and implementation being created and executed successfully.

Using the ASCA model as an example, it is evident that infrastructure is important for actual design, delivery, and evaluation of the program, while the foundation provides the philosophy and basis for delivery and management. The ASCA model has four components: foundation, delivery system, management system, and accountability (the details and diagram can be seen at https://www.schoolcounselor.org/school-coun selors-members/asca-national-model), in which the foundation provides the beliefs and philosophy, the management system and delivery system include the mission and standards, and accountability includes the evaluation and reports examining the performance of these two systems against the standards. From the ASCA model sample, it is concluded that successful program development must have a clearly defined mission based on the belief of the endeavor and a management organization to design, implement, monitor, and evaluate the program outcome. A sound systematic career development program for K-12 students should also include important stakeholders including teachers and administrators, parents, community members, and qualified professionals (Gysbers & Henderson, 2012). The developmentally appropriate program components should consider students' ages, needs, and abilities, or put in different perspective, the program should be developmentally compliant and not contradictory, instead, an integral part to academic training for school age youth (Mekinda, 2012). Last, but not least, the program needs to have concrete and measurable objectives as well as outcome evaluation plans. Evaluation of program development is like a follow-up examination after treatment; without such, the outcome of intervention is not known and there is no base for continuous improvement.

Although it is more likely that comprehensive career development programs are typically in K-12 and college settings, there is an increasing need for career prevention and intervention in community and business settings as there is more recognition of the need for integration and balancing of life and work roles for satisfying both organizational and individual needs. Compared to educational settings, the career development programs in organizations tend to have the following different characteristics: goals/purposes— benefitting both the institution and employees; the structure and personnel—usually within the human resources units of the organizations with a goal of maintaining and aspiring internal staff members; and mentoring—identifying and creating talents for organizational and individual growth (Brown, 2012). More details about career development in organizations and communities will be presented in Chapter 13.

The foundation and mission provide the guiding principles for the subsequent procedures in developing career development programs. These procedures are the specific measures to ensure the mission is accomplished with high quality and efficiency. Regardless of the setting, the process of designing a career development prevention and intervention program is similar. The next section will illustrate the detailed step-by-step procedure for developing a career development program.

PROCESS OF CAREER DEVELOPMENT INTERVENTION PROGRAMS

It is noted that the suggested process listed in the following sections is an ideal, logical, and sequential step-by-step approach. It means some steps could be taken out of order, depending on the context and situation where the program will be applied. In general, the process needs to attend to the needs of the population, the goals to be achieved, and contextual and practical factors that could impact the outcome of program effectiveness.

Creating Work Group

A task group or a steering committee is needed before the process even begins. In fact, two separate groups with distinct roles and functions might be necessary. The steering committee is needed for oversight of the program to ensure the mission and process are in alignment for overall positive impact and outcome, and a planning or task-oriented committee or group is needed to actually design and implement the program. The steering committee is usually composed of all stakeholders; for instance, in school settings, the committee should include teachers, administrative staff, school counselors, parents, community members, representatives from business, and possibly student representatives (American School Counselor Association, 2012; Gysbers & Henderson, 2001), or in the corporate world, the members should include executive branch, management team, representatives from different units, and community members.

The task group or committee is composed of personnel who will directly interact with the population to be served and who will be in charge of actual development and implementation of the program. These people are school counselors, teachers, human resource personnel, employee assistance program staff, or counselors working in the mental health agencies. In other words, these people should be professionals who have basic knowledge and skills of career development to work with students, workers, and individuals in the community.

Identify Target Population

The first step is to identify what population the program aims at serving. When considering the population, it is critical to consider the setting where the population will be served. The information of age, developmental levels, social/cultural/economic background, racial/ethnic background, and the context where the prevention or intervention will occur are important factors for program development. For instance, if you need to develop a comprehensive career development program for a school district, you need to gather information about the demographics of the district, the culture of the local community, the grade levels for which this program will be implemented, and each buildings' characteristics. Thus, the target population for the program could be all students in the school district, or could be sixth to eighth graders in the district, or could be for juniors and seniors. Depending on the population, the program could be varied in regard to goals, implementations, and activities to be chosen. A program targeted at recently laid-off workers will have different program intervention components than a program targeting a graduating class of college students, although the overall goal could to the same—finding a job.

Identify Goals and Objectives

The next step is to identify program goals and objectives. The goals are the overarching mission of the program, and the objectives are specific indicators that translate the goals to be observable and measurable. In other words, goals are general concepts, and objectives are concrete and action oriented. For instance, a goal for a career development program can be stated as, "All high school students in Wonderful School District will develop career awareness and readiness." This goal seems very appropriate and well-intended, but how do we know whether this goal is achieved or not? The

LEARNING ACTIVITY 10.1
WRITING PROGRAM OBJECTIVES

A community-based mental health agency is applying for funding to help its clients, who are mainly individuals who were recently laid off when a major employer in the community moved out of the area. You are preparing a proposal to secure the funding, and the goal is to help the community members deal with unemployment and ultimately get a job. Please write five specific objectives that are concrete, observable, and measurable.

objectives derived from this goal could be helpful to estimate if the goal is achieved. When the objectives are described to articulate observable and measurable behaviors or actions, one can judge the behaviors/actions to make the conclusion. Often these indicators can be evaluated through formal or informal measurement procedures. Thus, each goal typically will have multiple objectives. The goal stated in the example above probably needs to have the following objectives: "All students need to be able to describe their interests and values; all students need to be able to state the relationship between personal characteristics and world of work; all students need to develop skills in obtaining occupational information; all students need to develop skills in communication both in verbal and written format; all students need to develop skills in decision making; all students will have a specific career plan." These objectives are all related to the goal of career awareness and readiness but are subject to be evaluated for specific areas.

The process of developing goals and objectives needs to have three sources at least. One is the philosophy and mission, which will function as the guideline and framework for identifying goals and objectives. The second source should be the literature regarding the population being served and settings, which lays the theoretical foundation for program and evidence support for the goals and objectives. The third source should be data driven, or derived from the needs of the population and community. Therefore, input from all stakeholders should be incorporated. A common approach for gathering input from stakeholders is a needs assessment.

Needs Assessment: It is a tool to collect data pertaining to the existing resources, opinions of variety of people, challenges facing the population, areas for improvement, and desires. The needs assessment can be conducted through various procedures, for example, survey, interview, focus group, field observation, or examination of the existing documents and infrastructure. McDavid and Hawthorn (2006) suggested that understanding the political context is important for needs assessment because the results are used for decision making; therefore, avoiding biases or inaccuracy would be necessary for preventing pitfalls. They also suggest that needs assessments should proceed iteratively, meaning the process and results should be reviewed and modified as the program progresses. Based on McDavid and Hawthorn, these steps for conducting needs assessments are suggested:

- Gain demographic and socioeconomic-political facts of the organization and its surrounding context.

- Review the mission statement.

- Identify the characteristics of the target population.

- Find or design the assessment tool to collect data about the desires, expectations, and wishes from the stakeholders of the community.

- Analyze the existing infrastructure and resources.

- Summarize the data and evidence collected in comparison to the mission statement.

- Identify the gap, and report the findings to the planning committee.

An example of needs assessment is illustrated in Box 10.1. Clearly identified goals that are endorsed by the stakeholders provide useful direction for program development. Aligning the goals and objectives with the needs of the community can be done through needs assessment process.

Analysis of Resources and Barriers

The importance of analyzing the resources is mainly due to the fact that any program implementation requires both financial and human resources; therefore, if the design fails to assess fully the resources and potential barriers to implementation, the program will very likely encounter difficulties in the action phase. *Resources* refers to assets and support from the stakeholders and organization. For instance, sufficient budget, quality and supportive personnel, understanding of program mission by all stakeholders, trust of organization, and support of community could all be advantages for program design and implementation. Lacking these elements would be a challenge to developing career development programs, as a successful program design and implementation requires resources in both financial and personnel categories. Not only is it necessary to assess the resources, it is equally important to analyze the potential barriers, because if roadblocks are not anticipated in the design phase, it is likely the program will fail or malfunction. However, if an accurate analysis of the possible barriers is done early, it will help the design be more on target and be more prone to successfully dealing with obstacles.

To analyze the resources and barriers, the ecological counseling perspective (Conyne & Cook, 2004) could guide the process of identifying what could be the assets and what could be the barriers for implementing a career development program. The following lists are suggested for information gathering prior to conduct the analysis.

- Personal characteristics of the population to be served (e.g., age, socioeconomic status, cultural backgrounds, developmental levels, family dynamics, orientation toward life and work)

BOX 10.1
EXAMPLE OF NEEDS ASSESSMENT

We would like your views on providing services to students in the district. Please circle the number that you believe most closely represents your views:

Teaching career decision-making skills in classrooms

Very Important	Somewhat Important	Not So Important	Not Important at All
4	3	2	1

Providing comprehensive information to all students

Very Important	Somewhat Important	Not So Important	Not Important at All
4	3	2	1

Inviting business leaders to speak to school students

Very Important	Somewhat Important	Not So Important	Not Important at All
4	3	2	1

Organizing a career day twice a year

Very Important	Somewhat Important	Not So Important	Not Important at All
4	3	2	1

Assisting college application procedure by school counselors

Very Important	Somewhat Important	Not So Important	Not Important at All
4	3	2	1

Preparing students to have essential job-related skills

Very Important	Somewhat Important	Not So Important	Not Important at All
4	3	2	1

- Institutional characteristics such as history and shared values, policy, organizational structure, decision-making process, accountability system, communication loop, and budget source and allocation

- Community characteristics in regard to engagement of community members, financial status (e.g., tax levy, business development), ethnic and other demographic composition of the community, existing infrastructure, and relationship between the institution and community (e.g., school and business partnership, or corporate and community interaction)

- Macro-level elements at the time such as temporal, social, and cultural milieu, national policy, legislatures, and the economy

After this information is gathered, the working team should analyze whether these factors could be assets or could be barriers depending on their characteristics in relation to the mission and goals. The resources and barriers are not necessarily constant or stable because the factors themselves can change, and they may have varied meanings at different times and in different settings. Resources to one population and in one setting could be barriers to another population and setting; therefore, "cultural knowledge and awareness are important tools to assist accurate ecosystem, because what is perceived as assets might be regarded differently when viewed from other cultural backgrounds" (Tang & Russ, 2007, p. 42). Therefore, ecologically valid analysis of resources and barriers means culturally and contextually appropriate assessment. An ecologically valid assessment is based on full consideration of cultural and contextual factors to lay a solid foundation for success of implementation of the program. To increase ecological validity, evidence-based intervention informed by translational research would guide the design of the program component.

Design Program Content Related to Goals

The program components are designed to ensure the identified goals are accomplished with smoothness and effectiveness. In order to do so, the program design needs to consider both components to be valid in goal accomplishment and delivery channels to ensure desired outcomes achieved. For the components to be valid, it is necessary to review the goals identified and objectives developed for the program. For each objective, carefully examine the outcome indicators that could provide evidence for attaining the objective; then find out what materials are needed, what forms of intervention would be helpful, and what delivery modality could be conducive to ensuring the indicators or evidence could occur. For instance, if the goal is to have high school students like Rene have a clear plan to be ready for college, the objectives could be to identify areas of study in senior year, select three to five universities for considering application, review the scholarship and financial aid information with parents, and have a virtual or actual visit of targeted universities. The materials needed are academic disciplines associated to occupations; federal, state, private foundation, and university scholarships, including requirements; application forms; procedures; supporting documents; financial sheets summarizing and comparing tuition and living costs; and profiles of universities. The activities could be that school counselors introduce the individual career plan through classroom guidance in a variety of classes, that teachers reinforce the completion of the plan through classroom activities and assignments, and that school counselors collect the final plans at the end of junior year and put them in students' files. With the advancement of information technology, a lot of the information is accessible online, which significantly changes the information distribution, only to be more efficient as long as one knows how to take advantage of it.

It is also very important for program design to consult career development theories and updated literature pertaining to the program goals.

For smooth implementation, the program design needs to address delivery formats, timing, personnel, and budget. The delivery methods should be versatile and accommodate the environmental constraints. It is usually optimal to use the existing infrastructure rather than imposing a new one; however, if creating and changing an existing practice is better for serving the needs and for accomplishing the goals, it should be pursued. The reason for better using the existing infrastructure if possible is because things often work better following their organic mechanisms rather than outside influences. Timing is critical for implementation not only because sufficient time should be allocated for intervention but also because the wrong time of the day or year could jeopardize the program implementation. For instance, just a few days or even weeks before a fiscal year ending might not be an optimal time for any major program components being implemented. It is also not a good idea to ask teachers to incorporate career development program components in their classes when their students are undergoing major state competency testing in the same week. Personnel and budget probably are the most critical concerns for successful implementation. Without high-quality personnel or support from all stakeholders, the delivery efficacy could be compromised. It is no surprise that program design and implementation costs money—from materials, software, and personnel, to equipment for activities; therefore, the more detailed prior budgeting, the more helpful it is for future actual implementation.

Marketing Programs

A marketing program might contain different meanings for K-12 settings than for college settings, organization, or communities. In K-12 settings, the career development is an integral part of education (or at least should be according to ASCA); thus, marketing programs indicate the need for more participation by teachers and staff members to reach more or all students. For college settings, marketing the program probably is more like a campaign to make more students, student advisors, and faculty members aware of the existence of the program, as not many students or faculty members or even student affairs staff in college settings know about career development programs, so it becomes crucial to publicize as widely as possible for more people to understand the goal and benefits of career development programs. For business settings, marketing efforts probably need to target both administrative branches and employees because when marketing the concept of career development, it is valuable for the program be endorsed by both decision makers and the group of people the program aims at serving.

Marketing strategies include targeting the relevant public (e.g., taxpayers in the school district, school board members), students and their parents, and school personnel to make known the benefits of the program, strategic analysis of marketing plan, and evaluation of the outcome of marketing efforts (Bollendorf, Howrey, & Stephenson, 1990). Further, one can distribute flyers, brochures, and web links about the program to the target audience. Social media is an efficient and cost-effective platform for publicizing the information. Participation and regular involvement in school and community events, advocating for professionals of career development programs, and educating members of the community are helpful marketing strategies as well.

Implementation of Programs

If all the previous steps are well planned, this step should be self-withstanding. A well-designed plan with a detailed timeline, specific activities, and responsible persons for delivering will pave the way for successful implementation. The delivery of the program components should be diversified to meet different needs of diverse groups. For instance, for some components, such as information about pertaining topics and locating resources, it is wise to deliver the service through a large group format (e.g., school assembly, class) or through an online platform. For a skill development component, small group and classroom guidance activities would work more effectively.

As stated above, timing is critical for implementation. Any delivery of program components requires many parties' time to engage in activities, so finding an appropriate time when all involved personnel can be committed is important. Another factor related to timing is insurance of time allocated for implementation, that is, no other demands made on participants so that both the people delivering the program and the people receiving the intervention can focus on the program activities. It is ideal for the program to be implemented over a longer period of time with regular occurrence, steady frequency, and moderate time intervals to avoid crammed or sparse intervention.

Personnel is the key for successful implementation. Training might be necessary for relevant program team members and other professionals or paraprofessionals who will assist in the delivery of the program. For instance, in-service training for teachers is a good idea to orient all teachers with the program goals and objectives, program components, and their roles and responsibilities for program implementation. Outreach programs might be needed to educate parents and community members so that they can play a supporting role to assist students. In essence, program implementation needs highly competent professionals and a supportive community, strong leadership, and committed personnel to ensure a smooth and successful delivery of the program. Counselors, in either school or business settings, who are professionally trained, usually coordinate all these needs.

Evaluating Programs

Though program evaluation seems like the last step of the career development program process, it is actually part of the goal and objectives identification as well as the program component design because these three sectors need to align with each other for consistency and better outcome. In other words, the program components should be designed to support the goals and objectives, and evaluation is needed to examine whether the goals and objectives are achieved and whether the program components serve the program well and are effective in accomplishing the program goals. Further, evaluation is also an integral part of the entire process of the program design and implementation because results of evaluation are helpful data and a source of information for redesign and improving the program.

Evaluation is a structured process that gathers information to inform the stakeholders about the outcome of a given program (McDavid & Hawthorn, 2006). After all the efforts, activities, time, and resources being delivered, has the program achieved the intended objectives? According to McDavid and Hawthorn (2006), the key questions for program evaluation are whether the program achieves its intended objectives, whether the program is effective in achieving its intended outcome, and whether the program's observed outcome is consistent with its intended outcome. The other questions for program evaluation pertain to program efficiency. Efficiency is about cost effectiveness; in other words, not only should intended program goals be desired but also economic efficiency should be desired.

There are two types of evaluation: formative evaluations and summative evaluations. Formative evaluation focuses on the process of implementation, that is, how the program is being delivered, and the information mainly lends insights to program designers and implementation team for improvement purpose (McDavid & Hawthorn, 2006). According to McDavid and Hawthorn (2006), summative evaluation focuses on the intended outcome, that is, whether the target goals of the program have been achieved or not, and the evaluation of the outcome is also a check on the accountability of the program. In other words, can this program deliver the product it promises? A more bottom-line question is whether this program should continue or not. A comprehensive evaluation strategy often has both formative and summative evaluation. For instance, when evaluating a community career system program, the formative evaluation gathers information such as academic achievement, self-efficacy expectation and positive attributes, choice goals, and work readiness behavior in K-12 settings, and the summative evaluation focuses on the outcome pertaining to benefits to students, employers, and community (Lapan & Kosciulek, 2001). The evaluation about the process often collects data on participants' perceptions and feelings about the program in regard to implementation and its impact on them; however, evaluation about the outcome focuses more on the objective measures of program goals, such as whether the choices are made (not how they feel about their choices) or whether productivity is increased (not how workers feel about new employment assistance program components).

Systematic evaluation requires comprehensive assessment on impact, effectiveness, sustainability, and transportability and is often demanded by funding sources for program evaluation (Wright, 2014). The most well-known approach for systematic program evaluation is the CIPP model (Stufflebean, 2007). The CIPP model contains four parts: context, input, process, and product. The context evaluation assesses needs, assets, and problems within the environment where the program will be implemented; it concerns the question "what needs to be done?" The input evaluation assesses existing programs and proposed strategy in relation to sufficiency, feasibility, and political viability and budget of the selected approach; it concerns the question "how should it be done?" The process evaluation monitors, documents, and assesses program activities; it concerns

LEARNING ACTIVITY 10.2
EVALUATING PROCESS VS OUTCOME

Name the reasons why process evaluation is important for program evaluation. How can it be useful to the outcome evaluation for the program? Ask the class to search the Internet or the library resources on your campus and then identify an instrument that measures process and one that measures outcome. Have the class discuss their rationale for why they think the instrument can be used for process or outcome evaluation.

the question "is it being done?" The product evaluation assesses four different aspects: impact (i.e., the program's reach to the target population), effectiveness (i.e., the quality and significance of outcomes), sustainability (i.e., the extent to which a program's contributions would continue over time), and transportability (i.e., whether the program could be successfully applied or adapted to different environment); it concerns the question "did it succeed?" It is desirable for all of these elements to be incorporated in program evaluation if feasible; in reality, some parts of these guidelines might not be feasible due to resource restraints. The model provides a useful framework for what kind of data should be collected in program evaluation.

The data can be subjective or objective, process oriented or outcome based. The subjective data typically are formative evaluations about feelings, perceptions, and feedback about the program from all stakeholders. The objective data usually refer to the information collected or measured through objective assessment tools or observations, such as standardized inventories, actual performance on academic or work-related activities, behavior change, and so forth. For instance, The School Counseling Program Report Card—Student Version (Kimbel & Clemens, 2014), a tool for evaluating a comprehensive school counseling program, has these items for career development and planning. "My school counselor provides individual counseling or group counseling for planning for life after high school based on my academic achievement, making decisions about my career goals, making future training plans for my career choice, evaluating my educational plan to support my career choice, understanding the link between my career goals and my abilities, and gaining personal awareness related to my emerging career interests." These items are example of process-oriented data. Outcome-oriented data would be the number of career plans being completed, choices made by the number of students, and correspondence between students' interests and career plans. There are a variety of methods for data collection ranging from survey, interview, charting behaviors, focus groups, collecting data from records, and mixed methods (Wright, 2014). The procedure of data collection needs to follow the evaluation plan, which varies depending on the goals of the program. A common approach to evaluating the effectiveness of a program is collecting baseline data prior or at the beginning of the program and collecting the outcome data (same assessment indicators) at the end of program implementation, to determine if the desirable changes occurred. The process-oriented data can be collected throughout the program tenure, for example, at the beginning, middle, and end of the program delivery.

CAREER DEVELOPMENT PROGRAMS WITH DIVERSE POPULATIONS AND VARIOUS SETTINGS

This section reviews some examples of career development programs with different aims, serving various populations, in various settings to illustrate how career development programming can be done in reality and to gain understanding of the effectiveness of these programs. The types of programs include career development programs with at-risk youth in school settings, for employees in work settings, community partnership, and transition programs for K-12 students.

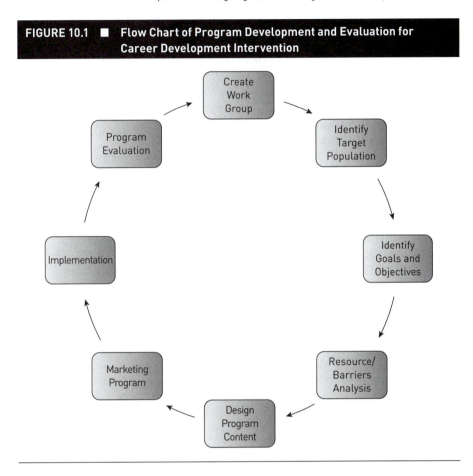

FIGURE 10.1 ■ Flow Chart of Program Development and Evaluation for Career Development Intervention

Youth With Challenges

Citizen Schools is a program for low-income youth in middle schools aiming at supporting academic performance, enrolling in top-tier high schools, and developing a pathway to college and eventually careers. The program components include structured homework and study time supervised by program staff and one-day-a-week apprenticeships in a community setting where volunteering professionals offer hands-on activities and instruction. Youth learn about possible career fields, gain problem-solving skills, collaborate, and have adult mentors. The results show that graduates of this program were more likely to enroll and graduate from top-tier high schools (Mekinda, 2014).

After School Matters is an after-school program for high school students primarily from low-income and minority backgrounds. It includes apprenticeship in communities for three hours a day, three days a week, for 10 weeks per academic term. This program intensity and duration aims at building mentor-like relationships with professionals who can provide guidance for work and life and developing both specific trade skills and across-the-board job-related skills. The program shows positive impacts on youth developing self-regulation skills and managing problem behaviors (Mekinda, 2014).

Career Academies has a long history and nationwide applications, and is an in-school program to integrate occupational and academic curricula through partnerships with local employers that provided work-based learning opportunities (Mekinda, 2014). This program targets a broader range of students with various academic readiness, so it is not just for at-risk students. The research findings show that youth, after participating in this program, had lower dropout rates and significant earnings gains in the long term (eight years later), which truly has positive impacts on labor force participation.

Job Corps, another long-existing program for low-income and disengaged youth (age range from 16 to 24), aims at promoting economic self-sufficiency, employability, and responsibility among youth. According to Mekinda (2014), this is the most intensive and comprehensive program with classroom-based vocational training that can lead to vocational certificate; a variety of services including meals, counseling, health care, and recreation; and the program is individualized and self-paced. The results of the program show that youth were more likely to attain GED, vocational certificate, more earnings, and a higher employment rate.

Career Exploration and Development for Adolescents with LD and EBD is a school-based curricular program that systematically infuses career development services to help students learning and emotional and behavioral disabilities. The four components are career assessment—informal and formal assessment of students' career attributes; authentic experiences—offering seasonal employment assistance via individual educational plan (IEP) planning; social capital—supporting students' development of social capital by strengthening personal connections between and among peers, parents, employers, and others in the community; and self-determination—teachers providing opportunities to learn about one's strengths and challenges, including disabilities, and to practice job-related skills suitable to their interests and strengths and challenges (Trainor, Smith, & Kim, 2012).

Work-Based Education is one of the most widely recognized approaches worldwide for addressing at-risk youth facing educational disengagement and unemployment. The program aims at fostering resilience in the face of adversity through components such as learning in the workplace, cooperative education, apprenticeship, job shadowing, school-sponsored enterprise, and blending secondary and postsecondary education (DeLuca et al., 2010). DeLuca et al. (2010) found that planning, structured and frequent communication, and peer and family support were critical to at-risk youth and that work-based education could be a protective factor for encouraging resilience among disengaged youth.

These programs have a common goal—to help youth develop career readiness by high school graduation, whether students will go to college or not. Despite the trend that a college degree is a must for high-wage jobs, there actually is a great demand for middle-skill jobs, i. e. more than a high school diploma but not a college degree is needed. In fact, increasing financial burden of college education for students and their parents do not provide predictable rewards (Schwartz, 2016). Career development programs, especially especially in K-12 settings, should not neglect the needs for those students whose career aspirations do not require a college degree to be successful. School counselors are in an important position to develop career development intervention programs that would help those students who do not want to go to college. School counselors could explore resources through Career Pathway programs in their state or at the federal level that may provide funding for schools to collaborate with local employers or postsecondary education institutions for more appropriate career development intervention programs for students' needs. School counselors could use the resources provided by the Career Pathways initiatives in the local region and collaborate with community colleges or other postsecondary education institutions to prepare these students to develop employability skills for the future workforce.

Enrichment Programs at Work Settings

The shared aims of career development programs in work settings are to increase quality work and life satisfaction and to enhance workers' career and personal growth. These career development programs at employees' institutions often target women or minority groups who were historically not considered the mainstream labor force until recently. These programs at institutions often aim at mentoring women and minority groups to leadership or senior roles, and the research shows that mentoring or similar programs do have positive impacts on women employees' self-confidence and competency (Woolnough & Fielden, 2014).

Programs with the goal of diversifying the workforce and retaining underrepresented groups in health professionals were examined for their effectiveness, and the findings revealed that career development and enrichment programs for minority members did help recruitment and retention of underrepresented groups in the health care workforce, and that funding is crucial for continued success of such programs (Evans, Johnson, Garma, & Kletke, 2013). The research also found that direct care workers in mental health professions (e.g., frontline workers directly interacting with clients without professional licenses or certifications) would provide better services to their clients and enhance the agencies' revenues if they were supported through educational and career development programs helping them develop job skills and increasing their compensation (Dailey, Morris, & Hoge, 2015). These examples illustrate the importance of supporting workers through specific programming for those people who have limited resources for career advancement.

Work and family balance is a much-needed area of prevention; however, fewer programs exist with this specific goal in either educational or work settings. The Synergy Project Model Intervention model, a program for young adults to manage future work and family conflicts, is one of the few programs addressing work and family issues (Cinamon, 2015). The program has six 90-minute sessions using a group format and addresses three content areas: exploration of personal meaning attributed to work and family roles; information about work, family, and work-family relations; and skills for role management, with a focus on establishing social networks (Cinamon, 2015, p. 418). The advantage of prevention seen in this approach is that young adults can gain information and learn skills to manage the conflict of different roles in the future.

Transition and Partnership

Helping individuals be prepared for transition from one phrase of life to another is essential for any career development program, as evidenced in the discussion of rationale in this chapter. Making the transition from school to work requires collaboration among professionals and community partnership. Involving parents in career exploration has positive impacts on helping children in the counseling process (Amundson & Penner, 1998). Universities can reach out to communities by providing career services to community members. The advantages of university and community partnerships are multiple. First, they serve the needs of the community, particularly the nonstudent adult population who needs career services (McKinnon, 2002); second, they benefit both the university and community by building a fluid and stronger relationship; the third benefit is enhancement of the training of counselors-in-training by working with real-life people and issues. All these efforts smooth the transition for youth and adults alike. Two school-based prevention programs to be reviewed next reveal how interprofessional collaboration and partnership is critical to facilitating a transition from school to work to life.

Achieving Success Identity Pathways is a psychoeducational program promoting stronger connection between students and their context, entailing teachers, parents, peers, and school policies, and it provides structured classroom-based group experiences for students to develop personal agency. The curricula has four components: (1) baseline estimation of one's status in comparison to peers' academic and social efficacy, stress, family support, connections with teachers and peers, persistence intentions, and emotional/physical well-being; (2) students write their life experiences, and teachers become aware of challenges faced by students; (3) exploration of interpersonal conflicts within classroom settings to learn behavior and impacts; and (4) youth develop career search skills, assess personal characteristics, and learn about postsecondary options (Solberg, Howard, Blustein, & Close, 2002). The program was found to have positive impacts on increasing academic performance and attendance rates.

Tools for Tomorrow is a psychoeducational intervention for innercity youth to develop skills for making school to work to life transitions. The program, designed to align with students' sociocultural and economic backgrounds and developmental levels, delivered in group format by a school counselor and teacher as a team, aims at increasing self-understanding, clarifying educational and career goals, having adult mentors, integrating cultural identities, and coping with family issues. It has three components: who am I, connecting school to career, and identifying resources and barriers. According to Solberg et al. (2002), this program increases school engagement, homework completion, and developmental tasks for career development, as well as improves students' decision making.

Summary: Ecological Validity

It is evident from materials presented in this chapter that career development is necessary because it can help more people get career guidance and counseling services. Programming with clearly identified goals and concrete intervention strategies possesses intent and capacity for prevention and intervention with diverse populations at various settings. It could be developmental and comprehensive as the ASCA model for all students at K-12 settings, or it could target at-risk youth partnering with local businesses for school engagement and job skills development, or if could be employee assistance/enhancement programs for better work and family life. Regardless of the aim and scope of programs, it is important to design the program to fit the needs of the population served and the environment surrounding the population. Sustaining a successful program is critical for making a positive impact on more people; however, sustainability is a challenge. Isaacson and Brown (2000) stated that reasons for career education failure were dependence on external funding, not being an integral part of the school district, lack of consideration of the realistic work load of teachers, misrepresentation of career education, and misunderstanding by parents and public who attribute it to vocational education. These lessons enlighten the importance of cultural and contextual concordance in program design and implementation. In essence, ecological validity of programs needs to be assessed in the process from design to evaluation.

Ecological validity means that career development programs needs to consider personal characteristics, inputs, and resources and barriers in relation to career development expectation and outcome; the school and community climate; support or lack of support from all stakeholders; and state and federal policy, legislature, and funding. Across the various level of ecological system, both personal and contextual factors in each system (e.g., demographic characteristics of the local community; school policy; funding; local, state, and national laws; resources; and barriers) should be carefully incorporated in career program development to avoid potential roadblocks hampering the program outcome. A high-quality program is also an iterative process, as continual improvement is needed. Therefore, formative evaluation and summative evaluation are necessary because they can be informative for evaluating program process and outcome. The analysis of multinational initiative of career task management (Hooley, Watts, Sultana, & Neary, 2012) reveals that lifelong learning, policy connection, theoretical framework, and contextual affordance are necessary elements for career services.

Keystones

- Career development programs can serve more people more efficiently, especially when resources are limited.

- Prevention is the primary goal of career development programs; through systematic and proactive intervention, people learn career tasks and to manage their work and life effectively.

- Comprehensiveness and lifelong learning are critical elements in career development programming principles, as the changing work environment demands people acquire attitudes and skills to be ready for any transitions throughout the life span, from school to work, from employment to unemployment, to reentry into workforce.

- The process of developing a career prevention/intervention program involves identifying the target population; identifying goals/objectives; analyzing resources and barriers; and designing program content, marketing plans, program implementation, and an evaluation plan.

- Cultural and contextual consideration is crucial in developing career development programs, as ecological validity is the key to accomplishing and sustaining the program.

References

American School Counselor Association. (2004). *ASCA national standards for students.* Alexandria, VA: Author.

American School Counselor Association. (2012). *The ASCA national model: A framework for school counseling programs* (3rd ed.). Alexandria, VA: American School Counseling Association.

Amundson, N. E., & Penner, K. (1998). Parent involved career exploration. *The Career Development Quarterly, 47*(2), 135-144.

Bloch, D. P. (1996). Career development and workforce preparation: Educational policy versus school practice. *The Career Development Quarterly, 45*(1), 20-40. doi:10.1002/j.2161-0045.1996.tb00459.x

Bollendorf, M., Howrey, M., & Stephenson, G. (1990). Project career Reach: Marketing strategies for effective guidance programs. *School Counselor, 37,* 273-280.

Brown, D. (2012). *Career information, career counseling, and career development.* Boston, MA: Pearson.

Brown, S. D., Lamp, K., Telander, K. J., & Hacker, J. (2013). Career development as prevention: Toward a social cognitive model of vocational hope. In E. M. Vera (Ed), *The Oxford handbook of prevention in counseling psychology* (pp. 374-392). New York, NY: Oxford University Press.

Carr, J. V. (1996). Comprehensiveness of career planning: The third C-comprehensiveness. *Journal of Career Development, 23,* 33-42.

Chronister, K. M., McWhirter, B. T., & Kerewsky, D. (2004). Counseling and ecological prevention practice. In R. K. Conyne & E. P. Cook (Eds.), *Ecological counseling: Innovative approach to conceptualizing person-environment interaction* (pp. 315-338). Alexandra, VA: ACA.

Cinamon, R. G. (2015). The synergy project: A group career counseling intervention to enhance work-family management. In P. J. Hartung, M. L. Savickas, W. B. Walsh, P. J. Hartung, M. L. Savickas, & W. B. Walsh (Eds.), *APA handbook of career intervention: Vol. 2. applications* (pp. 413-425). Washington, DC: American Psychological Association. doi:10.1037/14439-030

Conyne, R. K, & Cook, E. P. (Eds.). (2004). *Ecological counseling. An innovative approach to conceptualizing person-environment interaction.* Alexandria, VA: American Counseling Association.

Dailey, W. F., Morris, J. A., & Hoge, M. A. (2015). Workforce development innovations with direct care workers: Better jobs, better services, better business. *Community Mental Health Journal, 51,* 647-653. doi:10.1007/s10597-014-9798-4

DeLuca, C., Hutchinson, N. L., deLugt, J. S., Beyer, W., Thornton, A., Versnel, J., . . . Munby, H. (2010). Learning in the workplace: Fostering resilience in disengaged youth. *Journal of Prevention, Assessment & Rehabilitation, 36*(3), 305-319.

Donelly, M., & Given, F. (2010). Employment programs and professionals with a disability. *Work: Journal of Prevention, Assessment & Rehabilitation, 36*(2), 217-225.

Evans, R. M., Johnson, J. A., Garman, A. N., & Kletke, P. (2013). Meeting the challenge: Career development and targeted enrichment programs insuring a viable pipeline. *SAGE Open, 3*(2). doi:10.1177/2158244013484475

Feller, R. W. (2006). Developing comprehensive career plans for your clients. In D. Capuzzi, & M. Stauffer (Eds.), *Career and lifestyle planning: Theory and application* (pp. 178-203). Boston, MA: Allyn & Bacon.

Goodman, J., & Hansen, S. (2005). Career development and guidance programs across cultures: The gap between policies and practices. *The Career Development Quarterly, 54*(1), 57-65. doi:10.1002/j.2161-0045.2005.tb00141.x

Gottfredson, L. S. (2002). Gottfredson's theory of circumscription, compromise, and self-creation. In D. Brown & Associates (Eds.), *Career choice and development* (4th ed., pp. 85-148). San Francisco, CA: Jossey-Bass.

Gysbers, N. C., & Henderson, P. (2001). Comprehensive guidance and counseling programs: A rich history and a bright future. *Professional School Counseling, 4*(4), 246.

Gysbers, N. C., & Henderson, P. (2012). *Developing and managing your school counseling program* (5th ed.). Alexandria, VA: American Counseling Association.

Herr, E. L. (1999). Theoretical perspectives on the school-to-work transition: Reactions and recommendations. *Career Development Quarterly, 47*(4), 359-364. doi:10.1002/j.2161-0045.1999.tb00745.x

Herr, E. L., Cramer, S. H., & Niles, S. G. (2004). *Career guidance and counseling through life span: Systematic approaches* (6th ed.). Boston, MA: Allyn & Bacon.

Hooley, T., Watts, A. G., Sultana, R. G., & Neary, S. (2012). The 'Blueprint' framework for career management skills: A critical exploration. *British Journal of Guidance & Counseling*, 1-15. doi:10/1080/03069885.2012.713908

Isaacson, L. E., & Brown, D. (2000). *Career information, career counseling, and career development*. Boston, MA: Allyn & Bacon.

Kimbel, T., & Clemens, E. (2014). The development and validation of the school counseling program report card—student version. *Professional School Counseling, 18*(1), 111-124. doi:10.5330/prsc.18.1.c5671j65u272n0n9

Krumboltz, J. D. (1996). A learning theory of career counseling. In M. L. Savickas, & W. B. Walsh (Eds.), *Handbook of career counseling theory and practice* (pp. 55-80). Palo Alto, CA: Davies-Black.

Lapan, R. T., & Kosciulek, J. F. (2001). Toward a community career system evaluation framework. *Journal of Counseling & Development, 79*, 3-15.

Lent, R. W., Brown, S. D., & Hackett, G. (1994). Toward a unifying social cognitive theory of career and academic interest, choice, and performance [Monograph]. *Journal of Vocational Behavior, 45*, 79–122.

McCotter, S., & Cohen, S. (2013). Are middle school counseling programs meeting early adolescent needs? A survey of principals and counselors. *Journal of Counselor Preparation and Supervision, 5*(1). doi:10.7729/51.0015

McDavid, J., & Hawthorn, L. R. L. (2006). *Program evaluation & performance measurement: An introduction to practice*. Thousand Oaks, CA: Sage.

Mekinda, M. A. (2012). Support for career development in youth: Program models and evaluations. *New Directions for Youth Development*, (134), 45-54. doi:10.1002/yd.20014

Nota, L., Ginevra, M. C., & Santilli, S. (2015). Life design and prevention. In L. Nota, J. Rossier,

L. Nota & J. Rossier (Eds.), *Life design handbook* (pp. 183–199). Boston, MA: Hogrefe.

Romano, J. L., & Hage, S. M. (2000). Prevention and counseling psychology: Revitalizing commitments for the 21st century. *The Counseling Psychologists, 28*, 733-763.

Schultheiss, D. E. P. (2005). Elementary career intervention programs: Social action initiatives. *Journal of Career Development, 31*(3), 185-194. doi:10.1007/s10871-004-2226-1

Schwartz, R. B. (2016). The career pathways movement: A Promising strategic for increasing opportunities and mobility. *Journal of Social Issues, 72*, 740-759. doi:10.1111/josi.12192.

Solberg, V. S., Howard, K. A., Blustein, D. L., & Close, W. (2002). Career development in the schools: Connecting school-to-work-to-life. *The Counseling Psychologist, 30*(5), 705-725. doi:10.1177/0011000002305003

Stufflebean, D. L. (2007). *CIPP evaluation model checklist: A tool for applying the CIPP model to assess long-term enterprises* (2nd ed.). Kalamazoo, MI: West Michigan University. Retrieved from http://www.wmich.edu/sites/default/files/attachments/u350/2014/cippchecklist_mar07.pdf.

Super, D. E. (1990). A life-span, life-space approach to career development. In D. Brown & L. Brooks (Eds.), *Career choice and development: Applying contemporary theories to practice* (2nd ed., pp. 197-261). San Francisco, CA: Jossey-Bass.

Tang, M., & Russ, K. (2007). Understanding and facilitating career development of people of Appalachian culture: An integrated approach. *Career Development Quarterly, 56*(1), 34-46. doi:10.1002/j.2161-0045.2007.tb00018.x

Trainor, A. A., Smith, S. A., & Kim, S. (2012). Four supportive pillars in career exploration and development for adolescents with LD and EBD. *Intervention in School and Clinic, 48*(1), 15-21. doi:10.1177/1053451212443129

Woolnough, H., & Fielden, S. (2014). The impact of a career development and mentoring programme on female mental health nurses. *Gender in Management: An International Journal, 29*(2), 108-122. doi:10.1108/GM-05-2013-0049

Wright, R. J. (2014). *Research methods for Counseling: An introduction.* Thousand Oaks, CA: Sage.

Appendix A: ASCA National Standards for Students

ASCA National Standards for career development guide school counseling programs to provide the foundation for the acquisition of skills, attitudes, and knowledge that enable students to make a successful transition from school to the world of work, and from job to job across the life span.

CATEGORY 1: MINDSET STANDARDS

School counselors encourage the following mindsets for all students.

M 1. Belief in development of whole self, including a healthy balance of mental, social/emotional and physical well-being

M 2. Self-confidence in ability to succeed

M 3. Sense of belonging in the school environment

M 4. Understanding that postsecondary education and life-long learning are necessary for long-term career success

M 5. Belief in using abilities to their fullest to achieve high-quality results and outcomes

M 6. Positive attitude toward work and learning

CATEGORY 2: BEHAVIOR STANDARDS

Students will demonstrate the following standards through classroom lessons, activities and/or individual/small-group counseling.

Learning Strategies

B-LS 1. Demonstrate critical-thinking skills to make informed decisions

B-LS 2. Demonstrate creativity

B-LS 3. Use time-management, organizational and study skills

B-LS 4. Apply self-motivation and self-direction to learning

B-LS 5. Apply media and technology skills

B-LS 6. Set high standards of quality

B-LS 7. Identify long- and short-term academic, career and social/ emotional goals

B-LS 8. Actively engage in challenging coursework

B-LS 9. Gather evidence and consider multiple perspectives to make informed decisions

B-LS 10. Participate in enrichment and extracurricular activities

Self-Management Skills

B-SMS 1. Demonstrate ability to assume responsibility

B-SMS 2. Demonstrate self-discipline and self-control

B-SMS 3. Demonstrate ability to work independently

B-SMS 4. Demonstrate ability to delay immediate gratification for long-term rewards

B-SMS 5. Demonstrate perseverance to achieve long- and short-term goals

B-SMS 6. Demonstrate ability to overcome barriers to learning

B-SMS 7. Demonstrate effective coping skills when faced with a problem

B-SMS 8. Demonstrate the ability to balance school, home and community activities

B-SMS 9. Demonstrate personal safety skills

B-SMS 10. Demonstrate ability to manage transitions and ability to adapt to changing situations and responsibilities

Social Skills

B-SS 1. Use effective oral and written communication skills and listening skills

B-SS 2. Create positive and supportive relationships with other students

B-SS 3. Create relationships with adults that support success

B-SS 4. Demonstrate empathy

B-SS 5. Demonstrate ethical decision-making and social responsibility

B-SS 6. Use effective collaboration and cooperation skills

B-SS 7. Use leadership and teamwork skills to work effectively in diverse teams

B-SS 8. Demonstrate advocacy skills and ability to assert self, when necessary

B-SS 9. Demonstrate social maturity and behaviors appropriate to the situation and environment

CAREER DEVELOPMENT PREVENTION AND INTERVENTION IN K-12 SCHOOL SETTINGS

Mary L. Anderson

For this chapter, we turn our attention to providing career development services in schools throughout the K-12 curriculum. Ensuring the postsecondary success of students is increasingly crucial, especially in preparing students to meet the demands of the rapidly changing 21st-century workplace (Carey & Herr, 2012; Curry & Milsom, 2014). Education reforms and initiatives continue to be implemented to increase student achievement and address the challenges of a highly competitive and globalized workplace (Anderson & Vandehey, 2006; Niles & Harris-Bowlsbey, 2017). A core mission for professional school counseling programs is to equip *all* students to be college and career ready, and an important focus is on closing the gaps for marginalized and first-generation students (American School Counselor Association, 2014; White House, 2014). School counselors are positioned to assist students in visualizing their future aspirations and helping them take the steps required to successfully fulfill their goals (Hines, Lemons, & Crews, 2011).

LEARNING OBJECTIVES

After completing the reading and exercises provided in this chapter, you will be able to:

- understand career development within the framework of a comprehensive school counseling program;

- explain recent trends in education reform and initiatives;

- identify appropriate developmental and theoretical approaches for working with students in the schools;

- understand the use of assessment to develop students' awareness of interests, skills, and abilities and how these relate to the world of work;

- identify strategies to support students' career awareness and development across the elementary, middle, and high school levels; and

- identify multicultural and ethical implications when working with students and career development within the schools.

GOALS AND SCOPE OF CAREER DEVELOPMENT PROGRAMS IN K-12: THE AMERICAN SCHOOL COUNSELOR ASSOCIATION (ASCA) NATIONAL MODEL

The profession of school counseling continues to transition from a responsive, crises-orientated approach, to comprehensive programs with clearly defined functions and goals (Gysbers & Henderson, 2006). School counseling, which began 100 years ago as vocational guidance, has evolved from a position described as a list of duties, to a profession delivering services organized within a comprehensive framework (Gysbers, 2010). The reforms put forth with the American School Counselor Association National Model (American School Counselor Association, 2005, 2012a) and the Transforming School Counseling Initiative (The Education Trust, 1997) served to promote this new vision for the school counselor role (Milsom & Akos, 2005). Many factors continue to influence school counseling programs, including the globalization of careers, continued school reforms and initiatives, and an increased focus on accountability across the educational system.

The American School Counselor Association (ASCA) National Model (2012a) was designed to be comprehensive in scope, preventative in design, and developmental in nature, with a key emphasis on aligning school counseling with education reform movements focused on student achievement (American School Counselor Association, 2014). The ASCA Model (2012a) was founded on a vision for school counseling that is driven by student outcomes and evidenced-based standards for academic, career, and social/emotional development. When using this model, school counselors organize their time to ensure delivery of services for all students and intentionally design interventions for maximum program effectiveness. These services are defined as both direct and indirect; direct services include individual student planning, small group activities, classroom lessons, and responsive services and system support. Direct services may also include providing in-service presentations for teachers and informational workshops for parents and guardians. Indirect services support students in terms of school counselors interacting with others on their behalf, such as making referrals for additional services and consultation and collaboration with school administration, teachers, families, and community organizations. The fundamental purpose of a comprehensive model is to support the school's academic mission, while meeting the preventative and developmental needs of *all* students.

School counseling programs are essentially developmental, with an emphasis on strengths-based interventions to increase student competencies across the academic, career, and personal/social domains. Although these domains are portrayed as being separate, they are in actual practice delivered interactively and holistically (Gysbers, 2013). Within each domain, student competency standards provide benchmarks for student outcomes across the K-12 curriculum. Within the career domain, ASCA National Model standards relate to students' career awareness, employment readiness, and career goals (American School Counselor Association, 2004). As students progress through the elementary, middle school, and high school levels, school counselors design interventions to increase student competencies, building on foundations from previous levels.

ASCA recently updated their standards with the *Mindsets & Behaviors for Student Success: K-12 College- and Career-Readiness Standards for Every Student* (American School Counselor Association, 2014). These standards provide a more explicit focus on college-and career-readiness and identify the specific attitudes, knowledge, and skills that students should demonstrate across the K-12 curriculum. These mindset behaviors were developed based on research and best practices and are considered the next generation of the ASCA National Standards (Curry & Milsom, 2017). School counselors use the 35 mindset and behavior standards to inform their school counseling programs and to intentionally design interventions to promote college and career readiness. The mindset behavior competencies are organized by the domains of academic success, college and career readiness, and social/emotional development, with standards and grade-level competencies that align with the ASCA National Model (2012a). These are detailed in the Mindset Behavior Planning Tool template provided by ASCA on their website.

A comprehensive school counseling program is managed through ongoing assessments to determine student needs within the school and to evaluate the results of program interventions and activities. School counselors develop annual and weekly calendars to keep students, parents, teachers, and administration informed and to also encourage ongoing participation and engagement in the school counseling program. Student services are delivered through the school counseling core curriculum with structured lessons to address student competencies and skill development across the K-12 grade levels. A key aspect of contemporary school counseling programs is a focus on accountability, using measures to demonstrate the effectiveness of the program and the impact on student outcomes. Another important focus for positive outcomes is assisting students as they transition from elementary to middle school, on to high school, and finally transition to postsecondary careers and/or further training and education.

A central focus of the ASCA National Model (2012a) is on the role of the school counselor across the following themes: leadership, advocacy, collaboration, and systemic change. School counselors serve as leaders within the schools as they work for student achievement and collaborate with teachers, administrators, and school personnel. It is imperative that school counselors advocate for career development programs to be an integral component of the overall school curriculum, and this requires ongoing effective communication regarding goals and objectives with all stakeholders (Gysbers & Henderson, 2001; Niles, Trusty, & Mitchell, 2004). School counselors are committed to promoting equity and access for all students, which relates directly to their role as change agents. ASCA has established school counselor competencies (ASCA, 2012b) that detail the knowledge, skills, and attitudes necessary for school counselors to maintain the highest standards of the profession across the many aspects of the school counselor role. At the heart of the work is "preparing today's students to become tomorrow's adults," which has become the central mission of the American School Counselor Association (American School Counselor Association, 2004). Today's school counselors serve as leaders and advocates to ensure that students are offered the educational opportunities to obtain the skills and competencies needed to succeed in the current workplace (Curry & Milsom, 2017).

EDUCATIONAL REFORM AND INITIATIVES

There have been numerous educational reform movements that reflect a standards-based approach to education, such as No Child Left Behind Act (White House, 2014), the Blueprint for the Reauthorization of the Elementary and Secondary Schools Act (U.S. Department of Education, 2010), and the National Math and Science Initiative (National Math and Science Initiative, 2011). A common thread throughout these educational reforms is the focus on raising teacher accountability, student proficiency, and academic achievement for all students.

More recently, White House initiatives were put forth from the Obama Administration including the Every Student Succeeds Act (Executive Office of the President, 2015) and Reach Higher (White House, 2014) that resulted in a national movement focused on preparing students for career and college readiness (CCR). Former President Barack Obama established a North Star goal that by 2020 the United States will achieve the highest number of college graduates of any other country, and former First Lady Michelle Obama championed the charge through her Reach Higher initiatives focused on postsecondary education, especially for low-income, minority, and nontraditional students (White House, 2014). Many national and state organizations, along with school counselor educators, came together to provide leadership through forming collaborative partnerships and participation on state teams at the annual Reach Higher White House convenings (U.S. Department of Education, 2017). The four key areas of focus of the Reach Higher initiatives were exposing students to college and career opportunities, furthering understanding of financial aid eligibility, encouraging academic planning and summer learning opportunities, and supporting secondary school counselors in their work to assist students. In conjunction with ASCA, the former first lady also focused on recognizing the importance of school counseling and promoting the value of school counselors. She supported the profession of school counseling by speaking at events, such as the ASCA 2014 National Conference and the White House Day of Opportunity (White House, 2014), and she also established the annual School Counselor of the Year ceremony at the White House. The Reach Higher initiatives served to place school counselors at the center of the movement, emphasizing that they are optimally positioned within the schools to encourage student achievement, address barriers that students and families face, and propel students toward postsecondary college and career success. Along with initiatives for college and career readiness for students, there has also been an increased focus on state-mandated standards for school counselor training programs, along with professional development opportunities to enhance school counselors' competencies for assisting students in their academic, career, and postsecondary planning.

Additionally, the College Board National Office for School Counselor Advocacy recently put forth the Eight Components of College and Career Readiness (College Board, 2010). This document provides guidelines for school counselors to implement across grades K-12, with the central goal to ensure equity in process and results for all students. This is considered a systemic approach for school counselors to "build aspirations and social capital, offer enriching activities, foster rigorous academic preparation, encourage early college planning, and guide students and families through the college admission and financial aid process" (College Board, 2010, p. 2). The Eight Components of College and Career Readiness, along with the ASCA standards and Mindsets Behaviors, provide a foundation for goals and benchmarks for college and career readiness. Ideally, school counselors use these resources, along with state standards, to inform their programs. All these resources serve to define the knowledge and skills students should obtain within their K-12 education experience, preparing them to succeed in postsecondary college courses and in workforce training programs (Hatch, 2014).

Established in 1990 and reauthorized in 1997 and 2004, the Individuals with Disabilities Education Act (P.L. 101-476, IDEA) has provided a mandate for developing formal transition planning services to assist students with disabilities as they transition through the grade levels and prepare for postsecondary options. This mandate is focused on coordinated efforts among school counselors, teachers, and parents to assist students with acquiring the requisite skills and knowledge to successfully adapt to new environments. Developing a yearly individualized education program (IEP) that details academic and social goals, along with methods to achieve these goals, is a shared responsibility of school counselors and teachers to address the needs of students with disabilities. Transitioning from grade to grade and across educational levels can be especially challenging for students with changing environments and the different expectations and skill sets required. When students are approaching transitions, relevant goals focused on the transition need to be included within a student's IEP, and it is imperative that the individual student's needs are taken into consideration (Milsom, 2007).

THEORETICAL APPLICATIONS: WORKING WITH CHILDREN AND ADOLESCENTS

A key component of graduate training is learning about counseling theories, which includes conceptualizing client issues and designing interventions using theoretical approaches. Working with children and adolescents and career development within the K-12 school setting adapts well to a psychoeducational approach, and it is important to consider the developmental levels of children and adolescents when determining appropriate theories and strategies. While a thorough discussion of theoretical approaches is beyond the scope of this chapter, a few key theories are highlighted to provide a practical foundation for working with students in the schools. This discussion of theory is intentionally brief, yet the intent is to encourage further exploration and knowledge of theories that take into account both developmental and contextual factors. An important point when using theories is that cultural differences are an important consideration regarding the usefulness and appropriateness of theory and interventions. Intentionality and sensitivity to cultural differences are crucial when working with students and their families within the schools.

Developmental Theory

Developmental theories address the stages and tasks of development across the life span, including the physical, cognitive, moral, and social/emotional aspects. As these theories continue to evolve and advance, they provide a helpful framework for school counselors working in a K-12 school setting. Super's Life-Span, Life-Space theory (Super, 1990) is a widely recognized developmental approach, and concepts of the theory are highly relevant to working with students' career development in the schools. Super's approach incorporates theoretical perspectives from developmental theory, along with other prominent career theories, such as trait-and-factor, social learning, and psychodynamic (Niles & Harris-Bowlsbey, 2017). His theory emphasizes the *process* of career development over a person's entire life span and across different life/career roles. A key concept within the theory is *self-concept*, which refers to how people view themselves and their life situations. A person's self-concept develops through managing the tasks of the developmental stages and substages indicated for childhood through adulthood. The main stages of his theory include growth, exploration, establishment, maintenance, and disengagement. The stages most applicable to working with students in the schools are growth (relating to childhood) and exploration (relating to adolescence). Super's theory provides a helpful framework for conceptualizing the tasks of childhood (developing a sense of self and beginning knowledge of the world of work) and adolescence (increased self-awareness and clarity regarding occupational preferences). Using Super's theoretical framework, school counselors can design interventions that are developmentally appropriate at the elementary, middle school, and high school levels. These interventions may emphasize increasing students' self-awareness at the elementary level, facilitating exploration and educational planning at the middle school level, and moving on to more focused planning for postsecondary options at the high school level. Interventions are delivered through implementing the school counseling curriculum in the classroom and through small group activities, along with schoolwide events and programs.

Although school counselors take a program approach to meeting students' needs, they also have opportunities to work with individual students and parents. As mentioned previously, when applying theories and working with individuals, it is crucial to be sensitive to the culture and worldview of students and their families. Hess, Magnuson, and Beeler (2012) underscore the importance of exploring the meaning that students assign to an event or situation and taking the time to understand the student's perspective. This relates to career development issues, as well as other contextual issues that school counselors address when working with students and their families.

Gottfredson's Theory

Gottfredson's theory of circumscription, compromise, and self-creation (Gottfredson, 2002, 2005) provides a focus on career development processes that occur during childhood and adolescence. Her theory identifies stages related to how students develop career aspirations and also compromise by placing limits on their choices. A key concept of her theory is that people may unnecessarily limit their options, settling for a "good enough" choice, rather than striving for the best choice (Niles & Harris-Bowlsbey, 2017). According to Gottfredson (1981), young people limit their choices based on gender role stereotypes, prestige associated with occupations, and personality preferences within the world of work. She defined *circumscription* as the process of eliminating occupational alternatives, which takes place across four stages: orientation to size and power (ages 3-5), orientation to sex roles (ages 6-8), orientation to social valuation (ages 9-13), and orientation to the internal, unique self (ages 14 and above). These stages relate to students' cognitive development, from forming object constancy in the first stage, to becoming aware of the sex roles of men and women in the second stage, to determining a range of acceptable occupations based on social class and ability in the third stage. During the last stage, adolescents begin to generate goals and become more conscious of making choices. Another key concept from her theory is compromise, which relates to people giving up on occupations due to internal barriers with self-concept or to anticipating or experiencing external barriers.

Gottfredson's (2002, 2005) theory is helpful in addressing both the developmental and social contexts that influence students' career development choices. Her theory underscores the importance of early interventions, especially in exposing children to a variety of career options and working to promote active career exploration through schoolwide programs, classroom lessons, and small group interventions. It is imperative to work with students regarding perceived and actual barriers, especially as these relate to their career aspirations and dreams. Gottfredson (1981, 2002) suggested that children can reconsider the options available to them through new learning experiences and challenging sexual stereotypes associated with careers. These are areas that can be addressed throughout the school counseling curriculum.

LEARNING ACTIVITY 11.1

Consider the following questions. Write a response, and be prepared to share with a colleague: How influential were gender role expectations in your choices of a career path? Did you make any compromises regarding your career aspirations? Describe how you view these compromises at this point in your life/career journey.

Ecological Theory

Children and adolescents are impacted by the environments and contexts of their lives, and ecological theory (Bronfenbrenner, 1979) provides a model for understanding the different interrelated systems that are key influences on students' development. This theory has become prominent as school-based professionals and researchers continue to place a greater emphasis on the roles of family and community and their impact on

FIGURE 11.1 ■ Bronfenbrenner Ecological Model

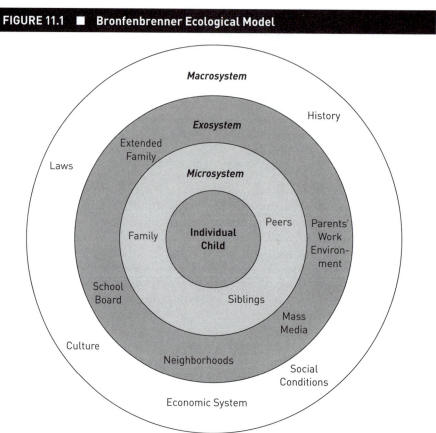

Niederer, Iris & Kriemler, Susi & Zahner, Lukas & Bürgi, Flavia & Ebenegger, Vincent & Hartmann, Tim & Meyer, Ursina & Schindler, Christian & Nydegger, Andreas & Marques-Vidal, Pedro & Puder, Jardena. (2009). Influence of a lifestyle intervention in preschool children on physiological and psychological parameters (Ballabeina): Study design of a cluster randomized controlled trial. BMC Public Health. doi:9. 94. 10.1186/1471-2458-9-94.

students' lives (Curry & Milsom, 2017). The ecological approach describes influential systems within four contexts: the *microsystem* where students interact daily, such as home and school; the *mesosystem* that refers to the relationships between systems, such as between family and the schools; *the exosystem*, that includes socioeconomic status, neighborhood, community, and extended family; and the *macrosystem* that addresses the larger context that may impact the person, including political ideologies, government laws/policies, cultural values, and the national economy.

School counselors may use the ecological framework when considering the influences impacting students in their schools, and Bronfenbrenner (1979) underscored the importance of the relationships that exist in the microsystem, as these hold the most influence on a child. These relationships are, in fact, reciprocal and play a key role in shaping college and career readiness development (Curry & Milsom, 2017). This theory provides a useful framework for determining interventions for specific student populations within the schools and addressing the negative impact of factors such as poverty, homelessness,

LEARNING ACTIVITY 11.2

Consider the contextual factors that influenced your own career development. What was happening in the different systems of Bronfenbrenner's Ecological Model as you grew up through childhood and adolescence? What were some key influences, assets, and challenges you faced within the different contexts?

parent drug use, and other hardships. As the school counseling field continues to evolve, the movement toward an ecological approach has proven helpful in addressing inequities through school counselor interventions focused on leadership, advocacy, and collaboration (McMahon, Mason, Daluga-Guenther, & Ruiz, 2014). Although a full discussion of this theoretical approach is beyond the scope of this chapter, key concepts of this theory may be used when addressing the developmental needs of students in the schools. Working within an ecological systems approach can be useful in developing interventions across the interrelated contexts of school, home, and community. Ideally, at the core of an ecological approach is creating a strengths-based focus through fostering respectful, collaborative relationships with all stakeholders and modeling the personal characteristics necessary to promote a healthy school environment (McMahon et al., 2014).

CAREER DEVELOPMENT PROGRAMS K-12

Career development interventions are crucial today, as students are preparing to enter a rapidly changing workforce landscape, with increasing demands for advanced skills and competencies. A comprehensive program can provide strategies and interventions to prepare students to succeed in reaching their postsecondary goals, and just as important, teach them the skills and mindsets necessary to become lifelong learners. It is key to engage students in their own career development, and school counselors serve as advocates for providing effective services, working collaboratively with teachers, staff, parents, and community members. Ideally, the school counseling curriculum should be integral to the school curriculum, advancing student competencies and supporting the mission of the school. School counselors may face challenges when working with teachers who are under pressure to ensure students achieve academic benchmarks. This is especially true today with high stakes testing and school ratings based on student test results. However, the movement toward college and career readiness places school counselors in an optimal position to advocate and provide leadership for career development programs.

With the current emphasis on college and career readiness, the school counseling curriculum and interventions should be coordinated as a comprehensive, systemic program that spans the K-12 grade levels. School counselors must be intentional in promoting positive student outcomes, using the ASCA standards and mindsets behaviors to plan interventions and to assess student outcomes. School counselors also refer to the National Career Development Guidelines (NCDG), which are organized across three domains: personal social development, educational achievement and lifelong learning, and career management (Kobylarz, 2004). These domains, with associated competencies, align well with the ASCA Student Standards and Mindsets Behaviors. Delivering interventions in a systemic manner ensures that all students have an opportunity to identify their strengths, interests, and skills; develop occupational goals; and formulate educational plans that lead to future postsecondary opportunities. A core value of a comprehensive school counseling program is ensuring equitable access to opportunities and rigorous curriculum for all students to participate fully in the educational process (American School Counselor Association, 2012a).

It is also critical that parents and guardians are invited to be involved and to encourage and reinforce the learnings from school-based interventions in the home (Gysbers, 2013). Research strongly supports the importance of family influence, which has been linked to positive student outcomes, including higher academic achievement, school attendance and grades, willingness to take on academic work, and aspirations for higher education (Greenwood & Hickman, 1991). The positive impact of connections with students and their families cannot be understated.

School counselors assist students with developing their educational plans and selecting courses of study related to students' individual career goals and postsecondary plans, and within this context, students may make decisions and finalize their postsecondary plans. Individual student plans can be developed collaboratively as school counselors work with students and their parents during the middle grades and can be reviewed as students continue their progress through their high school years. School counselors often work with students and parents to address the barriers and challenges they face, and this may include conveying important information, assisting with tasks such as completing the Free Application for Federal Student Aid (FAFSA) and college applications, and working with students and parents to take the steps of preparing and planning for postsecondary options.

CAREER SERVICES IN ELEMENTARY SCHOOL

In this section, we focus our attention on career development interventions at the elementary level. Historically, more attention has been given to career development at the secondary levels, and some may not recognize the importance of career interventions during the elementary years. However, research supports that younger children can benefit from career education and connecting academics with the world of work, and skill development in the early grades is essential to postsecondary success (Curry & Milsom, 2014). A comprehensive K-12 approach is imperative for both prevention and establishing a strong foundation for students before they move forward to middle and high school.

At the elementary level, school counselors work toward promoting a positive school environment to foster supportive relationships with students and enhance a sense of belonging in the schools. It is also an opportune time to assist children with developing a sense of self-efficacy around study skills and coping skills when faced with challenges. Career interventions with younger students are focused on topics such as enhancing students' awareness of self, interpersonal skill development, academic skill development, and expanding knowledge regarding occupations and careers. An important strategy is to design interventions targeting specific developmental grade levels and to engage students in a variety of hands-on activities. According to Super (1990), career development competencies develop out of children's natural curiosity, and school counselors may intentionally design activities that tap into children's love of play and fantasy. Examples of these types of interventions include using art projects, role plays, and games and also may also include field trips to expand occupational interests. A popular event is "bring your child to work day," and other events involving elementary school children's parents can provide a fun and engaging way to involve parents in sharing about their careers and avocations.

During the elementary years, there are fundamental career, academic, and personal social skills that are essential for building toward postsecondary success (Curry & Milsom, 2017). Elementary school counselors can use the ASCA Mindsets and Behaviors (2014) to develop learning objectives for career and college readiness interventions at each grade level. When designing lesson plans, it is helpful to identify specific mindset and behavior student competencies and also include plans for evaluation that assesses positive impact on students' attitudes, knowledge, or skills (American School Counselor Association, 2012a). School counselors may also use the Eight Components of College and Career Readiness to formulate goals to build a college-going culture and early awareness activities that encourage student confidence and college aspirations. Interventions may include creating connectedness to staff and fellow students, teaching skills to master their learning and social environment, and promoting helpful learning habits and positive attitude to be successful in school (College Board, 2010).

For the early grades, Niles & Harris-Bowlsbey (2017) suggest focusing on students developing increased self-awareness through activities that have children describing themselves through drawings, writing about things they like, and bringing favorite things to school to share with their classmates. They also emphasize the importance of appreciating

CASE ILLUSTRATION 11.1

Shawna is a second-grade student and is new to the school, after moving from a rural small town to the city to live with her grandmother. Shawna's grandmother communicated her concerns for both her daughter and her granddaughter when registering her at the school. She shared that Shawna's parents were recently divorced, and her mother is in the military and was recently deployed to Afghanistan. Shawna's father lives in another state with two younger stepchildren and his new wife. He works on an oil rig and stated that he could no longer be responsible for Shawna's care. While attending her previous school, Shawna's teachers noticed that she seemed withdrawn and had difficulties connecting with other children in her class. As her school counselor, when reviewing Shawna's records from her previous school, you notice that Shawna's reading and writing skills are below second-grade level.

Discussion questions:

1. As Shawna's school counselor, how would you assess her academic and career development needs?

2. Where would you begin to work with Shawna, and which theories/models would you use to conceptualize her issues?

3. Which staff and school personnel might assist you in working with Shawna; specifically, how might you collaborate to meet her needs?

the similarities and differences among students, and that highlighting cultural traditions and celebrating differences provide valuable contributions to the learning process. It is also crucial to focus at the elementary level on increasing occupational awareness and the relationship between work and education and provide activities that foster career exploration and a sense of self-efficacy and competence.

There are many engaging activities for the elementary grade levels, and resources listed at the end of this chapter will take you to examples provided by the ASCA and National Office for School Counselor Advocacy (NOSCA), among other sources. A key aspect of creating curriculum at the elementary level is to lay the groundwork by systematically addressing a range of career development competencies and also collaborating with middle school counselors to build on what students have gained during their elementary years (Dugger, 2016). To track areas covered in the curriculum, NOSCA provides a chart of key data elements for each of the Eight Components across the elementary, middle, and high school.

CAREER SERVICES IN MIDDLE SCHOOLS

The transition to middle school can be challenging for students, and the turbulent nature of this stage is commonly known to educators, school counselors, and parents. Students moving into adolescence experience a myriad of physical changes, growth spurts, and hormonal changes; these are important considerations regarding the lasting impact on students' self-concept, body image, and self-evaluations from a social perspective (Curry & Milsom, 2017). According to Niles & Harris-Bowlsbey (2017), it can be challenging for middle school students as they make strides toward independence, which may be accompanied by feelings of insecurity, conflict, fear, and anxiety. It can also be challenging for students to be active agents in the career development process with a tendency during the middle grades to be preoccupied with issues around belonging and being strongly influenced by peers (Niles & Harris-Bowlsbey, 2017).

It is crucial to provide support and encouragement to middle school students, and school counselors at this level may find that their role is more responsive and loosely defined. Yet, the importance of implementing a comprehensive approach to addressing students' academic, career, and personal/social needs cannot be overemphasized. During the middle grades, school counselors can implement career development interventions to promote students' developing self-concept and assist them in understanding their strengths, interests, and personal preferences. As school counselors encourage students to explore who they are and tap into their interests, students can also increase their knowledge about careers and begin making decisions regarding their short-term and long-term goals (American School Counseling Association, 2012a). When working with middle school students, it is helpful to use a multisystemic approach, which underscores the importance of collaborating with parents, teachers, administrators, and community members to promote career and college development (Curry & Milsom, 2017). It is especially important to collaborate with parents, as they may need assistance with how to best work with their children, and parents can become important allies in their child's career development process (American School Counseling Association, 2012a).

As children enter adolescence, they experience cognitive changes that provide them with new capacities for formal thought and regulation of behavior that are helpful in developing academic mindsets and learning strategies. When working with middle school students, it is important to recognize that students are cognitively ready to use their brains to process information differently, think more abstractly, problem solve, and use information to shape behavior (Farrington et al., 2012). According to Farrington et al. (2012), the middle grades are set apart as a key window of both opportunity and risk. They point out that on the one hand, students are developing the capacity to articulate an increasingly clear sense of themselves as learners, and on the other hand, students' failure to develop strategies and skills during the middle grades can create skill deficits and maladaptive patterns of withdrawal and disengagement. Based on their review of research and classroom practices, Farrington et al. (2012) suggest that it is key to make intentional choices about providing opportunities for students to develop the mindsets and learning strategies that will lead them to persevere toward their goals. With their increased capacities, middle school students can benefit from a variety of career interventions, including taking and processing informal and formal assessments, learning about occupational information, and using computerized programs designed to promote assessment and career exploration.

Some examples of informal assessments include skills and values card sorts, exercises regarding what students like to do, values clarification activities, art projects that visualize the present and future, and lifelines and genograms. The benefit of these types of informal activities is that they are engaging and nonthreatening, and they also provide a format for students to learn more about themselves, form collaborative relationships with their peers, and also promote a more personable relationship with their school counselor when processing the results.

To facilitate career exploration, many resources are available on the Internet, and school counselors can also use computer-assisted guidance systems, such as Career Cruising, Naviance, and the Kuder Career Planning Systems. A strong benefit of using these types of programs is that students can work through assessment activities, explore a variety of occupations, and have access to an array of information and resources. Students also have an ability to save their results and come back to continue working through the program. Additional features of computerized programs include video vignettes of people working in their occupations and interviews with people employed in different fields. These programs also include an educational planning component, which serves to connect students' career aspirations with the training and education required for pursuing occupations in specific fields. The value of using these types of programs is very evident with the importance of teaching students how to access information, along with processing the information they obtain (Dugger, 2016). School counselors may use computer-assisted guidance systems as part of the school counseling curriculum, which can be delivered over a series of classroom lessons. Teachers can collaborate by developing assignments to align or follow up on students' learning. For example, an English classroom assignment could be writing an essay describing information and comparing/contrasting students' top choices of occupations. School counselors can also "work back" from the top careers identified to define the steps to obtaining specific occupations. This provides a way of laying out students' educational plans and reinforcing persistence in working toward their goals.

Larger schoolwide events are also ideal for middle school students, and a popular option is having students attend a career fair. When collaborating on this event, school counselors work in conjunction with teachers, administration, parents, and members of the community. They may also collaborate with local community colleges or universities and surrounding school districts. This really takes a team effort and can be an energizing way to bring people together to provide first-hand career information for middle school students. In one example, four local school districts coordinated with a community foundation, a local university, and a regional educational service agency to put on a career fair for all the eighth-grade students in their districts. Planning began well in advance with meetings attended by representatives from each of the organizations, and each sponsored part of the event. The university provided the large auditoriums for the general welcome and classroom space for break-out sessions, along with donating lunch for the students, providing a campus tour, and giving a backpack to each student with paper, pencil, and a college souvenir. School districts and the regional educational service agency worked together to provide the busses to bring the students to the university campus, and to have t-shirts for each student color-coded by school district and printed with "Class of (graduation date)" on the back. Many community business owners and professionals from the various career pathways were invited to present to students and provide hands-on activities. The presenters received an orientation to the event beforehand and received helpful guidelines from school counselors for presenting to middle school students. They were encouraged to actively engage students and bring some freebies to give away as students left their sessions. The community foundation provided media coverage for the event and also brought in an inspiring "slam poetry" duo to end the day on an inspiring note. Success metrics included teachers administrating pre- and postsurveys for students with questions regarding their knowledge of careers and educational aspirations, along with an area to write additional comments. Data revealed positive student outcomes, and student comments were both fun to read and meaningful. The event was repeated the following year, and a total of over 700 students benefited from the career fair events, which were viewed as a "win/win" for all involved.

Other types of hands-on learning can take place through students conducting informational interviews with community members, job shadowing, and participating in service learning projects. All these programs can assist students in obtaining occupational information and coming closer to making decisions regarding their initial career goals. According to Akos, Konold, and Niles (2004), middle school students can benefit from career counseling interventions focused on decision making, especially with students at various developmental levels of readiness regarding making decisions. School counseling curriculum can be designed to follow up on hands-on learning experiences, promote decision-making skills, and to also provide individual meetings for students to process information and establish their education program and goals.

CAREER SERVICES IN HIGH SCHOOLS

The transition to high school is a critical point for students, and considerable attention has focused on the ninth-grade year and the unique needs of students as they adjust to high school (Curry & Milsom, 2017). Early research suggested that it is during this

LEARNING ACTIVITY 11.3

You have just been hired as a school counselor in a middle school, grades 5 through 8. The school counselor you replaced is retiring and had been there for years. His approach to working with students was responsive, with students lining up outside his office constantly wanting to talk with him about problems with teachers, conflicts with friends, and various other issues that came up each day. This counselor also agreed to requests by the principal to meet with students having discipline issues in the classroom. You are the only school counselor, and you notice that the teachers do not have much understanding or interest in what a school counselor actually does within the school. Consider this situation, and make an outline of steps you would take to address the following questions.

1. What are some unaddressed career development student needs in this middle school setting? How would you go about determining what those needs might be?

2. What student standards and mindsets behaviors would you want to focus on in moving toward a more intentional program approach? Where would you begin if you could just implement one strategy? Which grade level would you choose? Make an outline of your plans.

3. Who would be your allies in this situation? What steps would you to take to clarify your school counselor role and communicate this to key stakeholders?

transition that students diverge to either a path to successfully graduating from high school or to dropping out of school (Roderick, 1994). Farrington et al. (2012) reported that current research supports the earlier findings, and that a student's capacity to manage the high school transition plays a unique role in predicting school dropout. According to Farrington et al. (2012), when students begin high school, they experience dramatic increases in the complexity of their school environment, along with academic demands and increased sizes of their peer groups. They also emphasized that school transitions are typically where students can "get stuck" with a decline in grades, attendance, and attitudes toward school, and that urban and minority students are at particular risk.

Curry and Milsom (2017) stated that school counselors and teachers play an important role in providing support through school transitions, with interventions designed to keep students from falling behind. School counselors can intentionally design strategies to promote the ASCA mindsets and behaviors, establish a sense of belonging, and collaborate with teachers to hold high expectations for all students, along with consistent monitoring and ongoing support. A full range of transition interventions is beyond the scope of this chapter, however, research supports that targeted strategies during school transitions are key to students' persistence and success toward graduation. A review of the research and recommendations regarding noncognitive factors (sets of behaviors, skills, and attitudes) is available in the University of Chicago Consortium report conducted by Farrington and her colleagues (2012). They provided a thorough literature review of studies investigating the role of noncognitive factors, especially related to student transitions and increasing student attainment. They also worked to identify critical gaps in the knowledge base and in the link between research and actual practice in the schools.

According to Niles and Harris-Bowlsbey (2017), as with all developmental transitions, high school offers opportunities for actively engaging students in career development interventions to strengthen their academic motivation, bolster their self-esteem, and help them to make the connections between their school experiences and their future academic and career goals. These strategies fit well with concepts from Super's Life-Span, Life-Space theory (1990), with students moving through the *growth* stage (age 0-15) and into the *exploration* stage (age 15-24) during their high school years. According to Super, a characteristic of the growth stage includes the development of the *self-concept*, which evolves over time as a result of experiences. A characteristic of the exploration stage is "trying out," and for students this can include taking classes or having other work, extra-curricular, and/or volunteer experiences that lead to tentative choices. A key career development task for students during their high school years is the *crystallization* of career choices and formulating goals. This relates to *career maturity*, which refers to students' readiness for decision making. All these concepts are useful for high school counselors designing career development interventions, implementing the school counseling curriculum, and working with students to assist them with finalizing their educational plans and taking the necessary steps toward their postsecondary goals.

Within a comprehensive school counseling program, career and college readiness interventions at the high school level build on student competencies developed across the elementary and middle school grade levels. Ideally, students arrive at high school with the beginning foundations of self-awareness, career information and options, and skills related to decision making. At the high school level, the school counseling curriculum takes on a more direct focus with planning, especially related to academics, course selections, and determining postsecondary goals. While it is valuable to meet with students individually during this process, a comprehensive program approach includes schoolwide events, classroom lessons, and programs established for students, such as job shadowing and mentoring opportunities. These various methods of delivery can be very effective with providing important information and sharing resources with students and their families. Some examples of interventions are included here, however, the Additional Resources section of this chapter provides websites and links to many more strategies, ideas, and resources to inform a school counseling program.

School counselors implement a variety of strategies and interventions to address high school college and career competencies, from schoolwide programs like hosting FAFSA completion workshops and college nights to creating a "college-going culture" with displays, locker posters, and having "college Fridays" where teachers all wear t-shirts and gear from their alma maters. Classroom lesson plans focused on career development activities, occupational resources, and decision making are helpful for students, along with classroom visits focused on providing important information and deadlines. Informal and formal assessments can also be administered and interpreted in a classroom setting, however, it is important to be selective regarding choice of assessments based on your student population. When using formal assessments, follow-up is essential to process the meaning students take away from their results. Small group sessions can be helpful for students, and a number of other topics can be addressed in this format as well. As mentioned earlier in this chapter, school counseling programs are organized with a calendar in place for each grade level, listing interventions designed to improve student outcomes across the academic, career, and personal/social domains and moving students toward career and college readiness. School counselors develop these calendars over time, and it is crucial to include metrics for evaluation to make program adjustments when carrying calendars forward to the next academic year.

A new framework for grade level interventions and student expectations was established in Illinois by the Education & Career Development Planning committee. After extensive input from stakeholders and subject matter experts, benchmarks were established for career and college readiness for grades 8 through 12. Referred to as *Illinois PaCE*, this document is intended to provide guidance to students, families, educators, administrators, and community-based organizations on what types of experiences and information a student should have during their secondary school experience, with a focus on providing opportunities and students making informed decisions about postsecondary plans. The Illinois PaCE framework addresses three content areas: (1) career exploration and development; (2) college exploration, preparation, and selection; and (3) financial literacy and financing postsecondary education. The benchmarks describe what students need to know, how students need to be supported, and guidance for state agencies in targeting resources. This framework was actually established as The Postsecondary and Workforce Readiness Act (PWR), that went into effect on July 1, 2017 in Illinois. However, there is no mandate imposing its implementation. The expectation of the committee was to provide an organizing planning tool that can be used by families, schools, and state agencies. The PaCE framework document is another resource that can inform the school counseling curriculum (Illinois PaCE, 2018).

CASE ILLUSTRATION 11.2

Alex is a 14-year-old student. He came to your school counseling office with his mother for a scheduled appointment in late September—approximately four weeks after beginning the ninth grade. When attempting to speak with his mother, you realized that Alex was translating the conversation, and that his mother spoke little English. Through his translating, his mother shared that they are now homeless and living with a friend of their family. She expressed that she would like to receive assistance for Alex, and that he is losing interest in coming to school. School records show passing grades for Alex, with higher grades in math and science. Alex states he would be interested in learning more about auto mechanics as a future career and that he enjoys working on cars with his father.

Discussion questions:

1. What resources, programs, and information would be helpful for Alex and his mother? Take some time to research the possible resources in your local school districts to address his needs.

2. How would you conceptualize Alex's career development issues, using Bronfenbrenner's ecological model?

3. Which of the ASCA Mindsets and Behaviors would you focus on when working with Alex? What types of strategies could be helpful for him?

MULTICULTURAL AND ETHICAL CONSIDERATIONS

There are many important multicultural and ethical considerations for school counselors as they work with students and their families in the schools. A key point to remember is that, as school counselors are striving to meet the career development needs of all students, many students and their families experience inequities on a daily basis and face barriers in regard to access and resources. Despite educational reforms focused on student achievement, disparities continue to exist for low-income, first-generation, and minority students, which is evidenced by gaps in high school graduation rates and post-secondary attainment. Some of these gaps can be attributed to the education system, with inequalities such as African American students being half as likely as Whites to be enrolled in "gifted" programs and three times more likely to be enrolled in special education courses (Niles & Harris-Bowlsbey, 2017). Research indicates that a high school's environment influences students' development of career and college aspirations and academic preparation for college (La Rosa, Luna, & Tierney, 2006). School counselors are also key influences on students' career and college aspirations, and research suggests that school counselors' postsecondary expectations of students may influence whether they even seek the school counselor out for college information (Bryan, Holcomb-McCoy, Moore-Thomas, & Day-Vines, 2009).

It is imperative that school counselors consider the role of culture, ethnicity, race, gender, religion, socioeconomic status, sexual orientation, and other aspects of diversity when determining appropriate career and college readiness interventions and when working on postsecondary planning with students and their families. It is also important to understand that the different aspects of diversity intersect and interact and that the lived experiences of students and their families can be very complex (Curry & Milsom, 2017). The ASCA Ethical Standards for School Counselors (2010) state that school counselors "have a primary obligation to the students, who are to be treated with dignity and respect as unique individuals" (A.1.a). School counselors are to "respect students' and families' values, beliefs, sexual orientation, gender identification/expression and cultural background and exercise great care to avoid imposing personal beliefs or values rooted in one's religion, culture, or ethnicity" (A.1.f). These two ethical standards underscore the responsibility school counselors have for supporting development and affirming diversity for all students.

The ASCA Ethical Standards for School Counselors directly address working with underserved and at-risk populations, stating that school counselors "strive to contribute to a safe, respectful, nondiscriminatory school environment in which all members of the school community demonstrate respect and civility" (A.10.a). The new 2016 ethical standards include language that corresponds directly to a key aspect of the school counselor role: advocacy. Words like *implement, demand, collaborate, engage,* and *negotiate* all depict actions that school counselors are to take (Stone, 2016). According to Stone (2016), cultural competence without action remains hollow, that "knowledge of cultural competence in a vacuum without action is meaningless, empty rhetoric" (p. 6). She stated that culturally competent school counselors need to act to illuminate and then eradicate equity gaps, by challenging the status quo that denies equity for all students. She emphasized that school counselors are influential and that ethical school counselors will "take the charge to promote social justice" as they "help students learn to negotiate the systems in which they must move" (p. 7).

The ethical standards also apply to academic, career, and social/emotional plans, stating that school counselors collaborate with administration, teachers, staff, and decision makers to create a culture of postsecondary readiness (A.4.a); provide and advocate for individual students' preK–postsecondary college and career awareness, exploration, and postsecondary planning and decision making, which supports the students' right to choose from the wide array of options when students complete secondary education (A.4.b); identify gaps in college and career access and the implications of such data for addressing both intentional and unintentional biases related to college and career counseling (A.4.c); and provide opportunities for all students to develop the mindsets and behaviors necessary to learn work-related skills, resilience, perseverance, an understanding of lifelong learning as a part of long-term career success, a positive attitude toward learning, and a strong work ethic (A.4.d).

These ethical mandates may seem daunting, especially for a new school counselor. However, these serve to give weight to the key function of school counselors as leaders, advocates, and collaborators for systemic change (American School Counseling Association, 2012a). Advocacy takes on many forms and can take place on many levels. Working with students to address explicit and implicit barriers, assessing school data for disparities, developing strategies and programs to meet students' needs, ensuring all students have access to opportunities, resources, and information—these are all actions that school counselors take on a daily basis. School counselors are committed to equity for all students, and through implementing the ASCA National Model (2012a) they work toward socially just outcomes. A thorough discussion of the needs and interventions targeted to specific populations is beyond the scope of this chapter, however, it is important to stress that cultural competency and ethical action go hand-in-hand; you cannot have one without the other (Stone, 2016).

Summary: Challenges and Opportunities

In this chapter, we reviewed career developmental in the schools, highlighting key influences with school reforms and initiatives and the value of a comprehensive framework to address students' needs across the academic, career, and personal/social domains. Theories appropriate for working with students in the schools were discussed, with a focus on conceptualizing developmental and contextual influences. An overview of career development interventions and strategies was provided across the elementary, middle, and high school levels, with a focus on college and career readiness standards and competencies. Multicultural and ethical considerations were discussed, especially in terms of the school counselor's role and addressing inequities. Links to resources are included to provide the reader with further readings and research, along with ideas, lesson plans, and other helpful materials to inform your school counseling program.

School counselors today are ideally positioned in the schools to serve students in their career development, and this presents both challenges and opportunities. All school counselors know how they are stretched with high student ratios and conflicting expectations from administrators, teachers, students, and their parents. It can be heartbreaking to learn of students' stories and situations, and working with parents can also present its own challenges. However, with all that said, school counselors are constantly creating opportunities to make a difference in young people's lives, and working with their dreams, aspirations, and goals can be the most fulfilling work in the field of counseling. School counselors are always reaching out, forming collaborations, and staying connected with one another—all opportunities for continued professional growth and development! Keeping a balance and self-care also present both challenges and opportunities, and school counselors have the extra pressure to serve as role models for all they work with in the schools and the community. Wishing all the readers the very best as they carry forward this important work, advocate for the profession, and for the students whose lives they touch every day.

Keystones

- The fundamental purpose of a comprehensive school counseling model is to support the school's academic mission, while meeting the preventative and developmental needs of *all* students.

- Using Super's theoretical framework, school counselors can design interventions that are developmentally appropriate at the elementary, middle school, and high school levels. These interventions may emphasize increasing students' self-awareness at the elementary level, facilitating exploration and educational planning at the middle school level, and moving on to more focused planning for postsecondary options at the high school level.

- Working within an ecological systems approach can be useful in developing interventions across the interrelated contexts of school, home, and community.

- A key point to remember is that, as school counselors are striving to meet the career development needs of all students, many students and their families experience inequities on a daily basis and face barriers with access and resources.

- A central focus of the ASCA National Model (2012) is on the role of the school counselor across the following themes: leadership, advocacy, collaboration, and systemic change.

- A core value of a comprehensive school counseling program is ensuring equitable access to opportunities and rigorous curriculum for all students to participate fully in the educational process.

- School counseling programs are organized with a calendar in place for each grade level, listing interventions designed to improve student outcomes across the academic, career, and personal/social domains and move students toward career and college readiness.

- It is imperative that school counselors consider the role of culture, ethnicity, race, gender, religion, socioeconomic status, sexual orientation, and other aspects of diversity when determining appropriate career and college readiness interventions and when working on postsecondary planning with students and their families.

Additional Resources

American Institutes for Research: http://www .air.org/topic/higher-education-and-career-readiness/college-and-career-readiness

American School Counselor Association: http://www.schoolcounselor.org

ASCA Mindsets & Behaviors for Student Success: https://schoolcounselor.org/asca/media/asca/home/MindsetsBehaviors.pdf

ASCA Mindsets & Behaviors Program Planning Tool: https://www.schoolcounselor.org/asca/media/asca/ASCA%20National%20Model%20Templates/M-BProgramPlanningTool.pdf

College Board: www.collegeboard.org

College Counseling Sourcebook: http://store .collegeboard.com/sto/enter.do

The Education Trust: https://edtrust.org

Eight Components of College and Career Readiness: http://media.collegeboard.com/digitalServices/pdf/nosca/nosca-eight-components-tools-resources-counseling-091712.pdf

NOSCA's Own the Turf College and Career Readiness Counseling Toolkit: http://nosca.collegeboard.org

Southern Regional Education Board (SREB): www.sreb.org

Virginia Career View: http://www.vacareerview .org

YouCanGo!: http://youcango.collegeboard.org

References

Akos, P., Konold, T., & Niles, S. G. (2004). A career readiness typology and typal membership in middle school. *The Career Development Quarterly, 53*(1), 53–66.

Anderson, P., & Vandehey, M. (2006). *Career counseling and development in a global economy.* Boston, MA: Lahaska Press.

American School Counselor Association. (2004). *ASCA national standards for students.* Alexandria, VA: Author.

American School Counselor Association. (2005). *The ASCA National Model: A framework for comprehensive school counseling programs* (2nd ed.). Alexandria, VA: Author.

American School Counselor Association. (2010). *Ethical standards for school counselors*. Alexandria, VA: Author.

American School Counselor Association. (2012a). *The ASCA national model: A framework for school counseling programs* (3rd ed.). Alexandria, VA: American School Counseling Association.

American School Counselor Association. (2012b). *ASCA school counselor competencies*. Retrieved from https://www.school counselor.org/asca/media/asca/home/SCCompetencies.pdf.

American School Counselor Association. (2014). *Mindsets and behaviors for student success: K-12 college- and career-readiness standards for every student*. Alexandria, VA: Author.

Bronfenbrenner, U. (1979). *The ecology of human development*. Cambridge, MA: Harvard University Press.

Bryan, J., Holcomb-McCoy, C., Moore-Thomas, C., & Day-Vines, N. (2009). Who sees the school counselor for college information? A national study. *Professional School Counseling, 12*(4), 280-291.

Carey, E. N., & Herr, E. L. (2012). Career transitions; A new reality. *Career Developments, 28*, 5-9.

College Board. (2010). *Eight components of college and career readiness counseling*. Retrieved from http://media.collegeboard.com/digitalServices/pdf.

Curry, J., & Milsom, A. (2014). *Career counseling in P-12 schools*. New York, NY: Springer.

Curry, J., & Milsom, A. (2017). *Career counseling in KP-12 schools* (2nd ed.). New York, NY: Springer.

Dugger, S. (2016). *Foundations of career counseling: A case-based approach*. New York, NY: Pearson.

The Education Trust. (1997). *The national guidance and counseling reform program*. Washington, DC: Author.

Executive Office of the President. (2015). *Every student succeeds act: A progress report on elementary and secondary education. Executive Summary*. Retrieved from https://www.whitehouse.gov/sites/whitehouse.gov/files/documents/ESSA_Progress_Report.pdf.

Farrington, C. A., Roderick, M., Allensworth, E., Nagaoka, J., Seneca Keyes, T., Johnson, D. W., & Beechum, N. O. (2012). *Teaching adolescents to become learners. The role of noncognitive factors in shaping school performance: A critical literature review*. Chicago, IL: CCSR.

Gottfredson L. S (1981). Circumscription and compromise: A developmental theory of occupational aspirations. *Journal of Counseling Psychology, 28*, 545–579.

Gottfredson L. S (2002). Gottfredson's theory of circumscription and compromise. In D. Brown, L. Brooks, & Associates (Eds.). *Career choice and development* (4th ed., pp. 85–148). San Francisco, CA: Jossey-Bass.

Gottfredson L. S (2005). Applying Gottfredson's theory of circumscription and compromise in career guidance and counseling. In S. D. Brown & R. W. Lent (Eds.), *Career development and counseling: Putting theory and research to work* (pp. 71–100). Hoboken, NJ: Wiley.

Greenwood, G. E., & Hickman, C. W. (1991). Research and practice in parent involvement: Implications for teacher education. *Elementary School Journal, 91*, 279–288.

Gysbers, N. C. (2010). *Remembering the past, shaping the future: A history of school counseling.* Alexandria, VA: American School Counselor Association.

Gysbers, N.C. (2013). Career-ready students: A goal of comprehensive school counseling programs. *The Career Development Quarterly, 06,* 283-288.

Gysbers, N. C., & Henderson, P. (2001). Comprehensive guidance and counseling programs: A rich history and a bright future. *Professional School Counseling, 4*(4), 246.

Gysbers, N.C., & Henderson, P. (2006). *Developing and managing your school guidance programs* (4th ed.). Alexandria, VA: American Counseling Association.

Hatch, T. (2014). *The use of data in school counseling: Hatching results for students, programs, and the profession.* Thousand Oaks, CA: Corwin.

Hess, R. S., Magnuson, S., & Beeler, L. (2012). *Counseling children and adolescents in schools.* Thousand Oaks, CA: Sage.

Hines, P. L., Lemons, R. W., & Crews, K. D. (2011). *Poised to lead: How school counselors can drive college and career readiness.* Washington, DC: Education Trust.

Illinois PaCE. (2018). *Postsecondary and career expectations.* Retrieved at https://www.isbe.net/Documents/PaCE_Revisions.pdf.

Individuals with Disabilities Education Act of 1990, Pub.L.No 101-476, 20 U.S.C, 1400 et seq.

Kobylarz, L. (2004). *National career development guidelines: K-adult handbook.* Stillwater, OH: National Occupations Coordinating Committee Training and Support Center.

Retrieved from http://associationdatabase.com/aws/NCDA/asset_manager/get_file/3384/ncdguidellines2007.pdf.

La Rosa, D., Luna, M., & Tierney, W. G. (2006). *Breaking through the barriers to college: Empowering low-income communities, schools, and families for college opportunity and student financial aid.* Center for Higher Education Policy Analysis, University of Southern California.

McMahon, H. G., Mason, E. C., Daluga-Guenther, N., and Ruiz, A. (2014). An ecological model of professional school counseling. *Journal of Counseling & Development, 92,* 459-471.

Milsom, A. (2007). Interventions to assist students with disabilities through school transitions. *Professional School Counseling, 10*(3), 273-278.

Milsom, A., & Akos, P. (2005). CACREP's relevance to professionalism for school counselor educators. *Counselor Education and Supervision, 45*(2), 147-158.

National Math and Science Initiative. (2011). *The STEM crisis.* Retrieved from http://www.nationalmathandscience.org/solutions/challenges.

Niles, S. G., & Harris-Bowlsbey. (2017). *Career development interventions* (5th ed.). Upper Saddle River, NJ: Pearson.

Niles, S. G., Trusty, J., & Mitchell, N. (2004). Fostering positive career development in children and adolescents. *Leadership, advocacy and direct service strategies for professional school counsellors,* 102-124.

Roderick, M. (1994). Grade retention and school dropout: Investigating the association. *American Educational Research*

Journal, 31, 729-759. doi:https://doi.org/10.3102/00028312031004729

Super, D. E. (1990). A life-span, life-space approach to career development. In A. G. Watts, D. E. Super, & J. M. Kidd (Eds.), *Career choice and development: Applying contemporary theories to practice* (2nd ed., pp. 197-261). San Francisco, CA: Jossey-Bass.

Stone, C. (2016). Cultural competence and ethical action: Can't have one without the other. *School Counselor, 53*, 6-7.

U.S. Department of Education. (2010, March). *A blueprint for reform: The reauthorization of the elementary and secondary education act*. Retrieved from http://www2ed.gov/policy/elsec/leg/blueprint/publicationtoc.html.

U.S. Department of Education (2017). *Reach higher: Complete your education. Own your future. Reach Higher progress report*. Washington, DC: Author. Retrieved from https://www2.ed.gov/documents/press-releases/reach-higher-progress-report.pdf.

White House. (2014, October). *Reach higher*. Retrieved from https://www.whitehouse.gov/reach-higher.

CAREER DEVELOPMENT INTERVENTION IN POSTSECONDARY EDUCATION INSTITUTIONS

Kimberly Gilliam and Mei Tang

Victoria is a senior in a criminal justice studies program at a public four-year institution and wants to work for the FBI—her dream job. However, she just received a medical diagnosis that will prevent her from being a field agent for the FBI. How would you help Victoria?

Joe has always wanted to be a doctor. He is at the end of his freshman year and is failing all his science courses. Joe has realized he does not want to be a doctor; in fact, he never wanted to be a doctor. He just did not want to let his parents down. How would you help Joe?

Scott, a police officer, shot and killed someone in the line of duty and suffers from severe posttraumatic stress disorder (PTSD). He is attending college to earn a degree in something where he can still help people, but his PTSD diagnosis restricts his ability to work alone with people. How would you help Scott?

This is a sampling of the diverse types of cases a career counselor handles in higher education. Although many college students are traditional aged, straight from high school students (like Joe), an increasing amount of college students are nontraditional (i.e., not 18 to 22 years old, not living on campus, not enrolled full-time). In addition, college students present very different kinds of challenges in regard to career development needs because of their developmental stages. They are at the crossroads of searching for their own identities and finding careers to support their independence. College students are expected to land a job after graduation. In the 21st century, college students are a very diverse population and face unprecedented challenges as the world of work has been constantly changing in the last two decades. This chapter reviews the heterogeneous characteristics of today's college students and their career development needs. The structure and organization of college career development services and the service delivery models will be reviewed. The current practices of career services in regard to service scope and contents will be reviewed from multicultural perspectives. Some examples of college career development service and intervention models will be illustrated. This chapter also presents strategies for locating resources available on campuses to expand and enrich services for a diverse college population.

LEARNING OBJECTIVES

After completing the reading and exercises provided in this chapter, you will be able to:

- explain the heterogeneous characteristics of college students at various types of postsecondary educational settings;

- recognize the developmental and transition needs of college students pertaining to career development;

- describe the goals and scope of career intervention services at various postsecondary educational settings;

- identify appropriate career intervention models to optimize outcome for college students' career development tasks;

- name the essential features of providing career counseling services to college students;

- evaluate the effectiveness of various career intervention models at college settings in regard to their advantages and disadvantages;

- recognize ethical, multicultural, and professional duties for serving college students' needs; and

- locate a variety of resources on campus and outside to help students achieve their educational and career goals.

CHARACTERISTICS OF COLLEGE STUDENTS

The number of college students enrolled in various types of post-secondary degree-granting programs was estimated at 17.7 million in 2017 (National Student Clearing

House, 2017). The number of undergraduate enrollments is projected to reach 19.8 million by 2025 (National Center for Educational Statistics, 2016). White students are the largest percentage of the student population (approximately 55%), but there is an increased trend of minority students enrolled, and among the minority groups, Hispanic students show the fastest growth in enrollment. Another noticeable increase is the students enrolled in distance education. Nearly 25% of undergraduate students participated in distance education courses, and 12% take exclusively online courses. These statistics illustrate the emerging change of today's college students. In addition, use of technology and social media in classrooms are no longer innovative but normal, and not surprisingly, employers want college graduates to not only have credentials but also the ability and skills to apply their knowledge and solve problems and proper dispositions for productive and responsible citizenship (Goldberg, Guffrey, & Oliverio, 2016). The current student population consists predominantly of millennials, and Generation Z will be entering college in the future. Understanding their developmental needs in relation to career development would be beneficial to career services and intervention in college settings.

Heterogeneity of College Students

A variety of post-secondary institutions exist in the United States, offering a wide range of academic disciplines and diverse degree designations. People often associate college students with students at four-year colleges, but as a matter of fact, almost one third of undergraduate enrollment is in two-year colleges (National Student Clearinghouse, 2017). The open admission policy, relatively low tuition, and proximity to students' homes make two-year colleges or community colleges an attractive option for many students and parents. While the aim is providing accessibility and curriculum of introductory-level college courses for individuals who want to transfer to four-year colleges later, two-year colleges often offer programs and stand-alone degrees that prepare students to be ready for entering into the labor force with an associate's degree. These vocational education programs in community college settings have the curriculum more in alignment with job market demands and employer expectations. The career pathways movement signaled the need and effort of building stronger capacity of community college education through structured academic and career curriculum to achieve the goal of preparing youth for work demands, aiming at bridging the needs of students and employers (AACC, 2017). The rising cost of four-year college education and underemployment of many college graduates from non-STEM fields make career pathways movement and community colleges a promising endeavor to create opportunities and mobility for young people (Schwartz, 2016).

Various higher education institutions, including vocational-technical schools, community colleges, two-year colleges, and four-year colleges, have different goals for curriculum, different resources, and different characteristics of student bodies (Brown, 2012); therefore, counselors working in these settings need to be mindful of the diverse student population in order to provide appropriate career development intervention.

The diversity of college students in the 21st century is multifaceted. Though the majority of the college population is late teens and young adults, more nontraditional students are enrolled in colleges nowadays, particularly with the increasing trend of distance educational opportunities. Joe, as illustrated at the beginning of this chapter, might represent a traditional college student who is still in his late teenage years and still dependent on his parents for many reasons. However, Julie (Case Illustration 12.1) is an adult learner and probably has to support herself or even her own family while attending college. Thus, Joe and Julie not only have differences in their ages but also in their learning styles and expectation from classes. They may also have different needs for other aspects of life, such as financial aid, opportunities for extracurricular experiences, and services provided by the university.

College students also vary in their cultural backgrounds, which include but are not limited to racial/ethnic backgrounds, socioeconomic backgrounds, gender identity, sexual orientation, faith or religious backgrounds, ideological views, English-speaking preference or proficiency, and family experiences with higher education. College students also bring diverse preparation and expectations for higher education, such as their previous educational experiences, their physical and mental health status, whether learning disability is detected, and their world views.

The diversity presents in various forms; some are visible (e.g., sex, certain physical disability), and some are invisible (e g., ethnicity, gender identity). Counselors cannot make any assumptions based on visibility only. The diversity among students provides both assets and challenges for instruction in classrooms as well as for student services professionals, as one size could not fit all. Being mindful of students' heritage and values, needs and expectations of future careers, motivations, and readiness for college would aid career service professionals to provide more individualized services.

In regard to learning styles, this generation of college students presents the greatest challenges to instructional efficacy. Most college students on campuses nowadays are millennials or younger generations, growing up with digital devices and accessibility to volumes of information due to the Internet and technology advancement (Mechler, 2013). Their preferred learning platform is beyond classrooms and traditional lecturing, multimedia, multiplatform, multitasking, and probably multistimulated. Use of social media, blurred boundaries between home and professional settings in virtual learning environments, and heterogeneity in readiness of mastering newer technology demands educators have inclusive learning environments for the diverse needs of students so that they can all feel supported.

Developmental Needs

Traditional college students are at the emergence of adulthood in terms of developmental stages (Arnett, 2015). They are in the transition phase between reliance on parents and seeking independence; the lack of daily interaction and supervision by parents could mean a relief for some and homesickness for others. More freedom, less structure, and less close supervision in conjunction with desire to be independent, be self-sufficient, and make contributions to society could be hopeful for some and stressful for others. The millennial, or the digital age generation, might be the generation showing self-centeredness and care for the society at the same time (Ng, Schweitzer, & Lyons, 2010), and they may delay commitment to family and career as well (Zunker,

2012). While studying for obtaining academic degrees, college students are expected to prepare for marriage, family, first professional job, and community responsibilities (Gibson & Mitchell, 2006). For nontraditional-aged colleges students, seeking independence might not be the primary concern. Balancing work and school, or family and school, or even more demands from other roles than students could present different sources of worries.

Reality testing is another critical task for college students as they are getting ready to find their first professional job and embark on a journey to have a satisfying work and life. However, the discrepancy between vision and reality, in many forms, could indicate that college students need to balance their ideal vision with the reality of world of work. The reality testing could mean that the actual work settings are different from their expectation, that work demands and duties are different from what is envisioned or even conflicting their life roles, or rewards both in financial and internal satisfaction are lower than expected. Developing a realistic view and capacity for balancing work and life roles, thus, become an important task for college students while exploring their career options.

Career Development Needs

College students have common career development needs, as well as unique needs. Some needs are common for college students because of their shared developmental stages and their anticipated workforce participation postgraduation. Some needs are individualized because each student has her or his unique contextual and personal factors to be factored into career development planning and decisions. College students represent a diverse population, differentiated not only by their future goals but also by their level of preparation to effectively pursue their goals.

Despite the unique needs of each individual, college students typically need to develop further understanding about themselves and work environments to make informed decision for their postgraduation occupational choices. Thus, career development services could target career and self-awareness, exploration of self-understanding pertaining to career decisions, realities of the job market and future trends, and decision-making skills (Brown, 2012). Depending on the career maturity level and developmental stages, college students may need accurate and practical information about career options, and accordingly, an academic advising system that incorporates career planning. In addition to decision and choice, students need job-search-related skills to develop career readiness to enter into the workforce. In other words, career development could be developmental in nature (more general and applicable to everyone) or specific to an individual's career maturity and capacity (more individualized).

Barriers perceived by college students to their career development were found to include not being informed, not being capable, current and future financial concerns, significant others' influence on choice making, and students feeling that they may not get their first job due to their inadequate qualifications combined with the lack of opportunities (Swanson & Tokar, 1991). Students may not have accurate information about the labor market, resulting in discrepancies between career expectations and the labor market; for instance, while there were more job positions in the realistic, enterprising, and conventional areas based on the Holland's codes, more students were interested in pursuing jobs in the investigative, artistic, and social areas (Metz, Fouad, & Ihle-Helledy, 2009). Metz et al. (2009) found that career decision self-efficacy and coping with barriers contributed to the discrepancies between career aspirations and career expectations as well as the impacts of gender, minority status, and socioeconomic status.

College students encounter psychological and vocational concerns during their studies. It is not surprising that they may experience lack of readiness to make a decision, some dysfunctional beliefs, lack of information, or concerns about internal and external conflicts (Fouad et al., 2006). According to these studies, college students want help with decision making, making career decisions, and resolving conflict. Similarly, college students perceive that attending career fairs, interviewing people at the work site, and interacting individually with prospective employees were beneficial career services (Shivy & Koehly, 2002). However, it seems that there is a gap between awareness of services on campus and actual use of services; among the three highest areas of awareness—career fairs, job postings, and on-campus interviews (ranging from 43.4% to 69.3%)—only 15.2% of students (the highest percentage) or even lower used these three services. Therefore, it is important to have career development services available and accessible for all students.

CASE ILLUSTRATION 12.1
JULIE AS AN ADULT LEARNER

Julie, a 40-year-old, African-American female, lost her manufacturing job a year ago. She had worked in that factory in her hometown in a rural area for 20 years, and her extended family also lives in the same area. Julie was born and grew up in a rural area and has always feared an urban environment. One of the severance packages offered by her previous employer is to pay her tuition as long as she could be admitted to an accredited college. She is now enrolled in a state university, majoring in paralegal studies. Julie is divorced and has two teenage children who both are in high school. Her daughter can drive and is a big help to Julie in regard to household chores and transportation of her younger brother; however, Julie feels guilty that she couldn't attend to her children as she used to because her course work demands much more time and effort than she expected. She decided to obtain a college degree because she thought a college degree was a must to get a stable job. Now she is questioning her decision as she is struggling with balancing her roles as a mother of two teenage children and a college student. Julie enjoys the intellectual stimulation in the college classes but has difficulty handling a lot of the homework requiring use of technology that she is not familiar with or confident in using. She also can't find a comfortable way of interacting with her classmates, who are almost her daughter's age. She feels isolated, lacks a sense of identity, and feels like she needs to reinvent herself at 40 years old.

Discussion Questions

1. What are the issues Julie encounters?

2. What kind of career development program would you recommend Julie seek assistance from at her college?

3. How would you help Julie if you were her counselor? Or if you were her faculty advisor?

GOALS AND SCOPE OF CAREER SERVICES FOR COLLEGE STUDENTS

This section reviews the historical context and evolution of career services in college settings and provides an overview of the current goals and scope of services at campuses. Career development in community colleges, colleges, and universities is an integral part of the institution's structure from recruitment to retention to graduation rates. To this end, career service centers are usually housed in student affairs units, enrollment management units, or under the provost in academic affairs. Thus, career centers play an important role in student success; therefore, institutional success. These successes are not merely the academic performance but also student outcomes postgraduation and their career trajectories.

Historical Context and Evolution

The emergence of formalized career services on college campuses started at the time when many WWII veterans either resumed or began education and needed guidance to decide which academic program to enroll in as well as for occupational choices. Prior to this era in the 1940s and 1950s, career guidance was mainly absent or done by faculty members who mentored or guided students on career issues (Dey & Cruzvergara, 2014). Helping students find a match between their interests and abilities and an occupation choice as well as job placement have been the main focus from 1940 to 1970 for career services in college settings. Career services on most campuses was shifted in the 1970s and 1980s to a developmental model. Dey and Cruzvergara (2014) attributed this shift to the self-actualization movement of that era and the increased identity of career center staff as clinicians. The change from a focus on job placement to career counseling, career planning, and job-search preparation has also emphasized that students take ownership of their career development.

At the turn of 21st century, college career centers were transformed to providing comprehensive career services with a focus on promoting the relationship between institutions and employers because of the competition as the result of new technology (Dey & Real, 2010). Younger generations of students want to find meaning from their work experiences rather than just having a paid job; therefore, students want to find jobs in organizations where they feel they belong. Similarly, connecting to communities has become the goal and focus of career services in college settings in recent years. Many universities and colleges move career services toward "a customized connection model that promises specialized career development support to students and meaningful connections to internship and employment opportunities as well as mentoring and experiential learning" (Dey & Cruzvergara, 2014, p. 8). The goal of this emerging trend is to create career communities of learners and networks that facilitate students and alumni for lifetime professional development and sustainable employability accountability.

When the U.S. economy began to decline in 2008 and many Americans lost their jobs, higher education-based career centers had to change as well. The economic challenges caused higher demands on the career centers from the students, alumni, and upper level administration. Someone had to be accountable for helping students and alumni find employment. Parents, students, and administration held the career service centers responsible.

Table 12.1 ■ Summary of the Historical Changes in Career Services and Current Trends

	1990s	2000s	2010-2015
Dimension	Networking Proactive/interactive	Social networking Interactive/superactive	Global networking Hyperactive
Primary Purpose	Information Networking	Educate & prepare	Educate for a global marketplace
Service Delivery	Self-help (physical library)	Counseling and networking Web-based	Web-based
Typical Name	Career center	Career services	Career cyber center
Constituents Served	Students/alumni, employers, and faculty/staff	Students/alumni, parents, employers, and faculty/staff	Students/alumni, parents, employers, faculty/staff, and the community
Theoretical Orientation	Information management	Typology and eclectic	Typology and planned happenstance
Staff Identity	Organizer	Counselor/advisor	Educator
Employer Relations	Strategic	Competition	Experiential development
Assessment Focus	Program participation and revenues	Integrated technology, satisfaction surveys, demographic data, and revenues	Postgraduate tracking, global competency, and revenues

Dey, F., & Real, M. (2009). *Adaptation of Casella's model: Emerging trends in career services.* Retrieved from https://www.myacpa.org/sites/default/files/Casella%20Adaptation%20Presentation.pdf.

There is an ongoing transformation of career service centers, as institutions decide what service delivery model is most effective. Dey and Real (2010) contended this transformation is indicative of a paradigm shift where the focus is on delivering comprehensive services to students throughout their entire undergraduate education. Therefore, career centers are not just focusing on the traditional college freshmen looking to decide on a major.

A key factor in this paradigm shift is the desired increase in retention rates—retaining students through graduation. In a large-scale Columbia University study, it was found that about one third of entering freshmen leave college before they earn a degree (Hughes & Karp, 2004). One cause cited by the study was that students failed to develop academic plans for achieving their goals. Thus, they found it necessary for career service centers to define clear linkages between academic and career objectives and that this linkage was integral to increasing student motivation (Hughes & Karp, 2004).

Goals of Career Services in College Settings

As college students encounter both developmental and vocational tasks simultaneously while studying to obtain a college degree, career services at college settings should not take a pigeonhole or piecemeal approach to addressing their career development needs. In fact, almost all career development theories advocate for integration of various aspects of life in career decision making and intervention. There is no surprise that college career services would consider students' total development rather than focusing on only finding a job. The mission statement of the National Association of Colleges and Employers (NACE) also emphasizes the importance of promoting student learning and student development. According to NACE, the primary purpose of career services is to "assist students and other designated clients in developing, evaluating, and/or implementing career, education, employment and entrepreneurial decisions and plans" (NACE, 2016). Career services units on campus should provide leadership to the institutions on career development concerns and incorporate student learning in their missions. The specific goals suggested by NACE to help students are as follow:

- Develop self-knowledge related to career choice and work performance by identifying, assessing, and understanding their competencies, interests, values, strengths, and personal characteristics.

- Obtain educational and occupational information on their career and educational planning, and develop an understanding of the world of work.

- Select personally suitable academic programs and experiential learning opportunities that optimize future educational and employment options.

- Gain experience through student activities, community service, student employment, research projects, cooperative education, internships, entrepreneurial activities, international experiences, and other opportunities.

- Take responsibility for developing career decisions, graduate/professional school plans, employment plans, entrepreneurial plans, and/or job-search competencies.

- Prepare to find suitable employment by developing job-search skills, effective candidate presentation skills, and an understanding of how their competencies fit with occupational and job requirements, and organization cultures.

- Link with alumni, employers, industry representatives, professional organizations, community service organizations, and others who will provide opportunities to develop professional interests and competencies, integrate academic learning with work, and explore future career possibilities.

- Leverage existing and emerging technologies to facilitate the career development process.

- Pursue desired employment opportunities, entrepreneurial ventures, or entry into an appropriate educational, graduate, or professional program.

- Encourage lifelong learning and prepare students and other designated clients to manage their careers over a lifetime.

Pathways Models

According to the American Association of Community Colleges (AACC; 2017), the Pathways Model is an integrated, institution-wide approach to help students gain post-secondary credentials and be career ready in the labor market. From the beginning to the end, there is intentional assistance to support students complete their academic programs and career planning efficiently. The model also includes faculty ensuring that students are building the skills across their programs that they will need to succeed in employment and further education.

The four dimensions of the Pathways Model, together with essential practices under each, are the following:

1. *Clarify paths to students' end goals*: (a) Simplify students' choices with default program maps developed by faculty and advisors that show students a clear pathway to completion, further education, and employment in fields of importance to the region. (b) Establish transfer pathways through alignment of pathway courses and expected learning outcomes with transfer institutions, to optimize applicability of community college credits to university majors.

2. *Help students choose and enter a pathway*: (a) Bridge K-12 to higher education by assuring early remediation in the final year of high school through the application of courseware technology in strong K-12/higher ed partnerships, such as the TN SAILS model. (b) Redesign traditional remediation as an "on ramp" to a program of study, which helps students explore academic and career options from the beginning of their college experience, aligns math and other foundation skills coursework with a student's program of study, and integrates and contextualizes instruction to build academic and non-academic foundation skills throughout the college-level curriculum, particularly in program "gateway" courses.

3. *Help students stay on path*: (a) Support students through a strong advising process, embedded and ongoing in the pathway experience and supported by appropriate technology to help students make informed choices, strengthen clarity about transfer and career opportunities at the end of their chosen college path, ensure they develop an academic plan with predictable schedules, monitor their progress, and intervene when they go off track. (b) Embed academic and nonacademic supports throughout students' programs to promote student learning and persistence.

4. *Ensure that students are learning:* (a) Establish program-level learning outcomes aligned with the requirements for success in employment and further education in a given field and apply the results of learning outcomes assessment to improve the effectiveness of instruction across programs. (b) Integrate group projects, internships, and other applied learning experiences to enhance instruction and student success in courses across programs of study. (c) Ensure incorporation of effective teaching practice throughout the pathways.

(Retrieved from https://www.aacc.nche.edu/wp-content/uploads/2018/01/12 PathwaysModelDescriptionFinal1616.pdf.)

Thus, it is evident that the goals of career services in college settings have three major dimensions: assisting students to explore and develop self-understanding to make informed decisions for careers; coordinating between academic learning units, employer community, technology, and other resources on campuses to help students connect learning and work across the life span; and helping students become competent in job search and the world of work. These goals are helpful to strengthen students' employment opportunities yet require relevant and comprehensive services for the goals to be accomplished. The next session will present the information about the scope of services on college campuses.

Scope of Career Service Centers on Campuses

The diverse student population and its diverse needs requires the college career services to be comprehensive so that a variety of student needs can be met through purposeful prevention and intervention. The earlier section on goals and the next section on service delivery cover many prevention-focused programs that target helping students gain self-knowledge and engaging in exploration for informed career decision. One important function of career services is to help students secure employment upon graduation. NACE conducted a student survey in 2011 to determine what career services resources students used to find employment. Figure 12.1 demonstrates the utilization rates of various services of college seniors with internship experience ("intern") and without internship experience ("non-intern").

Figure 12.1 shows that students who completed at least one internship prior to graduation had a higher utilization rate for all services. Though employers typically cite networking as the most powerful tool in making the transition from school to work, the NACE 2011 survey indicates that students equally use a variety of job-search tools and methods. Therefore, it is essential that career service centers offer training to students on how to use all of the job search strategies available.

In the "Need-Based Segmentation Analysis of University Career Services: Implications for Increasing Student Participation" study, Garver, Spralls, and Divine (2008) identified the top 10 student priorities for career service centers:

1. Quality of companies to interview with

2. Provides a variety of different types of job opportunities

3. Helps students with job search strategies

4. Number of companies to interview with

5. Usefulness of resume critiquing services

6. Offers assessments to find the right major and potential job

7. Helpfulness in teaching how to research companies

8. Usefulness of mock interviews

9. Provides notification of application deadlines

10. Offers seminars about potential majors and careers

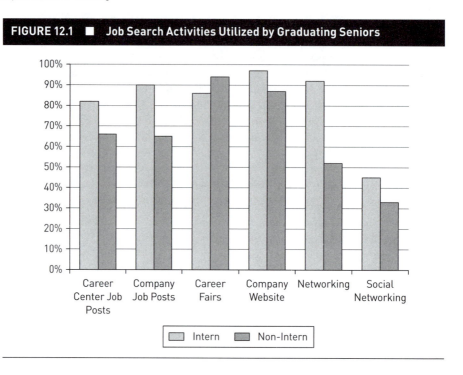

FIGURE 12.1 ■ Job Search Activities Utilized by Graduating Seniors

Based on these findings, the researchers suggest institutions use the information to provide better, more targeted services and programming. Students need practical assistance on locating accurate information about potential employers, preparing for job search, and making informed decisions. A support system—for example, networking with professionals, positive relationships with employers, and accountability help—would be beneficial, too.

Outcome Evaluation

Whether the goals of career services are achieved or whether students have their needs met is an important question for all shareholders in higher education. One of the common indicators for measuring outcomes of career services is student job placement. Placement rates, or as NACE calls it, "First Destination," data are one of the most frequently requested metrics by university administration, faculty, parents, legislators, and accrediting organizations to measure the overall performance of not only the career service center but the institution as a whole. As a result, many institutions' strategic plans include placement rate goals and initiatives (Lipka, 2008).

Collecting placement data can be troublesome for many career service centers, as graduating students do not always report their first destination plans. Additionally, response rates below 90% lead to skewed data because student who have plans are more likely to complete the survey than those who have no plans. Organizations such as NACE conduct regular surveys on graduating college students asking about salary statistics, employment by major, placement rates, and the resources used by students to conduct their job searches. The data is reported in aggregate to help career service center develop benchmark criteria.

Other outcome data collected by career service centers focus on program participation. For instance, when a career fair event is complete, the career service centers can collect the information about the rate of students' participation and result of participation. An exit survey could be administered to both students and attending employers about the career fair event to understand whether the event served their purposes and met their expectations. A follow-up survey could be administered to collect data such as the number of interviews at the event and the number of interviews after the event or attendance statistics by students and employers. A satisfaction survey could be used after a workshop to collect information about students' level of satisfaction of their participation.

Effectively communicating outcome data to employers enables each institution to brand itself and its student body. Most career service centers heavily market their student successes to employers. And, in turn, most employers want to be profiled and have name recognition on college campuses.

Establishing clearly defined goals and relating those goals to standardized metrics is key to obtaining meaningful data. NACE guidelines suggest that scaled surveys should always include clear descriptions of each interval or level. For example,

0 = I <u>don't feel confident</u> with my career decisions and/or career plans. I feel lost, and I need help deciding what to do with my major and my career.

5 = I feel <u>extremely confident</u> of my career decisions and career plans. I know what I want to do and how to make it all happen. At this time, I do not feel like I need any assistance.

Accurately measuring student and employer engagement with career service centers can be a valuable tool in marketing campaigns and can be used to enhance existing services or create new services. Moreover, institutions continue to have budgetary limitations and are requiring offices to mathematically demonstrate their usefulness to the institutional mission.

CAREER SERVICES MODELS FOR COLLEGE STUDENTS

Models

Comprehensive, systematic, and developmental should be the guiding principles of career services. The career intervention needs to be comprehensive due to the diversity of college students in terms of demographics and needs for career development. In order to have comprehensive and systematic career services that address a diverse student population, some common features are needed: academic and career development linkages, making the real-world connection (Herr, 1989), and increasing self-knowledge and knowledge of the world of work through assessment and structured education activities.

A variety of models have been asserted for comprehensive and systematic career services. Crites (1981) emphasized career services individualized to students' needs based on data and helping students go through process of exploration, narrowing options, and implementation. Similarly, Powell and Kirts (1980) proposed four components of comprehensive career services: providing orientation and overview of career services to new students for their awareness; promoting student learning about self-assessment activities; encouraging students to explore career options through group activities and courses; and training graduating students for job-search skills. It appears that this model targets all students from the beginning of their college study to the end of their higher education experiences, with a different focus at each phrase.

In college settings, centralized versus decentralized models of career services are applied in various forms. The centralized model indicates that the university career center is the one-stop place for all students on campus for their career development needs, from exploration of occupational choice, and internship/externship, to assessment, to job placement. The decentralized model typically means that career services are mainly provided within colleges or departments, and the university career center has less role in leading career services across campus. Garis (2014) classifies three dimensions on the continuum of centralized-decentralized services (the fourth one is funding source and does not pertain to the service model). The first one is the level of involvement the career center has in regard to career advising, counseling assessment, and information. The second one is to what degree the career center is involved in providing experiential education services such as externships; internships; cooperative education programs; and part-time, work-study, or volunteer or summer job programs. According to Garis, most colleges have a blended model, that is, colleges, academic programs, financial aid, and career centers are all involved to some extent on the continuum. The third dimension is employer relations services; many universities have a decentralize model for building and maintaining relationships with employers. Garis states that a comprehensive career service needs to have at least one component in the middle or more centralized on the continuum.

Service Delivery

Varieties of career service delivery channels have been implemented across different campuses in the last few decades. The centralized, decentralized, and hybrid models characterize the overall framework of service delivery as explained in the last section. There are actually many varieties of service delivery approaches to meet different needs and accomplish different missions.

Prevention and Intervention Activities: The specific approaches for delivery include structured, short-time, or brief education-focused programs such as workshops and seminars, and typical topics are usually related to career decision making, career planning, job-search skills, resumes, and interview tutoring. Structured counseling/intervention activities generally addresses common issues pertaining to a specific group who experience troubling emotions and specific career related issues (e.g., indecision, anxiety, first-generation college students), and these interventions are usually conducted through groups (Herr, Cramer, & Niles, 2004). Individual counseling or coaching focuses on issues ranging from consultation on specific needs to helping with resources, navigating college, critiquing resumes, conducting mock interviews, and making referral. Some college career centers offer walk-in services, and some do need appointments. Coaching "motivate[s] the client to develop and utilize the client's potential across his or her life span" (Gibson & Mitchell, 2006, p. 124), and involves the following steps: relationship establishment—use of relationship skills to build trusting relationships; assessment—information gathering to understand clients' strengths, weaknesses, and needs; goal identification—collaboratively identifying attainable goals; preparation to achieve goals—developing procedures to achieve goals; action to achieve goals—implementation of action plans; and continued reinforcement—lending support to clients, monitoring the progress, and providing advice. Often staff members with counselor training backgrounds or graduate students in training in counseling academic programs fulfill this line of services.

Dissemination of Information: Distributing career-related information widely so that students are aware of the needs for career planning and resources available on campuses is critical for the mission of career services. In the past, this consisted of a career resource library with many printed materials on display for students to review at the career center. In recent years, with the advancement of information technology, it is easier for students to obtain information via computer-assisted, web-based, or some form of online platform. Therefore, virtual career resource libraries are supplementing the traditional printed materials supplied by libraries, if not replacing it. There are two types of information typically in career resource libraries: educational information for graduate school, professional school, and other educational programs and occupational information like job trends, requirements, positions, and employers' profiles. Isaacson and Brown (2000) suggested that information could be distributed via orientation, catalogs, career information center, articles in student newsletters, computer-assisted programs, alumni newsletters, and flyers.

Experiential Learning: When one has the opportunity to actually observe or perform the activities involved in completing a work task, she or he has a better chance of understanding and retaining the knowledge. Similarly, the optimal way to understand work is through real-world experience. Experiential learning has been applied in classroom teaching for decades through methods like case studies, role plays, and projects. There are also types of experiential learning that go outside of classroom settings such as internships, externships, coop education, and work-study programs. These types of experiential learning experiences not only provide students opportunities to learn the subject matter and nature of future work but are also great networking channels. The academic departments typically coordinate internships and externships, and co-op education and work-study programs are more often administered through a centralized system.

Outreach: The outreach programs are core parts of career services at college settings. From the research findings, it is evident only a small percentage of college students use services provided in the career counseling center (see Fouad et al., 2006); therefore, it is necessary for career services professionals reach out to students. Offering career seminars in housing units, targeting special student group meetings to disseminate information and marketing programs, developing mentoring program using alumni or upper class students, and getting parent involvement in information and networking activities (Brown, 2012) have been suggested for outreach programs.

Faculty Advising: Faculty members have more interaction with students in and outside of classrooms and are often academic advisors for students. Faculty members also have appropriate knowledge and expertise in the field and are well positioned to help students from the beginning to the end in the learning process (Gibson & Mitchell, 2006). For some specialized professional training programs, for instance engineering and fine arts, faculty members could be more helpful than a career services professional with their resources to assist students in finding an internship or job placement. Collaborating with faculty members to design the class, disseminate the information, and to incorporate career planning in advising meetings would enhance students' learning experience and readiness for entry into workforce.

Credit Earning Courses: Having a course ranging from one credit to three credit hours for undergraduate students could be really beneficial for many reasons. The major advantages of career planning in undergraduate courses is serving a large number of students with intentionality and a proactive approach. Folsom and Reardon (2003) did a comprehensive review of career courses and found that completing the credit earning academic courses about career development had positive outcomes at the end; the positive outcomes included career maturity and development, locus of control, career decision making, vocational identity and thoughts, and course satisfaction and retention. They also found that a majority of the studies have positive impacts on selecting a major, time to graduate, academic achievement, job satisfaction, and increased retention. Some colleges incorporate career development content into college exploration or orientation types of courses. These courses typically are offered at the low class level for preventative purposes. A sample of a three-credit career development course is illustrated in Appendix A. In general, this type of course covers knowledge and application, in part to facilitate students understanding themselves and the world of work and developing skills for making career decisions, searching for jobs, and presenting oneself.

Integrated Services: Career services in college settings also could build partnerships and collaborative relationships with other educational entities within and beyond campuses. Hayden and Ledwith (2014) suggested that career services should strategically develop relationships with both on-campus and off-campus partners to enhance engagement of all stakeholders—students, faculty, employers, alumni, and community members. They recommended that career development staff provide guidance for faculty members to integrate the career center into their course work, for example, presentations on career development topics related to the academic discipline by career staff members, class assignments, or extra options to promote students use of career center services. Another on-campus partnership could be with academic advising units. "Academic and career offices are uniquely situated to collaborate on specific populations (e.g., first year or exploratory students) as a shared approach to more time-intensive student groups is potentially cost and resource effective" (Hayden & Ledwith, 2014, pp. 84). The off-campus collaborations suggested by Hayden and Ledwith (2014) include providing assistance to school counselors in K-12 settings to facilitate a continuum of prevention, forging strong partnerships with local community college staff to broaden options and accessibility at both institutions, and engaging community members in creating mutually beneficial experiences for higher education institutions and community agencies. One of the most practiced off-campus collaborations is probably partnerships with employers. By NACE standards, employers are a vital part of the educational process and primary customers of college career services. For a long time,

LEARNING ACTIVITIES 12.1
PROS AND CONS OF SERVICE DELIVERY MODEL

Out of delivery methods of career services listed in this chapter, make a pros and cons list for each. Consider these factors in your deliberating of pros and cons: student demographic backgrounds, costs, timing, efficiency, and accessibility. Read Case Illustrations 12.1 and 12.2, and then determine what services would be appropriate for Julie and Scott.

career services at college settings have focused on building strong relationships with local and national employers for the purpose of maximizing student placement upon graduation. However, the new trend is to shift sole placement focus to networking and developing partnerships in teaching students employment skills and industry specific information (Hoover, Lentz, & Garis, 2013).

Career Services Examples

The University of Florida was ranked number one in career services by the Princeton Review in 2010 and 2012. They have 26 career services staff members working in a *centralized* model across four departments: career networks, career development, director and operations, and information systems. The four departments are described in Figure 12.2.

FIGURE 12.2 ■ University of Florida Career Services Departments

Department	Description
Career Networks	Responsible for running employee relations, experiential educations programs, on-campus recruiting, web-recruiting services (CareerLink), and all career events
Career Development	Provides major and career-related counseling and classes, graduate student services, mock interviews, and career library
Director and Operations	Handles financial operations, publications, graphics and arts design, and facilities management
Information Systems	Manages all computer operations and develops computer strategies relevant to career services

Source: University of Florida

Integrating service, teaching, and research in a comprehensive career center is a feature that Florida State University (FSU) has established for providing career services in college settings. There are four major programs in place to implement the mission of the FSU career center, which is to "provide comprehensive career services, train career service practitioners, conduct life/career development research, and disseminate information about life/career services and issues to the university communities, the nation and the world" (Vernick, Garis, & Reardon, 2000). The four major programs are as follows:

- Curricular-Career Information Services: A self-help oriented system, creating resources supplemental to the work of professionals

- Career Experience Opportunities: Providing experiential education services, specific programs such as cooperative education, internship listing, internship referrals, externship programs, annual co-op/internship exposition, summer employment, and professionally relevant volunteer programs

- Career Placement Services: Obtaining full-time jobs after graduation, including web-based interaction for posting resumes and scheduling interviews, and career exposition for variety of disciplines

- Center for the Study of Technology in Counseling and Career Development: Active research center for career theory development, career planning research, design and teaching of the undergraduate career development course, development of career assessment instruments, and dissemination of research findings

Some specific programs at the career center include Career Portfolio, and online service to educate students develop professionally relevant skills throughout study in colleges, documenting their development in a portfolio to employers and graduate schools; undergraduate courses for credit; faculty members and graduate students team teaching; a lab for assignments and projects; and training and staff development in collaboration with counselor training master's program on campus.

The University of Texas (UT) at Austin offers a mostly *decentralized* career service center, with 17 decentralized college-level centers and centralized online job placement resources. The NACE 2012-2013 Career Services Benchmark Survey (National Association of Colleges and Employers, 2013) found that 85% of schools reported having centralized career service centers, which is a decrease from 87.5% in 2009-2010. Further, the survey revealed that while a large majority of students prefer a noncentralized, college-level career center, a majority of employers favored a centralized system. Employers prefer having one point of contact versus a contact in each individual college on a campus.

Career prep at community college settings is another example for building collaboration between high schools and colleges. It is designed to establish a consortium so that high school students start to get career preparation prior to entering college or to function as an extension of high school career guidance curriculum. The advantage is providing resources to bridge high school, college, and the world of work so that students have a boost at early stages of career development.

ESSENTIALS OF CAREER DEVELOPMENT PROGRAMS IN COLLEGE SETTINGS

The essential career development programs in higher education can be broadly broken down into two main areas: (1) career exploration and (2) professional development. NACE released the Professional Standards for College and University Career Services brief in 2014, indicating effective career service centers should help students to:

- Develop a career path based on their skills and interests

- Obtain educational and occupational information to aid in developing their path

- Select appropriate academic programs and other opportunities that maximize future educational and career options

- Prepare to find an internship or occupation after college by developing job search and presentation/interviewing skills

- Gain experience through extracurricular activities, community service, research projects, employment, and other aspects of the college experience

- Network with alumni, employers, organizations, and other groups that offer potential professional opportunities

- Utilize technology to enhance career development

- Find employment or a graduate school opportunity that fits their goals

- Prepare to manage their careers after college

To help students engage in career exploration and professional development, the essence is to facilitate their awareness and readiness as well as implementation to fulfill their career aspirations. A variety of the services and programs discussed in the last section could be helpful in implementing these elements. This section focuses on the contents and areas the programs should contain.

Career Exploration

Career exploration is made up of three domains: (1) knowledge of self, (2) knowledge of educational and occupational information, and (3) decision making. Career services professionals help students to develop the knowledge or skills necessary to master all three domains. In career exploration, the goal is to teach students the skills to learn about themselves, the world of work, and to make educated decisions, thus, increasing their comfortableness with or confidence in their career exploration decisions.

Knowledge of Self: Students gain knowledge of self by obtaining information on their interests, skills, values, and personality. One way career services professionals help students in higher education assess this knowledge is by administering career development assessments. Assessment results can be reviewed in individual or group counseling sessions. Career counselors administer and interpret a myriad of career assessments including interest and skill inventories, personality assessments, and career maturity or transition measures. Additionally, web-based career guidance systems are used in higher education settings due to the cost effectiveness and the comprehensiveness of the system. Typically, students also have a choice to enroll in a career planning course for academic credit. The courses may be online or in person with a class size limited to around 15 students. In these courses, students learn about themselves, the world of work, and various approaches to decision making (i.e., development models, trait-and-factor models, social learning theory models, etc.). Moreover, they experience *universality*—the feeling that they are not alone. Students tend to report that "all" their friends know what they want to do or "everybody knows what they want to do to except me," so being a part of a group where everyone has a similar goal is therapeutic. To encourage interpersonal growth and awareness, activities in the course focus on contextual factors that impact successful decision making such as family relationships and social, economic, and political situations. For example, it can be helpful for a student who is the first family member to leave the farm to complete a career and educational family tree. The picture of the family tree gives the student a visual representation of why they might be feeling conflicted. These courses help the deciding or exploring student feel more confident in their current decision and/or give him or her the necessary tools to explore majors and occupations.

Knowledge of Educational and Occupational Information: Career services centers teach students how to find information on occupations, graduate school programs, and the labor market. They provide resources in a physical career resource library and online. The online resources include the *Occupational Outlook Handbook, John Holland's Dictionary of Occupational Titles, America's Career Infonet, O*Net*, and national and state labor market information as well as graduate school program comparison sites. A variety of experiential learning programs could be beneficial to obtaining knowledge of work environment as well.

Additional options for students to learn about the world of work are conducting informational interviews and job shadowing. Informational interviews are done by contacting a professional from the job positions desired and asking questions about the nature of the job position and work environment. The typical information interview questions include the following:

- Please tell me what duties this job entails during a typical day.

- What is required in regard to credentials, qualifications, and personal traits one needs to have to succeed in this work?

- What opportunities does the organization provide for new employees?

- What is the compensation structure for this type of job in general?

Job shadowing provides students with opportunities to gain hands-on experience in a specific occupational field in which they are interested. The experience typically lasts one to five days and provides students with valuable information they can use in making career or educational decisions.

Decision-Making Skills: Once students have a clear understanding of self and the world of work, it is time to make a decision. It is critical to explain to students that this current decision is not a lifetime decision but rather a decision that encompasses what they know about themselves and the world of work right now. As they grow and gain additional information, their decisions may change. Many students put an excessive amount of pressure on themselves to choose the perfect major or career because they believe it is what they will be doing for the rest of their lives. So, normalizing indecision for their developmental level and recognizing those decisions can be changed (i.e., social learning theory) allows students to decrease their anxiety. By decreasing their anxiety, it relaxes their minds, which enables them to make decisions.

Peer tutoring and counseling have positive outcomes for student academic achievement, including increased confidence, and lowered anxiety, and could be a cost-effective method for career intervention for positive social interactions between students (McClain & Sampson, 2013). Peer tutoring was also found to help students identify transferrable skills, select majors, and provide emotional support. These positive outcomes eventually help students learn how to make career decisions and deal with the anxiety of indecision.

Professional Development Services

The essence of career services is to help students develop the capacity to pursue a career satisfying to them and to become productive citizens. After exploring self and options, one needs to implement his or her career planning and ultimately find a job upon graduation. Therefore, most professional job services are targeted at teaching college students job-search skills, providing resources for locating employment information, and assisting job interviews. Career services center usually take charge of and organize these services offered to all students and sometimes alumni. According to NACE (2013),

- 64% of colleges offer counseling using online media,

- 93% of schools assist students in finding internships with public and private sector employers,

- 90% of career service centers sponsor career fairs, and

- 62% of career service centers have formal on-campus interviewing programs.

Thus, career fairs are the most common and useful service to students, and according to Fouad et al. (2006), are also the most used services by college students. Career fairs can be across academic disciplines or can be focused on groups of academic disciplines sharing similar themes, for example, and education fair, STEM fair, or health-related fair. Career fairs provide accessibility to students and employers; though they are geared toward senior, lower class students could benefit from attending career fairs as well. They can observe the trend of hiring and the structure and flow of a career fair so that they can be more prepared in the future.

For job-search skills, how to find jobs and how to prepare for job interviews are the two primary needs of college students. The career services centers typically offer job postings and approaches to help students look for domain-specific jobs, for example, job-search correspondence or e-mail alerts. Nowadays, almost all career services centers have job placement information in a virtual environment. A section on the website of college career services centers is usually designed to list job information. Many off-campus online job placement services can be organized into clusters and the links made available for students to use.

Resume writing and job interviews are two important skills for students to do job search. Many college career centers offer critique of resumes to all students. Teaching how to write a professional-looking and impressive resume leading to an interview can be delivered through classes, workshops, and seminars. Preparing students to be ready for a job interview can be done through teaching communication skills in classes. A variety of interview models can be presented on the websites of career centers for students and alumni to learn. One common practice at career centers is to do a mock interview. The advantages of a mock interview is that students can practice interview skills in a safe and supportive environment, and they can learn how to improve from observing their own performances and from critiques and feedback provided by career professionals. Often times, these mock interview can be video recorded for feedback and learning purposes.

LEARNING ACTIVITIES 12.2
ARE WE DOING A GOOD JOB IN HELPING EVERYONE?

Divide the class into small groups. Each group needs to select a student population they want to work with. Each group will search on the Internet for three institutions of their choice to look for resources and services that target helping the student population of their choice. Examples of student populations could be veteran students, first-generation college students, student athletes, international students, students with disabilities, or so on. Each group will summarize their findings and report to the class. The class should then discuss what has been done and what is missing in regard to serving the students who may have different needs.

BUILDING MULTICULTURAL RESPONSIVE SERVICES

As stated in the introduction of this chapter, college students in the 21st century are a very diverse population. Students come from various cultural and socioeconomic backgrounds; they may have learning or physical or mental disabilities; they may come from privileged or underprivileged backgrounds; and they may or may not have resources to support their college education. Career services, therefore, should consider a variety of needs presented by college students when designing development programs and services.

Students With Disabilities

There has been an increasing number of students with disabilities on college campuses because of the need of a college degree to secure a job with adequate earnings and to subsequently gain independence. Career services professionals play an important role in helping these students navigate the education system, including student service entities on campus so that their learning and career development needs can be met. It is also critical for career services to be aware of the interaction between the culture of students with disabilities and the mainstream culture and how that interaction can impact social awareness and performance in career decision making. A gap exists in career services for students with disabilities, as most of them seek services through disability services offices where staff members are typically specialists for accessibility and accommodation services, not for career development needs; yet, college career center staff usually are not adequately trained for the transition and accommodation needs of students with disabilities. Therefore, integrating existing opportunities and resources to help students with disabilities to achieve their higher education goals and consolidating these services should be the goal of college career centers.

Being aware of the unique culture within each disability accommodation needs is a must. Some physical disabilities might be visible, and some are not. Some students know how to advocate for themselves, and some do not. Typical mental health diagnoses that college students present that may impact their career development include Autism spectrum disorders, anxiety, depression, attention deficit hyperactivity disorder, posttraumatic stress disorder, and eating disorders. Students with learning disabilities shared that a vision for the future, active development effort and assessment of their strengths and limitations, effects of disability to their function, and understanding of their disabilities would help them be prepared for the world of work (Hitchings & Retish, 2000). Therefore, in order to work successfully with these groups of students, it is important to build a collaborative relationship with on-campus partners, including disability services and counseling services, because each student will present with a unique set of needs.

Underprivileged/Marginalized Students

Students from underprivileged backgrounds often feel marginalized because the institutions frequently fail to recognize their differences from the dominant culture and inadequately address their needs (Sampson, Dozier & Colvin, 2011). These students may come from ethnic minority backgrounds, are students of sexual minorities, or are students from religious minority backgrounds. They may come from family backgrounds that value interdependence rather than independence. Research has found that gender and ethnic backgrounds had significant impact on differences in career aspiration and expectation (Metz et al., 2009). College students from low socioeconomic backgrounds, first-generation college students, ethnic minorities, and students with disabilities were found to have a low awareness of career services on campus, tended to have restricted time and finances, were more stressed about study and future careers, and underused the career services (Andrewartha & Harvey, 2017; Simpson & Ferguson, 2013). The fact that these students were underserved requires career development professionals to be more mindful of how to design culturally appropriate programs and to provide accessible services to these students so that underutilization of career services can be improved.

To make career development services accessible to underprivileged students, reaching out to these students and linking university career services and social justice are necessary. When designing the programs, career development professionals need to be thoughtful of cultural accommodation, inclusion, and accessibility. It is suggested that encouraging collaboration among academic units, career services, and community career education could be done to make higher education and employability more accessible for disadvantaged groups (McIlveen, Everton, & Clarke, 2005). The other ideas include offering more targeted support, such as industry-specific events, peer mentoring, and individual consultation for employability and equity (Andrewartha & Harvey, 2017). Provide staff members Safe Space training and make the career development service center be a safe and friendly place for LGBTQ students. Career service providers could be careful and thoughtful in selecting location, timing, and flexibility of services to ensure students from underprivileged backgrounds feel safe (Simpson & Ferguson, 2013).

Some examples of collaborative and inclusive practices are academic enrichment programs that provide minority students opportunities to gain research and clinical experiences and to work closely with advisors and mentors. It was found that advisors and mentors play an important role in minority students choosing and retaining in the STEM field (Sweeney & Villarejo, 2013). Community outreach, campuswide resources, encouraging minority students to use these resources, and collaborating with ethnic student organization on campus are all suggested as intentional efforts to reach out to minority students (Rush, 2012).

Student Athletes

Student athletes have unique needs because of their dual duties as learners in the academic discipline and active participants in competitive sports. Some other challenges encountered by this student population include time constraints as well as conflicts due to training, competition and travel, pressure to perform well in both academics and sports, and lacking career exploration or planning with the hope of becoming professional athletes (Brown, Glastertter-Fender, & Shelton, 2000). All these issues have significant impacts on their career development, particularly after they graduate from college. Even if they become professional athletes, the tenure in professional sports is not forever, and they still need to transition to a new field or occupation (Martinelli, 2000). The reality is that there are not enough spots in professional sports for every student athlete, and unfortunately, some student athletes may become injured or academic performance could negatively affect eligibility. Martinelli (2000) raised the following questions for framing career service to help student athletes in college settings: What are your alternative plans post sports? What are your transferrable skills? Who are your role models for healthy and successful transitions? How do student athletes handle pressure? What decision-making skills do they possess?

Anderson and Vandehey (2012) suggested that expanding exploration and job-skill development would benefit student athletes. The university career development staff needs to be flexible in terms of scheduling so that they can accommodate student athletes' nontypical schedule. It is also suggested that ongoing and early involvement in collaboration between academic, career development, and athletic units on campus would be helpful for student athletes to manage their dual roles, to have a plan for transitioning to the world of work, and to develop job readiness post sports.

CASE ILLUSTRATION 12.2
SCOTT: TORN BETWEEN ONE'S OWN AND PARENTS' EXPECTATIONS

Scott is an 18-year-old, second-generation Asian American, with both parents working as professionals. He is a freshman in a state university, majoring in biology, was a straight-A student in high school, and has recently experienced a lack of motivation to go to classes. He skipped classes, didn't turn in assignments, and did poorly on tests. His mood was low, and he didn't want to talk to his family or friends because he thought nobody understood him or his dilemma. His grades were declining, and he became really stressed because his parents expected Scott to earn only As. He had been achieving what his parents wanted until now when he couldn't concentrate on studying. Scott was worried that he might lose his scholarship because his grades were sliding. His parents would be furious if Scott lost the scholarship. Scott enjoys graphic design and wants to work in some kind of setting where he can use his skills in graphic design, but he is not sure how to find information about this line of work. During his entire time in high school, his parents constantly told him that he needed to go to college and to major in biology or chemistry so he could go to medical school and eventually become a doctor. Scott does not enjoy studying biology, and he does not want to be a doctor, but he can't contest his parents' plans for him because he is not sure if he can find a job in a design area, and he doesn't want to disappoint his parents. He came to the career development center hoping he could find more information about the job outlook for designer jobs.

Discussion Questions

1. What factors are influencing Scott's struggle?

2. How would you address Scott's issues with his parents? What roles do they play in Scott's career development? Do you need to consider his parents in your work with Scott?

Summary: Challenges and Opportunities

Because of the diversity in the college student population in the 21st century, there is no one-size-fits-all approach to higher education anymore. Teaching the millennial or even younger generations who grew up in the information loaded and digital era means educators in higher education institutions need to keep abreast of the increasing diversity of the student population, of the rapid changes of instructional technology and world of work, and of the instability of the work environment. As the roles and functions of career development professionals in higher education constantly shift to address the social and economic changes occurring in world, so do the goals and scopes of services. The career pathways movement with an aim to serve all students in postsecondary settings bridges the gap in education delivery and employment demand. Despite the challenges of more demands from administrators, from parents, from students, from employers, and from the community, opportunities exist. Because of the challenges of the ever-changing work environment due to technology advancement, economy, and the labor market, there is more acknowledgment by educators as well as employers that higher education needs to prepare college students not only to be job ready but also to be career ready, meaning that they need to gain capacity beyond employability for one job. In other words, college graduates should be ready and competent to address the challenges and changes in the real world; therefore, career development services has the opportunity to redefine its role in higher education as a more integral part rather than just job placement professionals. Career development services can be a collaborator with other units on campus to prepare students to develop competency in learning, problem solving, and effective communication.

Keystones

- College students in the 21st century come from diverse demographic backgrounds.

- The heterogeneity of college students requires career development intervention in higher education to address the variety of needs of students depending on their developmental stages, transition phrases, and individual characteristics.

- Career development needs of college students range from self-exploration and career planning to developing career readiness and employability.

- Career intervention in college settings has been evolving from job placement to providing a comprehensive service with a focus on educating students to develop competency in career readiness and adaptability in global economy.

- Various models of career intervention and services can be classified into centralized, decentralized, and hybrid models, which take many forms of service delivery, including prevention/intervention activities, dissemination of information, experiential learning, academic credit courses, faculty advising, outreach, and integrated services in collaboration with on-and off-campus units.

- The primary career development services include career exploration and professional development services with the goal of helping students gain self-understanding, knowledge of educational and occupational information, career decision-making skill, and job search skills.

- Building culturally responsive career services for every student, including students from underprivileged and marginalized backgrounds, requires career development professionals to engage in practice with a multicultural awareness, social justice, and inclusion perspective.

Additional Resources

Sources for career exploration, training, and jobs:

https://www.careeronestop.org

https://www.careeronestop.org/FindTraining/find-training.aspx?frd=true

National Association of Colleges and Employers:

https://www.naceweb.org

American Association of Community Colleges Career Pathways:

https://www.aacc.nche.edu/programs/aacc-pathways-project

https://www.aacc.nche.edu/wp-content/uploads/2017/09/TheMovementTowardPathways.pdf

References

AACC. (2017). AACC Career Pathways project. Retrieved from https://www.aacc.nche.edu/wp-content/uploads/2017/09/TheMovementTowardPathways.pdf.

Anderson, P., & Vandehey, M. (2012). *Career counseling and development in global economy* (2nd ed.). Belmont, CA: Brooks/Cole.

Andrewartha, L., & Harvey, A. (2017). Employability and student equity in higher education: The role of university careers services. *Australian Journal of Career Development*, *26*(2), 71-80. doi:10.1177/1038416217718365

Arnett, J. J. (2015). College students as emerging adults: The developmental implications of the college context, *Emerging Adulthood*, *4*, 219-222. doi:https://doi.org/10.1177/2167696815587422

Brown, C., Glastertter-Fender, C., & Shelton, M. (2000). Psychological identity and career control in college student student-athletes. *Journal of Vocational Behavior*, *56*, 52-62.

Brown, D. (2012). *Career information, career counseling, and career development* (10th ed.). Boston, MA: Pearson.

Crites, J. O. (1981). *Career counseling: Models, methods and materials*. New York, NY: McGraw-Hill.

Dey, F., & Cruzvergara, C. Y. (2014). Evolution of career services in higher education. *New Directions for Student Services*, *2014*(148), 5-18. doi:10.1002/ss.20105

Dey, F., & Real, M. (2010, September). Emerging trends in university career services: Adaptation of Casella's career centers paradigm. *NACE Journal*, *71*, 31–35.

Folsom, B., & Reardon, R. (2003). College career courses: Design and accountability. *Journal of Career Assessment 11*(4), 421-450.

Fouad, N. A., Guillen, A., Harris-Hodge, E., Henry, C., Novakovic, A., Terry, S., & Kantamneni, N. (2006). Need, awareness, and use of career services for college students. *Journal of Career Assessment*, *14*(4), 407-420. doi:10.1177/1069072706288928

Garis, J. (2014). Value-added career services: Creating college/university-wide systems. *New Directions for Student Services*, *2014*(148), 19-34. doi:10.1002/ss.20106

Garver, M., Spralls, S., & Divine, R. (2008). Need-based segmentation analysis of university career services: Implications for increasing student participation. *Research in Higher Education Journal*. Retrieved from http://www.aabri.com/manuscripts/09190.pdf.

Gibson, R. L., & Mitchell, M. H. (2006). *Introduction to career counseling for the 21st century*. Upper Saddle River, NJ: Pearson Merrill Prentice Hall.

Goldberg, K. I., Guffey, J., & Oliverio, P. (2016). Defining postsecondary degrees in the 21st century. *Journal of College Teaching & Learning (Online)*, *13*(2), 65.

Hayden, S. C. W., & Ledwith, K. E. (2014). Career services in university external relations. *New Directions for Student Services*, *2014*(148), 81-92. doi:10.1002/ss.20110

Herr, E. L. (1989). Career development and mental health. *Journal of Career Development*, *16*(1), 5-18. doi:10.1007/BF01354263

Herr, E. L., Cramer, S. H., & Niles, S. G. (2004). *Career guidance and counseling through lifespan: Systematic approaches* (6th ed.). Boston, MA: Allyn & Bacon.

Hitchings, W. E., & Retish, P. (2000). Career development needs of students with learning disabilities. In D. A. Luzzo & D. A. Luzzo (Eds.), *Career counseling of college students: An empirical guide to strategies that work* (pp. 217-231). Washington, DC: American Psychological Association.10.1037/10362-012

Hoover, M. Lenz, J., & Garis, J. (2013). *Employer relations and recruitment: An essential part of postsecondary career services.* Broken Arrow, OK: National Career Development Association.

Hughes, K. L., & Karp, M. J. (2004). *School-based career development: A synthesis of the literature.* Columbia University Academic Commons. Retrieved from https://doi.org/10.7916/D8SX6B8G.

Isaacson, L. E., & Brown, D. (2000). *Career information, career counseling, and career development.* Boston, MA: Allyn & Bacon.

Lipka, S. (2008, May 28). Researchers worry about inflated measures of student engagement. *The Chronicle of Higher Education.* Retrieved from http://chronicle.com/daily/2008/05/2998n.htm.

Martinelli, E. A., Jr. (2000). Career decision making and student-athletes. In D. A. Luzzo (Ed.), *Career counseling of college students: An empirical guide to strategies that work* (pp. 201-215). Washington, DC: American Psychological Association.

McClain, M. C., & Sampson, J. P. (2013). Using pair counseling to improve the cost-effectiveness of college career counseling. *The Professional Counselor, 3*(2), 82-92. doi:10.15241/mcm.3.2.82

McIlveen, P., Everton, B., & Clarke, J. (2005). University career service and social justice. *Australian Journal of Career Development, 14*(2), 63. doi:10.2255/1038-4162.14.2.0027

Mechler, H. (2013). Off our lawns and out of our basements: How we (mis)understand the millennial generation. *Journal of College and Character, 14*(4), 357-364. doi:10.1515/jcc-2013-0045

Metz, A. J., Fouad, N., & Ihle-Helledy, K. (2009). Career aspirations and expectations of college students: Demographic and labor market comparisons. *Journal of Career Assessment, 17*(2), 155-171. doi:10.1177/1069072708328862

National Association of Colleges and Employers. (2013). *Career services benchmark survey 2012-2013.* Bethlehem, PA: Author.

National Association of Colleges and Employers. (2014). *Professional standards for college and university career services 2014.* Retrieved from http://ulm.edu/careerconnections/naceprofessionalstandardsforcollegeanduniversitycareerservices.pdf.

National Association of Colleges and Employers. (2016). *Professional standards for college and university career services.* Retrieved from https://www.naceweb.org/uploadedfiles/files/2016/publications/product/professional-standards/2016-nace-professional-standards-for-college-and-university-career-services.pdf.

National Center for Educational Statistics. (2016). *The condition of education 2016.* Retrieved from https://nces.ed.gov/pubs2016/2016144.pdf.

National Student Clearinghouse Research Center. (2017, Spring). *Term enrollment estimates.* Retrieved from https://nscresearchcenter.org/currenttermenrollmentestimate-spring2017.

Ng, E., S. W., Schweitzer, L., & Lyons, S. T. (2010). New generation, great expectations: A field study of the millennial generation. *Journal of Business and Psychology, 25*(2), 281-292. doi:10.1007/s10869-010-9159-4

Powell, R., & Kirts, D. K. (1980). *Career services today: A dynamic college profession.* Bethlehem, PA: The College Placement Council.

Rush, L. C. (2012). Not business as usual: Reconsideration of the career needs, concerns, and the career interventions with African-American college students. *Career Planning and Adult Development Journal, 28*(1), 27.

Sampson, J. P., Dozier, V. C., & Colvin, G. P. (2011). Translating career theory to practice: The risk of unintentional social injustice. *Journal of Counseling & Development, 89*(3), 326-337. doi:10.1002/j.1556-6678.2011.tb00097.x

Schwartz, R. B. (2016). The career pathways movement: A promising strategic for increasing opportunities and mobility. *Journal of Social Issues, 72,* 740-759. doi:10.1111/josi.12192

Shivy, V. A., & Koehly, L. M. (2002). Client perceptions of and preferences for university-based career services. *Journal of Vocational Behavior, 60*(1), 40-60. doi:10.1006/jvbe.2001.1811

Simpson, A., & Ferguson, K. (2013). Location, timing, and flexibility: Positioning inclusivity in higher education career services. *Australian Journal of Career Development, 22*(1), 45-48. doi:10.1177/1038416213478806

Swanson, J. L., & Tokar, D. M. (1991). College students' perceptions of barriers to career development. *Journal of Vocational Behavior, 38*(1), 92-106. doi:10.1016/00018791(91)90020-M.

Sweeney, J. K., & Villarejo, M. (2013). Influence of an academic intervention program on minority student career choice. *Journal of College Student Development, 54*(5), 534-540.

Vernick, S. H., Garis, J., & Reardon, R. C. (2000). Integrating service, teaching, and research in a comprehensive university career center. *Career Planning and Adult Development Journal, 16,* 7-24.

Zunker, V. G. (2012). *Career counseling: A holistic approach* (8th ed.). Belmont, CA: Brooks/Cole.

Appendix A: Sample of Academic Course (3 credits for undergraduate students)

Module 1 Knowledge of Person and Work

Unit 1: Overview of Career and Life

Unit 2: Understanding Yourself

Part A: Personal Traits and Needs—Personality, Interests, Values

Part B: Person and Context—Family, Society, Culture

Unit 3: Understanding the World of Work

Part A: Work Nature and Requirements

Part B: Changing Work Environment

Module 2 Decision-Making Process and Skills

Unit 4: Decision-Making Model

Unit 5: The Process of Making a Decision

Unit 6: Career Decision-Making Self-Efficacy

Unit 7: Engaging in Exploration and Clarification

Module 3 Planning and Action

Unit 8: Identification and Development of Individual Plan

Unit 9: Building Skills for Job Readiness

Unit 10: Establishing Network & Support Resources

Unit 11: Enhancing Job-Search Skills

CAREER COUNSELING IN COMMUNITY SETTINGS

Rhonda Norman and Norman Townsel

Career counseling services occur across a wide variety of community settings. In recent years, advancing technology, along with newly emerging markets, created or reshaped many careers and occupations. Over the same period, workers have been subjected to the dynamic forces of an increasingly global economy. For instance, robots, automation, and software have made automotive manufacturing jobs scarce and travel agent careers almost obsolete (Rotman, 2013). In addition, the lasting shocks of the 2008 global recession resulted in record numbers of long-term unemployed workers and stagnant wages (Meyers, 2014). These developments have placed increasing pressure on career counseling practitioners to reexamine career counseling activities in the community as redesigned work environments, occupational insecurity, and work-related stressors continue to influence the career self-efficacy and outcome expectations of their clients (Dahling, Melloy, & Thompson, 2013).

Recent studies indicate that shifts in the makeup of available jobs and careers have created something of a mismatch with the current U.S. workforce. In 2010, at the height of the Great Recession, approximately 27% of college grads had a job that was closely related to their major (Rhee-Weise & Horn, 2013). While these numbers have improved over the past few years, recent college graduates in many fields are finding that these careers no longer require a four-year degree, resulting in much lower wages than anticipated. This is particularly true in technology majors, such as electrical or mechanical repair or radiology, or recent graduates majoring in communications, liberal arts, or business (Abel, Deitz & Su, 2014).

Career development services in the community have also continued to evolve. As discussed in previous chapters, early career development activities were primarily framed as vocational guidance and dominated by trait-factor or developmental theories of career choice and behavior. However, research over the past four decades has increasingly linked career development theory to learning, social cognition, mental and behavioral health, and multicultural perspectives. During this period, practitioners have increasingly acknowledged that work-related problems may be substantially more than an imperfect fit between person and job. It is also possible that psychological difficulties can occur as a result of debilitating work environments (Brown & Brooks, 1985). According to the National Institute for Occupational Safety and Health (NIOSH, 1999), working conditions play a primary role in causing job stress, regardless of the role of individual-level characteristics of employees. Maladaptive ways of managing stress are often related to behavioral health risks such as absenteeism, poor work performance, smoking, or substance abuse. More recently, the National Study of the Changing Workforce (NSCW) found employees in more effective and flexible workplaces are more likely than other employees to have less negative and stressful spillover from home to job, excellent overall physical health, low frequency of minor health and sleep problems, and better mental health.

As Herr (1992) suggested, the focus of career counseling is currently shifting from a focus on the job or occupation being chosen, to the individual making the choice. This focus on the individual is reflected in the groundbreaking career theories of learning (Krumboltz & Nichols, 1990), social cognition (Lent, Brown, & Hackett, 1994), cognitive information processing (Reardon, Lenz, Sampson, & Peterson, 2000), and cultural values (Brown, 2002). In fact, Blustein (2006) advocates that work-related issues be included in a comprehensive strategy for all counseling interventions, suggesting that counselors consider the following:

- The distinctions between vocational counseling and personal counseling are an artifact of language and do not conform to the realities of people's lives.

- Vocational problems have often been misconstrued as somehow less important or painful than relationship problems.

- Vocational counseling is as complex and challenging as is personal counseling.

- The process of human change across the various contexts of life contains many parallels and few distinctions. (p. 253)

The result of these and other innovative approaches is that career counseling has become increasingly relevant to more diverse populations, across a wide range community settings, for those seeking assistance in the face of current market realities.

LEARNING OBJECTIVES

After completing the reading and exercises provided in this chapter, you will be able to:

- explain the importance of career counseling in community settings,

- analyze the difference between career counseling in a mental health center and a private practice setting,

- identify three primary strengths of career services in employee assistance programs as compared to career services in mental health centers and the populations that could have access to the respective sites,

- critique the primary differences between career coaching and executive coaching,

- construct an example of a client who would benefit from job placement services, and

- outline the relationship between career counseling and multicultural competence and how it relates to effective career services in community settings.

GOALS AND SCOPE OF CAREER DEVELOPMENT PROGRAMS IN THE COMMUNITY

A wide variety of career development services are currently available in many communities. The goals associated with these services are largely influenced by whether they are being provided in a clinical or nonclinical setting. Clinical settings include those organizations that employ licensed and certified therapists and case managers to provide individual, family, and group counseling. Activities conducted in a clinical setting generally fall under the legal doctrine of medical necessity. Medical necessity requires that in order to receive reimbursement, services on behalf of the client must be derived from a clinical assessment and driven by planned interventions relevant to the health condition under treatment. Many mental health issues related to work and career fall under these requirements.

The goals of career development in nonclinical settings are much more varied. For example, the goals associated with career coaching are highly flexible. They may take the form of consulting for a specific client, to providing services for a private or corporate entity. Career coaching services encompass a broad spectrum of activities, from helping a client develop specific job skills, to helping increase a client's knowledge of available employment, or helping an employer redesign work tasks, to many other activities that will be discussed later in greater detail. In contrast, job placement services are typically much more narrowly focused, specializing in helping clients locate potential employment through arrangements or contracts with government agencies or private entities.

Regardless of the provider, the goals of career development in the community are largely tied to the contextual factors relevant to the particular individual being served. Certainly, there are those potential clients with opportunity and means, seeking to implement the "grand career narrative" as described by developmental theory. However, Blustein (2006) reminds us that for many individuals in the modern economy, work satisfaction may be secondary to providing food and shelter for themselves and their families. He suggests a contemporary approach to developing goals for career counseling constructed around a hierarchy of three core functions of work:

1. Work as a means for survival and power

2. Work as a means of social connection

3. Work as a means of self-determination

COMMUNITY SETTINGS

Career Counseling to Populations With Mental Health Issues

In most communities, unemployed individuals, or employees with limited income who are unable to access employee assistance program (EAP) services through an employer or a private practitioner, may choose to seek mental health services through a local community mental health center (CMHC). Created through federal legislation in 1963, CMHCs provide outpatient services, including specialized outpatient services for individuals who are chronically mentally ill or who have been discharged from inpatient treatment at a mental health facility; 24-hour-a-day emergency care services; day treatment, partial hospitalization, or psychosocial rehabilitation services; and screening for patients being considered for admission to state mental health facilities. CMHCs are eligible to be certified for Medicaid and Medicare reimbursement as long as they are providing specific public health services to the community. Most CMHCs are primarily state funded and maintain close working relationships with state and local employment agencies.

The United States Disabilities Report found 10.3% of individuals between the ages of 21 and 64 reported a disability, with an unemployment rate of 65.1% and as high as 85% (Caporoso & Kiselica, 2004; Erickson, von Shrader, & Lee, 2012). Participating in meaningful work, paid or unpaid, is a primary consideration for individuals with a mental health diagnosis (Niles & Harris-Bowlsbey, 2013). Mental health clients benefit from coaching and other career development interventions mainly in private practice and community mental health settings that embrace the integration of career counseling within the context of mental health treatment (Caporoso & Kiselica, 2004; Imbimbo, 1994). In my experience with integrating mental health and career counseling for over 20 years, several colleagues have been hesitant to embrace the integration due to competency issues in the area of career counseling and therefore choose to refer clients to a different practitioner to obtain the career-related services. Serving the client more effectively calls for the integration of mental health and career-related services.

CASE ILLUSTRATION 13.1

THE CASE OF SARAH, TRAUMA AND WORK-RELATED GOALS

Sarah is a 47-year-old African-American female, associate vice president within a fortune 100 company. She has been with the organization for 12 years and is keenly aware of the retirement of several senior members of the leadership team within the next five years. Sarah is a high performer, and her yearly evaluations have always "exceeded the standard," yet she is concerned that she may not be selected to replace one of the retirees because out of nine impending retirements, only one is female. She would like to be prepared when the openings become available, and therefore Sarah expresses a desire to participate in the executive coaching program sponsored by the company.

1. What would Sarah's proposal to her manager need to include?

2. What career related benefits could Sarah garner from her participation in the executive coaching initiative?

3. How could Sarah justify her participation in the executive coaching program when the evidence of effectiveness is limited?

Career Counseling to Populations With Substance Use Issues

Integration of career-related interventions in the treatment of substance-related disorders would be the optimum treatment approach in community settings. Substance use problems in the workplace negatively impact job performance and productivity. In 2013, over 9% of the U.S. population aged 12 or older (24.6 million Americans) used illicit drugs. At the same time, more than half of all Americans aged 12 or older report being current alcohol users, and heavy drinking was reported by 6% of respondents. Over 65% of full-time employed adults use alcohol (NSDUH). The National Institutes of Health (NIH) reports that more than 14,500 specialized drug treatment facilities provide counseling, behavioral therapy, medication, case management, and other types of services to persons with substance use disorders. Most federal, state, or community-funded treatment centers emphasize evidence-based interventions.

Evidenced-based interventions serve to ameliorate the lack of career identity or securing gainful employment for individuals who are struggling with substance use disorders (McAweeney, Jones, & Moore, 2008). Career-related services that are relevant for individuals with a substance use disorder include career counseling and assessment, referral for job acquisition skills, and job placement services (McAweeney et al., 2008; Niles & Harris-Bowlsbey, 2013). Follow-up counseling may be appropriate to focus on job-keeping skills, especially during the recovery process.

Unemployment has been substantiated in the literature as a risk factor that contributes to relapse amongst individuals with a substance use disorder (Giordano, Clark & Furter, 2014). Supported employment services and job placement services are heralded with clients accessing the needed support to obtain and maintain successful employment. Giordano et al. (2014) investigated the prediction of substance abuse relapse and found that work commitment was a protective factor in clients' relapse profiles. They cite a major concern regarding attaining and maintaining stable employment for those who are recovering from alcohol and drug-related issues, and it may be especially challenging if criminal charges are involved.

Career Counseling to Populations of Ex-Offenders

There are over 70 million people in the United States with criminal records ranging from misdemeanors to violent offenses (Vallas & Dietrich, 2014). Ex-offender status impacts people of color at a higher rate than the general population and disproportionately impacts Black men (Alexander, 2012). Michelle Alexander in her highly acclaimed book *The New Jim Crow* states that ex-offender status could be a new form of segregation that continues to marginalize specific populations and deny access to community resources.

Diverse populations have multiple contextual factors that impact their ability to find gainful employment. Ex-offender status, or having a criminal record, has implications when making a career choice or choosing a career pathway (Thompson & Cummings, 2010). The ex-offender is likely to face a tremendous amount of stigmatization from the community and from potential employers. In addition, there are certain professions that may be prohibitive due to licensure restrictions. Some ex-offenders have their driver's license suspended, which impairs their ability to travel to and from work. They may also be denied federal assistance such as student loans, food stamps, and housing assistance. Not having access to basic needs severely limits an ex-offender's ability to focus on seeking gainful employment and, moreover, exposes the individual to being at a higher risk of re-offending.

In 2016, the United States Sentencing Commission issued a report that studied the recidivism rate of over 25,000 federal prisoners who were released in 2005 (Hunt & Dummville, 2016). Being able to adjust to the community and find employment is most important within the first two years of being released from prison. The report highlights two major risk factors that impact recidivism of ex-offenders: (1) age, as being under 21 years of age increased the recidivism rate 67.6%; and (2) not having a high school diploma increased the recidivism rate to 60.4% (Hunt & Dummville, 2016). Career counselors and professionals can intervene and be helpful by providing employment and educational resources prior to and after being released from incarceration (Thul-Sigler, 2015).

There are resources available to assist ex-offenders find gainful employment. Chief among them are the American Jobs Center that was established in 1998 through the Workforce Investment Act (WIA), which serves to provide assistance with finding employment for the unemployed. There are other local sites that are positioned to assist, such as the local branch of the National Urban League and other local agencies. Some online sites may be helpful if the individual has access to technology. The National Hire Network (Hirenetwork.org) is a clearinghouse of information and an advocate for policy change for those who have criminal records. This site helps individuals and employers navigate the hiring process for those with criminal records. The Work Opportunity Tax Credit is a federal tax credit available to employers for hiring ex-felons and other targeted groups. The Federal Bureau of Prisons has a website that provides resources for employment and educational assistance with other helpful links. Please see the Additional Resources for this chapter for more information.

Managed Care Systems

Community settings may require clients who seek mental health or substance use treatment to access a managed care system. Managed care systems are a form of health care that controls costs by placing limits on fees and by restricting the recipients' choice of providers. Traditionally, managed care has been a means of employers providing medical

LEARNING ACTIVITY 13.1
HOW TO BECOME A CLINICAL COUNSELOR WHO INTEGRATES CAREER INTERVENTIONS

Interview a mental health counselor in private practice who specifically integrates career counseling within his or her scope of practice. Please use the following questions to assist with the interview.

1. How would you describe your career path into the counseling profession?

2. How did you become interested in career counseling?

3. What theory assists you in your work with integrating career and work-related issues in your clinical practice?

and behavioral health insurance coverage to employees and their families. Many EAP providers offer services as part of an employer's managed care contract. Though similar in design, the federal Medicare and Medicaid systems were not commonly referred to as managed care organizations. Beginning January 1, 2014, however, most citizens whose incomes do not exceed 138% percent of the federal poverty line qualify for Medicaid coverage if their home state adopted the Affordable Care Act (ACA) expansion.

Employee Assistance Programs

Several organizationally sponsored centers are available in the community to help employees cope with occupational stress and to meet career-related mental and behavioral health challenges. Noteworthy are employee assistance programs (EAPs), specifically designed to intervene with an employee experiencing personal problems in order to maintain that individual's productivity. Originally developed in the 1940s to 1950s to address problems related to substance abuse, EAPs emphasize assessment and modification of broadly defined "troubled" behaviors (Jerrell & Rightwell, 1982). The Employee Assistance Program Association specifically describes these behaviors as health, marital, family, financial, alcohol, drug, legal, emotional, stress, or other personal issues that may affect job performance. Most EAP providers offer brief, solution-focused interventions. In the United States, 78% percent of employers now offer EAPs.

Private Practice

Many private practitioners offer career counseling services as an area of specialization. Areas of specialization are activities where clinicians have gained enough training and experience to develop an expertise. For career counselors, these areas of expertise may include domains such as knowledge of career development theory, standardized assessment, multicultural or gender-specific interventions, or coaching.

Career Coaching

Career coaching is one of the more contemporary career interventions practiced in community settings. Historically, career coaching began to rise in the mid-1980s to mid-1990s as an internal consultation service provided by a manager who would assist an employee with their career planning goals (Chung & Gfroerer, 2003). Career coaching began to peak in response to changes in relation to the flattening and restructuring of organizational paradigm. Flattening eliminated many middle management positions, which left the manager coaching the employee on a myriad of career and organizational issues. Presently, the career coach as "manager" varies to a great degree, along with whether a career coach is internal or external to the organization. Many employee assistance programs provide the service of career coaching for designated employees as an employee benefit from the organization.

Career coaching is a solution-driven process, which involves working with clients to see what concrete steps they can take to achieve their career objectives (Cheeks, 2013; Chung & Gfroerer, 2003). Career objectives may include issues related to tenuous job security, career satisfaction, achieving balance in life roles, coping with occupational stress related to role overload, role ambiguity, difficult supervisors, and hostile relationships with coworkers (Amundson, Harris-Bowlsbey, & Niles, 2005). The primary goal of career coaching is to assist the client with a short- or long-term career transition. Additionally, coaching is provided to assist with the client's personal development, within a work-related context so that clients can (a) better identify skills, (b) make better career choices, (c) be more productive and valuable workers, (d) balance personal and work life, (e) implement and complete projects, and (f) develop leadership (Chung & Gfroerer, 2003).

A growing service that is usually external to the organization is executive coaching, which provides coaching services to upper level management (Kilburg, 1996). Kilburg (1996) defines executive coaching as a helping relationship formed between a client who has managerial authority and responsibility in an organization and a consultant who uses a wide variety of behavioral techniques and methods to help the client (p. 142). As the practice of executive coaching has been embraced by organizational structures the definition has transformed to include a tripartite relationship. The Executive Coaching Forum (2012) explains this relational definition as an experiential and individualized leadership development process that builds a leader's capability to achieve short- and long-term organizational goals, with the organization, an executive, and the executive coach working in partnership to achieve maximum impact. The provision of coaching services has increased tremendously within the last 10 years and has impacted the career development community in a multitude of ways.

Ethically, Chung and Gfroerer (2003) cite several major criticisms of coaching, chief among them are (a) lack of a nationally recognized professional organization that regulates the guidelines and training of career coaches, (b) lack of a unified code of ethics to guide the practice of career coaching, and (c) deficient evidence to substantiate the effectiveness of coaching. Because of not having a real way to quantify the impact on the career counseling field, there is a strong reliance on anecdotal examples of effectiveness, and this approach will continue to be problematic as we continue to emphasize evidence-based career interventions.

CASE ILLUSTRATION 13.2
JOHN'S PROMOTION

John is a 34-year-old Caucasian male who has spent most of his career working for a major car manufacturer. John had the responsibility of building engines on the assembly line until he was injured in a car accident, which has left him diagnosed with post-traumatic stress disorder and major depression. He was off work for three months and returned to work only to be laid off due to low demand after one month. He was told that the lay-offs were dictated by seniority, but John believes his diagnosis influenced his layoff. John has seven years with the company and therefore was given a severance package and outplacement services through a private company, away from the plant. John had envisioned himself retiring from the plant, but now his dream of early retirement has been lost.

John was seeing a counselor for his mental health needs while he was off work and would like to see one counselor for his mental health and career-related needs.

1. How would John go about finding the appropriate provider for both his mental health and career goals?

2. Once John finds a counselor, what do you think needs to be the primary goal of counseling?

3. John has a severance package, but once that package is depleted, he will need to apply for unemployment. What resource could help John access his unemployment benefits?

Job Placement Services

An additional intervention, highly used in career counseling by diverse clientele, is job placement services (Herman, Bramucci, & Fiala, 2010). Job placement services began in the early 1800s with commercial employment agencies offering placement services to graduates of teacher training programs, but by the late 1800s, the number of employment agencies had grown to over 200 in the United States (Herr, Rayman, & Garis, 1993). Career counselors, vocational rehabilitation counselors, and employment counselors have contributed significantly to the utilization of job placement services (Cross et al., 2015). In the mid 1980s, Burlew (1985) cited technological changes and an increase in immigrant populations as reasons that job development and placement are needed services. Today, we see that these two contextual factors are reasons that job development and placement services are a highly sought after career intervention (Cross et al., 2015; Herman et al., 2010).

Job placement services exist in a variety of forms in the career services market. Typically, job placement entities provide a specialized service to a particular population or industry. For example, veterans transitioning from the military to the civilian workforce have access to assistance from the Veterans Career Transition Program, a program initiated by Syracuse University's Institute for Veterans and Military Families (IVMF). Similar services are available for many other unique populations, such as individuals with disabilities, paroled prisoners re-entering the workforce, or retired workers seeking a second career. These organizations provide access to specific employers and offer specialized training and assistance. Job placement organizations may be privately or publicly funded, or they may exist as a partnership between government and the private sector.

Job placement services increased with the Workforce Investment Act of 1998 that gave birth to the "One Stop Centers" that would meet the needs of businesses for skilled workers and the associated training, as well as the education and employment needs of individuals (Herman et al., 2010). Formerly called the "One Stop Center," now the American Job Center is responsible for a significant portion of job placement services in the community (https://www.careeronestop.org/ExploreCareers/explore-careers.aspx).

Each state is responsible for the implementation of job placement services, and other resources will vary depending on the allocations to the specific state (Herman et al., 2010). The American Job Center is a resource appropriate for diverse populations, such as low income, unemployed, or underemployed, with some services provided free of charge.

In July of 2015, Congress passed the Workforce Innovation and Opportunity Act (WIOA). WIOA supersedes WIA of 1998 and provides better coordination with the Adult Education and Family Literacy Act, the Wagner-Peyser Act, and the Rehabilitation Act of 1973. This act provides the provisions for employees and employers that reflect the realities of the 21st century. It again enables a diverse workforce to gain access to career pathways, which is vital to shared prosperity and the growing economy.

LEARNING ACTIVITY 13.2

UNDERSTANDING THE AMERICAN JOBS CENTER'S RESOURCES

Critique the online website for the American Jobs Center at https://www.careeronestop.org/ExploreCareers/explore-careers.aspx. according to the NCDA online career development guidelines.

MULTICULTURAL APPROACHES TO CAREER DEVELOPMENT IN THE COMMUNITY

Multicultural competency in community-based career settings is imperative due to the diverse clientele. Trait-oriented career theories have traditionally assumed a level of access to vocational choice that has not always been available to all segments of the population.

Variable characteristics such as race, gender, sexual preference, socioeconomic class, and access to quality education have historically presented barriers to many occupations. Research in the late 20th century began to challenge the cultural validity of traditional trait-factor or developmental career theories as models for marginalized populations in the United States (Leong & Brown, 1995; Byars & Hackett, 1998).

As more recent theories of career counseling have incorporated the vocational experiences of diverse populations, greater emphasis has been placed on the importance of developing culturally competent career counselors. Sue & Sue (2012) suggest that cultural competence is dependent upon three critical attributes of the counselor:

- Being aware of one's own assumptions, values, and biases

- Understanding the worldview of culturally diverse clients

- Developing appropriate intervention strategies and techniques

Whether working in clinical or nonclinical settings in the community, clinicians must educate themselves in ways that provide them with techniques that maximize their cultural competence and increase their ability to serve the needs of diverse clients.

One such technique is metacognition. Metacognition refers to a counselor's ability to monitor his or her own thoughts and thought processes. This technique requires counselors to engage in ongoing self-reflection regarding the cognitive schema and thinking strategies used to understand and interpret client information (Byars-Winston & Fouad, 2006). The metacognitive process include such questions as the following:

- "What are the gaps in my knowledge about the client's context?"

- "Are there some career issues that I am willing to address more than others?"

- "Are there some issues that I am avoiding?"

Another such technique is viewing career development from an ecological or systems perspective. This perspective incorporates the interplay and relationships between the various systems of cultural influence that affect a client. It acknowledges that environmental and contextual variables such as gender, ethnicity, socioeconomic status, and cultural values play an important role in shaping career interest, career efficacy, and the interconnections between internal and external variables that have an impact on people's career development (Arthur & McMahon, 2005).

Blustein (2006) encouraged exploration of vocational guidance practices for poor and working-class populations, people with disabilities, at-risk youth, the unemployed, clients of color, and LGBT clients. Many private organizations and government agencies concerned with career guidance have adopted culturally specific programs to further such efforts. Currently, many marginalized populations have access to vocational information and assistance from a wide range of programs such as Out for Work, the Hispanic Employment Initiative, the Medical Minority Applicant Registry, and the National Urban League's Entrepreneurship Center. Clinical practitioners have access to several new methods of assessment and intervention with culturally relevant career topics, such as the development and enactment of identity (Abes, Jones, & McEwen, 2007; Cross, Grant, Ventuneac, & 2012), the perception of contextual supports and barriers (Lent, Brown, Hackett, & 2000), self-narratives and resume development (Toporek & Flamer, 2009), and the DSM-5 Cultural Formulation Interview (American Psychiatric Association, 2013).

MULTICULTURAL BOX 13.1
INTERSECTIONALITY AND OCCUPATIONAL IDENTITY

One of the most enduring concepts of psychological theory is the concept of the personal identity development. Early theories on racial identity surfaced in the 1960s and 1970s and suggested that like Erikson's life span model, racial minorities moved through a series of stages of racial salience: from naivety or low salience, to an "encounter" that triggered the individual to consider the negative consequences of racial minority status, to enveloping anger, to an eventual stage of commitment to fight for social change (Cross, 1978). However, later research indicated that unlike the concept of stage theory, racial identity attitudes tended to "recycle," depending upon the shifting experiences encountered by the individual (Parham, 1989).

Recent research suggests that rather than carrying a singular, relatively stable identity,

people carry multiple dimensions of social identities, reflecting the relationships and salience of race, gender, sexual orientation, social class, occupation, generational status, and other significant identity markers (Abes et al., 2007). Originating from the experiences of women of color, intersectionality suggests that individuals are considered from a viewpoint that recognizes the likelihood of marginalization by more than a single identity marker. Multicultural competence requires that the career counselor considers complexity and plans interventions accordingly.

Tips for consideration: What are some possible barriers facing a lesbian, African-American woman recently graduated with an education degree? What steps do you take to coach a transgender Latino male for a business interview?

Summary: Challenges and Opportunities

The focus of this chapter has been career counseling in community settings and the various centers that provide career services. Consideration

has been given to clinical and nonclinical environments and the integration of work-related issues for all counseling interventions. Highlighted are two major career counseling interventions in the community: career coaching and job placement services.

The challenge for career counseling in the community will be the development of multicultural competency skills to effectively meet the needs of a diverse community that is continually changing. Emphasis has been given to the primary centers for career counseling in the community, which include community mental health centers, private practice, and corporate settings. In addition, providing career services to individuals who are diagnosed with a mental health or substance use disorder adds another complex diversity dimension. Community settings are diverse environments; this necessitates the practitioner to develop multicultural competence that will be integrated at all levels of career counseling.

Keystones

- Career counseling has taken on greater importance since the great recession of 2008 and the integration of career related interventions in all counseling.

- Community mental health centers are primary centers providing career-related services to a diverse population of all socioeconomic levels.

- Private practice settings are significant providers of career interventions in the community who can provide the integration of work and mental health.

- Many organizations are providing career-related services through EAPs as part of the employee benefit package of the organization, with the purpose of improving or maintaining productivity.

- Career coaching and executive coaching are growing interventions used by organizations to remediate or develop employees and executives.

- Job placement services have been influential in assisting a diverse population with entering the workplace as well as being able to maintain employment with the added support.

- Multicultural competence will continue to be a challenge for career counseling in the community due to the vastly changing demographics of the United States with the immigrant and refugee population, which subsequently impacts the workplace.

Additional Resources

Information about the Work Opportunity Tax Credit: https://www.doleta.gov/business/incentives/opptax

Resources for former inmates from the Federal Bureau of Prisons: https://www.bop.gov/resources/former_inmate_resources.jsp

References

Abel, J., Deitz, R., & Su, Y. (2014). Are recent college graduates finding good jobs? *Current Issues in Economics and Finance, 20*(1), 1-8.

Abes, E. S., Jones, S. R., & McEwen, M. K. (2007). Reconceptualizing the model of multiple dimensions of identity: the role of meaning-making capacity in the construction of multiple identities. *Journal of College Student Development, 48*(1), 1-22.

Alexander, M. (2012). *The new Jim Crow: Mass incarceration in the age of colorblindness*. New York, NY: The New Press

American Psychiatric Association. (2013). *Diagnostic and statistical manual of mental disorders* (DSM-5), (5th ed.). Washington, DC: Author.

Amundson, N. E., Harris-Bowlsbey, J., & Niles, S. G. (2005). *Essentials elements of career counseling: Processes and techniques*. Upper Saddle River, NJ: Pearson Education.

Arthur, N., & McMahon, M. (2005). Multicultural career counseling: Theoretical applications of the systems theory framework. *The Career Development Quarterly, 53*(3), 208-222.

Blustein, D. (2006). *The psychology of working*. Mahweh, NJ: Lawrence Erlbaum Associates.

Brown, D. (2002). *Career choice and development* (4th ed). San Francisco, CA: Jossey-Bass.

Brown, D., & Brooks, L. (1985). Career counseling as a mental health intervention. *Professional Psychology: Research and Practice, 16*(6), 860-867. doi:10.1037/0735-7028.16.6.860

Burlew, L. D. (1985). A model for job development. *Journal of Counseling and Development, 63*, 575-577.

Byars, A. M., & Hackett, G. (1998). Applications of social cognitive theory to the career development of women of color. *Applied & Preventive Psychology, 7*(4), 255-267.

Byars-Winston, A. M., & Fouad, N. A. (2006). Metacognition and multicultural competence: expanding the culturally appropriate career counseling model. *The Career Development Quarterly, 54*(3), 187-201.

Caporoso, R. A., & Kiselica, M. S. (2004). Career counseling with clients who have a severe mental illness. *The Career Development Quarterly, 52*(3), 235-245.

Cheeks, D. (2013). 10 things you should know about career coaching. *Forbes*. Retrieved from http://www.forbes.com/sites/learnvest/2013/07/09/10-things-you-should-know-about-career-coaching.

Chung, Y. B., & Gfroerer, M. C. A. (2003). Career coaching: Practice, training, professional and ethical issues. *The Career Development Quarterly, 52*(2), 141-152.

Cross, K. E., Moore, C. L., Manyibe, E. O., Aref, F., Washington, A. L., Umadjela, A., Sanders, P. R., Payma, H. S., Pandey, J., & Cyprian, D. (2015). New immigrating racial and ethnic populations and "trends Impacts" on state vocational rehabilitation agencies. *Journal of Applied Rehabilitation Counseling, 46*(2), 20-33.

Cross, W. (1978). The Thomas and Cross models of psychological Nigrescence, a review. *Journal of Black Psychology, 5*(1), 13-31.

Cross, W. J., Grant, B. O., & Ventuneac, A. (2012). Black identity and well-being: Untangling race and ethnicity. In J. M. Sullivan, A. M. Esmail, J. M. Sullivan, A. M. Esmail (Eds.),

African American identity: racial and cultural dimensions of the black experience (pp. 125-146). Lanham, MD: Lexington Books/Rowman & Littlefield.

Dahling, J., Melloy, R., & Thompson, M. (2013). Financial strain and regional unemployment as barriers to job search self-efficacy: A test of social cognitive career theory. *Journal of Counseling Psychology 60*(2), 210–218. doi:10.1037/a0031492

Erickson, W., von Schrader, S., & Lee, C. (2012). *2010 disability status report, United States*. Retrieved from http://digitalcommons.ilr.cornell.edu/cgi/viewcontent.cgi?article=1561&context=gladnetcollect.

The Executive Coaching Forum. (2012). *The executive coaching handbook: Principles and guidelines for a successful coaching partnership*. Retrieved from http://www.executivecoachingforum.com.

Giordano, A. L., Clarke, P. B., & Furter, R. T. (2014). Predicting substance abuse relapse: The role of social interest and social bonding. *Journal of Addictions & Offender Counseling, 35*(2), 114-127. doi:10.1002/j.2161-1874.2014.00030.x

Herman, A. M., Bramucci, R., & Fiala, G. F. (2010). *The "plain English" version of the workforce investment act of 1998. U. S. Department of Labor Employment and Training Administration September 1998*. Retrieved from http://www.doleta.gov/usworkforce/wia/Runningtext.cfm.

Herr, E. (1992). Emerging trends in career counselling. *International Journal for the Advancement of Counselling, 15*, 255-288. doi:10.1007/BF02449904

Herr, E. L., Rayman, J. R., & Garis, J. W. (1993). *Handbook for the college and university career center*. Westport, CT: Greenwood Press.

Hunt, K. S., Dumville, R., & United States Sentencing Commission. (2016). *Recidivism among federal offenders: A comprehensive overview*. Washington, DC: United States Sentencing Commission.

Imbimbo, P. V. (1994). Integrating personal and career counseling: A challenge for counselors. *Journal of Employment Counseling, 31*, 50-59.

Jerrell, J., & Rightwell, J. (1982). Evaluating employee assistance programs: A review of methods, outcomes, and future directions. *Evaluation and Program Planning, 5*, 255-267.

Kilburg, R. R. (1996). Toward a conceptual understanding and definition of executive coaching. *Counseling Psychology Journal: Practice and Research, 48*(2),134-144.

Krumboltz, J. D., & Nichols, C. W. (1990). Integrating the social learning theory of career decision making. In W. B. Walsh S. H. Osipow (Eds.), *Career counseling: Contemporary topics in vocational psychology* (pp. 159-192). Hillsdale, NJ: Lawrence Erlbaum Associates.

Lent, R. W., Brown, S. D., & Hackett, G. (1994). Toward a unifying social cognitive theory of career and academic interest, choice, and performance. *Journal of Vocational Behavior, 45*(1), 79-122. doi:10.1006/jvbe.1994.1027

Lent, R. W., Brown, S. D., & Hackett, G. (2000). Contextual supports and barriers to career choice: A social cognitive analysis. *Journal of Counseling Psychology, 47*(1), 36-49.

Leong, F. L., & Brown, M. T. (1995). Theoretical issues in cross-cultural career development: Cultural validity and cultural specificity. In W. B. Walsh, S. H. Osipow (Eds.), *Handbook of vocational psychology: Theory, research, and practice* (2nd ed., pp. 143-180). Hillsdale, NJ: Lawrence Erlbaum Associates.

McAweeney, M., Jones, M., & Moore, D. (2008). Employment barriers for persons with substance use disorders and co-occurring disabilities: Supported employment strategies. *Journal of Applied Rehabilitation, 39*(2), 39-50.

Meyers, L. (2014). The lingering crisis of the great recession. *Counseling Today, 51*(4), 46-53.

Niles, S. G., & Harris-Bowlsbey, J. (2013). *Career development interventions in the 21st century* (4th ed.). Upper Saddle River, NJ: Pearson Education, Inc.

NSDUH-Substance Abuse and Mental Health Services Administration. (2014). *Results from the 2013 National Survey on Drug Use and Health: Summary of National Findings,* NSDUH Series H-48, HHS Publication No. (SMA) 14-4863. Rockville, MD: Substance Abuse and Mental Health Services Administration.

Parham, T. A. (1989). Cycles of psychological nigrescence. *The Counseling Psychologist, 17*(2), 187-226.

Reardon, R. C., Lenz, J. G., Sampson, J. P., & Peterson, G. W. (2000). *Career development and planning: A comprehensive approach.* Belmont, CA: Thomson Brooks/Cole.

Rhee-Weise, M., & Horn, M. (2013). Learning to do when unemployment rates are high. *New England Journal of Higher Education.* Retrieved from http://www.nebhe.org/the-journal/learning-to-do-when-unemployment-rates-are-high.

Rotman, D. (2013). How technology is destroying jobs. *MIT Technology Review.* Retrieved from http://www.technologyreview.com/featuredstory/515926/how-technology-is-destroying-jobs.

Sue, D. W., & D. Sue. (2012). *Counseling the culturally diverse: Theory and practice* (6th ed.). Hoboken, NJ: John Wiley & Sons.

Thompson, M. N., & Cummings, D. L. (2010). Enhancing the career development of individuals who have criminal records. *The Career Development Quarterly, 58*(3), 209-218. https://doi.org/10.1002/j.2161-0045.2010.tb00187.x

Thul-Sigler, A. (2015). Focusing on career development with inmates. *Career Convergence Magazine.* Retrieved from https://ncda.org/aws/NCDA/pt/sd/news_article/113485/_self/layout_details/false.

Toporek, R. L., & Flamer, C. (2009). The résumé's secret identity: A tool for narrative exploration in multicultural career counseling. *Journal of Employment Counseling, 46*(1), 4-17.

U.S. Department of Health and Human Services, National Institute for Occupational Safety and Health. (1999). *Stress . . . at work* (DHHS NIOSH Publication No. 99-101). Retrieved from https://www.cdc.gov/niosh/docs/99-101/pdfs/99-101.pdf.

Vallas, R., & Dietrich, S. (2014). *One strike and you're out: How we can eliminate barriers to economic security and mobility for people with criminal records* (Rep.). Washington, DC: Center for American Progress.

ADULT CAREER DEVELOPMENT

Jane Goodman

Traditionally career development was seen as a process in which young people developed the maturity, knowledge, and understanding to make a career *choice*—note the singular word, *choice*. Today, however, we recognize that career *choices* take place over the course of a lifetime, and therefore development is a continuous process. Helping adults with their career development draws on theories and practices used with young people but adds elements particular to adults, draws on their life experiences, and employs the understanding that this is an ongoing, not one-time, process. In this chapter, we will summarize career theories as they relate to adult career development, discuss theories that relate specifically to adults, and then focus on the role counselors play in helping adults make long- and short-term career decisions.

LEARNING OBJECTIVES

After completing the reading and exercises provided in this chapter, you will be able to:

- describe typical adult career development needs;

- summarize modern theories of career development as they apply to adults;

- demonstrate understanding of adult career development through responses to cases;

- use career counseling theories, exercises, and activities to meet the needs of a diverse groups of adults;

- recognize issues related to the stress of losing employment; and

- be able to describe a variety of retirement scenarios so as to help adults plan for and carry out the one(s) best suited to them.

TYPICAL ADULT DEVELOPMENT NEEDS

The more we learn about brain development, the more we learn that the brain remains plastic well into adulthood and even into old age. That means that adults learn, change, and, yes, develop throughout life. The idea of career maturity as a fixed destination does not jibe with these new understandings. Rather, career maturity needs to be defined as the ability to respond to the changing needs of the workplace, changing internal needs, and the changes necessitated by relationships with others. Theories of career development and career counseling are elucidated extensively elsewhere in this volume. Here we wish only to focus on how these need to be adapted to the needs of adults.

Erik Erikson (1950) was one of the first prominent theorists to discuss development beyond early adulthood. His tasks include occupational identity, generativity, productivity, and after age 60, integrity (vs. despair). Super (1980), Havighurst (1972), Levinson (1986), and others also discussed stages and developmental tasks of adulthood. All of these classical theorists, however, considered adulthood a time of consolidating and maintaining. The postmodern world, however, does not usually allow for adulthood to be static in that way. That is either exciting or challenging, depending on one's point of view—and for most it is probably sometimes one, sometimes the other, sometimes both.

JOB LOSS

Often the reason that adults are seeking career assistance is because they have lost their jobs. Organizations downsize, relocate, change focus, and retool in response to changing market needs, a changing economy, or changing demographics. Adults who have been performing successfully may still find themselves out of work as a result of these societal changes. Adults who have not kept up with technology, or who for other reasons have been not performing adequately, are even more likely to lose their positions. The experience of job loss can be profound. Responses have been described as resembling the stages of grief (Kubler-Ross, 1969) and can be troubling to both the adult experiencing them and to those around them. It is critical for career counselors to recognize these responses and help their clients recognize, understand, and manage them, perhaps even redirecting them. For example, the anger that is a common aspect of the grief experience is often directed inward. Although often unrealistic, people may be angry at themselves for somehow not seeing the unemployment coming, not avoiding the layoff. Counselors can help clients change the direction of that anger from self-blame to "They can't keep a good (wo)man down."

One of the more challenging aspects of career counseling with those who are newly unemployed is recognizing the need to perhaps stay immobilized while feeling this heavy grief. Spencer and Adams (1990) provided a compelling metaphor of this part of the grief process, calling it "the pit." Each individual has a unique need for time in the pit, and counselors need to both recognize and allow that, along with providing a helping hand for the climb out.

ADAPTABILITY

As he got older, Super modified his career development phases to see later adulthood as a time for flexibility rather than decline. Goodman (1994) discussed Super's (1980) coining of the term "career adaptability" to describe the inappropriateness of using the construct career maturity for adults as they needed to respond to changing internal and external conditions. Super and Knasel (1981) pointed out that a critical difference between youth and adults is that adults are engaged in work whereas youth's awareness is largely anticipatory. Hall (1986) made the case that mastery of adaptability led to adults seeing themselves as active participants rather than passive victims of circumstances. Strategies for developing adaptability have been suggested by Gelatt (1991, 2014, 2015) and Mitchell, Levin, and Krumboltz (1999), among others.

HB Gelatt's Positive Uncertainty

Originally proposed in 1991, the theory of positive uncertainty has found resonance with adults, who, in my personal experience, feel that it describes their lives and the struggle to make decisions in the face of a world where the pace of change is accelerating. Briefly, the theory says that one must decide **and** be prepared to change. Waiting for certainty will lead to paralysis; sticking with a decision in the face of change may lead to a loss of adaptability. Gelatt (2015, March 15) has added to and updated his theory through a series of blogs. He restated his strategies for adaptability as *Top Ten Tactics*:

Do different.

- Do different things and do things differently.
- Get off your paradigm—get out of your box, rut.
- See the big picture.
- Use a telescope—take the long view.
- Use a wide-angle lens—look for the larger implications.

Act like a child.

- Do something foolish, spontaneous, child-like.
- Put your imagination in high gear—and soar.

Take the pause that refreshes.

- Reflect—play the muse.
- Don't do something—just sit there.

Put on some different spectacles.

- Try rose-colored glasses—try the six thinking hats.
- Change your viewpoint—get a second and third opinion.

Look at past performances.

- Review and revise the past—consider it a set of raw materials.
- Write your future history—think backward.

Rewrite the rules.

- Slay some sacred cows—invent new rules of thumb.
- Eliminate obsolete standard operating procedures.

Seek serendipity.

- Look for surprises—expect the unexpected.
- Listen for the knock of opportunity—then answer.

Stick your neck out.

- Do something risky—play the giraffe.
- Try to fail at something—if you keep succeeding, move the target.

Dream some impossible dreams.

- Dream precisely—stop dreaming vaguely.
- Imagine your ideal future—and ask how.

Gelatt (2014) also suggested that change happens to you and doesn't wait for you. Furthermore, he states:

Although the future doesn't exist, never did and never will, I believe it is present right behind my eyes. Foresight is defined as "the perception of the significance and nature of events before they have occurred." Therefore, my foresight, my perception of the future, exists in my mind's eye. My image of the future may be the most important factor in determining what it will be.

Since the future doesn't exist, I have two choices: create it or let someone else. The future is not predetermined, not predictable, but it is persuadable. When it comes to the future, there are three kinds of people: those who make it happen, those who let it happen, and those who wonder what happened. I want to be the first kind.

Counselors who are working with adults around career issues can use Gelatt's ideas to help their clients be among those who "make it happen." They can help clients develop a sense of agency about their career plans, help them be active on their own behalf, and help them not only develop a vision of their preferred future but also acquire the tools to make that vision a reality. Those tools include decision-making strategies and implementation strategies. Implementation strategies may include networking; filling out applications; designing resumes for online submission as well as printed versions; identifying job openings; and preparing for telephone, Skype type, or in-person interviews; and follow-up strategies. These practical components have sometimes been seen as outside the realm of career counseling, but it is not enough to know where you are going, it is important to know how to get there.

Planned Happenstance

Mitchell et al. (1999) described adult career life as a series of events, some planned and some unplanned. They believed that adults who took advantage of the unplanned events were the ones who prospered. Their theory of planned happenstance described how individuals capitalized on chance events to create new opportunities. The inventions of such diverse products as Wite-Out, Velcro, and Penicillin are described rather as discoveries, deriving from making connections and chance observations. The happenstance part of the equation is clear. But what of the planned part? People frequently describe career opportunities as having been "in the right place at the right time." But few of us are as lucky as Cinderella, who could just wait for her prince to come. The rest need to live by being in many places, in hopes one of them will be the "right place." Mitchell et al. (1999) suggest five approaches to using chance events to improve the chances of career success:

1. Curiosity: exploring new learning opportunities

2. Persistence: exerting effort despite setbacks

3. Flexibility: changing attitudes and circumstances

4. Optimism: viewing new opportunities as possible and attainable

5. Risk Taking: taking action in the face of uncertain outcomes (p. 118)

Adult career planning, then, needs to add using and creating chance events to its repertoire of skills. Redefining indecision as open-mindedness has become another hallmark of this theory (Krumboltz, 1992). This use of classic reframing encourages adult career changers to embrace their uncertainty. Rather than thinking they are inadequate decision makers, they can see themselves as open to opportunity, learning, and growth. Changing perspective in this way is particularly useful for adults whose first career decision(s) may have been made more restrictively, by narrow information or following societal or parental restraints.

Ebberwein, Krieshok, Ulven, and Prosser (2004) also examined the qualities needed by adults for successful career adaptability. Using qualitative methods, they conducted extensive interviews with 18 people who were in career transition, nine women and nine men. They summarized the results of their research into three themes: adaptive

CASE ILLUSTRATION 14.1
THE CASE OF LATISHA FORBES

Latisha Forbes had been a librarian for the whole of her working life. Now 55, she had studied library science directly after completing her undergraduate degree. Her parents, as well as she, herself, had seen library work as appropriate for a woman. She also felt that she would be able to combine this work with her hoped-for roles as wife and mother, and indeed that plan panned out. She was able to have part-time work when her children were young and only returned to full-time employment when the youngest entered high school.

Suddenly, it seemed to her, things had changed. The university library where she worked had embraced technology enthusiastically, and although she had learned enough to manage her responsibilities, she found she no longer enjoyed what she did. Her youngest child would finish college in a year, she and her husband planned on working another 12 to 15 years before retirement, and she felt that was too long to stay in a job where she no longer looked forward to going to work. Latisha decided to see a career counselor to help in making a decision as to what to do next.

Her counselor had recently been to a workshop about planned happenstance, positive uncertainty, and open-mindedness, and thought these would provide a good framework for Latisha, whose original choices had been constrained by perceived necessity, her parents and advisors, and her own beliefs about appropriate roles for women. After developing rapport and learning a bit about Latisha's situation, the counselor began by explaining to Latisha the above-mentioned theories. Latisha understood the ideas but was uncomfortable with not being able to be certain about her choices. She wanted to know for sure that she was making a good decision. Dealing with her discomfort with ambiguity became a subtext of their sessions together as Latisha explored, for the first time in many ways, her interests, values, temperament, skills, and hopes for the future.

Discussion Questions

1. What assessment tools might you use to help Latisha explore her career options?

2. How would you prepare Latisha for the ageism she might encounter if she decides to search for another job?

3. How would you help Latisha examine her transferable skills from her previous experience?

---

responses, contextual challenges, and insights into the transition. Some of the adaptive responses included: approaching "job loss with a sense of urgency," picturing "the details of [the] next career move—even when no transition is in sight," getting "ready to make changes when career transitions seem imminent," treating "decisions about stop-gap employment cautiously," and setting "realistic goals and outlin[ing] steps to achieve them" (pp. 297-301).

Contextual challenges were described as follows: "Financial resources, or the lack of them, strongly influence how one copes with job transition." This was found to be the most important contextual factor. "Family life significantly interacts with work life." "An employer can have a significant impact on the experience of the transition (beyond getting it started, of course)" (pp. 301-303). Finally, insights into the transition were summarized thusly: "Needs and responsibilities sometimes conflict with the ideal occupation. . . . Adults in transition want counselors who attend to the big picture. . . . Personal transitions are rooted in significant changes in the world of work itself" (pp. 303-304).

The conclusions drawn by Ebberwein et al. (2004) are that planfulness pays off, even when there is not an obvious need in sight, and that the context can influence success in navigating a transition, for good or ill. We are reminded of the dental model (Goodman 1992). This model is predicated on the idea of the periodic career checkup, even when things are going well. It also suggests ongoing career maintenance where updating one's resume and nourishing a career network are the equivalent of flossing and brushing. Postmodern society has made it unusual for a person to choose a career and stay in it for the rest of one's working life. Adults need to understand this reality, which may be different from what they expected when they were younger. Engaging in continuing education, networking, and staying abreast of developments in one's career area and related career areas are all part of this ongoing career maintenance. Career management programs provided by some organizations often emphasize these skills. But most individuals do not have these kinds of programs; they need to be self-directed in keeping current with trends in the employment market as well as keeping their own employability active.

Managing Transitions

Schlossberg (Anderson, Goodman, & Schlossberg, 2012) developed her transition theory out of recognition, backed by research, that it was the transitions in people's lives that were more salient than their age or stage of life. Thus, an individual looking for a first job faced many of the same challenges and emotional experiences whether they were 20 or 60. Similarly an individual losing a job experienced many of the same thoughts and feelings whether a young married person or a worker close to retirement. She considered nonevents also to belong to the category of transitions. Thus, not getting a promotion or not getting into graduate school can be treated as transitions, because they require a redefinition of roles, hopes, and dreams. Counselors can use transition theory as an assessment process. Identifying where clients are managing their transitions well and where they need assistance can form the basis of a counseling plan of action.

Schlossberg found that there were four components, all beginning with an *S*, to consider when assessing someone's experience during a transition. These were the characteristics of the individual's *situation*, the psychological *self* of the individual, the *support* obtainable, and the *strategies* available to be employed. In assessing the *situation*, one needs to look at the trigger, timing, source of the transition, who is in control, what role change happens as a result, and what the person's previous experience with a similar transition is. In considering the *self*, the areas to look at are the individual's personal characteristics—for example, mental health or ego strength—and their psychological resources—that is, the balance of assets and liabilities that support or hinder their psychological well-being. Furthermore, when assessing the self in relation to adult career issues, it is important to consider the salience of work in individuals' lives; the balance among work, family, and community life; and individuals' resilience in the face of adversity. It is also useful to look at their sense of self-efficacy in regard to this transition and what meaning they are making out of what they are experiencing.

Support is the third in Schlossberg's quartet of coping resources. Support can be internal, for example, feeling positive about oneself, one's overall self-esteem; it can be external, that is; received from other people; or it can be provided by institutions, memories, or faith or spirituality. People can provide encouragement, information, referrals, practical help, and love and intimacy. Institutions can provide practical help, also, such as unemployment insurance, resume assistance, or job leads. One's spirituality or faith can provide a sense of comfort, belonging, and hope. From the foregoing it is clear that having adequate support is an essential component of successful weathering of a work-related transitions.

Finally, strategies form the fourth leg of Schlossberg's transition theory. Strategies can consist of changing the situation, for example, finding a job; changing the meaning of a situation, for example, not getting the promotion allows me to spend time with my family; and/or managing the stress of the transition. Assessing which strategies are already in the arsenal of the individual and which need to be added can be a critical component of the career counseling process. For those without good stress management skills, teaching these is also a useful part of successful service.

LEARNING ACTIVITY 14.1

1. List all the work and career transitions you can think of. Consider events and nonevents. For example, losing one's job, not getting into graduate school, or having one's spouse accept a transfer in a different city. Try to have at least 15 examples.

2. Consider what counseling interventions might be helpful for each transition, for example, grief counseling for the job loser or dual-career counseling for the spouse of the transferee.

3. How would the Schlossberg 4S help you to conceptualize these situations?

CASE ILLUSTRATION 14.2

JUAN BAEZ

Juan Baez is a 48-year-old man who has just lost the only job he has ever had. Juan was hired by a small manufacturing company, Tools, Inc., when he was 19, just out of high school. He worked his way up to being a shift manager and was making a good living at this trade. When Tools, Inc. went bankrupt, Juan was unprepared and had no Plan B. He began collecting unemployment compensation and was able to live on that and his wife's earnings along with some savings during the time the unemployment compensation lasted. When that ran out, he was in a near panic, as he had no idea what to do next. Juan was used to being independent and in charge of his life. He had worked his whole life and always felt confident in his ability to support himself and his family. His wife's income helped to buy luxuries, but he never felt they depended on it for living expenses. He is a proud man and finds asking for help to be very difficult.

Juan and his wife have one daughter. She has just finished college and is working in her first job as a teacher. She is living at home while she and her fiancé save money for a down payment on a house. She and Juan are close, and he says he will miss her when she gets married next year. Juan has a brother, who lives 1,000 miles away near his parents, who are elderly and need a lot of help, financial and instrumental. Juan feels bad that he has not helped much financially since he lost his job.

During his first months of unemployment, Juan stayed active in his softball league and with The Elks, where he was the coordinator of monthly luncheon programs. After a while, he let both of these go, telling the counselor he was embarrassed that he couldn't afford to be a part of the activities. His only other leisure activities were solitary ones, gardening and taking care of their house. Juan went to the unemployment office, and they referred him to a job-counseling center, where he met with a job counselor. She used the Schlossberg 4S model to assess Juan's assets and liabilities. Juan said that he felt he had no idea what to do next. Seeing a counselor was a big step for him, as he thought that made him seem weak, but he was desperate. He had no idea how to look for work and even less of an idea of what work he should be looking for. In thinking about Super's developmental levels, his counselor thought Juan, despite being an adult, was at the exploration stage.

Discussion Questions

1. What else does the counselor need to know to use the 4S model as an assessment tool?

2. What other information would be useful as she prepares to help Juan?

3. What personal issues do you see intertwining with Juan's career issues?

Guidelines for Individuals' Career Mastery

A search of national career development guidelines leads to the National Career Development Association website (https://ncda.org). There the guidelines are listed by topic but are not specifically delineated between youth and adults. This is perhaps recognition that all skills can be required and or mastered at different ages, but it implies less focus on adults than did the original guidelines, which specifically included an adult component.

The guidelines include three domains:

1. Personal social

2. Educational achievement and lifelong learning

3. Career management

Each domain includes goals, and each goal follows the structure of Bloom's taxonomy (Bloom, Engelhart, Furst, Hill, & Krathwohl, 1956), comprising knowledge acquisition, application, and reflection competencies. Knowledge acquisition is defined as, "They can recall, recognize, describe, identify, clarify, discuss, explain, summarize, query, investigate and compile new information about the knowledge." Application is defined as follows: "Youth and adults at the application stage apply acquired knowledge to situations and to self. They seek out ways to use the knowledge. For example, they can demonstrate, employ, perform, illustrate and solve problems related to the knowledge." Reflection is described thus, "Youth and adults at the reflection stage analyze, synthesize, judge, assess and evaluate knowledge in accord with their own goals, values and beliefs. They decide whether or not to integrate the acquired knowledge into their ongoing response to situations and adjust their behavior accordingly."

For example, under the personal social domain an overall goal is to develop understanding of self to build and maintain a positive self-concept. Within that goal are *knowledge*—to "identify your abilities, strengths, skills and talents"; *application*—to "demonstrate use of your abilities, strengths, skills and talents"; and *reflection*—to "assess the impact of your abilities, strengths, skills, and talents on your career development." Another goal under the personal social domain is to develop positive interpersonal skills including respect for diversity. The competencies subsumed under that goal are *knowledge*—to "recognize that the ability to interact positively with diverse groups of people is often essential to maintain employment"; *application*—to "explain how the ability to interact positively with diverse groups of peoples is often essential to maintain employment"; and *reflection*—to "analyze the impact of your ability to interact positively with diverse groups of people on your employment."

The domain of educational achievement and lifelong learning includes the goal of attaining a level of educational achievement that is needed to reach one's goals as well as participating in lifelong learning to function effectively in a diverse and changing economy. And the career management domain includes creating and managing a career plan as well as the skill of using accurate, current, and unbiased information for career planning.

MULTICULTURAL ISSUES

Effective career counseling requires one to be knowledgeable about one's own culture as well as about the cultures of those different from oneself. When working with adults, these cultural differences are both greater than and less than the differences when working with young people. The term *multicultural* is often used to describe race and ethnicity, but it can be seen to be much broader. Adults typically identify with several different groups. These may involve race and ethnicity, but they also include gender; age; religious beliefs (or lack thereof); level of education; urban, suburban, or rural; family structure; and others that are determined individually. With greater age comes more opportunities to establish multicultural identities. The United States, for one, has been described as a land of groups. Consider, for example, people who bowl, or scrapbook, or play golf, or own a certain breed of dog. All of these differences, whether central to identity or relatively trivial, affect an adult's worldview, approach to work, leisure, civic engagement, or family life. Career counselors working with adults need not only to understand their own cultural identities but also to have a heightened awareness of their clients' cultural identities in order to ensure that they are not interfering with the counseling relationship.

Super and Knasel (1979) proposed the use of the term *career adaptability*, but career maturity is still widely used in the profession. Adaptability has been defined as,

LEARNING ACTIVITY 14.2

1. List as many of your own cultural identities as you can. For example, you might be female, fortyish, single, heterosexual, Guatemalan born Hispanic, highly educated, urban, and caretaker of elderly parents.

2. Indicate the influence each of these identities has on your worldview and your career selection. For example, you might say as a city dweller you had a wide range of career choices; as a single person, you are able to enter into work that requires travel; or as a Spanish speaker, you can work in communities that require one to be bilingual.

On the restrictive side, being caretaker for your parents may mean that you are not geographically mobile.

3. For each of the identities listed in number 1, indicate how that might help or hinder a relationship with a client. For example, the motivation it took you to become highly educated might make it harder to empathize with someone with less motivation, and being a caretaker of your parents might make it easier to understand the challenges faced by a single mother in managing a work schedule.

"the ability to alter our responses without too much effort to fit into new or changing circumstances" (Rossier, 2015, p. 334). He stated that adaptability comprises four resources:

1. The ability to look ahead and be aware of one's own future (concern)

2. The ability to control one's career and life trajectories (control)

3. The ability to explore a variety of situations and roles (curiosity)

4. The self-confidence of one's ability of reaching his or her aspirations (confidence)

The life design framework, discussed in the approaches section that follows, is one way of facilitating individuals' adaptability (Savickas, 2012). Income level and social class are often ignored when diversity discussions are on the table. There has been a persistent myth that the United States is a classless society, but the disparity in income and restriction of the opportunity structure make it clear that this is not true. In 2013, 77% of adults from families in the top income quartile earned at least bachelor's degrees by the time they turned 24, up from 40% in 1970, according to a new report from the University of Pennsylvania's Alliance for Higher Education and Democracy and the Pell Institute for the Study of Opportunity in Higher Education. But 9% of people from the lowest income bracket did the same in 2013, up from 6% in 1970 (Korn, 2015). Although a bachelor's level college degree may not be the best goal for everyone, family income should not be the determinant of who goes to college and who does not. When helping adults make career decisions, it is important for counselors to look at past decisions and determine if they were made freely, with full access to the opportunity structure, or if they were constrained. Constraints may come from external barriers or from internal ones. Being the first in one's family or community to attend college, for example, may be

CASE ILLUSTRATION 14.3
THE CASE OF SAMUEL CHUNG

Samuel Chung came to Mary Garcia's counseling office one of the evenings that she held open for working adults. Sam was well dressed, in the "uniform" of a successful stockbroker: suit, white shirt, tie, with well-polished shoes and recently cut hair. He told Mary that he wasn't exactly sure why he was there. He had a good job and made good money, but he just wasn't sure that this work was right for him anymore. Mary thought about Hansen's (1997) tasks as she listened to Sam's story.

Sam told her that he was turning 50 in a few months. He was fairly recently divorced, and he had 2 children who had both graduated college and who had managed to find jobs. He joked that they both had jobs with health benefits, so he now felt free to pursue his own interests. His ex-wife had a good job, they were on decent terms, and he had no alimony to pay. Sam had never been a churchgoer, but he had recently joined a local men's group that met in a church, and he was considering joining the choir.

As Mary listened to Sam, she sensed a yearning to be engaged in work that connected more closely to the spirituality he was discovering in himself. She asked Sam to tell her what had drawn him to finance and being a broker. His reply told her a lot about the young man he had been. He said that he had majored in business in college, because his parents thought it was a good idea. He did well in his business classes and enjoyed them. He was offered a job with his present company after interviewing through the college placement office, and he had been there ever since. He had been successful, and he enjoyed the life that his high income allowed. Now, however, it just didn't feel like enough. He also said that the upcoming 50th birthday felt like an important milestone—kind of like it was his last chance to do something he wanted for himself. He just didn't know what it was.

Discussion Questions

1. What else would you like to know about Sam to help him with his current dilemma?

2. How would you apply the theories of adult development you have read about thus far, that is, how would you conceptualize his issues?

3. What would be your treatment plan for helping Sam?

both external—no funds or for people in rural areas no access—or it may be internal—no one I know has ever done this, why do I think I can? When past career constraints have been identified, it is incumbent on the career counselor to look at remediation, advocacy, and other empowering activities to provide an adult client with opportunities that may have been missed when they were younger.

MODERN THEORIES OF CAREER DEVELOPMENT APPLIED TO ADULTS

Although there are suggestions for how to proceed with career counseling in the previous sections, the focus has been on how to understand clients and their career issues. In this section of the chapter, we will focus on ways counselors can work with clients to manage their careers, make decisions as necessary, and understand the role that work has in their lives. It is important to keep in mind throughout this section that a critical difference between adults and young people is that adults are able to look back on their experiences to inform future decisions, that is, to be retrospective, whereas young people can only look ahead to an imagined future, that is, to be prospective.

Life Design

Savickas (2012) proposed linking constructionism and narrative approaches into a system called life design. In that system there is a process of assisting clients to clarify their identities through telling stories, often small or micro stories. Using these, the client and the counselor can construct the client's identity. They can then deconstruct, reconstruct, and coconstruct a new identity that is congruent with a new career identity. Let us look at each of these in turn as Savickas does.

Construction

Building on the work of Cochran (1997), Savickas (2003) suggests that counselors assist clients in telling their stories. Some of the questions that can be used to elicit these stories include the following:

1. Whom do you admire? Whom would you pattern your life after? Whom did you admire growing up? How are you like this person? How are you different from this person?

2. Do you read any magazines regularly? Which ones? Do you watch any TV shows regularly? Which ones?

3. What do you like to do in your free time?

4. Do you have a favorite saying or motto?

5. What is your earliest recollection?

These stories may then be used to help individuals understand their career history from a thematic perspective, understanding that can then lead to considering what next steps will work within, or as appropriate, counter to, these themes.

Deconstruction

Many adults have grown up with narrow ideas as to their possible career areas. These self-limiting ideas may come from parental dictates, teachers' comments, or cultural messages from the media or the community. Taking apart stories to uncover these biases is a way of freeing adults from inappropriate constraints. For example, a woman may have been told that physical labor is "not for girls," or a Hispanic man may have been told that he was not "college material." Even more positive stereotypes may be hindering as, for example, an individual may have been expected to go to a four-year college and become a professional, when his or her passion was for fixing cars or fine carpentry.

Reconstruction

As its name implies, putting stories back together to form a more complete and accurate narrative is the next task of the career counselor following Savickas's structure. The French term for construction, *bricolage*, often cited by Peavy (1997), one of the early proponents of constructionism, provides English speakers with an image of brick by brick building of a new narrative. The counselor's role is to identify themes, an overarching plot, and an explanatory macronarrative that can then help an individual make decisions from a knowledgeable, adult perspective, free of inappropriate constraints and informed by adult understanding.

Coconstruction

This stage of the work of the career counselor involves joining with the client to create a new narrative, one which paves the way for effective career choices that solve the problem presented by the client who has come to counseling. Savickas (2005) has said that that career selection offers us a chance to "actively master what we passively suffer."

Integrative Life Planning

Hansen (1997) formulated an approach to adult career counseling that she termed integrative life planning. She proposed a six-step process, described in detail in Chapter 5. Her six propositions foster a counseling process that looks at career in context—context of social life, personal life, and community life. Seeing these as steps to a satisfying life, rather than simply a satisfying career, leads the adult client to a broader view of career decision making, one that includes family and social responsibility. Let us look at each of these in turn.

Finding Work That Needs Doing

Entrepreneurship is said to be the fastest growing segment of the economy. Even within organizations, so called intrapreneurship, innovation, leadership, and the ability to be self-directed are prized attributes. For an adult choosing or needing to change jobs, the idea of creating work may be foreign or daunting. Counselors who can connect adult clients with programs to help them explore these options are doing their clients an important service. Many small businesses fail, usually because of lack of a meaningful business plan or because of undercapitalization. Expert advice can help adults make meaningful plans and explore if this is a good option for them. Free advice can often be obtained through SCORE (https://www.score.org). They describe themselves as follows:

> The SCORE Association "Counselors to America's Small Business" is a nonprofit association comprised of 13,000+ volunteer business counselors throughout the U.S. and its territories. SCORE members are trained to serve as counselors, advisors, and mentors to aspiring entrepreneurs and business owners. These services are offered at no fee, as a community service." (retrieved from https://www.sba.gov, August 21, 2015)

Many local educational institutions have low-cost classes on starting small businesses. The important message from Hansen's task is not just to look for job openings but also to see where a community's needs are and to look for a way that using one's skills can meet that these needs.

Weaving Our Lives Into a Meaningful Whole

Holistic thinking about life has been eloquently presented by Myers, Sweeney, and Wittmer (2000), who developed the Wheel of Wellness, a holistic model with 16 characteristics of healthy functioning. The researchers emphasized the characteristics of healthy functioning as a major component of wellness and outlined five major life tasks that can be identified with each component of the Wheel of Wellness. Somewhat parallel to Hansen's (1997) tasks, they identify five components of wellness: spirituality, self-direction, work and leisure, friendship, and love.

Connecting Family and Work

The decisions that adults make regarding work are usually more complex than younger people because they often have partners and children. They usually have recurring expenses such as mortgages and childcare or educational expenses for their children. They may have aging parents who need their help, instrumental or financial. Their partner may have work that needs to be considered when, for example, deciding about a transfer or new job in another location. Career counselors often offer dual-career counseling for couples who wish to have help in sorting out priorities and plans.

Another aspect of connecting family and work is that of having time for family while meeting demands of a work milieu that increasingly expects 24/7 involvement. A current car ad shows a man leaving the office at 5:00. It states, "When did it become an act of courage to leave work on time?" Technological accessibility, leaner workforces, fewer unionized workplaces, and a high unemployment rate have all contributed to many people working long hours and taking fewer vacation days. All of these issues contribute to creating a challenge for workers in balancing work and family life. Career counselors can help clients include balance issues in their decision-making process.

Valuing Pluralism and Inclusivity

Hansen's fourth task is more of a statement of values than a task. It reminds us that having a social conscience and a concern for other people and the world are an important component of life planning, and yes, career development. Expanding this idea to other areas of social justice, Peter Plant (2014) made the case that most career theories focus on a Western, middle-class view of career development as based on individual decision making and achieving autonomy. Sharma (2005) categorized life goals developmentally as, "achieving personal satisfaction, self-realization, and serving others." Plant (2014) exhorted us to define career choice "in terms of ecology rather than just economy" (p. 313).

The idea that adults consider the societal impact of their career choices may be radical, but it fits within a developmental perspective, acknowledging that life choices are not made in a vacuum, and that adults as they mature are more likely to look outward toward a communitarian point of view.

Managing Personal Transitions and Organizational Change

Personal transitions have been discussed at length in earlier sections, so let us now address organizational change. For many adults, a visit to a career counselor is not about wanting or needing to change jobs but more about how to handle the current job, as it morphs into something different. That the pace of change has accelerated is a cliché, but it is true nonetheless. Some large organizations have career centers or areas within human resources where employees may receive assistance in planning their careers or in managing the job they have. These programs may include individual counseling, group meetings, mentorship programs, tuition assistance, and the like.

Unions also provide career programs for represented workers, and there have been some joint union management programs, such as the programs supported by the so-called nickel an hour funds that provided educational assistance, and in some cases, counseling to represented workers. The unions supported these funds as they provided opportunities for their workers to achieve and perhaps advance; management supported them because they resulted in a better-trained workforce, one with the flexibility to meet the demands of technologically advanced manufacturing.

Exploring Spirituality and Life Purpose

Spirituality was mentioned in the section under holistic living; here is the focus of a life-planning task. Although young people certainly are interested in finding life purpose, the need for purpose and meaning seems to grow with adulthood. There is an old joke about why an elderly grandmother was reading the bible so much. Answer: "I'm studying for my finals." The recognition that life is finite seems to peak in late middle age, prompting many to consider their contribution or legacy. As lives develop, many people begin looking for ways to make a difference within their work life or outside of it. Jimmy Carter is often held up as a model of a past president, whose work on behalf of Habitat for Humanity and The Carter Center is almost universally respected and garnered him a Nobel Peace prize in 2002. Although we believe that it is cruel to always expect the newly unemployed to "make lemonade out of lemons," there can be an opportunity for meaning making after the grief and anger have subsided. Reflecting back on our discussion of Schlossberg's (Anderson et al., 2012) third S, the support dimension, we can see that although support can come externally, from people and other entities, it can also come internally, through spirituality, meaning making, and faith.

Chaos Theory

Bright and Pryor's (2008) work on applying chaos theory to transitions is particularly appropriate to adults as they navigate both transitions and the rapidly changing world of work. Focusing on the uncertainties of the future, they look at the skills needed for adults to manage this environment. They coined the term *shiftwork* to encapsulate all of the activities needed for adults to continually reinvent themselves, capitalize on chance opportunities, and find meaning in their occupational pursuits. They suggest that counselors work with clients to find patterns in complex situations, be open to changing circumstances, and accept with hope and optimism that unpredictability is part of the human condition. They support using stories—narrative—to tease out these patterns and develop an attitude of expected mastery of the complicated and ever-changing decision-making ground. We can see the connections to positive uncertainty, happenstance, and transition theory described earlier, but chaos theory adds an important component. It recognizes that it may not be possible to move with certainty through the decisions that adults will find necessary in a world of constant change. There is comfort in knowing that this uncertainty is real, not solely a psychological state, and that there are strategies for working within the uncertainty, although one cannot eliminate it.

Identity Renegotiation

The transitions discussed in all of the foregoing assume an individual is making choices in an autonomous fashion, responding to the vicissitudes of the world at large but largely independent from its influences. Blume's (2002, 2010) theory of identity renegotiation is based on situating identity within one's cultural milieu. He stated that all identities are based on an interaction with others, that is relationships, and that these are moderated, for better or worse, by one's cultural setting, that is, the context in which one operates. The implications of Blume's point of view for career counselors are profound. They lead us directly into multicultural considerations and require expanding the career counseling process from one of simply working with an individual toward making good choices—tentative or at least temporarily fixed. Instead, this concept requires counselors to learn about a client's context—social, cultural, ethnic, and so forth—in order to understand how this context mediates the client's identity. Because career transitions usually require a change of work identity, and often a change of many other aspects of identity, this understanding is critical. As we have discussed earlier, although identity was once seen as fixed, current thinking sees it as more fluid, mutable, and open to influence. Career counselors, then, must help their clients examine not only their own interests, values, goals, and so forth but also look at the world in which they express these values, including their family, their community, and the increasingly global society at large.

RETIREMENT

Atchley (2000) described several phases of retirement. Meant to be a broad brush, these stages are not always followed in sequence, nor is each of them always a part of an individual's experience. Nonetheless, they provide a schema that can be useful in helping a client plan for and navigate the retirement transition. Whether a client is looking for preretirement planning or looking for help in managing a retirement already in existence, career counseling is an appropriate intervention. Occasionally, individuals describe themselves as retired when in actuality they have lost their jobs. Job loss after a certain age—individually defined—can be more easily stomached and more easily explained to others as retirement. Atchley's phases are described in more detail in the following:

Phase 1: Preretirement

During this time, adults contemplate what they will do during retirement, often focusing on the financial aspects as well as planning how and when to disengage from their current paid work. Increasingly, out of desire or necessity, individuals are returning to paid work after retirement from a primary occupation. They may still describe themselves as retired, may be collecting a pension and/or social security, but have not completely disengaged from the workforce. When adults seek career counseling preretirement, it is important to check if they have a spouse or partner and if they have made joint retirement plans. The so-called out of sync career commitment curve (Goodman & Waters, 1985) describes what happens when two members of a couple are on different career trajectories, with one ready to wind down and one still planning on staying involved in work. It is also important to investigate visions of retirement and how they mesh or do not mesh. One person's vision of a cabin in the woods may not fit with the other member of the couple's vision of driving an RV across the country. One person's fantasy of volunteering at the local zoo may not fit with the other's plans to spend half of the year visiting family out of state.

Phase 2: Retirement

Atchley (2000) describes three types of retirement:

1. The honeymoon path, characterized by leisure activities, often including travel

2. Immediate retirement routine, characterized by continuing the active and involved nonwork activities established before retirement

3. The rest and relaxation path, characterized by very low activity—sometimes called the "rocking chair" phenomenon

Schlossberg (2004) describes six retirement paths:

1. Continuers—more of the same, but different

2. Adventurers—something new

3. Searchers—looking for your niche

4. Easy gliders—content to go with the flow

5. Retreaters—giving up

6. Combination paths

Each of these paths come from a different set of needs, possibilities, and plans, as well as all of the usual aspects of a career decision such as looking at interests, values, temperament, and so forth.

Phase 3: Disenchantment

For some, the end of the honeymoon period leads to a sense of disenchantment. This may be when the reality sets in that one is not on an extended vacation but that this is one's permanent reality. There can be a loss of status, of feeling productive, of identity, of a structure to one's day, of all of the aspects of a working life discussed in the section on job loss. Western, and particularly American, individuals often define themselves by what they do. "Who are you?" is usually answered by a job title or descriptor. After retirement people may say, or feel internally, "I know who I was, I don't know who I am now." Schlossberg (2009) adds the word *mattering* to this discussion, describing the status of feeling that what one does makes a difference to oneself, others, and the community. The state that Atchley describes as disorienting may lead individuals toward the next stage, reorientation, or may lead to prolonged dissatisfaction and even depression. Counselors are advised to consider the missing career aspects in the lives of depressed older adults.

Phase 4: Reorientation and Phase 5: Retirement Routine

Individuals at this stage are in a place to realign their needs and priorities and to make decisions about how to spend what may be as many as 20 to 30 years. They may decide to become involved in their communities through volunteer work, serving on local boards, becoming active in their faith community, and so forth. Successful retirees work this out and have satisfying retirement years. People who are not successful at reorientation may stay in the disenchantment phase and may be very unhappy. Career counseling can be an important component of successful reorientation.

Phase 6: Termination of Retirement

This seems like a logically impossible stage. Termination may come at death, but it may also come with disability or illness, leading to a need to focus on taking care of self rather than on activities related to an active retirement.

Summary: Challenges and Opportunities

Virtually all adults work, for much or all of their preretirement lives. The old structure of learn, then work, then play (c.f., Bolles, 1981) has given way to continuous change. This new way of living in relation to work creates challenges and opportunities for career counselors. Learning has become an ongoing necessity—many occupations even require continuing education to maintain a license or certificate. Times of unemployment may be interspersed with times of work, and older adults may continue employment or find new forms of work—paid or unpaid.

An interesting example of the vicissitudes of a career was provided by Bruni (2015). Bruni described the career arc of a successful political pollster and strategist, Joel Benenson. His first career? The stage. He credits Shakespeare with giving him "an understanding of the rhythm and nuance of language," invaluable in political strategy. He then co-owned a beer distributorship, during which, he said, he came in contact with people who lived paycheck to paycheck, an important understanding for a political strategist. Journalism occupied more of his career existence before he headed into politics. Benenson's message is as follows:

> Don't think about what you want to do for the rest of your life. Think about what you want to do next. Maybe you have a big goal out there and pursue it, but along the way, that line from A to B is not a continuum. The key will be identifying what you are passionate about in each of those steps along the way. (Bruni, 2015, p. 3)

The dental model (Goodman, 1992) has become even more the mode, and career counselors may find themselves working with adults in all aspects of career decision making at any age. The information in this chapter has been provided to offer some assistance in facing those challenges and being of the most possible help to adults who seek career counseling services.

Keystones

- Adult career development needs are not static as previously perceived; instead, these needs are varied and changing depending on both individuals and contextual factors.

- The modern theories of career development applicable to adults have common features of flexibility, adaptability, and active creativity.

- Counselors can help their adult clients develop a sense of agency about their career plans, help them be active on their own behalf, and help them not only develop a vision of their preferred future but also acquire the tools to make that vision a reality.

- Adult career planning, then, needs to add using and creating chance events to its repertoire of skills, self-directed in keeping current with trends in the employment market as well as keeping their own employability active.

- Counselors can use Schlossberg's transition theory to identify where clients stand in managing their transitions and form the basis of a counseling plan of action.

- It is important to recognize the intense stress of losing employment to adults and impacts on individuals, family, and career trajectory.

- Understanding and navigating pre- and postretirement scenarios would help adults plan for and carry out the one(s) best suited to themselves.

References

Anderson, M. L., Goodman, J., & Schlossberg, N. K. (2012). *Counseling adults in transition: Linking Schlossberg's theory with practice in a diverse world.* New York, NY: Springer.

Atchley, R. C. (2000). *Social forces and aging* (9th ed.). Belmont, CA: Wadsworth.

Bloom, B. S., Engelhart, M. D., Furst, E. J., Hill, W. H., & Krathwohl, D. R. (1956). Taxonomy of educational objectives: The classification of educational goals. *Handbook I: Cognitive domain.* New York, NY: David McKay.

Blume, T. W. (2002).Negotiating identity in couple sexuality. In L. Burlew & D. Capuzzi (Eds.), *Sexuality counseling* (pp. 89-109). New York, NY: Nova Science.

Blume, T. W. (2010). Counseling for identity renegotiation. *International Journal of Theory and Research, 10*, 92-105.

Bolles, R. N. (1981). *The three boxes of life and how to get out of them.* Berkeley, CA: Ten Speed Press.

Bright, J. E. H., & Pryor, G. L. (2008). Shiftwork: A chaos theory of careers agenda for change in career counseling. *Australian Journal of Career Development, 17*, 63-72.

Bruni, F. (2015, May 3). From Hamlet to Hillary. *New York Times*, p. 3.

Cochran, L. (1997). *Career counseling: A narrative approach.* Thousand Oaks, CA: Sage.

Ebberwein, C. A., Krieshok, T. S., Ulven, J. C., & Prosser, E. C. (2004). Voices in Transition: Lessons on career adaptability. *Career Development Quarterly, 52*, 292-308.

Erikson, E. H. (1950). *Childhood and society.* New York, NY: Norton.

Gelatt, H. B. (1991). *Creative decision making: Using positive uncertainty.* Los Altos, CA: Crisp.

Gelatt, H. B. (2014, June 18). *My open-minded assumption.* Retrieved from http://wp.me/p2tkyl-66.

Gelatt, H. B. (2015, March 15). *Top ten tactics.* Retrieved from https://hbgelatt.wordpress.com/2015/03/15/top-ten-tactics.

Goodman, J. (1992). The dental model for counseling. *American Counselor, 1*, 27-29.

Goodman, J. (1994). Career adaptability in adults: A construct whose time has come. *Career Development Quarterly, 43*, 74-84.

Goodman, J., & Waters, E. B. (1985). Conflict or support: Work and family in middle and old age. *Journal of Career Development, 12*, 92-98.

Krumboltz, J. D. (1992). The wisdom of indecision. *Journal of Vocational Behavior, 3*, 239-244.

Kubler-Ross, E. (1969). *On death and dying.* New York, NY: McMillan.

Hall, D. T. (1986). *Careers in organizations.* Pacific Palisades, CA: Goodyear.

Hansen, L. S. (1997). *Integrative life planning: Critical tasks for career development and changing life patterns.* San Francisco, CA: Jossey-Bass.

Havighurst, R. (1972). *Developmental tasks and education* (3rd ed.). New York, NY: Longram.

Korn, M. (2015, February 3). Big gap in college graduation rates for rich and poor, study finds. *The Wall Street Journal.* Retrieved from https://www.wsj.com/articles/big-gap-in-college-graduation-rates-for-rich-and-poor-study-finds-1422997677.

Levinson, D. J. (1986). A conception of adult development. *American Psychologist, 41*, 3-13.

Mitchell, K. E., Levin, A. L., & Krumboltz, J. D. (1999). Planned happenstance: Constructing unexpected career opportunities. *Journal of Counseling and Development, 2*, 115-124.

Myers, J. E., Sweeney, T. J., & Wittmer. M. (2000). The wheel of wellness, counseling for wellness: A holistic model for treatment planning. *Journal of Counseling and Development*, *78*, 3, 251–266.

Peavy, R. V. (1997). A constructive framework for career counseling. In T. Sexton & B. Griffin (Eds.), *Constructivist thinking in counseling practice, research, and training* (pp. 122-141). New York, NY: Teachers College Press.

Plant, P. (2014). Green guidance. In G. Arulmani, A. J. Bakshi, F. T. L. Leong, & A. G. Watts (Eds.). *Handbook of career development: International perspectives*. New York, NY: Springer.

Rossier, J. (2015). Personality assessment and career interventions. In P. J. Hartung, M. L. Savickas, & W. B. Walsh (Eds.), *APA handbook of career interventions, Vol 1* (pp. 327-350). Washington, DC: American Psychological Association.

Savickas, M. L. (2003, September 4). *The career theme interview*. Paper presented to the International Association of Educational and Vocational Guidance, Berne, Switzerland.

Savickas, M. L. (2005). The theory and practice of career construction. In S. D. Brown and R. W. Lent (Eds.), *Career development and counseling: Putting theory and research to work* (pp. 42-70). Hoboken, NJ: John Wiley & Sons.

Savickas, M. L. (2012). Life design: A paradigm for career intervention in the 21st century.

Journal of Counseling and Development, *90*, 13-19.

Schlossberg, N. K. (2004). *Retire smart, retire happy*. Washington DC: American Psychological Association.

Schlossberg, N. K. (2009). *Revitalizing retirement: Reshaping your identity, relationships, and purpose*. Washington, DC: American Psychological Association.

Sharma, S. (2005). Career guidance and counselling: Principles and techniques. In G. Arulmani, A. J. Bakshi, F. T. L. Leong, & A. G. Watts (Eds.), *Handbook of career development: International perspectives* (pp. 291-305). New York, NY: Springer.

Spencer, S. A., & Adams, J. D. (1990). *Life changes*. San Luis Obispo, CA: Impact.

Super, D. E. (1980). A life-span, life space approach to career development. *Journal of Vocational Behavior, 16*(30), 282-298.

Super, D. E., & Knasel, E. G. (1979). *Development of a model, specifications, and sample items for measuring career adaptability (vocational maturity) in young blue collar workers*. Cambridge, England: National Institute for Careers education and Counselling, and Ottawa, Ontario, Canada, Canada Employment and Immigration.

Super, D. E., & Knasel, E. G. (1981). Career development in adulthood: Some theoretical problems and a possible solution. *British Journal of Guidance and Counselling*, *9*, 195-201.

15

INTEGRATION OF THEORY AND PRACTICE

As we conclude this book, many thoughts and reflections emerge while preparing to write this last chapter. One recurring thought is what exactly do counselors in training need to understand about career development and intervention so that they help their clients more effectively and do no harm. The previous chapters have discussed work, career, life, and the multiple roles people play across different settings, interaction of intrapersonal factors, contextual factors for one's career development, multicultural issues pertaining to career development and intervention, career assessment, career counseling process and strategies, career intervention with diverse populations in various settings, and career development programs and evaluation. So, with an understanding of this information, will counselors in training be adequately knowledgeable and skillful to work competently at their future job settings either as mental health counselors, school counselors, substance abuse counselors, college counselors, or rehabilitation counselors? Well, to become a competent counselor, the graduate training is a minimum educational requirement, and career development is only one of the eight foundation areas that CACREP standards require; in other words, reading this book and taking career development in counselor education programs provides necessary but not sufficient training needed for becoming a professional counselor. It requires students and counselor educators to integrate and apply the learning about career development with other content in the curriculum, with their practicum and internship experiences, and with their self-discovery and professional development, in a word, *integrating* theories and practice to become an effective counselor who can serve clients from wellness, developmental, and prevention perspectives. Therefore, after completing the reading and exercises in this chapter, you will be able to

LEARNING OBJECTIVES

After completing the reading and exercises provided in this chapter, you will be able to:

- articulate the role of person and context interaction to career development and associated meaning,

- facilitate individuals to develop career readiness and resilience,

- translate career development theories to integrated practice serving diverse populations in various settings,

- identify needs for professional development and recognize the challenges of ethical obligations in a new era,

- engage in advocating for equity and social justice or for underserved populations,

- develop understanding and abilities to help clients in the context of uncertainty, and

- apply integrated services to promote wellness in work and health.

PERSON AND CONTEXT INTERACTION

From the work of Parsons to help immigrant youth in urban Boston at the turn of the 20th century, to the postmodern approaches based on construction theories, career intervention has always focused on optimization of individual capacity to live a satisfying life through a successful career. "Successful career" has different connotations in different times for different people; however, its essential characteristics imply individuals' harmonious relationships to their context, including other people in their lives and work environments. With the rapid changes in the society, understanding the changing environment is necessary and critical to appraise the interaction of person and environment. When career trajectory does not follow a certain pattern anymore, will career planning and decision making still be applicable? How can counselors help individuals be prepared for the changing environment and have a satisfying life? This section focuses on reviewing the relevant information to emphasize the importance of person and environment interaction in the 21st century.

Changing Environment

Many readers of this book probably do not have experience using a typewriter for homework. When the first iPhone was introduced to the market, many doubted its function and usefulness, particularly its touch screen function and combining many features in one tiny device. Just a few years later, almost all phones have "smart" features and use touch screens, and beyond, it totally changed how we live our lives—we get news from our smartphone, we connect with others via our smartphone, and we are reminded by our smartphones what we should do next. This is only one aspect of many technology changes that have had a significant impact on our lives and work as well. Yes, the work environment has changed. Many changes in the world of work, from labor force composition to structure of economy, have been discussed in Chapters 1 and 2 at some length. In a short, as Blustein (2006) stated, technology innovation transformed the work situation significantly enough to have impacts on a variety of sectors beyond employment loss of manufacturing jobs, and a combination of technology and globalization enabled jobs not bounded by national or language lines, thus creating more competition. Whether people like it or not, automation in various forms (e.g., the most known and probably quite influential ones, like self-driving cars) and other technology-induced change at work will be part of daily life in the foreseeable future. Learning modality is changed because of information technology, so it is more important to know where to locate and evaluate the information rather than memorizing the information. Similarly, technology affects how we perform our work and how we relate to colleagues. The changing environment requires workers to update their knowledge and skills constantly to keep up with new work demands. The younger generation growing up in the digital age has different skills and priorities than the older generations.

Virtual World of Learning, Working, and Socializing

As technology advances, so does the accessibility and user-friendly learning environment for more people. Online education was first doubted for its viability and then for its quality; with more and more online programs launched in so many disciplines and from some prestigious universities, the skeptics of online education have shifted focus to making it better. Currently, not only does learning occur in a virtual world, but work can also be done remotely from an organization's facility and socialization and friendships can be developed via a virtual world. Working from home has become increasingly accepted by both employers and employees. Another rising trend is seeking employment by both employers and prospective employers through virtual networks such as LinkedIn. The cloud technology enables the big data system that traces and records our entire life. Someone can earn a degree, get a job, and buy any product without stepping out of their bedroom.

What do all these changes mean to individuals in regard to career development? First of all, lifelong learning is a must rather than desirable because one will be left out if not able to adapt to the new work environment; second, the work environment and home environment, work and social life, become blurred or mingled due to the virtual world everyone is in now, therefore, the separation of work and personal life is questionable; third, job interviews are more than the interview day at the work location because of the available data through social media and iCloud technology—employers might obtain information about you via your Facebook page, your web surfing history, and even maybe your shopping records. The exact influence of the virtual world to individuals' career and life may be unknown now, but the virtual world certainly has already influenced how people work and live.

Generation/Cohort Effect

When stability and loyalty coexisted in the old economic structure when one could comfortably retire from their one-forever job, the labor force typically was composed of different generations of workers, with the older generation holding the wisdom and mentoring the younger generation; however, the fast changes in technology could create an unprecedented phenomenon, the older generation might need to consult the younger generation for job-related skills. Further, many workers have to postpone or delay retirement due to financial reasons (e.g., the financial crisis in 2008 caused many retirement funds to shrink dramatically); the other side of the coin is that many youth either voluntarily or involuntarily enter the labor force at a later age (e.g., one reason is more levels of education are required for some jobs). Nonetheless, the range of workers' generations has become more diverse, that is, at any given work setting, there might be multigeneration workers (e.g., baby boomers, generation X, and millennium) who may have different orientations toward needs and values in work. For instance, millennial workers who grew up in the digital age welcome the rapid changes of technology (as a matter of fact, probably enjoy it as they are used to or expect new devices to come to market in frequent time intervals), and having fun is important for them. The baby boomers are more comfortable working in traditional work settings as compared to the younger generation who like to work in more fluid settings where work and fun can be mingled. The generational cohort effect, that is, the distinctive opportunities and challenges due to historical eras to members of each generation (Cook, 2012), indicates that workers of each different generation has its unique ways of making career decisions and performance in work settings. As a result, the cohort effect has impacts on each generation pertaining to work-related behaviors or work ethics.

Work Ethics

Each generation when first entering the workforce is often negatively viewed by earlier generations already in the workforce (Davies, 2016) as not diligent enough, not respectful to rules, or not professional. Millennials, for instance, were viewed by their bosses, who are most likely boomers, as self-centered, immature, and multitasking constantly (e.g., see a *60 Minutes* episode on millennials at work: http://www.cbsnews.com/ news/the-millennials-are-coming). Millennials, growing up with messages from both home and school that they can be whoever they want to be and they are special and unique (some refer this generation as trophy child), find themselves unfit for the corporate culture when they land in the real work world. The incongruence of individual work expectation and work environment demands is overwhelming for both younger generation of workers and older generation of supervisors. Some companies even hire career consultants to retrain supervisors to work with millennial workers (e.g., how to talk to youth without being too harsh, how to coach rather than boss), and teach millennial workers to learn about professional behaviors (e.g., how to dress appropriately, communication is not just texting). The work ethics commonly held in conventional work settings such as reliability, professionalism, positivity, respect, integrity, and gratitude are valuable for work success and retention (Davies, 2016). These work ethics are teachable and learnable. Career development intervention, therefore, should address professional disposition and work ethics in early stages. Counselors can also educate professionals to be mindful of the diversity of work styles by different groups and the importance of creating inclusive climates in work settings. After all, each generation has assets to offer to the organization.

Identity and Meaningful Work

Self-Identity and Work

Due to the rapid changes in technology and subsequent changes in the economy and occupational structure, uncertainty and lack of loyalty in work settings has become the new norm. When a person works in one occupation at one particular organization for his or her entire life, career identity is solid, meaning that he or she can associate his or her self-identity with his or her career and can make meaning of work, such as sense of belonging and self-worth. However, when consistency or stability is no longer available, the identity a person used to associate to careers is seriously challenged. The meaning work provides for people to build connection and interpersonal relationships are also becoming unreliable. The loss of stability at work indicates that relationships based on work could be jeopardized; they then feel disengaged, isolated, and a loss of shared community values (Blustein, 2006). Therefore, one needs to look for an alternative narrative for career, work, and self. How can one make meaning of this constantly changing environment? How can one find connection despite lacking stability at work? Further, is it necessary or possible to construct one's self-identity through the meaning of work? If so, how does one manage identity crisis and find meaning amidst the uncertainty and instability of the job environment? If not, what will constitute one's identity in the absence of meaning out of work? While people are still struggling with millennials in work settings, generation Z is coming. This is the generation with unprecedented high cost of education and the greatest challenges of finding a job (Balentine, 2017). How can counselors help individuals navigate this world and find a meaningful career development path is a task all counselors and counselor educators need to address.

Hope and Resilience

To address these challenges of instability and a dismal outlook for many young people finding a more-than-a-minimum-pay job, counselors and educators in general do need to change the mindsets of matching person and environment. In other words, simply focusing on personal characteristics and work environment congruence is not sufficient for effective career counseling in the ever-changing context. Encouraging and helping individuals develop hope and resilience is necessary for dealing with the uncertainty and instability. A hope-based intervention proposed by Niles, Amundson, and Neault (2011) is an example of such an effort. The Hope-Centered Model of Career Development (HCMCD) recognizes the challenges encountered by people in the 21st century and articulates the importance of adaptability and self-awareness (Niles et al., 2011). The HCMCD suggests that developing one's capacity to respond to and reflect on the new or changing situation is essential to create visioning and goal setting. The model focuses on self-reflection, and posits that self-clarity would enable one to develop appropriate goals and planning and implementation as well as being vigilant of self-management of career and adaptability. The model emphasizes that creating hope is the cornerstone of career intervention and maintaining hopefulness even in the adversity of life events (Amundson & Thrift, 2008) is necessary.

Along with hopefulness, career resilience is another asset one can build to address the challenges amidst instability and to construct a positive relationship with the surrounding environment. Resilience, a capacity that mobilizes people to cope with difficult situations and persevere through hurdles in life, would be helpful for a successful career considering the nature of work and environment that presents anything but stability and orderliness. To develop career resilience, one needs to have an internal locus of control, sense of purpose, hope, and optimism; an attitude that encourages positivism and optimism and that discourages self-blaming and guilt (Borgen, Amundson, Reuter, & 2004). Determination, hope, creativity, and flexibility are the core components for career intervention in helping individuals develop career resilience.

Career Readiness or Employability

In recent years, both federal and state policies emphasize college and career readiness in K-12 and college education. The aim is to prepare youth for entering the labor force with qualified skills so that the United States has an effective workforce for the challenges of the 21st century. "The current focus on college and career readiness (CCR) in education policy emphasizes utilitarian elements of education and the need for learning to relate to the world of work" (Dougherty & Lombardi, 2016, p. 327). The essence of CCR is to increase employability of youth through educational programs that provide connection of learning to the real world of work. As a bridge between K-12 and college education, community colleges played a vital role in achieving the goal of college and career readiness (Grundmann, 2013). According to Conley (2010), college readiness indicates that students possesses cognitive strategies (e.g., critical thinking, analyzing, and evaluating information), fundamental knowledge of core disciplines like English and math, learning skills and techniques (e.g., self-efficacy, motivation, goals setting, and study skills), and transition knowledge and skills (e.g., navigating the transition to college). The outcome of CCR programs have promising impacts on academic readiness but are uncertain for longer term effects (Bragg & Taylor, 2014). Thus, preparing students to be capable of taking college credits and ultimately being ready for entering into the workforce to live a satisfying life is the new century's goal for education and career intervention, as the changed structure of

LEARNING ACTIVITY 15.1
CREATING A VISION FOR MYSELF

There are a lot of uncertainties about future work, for instance, concerns about automation replacing human labor entirely or much more than currently, worries about the tenure one can hold a job, and doubts about meaning of career planning if nothing is predictable. Divide the class into four small groups (or more if the class size is big), ask one group to search the occupational outlook online for the 10 year and 20 year predictions of occupational trends; ask one group to search the job announcements on the local newspaper; ask one group to search the job postings at online job service sites; and ask one group to search for job postings on social media such as LinkedIn. The class can decide which jobs they want to search. After the search is done, each group reports their results and their interpretation. Then in each group, members discuss what the implications of these results are to themselves as counselors in training and aa a family member (child, sibling, parent, spouse, and so on). After discussion, each student should create a road map for his or her future work and life.

the economy and occupations requires postsecondary education credentials for entering the workforce. Partnerships among educational institutions at various levels, formats, and with communities is vital for completing the mission of college and career readiness.

Self-Agency

Thus far, it should not be a surprise that taking ownership of one's own career path rather than reacting passively to the changing work environment is the direction of future career development. When the work environment was stable and predictable, one could realize his or her self-identity through occupational status and titles; when the work environment becomes unpredictable and one's job security is vulnerable, many of the meanings of work such as social connection and sense of fulfillment become questionable, too. The bonding contract between employers and employees has changed with no more lifelong contract (Blustein, 2006), and workers cannot count on job security any more. People have to manage their career path to remain marketable and competitive in the increasingly less stable world of work.

The new contract is described by Hall (1996) as relational and developmental, requiring employees to deliver a strong performance and continuously learn to adapt to new demands at work while organizations provide meaning, purpose, relationship, space for learning, rewards, and benefits. This ability to learn and redirect one's career across the life span is referred to as protean career (Hall, 1996), which specifically describes the self-management of one's career through learning and adaptation. Savickas (2005, 2015) has also propositioned the role of self-agency in individuals' career development when people have to cope with uncertainty occurring constantly in the work world through his ideas of career adaptability, career construction, and life design. All these ideas center around the idea that one can assume to actively master his or her career tasks rather than passively reacting to the life events.

In sum, in the context of stability and predictability long gone in the work world, the relationship between individuals and the work environment has changed, too. Organizations cannot provide a platform for people to achieve career success or to find meaningful connections. One needs to navigate through multilevel and multidimensional changing work environments and to take a control of her or his own journey by being her or his own action agent. More and more people find their sense of purposefulness and meaningful connection not necessarily from accomplishments in work settings but through shared values and meaning derived from working for the common good and ultimately through self-agency to make his or her career path meaningful.

INTEGRATION OF THEORY AND PRACTICE

Theories Have and Have Not

One of the strengths of career counseling is the multitude of career development theories in its 100 years of history. There are 37 theories or ideas that changed or shaped the career development intervention from its beginning in 1908 to 2013 according to

Savickas (2013) who used the Delphi technique to identify the essential knowledge base of career development. These theories and ideas explain why and how people make career choices, propose key concepts of influencing one's career behavior and choices, and suggest models of intervention to help individuals have satisfying careers. A recent examination of the published articles in *Career Development Quarterly* in 2013 found that the top ranked theories for both research and practice are Social Cognitive Career Theory, RIASEC Theory, and Career Construction–Life Design Theory (McClain, Kronholz, Hou, Osborn, & Sampson, 2015). However, the same study found that only 7% of articles examined the evidence-based practice, indicating that only a small portion of the scholarship in the field addressed the efficacy of theories and career intervention models. It is no surprise then that the most frequent challenges articulated by scholars are difficulties in communication among theorists, researchers, and practitioners (Sampson et al., 2016). In short, despite that many theories that have emerged and guided the practice of career intervention in the past 100 years, there still is lack of integration of theory and practice and insufficient evidence of how theories are actually applied or benefit the practice. In addition, most career development theories focus on explaining vocational behaviors pertaining to choice and decision-making process, rather than the process of conducting career intervention, or career theories lack in providing conceptual work to effective approaches of career counseling (Whiston, 2003). Further, career development theories primarily address the concerns and issues about choosing and advancing in career, so there seems to be a knowledge gap regarding the consequences of not working Blustein (2006).

Outcome Research

To better understand how career development theories are applied in practice and eventually influence the outcome of career intervention, more outcome research about efficacy and effectiveness of career counseling practice are needed. However, "researchers and theories in career counseling typically haven not taken the next step of translating the available research findings into cost-benefit analysis" (Herr, 2003, pp. 16). In other words, there is a scarcity of literature providing useful information about the utility of career development theories in counseling individuals for their career concerns and about the efficiency of career counseling regarding the immediate, midrange, or long-term outcome. Outcome research is needed because the information gained through examining the effectiveness and efficacy of career intervention based on career development theories would not only fill the gap in knowledge but also provide useful information to career counseling practice. More outcome research about career development theories would also enhance translation of theory to practice, therefore, increase integration of theory and practice, which now is lacking. After all, the goal of increasing outcome research is to improve theories in their utility to help people in actual practice.

Translation of Theory to Practice

The gap between theory and practice has been discussed in the previous sections, and it is apparent that more effort should be devoted to research that translates theories and research findings to enhance practice. Research about career development, therefore, should expand from understanding people's career behavior to exploring what theories, approaches, strategies, and models efficiently and effectively help individuals better master career tasks, achieve their career aspirations, and manage their work trajectories. Thus, integrating theory, research, and practice requires communication and collaboration among scholars and practitioners; further, more practitioner-researchers and researcher-practitioners are needed. To improve integration, Sampson et al. (2016) recommended that researchers can engage in creating and revising theory that integrates research and practice, conducting research that integrates theory and practice, communicating and collaborating more regularly with practitioners who are not typically involved in creating theory and conducting research; that both researchers and practitioners can promote delivering career services and creating career resources (practice) that integrate theory and research and take advantage of information technology to improve theory, research, and practice integration.

In addition to research, Sampson et al. (2016) also suggested that training needs to emphasize integration through teaching and supervising students and practitioners in delivering career services and that scholars could encourage and influence more submission of manuscripts that integrate theory, research, and practice. Further, more dialogue should occur among theorists, researchers, and practitioners to promote integration in training standards, practice, and funding priorities for awards and grants. In summary, encouragement and promotion of integration of theory, research, and practice and translational research should be emphasized in training, professional standards, and actual practice as a scholar or practitioner.

ETHICAL PRACTICE FOR PREVENTION AND INTERVENTION

Professional Development

The importance of professional development—meaning continual learning throughout the professional life span to be kept abreast of updated knowledge and skills regarding career development policies, theories, and intervention strategies—is evident in both professional license requirements and ethical codes of all professional organizations. Indeed, if any professional counselors want to keep up with new or innovative ideas and concepts and maintain ethical obligations to benefit clients to the best of their capacity, professional development is a must. In fact, the American Counseling Association (ACA), American School Counselor Association (ASCA), and National Career Development Association (NCDA) all have emphasized the importance of professional development as part of membership responsibilities and have also provided abundant information about the most recent learning materials and opportunities for earning continual education credits. With the advancement of technology, many professional development resources are available via platforms such as podcasts, webinars, and virtual conferences, in addition to the traditional conferences and publications (see more details in these websites: https://www.schoolcounselor.org/school-counselors-members/professional-development; https://www.counseling.org/continuing-education/overview; https://ncda.org/aws/NCDA/pt/sp/prodevelopment). As a result, there are multiple ways to seek professional development education and keep up with the most recent progress in the field.

Professional development is not merely for fulfilling requirements of renewing one's counseling license or certification; as stated above, it is an ethical obligation for counselors to learn about the developments of the profession so that they can provide the best and evidence-based practice supported by literature. Counselors need to be aware that counseling practice has room to improve as the science advances, and so too should counselors grow and better themselves as knowledge and skills are being innovated. Simply put, if counselors do not pursue professional development, they might unintentionally underserve their clients or even provide inadequate service.

Challenges Pertaining to Ethical Practice

Virtual Work Environment

The prevalence of the virtual world exits in every aspect of our lives, from distance learning to distance working, from online shopping to online dating; literally, one can earn a degree from online educational programs, can make a living by working from home, and can find social relationships through social media technology. The work environment is not exempt from this new norm, for example, conducting business meetings online, marketing via a virtual platform, and interviewing prospective employees via digital technology. The virtual work environment is not an extension of our normal work environment any more, it is a vital part of our work environment whether we like it or not. While the virtual work environment provides convenience and accessibility for many people, it certainly brings many challenges, too. One major concern of the virtual work environment is how similar or different the ethical obligations professionals have compared to the traditional physical work world. For the counseling profession, the ethical concerns become even more compelling due to the confidentiality and privacy requirements in the counseling relationship. For instance, how can counselors ensure the career assessment results are kept confidential if the assessment was taken online and results were either transmitted or stored by a third party (i.e., test publisher)? The virtual work environment presents a question about trust building as well. Will it be the same as in a face-to-face environment? Even if counselors do not work in a distance counseling environment, it does not mean ethical concerns do not exist because everyone is somehow visible in a virtual world, both at and off work.

The current ethical codes of ACA, ASCA, and NCDA all have sections on technology, distance counseling, and social media. The ACA code of ethics specifically states additional contents should be included in the informed consent form for distance learning, such as risks and benefits of using distance counseling, possibility of technical failure, response time, emergency procedure if in different time zone, possible denial of insurance, and social media policy. The other areas addressed in the ACA code include confidentiality maintenance limits, use of encryption standards within the websites and communication for security, client verification, professional boundaries and effectiveness of services (see http://www.counseling.org/docs/ethics/2014-aca-code-of-ethics.pdf?s fvrsn=4). The NCDA code of ethics has very similar contents regarding technology and distance counseling with more detailed information on web maintenance and technology development. It recommends that career professionals regularly ensure electronic links are working and professionally appropriate, assist clients in determining the validity and reliability of information found on websites and in other technology applications, and include disclaimers for accuracy and ethical alignment. It also has specific suggestions for managing job postings and searching websites or database (see https://ncda.org/aws/NCDA/asset_manager/get_file/3395). Due to the instant and wide distribution of any message or information on the Internet, as well as its permanent records instantly, the virtual world has created really unusual contests for counselors to keep their work and themselves alert for ethical obligation. To add more, social media is inevitably another layer of challenge because it permeates work and life with blurred boundaries.

Social Media

Whether to maintain a presence on social media is a personal choice; however, it is not easy to be totally out of social media even if one does not want to be involved unless one is not connected to the Internet at all. For counselors and counselor educators, it is almost impossible not to be present on the Internet if not social media. The difficulties for use of social media are that social media, although originally created as a social networking software/platform, has spilled over into the work world as a vehicle for publicity and networking/marketing; therefore, it is difficult to be entirely off social media. Another challenge is the impact of having a presence on social media, for instance, how to maintain a distinction between personal and professional presence (e.g., ACA code of ethics recommends keeping separate professional and personal presence). The NCDA requires career professionals to clearly identify themselves in regard to their professional expertise and to address questions within their scope of professional competencies. In essence, to maintain professional and ethical boundaries, counselors need to be cautious and alert regarding social media and, in fact, the virtual world we all are part of nowadays.

Equity and Social Justice

In Chapter 3, we discussed relevant issues to career development from multicultural perspectives. With all the changes in the economy and world of work, increasing disparity of resources available to people, existence of occupational stereotypes, occupational segregation, occupational discrimination, glass ceiling, and other social barriers, more people suffer from unemployment or underemployment. Even though career aspirations are about the same for everyone, minority groups perceive more barriers and fewer opportunities (Fouad & Byars-Winston, 2005). Access to resources and services for everyone is not only necessary but should be ethical obligations for professionals so that all can have quality career services.

Accessibility and Equity

Ensuring everyone has the access to quality services for their career development needs and to resources that would help them live up to their potentials is important for the overarching goals of career intervention—for people to have a satisfactory career by being an active member in the workforce and a contributing member to the society. Unfortunately, many factors in one's ecological system (e.g., disability at a microlevel, stereotypical and discriminatory views and practices at the mesosystem and exosystem, and public policy at the macrolevel) influence individuals' access to services and services quality (Cook,

Heppner, & O'Brien, 2002). As a matter of fact, the root of career intervention and counseling is the effort to help urban youth and recent immigrants (either form Europe or from rural areas) to secure a job that would support their living and adjustment to urban life. The mission to help more people gain entry into the workforce and achieve self-sufficiency and self-sustainability is still applicable in today's world. As a profession rooted in assisting disadvantaged populations to develop strengths and overcome social barriers, an ethical practice should address the disparity issues encountered by many people and target inclusion in services.

Equity and inclusion in services for everyone is a long-range aim and requires the profession to take an active role in creating and providing opportunities for people who lack resources. A comprehensive career development and intervention program at K-12 settings would benefit all students from various backgrounds. A specific program with specialized program components to help groups with special needs in school and community settings is also needed. School counselors need to play an important role and should assume a leadership role in advocating for students to achieve college and career readiness through collaborating with other school staff and families to assist all students to gain access and resources to be better served (Rivera, 2016). Counselors working in community settings should be mindful of the interrelationship of work and life issues and multiple layers and complexity of systematic factors that might influence clients' functioning and, therefore, help clients access resources and services that would assist them to function effectively to navigate the system for a better life, if needed, including gaining employment or empowering them for career resilience.

MULTICULTURAL BOX 15.1

Why is equality not enough? What is the difference between *equality* and *equity*? The distinction between these two similar terms may be more significant that you realize. While equality means that everyone is given the same treatment, equity means that each person is given the same opportunity, free from bias. What might this look like in an educational setting?

Jonny was born to a family with both parents working as professionals, grew up in a suburban house with a nice landscape, went to a well-funded public school, and is about to take the SAT and apply for college. Berry was born to a single mother who struggled to get a job, grew up in a neighborhood with street violence, went to an underfunded urban school, and is about to take the SAT and apply for college as well. Both Jonny and Berry were administered the same test and accepted to college, however, Jonny got good grades in most classes and found a paid summer internship during sophomore year, and Berry got below average grades in most classes and had to work multiple jobs to support himself despite the Pell grant he received.

Tips for consideration: What factors do you see that contribute to Jonny and Berry's academic performance? What do you think their job prospect is if their academic performance continues the same pattern? If Jonny and Berry received the exact same amount of assistance from their university career service center and their academic units, would this be equality or equity? What would be considered equitable service in this scenario?

For adults working in organizations, an inclusive and supportive work environment is so crucial not only for work performance but also for job satisfaction. However, there is a gap between workforce change (more women and ethnic minority workers) and the institutional culture of the workplace (gendered practice), therefore, changes to help employees have healthy lives and work effectiveness need to integrate work and home domains (Bailyn, 2011). "We will not achieve gender equity in the workplace if we do not challenge gender roles in the family" (Bailyn, 2011, p. 108). Career intervention for adults in institutions needs to make the service available and accessible (e.g., expansion of EAPs), and target equity to ensure quality.

Social Justice and Advocacy

Social barriers (as reviewed in Chapter 3 with details), prejudices, stereotypes, and biases limit the ability of nonmainstream groups to access resources and services. The limited access to education and training due to these social barriers further impedes peoples' access to full employment and subsequently deprives people from access to survival and power, social connection, and self-determination (Blustein et al., 2002, Blustein, 2006). To overcome these barriers requires action. One of the actions commonly recommended by professional organizations' ethical code of ethics and multicultural competencies is advocacy for social justice. Diversity and inclusion are the core values of career practitioners (Fickling, Chan, & Cooper, 2016). Career development practitioners are positioned to raise awareness among counseling profession, allied professionals (e.g., other health professionals, human resources professionals, organization administrators), and policy makers to create an inclusive and diverse workforce. For example, counselors in various settings could empower clients via individual counseling and career development programs. School counselors could collaborate with communities to create opportunities to mentor and support disadvantaged youth for job-related experiences and development of skills. Counselors working in organizations could educate both employers and employees to adopt inclusion policy and practice.

Public Policy

Public policy and legislation regarding career development has frequently shaped career intervention practice in both school and community settings, from who should do the work to the scope and nature of intervention throughout the entire history of career development intervention (Herr, 2003). Herr (2003) stated that career counseling is an integral part of national labor market policies to target preventing or reduction of unemployment, assisting unemployed workers adjust to fast changing labor market context, and helping people who are marginally employed because of lack of resources or preparation so that equality of access to work and training opportunities could be in place. The United States is not alone in trying to develop an effective workforce through policy and legislation. The European Commission also has policy that facilitates similar themes: improving career guidance for all levels of students and young people at risk; improving career guidance for adults who are unemployed through collaboration between public employee services, local training and educational institutions, and private and community-based guidance services; improving access to career guidance services (e.g., more flexible delivery methods,

LEARNING ACTIVITY 15.2
ADVOCACY AND INCLUSION

Many social barriers discussed in this chapter and Chapter 3 are related to individuals' personal inputs and backgrounds. In addition to these individual and institutional barriers, what else in the current context could limit one's opportunities to full participation in the workforce? Have the class discuss this question in small groups. Then regroup the small groups with representatives from each of the previous groups, have the new group first share the discussion points from the previous groups, then have them develop an action plan to address the issues of inequity and lack of inclusion to help the organizations to have inclusive practice and individuals have equitable services. The group will specify the steps they can take to start the advocacy process to implement this action plan.

establishing coherent policy and strategy); and improving systematic program quality and evaluation (OECD, 2004).

Coordination of career counseling policy and legislation at the national and state level is necessary for the application and integration of services to diverse population (Herr, 2003). Public policy and legislation will continually influence and shape the career development intervention; therefore, counselors need to be active in advocating for inclusion of career intervention as part of education and counseling initiatives. An example of an advocacy effort could be joining the professional organizations that support the mission of helping more people have access to quality services for career readiness.

The NCDA includes advocacy for clients and professionals in its mission statement. Because all career counselors and development specialists are affected by public policy, the government relations committee of NCDA works closely with other allied organizations to seek support for policies and legislative priorities of NCDA. The recent efforts included submitting an implementation recommendation for the Work Innovation and Opportunities ACT (WIOA) to provide workforce and training assistance to adults and disengaged youth through state one stop career centers; assisted in adding career counseling language and alerted membership on the larger roles of state and local schools to the Every Student Succeeds Act (ESSA); and provided career counseling questions to the House Education and the Workforce Committee to aim for authorization of the act and to improve career-technical programs (Carey, Dedmond, Wallwork, & Lehman, 2016).

PROMOTING WELLNESS THROUGH WORK AND HEALTH

Career and Health

The relationship between work and health is multiple and bidirectional (Swanson, 2015). Due to the interrelationship of physical and mental health, counselors working with diverse clientele either in school/college settings or mental health agencies cannot ignore the dynamics between career and health. The concurrence of mental illness and unemployment among adults is evident, and multiple studies have found the correlation between career related behaviors (e.g., career adaptability, career indecision, unemployment, dysfunctional career thoughts) and mental health issues such as depression and anxiety (Osborn, McCain, & Miller, 2016). Job performance, job satisfaction, and occupational stress are also intertwined with one's health (Ford, Cerasoli, Higgins, & Decesare, 2011). Mental disorder symptoms might be due to poor personal work environment fit (Herr, 1989), and vice versa, poor job performance could be because of mental health issues. For instance, a worker experienced symptoms of lack of appetite, sleep deprivation, and low energy, and it seemed that he had depression, but with further exploration, it was found that his boss was demanding, aggressive, micromanaging, and often assigned him to do the work he did not have the capacity or resources to accomplish. He had these symptoms because he was constantly worried that he would be fired. So, this person's seemingly pathological mental health symptoms were actually the result of his work environment. Ignoring the interrelationship between work and health can misguide counseling intervention and career intervention as well.

Balance of Multiple Life Roles

Throughout the life span, people have various life roles besides a worker role. At different life stage, certain roles play more dominance, for example, a focus on the student role during adolescent years and even young adulthood, more focus on the caregiver role when raising children or the primary person taking care of aging parents. When these various roles are in coordination, life and work is balanced, it is great. However, often there are conflicts between the different roles one plays simultaneously, and once the balance of life and work is tilted, it is stressful and can harm one's health. It seems that people can cope relatively well when family matters interfere with work demands but not so well when too much work overflows into home life (Haar, 2004). When an imbalance of work and life occurs, more dissatisfaction and negative feelings tend to emerge. On the other hand, people who are satisfied with their jobs tend to have more of a balance between work and home life and with support in the activities they engage in at work and home (Rudd & McKenry, 1986). People with balanced work and life roles also have decreased impairment at work (Casey & Grzywacz, 2008) and less intention to leave their jobs (Haar, 2004).

Role overload means that one has more responsibilities and duties than time and energy permits, in other words, time related demands exceed the time management resources an individual has (Schultz & Henderson, 1989). Such excessive demands for a long period of time make individuals susceptible to declining productivity and a sense of control or accomplishment. The rippling effect could then affect health, relationships, and life satisfaction in general. Thus, balancing work and life roles, being mindful of boundaries of work and life, especially in today's virtual work environment, is essential for living a healthy life and satisfactory work.

Transition Challenges

With the rapid changes in world of work, and innovative technology being developed at a fast pace as well, people not only encounter instability but also face constant demands of updating skills. Even in the normal cycle of career development, transitions from childhood to adulthood, from school to work, and from work to retirement are part of the path everyone has to go through. Throughout the life span, individuals voluntarily or involuntarily transition in and out of jobs, for instance, from school to work, from employment to unemployment, from being out of the workforce to reentry into the workforce. The declining stability in career trajectory further aggravates the transition challenges. The unpredictability and uncertainty of the future, along with unemployment, underemployment, and transitioning in and out of jobs, creates stress, anxiety, and possibly other mental health issues for workers and their families (Fouad & Bynner, 2008). The research has found that people losing jobs or having inadequate employment were more likely to be affected by mental and physical symptoms (Olesen, Butterworth, Leach, Kelaher, & Pirkis, 2013).

In addition, when transition is unexpected or involuntary, it worsens the psychological well-being of individuals. Any transitions, voluntary or involuntary, require a person to make decisions and choices, develop plans and strategies to successfully make the transitions (voluntary transition), and identify resources and acquire adaptability capacity (involuntary transition). Counselors need to work with individuals to develop readiness skill and expand capacity to navigate transition as it is almost inevitable in the current economic structure and to advocate for policy that influences transition at the organization and community level (Fouad & Bynner, 2008). In sum, transition is normal in the context of uncertainty existing in the world of work, therefore, being ready for changes and expanding one's career capacity is necessary.

INTEGRATED SERVICES

Integrated Training

One view commonly observed by many counselor educators is that many counseling students do not see the need to have training in career development intervention (Gilliam, 2012). Herr (2003) argued that an external threat to career development is lack of coordination and integration of the policies and legislation for career counseling practice. Herr further stated that one of the outcomes of such uncoordinated practice was personnel (i.e., no consistent titles for practitioners, who can do what) and training (i.e., what kind of training and who can provide the training). In a study about teaching a career development course, two CACREP standards, "career development theories and decision making models," and "interrelationships among and between work, family, and other life roles and factors, including the role of multicultural issues in career development" were perceived to have been met with high marks (Osborn & Dames, 2013). The study also found that there were at least 17 career theories covered in the course. These findings confirmed the argument by other scholars (see the section on theory and practice integration in this chapter) that there is a lack of focus on practice in training. Osborn and Dames (2013) also noticed that students' initial attitudes toward the career development class were negative but changed after the class. It is suggested that counselor educators provide feedback to accrediting and licensing bodies about the relevance of the career counseling practice and making course content personally relevant.

Integrated training thus becomes critical to educating future counselors who will provide services to diverse clientele, who need to conceptualize clients' issues from the ecological counseling perspective, and who should provide integrated services. To understand the importance of career development to health and wellness, it requires more than just one career development class. Interweaving career development content into other courses such as diagnosis, treatment planning, and school counseling are necessary. Counselor educators can collaborate with field placement sites to incorporate comprehensive and integrated services to promote wellness among the target population.

Integrated Services

Work plays a central role in people's lives. One of the roots of the counseling profession is vocational guidance with an aim to help struggling individuals cope with adversity and thrive. Effective counseling cannot separate personal issues and career issues when helping a person. As some scholars have argued, any counseling intervention needs to combine mental health and career issues in treatment (Herr, 1989; Niles & Yoon, 2011). The separation of mental health counseling and career counseling is artificial (Blustein, 2008) and hinders the complete view of a client as a whole person.

Integrated services require the counselor to conceptualize the client's presenting issues from a broad perspective, taking into consideration the various personal and contextual factors that would influence one's emotion and behavior. If school counselors and mental health counselors consider only mental health issues and neglect career issues in their case conceptualization, or vice versa, they may inadequately serve their clients. Therefore, it is necessary to equip counselors with tools for integrated services, and likewise, train future counselors to develop an integrated view of human behavior and competency in helping clients in continuous transitions across the life span. The ecological career counseling model proposed by Cook, O'Brien, and Heppner (2004) and Cook, Heppner, and O'Brien (2005) suggested that optimal career intervention should find the accordance of individual and contextual factors of a person's ecosystem, in other words, help individuals become change agents to use their resources to maximize their potential and minimize the barriers to living a fulfilling life. The ecological career counseling model would set the goal of intervention as empowering clients to become aware of the interrelatedness of each system and to become agents of their own to navigate the complex and changing dynamics of economy, workforce, and work settings. Achieving this goal requires counselors to be aware of resources and barriers clients encounter in their life space and to work together with clients to find the accordance of each layer of the system.

Professional Mandate

The counseling profession is distinct from other helping professionals with its roots in vocational guidance and helping people at disadvantages to adjust to contextual demands. Therefore, counselors are in a unique position among all the helping professionals to have the capacity to provide integrated services to clients because counselors are the only helping professionals who are professionally trained to have knowledge and skills to address both career and mental health issues as required by the training standards within the professional organization and accreditation standards (see ACA and CACREP). Individuals may not know what kind of counselors they need to seek

CASE ILLUSTRATION 15.1
ASHA IS LOST

Asha is 38 years old, working in a large insurance company as a division manager in charge of sales of long term care to customers. Asha has been in the insurance industry for 15 years and has always enjoyed working with customers and finds contentment in helping individuals have a solid financial plan for the future. Asha was promoted to be a division manager five years ago and had received good performance reviews by both the supervisor and the subordinates. Recently, Asha often felt very tired and had low energy to do anything, at work or at home, and seemed to be losing interest in social activities such as hanging out with colleagues or attending her children's sport activities. Asha noticed a change in her sleep patterns as well and had a hard time falling asleep at night and getting up in the morning. Her work demands have been changing in the last couple of years because a new database system was introduced to the company and a new director (Asha's boss) was appointed. The new boss was demanding and aggressive, and at the same time, had a micromanaging style. He often assigns Asha goals that are impossible to be accomplished and does not want to listen to any explanation. In her last performance review, Asha received an average score with some areas even less than satisfactory. Asha was very worried and became more distressed. Her spouse and two children started to noticed the change and were really concerned that Asha might have depression. The thought of having depression

further aggravated the situation to the extent that Asha tried to cover the symptoms by drinking a lot of coffee. It helped a little at the beginning, but was not really effective after awhile. Her sleeping problems worsened. Finally, Asha received an e-mail from her boss that Asha would be put on probation if her work performance continued to decline. As part of the probation plan, Asha was requested to seek professional counseling. Asha has seen three different counselors but did not feel any of the three counselors were truly helpful. Asha heard you are a counselor who can help people find good matching jobs and hoped that you service would be beneficial to her.

Discussion Questions

1. Why do you think the three counselors were not really helpful to Asha? What could be missing in the previous interventions?

2. How would you present yourself to Asha to gain her trust and work alliance?

3. How would you conceptualize Asha's case if Asha is a woman versus a man? Will Asha's racial and ethnic background make any differences in your conceptualization of Asha's case?

4. What would be your intervention goals and strategies for Asha?

help, and they may not recognize or separate their presenting issue as mental health or career related; or in most cases, the issues are not separable anyway. What are we doing if the counseling profession artificially categorizes clients to mental health clients or career clients? Professionals certainly can have specialized service of expertise, but understanding the interrelationship of personal and career issues and how they can affect one's mental health and wellness is what makes counselors distinct from other helping professionals. It is the professionals' responsibility to maintain the root and goal of counseling—wellness based, strength based, developmental, and preventive— through integrated training and services to diverse populations.

Summary: Challenges and Opportunities

As we conclude this chapter and this book, the United States, and in fact the entire world, has witnessed many changes in both socioeconomic and sociopolitical aspects. The technology community sends the messages that many human functions are gradually being done by machines or artificial intelligence, for instance, automatic driving cars, interpretation devices, and eventually, automation will replace a lot of jobs currently done by human labor. Globalization is seriously questioned and challenged for its impact on all workers, and unemployment and underemployment, refugees and terrorism, rights and voices of marginalized people, and the health care debate frequently appear on news and social media. For youth who need to enter into the workforce, they might wonder if they can get a job; for seniors who plan to retire, they might wonder if they can afford to retire. The questions (e.g., Can I get a job? Can I leave the job?) might be different, but the concerns are the same: security of life quality. How similar or different is the turbulence experienced by many people today compared to the industrialization era when vocational guidance emerged? What kinds of challenges and opportunities does the current situation imply to career intervention professionals? Career development and intervention has its roots and mission in helping people navigate the changing socioeconomic system to live a satisfying life. To accomplish this mission, understanding the interaction of individuals and the work environment is fundamental but not sufficient. Career intervention has evolved from vocational guidance (matching), to career planning, to career construction (Savickas, 2005). This evolution reflects the shift from helping individuals find a career to assisting individuals develop capacity to master one's own career

journey. Further, several scholars (Savickas, Pope, & Niles, 2011; Crockett, Byrd, & Erford, 2014) reviewed *Career Development Quarterly* in its 100 years of history and identified that the primary themes of the publication are contextual influences and multicultural issues, and the trend has been more international and female authorship in recent years. It is evident that inclusion, collaboration, equity, and social justice are the core values of the profession and will continue to be so. As counselors, regardless of work settings and in what professional specialty, gaining knowledge of the interrelationship between work and life and integrating theories, practice, and research to better serve clients with diverse backgrounds are professional requirements and ethical practice.

The challenges and opportunities are the two sides of same phenomenon: While instability and uncertainty in the work world engulf people, it also creates the opportunity for people to search further the meaning of work to individuals and to life and leads to further endeavors for identifying theories and intervention strategies that would help people in the chaos of the ever-changing work environment. More career intervention strategies in recent years focus on instilling hope and resilience, building capacity and self-construction, and engaging in lifelong learning and are responses to the challenges and beyond and create opportunities to integrate mental health counseling and career development, providing more holistic and integrated services to clients. After all, a person cannot be pigeonholed as a career client or mental health client, and neither should the counseling profession neglect its own root and mission. It is the time for professional counselors to provide much needed integrated services to variety of people with variety of issues.

Keystones

- With rapid changes in the work world and society in general, it is necessary to reexamine the impact of interaction of person and environment and associated meaning.

- The complex and reciprocal interrelationship between work and health should be considered and addressed in career development intervention.

- Career development theories need to go beyond understanding career-related behaviors; they should address career counseling processes and outcomes in regard to effectiveness of helping people.

- There are unprecedented challenges to ethical practice for career intervention professionals due to information technology and the virtual world for work and life.

- Both the roots and mission of career development are to help disadvantaged people become productive and contributing members of society; therefore, continual effort for equity, inclusion, and social justice is needed.

- To help individuals cope with uncertainty and unpredictability, counselors can work with clients to instill hope, build resilience, and develop adaptability with an aim to become self-agents of one's career development construction.

- An effective intervention needs to integrate theory, research, and practice as well as provide integrated services considering mental health and career issues concurrently.

References

Amundson, N., & Thrift, E. (2008). Emergence of more dynamic counseling methods. In R. V. Esbroeck, & J. Athanasou (Eds.), *The international handbook of career guidance* (pp. 325-339). doi:10.1007/978-1-4020-6230-8_16

Bailyn, L. (2011). Redesigning work for gender equity and work-personal life integration. *Community, Work and Family, 14*, 97-112. doi:10.1080/13668803.2010.532660

Balentine, J. (2017, August). Generation Z and the role of the career development professional in the workplace. *Career Convergence*. Retrieved from https://associationdatabase.com/aws/NCDA/pt/sd/news_article/142256/_PARENT/CC_layout_details/true.

Blustein, D. L. (2006). *The psychology of working: A new perspective to career development, counseling, and public policy.* Mahwah, NJ: Lawrence Erlbaum Associates.

Blustein, D. L. (2008). The role of work in psychological health and well-being: A conceptual, historical, and public policy perspective. *American Psychologist, 63*(4), 228-240. doi:10.1037/0003-066X.63.4.228

Blustein, D. L., Chaves, A. P., Diemer, M. A., Gallagher, L. A., Marshall, K. G., Sirin, S., & Bhati, K. S. (2002). Voices of the forgotten half: The role of social class in the school-to-work transition. *Journal of Counseling Psychology, 49*, 311-323.

Borgen, W. A., Amundson, N. E., & Reuter, J. (2004). Using portfolios to enhance career resilience. *Journal of Employment Counseling, 41*(2), 50-59. doi:10.1002/j.2161-1920.2004.tb00878.x

Bragg, D. D., & Taylor, J. L. (2014). Toward college and career readiness: How different models produce similar short-term outcomes. *American Behavioral Scientist, 58*(8), 994-1017. doi:10.1177/0002764213515231

Carey, N., Dedmond, R. Wallwork, L., & Lehman, C. (2016). NCDA and public policy. *Career Developments, 32*(3), 6-10.

Casey, P. R., & Grzywacs, J. G. (2008). Employee health and well-being: The flexibility and work-family balance. *The Psychologist-Manager Journal, 11,* 31-47.

Conley, D. T. (2010). *College and career ready: Helping all students succeed beyond high school.* San Francisco, CA: Jossey-Bass.

Cook, E. P. (2012). *Understanding people in context: The ecological perspective in counseling.* Alexandria, VA, US: American Counseling Association.

Cook, E. P., Heppner, M. J., & O'Brien, K. M. (2005). Multicultural and gender influences in women's career development: An ecological perspective. *Journal of Multicultural Counseling and Development, 33*(3), 165-179.

Cook, E. P., O'Brien, K. M., & Heppner, M. J. (2004). Career counseling from an ecological perspective. In Conyne & Cook (Eds.), *Ecological counseling: An innovative approach to conceptualizing environmental interaction.* Alexandria, VA: ACA.

Crockett, S. A., Byrd, R., & Erford, B. T. (2014). The career development quarterly: A 22-year publication pattern metastudy. *Career Development Quarterly, 62,* 327-339. doi: 10.1002/j.2161-0045.2014.00086.x

Davies, J. (2016, July). *Give employers what they want: Work ethic.* Presentation at the National Career Development Association Global Career Conference in Chicago, IL.

Dougherty, S. M., & Lombardi, A. R. (2016). From vocational education to career readiness: The ongoing work of linking education and the labor market. *Review of Research in Education, 40*(1), 326-355. doi:10.3102/0091732X16678602

Fickling, M. J., Chan, C. D., & Cooper, Y. (2016). Diversity, inclusion, and equity & career development. *Career Developments, 33*(1), 6-11.

Ford, M. T., Cerasoli, J. A., Higgins, J. A., & Decesare, A. L. (2011). Relationships between psychological, physical, and behavioral health and work performance: A review and meta-analysis. *Work and Stress, 25,* 185-204.

Fouad, N. A., & Byars-Winston, A. M. (2005). Cultural context of career choice: Meta-analysis of Race/Ethnicity differences. *Career Development Quarterly, 53*(3), 223-233. doi:10.1002/j.2161-0045.2005.tb00992.x

Fouad, N. A., & Bynner, J. (2008). Work transitions. *American Psychologist, 63*(4), 241-251. doi:10.1037/0003-066X.63.4.241

Gilliam, K. (2012). *Effects of professional socialization factors on career counseling self-efficacy and interest* (Doctoral dissertation). Retrieved from OhioLINK Electronic Theses and Dissertation Center.

Grundmann, O. (2013). Career readiness: An old idea revived? *Journal of College Science Teaching, 8.*

Retrieved from go.galegroup.com.proxy.libraries.uc.edu/ps/i.do?p=EAIM&sw=w&u=ucinc_main&v=2.1&it=r&id=GALE%7CA340945155&sid=summon&asid=4e7533b1adf54bb703394e1cb1b966c7.

Haar, J. M. (2004). Work-family conflict and turnover intention: Exploring the moderation effects of perceived work-family support. *New Zealand Journal of Psychology, 33*(1), 35-39.

Hall, D. T (1996). Introduction: Long live the career—A relational approach. In D. T. Hall (Ed.), *The career is dead—Long live the career: A relational approach to careers* (pp. 1-15). San Francisco, CA: Jossey-Bass.

Herr, E. L. (1989). Career development and mental health. *Journal of Career Development, 16*(1), 5-18. doi:10.1007/BF01354263

Herr, E. L. (2003). The future of career counseling as an instrument of public policy. *The Career Development Quarterly, 52*(1), 8-17.

McClain, M, Kronholz, J., Hou, P., Osborn, D., & Sampson, J. (2015). Exploring the integration of theory, research, and practice in career development: An overview. *Career Developments, 31*(4), 5-8.

Niles, S. G., Amundson, N. E., & Neault, R. A. (2011). *Career flow: A hope-centered approach to career development*. Columbus, OH: Pearson.

Niles, S. G., & Yoon, H. J. (2011). Career counseling: Current challenges and opportunities for mental health practitioners. In A. J. Palmo, W. J. Weikel, D. P. Borsos, A. J. Palmo, W. J. Weikel, & D. P. Borsos (Eds.), *Foundations of mental health counseling* (4th ed., pp. 135-153). Springfield, IL: Charles C Thomas.

Olesen, S. C., Butterworth, P., Leach, L. S., Kelaher, M., & Pirkis, J. (2013). Mental health affects future employment as job loss affects mental health: findings from a longitudinal population study. *BMC Psychiatry*. Retrieved from http://www.biomedcentral.com/1471-244X/13/144.

Organisation for Economic Co-Operation and Development (OECD)/European Commission. (2004). *Career guidance: A handbook for policy makers*. Paris, France: Author.

Osborn, D. S., & Dames, L. S. (2013). Teaching graduate career classes: A national survey of career instructors. *Counselor Education & Supervision, 52*, 297-310.

Osborn, D. S., McCain, S., & Miller, A. (2016). Career and mental health. *Career Developments, 32*(4), 6-10.

Rivera, L. M. (2016). Incorporating career development to achieve college and career readiness in every K-12 school. *Career Developments, 33*(1), 18-19.

Rudd, N. M., & McKenry, P. C. (1986). Family influences on the job satisfaction of employed mothers. *Psychology of Women Quarterly, 10*, 363-372.

Sampson, J. P., Bullock-Yowell, E., Dozer, V. C., Osborn, D. S., Lenz, J. G., & Ross, N. (2016). The state of the art in integrating theory, research, and practice in vocational psychology. In J. P. Sampson, E. Bullock-Yowell, V. C. Dozier, D. S. Osborn, & J. G. Lenz (Eds.), *Integrating theory, research, and practice in vocational psychology: Current status and future directions*. Tallahassee, FL: Florida State University. http://doi.org/10.17125/svp2016.ch20

Savickas, M. L. (2005). The theory and practice of career construction. In S. D. Brown &

R. W. Lent (Eds.), *Career development and counseling: Putting theory and research to work* (pp. 42–70). Hoboken, NJ: Wiley.

Savickas, M. L. (2013, July). *Essential ideas in the history of career intervention (1909-2013)*. Paper presented at the National Career Development Association Conference, Boston, MA.

Savickas, M. L. (2015). Career counseling programs: Guiding, developing, and designing. In P. J. Hartung, M. L. Savickas, & W. B. Walsh (Eds.), *APA handbook of career intervention: Vol. 1. Foundations* (pp. 129-143). Washington, DC: APA.

Savickas, M. L., Pope, M., & Niles, S. G. (2011). The Career Development Quarterly: A centennial retrospective. *Career Development Quarterly*, *59*, 528-538.

Schultz, J. B., & Henderson, C. (1985). Family satisfaction and job performance: Implications for career development. *Journal of Career Development*, *12*(1), 33-47.

Swanson, J. L. (2015). Work and psychological health. In P. J. Hartung, M. L. Savickas, & W. B. Walsh (Eds.), *APA handbook of career intervention: Vol. 2. Foundations* (pp. 3-27). Washington, DC: APA.

Whiston, S. C. (2003). Career counseling: 90 years old yet still healthy and vital. *Career Development Quarterly*, *52*, 35-42.

INDEX

Evidence-based practice, 380
Executive Coach Forum, 342
Ex-offenders, career counseling for, 339–340
Expectations, client, 159
Experiential learning, 228–229, 319

Facebook, 20, 247, 375
Family
    division of labor and, 46–47
    family-school balance, 309
    military, 343
    work and, 45–46, 365
    work-family balance, 273, 385, 387
Family Education Rights and Privacy Act, 186
Farrington, C. A., 293, 295
Federal Bureau of Prisons, 340
Federal Glass Ceiling Commission, 74
Feedback
    card sort and, 219
    clients and, 158–159, 169, 191, 326
    group work and, 219, 220
    work performance and, 38, 39
Feller, R. W., 248
Filmmaker Pro, 239
Find Your Interests, 101
Finklea, J. T., 20
Fitzgerald, L. F., 121
Flexicurity, 49
Flores, L. Y., 22, 83, 187
Flower of Identity technique, 217 (figure)
Focus 2 software, 240
Fogle, K. L., 228–229
Folsom, B., 320
Ford, M. T., 37
Formal assessment, 196–197. *See also* Assessment, career
Formal program evaluation, 269
Fouad, N. A., 47, 79–80, 325
Fractals, in chaos theory, 146
Free Application for Federal Student Aid (FAFSA), 290, 296
Friedman, T. L., 20

Garis, J. W., 318
Garver, M., 315–316
Gati, I., 171, 220–221, 242
Gelatt, H. B., 352–355

Gender
    assessment and, 193
    career development barriers and, 61–63, 70–71
    glass ceiling and, 74
    income gap and, 18
    occupational stereotypes, 72
    orientation to sex roles, 113
    workforce equity and, 385
    See also LGBTQ (lesbian, gay, bisexual, transgender, queer); Multicultural career development issues; Multicultural counseling; Women
General Aptitude Test Battery (GATB), 105
Generation/cohort effect, 375–376
Genetic factors, in career development, 42, 115, 118
Genogram, 217–218
George Barden Act (1946), 7, 8
Getting Hired, 245
Gfroerer, M. C. A., 342
Gibbons, M. M., 182
GI Bill (1946), 8
Gibson, R. L., 20–21
Ginsberg, E., 128
Giordano, A. L., 339
Glass ceiling, 74
Glassdoor, 244, 245
Globalization, 20, 33
Goals
    college career centers and, 313–315
    community settings AND, 337
    identification of, 167
    intervention programs and, 262–262, 266–267
    personal, 118, 119
Golan, R., 68
Goldman, L., 195
Goldsmith, W., 30
Goodman, J., 353
Google, 246, 247
Gorin, J., 186
Gottfredson, L. S., 112–114, 286–287
Greenleaf, A. T., 229–230
Group work, 219–220
Guerriero, J. M., 228
Guevara, K., 30
Guidance, career, 156